D1554540

THEATRICAL DIRECTORS

Theatrical Directors

A BIOGRAPHICAL DICTIONARY

EDITED BY

John W. Frick & Stephen M. Vallillo

Greenwood Press

Westport, Connecticut • London

Library of Congress Cataloging-in-Publication Data

Theatrical directors : a biographical dictionary / edited by John W.
  Frick and Stephen M. Vallillo.
     p.   cm.
  Includes bibliographical references and indexes.
  ISBN 0–313–27478–9 (alk. paper)
  1. Theatrical producers and directors —Biography—Dictionaries.
  I. Frick, John W. II. Vallillo, Stephen M.
PN2205.T54   1994
792′.0232′0922—dc20   93–1138

British Library Cataloguing in Publication Data is available.

Library of Congress Catalog Card Number: 93–1138
ISBN: 0–313–27478–9

First published in 1994

Greenwood Press, 88 Post Road West, Westport, CT 06881
An imprint of Greenwood Publishing Group, Inc.

Printed in the United States of America

The paper used in this book complies with the
Permanent Paper Standard issued by the National
Information Standards Organization (Z39.48–1984).

10 9 8 7 6 5 4 3 2 1

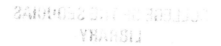

For Marsha and Maryann
and
For Rodney Who Died Too Soon

Contents

Preface

Theatrical Directors: A Biographical Dictionary is a reference book designed primarily for use by students and theatre generalists. *Theatrical Directors* contains biographical sketches, organized alphabetically, of nearly 300 individuals distinguished for their stage directing and includes not only contemporary directors, but those who are no longer working. Emphasis has been placed upon artists who have established international reputations, especially those whose work has significantly influenced American theatre. In addition, directors whose work may be little known outside of their home countries are included if their work has had a major impact upon the theatre of their homeland. Since this is a one-volume work, however, it is not intended to be exhaustive of the subject; rather, it concentrates upon those directors whose achievements, in the estimation of the editors and the Advisory Board, constitute a significant contribution to Western theatre, although in isolated cases, artists like Tadashi Suzuki have been included because of their extensive work in the United States.

In the selection of the artists included in *Theatrical Directors: A Biographical Dictionary*, the term ''director'' was interpreted liberally. Thus, this volume includes so-called traditionalists like Peter Hall and José Quintero; auteurs like Vsevolod Meyerhold and Lucian Pintilie; collaborators like Elia Kazan and Joseph Chaikin; experimentalists like Robert Wilson and Shuji Terayama; and extends to directors like Martha Clarke and Pina Bausch whose work borders upon dance, directors like László Moholy-Nagy whose principal contribution was theoretical, and producer-directors like Jed Harris, whose genius lay in mounting productions which achieved commercial success.

Each entry in *Theatrical Directors* is comprised of three separate sections.

The first provides a narrative summary of the major events of the director's life and an assessment of the importance of his or her accomplishments and their significance in the history of directing. More than a simple listing of biographical material or a chronicle of achievements, however, this section emphasizes and evaluates those characteristics which identify the director's work and which render it unique. Special attention has been paid to directorial innovations which may have advanced the ''state of the art'' and to those productions with particular historical significance.

The second section of the entry, ADDITIONAL PRODUCTIONS, is a chronological listing of important productions *not listed* in the narrative history including, where relevant, places of production, major collaborators, information on foreign or national tours, or variant versions of a playscript. In the case of plays that are reasonably well-known and accessible in the literature (i.e., *The Madwoman of Chaillot* or *Woyzeck*), it was felt that it was not necessary to include the playwright's name; but where there is more than one ''recognized'' version (*Antigone*, for example), the author's name has been included. Likewise, for ''minor'' versions of a play (the Georges de Bouhélier, Corneille, Voltaire, or Seneca versions of the Oedipus myth) or adaptations (Patrice Chéreau's adaptation of Chekhov's *Platonov*; Sanguinetti's adaptation of Ariosto's *Orlando Furioso* for Luca Ronconi), the name of the playwright or the adaptor has been listed. For the most part, the date provided is the date of the initial production. Taken in combination with the productions mentioned in the narrative portion of the entry, the total number of productions approximates an abridged production history of the director.

The final section of each entry, the SELECTED BIBLIOGRAPHY, provides a short list of sources which the contributor considers the most accessible and useful to the theatre student and the generalist. In cases where the sources listed are largely or exclusively in a foreign language, are published as articles in rare journals, or are housed in obscure repositories, the reader should interpret this as an indication of the difficulty which might be encountered in further research on the director.

Each entry is followed by the name of the writer(s), and a brief description of each contributor to *Theatrical Directors* is provided in the Contributors section. To assist the reader in further research, *Theatrical Directors: A Biographical Dictionary* contains two appendixes (one listing directors chronologically; a second listing directors by country in which primary work was done) and two separate indexes. The first, the Name Index, lists the directors, actors, designers, and major theatre companies contained in *Theatrical Directors*. The second, the Play, Film, and Television Title Index lists all plays and productions in the volume and will, hopefully, facilitate comparative studies of different directors' interpretations of the same script or aid in compilation of production histories. An asterisk after a name in an entry indicates that there is a separate entry on that person.

Since a project such as this one is never undertaken without a battery of people in support, we wish to thank the following for their help and encouragement: Mary Frances Belton, Theresa Lamb, Janet Crayne, Heidi Synnatzschke-Cochran, Peggy Holley, Betty Volkan, Jim Barns, Kim Varin, Margaret Merrill, Lynette Friesen, Karen Morris, James V. Hatch, Ursula Appelt, Karen Marshall, Jannette Hudson, Spencer Golub, Kate Davy, John Brokaw, Sharon Carnicke, Jean-Clio Godin, and John Lyons. We are especially indebted to the Advisory Board for its advice and guidance during the planning and compilation of *Theatrical Directors*; to all of the contributors for lending their time and expertise to the project; to Ewa Setaro for her help with entries which arrived written in Polish; to Paula Lester for translating from Finnish; to Rebecca Summerford for translating the French Canadian entries; to Kaz Braun for referring us to his colleagues in Poland; and to Tom Leff, Judy Lee Oliva, Stuart Lenig, Jan Cohen-Cruz, Joel Berkowitz, Paul Nadler, Mark Maniak, and Chris Jones for volunteering to write additional entries at the "last moment." Our final thank-you is reserved for our wives, Marsha and Maryann, for their patience and moral support throughout the project.

John W. Frick and Stephen M. Vallillo

THEATRICAL DIRECTORS

A

GEORGE (FRANCIS) ABBOTT [b. June 25, 1889, Forestville, New York]. After graduating with a B.A. from the University of Rochester, where he was involved in theatre, Abbott studied playwriting with Professor George Pierce Baker at Harvard in the early part of this century. Abbott's early success at writing earned him a $100 first prize in a one-act playwriting contest in Boston for his play *The Man in the Manhole* (1912). This led to a full production of the work at the Bijou Theatre and a job as an assistant there.

Although Abbott began his career as an actor, he is chiefly known as a writer, director, and producer of Broadway shows. His first production experience, in the office of John Golden, led to his directing a play he wrote with James Gleason called *The Fall Guy* (1925). Following the success of this work, Abbott directed *Broadway* (1926), written with Phillip Dunning, and a string of other famous works, including *Coquette* (1927) written with Ann P. Bridgers, *Three Men on a Horse* (1935) written with John Cecil Holm, and *On Your Toes* (1936) written with Richard Rodgers and Lorenz Hart. His preeminence on Broadway was assured through his direction and co-writing of such shows as *A Tree Grows in Brooklyn* (1951), *Pajama Game* (1954), *Damn Yankees* (1955), and *Fiorello*, which won the Pulitzer Prize in 1959.

Abbott's success was not limited to shows he cowrote. He was associated with some of the most significant shows on Broadway, including such musical hits as *Pal Joey* (1940), *Billion Dollar Baby* (1945), *Wonderful Town* (1953), *Once upon a Mattress* (1959), and *A Funny Thing Happened on the Way to the Forum* (1962), which earned him a Tony Award; and such plays as *Room Service* (1937) and *Take Her She's Mine* (1961). Abbott's work was so ubiquitous on

Broadway that in 1966 the Adelphi Theatre was renamed the George Abbott Theatre.

Abbott was often called upon when a director was fired from a production, and he acquired a reputation as a "play doctor." His technique relied heavily on improving the pacing of a production. For musicals, he employed the "crossover" scene, in which a scene could be played "in one," in front of a traveller curtain while a major scene change went on behind it. Abbott applied his touch to such shows as *Beggar's Holiday* (1946), *You Never Know* (1947), and *Out of This World* (1950).

Together with his work in the theatre, Abbott also wrote and directed several films for the major studios. His first directing credit was *The Bishop's Candlesticks* (1928). During the 1950s, Abbott directed the film versions of his Broadway hits *Damn Yankees, The Pajama Game*, and *Where's Charley?*

Although Abbott is now more than 100 years old and retired, he has at times offered his services as director or consultant. One of these projects was a workshop production of *Tropicana* (1985). Another project on which Abbott advised was *Jerome Robbins' Broadway* (1988). Although created and directed by Jerome Robbins,* this production was a collection of scenes from great Broadway shows, many of them originally directed by Abbott.

Known as one of this century's prominent showmen, Abbott credits his education with Professor Baker for his ability to mount a show. But, beyond the techniques that he learned through his education, Abbott was afforded the opportunity to stage plays and musicals that were distinctly American. Thus, through his experience, he developed a directing style that was characterized by the energy and quick pace of the American spirit.

ADDITIONAL PRODUCTIONS: (Plays directed, unless otherwise specified.) 1913: *The Misleading Lady* (acted the part of Babe Merrill); 1932: *Twentieth Century*; 1935: *Boy Meets Girl*; 1938: *The Boys from Syracuse*; 1941: *Best Foot Forward*; 1942: *Beat the Band*; 1944: *On the Town*; 1948: *Look Ma I'm Dancin'* (directed and coproduced); 1949: *Where's Charley?*; 1953: *Wonderful Town*; 1957: *New Girl in Town*; 1962: *A Funny Thing Happened on the Way to the Forum* (New York; London, 1963); 1965: *Flora the Red Menace*; 1967: *How Now, Dow Jones*; 1969: *The Fig Leaves Are Falling*; 1970: *Norman, Is That You?*; 1973: *The Pajama Game*; 1976: *Music Is*.

SELECTED BIBLIOGRAPHY: Abbott, George. *Mister Abbott*. New York: Random House, 1963; Atkinson, Brooks. *Broadway*. New York: Macmillan Publishing Co., 1974; Leiter, Samuel L. *From Belasco to Brook: Representative Directors of the English-Speaking Stage*. Westport, CT: Greenwood Press, 1991: 51–76; Taubman, Howard. *The Making of the American Theatre*. New York: Coward McCann, 1965.

                                                                    Tom Mikotowicz

JOANNE AKALAITIS [b. June 29, 1937, Cicero, Illinois]. Before being named by Joseph Papp as his artistic associate in 1990 and artistic director in 1991 at the New York Shakespeare Festival, JoAnne Akalaitis made her reputation as a performer and director with Mabou Mines, the theatre collective she helped to found with Philip Glass, Lee Breuer,* Ruth Maleczech, and David Warrilow in

1970. She studied acting at the Actors Workshop in San Francisco, and briefly with such teachers as Herbert Berghof, Bill Hickey, Joyce Aaron of the Open Theatre, and Spalding Gray, as well as with Jerzy Grotowski* in Paris. Her first attempt at directing was a stage adaptation of Samuel Beckett's radio play *Cascando* (1975). She replaced the flow and rhythm of the text with a series of repetitive activities and divided the Voice's speeches among five performers. This production signaled the start of her career at the forefront of avant-garde theatre.

While creating original performances, Akalaitis evolved her technique of amassing texts and visual images from extensive historical research and of discovering the "physical and emotional geography" of the production through a workshop rehearsal process. The most significant of these pieces include her examination about what it means to be female, *Dressed Like an Egg* (1977), based on the life of Colette; and *Dead End Kids* (1980), about the relationship between alchemy, science, technology, and the threat of nuclear destruction. Championing the aesthetics of "bricolage" found in performance art and the absence of linear narrative in the dances of postmodern choreographer Yvonne Rainer, Akalaitis linked together disparate scenes, fragments of texts, music, and dense visual imagery—including slide projections, film, and dance sequences. In these works, labeled "collages" by the critics, she aimed at creating multiple associations for each audience member which could lead to a personal and unique theatrical experience.

Although her award-winning productions of Franz Xaver Kroetz's *Request Concert* (1980) and *Through the Leaves* (1983) have established her as a director who can handle hyperrealism with chilling effectiveness, Akalaitis's direction of works by other playwrights has won her the title of "high priestess of postmodernism." In these productions, scenes from the plays remain autonomous entities layered against the design concept and sound score which have been developed from Akalaitis's intuitive responses to the play. These scenes evolve through improvisation into a plethora of visual images chosen for their contemporary resonances, even if they are jarringly anachronistic. Thus, Akalaitis never creates integrated, authoritative interpretations which place her in the position of intermediary between the audience and the text.

Akalaitis gained national recognition in regional theatres. At the Guthrie Theatre she was hailed first for her American southwest adaptation of Georg Büchner's *Leonce and Lena* (1987), with its silent black-and-white film based on Büchner's life of Lenz, a German romantic poet; and then for her definitive production of Jean Genet's *The Screens* (1989), which was indebted to the playwright's original notes to Roger Blin.* At the Goodman Theatre, her surrealistic, feminist examination of John Ford's *'Tis Pity She's a Whore* (1990), set in Italy of the 1930s, dominated by fascism and futurism, was a chilling indictment of patriarchal power.

Yet Akalaitis's highly experimental style has also generated controversy. She has been criticized for excessive use of visual imagery, for failing to provide her productions with an overarching concept, and for betraying the playwright's intentions. *Endgame* (1984)—set in an abandoned subway tunnel, cast with black actors in the roles of Hamm and his father, and accompanied by Philip Glass's high-tech electronic music—caused Samuel Beckett to file a lawsuit against this American Repertory Theatre production. Her production of *Cymbeline* (1989), set as a romantic Victorian fantasy for the New York Shakespeare Festival, was attacked by the critics because her postmodern style heightened, rather than unified, the play's mix of genres, periods, and implausible circumstances.

Although Akalaitis has been both praised and criticized as a director, her strength has been her willingness to continue experimenting and her commitment to create theatre that has a contemporary edge. Beyond aesthetic concerns, she aims at influencing her audience. By presenting them with abrasive, disjunctive, acutely vivid, yet often beautiful images in her productions, she hopes to stimulate them to ask the important questions, rather than provide them with the answers, to political and social ills of our time.

ADDITIONAL PRODUCTIONS: 1978: *Southern Exposure*; 1982: *Red and Blue* (Michael Hurson); 1983: *The Photographer/Far from the Truth* (Philip Glass and Robert Coe); 1986: *The Balcony* with Joan MacIntosh, *Green Card*; 1987: *Help Wanted* (adapted from play by Franz Xaver Kroetz); 1988: *American Notes* (Len Jenkin); 1989: *The Screens;* 1990: *The Mormon Project* (Eric Overmyer); 1991: *Henry IV, Part I* and *Henry IV, Part II* (designed by George Tsypin); 1992: *Woyzeck*.

SELECTED BIBLIOGRAPHY: Bartow, Arthur. *The Director's Voice*. New York: Theatre Communications Group, 1988: 1–19; Bharucha, Rustom. "Kroetz's Act without Words." *Theater* 13 (Fall/Winter 1981): 66–71; Bly, Mark. "JoAnne Akalaitis's *Leon and Lena (and lenz)*: A Log from the Dramaturg." *Theater* 21 (Winter 1989/Spring 1990): 81–95; Clubb, Dave. "Dead End Kidding." *Theater* 12 (Summer/Fall 1981):46–50; Cole, Susan Letzler. *Directors in Rehearsal: A Hidden World*. New York: Routledge, 1992: 75–90; Fuchs, Elinor. "Misunderstanding Post Modernism." *American Theatre* 6 (December 1989): 24, 26–31; Kalb, Jonathan. "JoAnne Akalaitis" (Interview). *Theater* 15 (Spring 1984): 6–13; Kalb, Jonathan. "The Underground Endgame." *Theater* 16 (Spring 1985):88–92; Mehta, Xerxes. "Versions of Performance Art." *Theatre Journal* 35 (May 1984): 164–98; Nouryeh, Andrea J. "JoAnne Akalaitis: Postmodern Director As Socio-Sexual Critic." *Theatre Topics* 1 (Fall 1991): 177–91; "Performing *Dead End Kids*: Statements by Mabou Mines Actors." *Theater* 13 (Summer/Fall 1982): 35–37.

Andrea J. Nouryeh

NIKOLAI PAVLOVICH AKIMOV [b. April 3, 1901, Kharkov; d. September 5, 1968, Moscow]. Trained as a painter at the New Art Studio in Leningrad, Nikolai Akimov began his theatrical career as a scene designer in Moscow in 1918. He made his mark as a designer with Petrov's productions of Ivanov's *Armored Train No. 14–69* (1927) and Afinogenov's *Fear* (1931), both at the State Academic Theatre in Leningrad.

Influenced by Evgeni Vakhtangov,* Akimov came to believe that the ideal director was his own designer and applied this belief to his own work. In May 1932, he made his debut as a director-designer with *Hamlet* (music by Shostakovich) for the Vakhtangov Theatre. Akimov staged this production as a reaction against the constructivist style that swept the post-Revolution theatre. In this rewritten and highly theatricalized production, Akimov staged Hamlet as a political intriguer who fakes his father's ghost, facing Gertrude who is the real power behind the throne.

Charged with formalism and refused more directing assignments in Moscow, Akimov became the director of the experimental studio of the Leningrad Music Hall and was appointed artistic director of the Leningrad Comedy Theatre in 1935. From this base, Akimov began doing avant-garde interpretations of classic works such as *Dog in a Manger* (1936) by Lope de Vega and *Twelfth Night* (1939). Again accused of formalism because of his liberal artistic and political views, Akimov was transferred to Leningrad's Lenin Soviet Theatre in 1949. In 1955, Akimov returned to the Leningrad Comedy Theatre, where he championed new Soviet playwrights, especially Evgeny Shvarts, whom he had first produced in 1940. Akimov staged Shvarts's last play, *An Ordinary Miracle*, in 1957. Akimov's production of Shvarts's satirical *The Dragon* (1963) ran afoul of the authorities, but he was allowed to continue his work. He was a faculty member of the Leningrad Theatrical Institute from 1955 until his death.

ADDITIONAL PRODUCTIONS: 1929: *Tartuffe* (with Nikolai Petrov and Vladimir Soloviev); 1939: *The Widow of Valencia* (Lope de Vega); 1940: *The Shadow* (Shvarts); 1953: *The Shadow* (Saltykov-Shchedrin) [at Lenin Soviet Theatre in Leningrad]; 1955: *The Affair* (Sukhovo-Kobylin) [at Lenin Soviet Theatre]; 1963: *Don Juan* (Byron); 1966: *Krecinskij's Wedding* (Sukhovo-Kobylin).

SELECTED BIBLIOGRAPHY: Akimov, Nikolai. "Pages from an Unwritten Autobiography." *U.S.S.R.* 24 (1961):53–57; Houghton, Norris. "Nikolai Akimov: Portrait of a Designer." *Theatre Arts* May 1936: 349–53; Law, Alma H. "Hamlet at the Vakhtangov." *The Drama Review* 21 (December 1977): 100–110; Rudnitsky, Konstantin. *Russian and Soviet Theater: 1905–1932.* Trans. Roxane Permar. New York: Abrams, 1988.

Edward Dee

BENNY SATO AMBUSH [b. June 17, 1951, Brookline, Massachusetts]. Throughout the 1980s, Benny Ambush firmly established himself as a preeminent figure among the newest wave of African-American theatre artists. After receiving a B.A. from Brown University, Ambush earned his M.F.A. in directing from the University of California, San Diego, in 1977. He then served as assistant director-in-residence at the Arena Stage in Washington, D.C., and as an NEA Directing Fellow at the Pittsburgh Public Theatre in 1980–81.

Prior to his eight-year tenure as artistic/producing director of the Oakland Ensemble Theatre (1982–90), Ambush held several positions in both arts administration and theatrical production, including serving as a consultant to the Zellerbach family fund Performing Arts Assistance Program and as a site evaluator and panelist for various programs of both the California Arts Council and the National Endowment for the Arts.

As theorist and advocate in the field of African-American theatre, Ambush served as panelist in the American Theatre Critics Association Conference, 1991, in New York and has written several articles on African-American theatre and cultural diversity. Internationally, Ambush has served as a United States Information Agency sponsored lecturer to Kenyatta University, Nairobi, Kenya.

Currently, Ambush is an associate artistic director with the American Conservatory Theatre in San Francisco. In this position, Ambush recently directed Dan Zellner's *Pigeon Egghead* (1991), which also aided in fostering the Bay Area Native American Theatre Company, Turtle Island Ensemble, by providing technical assistance, in-kind service, facility usage, and administrative help. Having the Bay Area's preeminent theatre provide this support has set the tone for other Bay Area partnerships with the Native American Theatre Company.

ADDITIONAL PRODUCTIONS: 1973: *The Experiment* (Rossie Lee Harris, Jr.) Providence, RI; 1976: *Slow Dance on the Killing Ground* (Hanley) San Diego, CA; 1978: *The Cotton Club Review* (Joanne McKnight) Washington, DC; 1979: *Games* (George Bass) Reston, VA; 1982: *Konvergence* (P. J. Gibson) Oakland, CA, *The Past Is the Past* (Richard Wesley) Oakland; 1987: *Tamer of Horses* (Mastrosimone) Oakland; 1989: *Master Harold . . . and the Boys* (Fugard) San Leandro, CA.

SELECTED BIBLIOGRAPHY: Ambush, Benny Sato. "Drawing the Line." *Callboard* August 1990; Ambush, Benny Sato. "Pluralism to the Bone." *American Theatre* 6 (April 1989): 5; Ambush, Benny Sato. "Minority Theatre in Plural America: A Snapshot Through a Black Looking Glass." *Callboard* June 1986.

Thomas-Whit Ellis

WINTHROP AMES [b. November 25, 1871, North Easton, Massachusetts; d. November 3, 1937, Boston, Massachusetts]. In 1904, Winthrop Ames left his position at the *Architectural Review* to become the manager of the Castle Square [light] Opera House in Boston. His trip to Europe in 1907 (documented in an eighty-five page notebook available on microfilm at the New York Public Library) exposed him to experimentations in theatre architecture, lighting design, scenic machinery, and the contemporary transition from realism to symbolism. His appointment as managing director of the New Theatre in New York City in 1908 allowed him to put these advanced ideas into practice.

His tenures at the New Theatre (1908–11), the 299-seat Little Theatre (1912–30), and the Booth Theatre (1913–32) were noted for his presentations of European plays. At the New Theatre, built on opera house scale, he spent lavishly on exquisite productions of symbolist dramas, among them *Sumurun*, and Maeterlinck's *The Betrothal* (1910), *Sister Beatrice* (1911), and *The Blue Bird* (1910). Ames was able to sell his productions as intellectual, not popular, entertainment and received a variance from the Gerry Society Laws that enabled him to feature children in the roles. Mary, Doris, and Pearl Eaton, the Fairbanks Twins, and many other theatre and film child stars made their New York debuts in these productions.

In the smaller theatres, he presented more popular works, among them drawing room comedies by A. A. Milne, melodramatic starring vehicles for George Arliss, such as *The Green Goddess* (1921), and plays by George S. Kaufman with Marc Connelly (*Beggars on Horseback*, 1924) and Edna Ferber (*Minick*,

1925). He retired in 1932 after successful seasons of Gilbert and Sullivan operetta revivals.

ADDITIONAL PRODUCTIONS: 1909: *The School for Scandal*; 1913: *Escape*; 1914: *Prunella* (Granville Barker); 1915: *Pierrot the Prodigal* (Michel Carre), *The Wrong Box* (Granville Barker); 1926: *White Wings* (Philip Barry).

SELECTED BIBLIOGRAPHY: MacArthur, David Edward. "A Study of the Theatrical Career of Winthrop Ames from 1904 to 1929." Diss. Ohio State U, 1962; Parker, H. T. "Winthrop Ames." *Theatre Guild Magazine* October 1929: 23 +. The Winthrop Ames Collection is held by the Billy Rose Theatre Collection, New York Public Library for the Performing Arts.

Barbara Cohen-Stratyner

ANDRÉ ANTOINE [b. January 31, 1857, Limoges, France; d. October 21, 1943, Pouligen, Brittany, France]. Antoine was a humble employee of the Paris Gas Company when, in 1887, he founded the theatre that was to affect profoundly the development of dramatic art over the next half-century. He had grown up in a working-class neighborhood in Paris, and although his formal education ended when he was twelve, he was self-motivated in seeking cultural enrichment by reading insatiably, visiting museums, joining the *claque* or serving as an extra at the theatre, and taking diction lessons. He also served a five-year military stint in Tunisia.

In 1886, he joined the Cercle Gaulois, an amateur group that presented a repertoire of—in Antoine's view—"lifeless nonsense." Antoine put together an adventurous bill of four previously unproduced one-acts, including Léon Hennique's adaptation of Emile Zola's *Jacques Damour*, but had to absorb all production costs himself when the club objected to that selection and withdrew its support. The single performance on March 30, 1887, in a rented hall in the Passage de l'Elysée des Beaux Arts drew critical attention, which encouraged Antoine to offer a second evening of theatre on May 30. He subsequently left his job at the gas company to devote himself to running the company that he named Théâtre Libre.

It was at the Théâtre Libre from 1887 to 1894 that Antoine introduced most of the innovations for which he is remembered. In those seven seasons, he staged 112 new plays, 69 of them by previously unproduced authors. In addition to launching such French dramatists as Eugene Brieux, François de Curel, and Henri Becque, he premiered major foreign plays, including Leo Tolstoy's *The Power of Darkness* (1888), Henrik Ibsen's *Ghosts* (1890) and *The Wild Duck* (1891), August Strindberg's *Miss Julie* (1893), and Gerhart Hauptmann's *The Weavers* (1893). He demanded that the translations accurately reflect the letter and spirit of the original.

Although he experimented with various styles, it was in the naturalist vein that Antoine made his mark by overthrowing stale conventions of the moribund commercial theatre. In a series of manifestoes, most notably a booklet published in May 1890, he called for plays with new ideas, performed by an ensemble of actors in safe, comfortable facilities at reasonable prices. He propounded a new style of acting—which he and his company demonstrated in practice—based upon direct observation of life, building complex characterizations through nuances of gesture and telling details of stage business, and using a "conversational" line delivery instead of declamation. Critics often referred to the "truth" and "naturalness" evoked by such means, as well as the use of silences and the emotional interaction of the characters. Such effects were achieved through meticulous rehearsals using actual props.

Antoine was also innovative in his use of stage space; his settings were often angled to convey a sense of continuity of the world of the play beyond the proscenium arch. His placement of furniture created the illusion of a fourth wall through which the audience could voyeuristically observe the action. He set new standards of historical and geographical accuracy in costuming. He was the first director in France to suppress the footlights and to darken the auditorium during performance. His most renowned use of motivational lighting on stage occurred in *La Mort du Duc d'Enghien* (1888), particularly during a scene in which lanterns provided the only sources of light and were so placed as to illuminate the faces of judges and victim.

The Théâtre Libre became a model for a number of small, independent, subscription-based theatres in Europe and the United States. After its bankruptcy in 1897, Antoine became a free-lance actor for two seasons. Hired as codirector at the Odéon in 1896, he soon resigned over differences with a colleague. He then opened the Théâtre Antoine, a commercial venture which he operated from 1897 to 1906. His production there of *King Lear* (1904) became the springboard for his being given a full appointment as director of the Odéon, where he remained until 1914. He continued to produce an eclectic repertoire and won a reputation as the first French director to take Shakespeare's plays seriously, commissioning new translations, achieving an uninterrupted flow of action by alternating full settings and scenes before a curtain, even visiting Rome in preparation for directing *Julius Caesar* (1906). In the final phase of his career, Antoine directed eight silent films.

ADDITIONAL PRODUCTIONS: 1887: *Jacques Damour* (Léon Hennique, from a Zola story, on a bill with three other one-act plays), *La Nuit Bergamasque* (Bergerat), *En famille* (Méténier), *Soeur Philomène* (Byl and Vidal, from a Goncourt novel); 1889: *La Casserole* (Méténier); 1892: *Blanchette* (Brieux); 1897: *La Parisienne* (Becque); 1899: *Poil de carotte* (Renard); 1902: *La Terre* (from Zola).

SELECTED BIBLIOGRAPHY: Antoine, André. *Memories of the Théâtre-Libre*. Trans. Marvin A. Carlson. Ed. H. D. Albright. Coral Gables: University of Miami Press, 1964; Carlson, Marvin. *The French Stage in the Nineteenth Century*. Metuchen, NJ: Scarecrow, Press, 1972; Chothia, Jean. *André Antoine*. Directors in Perspective series. Cambridge: Cambridge University Press, 1991; Gild, David. "Antoine's Production of *King Lear*." *Shakespeare Encomium*. Ed. Anne Paolucci. New York: City College, 1964: 135–49; Knapp, Bettina L. *The Reign of the Theatrical Director: French Theatre 1887–1924*. Troy, NY: Whitston Publishing Co., 1988; Waxman, Samuel Montefiore. *Antoine and the Théâtre-Libre*. New York: Benjamin Blom, 1926; reissued 1968; Whitton, David. *Stage Directors in Modern France*. Manchester: Manchester University Press, 1987.

Felicia Hardison Londré

ERWIN AXER [b. January 1, 1917, Vienna, Austria]. A pupil of Leon Schiller,* Axer founded the Contemporary Theatre of Warsaw in 1940 as part of the underground resistance to Nazi occupation. He has worked continuously in this theatre ever since as its artistic director and general manager. Consistently throughout his career, Axer has been recognized for his meticulous preparations of modern drama and especially for the introduction of newer works from the Continent and America. He typically prefers to direct playwrights such as Jean Giraudoux, Bernard Shaw, Harold Pinter, Thornton Wilder, Tennessee Williams, Arthur Miller, Friedrich Dürrenmatt, Max Frisch, and Bertolt Brecht,* and undertook to stage the Polish premieres of many of their plays.

Axer's directorial approach emphasizes the subtle interpretation of character psychology and its theatrical development. Stylistically, his productions tend toward a simplified realism in large part out of a preference for older-fashioned, rather than experimental, literature and for his willing subservience to the letter of the author's text. As a director, Axer's presence in production is always discreet, tasteful, and ever sensitive to the social and deeply philosophical implications of the drama. His artistic success has been augmented over the years by his ability to assemble one of the most technically proficient acting ensembles in Europe. With respect to his Polish contemporaries, Axer's work stands somewhere between the "monumental" theatre of spectacle as practiced by Schiller and Kazimierz Dejmek* and the "poor" theatre of Jerzy Grotowksi* and Józef Szajna.*

In addition to his artistic duties, Axer has been for many years an influential teacher of directing at Warsaw University's School of Theatre. His pupils have included Konrad Swinarski,* Jerzy Jarocki,* and Kazimierz Braun.*

ADDITIONAL PRODUCTIONS: 1955:*The Resistible Rise of Arturo Ui*; 1957: *The Germans* (Leon Kruczkowski); 1958: *The First Day of Liberation* (Kruczkowski); 1964: *The Firebugs* (Max Frisch); 1965: *The Mother* (Stanisław Ignacy Witkiewicz); 1967: *The Three Sisters*; 1970: *Maria Stuart* (Friedrich Schiller); 1971: *Iphigenia in Tauris* (Goethe); 1976: *Kordian* (Juliusz Słowacki); 1977: *Old Times*; 1978: *Lear* (Edward Bond); 1979: *Borys' Holiday* (Thomas Bernhard).

SELECTED BIBLIOGRAPHY: Drozdowski, Bohdan. *Twentieth Century Polish Theatre*. London: John Calder, 1979; Filler, Witold. *Contemporary Polish Theatre*. Warsaw: Interpress, 1977; Grodzicki, August. *Polish Theatre Directors*. Warsaw: Interpress, 1979; Szydłowski, Roman. *The Theatre in Poland*. Warsaw: Interpress, 1972. Also, see *The Theatre in Poland* (monthly journal) Warsaw: Institute International du Théâtre, 1958.

Thomas Leff

B

WILLIAM BALL [b. April 29, 1931, Chicago, Illinois; d. July 30, 1991, Los Angeles, California]. William Ball began his theatrical career as a designer, but soon turned to acting. As a young man, he appeared in Shakespeare festivals around the country, his most notable performance being with the Margaret Webster Shakespeare Troupe. He received a Bachelor of Arts degree from Carnegie-Mellon University and was awarded a Fulbright Scholarship to study repertory theatre in England. He returned to Carnegie to receive his master's degree in directing.

Ball's New York directing debut came in 1958 with *Ivanov*, a production which won both the Obie and Drama Desk awards for best direction. He subsequently directed at Houston's Alley Theatre, Washington's Arena Stage, and San Diego's Old Globe and staged several New York City Opera productions. His 1961 New York production of *Under Milk Wood* received honors similar to *Ivanov*'s, and his 1962 production of *Six Characters in Search of an Author* was highly praised as well. Ball restaged this production in 1964 in London with Sir Ralph Richardson heading the cast.

Ball's most important work, however, was done with the American Conservatory Theatre (ACT), which he helped found in 1965. Originating in Pittsburgh, the theatre made its permanent home in San Francisco two years later. Ball was named artistic director of the company and remained in that position until 1986, when he resigned because of artistic and financial disagreements with the theatre's board of directors. Ball directed many notable productions at ACT, but his philosophy and methodology were even more influential. He created a theatre similar to the Moscow Art Theatre or the Comédie Française, in which training was continuous and the needs of the ensemble superseded the desires of the individual actor. Ball frequently cast against type, used experienced actors in minor roles, and actors frequently appeared in two or more productions concurrently. He professed to be disinterested in creating popular productions, but was instead involved in the process of challenging, and thereby creating, great artists. Ball invented a term, "positation," which meant a willingness on the part of all parties to take risks in casting and productions, with the right to fail inherent as long as the process was honest and creative. Although he fashioned his behavior after the great European *régisseurs* (even down to a trademark hat), and shaped ACT to his personal liking, Ball was nevertheless an actor's director. He believed in saying "yes" to any idea that an actor had, and maintained that the task of the director was to support and develop the actor's creativity. His rehearsal work often consisted of asking the actors questions, constantly working with them to clarify their objectives for each moment in the play.

Ball established a training program at ACT which grew to be more notable than the ACT productions. The training provided young actors the opportunity to learn from more experienced, mature performers who in turn could reinvigorate their art. He based his curriculum on Konstantin Stanislavsky,* but believed that feeling could develop out of an action, the reverse of the Stanislavsky approach. Ball was critical of American Method acting, finding it too inhibited and closed off from the audience. The results of this thinking were clearly seen in many of his productions, which were very quick and physically exuberant. In 1979, Ball accepted a Tony Award voted to ACT for its repertory performance and advanced theatre training. After leaving ACT Ball worked as an actor, wrote, and taught, but he directed infrequently. He moved to Los Angeles, where he was involved in the development of television movies and miniseries.

ADDITIONAL PRODUCTIONS 1964: restages *Six Characters in Search of an Author* in London; 1965: *Tartuffe* (first ACT production); 1967: restages *Tartuffe* (first ACT San Francisco production); 1968: *Tiny Alice*; 1973: *The Taming of the Shrew* (later televised by PBS).

SELECTED BIBLIOGRAPHY: Ball, William. *A Sense of Direction: Some Observations on the Art of Directing*. New York: Drama Book Publishers, 1984; Fanshel, Fran. "It's All Bill Ball." *San Francisco Chronicle* 22 February 1967:24–29; Wilk, John R. *The Creation of an Ensemble: The First Years of the American Conservatory Theatre*. Carbondale and Edwardsville: Southern Illinois University Press, 1986; Winn, Steven. "Bill Ball: The A.C.T. Years." *San Francisco Chronicle* 11 October 1981:39–43.

Alan Kreizenbeck

EUGENIO BARBA [b. October 29, 1936, Brindisi, Italy]. In 1960, after receiving an M.A. in literature and history of religion, and only a few months after beginning studies at the theatre school in Warsaw, Poland, Barba left formal studies to spend three years (1960–62) assisting Jerzy Grotowski* at the Polish Theatre Laboratory. In 1964, Barba founded Odin Teatret with actors denied entry to Oslo's Theatre School. Odin's first productions were performed in an air-raid shelter. Two years later, Barba and Odin were invited to Holstebro,

Denmark, granted a farmhouse and, as the Nordisk Teaterlaboratorium, began receiving substantial government support as an experimental pedagogical institution. Barba's subsequent body of work remains inextricably bound to that of Odin Teatret.

In Holstebro, Barba created conditions conducive to a group whose life was devoted to creating theatre. Actor training was (and is) the backbone of Barba's approach. Holstebro's isolation made daily training possible, and consistently working with a core group of actors, Barba remained engrossed in their training. The company's third production, *Ferai* (1969), was well received at European theatre festivals; but immediately thereafter, the group concentrated even more on training and did not reemerge with a new production until 1972.

Barba's outlook reflects his difficult beginnings. His interest in theatre ethics, physiology, and historical insight are products of his years spent with Grotowski, a mutual devotion to Konstantin Stanislavsky* and Vsevolod Meyerhold,* and Odin's struggle to be perceived as a legitimate theatre. Barba seeks to build a relationship with the spectator by being viscerally evocative without necessarily clarifying a specific message. Consequently, in productions, Barba focuses the abilities of each actor into a precise expression of strong visceral sights and sounds, and texts are prepared in collaboration. *My Father's House* (1972–74) marked a turning point. With neither plot nor text, the play, which was based on private themes, was composed over a period of three years by Barba and the actors.

Barba wants theatre to look beyond ordinary life and beyond ordinary theatre. His plays do not move forward by means of plot or chronology; they expand by theatrical means. In *The Million* (1977–84), which compares Marco Polo's journeys to Odin to Odin Teatret's tours, stiltwalking skeletons and Japanese Lion-monkeys dance to a brass band while Polo puffs a cigar. Some plays, like *Anabasis* (1977–84), are processional or journey-like; while others, like *Brecht's Ashes* (1982–84), in which characters from Brecht's plays enact the themes embodied in his poems, are more literary. Still others, such as *Judith* (1987) or *Marriage with God* (1984–90), are one or two virtuoso character works based on historical characters.

Odin tours roughly half the year, performing in isolated villages in southern Italy and parts of South America. Barba takes professional theatre to places it has never been before. On these tours, Odin barters with locals, each group in effect exchanging performances. Enabled by travel, pedagogy, and barter, Barba developed the field of theatre anthropology—the study of pre-expressive behavior. Barba, through the International School for Theatre Anthropology (ISTA), studies what he calls the performer's extra-daily use of the body. He believes theatre anthropology is an empirical approach to performers' problems currently overlooked in Occidental performance study, which he feels concentrates more on theories.

By the late seventies, Barba and Odin had maintained roughly seven pieces in the public eye, while creating more. Though rarely seen in the United States,

Barba has presented work internationally at theatre festivals, founded ISTA, and conducted seminars with his collaborators I Made Bandem (Bali), Katsuko Azuma (Japan), and Sanjukta Panigrahi (India).

Barba's work has influenced thousands of small groups who are without government or financial support. His extensive writings enable those less exposed to his performances to become acquainted with his work. *Beyond the Floating Islands* is his most widely read book in which he records his theories.

Some people have a greater need to do theatre than to receive it, Barba observes. When discriminated against, these people form groups to express themselves. This, he calls the Third Theatre—metaphorically, an archipelago made of floating islands. He compares such groups to the floating gardens ancient Aztecs erected when banished to Lake Texcoco by the Toltecs. Like these Aztec communities, the Third Theatre arises out of survival needs. Barba's recent writings, *A Dictionary of Theatre Anthropology: The Secret Art of the Performer* and *The Dilated Body*, are significant because of the contributions they make toward the understanding of theatre anthropology.

ADDITIONAL PRODUCTIONS: 1965–66: *Ornitofilene*; 1967–68: *Kaspariana*; 1974–80: *The Book of Dances*; 1976–80: *Come and the Day Will Be Ours*; 1984–Present: *The Oedipus Story*; 1985–87: *The Gospel According to Oxyrhincus*; 1988–Present: *Talabot*; 1990-Present: *Memoria, The Castle of Holstebro*; 1991-Present: *Itsi-Bitsi*.

SELECTED BIBLIOGRAPHY: Barba, Eugenio. *The Dilated Body*. Rome: Zeami Libri, 1985; Barba, Eugenio. *Beyond the Floating Islands*. New York: PAJ Publications, 1986; Savarese, Nicola, and Eugenio Barba. *A Dictionary of Theatre Anthropology: The Secret Art of the Performer*. London: Routledge, 1991.

Seth Baumrin

HARLEY GRANVILLE BARKER [b. November 25, 1877, London, England; d. August 31, 1946, Paris, France]. In reaction to the theatrical excesses of leading actor-managers of the Victorian stage, such as Henry Irving* and Herbert Beerbohm Tree, a reform movement arose in the 1890s to produce artistically and socially relevant drama by new playwrights, as well as to revive older plays in versions that maintained a fidelity to the original text of the author. Out of this group of reformers—which included J. T. Grein, who was the founder of the Independent Theatre, William Poel* of the Elizabethan Society, William Archer of the Stage Society, and Bernard Shaw—Harley Granville Barker emerged as the most prominent actor, director, and producer of progressive theatre between 1900 and World War I.

Granville Barker's productions were strictly noncommercial and featured ensemble acting, long rehearsal periods, no star actors, unknown or difficult scripts, simple but effective settings, moderate ticket prices, and limited performance runs. For lack of a permanent theatre, these productions were first produced at matinees, or on Sundays, in established theatres. In 1904, Barker teamed up with the manager J. E. Vedrenne and refurbished the Royal Court Theatre, converting it into a 600-seat facility in which they could fully realize their ambitions. In three seasons at the Court, Barker presented over a dozen plays by Shaw, contemporary English works by John Galsworthy, John Masefield, St. John Hankin, and Barker's own play, *The Voysey Inheritance*. These productions, as well as productions of new drama from Scandinavia and the Continent, attracted a relatively small but devoted and influential audience of intellectuals, artists, writers, and educated elite from London's upper-middle and professional classes. In addition to directing and acting, Barker also collaborated on the translations or English versions of pieces by Arthur Schnitzler, Gerhart Hauptmann, Maurice Maeterlinck, and Henrik Ibsen as well as championed and produced the revival of ancient Greek tragedy in new translations by Gilbert Murray.

The success of Barker's productions lay in his emphasis upon the unification of all production elements in the service of a single artistic focus. This approach began first with a commitment to the work of the playwright. The text was treated with utmost respect and, if possible, the author was invited to participate, often as director, in the play's development during rehearsal. Ideas about staging, design, and interpretation were shared among the entire company, and actors were expected to acquaint themselves with the entirety of the drama, not merely their own roles.

While promoting a realistic style of performance, Barker insisted upon accurate and clear elocution of speech, a practice he first learned while at Poel's Elizabethan Society. Partly to economize and partly to draw more attention to textual values in performance, Barker sought to simplify production elements into a visually elegant if spare style that wouldn't hinder the natural flow of speech, action, and change of scene. This simplified visual style proved especially effective for the works of Shakespeare which, at that time, were typically overburdened with cumbersome scenery that required awkward and time-consuming set changes.

In 1908, Barker and Vedrenne moved their productions to the Savoy on the West End, where they hoped to increase their financial support while continuing to present the Court Theatre's program of new drama of quality. Although the project lost money—Bernard Shaw underwrote many of the productions at a significant personal loss—it was a critical success and firmly established playwrights like Shaw and Galsworthy with the broad theatregoing public. In 1909, the impresario Charles Frohman invited Barker to bring his program to the Duke of York's Repertory, where for two seasons the financial returns again remained meager, even if the artistic achievements were substantial.

In 1912, Barker returned to the Savoy to direct a series of independently produced works of Shakespeare. His seminal productions of *The Winter's Tale* and *Twelfth Night* were outstanding for their combination of an exacting attention to the original text, fluid staging, and inventive use of setting and costume, qualities reaffirmed in his *A Midsummer Night's Dream* a few years later. After the seasons with Frohman, Barker and his actress-wife Lillah McCarthy produced three more seasons at the new St. James Repertory until the exigencies of World

War I, and then Barker's sudden divorce from McCarthy, took him away from the theatre for what was essentially the rest of his life.

After the war Barker turned to criticism and scholarship, especially to build upon his work with Shakespeare. Eventually he published the famous *Prefaces to Shakespeare* which have provided a distinguished succession of directors with some of the most erudite yet sensible advice on producing the Bard's work. As much through his writing about the theatre and his own artistic and directorial philosophy as by the example of his earlier productions, Barker became especially influential at the Old Vic where the next generation of theatre giants (Tyrone Guthrie,* John Gielgud,* Ralph Richardson, and Laurence Olivier) would follow his lead. Barker also continued his advocacy of a National Theatre that was first articulated in the manifesto *A National Theatre: Scheme and Estimates*, which he coauthored with William Archer in 1907. Barker's dream finally came to fruition in 1949, three years after his death.

ADDITIONAL PRODUCTIONS: 1900: *The Death of Tintagiles* with the Stage Society; 1901: *The Man of Destiny*; 1902: *The Marrying of Ann Leete* (Barker); 1904: *Candida* at the Court, *Hippolytus* (Gilbert Murray adaptation), *John Bull's Other Island*; 1905: *You Never Can Tell, Man and Superman, The Wild Duck, Major Barbara, The Return of the Prodigal* (St. John Hankin); 1907: *Hedda Gabler, The Devil's Disciple, Caesar and Cleopatra, Arms and the Man*; 1909: *Strife* (Galsworthy); 1910: *The Madras House* (Barker), *Misalliance*; 1911: *Anatol* (Schnitzler), *The Master Builder*; 1913: *Androcles and the Lion*; 1940: *King Lear* at the Old Vic.

SELECTED BIBLIOGRAPHY: Barker, Harley Granville. *The Exemplary Theatre*. Freeport, NY: Books for Libraries Press, 1970; Barker, Harley Granville. *Prefaces to Shakespeare*. 6 vols. Princeton: Princeton University Press, 1946–74; Kennedy, Dennis. *Granville Barker and the Dream of Theatre*. New York: Cambridge University Press, 1985; Leiter, Samuel L. *From Belasco to Brook: Representative Directors of the English-Speaking Stage*. Westport, CT: Greenwood Press, 1991: 23–50; Purdom, C. B., ed. *Bernard Shaw's Letters to Granville Barker*. New York: Theatre Arts, 1957; Salenius, Elmer. *Harley Granville Barker*. Boston: Twayne, 1982.

Thomas Leff

JEAN-LOUIS BARRAULT [b. September 8, 1910, Vésinet, France; d. January 22, 1994, Paris, France]. Of Burgundian peasant stock, Barrault worked his way through school, focusing first on mathematics, then drawing, and finally discovering the theatre. Admitted by audition to the Atelier, the studio of Charles Dullin,* in 1931, he trained in mime under Etienne Decroux. There, in 1935, he staged his first production, his own adaptation of William Faulkner's *As I Lay Dying*, as a mime-drama titled *Autour d'une mère*. The dramatic expressiveness of his nearly nude body gave him a reputation as an artistic rebel and brought him several film roles, including one in *Hélène* (1936) opposite Madeleine Renaud, an established star of stage and screen ten years his senior, whom he would marry in 1940. To prove himself worthy of her, he daringly put together a surrealist production of Cervantes's *Numantia* (1937), which was soon selling out at the Théâtre Antoine. Admitted to the Comédie Française, he made his debut in *The Cid* in 1940. In 1943, he directed Claudel's *The Satin Slipper*, which David Whitton calls one of the outstanding directorial achievements of modern times. Barrault worked closely with the author on revisions and used all the visual and auditory resources of the theatre while keeping the emphasis on the physical expressiveness of the body. The production also served to buoy up the morale of the French resistance in German-occupied Paris.

In 1946, Barrault and Renaud left the Comédie Française to found the Compagnie Madeleine Renaud–Jean-Louis Barrault, which has operated continuously through numerous vicissitudes (as well as frequent international tours) up to the present. They also published production-related documents in a long series of *Cahiers Renaud-Barrault*. The company's first home was the Marigny, a boulevard theatre, which they opened with *Hamlet* (1946). There, they offered an eclectic repertoire ranging from the classics to the avant-garde. After ten seasons at the Marigny and two seasons (1957–59) in various venues, the company was installed in the state-subsidized Odéon. Barrault began his nine-year tenure there with the premiere of *Tête d'or* (1959), which Claudel had written in 1890, and he soon revived Claudel's 1906 play *Break of Noon*. It was Barrault's extraordinary rapport with the Catholic poet-dramatist that had brought about the release of these plays for production. Barrault's directorial proclivity for physicalization and his understanding of the rhythmic values of the Claudelian verse line based upon breathing patterns made him the ideal director for Claudel's work.

The events of May 1968 impacted both personally and professionally upon Barrault and Renaud. The entire costume stock and equipment owned by Barrault's company, amounting to nineteen full productions, was destroyed during the month-long occupation of the theatre. The story of the takeover of the Odéon by political agitators and of the government's failure to support him is recounted in Barrault's memoirs, *Souvenirs pour demain*.

As a result of the 1968 takeover, Barrault, in effect, had to start his company again from nothing. Dismissed from his post at the Odéon, he arranged to produce *Rabelais* (1968) at the Elysée-Montmartre. Despite difficulties, he achieved a joyful comeback with the knockabout bawdry of the production, which also toured to several California universities. From 1972 to 1981 the company performed in the Gare d'Orsay, a former railway terminal that is today a museum of nineteenth-century art. Finally, the Compagnie Renaud-Barrault moved into the Théâtre du Rond Point on the Champs-Elysées, virtually across the street from the Marigny, where it had begun.

Barrault has written voluminously on his ideas about theatre. He has defined directing as "making humanity in scenic space." With his unremitting emphasis on the human factor, he begins by eliciting the actor's entire range of expression from silence to gesture to dance. He elucidated his quasi-mystical appreciation of the human body in a 1980 demonstration performance, *The Language of the Body*, in which he stated: "I am attached with all my being, with my carnal soul, to the larger world, to nature's great body. This gives me an intense feeling of desire, of love, of giving myself, of universal interaction, a profound sensation of plenitude. My heart beats to the rhythm of the world.''

ADDITIONAL PRODUCTIONS: 1946 (revived 1962): *Hamlet* (music by Arthur Honegger, designed by André Masson), *Les Fausses confidences* (Marivaux, revived 1961), *Le Procès* (adapt. André Gide from Kafka's *The Trial*); 1948 (revived 1961): *Partage de Midi* (Claudel; costumes by Christian Bérard, with Edwige Feuillère); 1953: *Christophe Colomb* (Claudel); 1956: *Le Personnage combattant* (Jean Vauthier); 1970: *Jarry sur la butte* (adapt. by Barrault from Jarry's plays; music by Michel Legrand); 1975. *Les Nuits de Paris* (adapt. by Jean-Claude Carrière from Restif de la Bretonne).

SELECTED BIBLIOGRAPHY: Barrault, Jean-Louis. *Comme je le pense*. Paris: Gallimard, 1983; Barrault, Jean-Louis. *Memories for Tomorrow*. Trans. Jonathan Griffin. New York: E. P. Dutton and Co., 1974; Barrault, Jean-Louis. *Reflections on the Theatre*. Trans. Barbara Wall. London: Rockliff, 1951; Barrault, Jean-Louis. *Saisir le présent*. Paris: Robert Laffont, 1984; Barrault, Jean-Louis. *Une Troupe et ses auteurs*. Paris: Jacques Vautrain, 1950; Frank, André. *Jean-Louis Barrault*. Paris: Seghers, Théâtre de tous les temps, 1971; Le Bon, Joël. *Renaud Barrault: Paris, notre siècle*. Paris: Editions de Messine, 1983; Whitton, David. *Stage Directors in Modern France*. Manchester: Manchester University Press, 1987: 137–59.

Felicia Hardison Londré

ANDRÉ BARSACQ [b. January 24, 1909, Theodosia, Crimea; d. February 3, 1973, Paris]. Son of a French father and a Russian mother, André Barsacq moved to France in 1919 and began studying architecture in 1925, but was soon enticed into the theatre by Charles Dullin.* His set design for Dullin's *Volpone* (1928) was a high point of French theatrical design during that period. Continuing to design for theatre and films, he nevertheless longed to become a director and finally realized his dream when he founded, along with Jean Dasté* and Maurice Jacquemont, the Théâtre des Quatre Saisons in 1936. In 1940, Dullin moved to a larger theatre and offered his famous Atelier to his former pupil; Barsacq accepted and continued to direct the prestigious Parisian private theatre until his death.

Barsacq the designer was particularly interested in the interplay of set and architecture. As a director, he is most often remembered as the one who launched the career of Jean Anouilh, directing eleven of Anouilh's early plays. Barsacq was constantly committed to the discovery and production of new playwrights, revealing to French audiences the first efforts of Marcel Aymé, Félicien Marceau, Françoise Sagan, Jean-Claude Carrière, Rémo Forlani, Ugo Betti, Friedrich Dürrenmatt, Bernard Kops, and David Mercer. He likewise paid homage to his Slavic roots, producing his own adaptations of *The Inspector General* (1948), Ostrovsky's *The Forest* (1970), *The Idiot* (1966), *Crime and Punishment* (1966), *A Month in the Country* (1963), and *The Flea* (1959).

Combining the tasks of producer, theatre manager, director, and designer, Barsacq was a total man of the theatre; but he saw his role primarily as that of facilitator, effacing himself without false modesty behind the work of the playwright and the actors. In that way, as in others, he was perhaps the true successor to Jacques Copeau* and the Cartel; he clung to eclecticism and shunned theatrical fads such as the absurdists of the fifties and the popular theatre movement of the sixties. He tried to revive the Cartel to protect private theatres such as his against the competition of television and state-subsidized theatres and, in the process, founded the Syndicat des Metteurs en scène and became its honorary president.

ADDITIONAL PRODUCTIONS: 1938: *Thieves' Carnival*; 1944: *Antigone* (Anouilh); 1947: *Ring Round the Moon*; 1949: *Le Pain dur* (Paul Claudel); 1950: *Traveler without Luggage*; 1952: *La Tête des autres* (Marcel Aymé); 1955: *The Sea Gull*; 1956: *L'Oeuf* (Marceau); 1958: *La Bonne Soupe* (Marceau); 1960: *Le Château en Suède* (Françoise Sagan).

SELECTED BIBLIOGRAPHY: Barsacq, André. "La Crise théâtrale et ses remèdes." *Théâtre Populaire* 52 (4th quarter 1963):8–13; Christout, Marie-Françoise. *André Barsacq: Cinquante ans de théâtre*. Paris: Bibliothèque Nationale, 1978; Simon, Alfred. *Dictionnaire du théâtre français contemporain*. Paris: Larousse, 1970.

                                                                          Dan M. Church

JOHN ADIE BERNARD BARTON [b. November 26, 1928, London, England]. At Eton in 1947, John Barton began his illustrious career as Shakespearean producer, director, and actor in *Henry IV, Part I*. His years at Cambridge, starting in 1948, afforded him a thorough apprenticeship in most areas of theatre-making. He was involved with dozens of plays there as producer, director, actor, playwright, and accountant for the Amateur Dramatic Company. Dominating the college's theatrical life as a student and as a don, he emphasized the need to raise acting and production standards, a goal he brought with him to the Royal Shakespeare Company (RSC).

When Cambridge classmate Peter Hall* became director of the RSC, he invited Barton to join the new company to teach Shakespearean verse and text. Thus, in 1960, Barton's long-standing association with the RSC began. He soon earned renown as one of Britain's foremost Shakespeare directors, and he also earned a reputation as dramaturg, adapter, playwright, and acting teacher. A scholar as well as a practitioner, his textual adaptation work, which included writing hundreds of lines of blank verse he interpolated into many of the texts, has become one stamp of a Barton production.

In 1963, Barton adapted the *Henry VI* plays and *Richard II* into a three-part epic, *The Wars of the Roses*, on which he collaborated with Peter Hall and whose 1965 BBC telecast he supervised. In 1964, he adapted *The Henriad*, which he co-directed with Hall and Clifford Williams.* His most massive undertaking was *The Greeks* (1980). He adapted and directed the ten-play epic in three parts, from nine Greek classical plays and one, *Achilles*, which he wrote. His 1974 *King John* amalgamated three plays and 600 original Barton lines. He justifies his adaptations by citing the theory of continuous copy—the Elizabethan practice of adjusting texts to specific performance needs.

An ironist, influenced by the Moscow Art Theatre's Chekhov productions in mid–1950s London, he seeks the dark side of comedy and the humorous side of tragedy. His *Love's Labour's Lost* (1965 and 1978), *Twelfth Night* (1969), and *All's Well That Ends Well* (1967) solidified his reputation as a director of Shakespeare's comedies. Presentational in his staging and naturalistic in his direction to actors, he is a lover of myth and ritual, as well as high theatricality. He uses ceremony liberally: six coronations in *King John*; a ceremony of monks robing, crowning, and uncrowning Richard II from a uniformly clad group of actors; hand and Bunraku puppets in *Dr. Faustus* (1973–74); giant hobbyhorses in *Richard II*; and bird-of-prey-like capes and masks are only a few devices he has used. A master of controversial moments, he had his Achilles (*Troilus and Cressida*, 1968) enter in drag, sporting a blond wig. His productions appear nonpolitical, though his agenda is clearly humanist. The best known characteristic of Barton's productions is the high quality of verse-speaking. His methods, which have contributed in large part to the RSC "style," are documented in his nine-part television series, "Playing Shakespeare," and his book of the same name. Created a Commander of the British Empire, he continues to write, direct, and teach.

ADDITIONAL PRODUCTIONS: 1960: *The Hollow Crown* (J. Barton); 1964: *The Henriad* (codirectors, Peter Hall and Clifford Williams); 1965: telecast, *The Wars of the Roses*; 1967: *The Peloponnesian Wars* (J. Barton), *Coriolanus*; 1970: *Measure for Measure*; 1971: *Richard II*, *Othello*; 1976: *The Winter's Tale* (codirector, Trevor Nunn*); 1977: *The Pillars of the Community* [Ibsen's *Pillars of Society*]; 1978: *The Merchant of Venice*; 1982: telecast of "Playing Shakespeare" (J. Barton); 1983: *The School for Scandal* (codirector, Peter Stevenson), *The Vikings* (adapted by J. Barton and Adrian Mitchell); 1985: *Dreamplay* [Strindberg's *A Dream Play*]; 1986: *The Rover* (Aphra Behn); 1988: *The Three Sisters*; 1990: *Peer Gynt* in Oslo; 1992: *As You Like It*, *Measure for Measure* in Oslo.

SELECTED BIBLIOGRAPHY: Barton, John. *Playing Shakespeare*. London: Methuen, 1984; Beauman, Sally. *The Royal Shakespeare Company: A History of Ten Decades*. Oxford: Oxford University Press, 1982; Greenwald, Michael L. *Directions by Indirections: John Barton of the Royal Shakespeare Company*. Newark: University of Delaware Press, 1985; Hubbard, Linda S., and Owen O'Donnell, eds. *Contemporary Theatre, Film and Television: A Continuation of Who's Who in the Theatre*. Vol. 6. Detroit: Gale Research, 1989; Wells, Stanley. *Royal Shakespeare: Four Major Productions at Stratford-upon-Avon*. Manchester: Manchester University Press, 1976.

Lila Wolff-Wilkinson

GASTON BATY [b.May 26, 1885, Pélussin, France; d. October 13, 1952, Pélussin, France]. Baty alone among the members of the Cartel was not an actor, but was instead an intellectual and a scholar of literature and art history. However, he became interested in the theatre at an early age and, during his student years and later while working for his father, traveled throughout Europe, using that opportunity to see many theatrical productions, particularly those of Fritz Erler, Georg Fuchs, and Max Reinhardt.* He visited Paris only rarely until he went there in 1919 to work with Firmin Gémier,* whom he had met in Lyon.

It was Gémier who took the young Baty under his wing and gave him the opportunity to direct his first plays at the Cirque d'Hiver and the Comédie-Montaigne. Baty soon formed his own acting company, La Chimère, using a succession of Parisian theatres (and even building his own makeshift house on the Boulevard St-Germain) before finding a home in 1924 in the tiny Studio des Champs-Elysées above the larger Comédie des Champs-Elysées shared by Louis Jouvet* and Georges Pitoëff.* He remained there until 1928, when he settled in the larger Théâtre Montparnasse (now Montparnasse-Gaston Baty), a house he occupied from 1930 until 1947. At that point, he abandoned the flesh-and-blood theatre for puppet theatre (a love of his since his youth in Lyon); but he was lured back during the last year of his life to found the state-subsidized Comédie de Provence.

More than any other French director of the period, Baty was a theoretician of the theatre. He published voluminously, primarily in the three periodicals (*La Chimère Bulletin d'art dramatique*, *Masques*, *Bulletin du Studio des Champs-Elysées*) that he founded, and in three books written at various points in his career. Despite the attacks of many critics, Baty remained remarkably constant in his controversial ideas; in fact, most of his theatrical credo is at least implicit in his 1921 article "Sire le Mot." There he claimed that renewal of theatre meant reclaiming it from "literature," which had stripped it of nonverbal means of expression that could, according to Baty, create a poetic world far beyond the capacities of words alone. Often called "escapist," Baty's theatre used nonrepresentational stage effects to create a poetic atmosphere of fantasy, supernatural, or even religious images. When he turned to puppets, it was because they were capable of attaining a level of nonrealistic expression beyond the reach of human actors.

Unfortunately, Baty found few French playwrights whose works corresponded to his ideas. The writers whose plays he directed—Jean-Victor Pellerin, Simon Gantillon, Jean-Jacques Bernard, and Marcelle Maurette—were only modestly successful at the time and are mostly forgotten today. His productions of meritorious foreign plays, *The Threepenny Opera* (1930), *Arms and the Man* (1921), *The Emperor Jones* (1923), and *The Dybbuk* (1928), garnered little critical acclaim. When he turned to the classics (e.g., the first version of *Hamlet*, *The Imaginary Invalid*, *Phédre*), his interpretations were almost invariably decried as betrayals. Among his most successful productions were his own adaptations of *Madame Bovary* (1936) and *Crime and Punishment* (1933).

ADDITIONAL PRODUCTIONS: 1920: *Le Simoun* (Henri-René Lenormand); 1921: *Martine* (Jean-Jacques Bernard); 1924: *Maya* (Simon Gantillon, revived in 1927); 1936: *Les Caprices de Marianne*: 1946: *Lorenzaccio*, *Bérénice*.

SELECTED BIBLIOGRAPHY: Baty, Gaston. *Le Masque et l'encensoir*. Paris: Bloud et Gay, 1926; Baty, Gaston. *Rideau baissé*. Paris: Bordas, 1949; Baty, Gaston, and René Chavance. *Vie de l'art théâtral des origines à nos jours*. Paris: Plon, 1932; Borgal, Clément. *Metteurs en scène*. Paris: Fernand Lanore, 1963; Simon, Arthur. *Gaston Baty, théoricien du théâtre*. Paris: Klincksieck, 1972; Whitton, David. *Stage Directors in Modern France*. Manchester: Manchester University Press, 1987.

                                                                              Dan M. Church

PINA BAUSCH [b. July 27, 1940, Solingen, Germany]. Bausch is one of the preeminent choreographers to emerge from postwar Germany, and a major dance-theatre proponent. She began her dance training in 1955 under the direction of Kurt Jooss at the Folkwang School in Essen. After graduating five years later she attended the Juilliard School of Music as a exchange student and was exposed to a variety of modern dance styles. She studied the technique of Martha Graham and Paul Taylor and performed with the Metropolitan Opera Ballet and with New American Ballet at the Spoleto Festival in 1961. On her return to Germany in 1962 she became a soloist in Kurt Jooss's newly formed Essen Folkwang Ballet, finally becoming director there in 1969.

By 1973 her work had received widespread recognition, and she assumed the directorship of the Wuppertal Tanztheatre (dance-theatre), formerly the Wuppertal Opera Ballet. The change in name reflected Bausch's revolutionizing of the traditional repertory from romantic ballets to aesthetically demanding dance-theatre works. Her unconventional productions, such as *Rite of Spring* (1975), which incorporated speech and pantomime, have been hailed as pioneering experiments in the dance-theatre movement of the 1980s. Along with other practitioners such as Suzanne Linke and Reinhild Hoffman, Bausch has attempted to experiment with the expressive potential of the body and blurred the traditional boundaries between theatre and dance. Bausch's performers are professionally trained dancers, who combine traditional dance movements with speaking, singing, and everyday gestures. Her productions typically contain elaborate props and sets (Rolf Borzik and Peter Pabst have been principal scene designers), and live musicians often form part of the onstage action.

Bausch's unconventional performance aesthetic has its roots in the traditions of German expressionistic dance, as well as American formalist dance of the 1960s. She has forged a distinctive style in which ritualized movements, repetitive gestures, and everyday movements are used to convey powerful emotional states, suggesting emotional conflicts, fears, and personal turmoil. Her dancers exhibit a range of human motion: they run, fall, hop, gesticulate, and bounce into one another. In a Pina Bausch dance-theatre piece, overlapping non-narrative movement sequences are strung together, creating a continuous, unrelenting series of arresting stage images. Bausch's technique suggests that physical behavior does not occur spontaneously; rather it is often cruelly controlled by external, social circumstances.

The mise-en-scène in Bausch's productions is specifically designed to incorporate the chaos and messiness of the outside world; in *Arien* (1979), for instance, six inches of water covers the stage, while in *Palermo, Palermo* (1990) a huge concrete wall tumbles down before the audience's eyes. A hallmark of Bausch's pieces is her use of Brechtian distancing effects, which prompt the audience to question its role as a spectator and consumer. In *Viktor* (1988) the performers are auctioned off to the audience like goods, while in *Kontakthof* a performer posing as photographer takes carefully composed pictures of the production, later offering them to the audience. Bausch continually attempts to break down the artificially created fourth wall between spectators and performers, as in the scene from *Kontakthof* (*Contacting Square*, 1978) where a row of dancers facing the audience talk into a tape recorder revealing private dreams and secrets.

Themes of alienation and angst permeate Bausch's work; she is fascinated, in particular, with the ways in which social roles and codes of behavior distort communication between women and men. Her use of repetitive images of degradation, even violence, suggests the inevitability of male-female relationships, as in *Cafe Müeller* (1978), where a somnambulant-like woman clings to her male partner, who repeatedly drops her to the floor. A controversial aspect of Bausch's work is its inherent nihilism, since her pieces suggest no alternatives to these damaging patterns of social interaction. But Bausch views her task as one of presenting dilemmas, rather than offering solutions. In a 1986 interview in the yearbook *Ballett*, quoted in *Dance Theatre Journal* (1988), Bausch says, "I only know that the time in which we live, the time with all its anxieties is very much with me. This is the source of my pieces."

ADDITIONAL PRODUCTIONS: 1976: *The Seven Deadly Sins*; 1977: *Bluebeard—while listening to a tape recording of Bela Bartok's opera "Duke Bluebeard's Castle," Komm, tanz mit mir (Come dance with me)*; 1979: *Legend of Chastity, Airs*; 1980: *1980—a piece by Pina Bausch*; 1982: *Carnations*; 1984: *Gebirge: Auf Dem Gebirge Hat Man Ein Geschrei Gehort (On the Mountain a Cry Was Heard)*.

SELECTED BIBLIOGRAPHY: Baxmann, Inge. "Dance Theatre: Rebellion of the Body, Theatre of Images, and an Inquiry into the Sense of the Senses." *ballett international* January 1990:55–60; Goldberg, Marianne. "Artifice and Authenticity: Gender Scenarios in Pina Bausch's Dance Theatre." *Women & Performance* 8 (1989): 104–17; Hoghe, Raimund. "The Theatre of Pina Bausch." *The Drama Review* 24 (March 1980):63–74; Langer, Roland. "Compulsion and Restraint, Love and Angst: The Post-War German Expressionism of Pina Bausch and Her Wuppertal Dance Theatre." *Dance Magazine* June 1984:46–48; Manning, Susan Allene. "The Feminine Mystique." *Ballet News* October 1985:11–17; Partsh-Bergsohn, Isa. "Dance Theatre from Rudolph Laban to Pina Bausch." *Dance Theatre Journal* 6 (Fall 1988): 37–39; Sikes, Richard. "But is it dance . . . ?" *Dance Magazine* June 1984: 50–53.

Julie Malnig

JULIAN BECK [b. May 31, 1925, New York, New York; d. September 14, 1985, New York, New York], and JUDITH MALINA [b. June 4, 1926, Kiel, Germany]. Judith Malina and Julian Beck started the Living Theatre in 1951 to express their political beliefs and to inspire audiences to effect societal change. Beck and Malina named their theatre the Living Theatre to symbolize the dynamic relationship between art and life they hoped to achieve.

The Living Theatre was an ensemble of theatre artists committed to the same artistic and political goals. Collectively organized, they lived and worked together, sharing responsibilities, accolades, and profits. They rejected the commercialism of mainstream theatre, its star system, and its emphasis on entertainment devoid of meaning. The Living Theatre's work focused upon actors and their ability to communicate ideas without elaborate productions or commercial considerations. Central to the goals of the Living Theatre was the creation of a vital actor-audience relationship. The company broke down the physical and emotional barriers between audience and actor, believing that involving audience members in the production would inspire them to effect political and social change outside of the theatre. To help achieve this audience involvement, the Living Theatre experimented with form, language, improvisation, and audience participation while promoting social awareness and anarchy.

The Living Theatre struggled for a number of years, passing the hat at performances and existing without publicity. In 1959, the company obtained critical recognition with a production of Jack Gelber's *The Connection*, which depicted a group of drug addicts and their relationship to their drug and to their pusher. In directing the production, Malina wanted the audience to viscerally experience the horrors of drug addiction. She directed the actors to treat the audience as pushers, to ask them for fixes and to enact overdoses in front of them. The audience was so affected by the production that on several occasions audience members fainted during the show. This was the kind of impact Malina and Beck sought. In presenting *The Connection*, the Living Theatre offered no moral judgments or practical solutions; rather, it provoked questions about the nature and cause of addiction to which the company hoped the audience would respond.

Malina, Beck, and company continued to produce innovative shows, such as *The Marrying Maiden* (1960), in which the arrangement of six scenes was determined each night by rolling dice. They achieved their biggest success in 1963 with *The Brig*, a play about a military prison, written by Kenneth Brown. As anarchists, Beck and Malina believed in revolution, but as pacifists they believed in the sanctity of life. In *The Brig*, they found a play that could express both of these ideas. *The Brig* demonstrated the brutality of guards in a military prison who attempt to rehabilitate the prisoners by dehumanizing them. Subject to random strip searches, physical abuse, and totally controlled behavior, from the pattern of their speech to the rhythm of their smoking, the prisoners became automatons. In directing the play, Malina again attempted to recreate reality insofar as was possible. She organized rehearsals, using rules similar to those in a brig, to create tension, and required that actors exchange roles (from guard to prisoner) every night, often switching during a performance. Following Antonin Artaud, Malina and Beck believed that the more the prisoners' pain was made tangible to the audience, the greater the chance the audience would demand change.

Despite the success of *The Brig*, the Living Theatre's financial troubles continued, and in 1963 the Internal Revenue Service demanded back taxes, which forced the closing of the theatre. The company moved to Paris, beginning a four and a half year period of exile. In Paris, the Living Theatre experimented with nonscripted, collaborative productions (such as *Mysteries and Smaller Pieces*, 1964) in which the actors helped to develop the material. Based on a series of acting exercises, *Mysteries* attempted to blur the distinction between acting and living, consequently, no costumes, sets, or lights were used. The Living Theatre's biggest success during this period was *Paradise Now* (1968), produced in Avignon, France.

Beck and Malina devised the initial concept—a map reveals the way to Paradise—and from this idea the company developed the production. *Paradise Now* suggested that paradise was in the reach of everyone who followed the map. Unlike *The Brig*, which depicted how violent behavior endangered life, *Paradise Now* involved the audience in discovering ways to improve life.

Paradise Now required direct audience participation. By interacting with the audience, by allowing them to decide the actions of the play, the company attempted to create real (as opposed to recreated) events. Again, the company's objective was the meaningful involvement of the audience in the issues. The audience would believe the events and be persuaded by the issues if they had helped to create them.

In 1968, the Living Theatre was invited to tour the United States. The company traveled throughout the country, performing the pieces they had developed in Europe. Following this tour, they performed in Brazil and then again in America. Whether producing scripted plays, such as *The Brig*, or developing company pieces, such as *Mysteries*, Beck and Malina and their company foregrounded their political beliefs, hoping to effect societal change.

ADDITIONAL PRODUCTIONS: 1951: *Childish Jokes* (Paul Goodman), *He Who Says Yes and He Who Says No*, *The Dialogue of the Mannequin and the Young Man* (Federico García Lorca), *Doctor Faustus Lights the Lights* (Gertrude Stein), *Beyond the Mountains* (Kenneth Rexroth), *An Evening of Bohemian Theatre*; 1952: *Ubu the King* (Alfred Jarry); 1954: *The Spook Sonata*, *The Idiot King*, *Orpheus* (Jean Cocteau); 1955: *Tonight We Improvise* (Luigi Pirandello), *Phèdre* (Jean Racine), *The Young Disciple* (Paul Goodman); 1959: *The Cave at Macpelah* (Paul Goodman); 1960: *The Women of Trachis* (Ezra Pound); 1961: *The Apple* (Jack Gelber); 1962: *Man Is Man*; 1963–68: *The Connection, Many Loves*; 1968–69: *Frankenstein, The Maids, Antigone*; 1970: *The Legacy of Cain, Plaza Project 1: Rituals and Transformations*; 1971: *School Project 1: A Critical Examination of Six Dreams about Mother*; 1972: *University Project 1: Seven Meditations of Political Sado-Masochism*; 1974: *Strike Support 1: Strike Support Ovatoium*; 1975: *Six Public Acts, The Money Tower*; 1978: *Prometheus*; 1980: *Masse Mensch*; 1982: *The Yellow Methuselah*; 1986: *The Living Theatre Retrospectacle*; 1988: *Poland 1931*.

SELECTED BIBLIOGRAPHY: Banham, Martin, ed. *The Cambridge Guide to World Theatre*. Cambridge: Cambridge University Press, 1988; Beck, Julian. *The Life of the Theatre*. San Francisco: City Lights Books, 1972; Biner, Pierre. *The Living Theatre*. New York: Avon Books, 1972; Malina, Judith. *The Diaries of Judith Malina: 1947–1957*. New York: Grove Press, 1984; Malina, Judith. *The Enormous Despair*. New York: Random House Books, 1972; Neff, Renfreu. *The Living Theatre: USA*. New York: Bobbs-Merrill Company, 1970; Roose-Evans, James. *Experimental Theatre: From Stanislavsky to Today*. New York: Avon Books, 1970.

Geraldine Maschio
Sullivan White

DAVID BELASCO [b. July 25, 1853, San Francisco, California; d. May 14, 1931, New York, New York]. Today the name of David Belasco and the phenomenon of American theatre naturalism in the early years of the present century are nearly synonymous. According to Lise-Lone Marker, "meticulous realism remained throughout his career the key to the inner reality of a play." While Belasco's pursuit of realistic effects was largely in the service of a dated melodramatic repertory, it led him into the vanguard of American theatrical technology and practice. Additionally, many of his productions were imbued with atmospheric effects which anticipated those of the seemingly antithetical New Stagecraft movement.

Only death could end a career that spanned sixty years of virtually uninterrupted activity. Stagestruck from childhood, in 1871 Belasco became an itinerant actor, playing in California and Nevada in the typical melodramas of the day, frequently in support of such old-style stars as Edwin Booth, James Murdoch, and Charlotte Cushman. He served as stage manager at Baldwin's Theatre in San Francisco from 1878 to 1882; then, he journeyed to New York, where he became a stage manager and dramatist with Steele MacKaye* and the Frohmans at the Madison Square Garden and the Lyceum theatres, a period that lasted until 1889. While at the Lyceum, he coauthored a successful series of contemporary dramas and staged a production of Sophocles' *Electra* (1888) for the American Academy of Dramatic Arts. He retained his association with the Frohmans until 1901. His first major independently produced and written hit was *The Heart of Maryland* (1895). In 1907, Belasco opened his own Belasco Theatre with *A Grand Army Man*, and for the next twenty-five years he worked in this extensively equipped and lavishly decorated house.

Well established early in his career, the Belasco style changed little over the years. A typical Belasco production offered a setting of the utmost realism, and his sets were frequently filled with a myriad of detail and embellishment. Surviving promptbooks contain pages of specifications for scenery, properties, and costumes. Belasco believed that painted or canvas objects would not suffice when the real items could be found or recreated. Well-known Belasco efforts in this vein include the genuine Japanese furniture imported for *The Darling of the Gods* (1902) and the completely recreated Child's Restaurant for *The Governor's Lady* (1912). Belasco defended his scenic practices, maintaining that a "correct setting" assisted actors in sustaining the illusions which must live in their imaginations.

For all his scrupulous attention to realistic detail, Belasco's productions were also highly atmospheric. His naturalism was closely connected to an appreciation for nature as it was manifested in the romantic and melodramatic repertory popular during his youth and which he favored as a producer. His ability to create atmospheric effects was due to his interest in the use of light on the stage. Belasco and Louis Hartmann, his lighting designer of many years, developed the first incandescent spotlights and experimented with indirectly focused light, projected images, and complex changes. Belasco claimed that his own *Madame*

Butterfly (1900) was "the first play to develop electricity in its use for stage effects, from the merely practical to the picturesque and poetical" (*New York Herald*, 3 January 1903). It was not unusual for Belasco and Hartmann to spend months preparing effects for a single show in a laboratory which they maintained for this purpose, and to rehearse these effects with a cast for weeks. "A typical Belasco sunset" was one legacy of these experiments, as the sunrise at the finale of his *The Girl of the Golden West* (1905) dramatically exhibited.

Due to the nature of his repertory and his love of strong acting, Belasco's theatre was organized around star performers in pivotal roles. Of a long and distinguished list of star players, mention here of only two must suffice. The "tigerish" Mrs. Leslie Carter was a sensation in *The Heart of Maryland* and *Du Barry* (1901), both written for her by Belasco. For his Shylock in Belasco's only venture into Shakespeare (1922), David Warfield drew the praise of Konstantin Stanislavsky.* Earlier Warfield vehicles included *The Auctioneer* (1901) and *The Return of Peter Grimm* (1911). Although autocratic, Belasco was sensitive to the needs and suggestions of his stars. Unwilling to settle for slavish or mechanical imitation, Belasco encouraged his actors to develop their own unique performances.

Belasco granted many interviews, wrote essays and a full-length memoir, and made detailed promptscripts which have been preserved. He adopted theatrical personal habits, including the wearing of a white turned collar which led to his well-known appellation as "The Bishop of Broadway." Although Belasco was always popular with his audiences, the response to his work by critics and professionals varied according to their perspectives.

ADDITIONAL PRODUCTIONS: 1903: *Sweet Kitty Bellairs* with Henrietta Crosman (Belasco); 1908: *The Fighting Hope* with Blanche Bates (William J. Hurlbut); 1909: *The Easiest Way* with Frances Starr (Eugene Walter); 1911: *The Woman* (William C. de Mille); 1917: *Polly with a Past* with Ina Clair (George Middleton and Guy Bolton); 1926: *Lulu Belle* with Lenore Ulric (Edward Sheldon and Charles MacArthur); 1928: *Mima*.

SELECTED BIBLIOGRAPHY: Belasco, David. *The Theatre through Its Stage Door*. New York: Harper and Row, 1919; Leiter, Samuel L. *From Belasco to Brook: Representative Directors of the English-Speaking Stage*. Westport, CT: Greenwood Press, 1991: 1–22; Marker, Lise-Lone. *David Belasco: Naturalism in the American Theatre*. Princeton, NJ: Princeton University Press, 1975; Timberlake, Craig. *The Life and Work of David Belasco*. New York: Library Publishers, 1954; Winter, William. *The Life of David Belasco*. New York: Moffat, Yard and Company, 1918.

Maarten A. Reilingh

CARMELO BENE [b. September 1, 1937, Campi Salentini, near Lecce, Italy]. Producer, director, author, and actor, this flamboyant figure is known as "The Transgressor," the *enfant terrible* who single-handedly shook postwar Italian theatre out of its comfortable lethargy and thrust it into the era of the avant-garde. He has also been called the Italian Kean of the 1960s and 1970s for his unorthodox behavior, both on and off stage.

The son of the owner of a tobacco factory, Bene discovered at an early age that he possessed a beautiful tenor voice, and consequently began to study singing. Incessant smoking, however, soon ruined his vocal cords. After leaving the provinces, he enrolled at the University of Rome as a law student while, at the same time, he frequented the Academy of Dramatic Art, where he became obsessed with Albert Camus's drama *Caligula*. Learning that Camus was stopping in Venice, Bene went there and managed to meet him. Impressed by the singular personality of the youth, Camus granted him the rights to present his play in Italy. Bene made his acting debut as Caligula at the Teatro delle Arti in Rome in 1959 to great critical and public acclaim.

Since Italy had no Ionescos nor Becketts, theatre at that time consisted mainly of respectful revivals of Luigi Pirandello,* Gabriele D'Annunzio, and Carlo Goldoni, together with translations of current French and American successes. Bene proceeded to present a series of provocative, often shocking productions of classics from the repertoire heretofore regarded as sacrosanct. He was called a charlatan and an exhibitionist by some, a genius by others; but his productions became the most talked-about in Italy.

In 1962, Bene opened a small basement theatre in the Trastevere quarter of Rome, where he presented a version of *Pinocchio* in a "phallic key" (1962), *Hamlet* (1962), Christopher Marlowe's *Edward II* (1963), *Salomé* (1963), *Manon* (1965), his own *Nostra Signora dei Turchi (Our Lady of the Turks*, 1966), and *Don Quixote* (1968). During one infamous production, he urinated on the spectators in the front row, while on another occasion, irritated at an unresponsive audience, he had all the exits to the theatre locked, while he himself left.

In Bene's version of *Macbeth* (1984), all of Shakespeare's precisely described locations were swept aside, and the tale unfolded in an enormous vacuum, in no specific space or time. Lines were altered or excised, and the witches were eliminated, as were Malcolm, Donalbain, and most of the minor characters. In the "Is this a dagger which I see before me" speech, Macbeth held the knife, not on high, but between his legs, caressing it while delivering the soliloquy.

Bene was named director of the theatre division of the Venice Festival, a post which he held until 1990. Time and official recognition seem to have mellowed him to a degree, and today he is regarded as a less controversial figure, almost as a member of "the establishment."

Bene is also a filmmaker. He made his movie debut in 1967 in the role of Creon in Pasolini's *Oedipus Rex*, and since then, he has continued to be active in both films and theatre, often making film versions of his stage productions. His tour de force version of Manzoni's drama *Adelchi*, done in 1984 as an oratorio, was subsequently presented on Italian television.

ADDITIONAL PRODUCTIONS: **Theatre** (director and actor): 1961: *Dottor Jekyll* (Stevenson/Bene); 1964: *La Storia di Sawney Bean* (Roberto Lerici); 1966: *Il rosa e il nero* (adapted from *The Monk* by M. G. Lewis); 1974: *S.A.D.E.* (Bene); 1980: *Manfred* (Lord Byron, music by Robert Schumann); 1983: Readings from Hölderlein and Leopardi; 1984: *Egmont* (Goethe/Beethoven); 1986: *Faust o Margherita* (Bene and Franco Cuomo), *Hyperion* (Friedrich Hölderlein/Bene), *Otello* (Shakespeare/Bene), *Lorenzaccio* (Alfred de

Musset/Bene); 1987: *Hommelette for Hamlet* (Bene adaptation). **Films:** (Director and actor): 1968: *Nostra Signora dei Turchi*; 1969: *Capricci*; 1970: *Don Giovanni*; 1971: *Necropoli*; 1972: *Salomé*; 1973: *Un Amleto di meno (One Hamlet Less)*; 1983: *Mi presero gli occhi (They Took My Eyes)*; 1984: *Adelchi*; 1988: *La cena delle beffe (The Jest*, Sem Benelli); 1989: *Achilleide Omerica Postomerica Kleistiana, Tamerlano il Grande* (Christopher Marlowe).
SELECTED BIBLIOGRAPHY: Bartalotta, Gianfranco. "L'Amleto di Carmelo Bene." *Teatro contemporaneo* Feb.-May 1983: 361–92; Cardone, Salvatore. "La regia negata: Carmelo Bene (1959–1968)." *Rivista Italiana di Drammaturgia (RIDD)* September 1980: 57–94; Gedda, Lido. *La scena spogliata. Scritti sul teatro italiano del riflusso.* Torino: Tirrenia Stampatori, 1985; Grande, Maurizio. *La riscossa di Lucifero. Ideologie e prassi del teatro di sperimentazione in Italia (1976–1984).* Roma: Bulzoni Editore, 1985; Tessari, Roberto. *Pinocchio: Summa atheologica di Carmelo Bene.* Firenze: Liberoscambio, 1982.

Robert Connolly

SIMONE BENMUSSA [b. July 10, 1938, Tunis, Tunisia]. Graduating from the Sorbonne with a degree in aesthetics, Simone Benmussa ardently desired a chance to effect how culture creates meaning. She began working for Jean-Louis Barrault* and Madeleine Renaud in 1959 as editor of their journal, *Les Cahiers Renaud-Barrault*, curator of exhibitions, and all-around impresario. While the Renaud-Barrault enterprise, which produced almost all of her plays, still provides a home base, from 1976 on Benmussa has also established her artistic independence, directing, adapting, and designing some twenty productions, as well as inventing an original form of theatrical experience within museum spaces.

Her first major production, Hélène Cixous's *Portrait of Dora* (1976), evinced the characteristics which have marked all her directing efforts: the creation of a *dream space* in which characters emerge as though out of touch with reality, and the ability to engage the public in this space through a refined scenography. *The Singular Life of Albert Nobbs* (1979), her first adaptation, confirmed her vocation to transform slightly offbeat, slippery, and nondramatic texts into theatre pieces in which she could, through voice-overs, scenic commentaries, and ethereal acting, suggest the gaps between what passes for "real" and the reality of mindscapes.

Like *Dora, Albert Nobbs*, by making felt the difference between women's reality and the way reality is framed and interpreted by men (the narrator in the first instance; Freud in the second), also situated Benmussa at the forefront of theatre artists able to create forms which challenge accepted perceptions of gender. Benmussa's 1990 treatment of Goffredo Parise's *L'Absolu naturel* likewise corrosively undercut Parise's misogyny by portraying his victimized hero as silly.

Benmussa brought women's oppression to life in the first of her successful theatricalized spaces. In *La Traversée du temps perdu* (1978), as spectators wound their way among the objects of a nineteenth-century bourgeois residence, offstage voices of unmarried daughters, deprived of a personal life in order to keep family economics running smoothly, commented lucidly on their loss. Their "real" was thus contrasted with the materiality that enclosed them in a system of meaning which made sense by sacrificing them.

The intimacy and delicacy of Benmussa's work align her with another contemporary director, Claude Régy. Both particularly enjoy staging Nathalie Sarraute's pieces. Benmussa's productions of Sarraute's *For No Good Reason* (1985) and *Childhood* (1984) allowed her to practice what for her has become a theatrical necessity: keeping alive the circulating shadows.

ADDITIONAL PRODUCTIONS: 1976: *Portrait of Dora* with films by Marguerite Duras; 1977: *The Singular Life of Albert Nobbs* (adaptation of George Moore) with Susannah York (1978), Glenn Close (1982); 1979: *Apparences* (adaptation of Henry James); 1981: *Virginia* (adaptation of Edna O'Brien) with Catherine Sellers; 1983: *Freshwater* (Woolf); 1984: *The Human Voice* (Cocteau) with Susannah York; 1989: *Michelet ou le Don des larmes* (adaptation by E. de Fontenay).

SELECTED BIBLIOGRAPHY: Benmussa, Simone. *Benmussa Directs: Portrait of Dora, The Singular Life of Albert Nobbs.* New York: John Calder, 1978; Case, Sue-Ellen. *Feminism and Theater.* New York: Methuen, 1988; Diamond, Elin. *Feminist Stagings: Unmasking Mimesis.* London: Routledge, 1993; Diamond, Elin. "Refusing the Romanticism of Identity: Narrative Interventions in Churchill, Benmussa, Duras," *Theatre Journal* 27 (October 1985): 273–86; Julian, Ria. "Julia Foster and Susannah York in *The Singular Life of Albert Nobbs.*" *Plays and Players* August 1978:19–22; Lamont, Rosette. "Probing the Drama of the Commonplace." *New York Times* 26 May 1985: 5, 16; Temkine. Raymonde. *Le Théâtre au present.* Paris: Bouffoneries/Contrastes, 1987.

Judith G. Miller

MICHAEL BENNETT [b. Michael Bennett DiFiglia, April 8, 1943, Buffalo, New York; d. July 2, 1987, Tucson, Arizona]. Knowing that dance and theatre would be his life, Michael Bennett made a decision in 1960 to play the role of Baby John in the European tour of *West Side Story* rather than finish high school. This experience provided him the opportunity to observe the process of director-choreographer Jerome Robbins,* the man that Bennett would choose to emulate, and to meet performer Robert Avian, who would become his lifelong friend and collaborator. Between 1962 and 1966 Bennett performed and choreographed for musical theatre and staged dances for television.

Bennett won instant recognition when his first two choreographic efforts on Broadway earned him Tony Award nominations, even though *A Joyful Noise* (1966) closed after only twelve performances, and *Henry, Sweet Henry* (1967) closed after eighty. Because of his extraordinary talent for seeing the whole picture of a production, he was often called to fix shows that were in trouble and he soon earned the reputation of "show doctor." He was regarded as a concept artist rather than the inventor of steps, and his signature can be found in the integration of theatrical elements, the seamless tying together of scenes, and the use of the individuality of the performers, especially chorus members.

Bennett began perfecting this process while staging *Promises, Promises* (1968), *Company* (1970), and *Follies* (1971), and soon redefined the formula for the American musical. He was a perfectionist who relentlessly pursued the realization of his creative concepts, and as he began seeking more artistic control over projects, he created numerous love-hate relationships with performers and collaborators.

Bennett's use of the ensemble brought a new public appreciation of chorus gypsies. He himself started as a Broadway gypsy, and he believed that gypsies should be challenged to become actors who, through singing and dancing, play a role in the balance of the production and the progression of the plot. Thus, he often approached his staging through characterization, rather than choreography.

In 1974, several dancers asked to meet at Bennett's rehearsal space to discuss the state of theatre, their lives, dreams, and frustrations. This gathering, and a subsequent session (which were both taped), became the seed of the idea for *A Chorus Line*. The *Chorus Line* project, which dealt with a subject dear to Bennett, set a new precedent in the development of a musical. Rather than a standard Broadway scenario, which routinely began with the scripting of book and music, and progressed through auditions, a five-week rehearsal period, out-of-town tryouts or New York previews, and the Broadway opening, *A Chorus Line* (as it would later be named) was developed through a series of workshops held at the Public Theatre and supported by Joseph Papp's New York Shakespeare Festival. Within this workshop environment, Bennett had no pressure from financial backers and was afforded the luxury of creative time with performers and collaborators. The show had its first public preview in April of 1975, and then moved to Broadway's Shubert Theatre that same year where it played until March 1990, making it (at this writing) the longest running show in Broadway history. The universal appeal of this backstage story can be found in the essence of each character's struggle as he or she places his talent and life "on the line." The professional world honored the show with the New York Drama Critics Circle Award, the Tony Award, the Pulitzer Prize, and a special award to Bennett from *Dance Magazine* for his outstanding contributions.

Bennett's next productions, *Ballroom* (1979) and *Dreamgirls* (1981), failed to achieve the success of *A Chorus Line*, but were nonetheless vehicles for Bennett's talents. Bennett liked to visually tie things together and often employed the same devices used in film to achieve his theatrical staging. Collaborating with the same production team which created *A Chorus Line* (set designer Robin Wagner and lighting designer Tharon Musser), Bennett developed *Dreamgirls* into a technical wonder. The sets and lights were choreographed as carefully as the dances and, consequently, became dramatic forces essential to the telling of the story.

Between 1983 and 1987, Bennett was involved with projects that he would ultimately abandon, and more of his time was required to fight the AIDS virus which eventually took his life.

ADDITIONAL PRODUCTIONS: 1969: *Coco* (choreographer); 1971: *Twigs*; 1973: *Seesaw*; 1971: *God's Favorite*.

SELECTED BIBLIOGRAPHY: Challender, James Winston. "The Function of the Choreographer in the Development of the Conceptual Musical: An Examination of the Work of Jerome Robbins, Bob Fosse, and Michael Bennett on Broadway between 1944 and 1981." Diss. Florida State U, 1986; Flinn, Denny Martin. *What They Did for Love: The Untold Story behind the Making of "A Chorus Line."* New York: Bantam Books, 1989; Gerard, J. "Michael Bennett and Broadway." *Times Biographical Service* 17 (November 1986): 1313–15; Kelly, Kevin. *One Singular Sensation: The Michael Bennett Story.* New York: Doubleday, 1990; Mandelbaum, Ken. *"A Chorus Line" and the Musicals of Michael Bennett.* New York: St. Martin's Press, 1989; Viagas, Robert, Thommie Walsh, and Baayork Lee. *On the Line: The Creation of "A Chorus Line."* New York: William Morrow, 1990.

Colleen Kelly

INGMAR BERGMAN [b. July 14, 1918, Stockholm, Sweden]. Bergman began directing when, as a student at the Royal Dramatic Theatre (Dramaten), he staged plays (principally Shakespeare and Strindberg) with fellow students. In 1943 he attracted national recognition when he directed the pacifistic *U39* by Rudolf Värnlund and the resistance drama *Niels Ebbesen* by Kaj Munk at the Swedish Playwrights Studio. The major influences upon Bergman, early in his career, were Olof Molander* and Alf Sjöberg,* leading directors at the Dramaten during the 1930s.

Bergman's professional career began in 1944 when he was appointed head of the Municipal Theatre of Helsingborg, which he transformed into "the unquiet corner of the town." There, he gathered a company of young, talented actors and during two seasons directed nine productions (including an outspoken, anti-Nazi *Macbeth*) and stressed contemporary Swedish plays like the bitter romantic comedy *The Saga* (Hjalmar Bergman) and the furious misanthropical *Rabies* taken from an Olle Hedberg novel.

At the City Theatre of Göteberg, which was better equipped than Helsingborg and where the manager, Torsten Hammarén, taught him to organize his work, Bergman staged a resoundingly successful *Caligula* and was much praised for his rhythmic, atmospheric interpretation of *A Streetcar Named Desire* (1949). At roughly the same time, he began staging his own plays, "modern moralities" like *Rachel and the Cinema Doorman* (1946), *Early Days* and *To My Terror* (1947), *The Murder at Barjärna* (1952), and *Painting on Wood* (1955), from which *The Seventh Seal* was derived. Shortly thereafter, following his writing of the screenplay for Sjöberg's film *Torment*, Bergman began making his own films and virtually ceased writing stage plays, claiming that particular kind of creativity had been incorporated in his filmmaking.

Bergman's most productive period occurred while he was at the Malmö Theatre, a "people's theatre" equipped with a 1700-seat auditorium and a vast stage which Bergman reputedly used better than anyone before or after him. Playing on the tension between the large stage space and the relative intimacy of the forestage, Bergman, in productions like August Strindberg's *The Crown Bride*

(1952) and *The Ghost Sonata* (1954), created a "great rhythm" between vastness and isolation and concentrated closeups. At Malmö, Bergman experimented with dynamic movements created in relation to "the magic point"—the point in a theatre from which an actor is "best seen and heard"—in Strindberg's historical *Erik XIV* (1956), *Peer Gynt* (1957), and *Ur-Faust* (1958), the latter two featuring Max von Sydow. Bergman's greatest triumph at Malmö, however, was *The Misanthrope*, staged as an intimate psychological duel between von Sydow's energetic but disgusted idealist and the sensuous, seductive Celimène of Gertrud Fridh.

Of equal significance, Bergman began working regularly with an ensemble composed of some of the best actors in Sweden including von Sydow, Benkt-Åke Benktsson, Naima Wifstrand, Ingrid Thulin, and Bibi Andersson, all of whom had worked in Bergman's films. Working within this ensemble, Bergman established himself as an actor's director. His work was characterized by his capacity for listening, feeling, and serving as a form of radar, capable of sensing whether an actor felt secure, tense, or unhappy.

Bergman repeated his success at Malmö in his later work, much of it devoted to four playwrights: Molière, Ibsen, Strindberg, and Shakespeare. In his first Molière, *Don Juan* (1955), Bergman stunningly unmasked the great seducer, as the audience was made to look at him through his valet Sganarelle. Equally impressive were Bergman's *Hedda Gabler* (Stockholm, 1966), in which his exploitation and exploration of Ibsen's dramaturgical mechanisms threw new light on the classic, and his interpretation of *The Wild Duck* (Stockholm, 1972), where he manipulated the setting so that the attic, the place of fantasies and the play's tragic culmination, seemed to be situated in the audience. Ibsen was also represented in what many regard as Bergman's most ambitious project: in Munich in 1981, he staged three parallel productions on the same evening—*A Doll's House*, *Miss Julie*, and a stage version of his own television play, *Scenes from a Marriage*.

Throughout his career, Bergman has also remained devoted to Strindberg, staging *A Ghost Sonata* on several occasions, *To Damascus* parts 1 and 2, and four versions of *A Dream Play* (for television, 1963; Stockholm, 1970 and 1986; Munich, 1977), in which he explored the nature of the poetic dream sequences and ways of abstracting settings.

More recently, Bergman has been attracted to Shakespeare's dramaturgy. Following his return to Sweden after an eight-year exile in Munich, Bergman staged *King Lear* and *Hamlet*, both noted for their reduction of scenery, superb lighting, choreographic movements, and fluent changes of scene which created a great dramatic rhythm.

A deeply musical director, Bergman has staged *The Merry Widow* (1954), and in 1961, he directed Stravinsky's *The Rake's Progress* in a stylish, demonic performance at the Royal Opera in Stockholm. His television version of *The Magic Flute* (1975) has been an international success. He collaborated with composer Daniel Börtz on an opera based upon Euripides' *Bacchae*, which had its first performance in Stockholm in 1991.

ADDITIONAL PRODUCTIONS: 1944: *Jacobowsky and the Colonel*; 1945: *The Pelican* (Strindberg); 1951: *The Rose Tattoo*; 1953: *The Castle* (Kafka), *Six Characters in Search of an Author* (also 1967); 1956: *Cat on a Hot Tin Roof*; 1961: *The Sea Gull*; 1963: *Who's Afraid of Virginia Woolf?*; 1965: *Tiny Alice*; 1966: *The Investigation*; 1969: *Woyzeck*; 1973: *The Misanthrope*; 1978:*The Three Sisters*; 1979: *Tartuffe*; 1982:*The Master Builder*; 1984: *John Gabriel Borkman*; 1985: *Miss Julie*; 1989: *Long Day's Journey into Night*, *The Marquis de Sade* (Yukio Mishima).

SELECTED BIBLIOGRAPHY: Marker, Lise-Lone, and Frederick Marker. *Ingmar Bergman: Four Decades in the Theatre*. Cambridge: Cambridge University Press, 1982; Sjögren, Henrik. *Ingmar Bergman på Teatern*. Stockholm: Almqvist and Wiksell, 1968; Sjögren, Henrik. *Regi: Ingmar Bergman*. Stockholm: Almqvist and Wiksell, 1969; Sjögren, Henrik. *Stage and Society in Sweden*. Stockholm: The Swedish Institute, 1979.

Henrik Sjögren

BJØRN BJØRNSON [b. November 15, 1859, Christiania, Norway; d. April 14, 1942]. The son of playwright Bjørnstjerne Bjørnson, Bjørn Bjørnson is best known as the founder of the Norwegian National Theatre. After studying in Europe with such teachers as Anton Bruckner, Max Streben, Tommaso Salvini, and Heinrich Laube, in 1880 Bjørnson became a member of the acting company of Georg II, Duke of Saxe-Meiningen.* From 1884 to 1893, Bjørnson served as artistic director of the Christiania Theatre in Norway. Bjørnson brought many of the Meininger innovations with him, including scenic realism, effective crowd scenes, and a less declamatory approach to acting. He also introduced and developed a number of younger Norwegian actors, including Johanne Dybwad,* Egil Eide, and Halfdan Christensen.

Bjørnson actively campaigned for the establishment of a Norwegian National Theatre, and was involved with the design of the theatre complex. He served as its first artistic director from 1899 to 1907. The first years of the National Theatre were the years of his greatest achievements. Ibsen's *An Enemy of the People* (1899), *Peer Gynt* (1902), and *Brand* (1904), and Bjørnstjerne Bjørnson's *Beyond Our Powers I* (1899) and *Paul Lange and Tore Parsberg* (1902) were among the more important productions. Later, he also directed in Denmark, Sweden, and Germany. From 1923 to 1927, he again served as artistic director at the National Theatre, although less successfully than before.

Bjørnson's directing was known for its emotional simplicity and directness, as he led the theatre toward realism. He frequently acted in his own productions and, in rehearsal, was known to insist that actors copy his line readings. He also instilled a Meininger-like discipline, with a system of fines for missing rehearsals. His energy and good humor were his greatest assets as a theatre administrator, enabling him to overcome occasional deficiencies in judgment and organization. Although at times his work was criticized as superficial and unfelt, his productions were filled with a characteristic movement, color, and vitality. He was a particularly effective director of Shakespeare, Ibsen, and the plays of his father, Bjørnstjerne Bjørnson.

ADDITIONAL PRODUCTIONS: 1884: *Richard III*, *The Wild Duck*; 1887: *Rosmersholm* with August Lindberg; 1892: *Peer Gynt*; 1900: *Aunt Ulrikke* (Gunnar Heiberg), *Ghosts*; 1901: *Cyrano de Bergerac*; 1902: *Emperor and Galilean I*; 1903: *A Midsummer Night's Dream*; 1904: *Mary Stuart in Scotland* (Bjørnstjerne Bjørnson); 1907: *Oedipus Rex*; 1919: *Danton's Death*.

SELECTED BIBLIOGRAPHY: Bjørnson, Bjørn. *Det Gamle Teater*. Oslo: Gylendal, 1937; Erbe, Berit. *Bjørn Bjørnson's vej mod realismens teater*. Nordisk Institutt, Universitet i Bergen, 1973; Jynge, Andreas. *Ibsen's Brand paa Nationaltheatret i Kristiania*. Kristiania 5th., 1904; Rønneberg, Anton. *Nationaltheatret qjennom femti år*. Oslo: Gylendal, 1949; Waal, Carla. "Johanne Dybwad, Norwegian Actress." Diss. Indiana U, 1964.

Eric Samuelsen

ROGER BLIN [b. March 22, 1907, Neuilly-sur-Seine, France; d. January 20, 1984, Paris, France]. Roger Blin, arguably the most important director in the theatre of the avant-garde, discovered and introduced the dramatic work of Samuel Beckett and directed major plays by Jean Genet. Blin's productions of Beckett include *Waiting for Godot*, with Jean Martin, Lucien Raimbourg, and Pierre Latour (1953); *Endgame* (1957); *Krapp's Last Tape*, with R. M. Chauffard (1960); and *Happy Days*, with Madeleine Renaud (1963). He revealed Genet's mature theatrical work in definitive stagings of *The Blacks* (1959) and *The Screens* with Maria Casarès (1966). Though Blin made his mark in large part through his directing, he overcame a stutter to work first and extensively throughout his career as an actor. He created such memorable stage roles as Pozzo in *Waiting for Godot* and Hamm in *Endgame*, and played over one hundred parts in film and television productions.

As his work with Beckett and Genet indicates, Blin's principal contribution to the theatre was his searching out and cultivating unknown and unusual authors, actors, and designers, and presenting these artists to the public. While a humanities student at the Sorbonne, he associated himself with anti-establishment figures in Paris, befriending Antonin Artaud and Jean-Louis Barrault* and working with the experimental theatre company, "le groupe Octobre." Blin began directing in 1949. His production of *La Parodie* in 1952 was one of the first stagings of Adamov's work, judged "difficult" in the context of Anouilh, Salacrou, and the "théâtre de boulevard" to which audiences were accustomed.

Blin's ability to translate onstage both the asceticism of Beckett and the baroque qualities of Genet manifested itself in landmark productions during the fifties and sixties. His production of *Waiting for Godot* in 1953 was the first real success of avant-garde theatre. With Blin's staging of *Happy Days* three years later, Beckett's popularity hit a new high, due in part to the acclaimed performance of Madeleine Renaud. During the same period, Blin instructed a group of young black drama students and directed them in Genet's *The Blacks* (1959). His production of *The Screens* (1966), which criticized French colonialism when the country had just lost its war with Algeria, created a scandal in Paris.

With his staging of *Waiting for Godot*, Blin had formed a directing style that would continue for the rest of his career. According to his biographer, Odette Aslan, he considered himself the intermediary between contemporary scripts and their audience, rather than a creator of highly personalized productions. When directing, Blin never wrote down ideas before meeting with the designers and actors. A practitioner of "théâtre pauvre," he believed that actors could create an appropriate atmosphere under any conditions. Blin worked closely with designers—often with André Acquart and with Matias—in conceiving minimal sets, lighting, and costumes, and he routinely participated in their construction. Continuously onstage during rehearsals, he showed how a part might be played, gave suggestions, and listened. This directing style necessitated working with actors who could react to and, if necessary, contest his viewpoint.

After the mid-1960s, Blin continued his work of discovering and revealing new talents, directing and helping to polish scripts by young foreign writers. These works included *Les Charognards* (*The Carrion Eaters*, 1968) by American author Roman Weingarten and *Les Nonnes* (*The Nuns*, 1969) by the Cuban Edouardo Manet. Although, as Aslan points out, Blin was not a producer of "théâtre engagé," he did choose to direct certain plays with politically provocative themes, such as the Weingarten work, Fugard's *Boesman et Lena* (1976), and Osamu Takahashi's *Minimata and Company* (1978). These plays were balanced by works of a more universal, Beckettian character, including plays by Sławomir Mrożek, François Billetdoux, and Carlos Semprun Maura.

ADDITIONAL PRODUCTIONS: 1961: *The Blacks* in English, London; 1967: *The Screens* in German, Essen; 1971: *La Nuit des Assassins* (*The Night of the Assassins*, José Triana); 1972: *Macbeth*; 1974: *Les Emigrés* (Sławomir Mrożek); 1975: *A Dream Play*; 1979: *M'appelle Isabelle Langrenier* (I'm Called Isabelle Langrenier, Jean-Louis Bauer); 1980: *Ai-je dit que je suis bossu?* (*Did I say I was hunchbacked?*, François Billetdoux); 1981: *Le Président* (Thomas Bernhard), *Le Bleu de l'eau-de-vie* (*The Blue of the Brandy*, Carlos Semprun Maura); 1983: *Triptyque* (Max Frisch). A number of revivals of *Godot* and of *Endgame, Krapp's Last Tape*, and *Happy Days*.

SELECTED BIBLIOGRAPHY: Aslan, Odette. "Genet, His Actors and His Directors." *Genet: A Collection of Critical Essays*. Ed. Peter Brooks and Joseph Halpern. Englewood Cliffs, NJ: Prentice-Hall, 1979; Aslan, Odette. *Roger Blin and Twentieth-Century Playwrights*. Trans. Ruby Cohn. Cambridge, England: Cambridge University Press, 1988; Fletcher, John. "Roger Blin at Work." *Casebook on "Waiting for Godot."* Ed. Ruby Cohn. New York: Grove Press, 1967: 21–26; Genet, Jean. *Les Nègres*. Isère: Marc Barbazat, 1963; Genet, Jean. *Lettres à Roger Blin*. Paris: Gallimard, 1966; *Reflections on the Theatre, and Other Writings*. Trans. Richard Seaver. London: Faber, 1972; Knapp, Bettina. "An Interview with Roger Blin." *Tulane Drama Review* 7 (Spring 1963): 111–25.

Cynthia Running-Johnson

WILLIAM EDVARD BLOCH [b. March 30, 1845, Copenhagen Denmark; d. November 1, 1926, Copenhagen, Denmark]. In 1881, after working as a fire insurance clerk and a spare-time writer of comedies, Bloch was appointed stage director at the Royal Theatre in Copenhagen. There, between 1881 and 1893, and again between 1899 and 1909, Block reformed Danish staging by introducing a coherent system of naturalistic acting and directing. His productions of plays by Henrik Ibsen and Ludvig Holberg were epoch-making.

Bloch, the playwright, was influenced by contemporary French drama and soon evolved into Bloch, the director. In Bloch's theatre, the artistic task of the director began where the task of the author ended. The stage, in his opinion, should never be strictly a mirror of life, but rather an "indirect revelation" created through an ever-changing interplay of outer and inner reality, tuned like a piece of music. Consequently, the style of his productions often came closer to impressionism than to strict naturalism.

In his preparation, Bloch nevertheless treated every detail as important to the organic totality of the performance, staging his productions with the precision of a scientist. He supervised rehearsals from a desk placed stage left, and increased the number of rehearsals from the eight or ten common earlier to an average of twenty-five. Every character, however small, had a life story of its own; and every action, however minute, had a clear psychological motivation. Bloch always respected the personal interpretation of the actor, provided it was based on authentic feeling.

Between 1881 and 1893, Bloch established himself as the leading modern director in Denmark with his stagings of contemporary plays, especially those of Ibsen. In his creation of lifelike atmosphere, Bloch was perhaps the most compatible (of Ibsen's contemporaries) with Ibsen's realistic and naturalistic plays. For *The Wild Duck* (1885), Bloch recreated a photographer's studio in detail, and his renowned direction of *An Enemy of the People* (1883) reflected Ibsen's demands for detailed direction. The crowd scene alone was a meticulous mosaic of coordinated, individualized actions and utterances, orchestrated in a musical sweep. The performance was hailed as a model of naturalistic staging, prompting Aurélien Lugné-Poe* in 1893 to use Bloch's promptbook as a guide to his own production at the Théâtre l'Oeuvre in Paris. Bloch's rendering of Ibsen's more symbolic plays—*The Lady from the Sea* (1889), *Hedda Gabler* (1891), and *The Master Builder* (1892)—were more limited, reflecting the aesthetic conservatism of the Royal Theatre audience.

During his second period as stage director (1899–1909), Bloch concentrated on reinforcing the then-unbroken stage tradition of the eighteenth-century comedies of Ludvig Holberg. Individualizing their stock of characters, he transformed the comedies into logically knit genre paintings with historically correct scenery and costume. His seven Holberg productions, most notably *Master Gert Westphaler* (1990), *Jeppe on the Hill* (1903), and *The Lying-In Room* (1904), created a naturalistic Holberg tradition which was to last for decades.

Between 1896 and 1901, Bloch published his principles on acting and directing in the periodical *Tilskueren* (*The Spectator*). He strongly opposed the traditional view of acting as secondary to the words of the playwright, maintaining that acting should surpass language. Further, Bloch emphasized that the right place for the director during rehearsals was on the stage, rather than in the stalls, and he stressed that the director should convince with reason and never rely strictly upon his authority. Bloch believed that the ideal stage director should ''vanish behind the finished production.'' Consequently, his name never appeared in the playbills, and once, when applauded while on a tour, he concealed himself in a cupboard.

ADDITIONAL PRODUCTIONS: [At the Royal Theatre, Copenhagen]: 1900: *Erasmus Montanus* (Holberg); 1901: *Eleventh of June* (Holberg); 1905: *Sorcery or False Alarm* (Holberg); 1907: *The Political Tinker* (Holberg). Promptbooks are in the Royal Theatre archives.

SELECTED BIBLIOGRAPHY: Davidsen, Elisabeth. *Henrik Ibsen og Det kongelige Teater*. København: Akademisk Forlag, 1980; Jacobsen, Kirsten, ed. *William Bloch om skuespilkunst og sceneinstruktion*. København: Det teatervidenskabelige Institut, 1979; Marker, Frederick J., and Lise-Lone Marker. *The Scandinavian Theatre: A Short History*. Oxford: Basil Blackwell, 1975: 132–75; Marker, Lise-Lone, and Frederick J. Marker. ''William Bloch and Naturalism in the Scandinavian Theatre.'' *Theatre Survey* 15 (1974): 85–104; Nathansen, Henri. *William Bloch*. København: Arnold Busck, 1928; Neiiendam, Robert, and Jytte Wiingaard. ''Bloch, William Edvard.'' *Dansk Biografisk Leksikon*. 3rd ed. København: Gyldendal, 1979: 256–57; Wiingaard, Jytte. ''Ibsen og Holberg.'' *Dansk teaterhistorie* 2 København: Gyldendal, 1992; Wiingaard, Jytte. *William Bloch og Holberg*. København: G.E.C. Gad, 1966.

Janne Risum

AUGUSTO BOAL [b. March 13, 1931, Rio de Janeiro]. Augusto Boal is best known as the creator of Theatre of the Oppressed, a body of theatrical techniques that physically activate spectators and empower them to rehearse alternatives to their collective oppressions. Boal honed his theatrical skills as director of the Arena Theatre in São Paulo (1956–71). While most directors in Brazil were modeling their companies on European theatre, Boal focused on the relationship between his productions and Brazilian audiences.

Boal's work at the Arena went through four stages. In 1956–58, Boal rooted the actors' work in Stanislavsky and specialized in American and European realism (Steinbeck's *Of Mice and Men*[1956–58], O'Casey's *Juno and the Paycock* [1956–58]). He believed such work would address a Brazilian public by dealing realistically with universal themes. Between 1958 and 1964, Boal presented Brazilian experience onstage directly, via productions of new Brazilian plays such as Oduvaldo Viana Filho's *Chapetuba F. C.* and his own *Revolution in South America*. From 1964 to 1968, Boal again directed world classics— Machiavelli's *The Mandrake*, Molière's *Tartuffe*—but in irreverent adaptations meant to reflect contemporary Brazilian concerns. In 1968–71, Boal and his collaborators created musical works, such as Boal and Guarnieri's *Arena Tells about Zumbi*, in a new genre they called ''the Joker System,'' which was characterized by the mixing of fact and fiction; the shifting of roles during the play so that all actors played all characters; and the introduction of the ''joker'' figure, who was both a narrator who addressed the audience directly and a ''wild card'' actor, able to jump in and out of any role in the play.

In 1964 and 1968 Brazil experienced two military coups. Boal worked to restore democracy through both theatrical and political means. While touring agitprop plays for peasants and workers, Boal devised "forum theatre," a Theatre of the Oppressed technique in which spectators explore their own solutions to collective problems rather than be told what to do by actors who do not share their circumstances. In forum, a scenario is played up to a crisis, at which point spectators are invited to intervene, physically replace the protagonist, and try out their own solutions. In 1971, because of his work against the military regime, Boal was jailed and tortured. After three months, he was released with the warning that, if arrested again, he would end his days in prison.

Based in Argentina from 1971 to 1976, Boal further developed Theatre of the Oppressed. Invited to participate in a national literacy campaign in Peru in 1973, Boal invented "image theatre," a technique that privileges physical expression and thus provides a form of aesthetic communication that transcends spoken language and educational difference. On returning to Argentina, forbidden to do political theatre under an increasingly repressive regime, Boal devised "invisible theatre." Staged in public spaces and masquerading as real life, these theatrical scenarios addressing social issues caught people's attention and led to energetic discussions. Finally, unable to do theatre at all because of military rule, Boal wrote *Theatre of the Oppressed* (1974), *Latin American Techniques of Popular Theatre* (1975), and *200 Exercises and Games for Actors and Non-Actors* (1975).

From 1976 to 1986 Boal was in exile in Europe, where, as a result of the translation of *Theatre of the Oppressed* into twenty-five languages, his reputation expanded. He directed plays and led workshops in Portugal and France, and in 1979 established a Parisian company and Center for Theatre of the Oppressed. At first frustrated by the themes of loneliness and alienation the Europeans brought to his workshops, Boal came to realize the depth of pain caused by these internal oppressions. He thus began to develop a body of therapeutic theatrical techniques.

In 1986, after a change in governments, Boal returned to Brazil to design a theatre program for poor schoolchildren. When funding fell through, he nevertheless founded a Rio de Janeiro Center for Theatre of the Oppressed. In October 1992, Boal was elected to a city council position in Rio. He now plans to develop "legislative theatre," the use of forum to generate a dossier of laws that people believe will help solve the problems they are facing.

Boal still travels extensively, teaching and directing. His work has been adapted in places including Burkino Faso, Estonia, Puerto Rico, Canada, Sweden, England, India, and Germany.Boal was the keynote speaker for the 1992 Association for Theatre in Higher Education (ATHE) Conference and plans are underway for a Center for Theatre of the Oppressed in New York City.

ADDITIONAL PRODUCTIONS: 1956–58: *They Knew What They Wanted*; 1968–71: *São Paulo Fair of Opinion*. Boal is best known for facilitating (though not exactly *directing*) hundreds of plays through Theatre of the Oppressed workshops, in which people create scenarios from their own experiences using forum, image, and invisible theatre. He has continued to direct several conventional plays each year, ranging from musicals to Racine's *Phèdre*.

SELECTED BIBLIOGRAPHY: Boal, Augusto. *Games for Actors and Non-Actors*. London and New York: Routledge, 1992; Boal, Augusto. *Tecnicas Latinoamericanas de Teatro popular*. Buenos Aires: Ediciones Corregidor, 1975; Boal, Augusto. *Theatre of the Oppressed*. New York: Theatre Communications Group, 1985; Boal, Augusto. *Methode Boal de theatre et therapie: L'arc-en-ciel du desir*. Paris: Ramsay, 1990 (Projected English-language publication, London and New York: Routledge, 1994); Schechter, Joel. *Durov's Pig*. New York: Theatre Communications Group, 1985; Schutzman, Mady, and Jan Cohen-Cruz, eds. *Playing Boal: Theatre, Therapy, Activism*. London and New York: Routledge, projected 1993; *The Drama Review* 34 (Fall 1990), Special Issue on Boal, includes bibliography pp. 84–87.

Jan Cohen-Cruz

ANNE BOGART [b. September 25, 1951, Newport, Rhode Island]. Bogart is foremost among a group of young, experimental theatre directors whose work employs a combination of movement, gesture, song, and spoken word. Her works are typically large-scale epic pieces, many of them reworkings of classic dramatic texts. To achieve her unique performance style, Bogart has developed a corps of performers who are equally adept in acting and dance. Bogart has been influenced by the work of several major European theatre directors, including Peter Stein,* Giorgio Strehler,* and Ariane Mnouchkine,* as well as American experimental theatre director Richard Schechner,* whose application of anthropology and history to theatrical performance fueled some of her own artistic discoveries. Bogart has served as primary director for the experimental Music-Theatre Group in Lenox, Massachusetts, and from 1989 to 1990 she was the artistic director of the Trinity Repertory Company in Providence, Rhode Island.

Bogart's early work, characteristic of much of the experimental theatre of the 1960s, occurred in actual dwellings, such as apartments and coffeehouses, where staged events, controlled by the director, were interrupted by actions from real-life dramas. Works such as *Inhabitat* (1979) and *Out of Sync* (1982), in which audience members became participants, initiated Bogart's continuing exploration of issues of audience perception and the boundaries between artifice and reality. Subsequent works began reshaping classic texts, such as *Spring Awakening* (1984), based on Frank Wedekind's 1891 drama, and Bogart's Bessie Award–winning *South Pacific* (1984). Set in a rehabilitation clinic for war veterans, the piece deconstructed the 1949 American musical to probe issues aroused in the original work, including the nature of patriotism, racism, and the relationship of the individual to authority. *South Pacific*, like other Bogart creations, tackled large historical themes, filtered through a late twentieth-century sensibility.

A distinguishing characteristic of Bogart's work is its sociopolitical content. Relationships between men and women form a central theme. In her 1982 production *Women and Men: A Big Dance*, a high school dance serves as a metaphor for how social and sexual relationships are forged in American culture. In her typically innovative directing, Bogart locates meaning not through sequential narrative, but rather through a collage of repetitive gestures, patterns of speech and dialogue, and tableaux vivants which evoke mood and create meaning through associative images. As in other Bogart pieces, the repetition and accumulation create a psychological distancing effect, precluding viewer sentimentality; according to critic Sally Banes, the images "lose their specificity and gain the scale of a zeitgeist" (Banes, "Barefoot in the Gym").

In *History, An American Dream (1983)*, another large-scale work, Bogart explored the interlocking theme of women, men, and militarism. The piece demonstrated her interest in the relationship between architectural elements and meaning. Bogart experimented with differing levels of physical reality to help the audience consider the history of war from a fully dimensional historical perspective. The audience is seated at the altar as a cast of historical, mythic figures from Emma Goldman to Joseph McCarthy perform above from a balcony, making imploring speeches to the audience. A large-scale performance ensues in the nave, of women and men in stylized actions depicting scenes of love, conflict, and separation from one another because of the war. Speaking directly to the audience is a contemporary woman narrator, reflecting wryly on the activities of the couples. Bogart suggests that past and present exist simultaneously, that history is a living force guiding our behavior in the present.

ADDITIONAL PRODUCTIONS: 1979: *Hauptstadt, Inhabitat*; 1980: *Out of Sync*; 1982: *The Ground Floor and Other Stories, Women and Men: A Big Dance*; 1983: *History, An American Dream*; 1984: *Spring Awakening, South Pacific*; 1985: *The Making of Americans*; 1987: *Assimil*; 1988: *No Plays, No Poetry*; 1989: *Cinderella/Cendrillon*.

SELECTED BIBLIOGRAPHY: Abbe, Jessica. "Anne Bogart's Journeys." *The Drama Review* 24 (June 1980): 85–100; Banes, Sally. "Barefoot in the Gym, *Women and Men: A Big Dance*." *The Village Voice* 21 December 1982; Bogart, Anne. "Stepping Out of Inertia." *The Drama Review* 27 (Winter 1983): 26–28; De Vries, Hilary. "Anne Bogart Changes Course at Trinity Rep." *New York Times* 8 October 1989; sec. 2:5, 28; Lampe, Eelka. "From the Battle to the Gift: The Directing of Anne Bogart." *The Drama Review* 36 (Spring 1992): 14–47; Lassiter, Laurie. "*History, An American Dream*" [review]. *Women & Performance* 1.2 (Winter 1984): 150–53; Lassiter, Laurie. "*The Making of Americans*" [review]. *Women & Performance* 3 (1986): 101–3; Sheehy, Catherine. "Paradise's Back Door: An Interview with Anne Bogart." *Theater* 22 (Fall/Winter 1990–91): 6–13; Shewey, Don. "Bogart in Space." *The Village Voice* 18 December 1984:126; Stuart, Jan. "Bogart in Bali Ha'i." *American Theatre* 1 (February 1985): 28–29.

Julie Malnig

MICHAEL BOGDANOV [b. December 15, 1938, London, England]. Following studies in literature at Trinity College, Dublin (M.A.), in Munich, and at the Sorbonne, Bogdanov worked for several years as a director for Telefis Eireann. In 1968, he directed his own musical adaptation of Molière's *Le Bourgeois Gentilhomme*, entitled *The Bootleg Gentleman*, at the Oxford Playhouse. Then, after a season as an assistant director at the Royal Shakespeare Company (1970), he was associated with several provincial companies, including the Tyneside Theatre Company (1971–73), the Phoenix Theatre, Leicester (1974–77), and the Young Vic (1978–80). In 1980, he was appointed associate director of the Royal

National Theatre, but broke with this company in 1986 to cofound with the actor Michael Pennington the English Shakespeare Company (ESC). From 1988 to 1991, Bogdanov also served as intendant of the Hamburg Deutsches Schauspielhaus.

Bogdanov's reputation rests principally on his radically modernized Shakespearean productions, particularly his monumental, seven-play "The Wars of the Roses" cycle which toured worldwide in 1988–89. His approach is to find within Shakespeare's plots, language, and characters, associations which parallel incidents and events, attitudes and tensions in our own time or our recent past. He then foregrounds these associations by using modern costumes and properties and various visual and musical references. The historical world of the play, its character relationships and thematic concerns, are thus juxtaposed against contemporary culture and, especially, politics.

Costumes in the "The Wars of the Roses" ranged over the entire modern period, moving roughly from the Regency period in *Richard II*, through the *fin de siècle* in the five Henry plays, to the present day in *Richard III*. Within a generally Edwardian mode of dress, there might be characters in more ancient or more contemporary costumes. Similarly, while in the battle scenes modern pistols and rifles were most often used, Hal and Hotspur and Richmond and Richard, dressed in medieval chain mail, fought their duels with broadswords. Seemingly freewheeling, but always compelling and surprising, this progression and juxtaposition of styles—Regency, Edwardian, medieval, contemporary—ironically suggested that "The Wars of the Roses" was not just about the power struggles between the Houses of Lancaster and York, but about the political development of modern Britain as well.

Bogdanov is undoubtedly at his most inventive creating, often by fairly economic means, "speaking pictures" of an explicit social world with which audiences can readily identify. For his 1986 *Romeo and Juliet*, for example, he staged the Capulet banquet as a boisterous yuppie bash, complete with rock music and drunken guests plunging fully clothed into a downstage swimming pool. In *Henry V*, the embarkation from Southampton was staged as if the departing soldiers were working-class football fans, waving Union Jacks and chanting " 'Ere we go, 'ere we go," eager to cross the Channel and, as one of their banners read, "Fuck the Frogs." *Coriolanus* (1990–91) was relocated to modern-day Eastern Europe with a mise-en-scène that suggested parallels to a Solidarity-style uprising.

Bogdanov's modernized versions of Shakespeare have been reproved by some critics for their heavy-handed efforts to make the plays relevant, but many scholars, critics, and audience members have commended him for returning Shakespeare to a populist theatre tradition that compels all parts of the house to confront the meaning of his plays in performance.

ADDITIONAL PRODUCTIONS: 1976: *Richard III*, *Hamlet*, *The Tempest*, *Romeo and Juliet* (Imperial Theatre Tokyo); 1977: *Sir Gawain and the Green Knight*, *The Hunchback of Notre Dame*; 1978: *Hiawatha*, *The Taming of the Shrew*; 1978–79: *Richard III*, *Hamlet*, *The Tempest*; 1980: *The Romans in Britain*; 1983: *Hamlet* (Abbey Theatre); 1985: *Don-*

nestag aus Licht (Royal Opera House), *Measure for Measure* (Stratford Festival); 1986–
87: *Julius Caesar, Reineke Fuchs* (Deutsche Schauspielhaus, Hamburg); 1990–91: *The
Winter's Tale* (toured worldwide).
SELECTED BIBLIOGRAPHY: Berry, Ralph. *On Directing Shakespeare*. London: Hamish
Hamilton, 1989: 217–27; Bogdanov, Michael, and Michael Pennington. *English Shake-
speare Company*. London: Nick Hern Books, 1990; Gibney, Liz. "Michael Bogdanov."
Plays International June 1990: 32–33; Kift, Roy. "Hamburger Bar." *Plays and Players*
April 1991: 16–17; Trilling, Ossia. "Ich bin ein Hamburger." *Plays and Players* April
1989: 7–9; Welsh, Jack. "Interview with Michael Bogdanov." *Western European Stages*
Fall 1990: 37–44.

Daniel J. Watermeier

RICHARD BOLESLAVSKY [b. February 4, 1889, Plock-Debowa Gora, Poland;
d. January 17, 1937, Los Angeles, California]. Christened Boleslaw Ryszard
Srzednick, Richard Boleslavsky began an international career as actor, director,
author, and master teacher when he was invited to join the Moscow Art Theatre
(MAT) apprentice company in 1906. He became an immediate favorite of his
mentor, Konstantin Stanislavsky,* and was admitted into the MAT company in
1908, where he played Laertes in Gordon Craig's *Hamlet* and Belyayev in *A
Month in the Country*. His major directorial contributions centered on his work
at the First Studio, where he staged its inaugural production, *The Good Hope*
in 1913. Boleslavsky was a natural leader and a successful experimenter with
the fledgling System of actor training. He employed the System's techniques of
actor investment in the psychological nature of character and true ensemble
playing in all his directorial efforts. In the period between 1913 and 1915,
Boleslavsky continued to receive acclaim as director and actor in both stage (*The
Festival of Peace, The Wanderers* by Vladimir Volkenstein) and film (*Mimo
Zhizni* and *Tanets Vampira*). After war service, he returned to the First Studio
in November 1918 to stage Juliusz Słowacki's *Balladyna*, where he attempted
to synthesize inner realism in acting style with expressionistic stage conceptualization.

Boleslavsky spent the next years (1920–22) in exile in Warsaw, Paris, Vienna,
Prague, and Berlin. During these year he was elected director and head of an
ensemble known as the Kachalov Group, after the famous Russian leading man
Vassily Kachalov. The group was largely comprised of exiled former members
of the Moscow Art Theatre. Boleslavsky was responsible for the staging of
Hamlet and *Revue Russe*, a collection of skits and scenes from Russian life and
society. The *Revue* was optioned by Elizabeth Marbury and the Shubert brothers
and opened at New York's Booth Theatre on October 5, 1922.

Boleslavsky's most significant contributions came in the next six years in New
York. From his first New York production of an evening of one acts at the
Neighborhood Playhouse on October 16, 1923, to his final New York staging,
the Broadway production *Judas* in 1929, Boleslavsky directed twenty-nine plays.
Ten of these projects were produced by the American Laboratory Theatre. The
most influential Lab productions include *Twelfth Night* (1925); *The Sea Woman's
Cloak* by Amelie Rives Troubetskoy (1925); Thornton Wilder's *The Trumpet*

Shall Sound (1926); a dramatization of *The Scarlet Letter* (1926); and Clemence Dane's *Granite* (1927).

His experiments with the Lab Theatre and its actor-director training program serve as the necessary link between Stanislavsky and America's initial translation of the System. Among the roughly five hundred students who attended classes were Harold Clurman,* Lee Strasberg,* Stella Adler, and Francis Fergusson. Fundamental theoretical considerations included units of action, the "spine" of the play, and emotion memory exercises. Boleslavsky enjoyed two Broadway successes during this same period with *The Miracle* (assistant director, 1924); and *The Vagabond King* (1925, and London, 1927). He gained a national reputation for these productions with breathtaking crowd scenes and exuberant playing style.

Lured to Hollywood in 1930, Boleslavsky supported a disastrous start to his film directing career by writing a series of articles for *Theatre Arts Monthly* (1930–32) that would eventually become his text *Acting: The First Six Lessons* (1933). His two autobiographical novels, *Way of the Lancer* and *Lances Down*, were both published in 1932. Ironically, it was his writing skills, not his directorial talents, that impressed producer Irving Thalberg, who hired Boleslavsky in 1932 to direct the film *Rasputin and the Empress*, starring the three Barrymores, Ethel, John, and Lionel. Over the next four years until his death in 1937, Boleslavsky completed fifteen major films, most notably *Men in White* (1934), *Les Misérables* (1935), and *Theodora Goes Wild* (1936) with Irene Dunne (nominated for Best Actress Academy Award, 1936). Boleslavsky is credited with integrating Stanislavsky's System into the American film genre, perhaps its most sympathetic medium. His movie direction was distinguished by specific action analysis, elaboration of the dramatic spine, and the actors' inner intensity.

ADDITIONAL PRODUCTIONS: 1923: *Sancho Panza* (Melchoir Lenyel); 1924: *The Saint* (Stark Young); 1927: *Ballyhoo* (Kate Horton); 1928: *Martine* (Bernard) designed by R. E. Jones; 1937: *The Last of Mrs. Cheney.*

SELECTED BIBLIOGRAPHY: Blum, Richard A. *American Film Acting: The Stanislavsky Heritage.* Ann Arbor: UMI Press, 1984; Boleslavsky, Richard. *Acting: The First Six Lessons.* New York: Theatre Arts Books, 1937; Boleslavsky, Richard. "Fundamentals of Acting." *Theatre Arts Monthly* February 1927: 121–29; Boleslavsky, Richard. "The Laboratory Theatre." *Theatre Arts Monthly* July 1923: 244–50; Boleslavsky, Richard. *Lances Down.* Indianapolis: Bobbs-Merrill Co., 1932; Boleslavsky, Richard. *Way of the Lancer.* Indianapolis: Bobbs-Merrill Co., 1932; Roberts, J. W. *Richard Boleslavsky: His Life and Work in the Theatre.* Ann Arbor: UMI Press, 1977; Strasberg, Lee. *A Dream of Passion.* New York: Plume, 1988; Willis, Ronald A. "The American Lab Theatre." *Tulane Drama Review* 9 (Fall 1964): 112–16.

Richard Warner

GILDAS BOURDET [b. April 22, 1947, Laforêt-Fouesnant, France]. Gildas Bourdet's theatrical history is only recently separable from that of La Salamandre which, once installed in the Lille region in the mid–1970s, became the premier professional company north of Paris. Founded in 1969, La Salamandre was catapulted into fame when it collectively created a high-spirited burlesque, *Vie* *de Jean-Baptiste Poquelin, dit Molière* (1973). This production set the work pattern and the tone for two more collective creations—*Martin Eden* (1976) and *Attention au travail* (1979). It also consolidated Bourdet's position as director-designer within the group.

Bourdet's lushly detailed, poeticized sets and highly charged stagings function contrapuntally to reveal the operation of power and the ravages of powerlessness within the context of both the plays he directs and the world in which his audience lives. Thus, in *Britannicus* (1979), Bourdet had a regal Agrippina, in full-skirted seventeenth-century splendor, thrash about in naturalistic fury on the floor of Nero's marble antechamber, while an allegory of Louis XIV's rise to power, signaled by a museum nameplate, stared over the heads of the audience. The message was clear, if multilayered: human beings are always gripped by social forces outside their control, and while the signs of dominance may change, the reality of the system does not.

Bourdet's sympathy for the "dominated" and his related critique of late capitalism were apparent in his adaptation of Gorky's *The Lower Depths* (1982), in which the characters all spoke in the dialect of Lille's disinherited squatter class. In his treatment of Claudel's *Le Pain dur* (1984), the lead actor self-consciously wore the mask of the tyrant that his character Turelure had become, thereby emphasizing the role of social conditioning in the creation of monsters.

In his own plays of the 1980s, particularly *Le Saperleau* (1982), the triangular farce for which he invented a language, and his working-class drama, *The Gas Station* (1985), Bourdet skewered the sanctity of the family and, also, highlighted boulevard theatre's tendency to deal complaisantly with violent acts of adultery and abandonment.

All his productions, be they of classics (Molière's *The Imaginary Invalid*, 1991) or of relatively recent and challenging texts (Romain Weingarten's *L'Été*, 1990), bear witness to his acute sense of comic timing, his appreciation of popular culture—particularly blues music and cinematographic framing devices—and his ability to find a new, uncanny interpretive twist. To wit, Molière's farce became, in Bourdet's hands, a meditation on death rather than a satire of hypochondria. Bourdet specializes in recuperating through comedy portrayals of extreme alienation, while never denying alienation's omnipresence.

With the disbanding of La Salamandre in 1990, Bourdet began a new phase of his career as visual artist cum writer-director. He now splits his time between free-lance directing and screenwriting.

ADDITIONAL PRODUCTIONS: 1984: *La Finta Giardiniera* (Mozart); 1986: *Les Crachats de la lune* (Bourdet); 1987: *Dialogues of the Carmelites* (Bernanos); 1988: *Endgame*, *L'Inconvenant* (Bourdet); 1989: *False Confidences* (Marivaux); 1992: *Professor Bernardi* (Schnitzler).

SELECTED BIBLIOGRAPHY: Benhamou, Anne-Françoise. *Britannicus et la Salamandre*. Paris: Solin, 1981; Godard, Colette. *Le Théâtre depuis 1968*. Paris: Lattes. 1980; Malbert, Daniel. "Gildas Bourdet: homme orchestre." *Le Français dans le monde* Feb.-March 1986: 12–18; Miller, Judith G. "Novels into Theatre: Adaptation as a New Mode of

Reading." *Theatre Journal* 33 (December 1981): 431–52; Pavis, Patrice. *Dictionnaire du théâtre*. Paris: Messidor/Editions sociales, 1987; Temkine, Raymonde. *Le Théâtre au présent*. Paris: Bouffoneries/Contrastes, 1987; Wehle, Philippa. *Dramacontemporary: France*. New York: Performing Arts Publications, 1986.

Judith G. Miller

ANTOINE BOURSEILLER [b.1930, Paris, France]. Antoine Bourseiller has moved from private to public theatre, from Paris to the provinces, and from dramatic to lyric modes since his entry onto the dramatic scene in the late 1950s. His controversial dramatic productions, ritualistic and abstract in character, have been variously described as surrealistic, expressionistic, and Brechtian.

Bourseiller began by directing lesser-known seventeenth century plays, including Tristan Lhermitte's *Marianne* and *La Mort d'Agrippine* by Cyrano de Bergerac (1960), in spare and technically simple stagings. In 1960, he was awarded the Prix du Concours des Jeunes Compagnies. Soon afterward, he temporarily replaced Maurice Jacquemont at the Studio des Champs-Elysées. Bourseiller's successes at the Champs-Elysées included *Va donc chez Törpe* (1961) by François Billetdoux, Brecht's *In the Jungle of Cities* (1962), and L'Isle-Adam's *Axël* (1962). As director of the Poche-Montparnasse from 1964 to 1966, he staged the first Parisian productions of plays by LeRoi Jones (*Le Métro-fantôme*, 1965) and by the Polish writer Sławomir Mrożek. His *Don Juan* at the Comédie Française in 1967, with its fantastic sets and costumes and its unusual interpretation of the main characters, set off a battle among critics. In 1966, Bourseiller left Paris to direct one of the national "centres dramatiques"— the Centre dramatique du Sud-Est in Marseille, where he remained until 1975. He then headed the Théâtre Récamier until 1978, and from 1980 to 1981, he directed the Théâtre d'Orléans.

In 1980, Bourseiller stopped working in dramatic theatre and began a second career as a director of lyric theatre. Since 1982, he has been the head of the Opéra de Nancy et de Lorraine, where he remains committed to dramatic exploration and experimentation. Four of his operas, *Cantate d'Octobre* (Prokofiev, 1985), *Donna Abbandonata* (Bourseiller, 1987), *Lady Macbeth de Mtsensk* (Shostakovich, 1989), and *Don Juan* (Mozart, 1991), have received the Prix du Syndicat National de la Critique for the best production outside Paris.

ADDITIONAL PRODUCTIONS: 1960: *As You Desire Me* (Pirandello); 1967: *Silence, l'arbre remue encore* (*Silence, the Tree Is Still Moving*, François Billetdoux); 1969: *America Hurrah* (Jean-Claude van Itallie); 1973: *Phèdre*; 1974: *Jean Harlow contre Billy the Kid* (Michaël MacClure); 1975: *The Balcony*; 1976: *Kennedy's Children* (R. Patrick); 1977: *La Tour* (von Hofmannsthal); 1978: *Six Characters in Search of an Author*; 1981: *Woyzeck*; 1984: *Boulevard Solitude* (Hans Werner Henze).

SELECTED BIBLIOGRAPHY: "Biographie d'Antoine Bourseiller." Opéra de Nancy et de Lorraine, 1992; Poirot-Delpech, Bertrand. *"Dans la jungle des villes," "Le Métro fantôme,"* and *"Va donc chez Törpe." Au soir le soir*. Paris: Mercure de France, 1969: 85–88, 72–75, 170–72; Simon, Alfred. *Dictionnaire du théâtre français contemporain*. Paris: Larousse, 1970.

Cynthia Running-Johnson

ANTON GIULIO BRAGAGLIA [b. February 11, 1890, Frosinone, Italy; d. July 15, 1960, Rome, Italy]. Bragaglia became involved with the futurists in 1910, collaborating on artistic and theatrical events, journals, and daily papers. In 1916, he made an important Italian avant-garde film, *Perfido incanto*, and two years later, he founded Casa d'Arte Bragaglia, a cultural center where he introduced new ideas in art, music, and theatre. There, he presented for the first time in Italy such artists as Gustav Klimt, Max Beckmann, and the dadaists and helped launch Giacomo Balla, Fortunato Depero, Umberto Boccione, Giorgio De Chirico, and Enrico Prampolini.

Bragaglia began experimenting as a theatre director in 1916, using new techniques such as psychological lighting effects, revolving stage, and side lighting in productions of plays by Rosso di San Secondo. In 1922, he founded the experimental Teatro degli Indipendenti in Rome, where for fourteen years, he tried out his new ideas on modernist works from Europe and the United States (August Strindberg, Frank Wedekind, Arthur Schnitzler, Miguel de Unamuno, Guillaume Apollinaire, Alfred Jarry, Maurice Maeterlinck, Filippo Marinetti,* Luigi Pirandello,* Eugene O'Neill, Bertolt Brecht*), new productions of the classics, ballet, and pantomime—200 works in all. Bragaglia often worked with untrained actors, and unfortunately, while his ideas looked good on paper, they were seldom satisfactory in practice, possibly due to lack of space and adequate resources. From 1937 until 1943, he was hired by the Fascist regime to be artistic director of the Teatro delle Arti in Rome, where he revitalized the classics (Angelo Beolco a.k.a. Ruzzante, Giovanni Verga); introduced previously unknown Italians (Vitaliano Brancati, Diego Fabbri, Alberto Savinio); and brought recognition to foreign writers(Sean O'Casey, Thornton Wilder, Federico García Lorca, Armand Salacrou, Fernand Crommelynck).

Bragaglia was a prolific writer and contributor to journals. Among his favorite topics were Italian popular theatre, *commedia dell'arte*, and set design, and among the revolutionary ideas he strongly advanced in his writings and in his experimental work were that the three unities led to a stultifying "theatre of talk"; theatre's visual aspect, its spectacle, is more important than its literary aspect; and stage technology and set design should be brought up to date with film technology. Bragaglia further advocated that scenic architecture—mobile architectural volumes—should replace painted sets; that lighting can be used for psychological effect and to create drama and rhythm; that the *régisseur* or *corago*, as the dominant figure in a production, should have author's rights since he controls all aspects of the play—decor, lighting, sound, costumes, makeup, rhythm of the action, movement, vocal inflections, psychological insights.

ADDITIONAL PRODUCTIONS: 1916: *Per fare l'alba* (Rosso di San Secondo); 1919: *La Bella addormentata* (Rosso di San Secondo). At Theatre of Independents:1923: *Siepe a Nord-Ovest* (Massimo Bontempelli), *Bianco e rosso* (Marinetti), *L'Uomo dal fiore in bocca*, and *All'uscita* (Pirandello); 1925: *Fantocci elettrici* (Marinetti), *Il Fiore necessario* (Rosso di San Secondo), *L'Inventore del cavallo* (Achille Campanile), *Pierrot fumiste* (Jules Laforgue); 1926: *Don Chisciotte* (Bragaglia), *Tintagile* (Maeterlinck); 1927: *L'Im-*

peratore (Luigi Bonelli); 1930: *Il suggeritore nudo* (Marinetti). At Teatro Delle Arti: 1939: *Beyond the Horizon, Anna Christie, Our Town*; 1940: *La Nuova colonia* (Pirandello); 1941: *Mourning Becomes Electra, Luciella Catena* (Ferdinando Russo); 1942: *Caterina Ivanovna* (Andreyev); 1943: *Don Giovanni involontario* (Brancati).

SELECTED BIBLIOGRAPHY: Alberti, Alberto Cesare. *Poetica teatrale e bibliografia di Anton Giulio Bragaglia.* Roma: Bulzoni, 1978; Alberti, Alberto Ceasare. *Il teatro nel fascismo: Pirandello e Bragaglia.* Roma: Bulzoni, 1974; Bookman, Judith. "Bragaglia, a Dynamo of the Theatre." *The Drama Magazine* October 1930:5–6, 10–12; Bragaglia, A. G. *Del Teatro teatrale ossia Del teatro.* Roma: Tiber, 1929; Bragaglia, A. G. *Il Teatro della rivoluzione.* Roma: Tiber, 1929; Mariani, Valerio. *Storia della scenografia italiana.* Firenze: Rinascimento del libro, 1930; Verdone, Mario, ed. "Anton Giulio Bragaglia." *Bianco e nero: Rassegna Mensile di Studi Cinematografici e Televisivi* 26 (Special Edition, 1960): 5–6.

Jane House

OTTO BRAHM [b. February 5, 1856, Hamburg, Germany; d. November 28, 1912, Berlin, Germany]. After terminating an apprenticeship at a bank, Brahm studied German literature in Berlin in 1876, where he soon encountered a circle of students centered around Wilhelm Scherer, one of the most influential literary scholars of the positivist movement. Here he received the sound training in text analysis that later would have an enormous impact on his directing principles. After receiving a Ph.D. in German literature in June of 1879, Brahm worked as a journalist starting in 1882.

It was not until 1889 that he actually became involved in the theatre, when he initiated the foundation of the Theaterverein Freie Bühne, a private theatre club whose productions were limited to plays by contemporary authors whose work had not yet been accepted by public theatres. This private theatre club promoted the plays of Henrik Ibsen, August Strindberg, and Leo Tolstoy, as well as those by contemporary German authors of the naturalistic style, especially Gerhart Hauptmann, whom Brahm had met that same year. In 1893 Brahm became theatre director of the Deutsches Theater in Berlin, where he opened his first season with a production of Friedrich Schiller's *Kabale und Liebe*. The audience was visibly offended by Brahm's staging of the classical drama because he updated it and produced it like the plays of Ibsen or Strindberg, thus straying from the usual production style of classical drama with its characteristic pose and pathos. After this failure Brahm essentially stopped staging classics and focused on contemporary plays for the rest of his career.

In 1894 the performance of the naturalist drama *Die Weber* by Gerhart Hauptmann led to one of the biggest scandals in the history of the German theatre. Enraged by what it considered obscenities, the audience interrupted the performance frequently. That evening the German Kaiser cancelled his box at the Deutsches Theater and prohibited his officers from seeing other shows there.

In 1905 Brahm became director of the Lessingtheater in Berlin, where he continued staging plays by the naturalists and Scandinavian playwrights. In the same year the Deutsches Theater of Max Reinhardt* began its ascendency as a major force in theatre. Audiences drifted away from Brahm's naturalistic productions and came to prefer the more fantastic and elaborate shows of Reinhardt.

Two distinctive achievements can be attributed to Otto Brahm: first, his role as mediator between contemporary playwrights such as Hauptmann and Arthur Schnitzler and the stage (and his influence on the production of their scripts); and second, his naturalistic style of directing, which relied on scientific dramaturgy. It was his literary analysis of the script that determined all elements of the production and achieved a closure and depth that was unknown before; it thus marked the beginning of directing in the modern sense. When Brahm said, "The modern theater will be naturalistic, or it will not exist at all," he had several specific ideas in mind. First, he was referring to the development of a new acting method—the psychological and realistic "Menschendarstellung" (portrayal of human beings). Actors were supposed to find these new means of portrayal on their own, as Brahm refused to interfere at rehearsals and rejected the pose, pathos, broad gestures, and declamatory language of the traditional acting style. Second, the scenery aimed to create a continuum between reality and the set. Brahm preferred naturalistic drama because this style readily suited those plays. In a sense, the art of directing began with Brahm, and his work helped shaped the theatre of the twentieth century.

ADDITIONAL PRODUCTIONS: 1894–95: *Nora, Ghosts*; 1896: *Liebelei*; 1897–98: *Hedda Gabler*; 1898: *Fuhrmann Henschel*; 1901: *Der rote Hahn*; 1904: *Der einsame Weg*; 1905: *Das gerettete Venedig* with E. G. Craig, *Demetrius*; 1909: a cycle of 13 plays by Ibsen.

SELECTED BIBLIOGRAPHY: Brahm, Otto. *Kritische Schriften*. Berlin: S. Fischer, 1915; Brahm, Otto. *Theater—Dramatiker—Schauspieler*. Berlin: Henschelverlag, 1961; Claus, Horst. *The Theatre Director Otto Brahm*. Ann Arbor: UMI Research Press, 1981; Miller, Anna Irene. *The Independent Theater in Europe 1887 to the Present*. New York: R. Long and R. R. Smith, 1931; Newmark, Maxim. *Otto Brahm—The Man and the Critic*. New York: G. E. Stechert and Co., 1938; Siedlin, O., ed. *Der Briefwechsel Arthur Schnitzler—Otto Brahm*. Tubingen: M. Niemeyer, 1975; Sprengel, P., ed. *Otto Brahm—Gerhart Hauptmann. Briefwechsel 1889–1912*. Tubingen: M. Niemeyer, 1985.

Kai Hammermeister

ANDRÉ BRASSARD [b. August 28, 1946, Montreal, Quebec]. Following high school, André Brassard planned to audition for entrance into the National Theatre School of Canada, but that same year (1965) the troupe Saltimbanques, one of the most avant-garde companies in Montreal at that time, asked him to direct a production of *The Trojan Women*. Brassard abandoned his study plans and threw himself into a theatrical career. After that, he never ceased directing.

Brassard created his own group, the Mouvement Contemporain (1966–1969) with whom he produced the works of Beckett, Arrabel and Genet. The group also premiered several short plays by the dramatist Michel Tremblay. In 1968, Brassard gained success and fame with the premiere of *Les Belles-Soeurs* by Tremblay. This production, which was fairly realist in its workmanship, was an important moment in Quebec's theatrical history, corresponding to the rise of "théâtre québécois" (Quebec theatre). The production also marked the beginning of a long collaboration between Brassard and Tremblay and from 1968 on, all of Tremblay's plays were premiered by André Brassard.

Brassard's career, which lasted for more than 25 years, was strongly tied to the evolution of theatre and theatrical direction in Quebec. A dominant figure on the theatrical scene in Quebec, Brassard mounted productions in all the great theatres in Quebec and directed the biggest names in contemporary Quebec theatre. His work extended equally to the English milieu (Stratford, Toronto, Ottawa) and his productions were often revived in Europe and the United States.

Brassard's first productions were essentially realist, as much in the performance as in the design, Later, his esthetic evolved toward stylization and symbolism, approaching even minimalism. This purified esthetic, which centered on interpretation and metaphoric effect, had its climax in 1992 with a remarkable production of *Waiting for Godot* at the Théâtre du Nouveau Monde in Montreal.

Brassard's approach was at the same time pragmatic and intuitive. He conceived each of his productions around a primary idea, often an image, that inspired his reading of the dramatic text. This image was often presented on stage: for example, a grotesque statue of the Virgin Mary in *Damnée Manon, Sacrée Sandra* (Michel Tremblay, 1977), the huge kitchen table in *Bonjour, là, bonjour* (Michel Tremblay), the bust of Nero in *Britannicus* (Racine, 1982), the model of the junior high school in *Les Feluettes* (Michel Marc Bouchard, 1987), or the condensed, almost imprisoned, universe of *La Charce de l'original épormyable* (Claude Gauvreau, 1991).

The presence of this central element, whether an object or the organization of theatrical space, is a constant in Brassard's work. It justifies the eclecticism of his dramatic choices which ranged from Tremblay to Racine, from Brecht to Shakespeare, from Genet to Claude Gauvreau, from Beckett to Réjean Ducharme. Brassard also contributed equally to the success of little-known young actors such as Michel Marc Bouchard, Anne Legault, and Normand Chaurette. The other constant in Brassard's work lies in the importance accorded to the actors' direction. The performance is rarely physical. In general, it is centered on the interpretation of characters and incorporates little movement. The characters are often seated or immobile and their movements are almost always distorted by scenic elements (for example, the use of an often steeply inclined floor as in *La Trilogie des Brassard*, by Michel Tremblay, in 1991) or by a very exaggerated gesture (as in *Waiting for Godot*), which contribute to the creation of dramatic tension. The intensity of the interpretation, united with his attention to movement, confers a certain solemnity to most of André Brassard's productions, without, however, injuring their accessibility. Accessibility is one of the major characteristics Brassard shares with Tremblay—he is viewed and appreciated by a very large public while his talent is equally recognized and often rewarded by the critics. Over the course of his career he has received numerous prizes including Prix Victor Morin, Prix Gascon-Roux, and best direction and best production from the Association québécoise des critiques de théâtre.

Bassard also directed three films, two of which (*Françoise Durocher—wait-*

ress, 1972; and *Il était une fois dans l'Est*, 1973) were directly inspired by the work of Michel Tremblay. But his third and last film, *Le Soleil se lève en retard* (1976) is by far the most accomplished. He also directed two lyric works, *Demain Matin, Montréal m'attend* and *Nelligan* (1991).

André Brassard taught from time to time in Quebec's most prominent theatre schools. From 1982 to 1989, he was artistic director of the French theatre at the National Arts Center in Ottawa and, since 1991, has been director of the French department at the National Theatre School of Canada.

ADDITIONAL PRODUCTIONS: 1970: *A toi pour toujours, ta Marie-Lou* (Michel Tremblay); 1982: *Pericles*; 1990: *Bousille et las justes* (Gratien Gélinas); 1991: *Iphigénie* (Racine); 1992: *Six Characters in Search of an Author*.

SELECTED BIBLIOGRAPHY: *André Brassard: Stratégies de mise en scène*. Montréal: VLB Editeur, 1990; Brassard, André. Interview with Hélène Beauchamp. *Le Théâtre canadien-français*. Ed. Paul Wyczynski, Bernard Julien, and Hélène Beauchamp [Rank]. Fides, Archives des Lettres canadiennes, tome V, 1976:849–51; Hart, Daniel. "En attendant Godot." *Veilleurs de nuit* 4 (1992): 80–81; Lefebvre, Paul. "Britannicus." *Jeu* 27 (1983): 163–64: Lévesque, Solange, Diane Pavlovic, and Isabelle Raynauld. "Les Feluettes." *Jeu* 49 (1988):151–75; Vigeant, Louise. "Les Sorcières de Salem." *Jeu* 52 (1989): 215.

Jean-Marc Larrue

KAZIMIERZ BRAUN [b. June 29, 1936, Kielce, Poland]. Among the new wave of Polish directors in the 1950s and 1960s, Kazimierz Braun has shown himself to be an especially creative force. His productions of Cyprian Norwid's plays renewed interest in one of Poland's most important romantic writers. Braun is noted for directing classics of Polish dramatic history: Norwid's *The Actor* (1965), *Cleopatra* (1969), *Behind the Scenes* (1970); Juliusz Słowacki's *Fantazy* (1966); Stanisław Wyspiański's *The Wedding* (1965) and *November Night* (1967); S. I. Witkiewicz's *The Shoemakers* (1987); Witold Gombrowicz's *Operetta* (1977); and the first ever full-length production of Adam Mickiewicz's *Fore-father's Eve* (1979). Braun has also collaborated with Poland's finest contemporary playwrights including Sławomir Mrożek: *Strip-Tease* (1961); *Happy Event* (1974); and, especially, Tadeusz Różewicz: *Interrupted Act* (1970), *White Marriage* (1975), *Birthrate* (1979), *The Old Woman Broods* (1983), and *The Trap* (1984).

Noteworthy for his unconventional use of space, Braun often moves out of the theatre and into lobbies, basements, museums, and churches, or frequently places the audience on stage and uses the auditorium as a site for action. Although he studied with Erwin Axer* and Bohdan Korzeniewski, Braun discarded their styles (literary realism and mass spectacle) for a Theatre of Communion which emphasizes the interactive relationship between spectator and performer. Braun's productions feature intimacy and, at some level, audience participation. He considers Adolphe Appia and Juliusz Osterwa* his theatrical ancestors.

Braun has written or adapted eleven plays, including *The Immigrant Queen* (1989) about Helena Modjeska, *The Comet's Sign* (1986), *The Plague* (after

Camus, 1983), *The Iliad* (after Homer, 1979), and *Anna Livia* (after James Joyce, 1977). His playwriting is noted for its poetical-political style. *The Comet's Sign* uses imagery of Christ's resurrection to implicate, then absolve, public complicity with forces of oppression. *Valesa* (written under the pseudonym Jerzy Tymicki, 1982) and *The Plague* draw specific analogues to Martial Law during the mid-1980s. After the enormous public success of *The Plague*, Braun was suddenly dismissed by the Communist regime from his post as artistic director at the Teatr Wspoczesny in Wrocław. In 1985 he emigrated to the United States, where he continues to direct, write, and teach.

Braun has published nine scholarly books and over 200 articles. Three books, *The Great Reform of the Theatre* (1984), *The Second Reform of the Theatre* (1979), and *Cyprian Norwid's Theatre without Theatre* (1975), have been especially influential.

ADDITIONAL PRODUCTIONS: 1962: *Right You Are If You Think You Are*; 1964: *Andorra* (Max Frisch); 1966: *Inadmissible Evidence*; 1967: *The Visit*; 1969: *All My Sons*; 1972: *The Deliverance* (Stansiław Wyspiański); 1976: *Mother Courage*; 1986: *Rhinoceros*.
SELECTED BIBLIOGRAPHY: Demska, Krystyna. "Birth Rate." *Theatre in Poland* 1980: 10–16; Dzieduszycka, Małgorzata. "Anna Livia." *Theatre in Poland* 1977: 3–11; Raczek, Tomasz. "The Plague." *Theatre in Poland* 1984: 22–29; Szydłowski, Roman. *The Theatre in Poland*. Warsaw: Interpress, 1972.

Thomas Leff

BERTOLT (EUGEN BERTHOLD) BRECHT [b. February 10, 1898, Augsburg, Germany; d. August 14, 1956, Berlin]. Although better known as a playwright and theoretician, Brecht was one of the century's most influential directors. The mainstream German theatre of the 1920s resisted his attempts to "refunction" it: Brecht was fired from his first assignment, a 1922 production of Arnolt Bronnen's *Patricide*. Thereafter, his early directing was primarily limited to his own plays. He codirected many of these productions and worked actively but unofficially on several more, including his 1928 *Threepenny Opera* for which Erich Engel is the director of record. This taste for collective creation let Brecht work with the greatest artists of his time, among them the designer Caspar Neher, a boyhood friend, and Helene Weigel, Brecht's wife.

Brecht fled Hitler's Germany in 1933. He was able to direct very little in exile, and largely unable to test either his so-called great plays or major theoretical statements against theatrical practice. Fortunately, after his return to East Berlin, Brecht was able to evolve both plays and theory further in productions at the Berliner Ensemble, which he and Weigel founded in 1949; neither the plays nor the theory can be understood without reference to these productions. The Ensemble's adaptations of classic plays also taught a generation of German directors that directorial interpretation has the right to intervene in the text itself. The Ensemble's tours to Paris in 1954 and 1955 and to London in 1956 helped change the face of the European theatre. Brecht's model was carried forward after his death by younger Ensemble members he had trained—including the directors

Manfred Wekwerth and Peter Palitzsch and the designer Karl von Appen—to influence a second generation of directors in the 1960s.

Brecht is best known for the theory and practice of "epic theatre." First developed in the 1920s, epic theatre uses the theatrical apparatus as a narrator to tell a story, the play, while also commenting on it. This commentary proceeds through a "separation of the elements" of production, which need not illustrate the play's characterization or milieu, but can comment on the action through open aesthetic self-presentation. Brecht commented on the practical identity of one man with another in his 1931 *A Man's a Man*, for example, by putting the British soldiers on stilts and clothing them in grotesquely padded uniforms and whiteface.

Brecht's postwar work made sparing use of these techniques, but by then Brecht had refined another key concept, *Verfremdung*. Although "alienation" has become standard, "defamiliarization" is a better translation, for the goal is to encourage spectators to look at familiar instances of social interaction in a fresh, hopefully critical, perspective. *A Man's a Man* made early use of his concept, but *Mother Courage* provides perhaps the most famous example: Courage learns nothing as the war beats her down; we are supposed to learn that war is a business in which we don't want to engage. Brecht assisted the spectators of his 1949 production by defamiliarizing whole scenes with songs whose lyrics commented on the surrounding action. For further emphasis, the action stopped, the lighting changed, a special sculpture flew in, and the actor stepped downstage out of his or her blocking to deliver this commentary.

The Ensemble's acting style was highly differentiated but emotionally underplayed. The spectators first confronted with it were, however, used to a hot, vastly overacted, psychological theatre; their initial response gave Brecht's theatre an undeserved reputation for emotional coldness that still persists. Brecht's ability to show how interpersonal behavior is influenced by social situation has influenced realistic and antirealistic directors and writers alike. The influence of his "separation of the elements" is already visible in Wilder's *Our Town*, virtually a catalogue of epic theatre techniques, and has recently resurfaced in postmodern practices like those of Robert Wilson,* with its nearly absolute separation of production and text.

ADDITIONAL PRODUCTIONS: 1924: *Edward the Second* (adapted by Brecht and Lion Feuchtwanger), with Neher; 1929: *Lindbergh's Flight* and *The Baden Learning Play*; 1932: *The Mother*, world premiere, with Weigel, codirected by Emil Burri; 1947: *The Life of Galileo*, world premiere, with Charles Laughton as Galileo and codirector; 1948: *Antigone* (Hölderlin translation, adapted by Brecht), world premiere, with Weigel and Neher, *Puntila and Matti, His Hired Man*, sets by Teo Otto; 1949: *Mother Courage and Her Children*, codirected by Erich Engel, with Weigel and Otto, opening production of the Berliner Ensemble; 1950: *The Tutor* (J.M.R. Lenz, adapted by Brecht), codirected and designed by Neher; 1954: *The Caucasian Chalk Circle*, with Appen and Wekwerth.

SELECTED BIBLIOGRAPHY: Brecht, Bertolt. *Brecht on Theatre*. Ed. John Willett. New York:Hill and Wang, 1964; Brecht, Bertolt. *Collected Plays*. Ed. Ralph Manheim and John Willett. New York: Vintage-Random House, 1971; Braun, Edward. *The Director and the Stage: From Naturalism to Grotowski*. New York: Holmes and Meier, 1982:

162–79; Fuegi, John. *Bertolt Brecht: Chaos, According to Plan*. Cambridge, England: Cambridge University Press, 1987; Jones, David Richard. *Great Directors at Work: Stanislavsky, Brecht, Kazan, Brook*. Berkeley: University of California Press, 1986; Patterson, Michael. *The Revolution in the German Theatre 1900–1933*. Boston: Routledge, 1981; Rouse, John. *Brecht and the West German Theatre: The Practice and Politics of Interpretation*. Ann Arbor: UMI Research Press, 1989; Willett, John. *The Theatre of Bertolt Brecht: A Study from Eight Aspects*. London: Methuen, 1959.

John Rouse

LEE BREUER [b. February 6, 1937, Philadelphia, Pennsylvania]. Although he has acted onstage, Breuer is primarily known as a founding member and director of the avant-garde theatre collective Mabou Mines. After graduating from the University of California at Los Angeles in 1958, he met actress Ruth Maleczech, who became his wife. Together they worked with the San Francisco Actor's Workshop, directing and acting in experimental works. Breuer also tried to write novels, but when he was given the opportunity to direct Brecht's *The Caucasian Chalk Circle* in 1959, director Alan Schneider* saw the production and recommended that the Actor's Workshop hire Breuer. There, he assisted the director Herbert Blau and staged such plays as Beckett's *Happy Days* and *The Maids*.

After approximately four years with the company, he and Maleczech left for Europe in 1965. They traveled to Germany to study with the Berliner Ensemble, then to Poland to study with Jerzy Grotowski* and the Polish Theatre Lab, and finally to Paris. While there, Breuer directed a successful production of Beckett's *Play* (1969) with Maleczech, and his friends from San Francisco, JoAnne Akalaitis* and David Warrilow, performing and Phillip Glass playing original music. In Paris, Breuer also postponed the novel he had been writing for ten years and wrote his first play, *B. Beaver Animation*.

After returning to America in 1970, Breuer and his colleagues Akalaitis, Glass, Maleczech, and Warrilow founded Mabou Mines, based in New York City. His first production with the group, *The Red Horse Animation* (1970; revised 1972, performed at the Guggenheim and Whitney museums, respectively), was the first of a trilogy of plays. The second was *B. Beaver Animation* (1974), staged at the Museum of Modern Art and the Theatre for the New City, followed by *The Shaggy Dog Animations* (1978), presented at the New York Shakespeare Festival's Public Theatre. Using animal characters, Breuer's metaphorical productions employed multicultural theatre techniques from Japanese Kabuki, Noh drama, and Bunraku; filmic elements such as quick cuts from scene to scene to create a "live-action cinema"; and autobiographical material culled from his writings.

During the 1980s, Breuer remained very active. He wrote and directed such works as *Sister Suzie Cinema* (1980), *Prelude to a Death in Venice* (1980), and a workshop production of his planned epic work *The Warrior Ant* (1986; revised 1989 at the Brooklyn Academy of Music).

Also, during the 1980s, Breuer attempted to give new life to the classics. His production of *The Tempest* (1983), produced for the New York Shakespeare Festival, tried to bring a pop-art sensibility to Shakespeare's characters. Breuer's Broadway production of *The Gospel at Colonus* (1988), an adaptation of Sophocles' *Oedipus at Colonus*, was set in the milieu of a black Pentecostal Church, employing spiritual, revival-meeting songs together with a written text. In this musical work, first performed for the Brooklyn Academy of Music's Next Wave Festival in 1983, Breuer's approach incorporated race as culture. He successfully used contemporary American religious rituals to reinvigrorate a classic text.

Breuer's production of *Lear* (1990) was heralded as a gender-bending, interracially cast production. Viewing gender as culture, Breuer set Shakespeare's classic in the Deep Southern town of Smyrna, Georgia, in the 1950s. The character of King Lear was transformed into a southern grandmother, played by Ruth Maleczech, who wants to divide her estate among her three sons. Contemporizing the action while leaving Shakespeare's text mostly intact, Breuer created a production that worked on several levels of understanding: male versus female, black America versus white America, and power versus love.

Currently, Breuer continues to travel to such places as India to study performance traditions. His main focus in directing is intercultural, employing performance techniques from other countries. He is working on the epic play called *The Insect That Loved the World*, which began with *The Warrior Ant* in 1986. In addition, Breuer publishes poetry and criticism, as well as teaches and lectures at universities.

ADDITIONAL PRODUCTIONS: 1968: *Mother Courage* (Paris), *The Messingkauf Dialogues* (Edinburgh Festival); 1970: *Play* (New York); 1980: *The Lost Ones, Prelude to a Death in Venice* (Producer; two Obie Awards); 1983: *The Saint and the Football Players* (choreographed and directed for the American Dance Festival); 1984: *Hajj*.

SELECTED BIBLIOGRAPHY: Breuer, Lee. *Animations: A Trilogy for Mabou Mines—The Red Horse, The B.Beaver, The Shaggy Dog*. Ed. Bonnie Marranca and Gautam Dasgupta. New York: Performing Arts Journal Publications, 1979; Breuer, Lee. *Sister Suzie Cinema: The Collected Poems and Performances 1976–1986*. New York: Theatre Communications Group, 1987; Breuer, Lee. "Lee Breuer and Interculturalism." Interviewed by Gabrielle Cody. *Performing Arts Journal* 11.3/12.1(1989):59–66; Cole, Susan Letzler. *Directors in Rehearsal: A Hidden World*. New York: Routledge, 1992:199–216; Fiscella, Laurie, Lassiter. "Mabou Mines, 1959–1989: A Theatre Chronicle." Diss. New York U, 1989; Neely, Kent. "Lee Breuer's Theatrical Technique: From *The Animations* to *Gospel at Colonus*." *Journal of Dramatic Theory and Criticism* 3(Spring 1989):181–90; Runnels, Marti Ray. "Lee Breuer and His Cross-cultural American Classicism." Diss.Texas Tech U, 1989; Wetzsteon, Ross. "Wild Man of the American Theatre: Lee Breuer Turns His Life and Off-Broadway Upside Down." *Village Voice* 19 May 1987:19–26.

                                                                    Tom Mikotowicz

PETER BROOK [b. March 21, 1925, London, England]. Peter Brook is arguably the preeminent director of the second half of the twentieth century. Never having served an apprenticeship nor struggled to make a name in fringe theatre, he has been in the top echelon of his field since he began professional work at the age of twenty. His work ranges from Shakespeare to boulevard farce to film to opera to collaboratively developed pieces played before a variety of audiences including schoolchildren, Chicano farmers, rural Africans, Australian aborigines, and the West End/Broadway establishment. The only Brook "style" is experiment, and his work is a personal as well as an artistic journey—a process which tries everything, but supersedes a final solution. Brook has inspired many Boswells, who have observed and written about his process; and critics and scholars have praised, damned, and debated his productions.

Brook has always been precocious. At five, he staged a three-hour puppet version of *Hamlet*. After Oxford, he began staging plays professionally in London and at the Birmingham Repertory Theatre. *Love's Labour's Lost* (1946) marked his Stratford-upon-Avon debut, and he subsequently became artistic director at the Royal Opera House, Covent Garden, at twenty-three; co-artistic director with Peter Hall* and Michel Saint-Denis* at the then new Royal Shakespeare Company; lecturer; published author; film and Broadway director in his thirties; and Commander of the British Empire at forty.

Brook has long believed the only way to create a "total theatre" experience is to simultaneously direct, dramaturg, design, and compose. High production values were part of this imagistic aesthetic, yet he strove to achieve maximum effect with minimum means. His stage silences and pauses (notably in his *Measure for Measure*, 1950) were daring at that time, while some of the impact he achieved came from his dramaturgy: in his renowned 1962 *King Lear* (with Paul Scofield, Diana Rigg, Irene Worth, Alec McCowen, and Ian Richardson at Stratford-upon-Avon and London), he cut the scene in which the blind Gloucester receives sympathy from servants, and in his 1955 *Titus Andronicus*, red ribbons used instead of stage blood caused audience members to faint. Imaginative evocation of horror, he showed, was stronger than literal portrayal of it. Brook aimed to disturb audiences, not move them, and he believed that effect could come only from actors' total commitment to the process.

Early in his career, Brook developed long-term working relationships with individual actors—Paul Scofield, John Gielgud,* and Irene Worth among them—and established a new ensemble for each production. He remains a guru to many—a Pied Piper whose followers go where he leads, work as he requires.

From the mid–1960s, however, his work process has required a fixed company. For his 1964 Theatre of Cruelty workshop, he gathered a group of actors, many of whom still work with him today, and he increasingly turned to improvisation, vocal, physical, and psychodramatic exercises which mandated the privacy and consistency required for group process. Influenced by Antonin Artaud and Bertolt Brecht,* his work focused on what David Williams (*Peter Brook: A Theatrical Casebook*) calls "Theatre of Disturbance." These were the years of *Lear*, *Marat/ Sade* (awarded three Tonys), and his unsuccessful attempt at agitprop theatre, the anti–Vietnam War play, *US* (1966). The 1970 "circusy" *Midsummer Night's Dream* (with Alan Howard, Sarah Kestelman, John Kane, Ben Kingsley, Mary Rutherford, and David Waller; designed by Sally Jacobs; music by Richard

Peaslee), an ensemble piece now regarded as a classic production, earned Brook a Tony as best director.

In 1971, in order to work with an international group, Brook founded the International Center of Theatre Research in Paris. During its first year, the company investigated the nature of pure sound and its evocative potential. An invented language, Orghast, led to *Orghast in Persepolis*, performed in Iran; while an African journey culminated in *The Conference of the Birds*, which subsequently toured America. The company was headquartered in an abandoned Paris theatre, the Bouffes du Nord, where it continued to create new projects and revivals of earlier ones.

The Cherry Orchard and an adaptation of Bizet's *Carmen* occupied Brook's time in the early 1980s, touring Europe and later, New York. Mid-decade, the group traveled to India to prepare a project on which Brook and writer Jean-Claude Carrière had been working for ten years—an adaptation of the sacred Hindu text *The Mahabarata*, which premiered at Avignon in 1985 and subsequently toured globally.

Between the ongoing experimental work with the company, Brook directed elsewhere, lectured, and wrote a second book. Multilingual, he has translated many of his texts (including the nine-hour *Mahabarata*, originally written by Carrière in French) between French and English.

Brook is controversial, a mass of dualisms, which doubtless informs his work. He has been called politically radical, a cultural colonialist, and apolitical; idealistic and nihilistic; iron-willed and indecisive; a stylist and an antistylist; an intellectual and a populist; a slave driver and an inspiration. Nonetheless, the volume and variety of his work; his attempts to develop universally accessible communication through performance, to bridge intellectual and popular theatre; and his efforts to push theatre in new directions make him unique in twentieth-century theatre history.

ADDITIONAL PRODUCTIONS: 1946: *Love's Labour's Lost* (with Paul Scofield at Stratford-upon-Avon); 1947: *Romeo and Juliet*; 1948: *Boris Godunov* (Covent Garden); 1952:film, *The Beggar's Opera* (with Laurence Olivier); 1953: *Faust* (Metropolitan Opera); 1954: *House of Flowers* (Truman Capote and Harold Arlen with Pearl Bailey on Broadway); 1960: *The Balcony* (with Roger Blin,* in Paris); 1961:film, *Lord of the Flies* (William Golding); 1964: *The Persecution and Assassination of Jean-Paul Marat as Performed by the Inmates of the Asylum of Charenton under the Direction of the Marquis de Sade* (Peter Weiss, with Patrick Magee, Ian Richardson, Glenda Jackson; designed by Sally Jacobs; music by Richard Peaslee); 1968: *Oedipus* (Seneca, adapted by Ted Hughes), *The Tempest*; 1971: *Orghast at Persepolis* (in Iran with an international company); 1973: *Conference of the Birds* (music by Elizabeth Swados); 1974: *Timon of Athens*; 1975: *Les Iks*; 1981 and 1983: *La Cérisaie* (Chekhov).

SELECTED BIBLIOGRAPHY: Brook, Peter. *The Empty Space*. New York: Penguin, 1968; Brook, Peter. *The Shifting Point*. New York: Harper and Row, 1987; Heilpern, John. *Conference of the Birds: The Story of Peter Brook in Africa*. London: Methuen, 1989; Leiter, Samuel L. *From Belasco to Brook: Representative Directors of the English-Speaking Stage*. Westport, CT: Greenwood Press, 1991: 219–64; Selbourne, David. *The*

Making of "A Midsummer Night's Dream." London: Methuen, 1982; Smith, A.C.H.
Orghast at Persepolis. New York: Viking Press, 1972; *Theater* 19 (Spring 1988) [Entire
issue devoted to Brook]; Williams, David. *Peter Brook: A Theatrical Casebook.* London:
Methuen, 1988.

Lila Wolff-Wilkinson

ARVIN BRAGIN BROWN [b. May 24, 1940, Los Angeles, California]. Artistic
director of the Long Wharf Theatre in New Haven, Connecticut, Arvin Brown
has been one of the most successful and prolific regional theatre directors for
over four decades.

Having grown up in Los Angeles, he attended Stanford University with the
intention of becoming a novelist, but graduated in 1961 still unsure of his career
plans. The following year, having received a Fulbright Fellowship to study at
the University of Bristol, England, he directed his first play, Strindberg's *The
Stronger*, and became acutely interested in the directing process. He earned his
master's degree in English at Harvard in 1963 and entered the Yale School of
Drama the following year to study directing. Two classmates, Jon Jory and
Harlan Kleiman, left school to form a small theatre in a former New Haven meat
market, naming it the Long Wharf. Persuaded to join them, Brown was hired
to supervise their children's theatre productions, and in 1966 he directed his first
full-length play, *Long Day's Journey into Night*, with Mildred Dunnock and
Frank Langella for Long Wharf's main stage.

With the theatre suffering from financial problems, Jory and Kleiman left,
and Brown was appointed artistic director in 1967. In 1970, M. Edgar Rosenblum
joined him as executive director. Since that time, the theatre's future has never
been in financial jeopardy, and Brown has directed and/or supervised over 200
plays, more than 40 of which have moved to Broadway.

Regarded as an "actor's director," Brown emphasizes the importance of the
text, the author's original intentions, and his actors' impulses. Rehearsals are
truly collaborative and relaxed. Consequently, a large number of actors (including
Al Pacino, Kathleen Turner, John Lithgow, Richard Dreyfuss, Joanne Woodward, Hume Cronyn, Jessica Tandy, Colleen Dewhurst, Jason Robards, Linda
Hunt, and Stacy Keach) have returned repeatedly to the Long Wharf to work
with him. His directorial style has been described as having a "muscular reality";
his approach to a play is generally more visceral than cerebral; and his directorial
technique has been described as "unobtrusive" and "subtle." Leaving an Arvin
Brown production, one is struck not by an emphasis on directorial *concept*, but
rather the actors' *performances*, as he prides himself in a final product in which
the directing seems to be "invisible."

Brown's selection of his seasons has been eclectic, as he has chosen plays he
has wanted to direct rather than the plays he thought he should direct. These
have ranged from smaller chamber plays, which accommodated the small Long
Wharf main stage in his early years, to a new interest in musical theatre and
opera, as well as to British imports, world premieres, and revivals of the classics.

In 1978, Stage II was established at the Long Wharf especially for the development of new plays. Also in that year, Broadway honored his theatre with a special Regional Theatre Tony Award. According to his peers, as a director Brown is "extraordinarily perceptive and precise," "generous," "a fine gentleman," "a divinely patient man," and "a brilliant director." In 1967, he married the actress Joyce Ebert, who remains one of the leading players at the Long Wharf.

ADDITIONAL PRODUCTIONS: 1968: *The Indian Wants the Bronx* (Israel Horowitz, London premiere); 1970: *Hay Fever* (Brown's first Broadway production); 1971: *Solitaire/ Double Solitaire* (Robert Anderson, Edinburgh Festival); 1974: *The National Health* (Peter Nichols); 1975: *Ah, Wilderness*; 1978: *Amahl and the Night Visitors* (NBC Television); 1980: *American Buffalo* (with Al Pacino); 1983: *A View from the Bridge*; 1985: *Requiem for a Heavyweight, A Day in the Death of Joe Egg* (two Tony nominations and Vernon Rice Award for Directing); 1986: *All My Sons* (Tony Award, Best Revival on Broadway); 1988: *In a Grove* (produced with National Theatre of the Deaf and presented in Republic of China); 1989: *Porgy and Bess* (Metropolitan Opera).

SELECTED BIBLIOGRAPHY: Backalenick, Irene. "Long Wharf Celebrates Its 25th Anniversary." *Theatre Week* 6 November 1989:27–31; Bartow, Arthur. *The Director's Voice*. New York: Theatre Communications Group, 1988:20–35; Brown, Arvin. "The Art of the Possible." *American Theatre* 2 (September 1985): 17–18; Brown, Arvin. "Hands across the Sea." *American Theatre* 3(March 1987):24–25; Brown, Arvin. "What Does an Artistic Director Do?" *New York Theatre Review* January 1979: 14–15; Klein, Alvin. "Long Wharf Director Sets a Fast Pace." *New York Times* 6 January 1985; sec. 2:23; Morrow, Lee Ann, and Frank Pike. *Creating Theatre*. New York: Vintage, 1986: 85–136; Novick, Julius. "He Trusts Plays, He Trusts Actors." *New York Times* 12 October 1975; sec. 2:1 + .

Robert Chapel

MAURICE BROWNE [b. February 12, 1881, Reading, England; d. January 21, 1955, Torquay, England]. During his varied career, Maurice Browne worked as a teacher, poet, actor, playwright, producer, and director. However, he is probably best known as the founder of the Little Theatre Movement in the United States.

Born in England, Maurice Browne was educated at Cambridge University. After graduation, Browne traveled extensively, wrote poetry, and taught at various colleges. He also had a short career as a publisher before following actress Ellen Van Volkenburg to Chicago in 1910.

In 1911 the Irish Players of the Abbey Theatre performed *The Playboy of the Western World* in Chicago. Browne was so inspired that even with no money, experience, actors, or theatre, he decided to start his own company. He and Van Volkenburg wanted to develop an experimental theatre where new ideas and techniques could be developed independent of box office revenue. They relied on subscriptions and a few endowments for their income. Irish playwright Lady Gregory encouraged the pair, suggesting that they use only amateur actors and not confuse literary and theatrical values.

The first productions, in 1912, were staged in a ninety-one seat theatre with a tiny stage on the fourth floor of the Fine Arts Building. Although the house was rarely full, it attracted the artistic and political radicals of Chicago and elsewhere, and as a result its influence was far-reaching. Continually close to financial disaster, the Chicago Little Theatre survived for five years. Personal conflicts within the company and the advent of World War I finally proved its undoing. Browne and Van Volkenburg moved to the West Coast and worked at various theatrical enterprises. From 1927 Browne worked in London, where he acted, managed several theatres, and produced *Journey's End* (1929).

Browne's ideas about theatre and directing were greatly influenced by Gordon Craig and others of the "New Movement" of theatre in Europe. Browne felt that the theatre should have a religious and ritualistic nature where meaningless movement was eliminated. Trying to move away from the realism of drama and its dependence on the human body, Browne became increasingly involved with mime and puppetry. He believed that theatre was a collective art form in which each person should subordinate both personality and art to the whole. There were no stars, parts were often alternated, and the names of individual actors were not listed in the program. Browne also felt, however, that it was essential that the director have the freedom to mold the entire production to his concept. Although realistic plays from European sources were fundamental to the repertory, improvisation was very important, and the text was often subordinated to movement and light.

Browne and the Chicago Little Theatre were very influential on the organization of both the Provincetown Players and the Washington Square Players.

ADDITIONAL PRODUCTIONS: 1912–17: *Womankind* (W. W. Gibson), *On Baile's Strand*, *Anatol* (Schnitzler), *Passion Play in Silhouette*, *The Trojan Women*, *Medea*, *The King of the Jews*, *Deirdre of the Sorrows* (Synge), *Hedda Gabler*, *Mrs. Warren's Profession*, *Rosmersholm*; 1920: *Medea*; 1921: *Iphigenia in Aulis* (with Margaret Anglin); 1922: *Mr. Faustus*.

SELECTED BIBLIOGRAPHY: Browne, Maurice. "The New Rhythmic Drama," Parts 1 and 2. *The Drama* 4 (November 1914): 616–30, 5 (February 1915): 146–60; Browne, Maurice. "The Temple of a Living Art." *The Drama* 3 (November 1913): 160–78; Browne, Maurice. *Too Late to Lament*. Bloomington: Indiana University Press, 1956; Chinoy, Helen Krich. "The Professional and the Art, Directing in America, 1860–1920." *The American Theatre: A Sum of Its Parts*. New York: Samuel French, 1971: 125–51; Feinsod, Arthur. *The Simple Stage: Its Origins in the Modern American Theater*. Westport, CT: Greenwood Press, 1992: 77–106; Head, Cloyd. "The Chicago Little Theatre." *Theatre Arts* 1 (May 1917): 110–16; Henderson, Mary C. *Theatre in America*. New York: Harry N. Abrams, 1986: 105–6, 266–67; Lock, Charles. "Maurice Browne and the Chicago Little Theatre." *Modern Drama* 31 (March 1988): 106–16.

Candice M. Coleman

RENÉ AUGUSTO BUCH [b. December 19, 1925, Santiago de Cuba, Cuba]. Cofounder of New York City's Repertorio Español, René Buch stands as one of the foremost Spanish-language directors active in the United States today. Since 1968, Buch and his company have brought Spanish classics, modern Latin American plays, and original musical revues to both English- and Spanish-speaking audiences.

Active as a playwright in his native Cuba, Buch was strongly influenced by the company of Louis Jouvet* when it was stranded in Havana during World War II. After moving to the United States and receiving his M.F.A. from Yale Drama School in 1952, Buch devoted most of the next two decades to journalism. Only in 1969, however, when he founded the Greenwich Mews Spanish Theatre with Gilberto Zaldivar, did he begin to devote himself primarily to theatre. His staging of Nelson Dorr's *Las pericas* that year, along with his previous production of Calderón's *La dama duende* in 1968, helped establish the emerging company's reputation. In 1972, the troupe was renamed Repertorio Español and moved into the 149-seat Gramercy Arts Theatre.

Buch's productions with Repertorio Español, which he serves as artistic director, have included works presented alternately in English and Spanish, although the bulk of his work has been for Spanish-speaking audiences. In addition to Golden Age plays by Calderón and Lope de Vega, Buch has staged most of García Lorca's works, other classics of the modern international repertory, works by emerging Latin American playwrights, and original pieces such as Buch's adaptation of the fifteenth-century dramatic dialogue, *La celestina*. True to its name, the company has maintained many of its productions in active repertory, restaging and reconceiving them as necessary. Buch has also directed at regional theatres outside of New York, including Calderón's *Secret Injury, Secret Revenge* (1982) for the Milwaukee Repertory and *Fuente Ovejuna* (1991) for Washington's Folger Theatre.

Buch sees the actor as the center of the play, and his productions have depended on the physicality and ingenuity of his performers while, in the tradition of Jouvet, remaining true to the text. With the frequent collaboration of designer Roberto Weber Federico, Buch has striven for simple, striking staging concepts. His rhythmically precise work has received frequent praise from the critics in New York for its understated dramatic intelligence.

ADDITIONAL PRODUCTIONS: 1971: *Life Is a Dream*; 1972: *Who's Afraid of Virginia Woolf?*; 1973: *Blood Wedding*; 1974: *La celestina*; 1976: *La malquerida* (Benavente); 1981: *The Cherry Orchard*; 1983: *Cafe con leche* (Gloria Gonzalez); 1984: *Habana* (Buch and Pablo Zinger); 1986: *El burlador de Sevilla*; 1988: *A Burning Beach* (Eduardo Machado).

SELECTED BIBLIOGRAPHY: Bartow, Arthur. *The Director's Voice*. New York: Theatre Communications Group, 1988: 36–50; Strand, John. "Back with a Vengeance." *American Theatre* 8 (May 1991): 24–30.

Harley Erdman

PAUL BUISSONNEAU [b. December 24, 1926, Paris, France]. Paul Buissonneau is a producer, director, actor, artistic director, set designer, writer, marionettist, and professor of mime. He studied theatre in France with Hubert Gignoux, Yves Joly, and Léon Chancerel with whom he continued to work. He made his debut as the manager of a travelling company, the Théâtre de la Ville et des Champs (City and Country Theatre). In 1946, he joined the Compagnons de la Chanson and was part of their international tour with the popular singer Édith Piaf, which led him to Quebec where he settled in 1950.

In 1952, Buissonneau took charge of La Roulotte, a travelling theatre charged with enlivening between 35 and 40 parks and playgrounds. He directed children's entertainments, offering at the end of each evening a popular tale based in the arts of mime and the masque. Buissonneau's artistic spirit was the vehicle that allowed him to find his own unique style, which was full of ingenuity and fantasy, and his creations virtually astounded his audiences. In this adventure, which lasted 25 years, Buissonneau involved a number of young artists—actors, designers, costumers and technicians—who were initiated into the theatre and for whom La Roulotte became a training school.

In 1955, Buissonneau founded the Théâtre de Quat'Sous. With this company, he directed ten plays, among them *Orion le tueur* (Fombeurre and Grenier), *La Bande à Bonnot* (H. F. Ré), *Voulez-vous jouer avec moâ* and *Malbrough s'en va-t-en-guerre* (M. Achard), *La Tour Eiffel qui tue* (Hanoteau), which he revived in 1976, and *Les Oiseaux de lune* (Marcel Aymé). These fresh and bold productions were produced in some of Montreal's most prominent theatres (Gésu, Comédie Canadienne, Orphéum, la Poudrière). In 1960, he wrote *Le Manteau de Galilée*, which he presented at the Orphéum. He revived the production in 1964 at the Place des Arts. In the interim, on a scholarship from the Conseil des Arts du Canada (Canadian Council of Arts) in 1961, he studied with Maximilien Decroux and apprenticed at the Grenier in Toulouse.

On his return in 1963, he made the Théâtre de Quat'Sous a non-profit organization and, with Yvon Deschamps, Claude Léveillée, and Jean-Louis Millette, bought a synagogue at 100 est ave. des Pins, which was transformed into a 160-seat theatre. The theatre was inaugurated in Autumn 1965. In the meantime, he was responsible for two summer seasons at the Centre d'art de Repentigny (Repentigny Art Center) and produced in its pavillion *Le Cirque aux illusions* (René Aubert) and *La Jument du Roi* (J. Canole).

As artistic director of the Théâtre de Quat'Sous, a post which he occupied from 1965 to 1984, Buissonneau played an important role in the development of the collective creation of a rising generation of Quebec dramatic artists. In May 1968, he directed *L'Osstidcho*, which reunited singers Robert Charlebois, Louise Forestier, Mouffe, Yvon Deschamps, and the Jazz Libre du Quebec quartet (Quebec Free Jazz Quartet). He introduced texts by Jean Morin, Robert Gurik, Marie Savard, Serges Sirois, and Michel Tremblay. In the 1980s, he presented a new generation of authors: Marc Drouin, Normand Chaurette, René Daniel Dubois, and André Ducharme. At the same time, he produced and directed authors from the international repertoire. He chose authors who stimulated his imagination and allowed him considerable freedom of expression. But his activities were not completely restricted to the Théâtre de Quat'Sous. He guest directed at a number of different theatre companies, including Théâtre du Noveau Monde and the Rideau Vert (Green Curtain), among others, and in dramatic training schools including the Conservatoire and Cegep Lionel-Groulx.

During his career, Buissonneau directed almost sixty plays and created twenty sets, while remaining active as marionettist, producer, television actor (the character Piccolo), and film actor.

ADDITIONAL PRODUCTIONS: 1965: *La Florentine* (J. Canole); 1966: *La grande roue* (G. Hanoteau); 1967: *Luv* (Murray Schisgal), *The Knack* (Ann Jellicoe), *La promenade du dimanche* (Georges Michel); 1968: *Le Chemin du Roy* (Françoise Loranger), *Peuple à genoux* (collective creation); 1969: *Vive l'empereur* (Jean Morin), *Demain, une fenêtre sur rue* (J. C. Grumberg), *Il faut jeter la vieille* (Dario Fo), *La Clameur de la foule* (Edouardo Manet); 1970: *N'écrivez jamais au facteur*, (M. Faure), *Le diable en été* (M. Faure); 1971: *D.D.T.* (in collaboration with M. Faure), *Les balançoires* (Jean O'Neil); 1972: *Arbalète et vieilles rapières* (Georges Michel); 1973: *Aujourd'hui peut-être* (Serges Sirois); 1974: *Le Chinois* (M. Faure), *Eux (Edouardo Manet); 1975: Exercises de style* (Raymond Queneau); 1978: *Théâtre de Chambre* (Jean Tardieu), *The Lesson* (E. Ionesco), *La cantatrice chauve* (E. Ionesco), *La crique* (Guy Foissy); 1981: *Exercise de diction et de conversation française pour étudiants américains* (E. Ionesco); 1983: *The Resistible Rise of Arturo Ui* (Bertolt Brecht); 1989: *La terre est une pizza* (Gilles Carle), *The Chairs* (E. Ionesco).

SELECTED BIBLIOGRAPHY: Laplante, Jean de. *Les parcs de Montréal, des origines à nos jours*, 151–53; Montréal: Méridien; *Le théâtre canadien-française*. Ed. Paul Wyczynski, Bernard Julien, and Hélène Beauchamp-Rank. Montreal: Fides, Archives des Lettres canadiennes, tome V, 1976: 840–41; MacDuff, Pierre. *The Oxford Companion to Canadian Theatre*, 533–34, ed. Benson and Connoly. London: Oxford University Press, 1989.

Renée N. Gurik

EMIL FRANTIŠEK BURIAN [b. June 11, 1904, Pilsen, Bohemia; d. August 9, 1959, Prague, Czechoslovakia]. The offspring of professional concert and opera singers, and himself a graduate of composition from the Prague Conservatory, E. F. Burian became a preeminent avant-garde theatre artist in Czechoslovakia during the 1920s and 1930s, eventually establishing his own theatre, which achieved international recognition. Although he composed several operas and ballets and provided incidental music for most of his own productions, Burian's major achievements occurred as a director, one who was committed to theatre as a creation of poetic synthesis devoted to Marxist sociopolitical reform. The duality of this ideal frequently caused Burian trouble when one element seemed sacrificed to the other, but it also led to a series of notable productions in which aesthetic and ideational values reinforced each other with striking effect.

In the 1920s, Burian's efforts were channelled mainly into music and acting. He was associated primarily with productions directed by his two peers, Jiří Frejka* and Jindřich Honzl,* in the Liberated Theatre, Theatre Dada, and the Modern Studio; but he also developed a unique form of choral song and poetic recital called Voiceband, with which he toured successfully both in Czechoslovakia and throughout Europe. His early directing experience occurred in Brno and Olomouc between 1929 and 1932. Working within relatively conventional theatre organizations in those cities made Burian aware that if he wanted to do his own distinctive type of theatre, he would have to start his own company. He did so in 1933 in Prague, calling his theatre D34. The letter *D* stood for the Czech word for theatre (*divadlo*), while the numbers represented the forthcoming theatre season and thus changed each year. At first his repertoire reflected the sociopolitical, even agitprop end of Burian's creative spectrum, and his approach was compared to that of Erwin Piscator*; but gradually Burian's innately poetic, musically based creativity made its presence felt, which led some critics to compare his work to that of Aleksandr Tairov.*

Burian would rarely stage a play exactly the way it was written, unless he wrote or orchestrated the text himself. Burian preferred to work with texts that lent themselves to his editing and adaptation, frequently taking nondramatic literary material and weaving it together with his musical, choreographic accompaniment. He was particularly drawn to folk poetry and tales, which he dramatized with great sensitivity to their lyrical stage values. These he imbued with strong relevance to contemporary issues, such as the growing threat of fascism and war (e.g., in *Vojna* [*War*], 1935). The fact that he rarely worked in large, well-equipped theatres did not hamper Burian's flair for precisely modulated and orchestrated staging, which reached its peak in productions identified with his Theatergraph, a unique system of complex lighting, film and slide projection onto scrims and opaque surfaces which enclosed the actors. With this instrument, Burian found fullest expression for his poetic, metaphoric sense of space, time, and imagery (e.g., *Spring's Awakening*, 1936, and *Eugene Onegin*, 1937).

A sophisticated, cosmopolitan artist, Burian was not always able to adapt to the restrictive implications of his Communist affiliation. Deeply distressed at the maltreatment of his Soviet hero, the great director Vsevolod Meyerhold,* Burian produced several plays (above all *Hamlet III*, his own version of the Hamlet story staged in 1937) in the mid-thirties that conveyed his artistic defiance of all political oppression. Nevertheless, Burian did not shift ideological allegiances. He was interned in a concentration camp during the last four years of the war, but resumed his career immediately after its end and reactivated his theatre, then D46. For the rest of his life, Burian strove to find a formula that would enable him to combine his poetic creativity and his fidelity to the Communist regime. His productions essentially alternated between revivals of his prewar poetic theatre productions and attempts at a new psychological realism that would explore the state of man in a socialist society. Never quite at home with the realistic form, he died before finding a satisfactory solution.

ADDITIONAL PRODUCTIONS: 1929: *Mandragola, The Emperor Jones*; 1930: *Threepenny Opera*; 1935: *Maj* [*May*] (K. H. Mácha), *The Good Soldier Schweik* (Jaroslav Hašek); 1936: *The Barber of Seville*; 1938: *The Sorrows of Young Werther* (J. W. Goethe), *První Lidová Suita* [*The First Folk Suite*] (E. F. Burian), *Věra Lukášová* (E. F. Burian); 1940: *Manon Lescaut* (V. Nezval); 1941: *Loretka* (V. Nezval); 1945: *Romeo and Juliet*; 1946: *Cyrano de Bergerac*.

SELECTED BIBLIOGRAPHY: Burian, E. F. *Pražská Dramaturgie [Prague Dramaturgy]*.
Prague: Kompas, 1938; Burian, Jarka. "E. F. Burian: D34-D41." *The Drama Review*
20 (Dec. 1976); 95–116; Burian, Jarka. "High Points of Theatre in the First Czechoslovak
Republic." *Modern Drama* 27 (March 1984): 98–111; Kladiva, Jaroslav. *E. F. Burian*.
Prague: Jazz Petit, 1982; Obst, Milan, and Adolf Scherl. *K Dějinám České Divadelní
Avantgardy [The Czech Theatrical Avant-garde]*. Prague: Československá Akademie Věd,
1962; Rutte, Miroslav, and František Bartoš. *The Modern Czech Scene*. Prague: Vladimír
Zikeš, 1938; Vočadlo, Otakar. "The Theater and Drama of Czechoslovakia." *The Theater
in a Changing Europe*. Ed. T. H. Dickinson. New York: Henry Holt, 1937.

Jarka M. Burian

RICHARD HUBBER BURNSIDE [b. August 13, 1870, Glasgow, Scotland; d.
September 14, 1952, Metuchen, New Jersey]. Son of the manager of Glasgow's
Gaiety Theatre, R. H. Burnside performed in theatre and variety as a child
throughout Scotland and England. In adult publicity, he recalled being a call
boy at the Savoy Theatre, London, and appearing in the original production of
Charley's Aunt. He became the stage manager and director for Lillian Russell,
who brought him to America to stage *The Queen of Brilliants*, *The Grand
Duchess*, and *La Perichole* (all in the 1894–95 season), and *Lady Teasle* (1904).

Burnside became famous in the United States for his work as director and
author of over two hundred shows. His American career included three concurrent
sets of productions—musical comedies for producer-theatre owner Charles A.
Dillingham, musicals for vaudevillians David Montgomery and Fred Stone, and
extravagant revues for the Hippodrome Theatre. His Dillingham collaborations
began with the Victor Herbert operetta *The Red Mill* in 1906 and included many
plotted musicals built around the newly popular exhibition ballroom dance stars
and tunes, among them Irving Berlin's first complete scores, *Watch Your Step*
(1914) and *Stop! Look! Listen!* (1915). The productions for Montgomery and
Stone, such as *The Lady of the Slipper* (1912) and *Chin Chin* (1914), were
modernized fairy tales, designed for the pair's eccentric dance and comedy
talents. After Montgomery's death, Burnside staged many popular musical comedies for Stone's family act, *Stepping Stones*. The full-evening vaudevilles at
Dillingham's massive Hippodrome (1915–23), with names like *Everything*, *Good
Times*, and *Better Times*, included more than two dozen production numbers
with casts of over 500 choristers, actors, comics, singers, equestrians, trick
bicycle riders, divers, and animals. Many revues featured aerial effects or used
the famous water tank in and on which he staged ice skating, roller dancing,
and swimming acts starring Annette Kellermann. Burnside, also a gifted lyricist,
staged production numbers around songs co-written by then-new talents Raymond
Hubbell, Harry Tierney, Irving Berlin, and John Golden.

Burnside was also a successful creator of pageants and community spectacles,
including *Freedom*, the Philadelphia Sesqui-Centennial (1926), and of benefits.
He was briefly involved in motion pictures in the early 1920s, producing for
Famous Players-Lasky in New York. His final professional stage activity was a
repertory company of Gilbert and Sullivan revivals in 1942–45.

ADDITIONAL PRODUCTIONS: 1903: *Sergeant Kitty*; 1907: *Fascinating Flora*; 1908: *The War of the Worlds*; 1909: *A Trip to Japan*; 1915: *Hip Hip Hooray!*; 1916: *The Big Show*; 1917: *Jack O'Lantern*; 1919: *Happy Days*; 1920: *Tip Top*; 1923: *The Stepping Stones*; 1929: *Great Day, How's Your Health*; 1933: *Hold Your Horses*; 1940: *Walk with Music*. RESOURCE NOTE: The suitably mammoth R. H. Burnside collection of scripts, staging notebooks, manuscripts, original designs, scrapbooks, and scores can be found in the Billy Rose Theatre Collection and the Americana Collection, Music Division, New York Public Library for the Performing Arts, and the Manuscript Collections, New York Public Library.

                                                                      Barbara Cohen-Stratyner

C

JOHN CAIRD [b. September 22, 1948, Montreal, Canada]. In the opinion of director John Caird, the idea "that the director is considered an undeniable force and source of wisdom is rubbish" (*Plays and Players,* 11). Caird is noted for his original interpretations of Shakespeare and Jonson, his work with Trevor Nunn* on Royal Shakespeare Company (RSC) hits *Nicholas Nickleby* (1980) and *Les Misérables* (1986), and his advocacy of the collaboration process in directing.

Born into a professor's family, Caird grew up in a university environment. He trained as an actor at the Bristol Old Vic School, but soon discovered that he had little aptitude or patience with "soldiering" across the stage. He found himself fascinated by dramatic literature, criticizing productions and puzzling over the dismal level of acting. Through directing he found a means of controlling the end product.

Though somewhat less known than his friend and collaborator Trevor Nunn, Caird has guided some of the most exciting British theatre of the past decade. Nunn discovered Caird, starting him at the Royal Shakespeare Company in 1977 as a director of laboratory productions. There, Caird had the opportunity to work with both classic texts and fledgling writers. He rejected the autocratic directing model, scoffing at the notion that the director knows all, and he developed a collaborative working method, involving writers and actors intimately in the process of creating the works. One of his techniques asks actors to prepare research material about the play's period and conventions and demands that *everyone* make oral reports. The technique unifies and trains the cast. Everyone teaches; everyone learns.

Experiences in lab theatres allowed Caird to develop his skills and talent. In the RSC's Pit and Warehouse spaces, Caird codirected productions of *Merry Wives of Windsor* (1979) and *As You Like It* (1978) with Nunn. He achieved international notice as co-director (with Nunn) of the successful eight-and-a-half hour production of *Nicholas Nickleby,* the RSC's 1980 commercial breakthrough which started the current wave of high-budget British imports. The production took shape when the RSC experienced a funding shortfall and needed a large-scale production to engage and reenergize the financially strapped company. Artistic director Trevor Nunn called upon Caird to co-direct the mammoth project, which had both directors literally directing as author-adaptor David Edgar rewrote scenes. The work codified the RSC's Brechtian approach to staging during the 1960s–70s. Caird and Nunn focused on actor-centered staging, increasing the flexibility of the thirty-two actors to allow them to play 135 speaking roles. The set, a rambling, precarious, structuralist assemblage of ramps and platforms by master RSC designer John Napier, engaged Caird's laboratory theatre imagination.

Caird also continued to work in small productions. After the success of his 1982 production of Andrew Lloyd Webber's *Song and Dance,* an evening of choreography and music, he went back to the RSC's Pit to stage a small epic, Peter Flannery's three-hour *Our Friends from the North* (1982), which detailed the corruption of British government from 1964 to 1982 through the eyes of grafters, politicians, and radicals. In fact, Caird's productions of *Caucasian Chalk Circle* (1979), *Our Friends from the North, Les Misérables,* and *A Question of Geography* (1988) suggest an underlying emphasis on themes of corruption and dehumanizing political systems.

In the 1980s, Caird championed the long-neglected work of Ben Jonson who, Caird claimed, had been written off by the British theatrical establishment as a one-play writer. He directed Jonson's *Every Man in His Humour* (1986) and *The New Inn* (1987).

In 1986, Caird and Nunn scored a second hit with *Les Misérables,* a musical adaptation of Victor Hugo's famous novel. Caird and Nunn were late additions to the play which had previously been performed in France. They reinvented the production for English audiences, creating a horrific revolutionary France as a means to unveil Hugo's political and theological views. Caird and Nunn shared the Tony Award (1986) for their efforts.

Caird's 1989 *A Midsummer Night's Dream* surprised critics with its bicycle graveyard-styled Athenian wood, its punky, autograph-giving Puck, and fox-trotting resolution. In 1990, the RSC considered Caird to replace outgoing artistic director Terry Hands, but the job fell to Adrian Noble.* Caird departed the RSC in February 1991, starting his own independent production company. In 1991, he joined forces with composer and lyricist Stephen Schwartz to create *Children* *of Eden,* an allegory beginning with the biblical fall of man and moving to contemporary ecological crises.

ADDITIONAL PRODUCTIONS: 1977: *Dance of Death*; 1978: *Savage Amusement* (Peter Flannery); 1981: *Naked Robots* (Jonathan Gems), *The Twin Rivals* (Farquhar); 1982: *Peter Pan* (with Nunn); 1989: *As You Like It.*

SELECTED BIBLIOGRAPHY: Cook, Judith. *Director's Theatre.* London: Holden and Stoughton, 1989: 43–52; Engstrom, John. "Dickens on Broadway" (interview with John Caird about *Nicholas Nickleby*). *Horizon* September 1981: 57–61; "New Musical's Opening Off Off Off Broadway." *New York Times* 6 January 1991; sec. L: 40; Roper, David. "A Young Man's Game?" (interview). *Plays and Players* June 1982: 10–12; Rubin, Leon. *The Nicholas Nickleby Story.* Hammondsworth, Middlesex, England: Penguin Books, 1981.

Stuart Lenig

VINNETTE CARROLL [b. March 11, 1922, New York, New York]. Broadway's first black female director, Vinnette Carroll has dedicated her life to nurturing the talents of black actors and the growth of black audiences. Carroll spent much of her formative years in her parents' native country of Jamaica, where she developed a keen sense of ethnic pride. Her education included a firm grounding in black history with an appreciation of the classics of Western literature and music. With the exception of a dissertation, she had completed all requirements for a doctorate in psychology when she accepted a scholarship to study acting with Erwin Piscator* at the New School for Social Research, 1948–50. While continuing her studies with such famed instructors as Lee Strasberg* and Stella Adler, Carroll acted professionally and taught at New York's High School for the Performing Arts. Her attentions turned to directing, although the profession provided little precedent for such an aspiration by African Americans, especially black women. The 1957 Harlem YMCA Drama Guild production of *Dark of the Moon,* Carroll's most notable project of this early period in her career, featured such fledgling African-American actors as James Earl Jones, Cicely Tyson, and Rosalind Cash.

Carroll's first commercial breakthrough came with the 1962 production of Langston Hughes's *Black Nativity.* Influenced by her growing appreciation for the inherent theatricality and cultural esteem of the African-American Baptist church, the production fused Hughes's narrative with the vibrancy of the church's gospel music and oral traditions. The enthusiastic reception of the production in no small part led to its inclusion as *the* Christmas holiday production of many black performing arts groups throughout the nation. Carroll utilized this new theatre form, sometimes known as the "song play," in such subsequent productions as *Trumpets of the Lord* (adapted from James Weldon Johnson's *God's Trombones,* 1962), and *The Prodigal Son* (Langston Hughes, 1963).

Carroll has staged works in such cities as Los Angeles, Miami, London, and Paris. However, she is best known for her long association with New York's

Urban Arts Corps (UAC), founded in 1968 with the assistance of the New York Council on the Arts. Carroll served as the artistic director of the company which developed the professional skills of minority performers, writers, and composers. With a constituency primarily of black artists, UAC conducted classes to hone their talents and employed a workshop format to develop plays. Usually, Carroll conceived of the projects and created plays using source material from folktales, the Bible, and Western classic and contemporary literature. She and composer Micki Grant, Carroll's collaborator on many productions, merged the narrative, written in a black idiom, with music and dance into a seamless tapestry using distinctive black theatrical forms and traditions. In their best known productions—*Don't Bother Me, I Can't Cope* (1971) and *Your Arms Too Short to Box with God* (with music and lyrics by Grant and Alex Bradford based on the Gospel of St. Matthew, 1975)—these elements are derived from the rituals and musical styles of the African-American church. Due to their popularity, a few of these productions have played on Broadway as well as toured extensively throughout the nation and Europe. This refined form of the song play has since been widely imitated in many contemporary productions such as *Mama, I Want to Sing* and *Don't Get God Started*.

A self-described "Earth Mother," Carroll created a rehearsal atmosphere of warmth and compassion for her actors, while maintaining a high level of professionalism. She has served as a prominent force in the careers of such black actors as Phylicia Rashad, Ben Vereen, Glynn Turman, Al Freeman, Jr., and Debbie Allen. Her productions offered dignified and uplifting roles to African-American actors weary of the usual stereotypes of the American theatre. Black audiences, rarely welcome in commercial theatre houses, attended Carroll's productions in large numbers to enjoy plays which reflected their lives and culture in a familiar style.

ADDITIONAL PRODUCTIONS: 1969: *But Never Jam Today* (adapted by Carroll from Lewis Carroll's *Alice's Adventures in Wonderland* and *Through the Looking Glass*); 1972: *Step Lively Boy* (adapted by Carroll with music and lyrics by Grant from Irwin Shaw's play, *Bury the Dead*); 1974: *The Ups and Downs of Theophilus Maitland* (adapted by Carroll with music and lyrics by Grant based on a West Indian folktale), *All the King's Men* (adapted by Carroll from play of the same title by Robert Penn Warren); 1979: *When Hell Freezes Over* (Carroll).

SELECTED BIBLIOGRAPHY: Jack, Carolyn. "Carroll Has a Mission, A New Home." *American Theatre* 5 (November 1988): 42–43; Mapp, Edward. *Directory of Blacks in the Performing Arts*. 2nd ed. Metuchen, NJ: Scarecrow Press, 1990; Mitchell, Loften. *Voices of the Black Theatre*. Clifton, NJ: James T. White and Co, 1975; Peterson, Bernard L., Jr. *Contemporary Black American Playwrights and Their Plays*. Westport, CT: Greenwood Press, 1988; Tanner, Jo A. "Carroll, Vinnette." *Notable Women in the American Theatre*. Ed. Alice Robinson, Vera Mowry Roberts, and Milly Barranger. Westport, CT: Greenwood Press, 1989: 111–14; Woll, Alan. *Black Musical Theatre*. Baton Rouge: Louisiana State University Press, 1989.

Addell Austin Anderson

JOSEPH CHAIKIN [b. September 16, 1935, Brooklyn, New York]. A major director of experimental, noncommercial theatre, Joseph Chaikin can best be described as a strong leader of collaborative endeavors. As founder and director of New York's Open Theater (1963–73) and Winter Project (1976–83), Chaikin created artistic collectives of actors, writers, designers, and musicians who would explore such universal issues as creation, dreams, and death. Although Chaikin always made the final directorial decisions, he allowed his company the freedom to create and provided a space in which that creativity could flourish.

Chaikin was born in Brooklyn, New York, but grew up in Des Moines, Iowa, where he studied philosophy and drama at Drake University. As a child, he suffered from rheumatic fever, which severely weakened his heart. He would undergo numerous heart surgeries in later life, the last of which, in 1984, caused a severe stroke that gave him aphasia.

Chaikin moved to New York City in 1955 and studied Method acting with Herbert Berghof, Mira Rostova, and Nola Chilton. In 1959, he joined the Living Theatre, where he became a leading actor in such plays as *The Connection* (1959), *In the Jungle of the Cities* (1960), and *Man Is Man* (1962).

Chaikin's portrayal of Galy Gay in *Man Is Man* was pivotal to his career. Although it won him his first major critical acclaim, it also convinced him to forgo commercial success in favor of artistic and political concerns. He also learned that psychological acting techniques do not work in non-naturalistic theatre. Consequently, he organized a workshop within the Living Theatre to explore different modes of acting. The group struck out on its own and, with Chaikin as its leader, became the Open Theater.

The Open Theater began as a laboratory for improvisational and ensemble exercises. Its first two productions, written by resident playwrights Megan Terry (*Viet Rock*) and Jean-Claude van Itallie (*America Hurrah*), opened in 1966 and were commercial and critical successes. Chaikin's first directing credit was the *Interview* section of the three-part *America Hurrah*.

Despite the company's Obie Award ''for maintaining a laboratory where a company of actors, directors, and playwrights confront the limits of contemporary theatre experience,'' Chaikin was dissatisfied with the commercialism of their work which, he felt, stifled creativity and inhibited risk-taking. His workshops began to focus on creating full-length performance pieces that were seamless collaborations of actor, director, and playwright. The first, *The Serpent: A Ceremony* (1968), explored the company's personal reactions to the Book of Genesis. *Terminal* (1969) considered death and dying; *The Mutation Show* (1971) examined change and human transformation; and *Nightwalk* (1973), the group's final effort, dealt with sleep and awareness.

Fearing that their work would become institutionalized, Chaikin disbanded the Open Theater and embarked on other projects. In 1976, he founded the Winter Project, a similar collaborative group which included former members of the Open Theater, to explore basic theatre questions, including the use of music and actor-audience relationships.

Although Chaikin has directed more traditional projects—among them *The Sea Gull* (1975) for the Manhattan Theatre Club; *Electra* (1976) for the Mark Taper Forum; and *The Dybbuk* (1977) for the New York Shakespeare Festival— it was his revolutionary work with the Open Theater and the Winter Project that brought him international attention. Unlike most American directors, Chaikin is a true collaborator who relies on his actors to develop the ideas and images that constitute the performance. He also works closely with a dramaturg, generally several contributing playwrights, and the various designers and musicians on a project, eagerly incorporating their suggestions.

Chaikin characterizes his role in the creative process as that of investigator, an explorer who uses the tools of theatre to shape and edit the final product. His most valuable tools are intelligent, sensitive performers who also are investigators—of character, situation, and ideas. The performer, while being totally engaged in his explorations, however, must also be aware of communicating to the audience. Chaikin's collaborations are not group therapy; they are highly developed, polished performances of wholly original work.

Chaikin is equally well known for his playwrighting-performing-directing collaborations with Sam Shepard, which include *Tongues* (1978), *Savage/Love* (1979), and *The War in Heaven,* completed and performed after Chaikin's 1984 stroke. Despite his disability, he remains active as a writer, performer, and director.

ADDITIONAL PRODUCTIONS: **Open Theater Productions:** 1966: *Interview* in *America Hurrah* (New York and London); 1968: *The Serpent: A Ceremony* (Obie Award, Outstanding Achievement); 1969: *Terminal*; 1971: *The Mutation Show* (Obie Award, Best Theatre Piece of the Season; Drama Desk Award, Best Director). **Winter Project Productions,** all performed at LaMama Experimental Theatre Club, New York: 1980: *Tourists and Refugees*; 1981: *Tourists and Refugees No. 2*; 1982: *Trespassing*; 1983: *Lies and Secrets*. Other: 1979: *The Dybbuk* (Habimah Theatre, Tel Aviv, Israel); 1982: *Solo Voyages* (Interart Theatre, New York); 1987: *The Bald Soprano* and *The Leader* (Cubiculo Theatre, New York).

SELECTED BIBLIOGRAPHY: Blumenthal, Eileen. *Joseph Chaikin: Exploring at the Boundaries of Theatre*. New York: Cambridge University Press, 1984; Blumenthal, Eileen. "Taking Speech to Its Limits." *New York Times* 7 June 1987; Bonarski, Andrzej. "Interview with Joseph Chaikin." *Performing Arts Journal* 1.3 (1977): 117–23; Chaikin, Joseph. *The Presence of the Actor*. New York: Atheneum, 1972; Daniels, Barry V. "Letters of Joseph Chaikin." *The Drama Review* 31 (Spring 1987): 89–100; Loney, Glenn. "Joe Chaikin: Bringing It All Back Home." *Other Stages* 23 April 1981; Toscan, Richard. "Joseph Chaikin: Closing the Open Theatre." *Theatre Quarterly* 4 (November 1974–January 1975): 36–43.

Martha Schmoyer LoMonaco

GOWER CHAMPION [b. June 22, 1919, Geneva, Illinois; d. August 25, 1980, New York, New York]. Born in Geneva, Illinois, a middle-class suburb of Chicago, Champion moved to Los Angeles with his mother, Beatrice, and older brother, John Jr., after his parents' divorce. Although most of his successes were on the New York stage, Champion always considered himself a Californian and returned there to recover from successes or failures.

Stylistically, Champion was perhaps the most enigmatic of the four great director-choreographers of the 1960s through 1980s. Jerome Robbins* was narrative and balletic; Bob Fosse* could be described as angular and filled with dazzle; Michael Bennett,* on the other hand, was characterized by a full-out Broadway jazz style of dancing. Champion was much more controlled than Bennett, yet far more lyrical than Fosse, and much more abstract than Robbins. Champion's choice of material ranged from bubble-headed teenaged satires such as *Bye, Bye, Birdie* (1960) to stories of schizophrenia and alcoholism, as in the disastrous *Prettybelle* (1971). Perhaps because whatever he did, he did honestly and without pretension, critics were kind to him, even when panning his productions.

Before he graduated from high school, he and his first dancing partner, Jeanne Tyler, won the "Veloz and Yolanda Waltz to Fame," which included as first prize an appearance at the prestigious Coconut Grove. One engagement led to another and the team, known as Gower and Jeanne, America's Youngest Dance Team, soon appeared at the best nightclubs and in two Broadway shows. World War II halted their career as Champion entered the coast guard and toured in the military revue *Tars and Spars*. After the war he tried to work in both film and Broadway but soon paired with Marjorie Belle, the daughter of one of his early dancing teachers, Ernest Belcher. As the dance team of Marge and Gower Champion they were successful in nightclubs and a series of films including the 1951 remake of *Show Boat*.

Champion had always wanted to direct, however, and accepted a number of television jobs while choreographing two revues and a musical, *Make a Wish* (1951), on Broadway. His opportunity to choreograph and direct a book musical came with *Bye, Bye, Birdie,* which opened in 1960. This success was followed with *Carnival* the next year. London productions followed, and his reputation as a first-class director-choreographer seemed set. In 1963, a disastrous Lillian Hellman play, *My Mother, My Father, and Me,* and an equally disappointing film, *My Six Loves,* seemed to set his career back, but in 1964 he staged the phenomenally successful *Hello, Dolly!,* which was, perhaps, his signature piece. Full of stylized movement and larger-than-life characterizations, particularly by Carol Channing and David Burns as Dolly Levi and Horace Vandergelder, it established the Champion style as sharp, witty, and precise, full of invention and good humor.

After *Hello, Dolly!* Champion's career seemed to take a number of odd turns. He chose bad material, such as *Rockabye Hamlet* (1976), a razzle-dazzle rock version of Shakespeare's *Hamlet,* or was unable to bring good material to full life as in *Mack and Mabel* (1974), which he tried to present as a study in abuse and drug addiction. His successes, *I Do! I Do!* (1966) and *Sugar* (1972), became thinner, and his failures became more dismal, possibly because of marital difficulties. He and Marge separated and finally divorced in 1973. Champion began to accept less and less prestigious projects, and his reputation began to fade. He married Karla Russell, a friend of long standing, in 1976 and spent much time at home. He did "doctor" a number of shows, and he even appeared with Liza Minelli as a replacement for six weeks in *The Act* in 1977.

His friend Michael Stewart (author of *Hello, Dolly!* and *Carnival*) got the director involved in a musical based on the classic film *42nd Street*. Although Champion was extremely ill with Waldenstrom's Syndrome, a rare cancer of the blood, the production successfully premiered on August 25, 1980. Champion never saw the opening, he died the afternoon of the premiere.

ADDITIONAL PRODUCTIONS: 1948: *Lend an Ear* (choreographer only), *Small Wonder* (choreographer only); 1955: *Three for Tonight*; 1968: *The Happy Time*; 1978: *A Broadway Musical*.

SELECTED BIBLIOGRAPHY: Payne Carter, David. *Gower Champion and the American Musical Theatre*. New York: Backstage Books, forthcoming; Payne Carter, David. "Gower Champion and the American Musical Theatre." Diss. New York U, 1987.

David Payne Carter

TISA CHANG [b. April 5, 1941 in Chungking, China]. Tisa Chang came to the United States in 1947 when her father became the consul general to New York City from the Republic of China. She studied ballet and traditional Chinese dance, received a scholarship from the Martha Graham Dance Company, and studied acting with Uta Hagen. After performing on Broadway, on television, and in films, Chang began to direct at La Mama ETC (Experimental Theatre Company).

In 1975, Chang formed the Chinese Theatre Group at LaMama, which was incorporated as the Pan Asian Repertory Theatre in 1977. The Pan Asian Rep has been enormously successful, providing sustained and significant professional opportunities for Asian-American theatre artists and implementing in 1986 a Senior Artists program to maintain a nucleus of an acting company.

Chang's early productions were often bilingual adaptations of classic Asian dramas. She later began to direct plays written in English by contemporary Asian-American playwrights, many containing social and political content which addressed Asian-American identity. Chang has worked in a wide range of directing styles from the naturalistic to the surrealistic, and from comic to historical to epic. She has featured multiethnic casts and traditional Asian acting techniques, such as Kabuki.

Chang's directing has been consistently praised for its clarity and creativity, and as the artistic-producing director of the award-winning Pan Asian Rep, her contribution to a multicultural theatre community has been significant.

ADDITIONAL PRODUCTIONS: 1977: *The Legend of Wu Chang*; 1979: *And the Soul Shall Dance* (Wakako Yamauchi); 1980: *Sunrise* (Cao Yu), *Monkey Music* (Margaret Lamb), *An American Story* (Ernest Abuba); 1981: *Flowers and Household Gods* (Momoko Iko), *Bullet Headed Birds* (Philip Kan Gotanda); 1982: *Station J* (Richard France); 1983: *Teahouse* (Lao She), *A Midsummer Night's Dream, Empress of China* (Ruth Wolff); 1985: *Eat a Bowl of Tea* (Abuba), *Ghashiram Kotwal* (Vijay Tendulkar); 1987: *Wha . . . i, Whai, a Long Long Time Ago* (Che Inhoon); 1988: *Boutique Living and Disposable Icons* (Iko).

SELECTED BIBLIOGRAPHY: *Contemporary Theatre, Film, and Television,* Vol. 1. Detroit: Gale Research Co., 1984: 102–3; *New York Post* 19 November 1980; *New York Times* 14 October 1977, 8 November 1977, 30 June 1979, 8 April 1980, 29 July 1980, 13 November 1980, 21 April 1981, 25 November 1981, 15 April 1982, 23 March 1983, 20 April 1983, 24 June 1983, 28 April 1984, 19 April 1985, 15 November 1985, 3 May 1987, 30 June 1988; *Newsday* 19 August 1981; Robinson, Alice M., Vera Mowry Roberts, and Milly S. Barranger, eds., *Notable Women in American Theatre: A Biographical Dictionary.* Westport, CT: Greenwood Press, 1989: 119–21; *The Villager* 21 July 1980.

Stacy Wolf

PETER CHEESEMAN [b. January 27, 1932, Portsmouth, England]. Spurred by the success of the Theatre Workshop of Joan Littlewood,* the growing regional repertory theatre movement in England turned to dramatizations of local events and issues as a way of establishing ties to local audiences. Central figures in this movement, Peter Cheeseman, who began his professional directing career at the Playhouse in Derby in 1959, and his partner Stephen Joseph, found a home for their touring Studio Theatre Company in a converted cinema, the Victoria Theatre, at Stoke-on-Trent. The Victoria Theatre thereafter became one of the leading professional repertory companies in Britain, creating documentary plays based on research into local issues, developing them with writers on the theatre's staff (including Peter Terson), and performing them in-the-round (a form developed by Cheeseman more than any other British director).

Cheeseman wanted to bridge the cultural gap which separated the artist from the majority of the community—a gap which he believed had been created by style, not by subject matter. He hoped to develop a popular style, form, and language that would reflect and attract local audiences. By encouraging group research, adapting novels of writers (such as Arnold Bennett) associated with pottery towns like Stoke, and urging playwrights to take "objective" stances in their plays, Cheeseman guided the theatre to success with a broad range of audiences with plays about working-class themes.

In addition to his work with the Victoria Theatre (he has directed nearly half of its productions), Cheeseman has directed for British television.

ADDITIONAL PRODUCTIONS: **Group Created Documentaries:** 1969: *The Jolly Potters, The Knotty* (a musical documentary about the building of the Staffordshire Railway); 1970: *Six into One* (about the local reorganization of six towns into one city), *The Staffordshire Rebels;* 1974: *The Fight for Shelton Bar* (about a local industrial dispute); *The Mighty Reservoy, A Night to Make the Angels Weep* (Peter Terson).

SELECTED BIBLIOGRAPHY: Cheeseman, Peter. "A Community Theatre-in-the-Round" and "Production Casebook on *The Staffordshire Rebels.*" *Theatre Quarterly* 1.1 (1971): 71–102; Elsom, John. *Post-war British Theatre.* Revised edition. London: Routledge and Kegan Paul, 1979.

Mark S. Weinberg

MICHAEL CHEKHOV [b. Mikhail Alexandrovich Chekhov, August 16, 1891, St. Petersburg; d. September 30, 1955, Los Angeles, California]. The nephew of the playwright Anton Chekhov, Michael Chekhov spent much of his career developing a radically new acting technique built on the principles of Konstantin Stanislavsky* and the movement-and-sound studies of Rudolf Steiner, a turn-of-the-century German spiritualist. A celebrated character actor in the Moscow Art Theatre's First Studio, Chekhov sought to create a theatre that more fully integrated the internal workings of the performer with his physical presence. As a director and teacher in Europe and America, he proselytized for a "future theatre" that could stimulate the spectator's imaginative sense of the fantastic and universal wonder. In April 1921, Chekhov inaugurated his own private studio with performances of the folk-based comedies *The First Distiller* and *Shemyaka's Journey*. Emphasizing constant improvisation and yogic psychophysical exercises, the instruction at the Chekhov Studio seemed out of place in the materialist Soviet culture. Two years later, Stanislavsky presented Chekhov with a professionally staffed playhouse, called the Second Moscow Art Theatre. There, Chekhov trained his enthusiastic actors in Steiner's Eurythmy, the "science of visible speech," and other innovative regimens. Starring in an experimental *Hamlet* (1924), Chekhov demonstrated the efficacy of his revolutionary technique as Shakespearean dream images unfolded before astonished Soviet audiences.

Fearing for his artistic freedom and safety in 1928 when socialist realism was declared a Russian state policy, Chekhov entered into a lifelong exile. In Berlin, he directed the Hebrew-language Habima Players in a lighthearted *Twelfth Night* (1930). He also mounted and starred in a modernized and reduced version of *Hamlet,* in which Claudius and Gertrude doubled as the Player King and Queen. During the early thirties in Paris and the independent Baltic republics, Chekhov reproduced much of the classical repertoire from the disbanded First Studio. His most original production was his mystical fantasy, *The Castle Awakens* (1931, in collaboration with Viktor Gromov), based on Russian folktales and Steiner's occult theories of movement, sound, and color.

Invited to perform and direct on Broadway in 1935, Chekhov and his Russian troupe, the Moscow Art Players, performed a mixed repertoire of First Studio pieces and modern Soviet plays, like Mikhail Bulgakov's *The White Guard.* Members of the Group Theatre were so impressed with Chekhov's directing and performance that they invited him to discuss a collaboration. Instead, Chekhov accepted an offer from the young actress Beatrice Straight to head a school and theatre at her family estate in Dartington, Great Britain. Freed of political and commercial restraints, Chekhov finally managed to organize his acting technique into a pedagogical format.

After the Chekhov Theatre Studio relocated to Ridgefield, Connecticut, in 1939, Chekhov directed George Shdanoff's adaptation of Dostoyevsky's novel *The Possessed* on Broadway. His actors' inexperience coupled with the heavy Russian mood of the production resulted in Chekhov's first American failure. Extensive tours of the Chekhov Theatre Studio's productions of *Twelfth Night, Cricket on the Hearth, Doublemaker-Troublemaker* (a children's play by Chekhov and Arnold Sundgaard), and *King Lear,* however, were well received in small communities across America. In 1942, Chekhov performed for the first time in English in *An Evening of Anton Chekhov's Sketches*. After the Chekhov Theatre Studio disbanded, Chekhov began a new career as a Hollywood character actor, where he appeared in eleven motion pictures, including Alfred Hitchcock's

Spellbound. Chekhov directed his last stage play, *Inspector General,* in 1946 at the Actor's Lab, starring Morris Carnovsky.

ADDITIONAL PRODUCTIONS: 1924: *Hamlet* [in collaboration with Vladimir Tatarinov and Alexei Cheban]; 1930: *Twelfth Night*; 1931: Strindberg's *Erik XIV*; 1931: *Deluge*; 1935: *Inspector General*; 1939: *The Possessed* with Beatrice Straight; 1940: *King Lear* with Yul Brynner.

SELECTED BIBLIOGRAPHY: Chekhov, Michael. *Lessons for the Professional Actor.* New York: Performing Arts Books, 1985; Chekhov, Michael. *On the Technique of Acting.* New York: HarperCollins, 1991; Chekhov, Michael. *To the Director and Playwright.* New York: Harper, 1962; Gordon, Mel. *The Stanislavsky Technique: Russia.* New York: Applause Theatre Books, 1988; *The Drama Review* 27 (Fall 1983) [Michael Chekhov Issue].

Mel Gordon

PATRICE CHÉREAU [b. November 2, 1944, Lézigné, France]. As a young boy, Patrice Chéreau sketched imaginary stage settings for the plays he was reading. This early interest in the visual aspects of theatre points to one of the most salient features of Chéreau's work as a director: the extraordinary richness and subtlety of scenography that tends to dominate his mise-en-scènes despite his undoubted and frequently praised ability as a director of actors.

Since the late 1960s, Chéreau has collaborated with scenographer Richard Peduzzi and costume designer Jacques Schmidt on almost all his productions (from time to time, Chéreau has been formally credited with aspects of the design). This unusually long-lived collaboration has enabled Chéreau to refine his favorite scenographic idioms from one production to the next. Another by-product of his long association with Peduzzi and others is that the continuity of scenographic motifs and other visual ideas in Chéreau's mise-en-scènes is far more apparent than in the productions of other directors.

In a Chéreau mise-en-scène, the human figure appears dwarfed by architectural forms and scenic motifs that tell a story of their own. Chéreau's visual narrative is akin to the techniques of *écriture scénique* (scenic writing) first introduced in France in the post-Brechtian productions of Roger Planchon* in the late 1950s and early 1960s. This technique is especially useful in the staging of classic texts, and like Planchon, Chéreau often uses the visual text to articulate a twentieth-century, historicizing critique of the society in which the classic text emerged. Frequently, Peduzzi's imposing walls seem to represent the forces of society and culture overshadowing, if not actually crushing, the characters who assemble beneath. It is all the more startling, therefore, to see Chéreau's actors employ such an extensive range of lyrical emotion in these suffocating and almost glacial spaces. This juxtaposition of lyrical performance and imposing scenography served Chéreau particularly well in his controversial staging of Wagner's *Ring* (1976–80) as well as in his production of Berg's *Lulu* (1979).

Chéreau served as artistic director of the Théâtre de Sartrouville from 1966 to 1969. He then worked for a time at the Piccolo Teatro de Milano, where he staged both Tankred Dorst's *Toller* and Pierre Marivaux's *La Finta Serva (La*

Fausse Suivante) in 1970–71. Both productions were later remounted in French versions. In 1972, Roger Planchon invited Chéreau to join him and Roger Gilbert as co-directors of the Théâtre National Populaire/Villeurbanne. Among his greatest successes at Villeurbanne was a 1973 production of Marivaux's *La Dispute* that established the play as a staple of the contemporary repertory in France and abroad. The production toured extensively in Europe, and Chéreau twice revised the staging between 1973 and 1976.

His last production as a codirector of the Théâtre National Populaire was an uncut version of *Peer Gynt* (1981) that played over two evenings. In 1982, he was appointed codirector (along with Catherine Tasca) of the Théâtre des Amandiers at Nanterre. During his time at Nanterre, Chéreau staged a series of world premieres of plays by Bernard-Marie Koltès, in addition to a well-received *Hamlet* in 1988 (Prix Molière for Best Director).

ADDITIONAL PRODUCTIONS: 1969: *Don Juan*; 1970: *Richard II*; 1972: *Le Massacre à Paris* (Christopher Marlowe); 1973–76: *La Dispute* (three versions); 1975: *Lear* (Edward Bond); 1977: *Loin d'Hagondange* (Jean-Paul Wenzel); 1983: *The Screens, Combat de nègres et de chiens* (Koltès); 1985: *Fausse Suivante, Quartett* (Heiner Müller); 1986: *Quai Ouest* (Koltès); 1987: *Dans la solitude des champs de coton* (Koltès); *Platonov* [Chekhov, adaptation Chéreau]; 1988: *Le Retour au désert* (Koltès).

SELECTED BIBLIOGRAPHY: Aslan, Odette, ed. *Chéreau*. Vol. 14 of *Les Voies de la création théâtrale*. Paris: Centre National de la Recherche Scientifique, 1986; "Chéreau, Patrice." *1990 Current Biography Yearbook*. New York: Wilson, 1990: 113–17; Nussac, Sylvie de, ed. *Nanterre Amandiers: Les Années Chéreau, 1982–1990*. Paris: Imprimerie Nationale, 1990; Pavis, Patrice. *Marivaux à épreuve de la scène*. Paris: Publications de la Sorbonne, 1986.

James Carmody

LIVIU CIULEI [b. July 7, 1923, Bucharest, Romania]. An actor, scene designer, architect, and filmmaker as well as theatre director, Liviu Ciulei is the most renowned and important figure in the history of the Romanian theatre. The son of a wealthy engineer, Ciulei earned a degree in architecture before entering the Institute of Theatre. Upon completion of his theatre training in 1945, his father built the Odeon Theatre for him and appointed him director. When the Communist government solidified its power in 1948, the Odeon was closed, and Ciulei started his career over as a scene painter at the Municipal Theatre in Bucharest. Proving himself accomplished as actor, director, and scene designer, in 1962 he assumed the position as director of the Municipal Theatre, by then renamed the Lucia Sturdza Bulandra Theatre.

Although Ciulei reached maturity during a period when a dying Stalinism reduced art to the stylistically conservative, ideologically doctrinaire, and rigidly conventional, he managed, through his knowledge of the visual arts and world culture in general, to keep alive a modernist sensibility. Although most new Romanian plays continued to avoid questioning either Communist party doctrine or the official version of life in the country, directors and designers were able to mount productions of classical plays that suggested to Romanian audiences ideas and attitudes that could only be expressed obliquely.

In the late 1960s a brief thaw in Romanian cultural policy allowed a flourishing in the nation's theatres that attracted international attention. Ciulei's productions of *Danton's Death* in 1966 and *Macbeth* in 1968 were seminal works in what Romanian artists and intellectuals initially hoped would be a more cosmopolitan and liberalized culture; but by the time Ciulei was dismissed as director of the Bulandra in 1972, hopes of liberalization had disappeared as the madness of the Ceausescu dictatorship drove most of the major Romanian theatre artists to find work abroad.

Throughout the 1960s and early 1970s, Ciulei's work in both theatre and film established his international reputation as a major artist in both media. His films *The Waves of the Danube* (1960) and *The Forest of the Hanged* (1965) both won major international prizes, with *The Forest of the Hanged* earning the award for best directing at the Cannes Film Festival. His West German productions (*Danton's Death, As You Like It, Richard II, The Sea Gull*, and *The Threepenny Opera*), his tours abroad with his Romanian company, and his appearances at major international festivals made him one of the best known, most sought after, and most discussed European theatre directors.

His American debut in 1974 at Washington's Arena Theatre with Georg Büchner's *Leonce and Lena* (visually inspired by the paintings of Jasper Johns) attracted both widespread attention and generous praise. It was not until 1977, however, that Ciulei made his New York debut with Frank Wedekind's *Spring's Awakening*, staged with students of the Julliard Theatre Center. The New York critics were impressed both by the visual expressiveness of the production and by the extraordinary performances Ciulei drew from the student actors. Critic Richard Eder of the *New York Times*, was particularly impressed by the deep cultural dimension of Ciulei's work, his obvious understanding of the complexities of the dramatic text, its cultural background, and his awareness of how the play reverberated, not only historically, but in the present as well.

Although no longer the artistic director of the Bulandra Theatre, Ciulei continued to work there as well as throughout Western Europe and the United States. His 1979 Romanian production of *The Tempest* was a brave statement of the seeming impotence of artists and intellectuals to effect change in an apparently mad world. In 1980 he directed Paul Foster's *Elizabeth I* and Goldoni's *Il Campiello* for the Acting Company of John Houseman.*

In 1981 almost everyone was astonished when Minneapolis's Guthrie Theatre announced the appointment of Ciulei as its artistic director. During his tumultuous five-year tenure at the Guthrie, the upper midwest became the unlikely setting for some of America's most radical theatre productions. Bringing in guest directors like Andrei Serban,* Richard Foreman,* Peter Sellars,* and Lucian Pintilie,* Ciulei alternately provoked, delighted, and enraged Minneapolis audiences. The idea of the Guthrie under Ciulei and his co-director Garland Wright* was to "entertain upper Midwest audiences with artistic productions of an eclectic repertory, while remaining close to the classics."

While some conservative audience members were mildly dismayed by the Guthrie repertory, others were incensed by Ciulei's interpretation of "remaining close to the classics." From his earliest work with classical texts, Ciulei has always proceeded in two seemingly contradictory directions. While he is deeply knowledgeable about both the history of the text and the world out of which it came, his goal is to replant the work firmly in the present. Thus, he builds on the past but injects new thinking, new images, a new sensibility into the old texts. He also remains that rarest of combinations, actor and designer, and his productions always reflect both a high level of visual expressiveness and textured, detailed acting.

Following his tenure as artistic director of the Guthrie, Ciulei continued working there as a guest director. He has also continued to work with Washington's Arena Theatre, the McCarter Theatre, and the American Repertory Theatre.

ADDITIONAL PRODUCTIONS: 1961, 1967, 1981: *As You Like It*; 1968: *The Sea Gull*; 1970, 1974: *Leonce and Lena*; 1975: *Long Day's Journey into Night*; 1978, 1985: *Hamlet*; 1979, 1981: *The Tempest*; 1987: *The Bacchae*; 1988: *Coriolanus*; 1989: *Platonov*; 1990: *Cerceau* (Slavkin).

SELECTED BIBLIOGRAPHY: Berlogea, I. "Shakespeare in Romania." *Shakespeare Quarterly* 30 (Winter 1979): 281–82; Cole, Susan Letzler. *Directors in Rehearsal: A Hidden World*. New York: Routledge, 1992: 171–86; Lipsius, Frank. "Ciulei's Way." *Connoisseur* 214 (August 1984): 80–83; Steele, Mike. "The Romanian Connection." *American Theatre* 2 (July/Aug. 1985): 4–11.

Miles Coiner

MARTHA CLARKE [b. June 3, 1944, Baltimore, Maryland]. Raised in a family environment that nurtured her creative and artistic endeavors, Martha Clarke began a career in dance at the Juilliard School (studying with Antony Tudor) and later joined Anna Sokolow's dance company. At the age of twenty, she married sculptor Philip Grausman, had a son, and retired from performing. This early retirement, however, was short-lived, and Clarke's creative drive soon found an outlet in 1972 when she joined Pilobolus Dance Theater. Receiving encouragement and support from professionals such as Charles Reinhart of the American Dance Festival, Joseph Papp of the New York Shakespeare Festival, and Lyn Austin of the Music-Theater Group, in the late seventies Clarke formed her own company, Crowsnest, and began developing pieces that integrated dance, theatre, and music—pieces that embodied powerful, visceral images that are now the signature of her work. It was Austin who invited Clarke to direct and who provided financial support for the development of works such as *A Metamorphosis in Miniature* (1982), *The Garden of Earthly Delights* (1984, 1987), *Vienna: Lusthaus* (1986), and *The Hunger Artist* (1987).

Clarke's aesthetic finds shape through the collective efforts of the performers and the director, and attains its performance life through collaboration with the design team. Its structure is not a traditional through-line, but rather dramatic fragments which blend and overlap. Its content—abstract images of the human condition—is sometimes lyrical and often volatile. Clarke's unconventional rehearsal process is occasionally frustrating for performers and designers, as Clarke will continue to define and change the work through opening, and it has been said that those who work with her "swear by her when they are not swearing at her" (Tallmer, 1990, B3).

Metamorphosis, with actress Linda Hunt, brought Clarke her first Obie in 1982, but it was *The Garden of Earthly Delights,* a sixty-minute, four-part progression based on a triptych by Renaissance painter Hieronymous Bosch, that earned Clarke a Drama Desk Award and the attention of colleagues, critics, and the general public. The journey ("Eden," "The Garden," "The Seven Sins," and "Hell") was a stylized fantasy that ranged from innocent love to demonic torture. Performed to a score by Richard Peaslee, the actors explored the boundaries of human existence—earthbound one moment and airborne the next. Clarke's explicit delving into eroticism and decadence drew a variety of responses from critics and audiences. In productions such as *Vienna: Lusthaus* (Off-Broadway Obie award) and *Miracolo d'Amore* (1988), nude performers represented both beauty and bestiality. Audiences often found themselves engaged, confused, and offended, but as Clarke intended, they responded strongly. Although she claims to be apolitical, she nevertheless creates theatre that alters the sensibility of the viewer. Her 1990 production of *Endangered Species* was as much about our own endangerment as it was about the animals she employed. It was during the preparation of this piece that Clarke received a MacArthur Foundation "genius" grant.

SELECTED BIBLIOGRAPHY: Bartow, Arthur. *The Director's Voice.* New York: Theatre Communications Group, 1988: 51–66; Berman, Janice. "An Italian Village with Vast Emotion." *Newsday* 24 June 1988; Erstein, Hap. "A Vision of Vienna's Collective Id." *Insight/Washington Times* 6 October 1986; Kriegsman, Alan. "Martha Clarke, Tending to Her 'Garden.' " *Washington Post* 31 January 1988; Ostlere, Hilary. "Martha Clarke: Alas, No Giraffe." *Dance Magazine* October 1990: 46–49; Tallmer, Jerry. "All Clarke's Creatures." *New York Post* 3 October 1990.

Colleen Kelly

HAROLD EDGAR CLURMAN [b. September 18, 1901, New York, New York; d. September 9, 1980, New York, New York]. Director, critic, author, and teacher, Harold Clurman was, at the time of his death, the elder statesman for the American theatre. In his fifty-five year career, Clurman directed over forty plays; served as a major drama critic, first for *The New Republic* and from 1953 on for *The Nation*; wrote numerous articles as well as seven books including his treatise *On Directing*; and co-founded, managed, and guided the Group Theatre.

The son of a physician, Clurman grew up on Manhattan's Lower East Side. He became enamored of theatre when, at the age of six, he saw the great Yiddish actor Jacob P. Adler perform in *Uriel Acosta*. Clurman later married and divorced Adler's daughter, Stella, a major actress and teacher.

He attended Columbia University from 1919 to 1921, but left for Paris to study at the Sorbonne, where he received a diploma in 1923, and at the school of Jacques Copeau* at the Théâtre du Vieux Colombier. Clurman returned to New York in 1924 and landed his first theatre job as a bit player in Stark Young's *The Saint* at the Provincetown Playhouse. In 1925 he was hired by the Theatre Guild, where he progressed from actor to stage manager to play reader. While there, he formed friendships with Lee Strasberg* and Cheryl Crawford who, with Clurman, would become the directors of the Group Theatre.

The Group grew out of a series of meetings held in Clurman's New York apartment. Every Friday night at 11:20 P.M., for twenty-five weeks in 1930–31, a group of actors, including Franchot Tone, Morris Carnovsky, and Sanford Meisner, were mesmerized by Clurman's impassioned plans to found a collaborative theatre based on the work of Konstantin Stanislavky* that would convey "the life of our times." Clurman quickly became the spiritual leader of the Group, sustaining it through the turbulent decade of its existence, 1931–41.

Clurman did not immediately direct for the Group, but guided and co-produced their plays, workshops, and classes from 1931 to 1935. In 1935, he made his directorial debut with Clifford Odets's *Awake and Sing,* perhaps the Group's finest offering. Clurman directed four other Odets plays and two by Irwin Shaw before the company's demise. He recorded the history of the Group Theatre in his book *The Fervent Years.*

Clurman spent 1941–45 in Hollywood as a script consultant and producer. He directed one film, *Deadline at Dawn* (1945), before returning to New York. His career reignited in 1950 when he directed Carson McCullers's *Member of the Wedding* on Broadway, winning the New York Drama Critics Circle's Donaldson Award for excellence in directing. Clurman directed eighteen Broadway productions during the 1950s including the premieres of *Bus Stop* (1954–55), *Orpheus Descending* (1956–57), and *A Touch of the Poet* (1958–59). In the 1960s, his directorial work subsided. Notable productions included two shows in Tokyo—*Long Day's Journey into Night* with American actors (1965) and *The Iceman Cometh* with Japanese performers (1968)—and his final effort, *Uncle Vanya* (1969), in Los Angeles.

Clurman's theories are documented in his book *On Directing.* He views the director as an organizer, teacher, politician, psychic detective, technician, and creative being who is schooled in literature, the arts, and human psychology. After a careful study of the script, a director must articulate in simple terms the play's main action which, borrowing from Stanislavsky, Clurman calls the "spine." Once determined, the spine needs to be realized through style—the particular mood, emphasis, and dimension chosen by the director. Whatever choices are made must be consistent and result in a coherent production. Ultimately, the production should serve the script and be guided by the author's plot and dialogue.

Clurman taught directing as well as modern theatre practice at Hunter College of the City University of New York, where he was appointed professor of theatre

in 1967. Among numerous awards, Clurman received the first George Jean
Nathan Award for dramatic criticism in 1959, was elected a Chevalier of the
French Legion of Honor, and, in 1979, had a new theatre named after him on
West 42nd Street in New York's Theatre Row.

ADDITIONAL PRODUCTIONS: Group Theatre Productions: 1935–36: *Paradise Lost*;
1937–38: *Golden Boy*; 1938–39: *Rocket to the Moon, The Gentle People*; 1939–40: *Night
Music*; 1940–41: *Retreat to Pleasure*. Others: 1949: *Montserrat* (Habimah Theatre, Tel
Aviv); 1955–56: *Tiger at the Gates*; 1956–57: *The Waltz of the Toreadors*; 1965: *Incident
at Vichy*.

SELECTED BIBLIOGRAPHY: **Books by Harold Clurman**: *All People Are Famous*. New
York: Harcourt Brace Jovanovich, 1974; *The Divine Pastime*. New York: Macmillan,
1974; *The Fervent Years: The Group Theatre and the Thirties*. New York: Harcourt
Brace Jovanovich, 1975; *Ibsen*. New York: Macmillan, 1978; *Lies Like Truth: Theatre
Reviews and Essays*. New York: Macmillan, 1958; *The Naked Image: Observations on
the Modern Theatre*. New York: Macmillan, 1966; *On Directing*. New York: Collier,
1972. **Works about Clurman**: Blakely, Don Frederick. "Harold Clurman as Theatrical
Director and Critic: His Philosophic, Artistic, and Critical Theories." Diss. Wayne State
U, 1968; Chinoy, Helen Krich. "Reunion: A Self-Portrait of the Group Theatre." *Ed-
ucational Theatre Journal* 28 (December 1976); Cole, Toby, and Helen Krich Chinoy.
Directors on Directing. Indianapolis: Bobbs-Merrill, 1963; 272–78, 380–89; Gussow,
Mel. "A Long Life in the Theater." *New York Times* 6 May 1979.

Martha Schmoyer LoMonaco

PETER COE [b. April 18, 1929, London, England; d. May 25, 1987, London,
England]. At the age of twenty-two, Wunderkind Peter Coe had three successful
productions (*The Miracle Worker, The World of Suzie Wong,* and *Oliver!*) running simultaneously in London. Coe, whose career included dramatic adaptations
of literary works and artistic direction of an array of major regional theatres in
Canada, Great Britain, and the United States, was celebrated not only on the
legitimate stage, but also as a popularizer of classics.

Coe trained at the London Academy of Music and Dramatic Art. While serving
as the first resident director of London's Mermaid Theatre, he had a major success
with his own musical version of Henry Fielding's eighteenth-century play, *Lock
Up Your Daughters* (1959). Artistic and associate directorships included a lasting
relationship with the prestigious Chichester Festival in England, where he directed and adapted plays until the end of his career. In 1975, he was artistic
director of the Bubble Theatre, writing and directing five productions. In 1980,
he was appointed director of the Citadel Theatre in Edmonton, Alberta, Canada,
and one year later, he assumed the helm of the troubled Stratford, Connecticut,
American Shakespeare Theatre, where he produced *Henry V* (1981) with Christopher Plummer, a poorly received *Henry IV* (1982), and a disastrous *Hamlet*
(1982) with Christopher Walken.

Coe was credited with the success of the 1982 revival of *Othello* (although
Zoe Caldwell also directed pre-Broadway tryouts) starring James Earl Jones as
Othello and Christopher Plummer as Iago. Coe's innovative production shifted

focus to Iago's machinations, allowing Plummer to become the multifaceted center of the play.

From 1983 until his death in 1987, Coe was artistic director of the Churchill Theatre south of London. Although thrice nominated for a Tony Award (for *Oliver!*, 1963; Hugh Leonard's *A Life*, 1981; and again for *Othello*, 1982), Coe won only once, for *Othello*.

ADDITIONAL PRODUCTIONS: 1960: *Oliver!* (Lionel Bart); 1964: *Golden Boy* (Clifford Odets); 1966: *In the Matter of J. Robert Oppenheimer* (Heinar Kipphard); 1980: *Mister Lincoln* (Herbert Mitgang); 1984: *Great Expectations* (adapted by Coe); 1986: *Jane Eyre* (adapted by Coe).

SELECTED BIBLIOGRAPHY: *Contemporary Theatre, Film and Television*. Detroit, MI: Gale Research Co., 1988, 3: 104–5; Gill, Brendan, Rev. of *Othello. New Yorker* 15 February 1982: 108–9; Rev. of *Jane Eyre. Plays and Players* October 1986: 27; McEnroe, Colin. "Coe's Muse Is the Bard Himself." *The Courant* (Hartford, Connecticut) 12 April 1981; Taylor, Markland. "At AST, the Question is 'to be or not to be.' " *The Register* (New Haven, Connecticut) 8 August 1982.

Stuart Lenig

GEORGE M. COHAN [b. July 3, 1878, Providence, Rhode Island; d. November 5, 1942, New York, New York]. George M. Cohan, well known as a performer, songwriter, and playwright, produced and directed over forty of his own musicals, comedies, and dramas. After he directed his family's vaudeville sketches, his first full-length musical comedy, *The Governor's Son*, appeared in New York in 1901. Cohan produced seventeen musicals and revues, and he also produced nonmusical plays throughout his career. Although these plays contain the fast pacing, humor, and contemporary feeling that characterize his work, his directing style was established with his musicals.

Cohan brought the pacing, humor, and structure of popular entertainments to the legitimate stage. His rapid and humorous staging mirrored the urban pulse of New York; and his combination of vaudeville, musical comedy, and a Broadway perspective made Cohan's work uniquely his own.

For Cohan, speed and action were essential. Consequently, his shows were fast-paced, filled with movement and action and, in the case of his musicals, complete with songs and dances for variety. Although Cohan was also a skilled director of realistic stage action who guided his actors into quiet, natural performances, this fast-paced musical staging remains his principal legacy. The speed and variety Cohan used in his musical productions influence American musical theatre to this day.

ADDITIONAL PRODUCTIONS: 1904: *Little Johnny Jones* (his first musical production in Times Square theatre district); 1906: *Forty-Five Minutes from Broadway*; 1909: *The Man Who Owns Broadway*; 1910: *Get-Rich-Quick Wallingford* (first successful nonmusical play); 1913: *Seven Keys to Baldpate*; 1914: *Hello Broadway* (first of his topical revues); 1920: *The Tavern*; 1922: *Little Nellie Kelly*; 1928: *Billie* (his last musical production); 1933: *Pigeons and People*; 1940: *The Return of the Vagabond*.

SELECTED BIBLIOGRAPHY: Cohan, George M. *Twenty Years on Broadway and the Years It Took to Get There*. New York: Harper and Brothers, 1924; Glann, Frank Warren. "An Historical and Critical Evaluation of the Plays of George M. Cohan 1901–1920." Diss. Bowling Green State U, 1976; McCabe, John. *George M. Cohan: The Man Who Owned Broadway*. Garden City, NY: Doubleday and Company, 1973; Morehouse, Ward. *George M. Cohan: Prince of the American Theater*. Philadelphia: J. B. Lippincott Company, 1943; Smith, Cecil, and Glenn Litton. *Musical Comedy in America*. Expanded ed. New York: Theatre Arts Books, 1981; Vallillo, Stephen M. "George M. Cohan's *Little Johnny Jones*." *Musical Theatre in America*. Ed. Glenn Loney. Westport, CT: Greenwood Press, 1984: 233–44; Vallillo, Stephen M. "George M. Cohan, Director." Diss. New York U, 1987.

Stephen M. Vallillo

MIRIAM COLÓN [b. August 20, 1935, Ponce, Puerto Rico]. After graduating from high school, Miriam Colón came to New York in 1952 to study acting at the Dramatic Workshop of Erwin Piscator.* In 1953, she became the first Puerto Rican to be accepted to study at the Actors' Studio. Since her Broadway debut in 1953, she has continued to work as an actress on stage, in films, and in over 250 television shows. These performances made her aware of the limited and stereotyped roles available for Hispanics and the need for an alternative theatre for Latinos.

Although she continues to act, Colón turned to producing in 1966 while she was playing Juanita in a Spanish-language production of *La Carreta (The Oxcart)* by Puerto Rican playwright Rene Marquis. The three-month run at the Greenwich Mews Theatre convinced her there was an audience for a theatre emphasizing the heritage of Puerto Rico. *The Oxcart* toured New York City parks and playgrounds and became the foundation of the Puerto Rican Traveling Theatre, a bilingual theatre company performing all plays with multiracial casts in English and Spanish on alternating days. With Colón as its executive director, the Puerto Rican Traveling Theatre continues as one of the major Hispanic theatres in New York City, and often premieres translations of plays by Puerto Ricans and *Nuyorcians* (those of Puerto Rican descent, but born and raised in New York City).

Colón began her directing career at the Puerto Rican Traveling Theatre with *The Golden Streets* by Piri Thomas in 1970. Her most important production as a director was *Simpson Street*, a realistic portrayal of Nuyorcian life in the South Bronx. The Puerto Rican Traveling Theatre toured this production (in Spanish under the title *La calle Simpson*) to Puerto Rico in 1977.

ADDITIONAL PRODUCTIONS: 1972: *The Passion of Antigona Perez* (Luis Rafael Sanchez) with Colón in the title role; 1975: *Ceremony for an Assassinated Black Man* (Fernando Arrabal); 1979: *Simpson Street* (Edward Gallardo).

SELECTED BIBLIOGRAPHY: Bosworth, Patricia. " 'Look, Let's Have Justice Around Here.' " *New York Times* 12 September 1971: D 5; Mirabella, Alan. "Miracle Maker: Miriam Colón Celebrates 20 Years of Traveling Theater." *New York Daily News* 19 April 1987, magazine section: 20–27; Perez, Miguel. "All the City Is Her Stage." *New York Daily News* 7 August 1982: 16; Rigdon, Walter, ed. *Notable Names in the American*

Theatre. Clifton, NJ: James T. White and Company, 1976: 636; Robinson, Alice M., Vera Mowry Roberts, and Milly S. Barranger, eds. *Notable Women in the American Theatre.* Westport, CT: Greenwood Press, 1989: 153–55; *Who's Who in the Theatre* 16th ed. Detroit: Gale Research Company, 1977: 501–2.

David J. Pasto

JACQUES COPEAU [b. February 4, 1879, Paris, France; d. October 10, 1949, Beaune, France]. Through his life's work of theatre reform, Jacques Copeau transformed stage architecture, theatrical directing, and actor training for generations to come. His seminal work in France, sharing much with that of Adolphe Appia, Gordon Craig, Konstantin Stanislavsky,* Vsevolod Meyerhold,* and Granville Barker,* was carried on in Europe and abroad by pupils and disciples, most notably the Cartel—Louis Jouvet,* Charles Dullin,* Georges Pitoëff,* Gaston Baty,* Michel Saint-Denis,* and Jean Vilar.*

Copeau began his career in 1901 writing for *Hermitage* and *La Revue d'Art Dramatique.* In 1907, he became the drama critic of the *Grande Revue,* and in 1909 he founded, with André Gide, Henri Ghéon, Jean Schlumberger, and others, the important *Nouvelle Revue Française.* Copeau spoke out with bold indignation against the overcommercialization of the artificial boulevard theatre and its star system. Throughout his career, this man of principle refused the least concession to practical necessity and material success.

In 1913, Copeau opened his Théâtre du Vieux-Colombier in the renovated Théâtre de l'Athénée-Saint-Germain. Twice more, later in his lifetime, Copeau rehabilitated this theatre to conform to his radical notion of a presentational stage designed along austere, classic lines. While Copeau acknowledged that the revolutionary realism of André Antoine* emancipated theatre from petrified conventions, he rejected naturalistic verism. His call for an antirealist theatre demanded the creation (through the genius of the director *in service to the text,* and not via stage accoutrements) of an environment conducive to the valorization of the poetry of the text. All artifice and ornamental decor, the proscenium, and footlights were rejected in favor of the bare stage. Indirect lighting and an enlarged forestage were added to create freedom of movement for the actors and to present them in a more direct relationship to the audience. From his public, Copeau demanded a collaborative effort and tangible proof of interest.

The theatre space embodied Copeau's new concept of theatre. Its permanent setting, modifiable by the addition of modular elements, served equally the French and foreign classics, and new works (e.g., of Schlumberger, Ghéon, René Duhamel, François Porché, and Benjamin) that made up the eclectic repertory of the Vieux-Colombier. Copeau's brilliant interpretation of the classics, most notably Molière, renewed their vitality and humanity.

After a successful 1913–14 season, Copeau's projects were interrupted by the war. Between 1917 and 1919, he worked in the United States, directing his troupe, the Vieux-Colombier of New York, in the redesigned Garrick Theatre. His often-thwarted efforts to supplant standard Broadway fare with serious drama discouraged Copeau deeply, but nonetheless left their mark on American art and educational theatres. In 1920, again in Paris after the war, Copeau (while reopening his theatre) began work on the *Cahiers du Vieux-Colombier,* meant to establish an esprit de corps within his public. That fall, he reopened the school of the Vieux-Colombier (begun in 1911 at Limon) in collaboration with Jouvet, Suzanne Bing, and others. His free school was to be a laboratory for research and experimentation, and to serve as a reserve of well-prepared actors to feed and refresh his theatre. The broad curriculum formed a *whole* artist intimate with every function of the theatre. Detailed training of voice, body, and imagination; textual analysis; and improvisation were central to the process. An enemy of dogma, Copeau nurtured the renewal of spontaneity and true dramatic sentiment through a return to the great theatrical traditions of Noh and commedia dell'arte. He sought to create a sense of collaborative work, subordination of the individual to the ensemble, and the ensemble to the text.

Despite four successful seasons and tours in England, France, and elsewhere in Europe, Copeau closed his Théâtre of the Vieux-Colombier in May 1924 and left Paris for Burgundy to devote himself entirely to actor training and his Company of the Copiaus. Thereafter, he shunned most theatre enterprises in Paris, although he was associated with the Comédie Française from 1936, directing its programs from May 1940 to March 1941. He spent his last years reworking writings that would become his *Régistres.*

ADDITIONAL PRODUCTIONS: 1896: *Morning Fog* (Copeau); 1913: *A Woman Killed with Kindness, The Love Doctor,* Barbarine** (Musset), *Household Bread** (Renard), *The Miser**; 1914: *La Jalousie du Barbouillé,* The Exchange* (Claudel), *Father Leleu's Will** (Martin du Gard), *The Brothers Karamazov** (adapted by Copeau and Jean Croué); *The Rogueries of Scapin,* The Merry-Go-Round** (Becque), *The Carriage of the Holy Sacrament** (Mérimée); 1918: *The Surprise of Love** (Marivaux); 1919: *The Marriage of Figaro**; 1920: *The Winter's Tale, Crommedeyre-le-Vieil** (Romains), *The Doctor in Spite of Himself,* Le Paquebot Tenacity** (Vildrac); 1922: *Love's Golden Book* (Tolstoy), *Saul* (Gide); 1923: *The Princess Turandot* (Gozzi), *Dardamelle* (Mazaud), *Bastos the Bold* (Régis and de Veynes), *Native House* (Copeau). *Indicates often-staged plays in Copeau's repertory; first performance dates given.

SELECTED BIBLIOGRAPHY: Copeau, Jacques. "Dramatic Economy." Trans. Joseph M. Bernstein in *Directors on Directing.* Ed. Toby Cole and Helen Krich Chinoy. New York: Bobbs-Merrill Co., 1963: 214–25; Copeau, Jacques. "An Essay on Dramatic Renovation: The Theatre du Vieux-Colombier." Trans. Richard Hiatt, *Educational Theatre Journal* 19 (December 1967): 447–54; Katz, Albert. "Copeau as Régisseur, an Analysis." *Educational Theatre Journal* 25 (May 1973): 160–72; Katz, Albert. "The Genesis of the Vieux Colombier: The Aesthetic Background of Jacques Copeau." *Educational Theatre Journal* 19 (December 1967): 433–46; Katz, Albert. "Jacques Copeau: The American Reaction." *Players* 45 (February 1970): 133–43; Knapp, Bettina L. "Jacques Copeau— The Theatre du Vieux Colombier (1913–1924)." *The Reign of the Theatrical Director, French Theatre: 1887–1924.* Troy, NY: Whitston Publishing Co., 1988: 171–227; MacGowan, Kenneth, and Robert Edmond Jones. "The Theatre of the Three Hundred."

Continental Stagecraft. New York: Harcourt, Brace and Company, 1922: 171–83; Rudlin, John. *Directors in Perspective: Jacques Copeau*. Cambridge, England: Cambridge University Press, 1986.

M. Clare Mather

ORAZIO [GIOVANGIGLI] COSTA [b. August 6, 1911, Rome, Italy]. A leading Italian theatre director of the postwar generation in antinaturalistic, poetic theatre, Orazio Costa is known for his connection to dramatic works with spiritual significance. Costa is also an actor, teacher, theorist, and critic. After receiving a bachelor's degree in Italian literature at the University of Rome, he studied at the Eleonora Duse* performance school. In 1935, Costa completed a degree in directing at the Academy of Dramatic Arts in Rome, studying the Konstantin Stanislavsky* Method with Tatiana Pavlova.

He was among the first generation of directors to graduate from the academy founded by Silvio D'Amico. D'Amico's influence on his work included emphasizing the necessity of spirituality and faith in the theatre. Following graduation, Costa traveled to Paris, where he served as assistant and student to Jacques Copeau.* Copeau's respect for the text and integrity in production are important elements in Costa's theory and practice.

In 1939, Orazio Costa debuted as a director at Silvio D'Amico's Compagnia dell'Accademia in Rome with *Mistero della Nativita': Passione. Morte e Resurrezione di Nostro Signore (The Mystery of the Nativity; Passion, Death and Resurrection of Our Lord)*. He began teaching directing at D'Amico's Academy in 1944. Costa influenced many students including Paolo Grassi* and Luigi Squarzina.* For Costa, the theatrical director is the conscience of the production. In his opinion, it is the director's obligation to control all elements of the production including the actors. Costa was among those responsible for raising the level of directing in Italy.

In 1948, Costa founded the Piccolo Teatro della Citta' di Roma, which he also managed until 1954. He is best known for directing the works of Diego Fabbri, Ugo Betti, and Henrik Ibsen, whose symbolic and universal ideas he prefers over the real and material. Orazio Costa is interested in returning the theatre to the religious experience on which it had originally been based. His theatre is in the dimension of ritual, intense and affecting.

Like Copeau, Orazio Costa favors the text and the word. Theatrical movement comes from the changes and development within the work and is not arbitrary. Images of production are developed from its interior tone, are directly related to the text, and are not autonomous. Costa has written many articles about the production choices made from his interpretive analogies and has also developed a pedagogy for acting which has been implemented in Italian dramatic schools. His younger brother, Tullio, and sister, Valeria, designed sets and costumes for many of his productions.

ADDITIONAL PRODUCTIONS: 1940: *Attilo Regolo* (Pietro Metastasio); 1942–43: *Little Eyolf, Hedda Gabler*; 1944–45; *Il vento notturno* (Ugo Betti); 1948–49: *Filippo, Oreste* (Vittorio Alfieri); *Spiritismo nell' antica casa* (Betti); 1950: *Il Poverello* (Copeau); 1952: *Agamemnon* (Aeschylus), *Agamemnon* (Alfieri), *I Dialoghi delle carmelitane* (Georges Bernanos); 1953: *L'Aiuola bruciata* (Betti); 1955: *Processo a Gesu'* (Diego Fabbri).

OPERAS: 1948: *Le Bacchanti* (Giorgio Federico Ghedini); 1949: *L'Incoronazione di Poppea* (Monteverdi); 1952: *Don Giovanni*; 1954: *Arianna* (Benedetto Marcello).

SELECTED BIBLIOGRAPHY: Antonucci, Giovanni. *La regia teatrale in Italia. e altri scritti sulla messinscena.* Roma: Abete, 1978; Cibotto, G. A. *Interventi sul teatro italiano contemporaneo.* Preganziol (TV): Matteo Editore, 1979; Coccheri, Paolo. "La formazione dell'attore negli Anni Ottanta: metodologia e ricerca." *Quaderno Teatro* 5 August 1982; Colli Giangiacomo. *Una Pedagogia dell'attore l'insegnamento di Orazio Costa.* Roma: Bulzoni, 1989; Lucignani, Luciano. "Orazio Costa Regista." *Teatro* 1950: 39–41; Meldolesi, Claudio. *Pondamenti del teatro italiano: la generazione dei registri.* Firenze: Sansoni, 1984; Verdone, Mario. *Teatro Contemporaneo.* Vol. 3. Roma: Lucarini, 1986: 87–106.

Shirley Vendrasco Burke

TONY CURIEL [b. September 2, 1954, Pomona, California]. After earning a Bachelor of Arts degree in drama from the University of California at San Diego in 1978, Curiel completed a master's degree in 1981 at Stanford where he directed *Curse of the Starving Class* as his thesis production. Following a two-year association with El Teatro Campesino, a San Francisco–based theatre devoted to Chicano theatre, he was hired in 1983 as assistant to the artistic director.

Reflecting his interest in new play development, Curiel's work includes directing staged readings and original cabaret shows, as well as participation in the South Coast Repertory Hispanic Workshop. Curiel believes that it is important to recognize a script's "cultural subtext" and that a director who is in tune with the consciousness of the playwright can help create "intangible vibrations' which resonate throughout a production.

In addition to El Teatro Campesino, Curiel has directed at the Los Angeles Theatre, Burt Reynolds Jupiter Theatre, San Diego Repertory Theatre, Joseph Papp's Public Theatre, the Asian American Theatre Company, and San Jose Repertory Theatre. He serves as theatre consultant to the California Arts Council and is a founding member of the National Coalition of Professional Hispanic-American Theatre Companies.

Recruited in 1989 to help implement the first graduate program in Hispanic-American theatre in the United States, Curiel joined the faculty at the University of California at San Diego (UCSD) as a practicing artist. At UCSD he teaches acting, directing, and Chicano theatre courses. He resides with his family in San Diego and continues to hold his position with El Teatro Campesino.

ADDITIONAL PRODUCTIONS: 1983 (1985, 1987, 1989, 1991): *La Pastorela* (adapted by Luis Valdez*); 1984 (1986, 1988): *La Virgen del Tepeyac* (adapted by Luis Valdez); 1985: *The Dark Root of a Scream* and *Soldado Razo* (Luis Valdez), *Bernabe* (Luis Valdez), *La Tienda, Los Novios,* and *Los Compadres* (public service announcement videos for Planned Parenthood); 1986 (1987): *I Don't Have to Show You No Stinking Badges* (Luis

Valdez); 1988: *The Doa Lady* (Milcha Sanchez-Scott), *Y Se Van A Divorciar de Nosotros Tambien*? (video); 1989: *Burning Patience* (Antonio Skarmeta), *The Mission* (by Culture Clash); 1991: *Prospect* (Octavio Solis).

SELECTED BIBLIOGRAPHY: Curiel, Tony, ed. *El Teatro Campesino: The First Twenty Years* (Special Edition commemorating El Teatro Campesino's twentieth anniversary, 1985); Curiel, Tony. *La Mariposa* in *Macmillan Basal Second Reader*. New York: Macmillan, 1986; Valdez, Luis. *Bernabe, the Dark Root of a Scream and Soldado Razo* in *West Coast Plays* 19/20 (1986).

Sherry Engle Johnson

D

PIERRE DAGENAIS [b. May 29, 1923, Montreal, Canada; d. December 24, 1990, Montreal, Canada]. Playwright, novelist and satirist, Pierre Dagenais is renowned as a director, actor, and producer. Holder of a Bachelor of Arts degree from Stanislas College in Montreal, he abandoned his studies at the University of Montreal in order to devote himself to the theatre. Since there was no arts academy there at the time, Dagenais studied diction and interpretation with Madame Jean-Louis Audet. At the age of nineteen, Pierre Dagenais began a dramatic career as rich as it was dazzling, and founded the Equipe, one of the most remarkable companies in the history of Quebec theatre. Dagenais directed twelve of the thirteen productions presented by the Equipe between 1943 and 1948, when the company disbanded, and he performed in most of these productions as well. For *Le Temps de vivre* (1948), he wrote the script, performed, and directed.

The first production of this avant-garde troupe, Julian Luchaire's *Altitude 3200*, was presented on the stage of the National Monument in Montreal in January 1943. The critics were unanimous in emphasizing the audacity and the quality of the production, and saluted the young Dagenais as one of the most promising theatrical talents in the country. The following year, the troupe produced the plays *Marius* and *Fanny* (at the National Monument in Montreal) at the same time that films of these Marcel Pagnol works were triumphing in the film theatres. This Québecois interpretation of the Marseillais universe was both a critical and a popular success. In 1945, Dagenais and his Equipe proved their boldness again in an impressive outdoor production of Shakespeare's *A Midsummer Night's*

Dream, in the Hermitage in Montreal. In 1946, the company presented *No Exit* (*Huit-Clos*) by Jean-Paul Sartre, which the author himself attended. In 1948, Dagenais directed his own work, *Le Temps de Vivre,* at the National Monument in Montreal. Around the same time, Dagenais also worked in English, in particular with the Montreal Repertory Theatre in 1946 and 1947.

Despite their artistic qualities and their innovations, Dagenais's productions at the Equipe rarely drew crowds. The company's deficit grew so large that Dagenais was imprisoned for unpaid debts. In 1948, these financial problems caused the disbanding of the Equipe. After this, Dagenais's theatrical activity was limited to a few noteworthy productions (among them *Brutus* by Paul Toupin in 1951) and to several appearances and collaborations in French and in English in Montreal and in Ottawa.

Pierre Dagenais next turned to radio and television where he had important successes as both actor and author, including the television productions *Le Faubourg à m'lasse* (1948–53), *L'Ami Pierre* (1956–60), and *Les Contes de la pluie et du beau temps* (1952), as well as radio plays including *Avant-première,* and *L'Arrestation du Père Noel* in 1953. He wrote eighteen television plays between 1954 and 1973.

Pierre Dagenais holds a preeminent place in Quebec theatre. Innovative and bold, his productions contrasted with the realism then dominating Quebec stages. Dagenais rejected the theatrical practices and aesthetics of his time and explored new creative avenues. Inspired by the pageant tradition, he enlarged the traditional theatrical space to unconventional locations, even to the outdoors. He also contributed to a renewal of the actor's craft by demanding of his players a more internalized and simple performance, leaving no room for improvisation. Finally, he raised direction to the level of a rigorous art, exacting and very controlled. The modern director's role in Quebec, in which the production is considered an artistic creation and the director is seen as the primary force behind the artistic process rather than an unifier-coordinator (in the manner of Émile Legault*) is primarily due to Dagenais's efforts.

Pierre Dagenais died in 1990, following a long illness. He left a plentiful and varied body of work which also includes novels, satires, and the autobiographical *. . . et je suis reste au Quebec* (1974).

ADDITIONAL PRODUCTIONS: 1946: *King Lear* (in English), *Les Fiancés du Havre* (Armand Salacrou); 1947: *The School for Wives* (*L'École des femmes*).

SELECTED BIBLIOGRAPHY: Beauchamp, Hélène. "Pierre Dagenais." *Le Théâtre canadien-français.* Ed. Paul Wyczynski, Bernard Julien, and Hélène Beauchamp-Rank. Montreal: Fides, Archives des Lettres canadiennes, tome V, 1976: 821–24; Dagenais, Pierre. *Contes de la pluie et du beau temps.* Montreal: Cercle du livre de France, 1953; Dagenais, Pierre. *. . . Et je suis reste au Quebec.* Montreal: La Presse, 1974; Dagenais, Pierre. *Isabelle* (play). Montreal: Édition Pierre Dagenais, 1966; Dagenais, Pierre. *Le Feu sacré* (novel). Montreal: Beauchemin, 1970.

Jean-Marc Larrue

(JOHN) AUGUSTIN DALY [b. July 20, 1838, Plymouth, North Carolina; d. June 7, 1899, Paris, France]. Daly began his forty-year theatre career in 1859 as a drama critic and playwright. In the next decade, he turned to management when he leased New York's Fifth Avenue Theatre. In 1873, this theatre was destroyed by fire, and Daly occupied a second house which he also called the Fifth Avenue Theatre. In 1879, he moved uptown into his own theatre (renamed Daly's Theatre) where he was to stay until his death, although he occasionally operated additional theatres in the city. Several international tours culminated in the opening of a second Daly's Theatre in London in 1893. His success on both sides of the Atlantic set production standards and methods of lasting influence.

Today, Daly is remembered as America's first *régisseur* because he was among the first nonactors to control all artistic aspects of a production according to his own specific vision. He was, first and foremost, an exacting disciplinarian who aimed to achieve the highest levels of ensemble playing from his actors. Using whatever time was available (including the early morning hours after a performance), Daly would conduct rigorous rehearsals in which he would drill all performers until they fit into his plan for production. He gave very precise directions, frequently by demonstration, which he expected to be carried out exactly. Daly attempted to subvert the system of hiring actors to play particular lines of business. In his company he had no stars, and he insisted that all members of his company be prepared to take any role he might assign. As a consequence, many performers of star quality, such as Otis Skinner, Clara Morris, and Fanny Davenport, left his company after achieving initial success.

Eventually, Daly developed an acting nucleus for his company. Known as "The Big Four," leads Ada Rehan and John Drew, and the veterans Mrs. G. H. Gilbert and James Lewis acted together for the first time for Daly in *Needles and Pins* in 1880 and stayed with him until his death. The Daly company style was one of finesse and polish. Called "Touch and Go" by members of the profession, it was particularly suited to the romantic comedies and melodramas which he frequently offered. They also excelled in the old comedies of Shakespeare, Goldsmith, and Sheridan to which Daly turned with increasing frequency later in his career. Of Rehan and Drew together, L. Clarke Davis noted, they "give and take like masters of the foils with such skill and grace as to compel admiration and delight."

Daly always specified and supervised all technical effects. All Daly productions were set in closely coordinated environments which, over the years, became increasingly elaborate. For example, his production of *The Taming of the Shrew* (New York, 1887 and Stratford-upon-Avon, 1888) featured a banquet scene backdrop based upon a painting by Veronese.

Another Daly attribute was organization. While he always provided the guiding vision, he delegated responsibility to a corps of assistants who supervised rehearsals and coached actors in his absence. Witnesses claim to have observed as many as four rehearsals conducted simultaneously in different parts of the theatre.

Daly often was his own playwright, and he would not hesitate to rewrite someone else's line. If a play was not successful, he would write or adapt a new one and rush it into production, or he would revive an earlier success. Most of Daly's plays were written with the unacknowledged collaboration of his brother and were adaptations of popular foreign works. His most famous original plays are *Under the Gaslight* (1867), a sensational melodrama which features a hero tied to the railroad tracks; and *Horizon* (1871), which gave a realistic portrayal of the contemporary American West.

ADDITIONAL PRODUCTIONS (all titles are Daly or Shakespeare unless noted): 1870: *Frou-Frou* (Meilhac and Halévy); 1871: *Horizon* with Agnes Ethel at the Olympic Theatre, *Divorce* with Fanny Davenport; 1875: *Pique* with Davenport and Maurice Barrymore; 1885: *The Magistrate* (Pinero) with Ada Rehan; 1887: *The Railroad of Love* with "The Big Four"; 1888: *Midsummer Night's Dream* with Otis Skinner; 1898: *The Merchant of Venice*.

SELECTED BIBLIOGRAPHY: Daly, Joseph Francis. *The Life of Augustin Daly*. New York: Macmillan, 1917; Felheim, Marvin. *The Theatre of Augustin Daly*. Cambridge, MA: Harvard University Press, 1956; Schaal, David. "Rehearsal-Direction Practices and Actor-Director Relationships in the American Theatre from the Hallam's to Actor's Equity." Ph.D. Diss., University of Illinois, 1956; Schaal, David. "The Rehearsal Situation at Daly's Theatre." *Educational Theatre Journal* 14 (March 1962): 1–14.

Maarten A. Reilingh

JEAN DASTÉ [b. September 18, 1904, Paris, France]. An actor, stage director, and theatre company director, Jean Dasté is known principally for his role in the decentralization of French theatre since the 1920s. Student (and later son-in-law) of Jacques Copeau,* he worked with several traveling troupes before becoming head of the newly created Comédie de Saint-Etienne, one of the first national "centres dramatiques," in 1947.

Dasté, of working-class origins, studied acting from ages eighteen to twenty at Copeau's Ecole du Vieux-Colombier in Paris. In 1925, he followed his teacher to the province of Burgundy, where Copeau had founded an experimental school and itinerant troupe. It was this experience, lasting until 1929, that in Dasté's words "hooked" him on the idea of a "théâtre populaire."

Dasté became part of another traveling company, La Compagnie des Quinze, in 1929. Seven years later, after playing major film roles (in Jean Vigo's *Zéro de conduite,* 1933, and *L'Atalante,* 1934) as well as performing in theatre, Dasté cofounded La Compagnie des Quatre-Saisons with Maurice Jacquemont and André Barsacq.* The goal of the group was to work in a different province each year, to get to know the people of the region, and to compose for that audience. The company performed mainly outdoors, traveling with a collapsible and portable set, and toured in the United States as well as France. After Jacquemont decided to pursue his career in Paris, Dasté, one of the few important theatre professionals of the era to remain faithful to the idea of extending drama to the provinces, founded his Théâtre Ambulant de la Saison Nouvelle (1941–44).

Dasté was invited to form a permanent troupe in Grenoble in 1945. When the troupe folded in 1947 because of insufficient funding by the city, it was immediately offered a place in Saint-Etienne, near Lyon. Part of the official politics of dramatic decentralization under the direction of Pierre Bourdan and Jeanne Laurent, the Comédie de Saint-Etienne became the second theatre outside of Paris to be funded in major part by the national government. As it had done in Grenoble, the troupe produced a mixture of contemporary pieces, Japanese Noh theatre, classic works, and collective creations. The French premiere of *The Caucasian Chalk Circle,* by Bertolt Brecht,* with its increased use of masks, its emphasis upon certain humorous elements in Brecht, and its accentuation of the play's folktale aspect, which took place at Saint-Etienne in 1956, has been called the most influential production of that decade.

Dasté directed the Comédie de Saint-Etienne for twenty-two years, until 1969. Since that time, he has remained active as a performer, playing roles on television and in film (including François Truffaut's *La Chambre verte,* 1982) and doing poetry recitations.

ADDITIONAL PRODUCTIONS: 1945: *Noah* (André Obey), *Sept Couleurs* (collective creation); 1946: *Le Bal des voleurs* (*The Thieves' Carnival*), *L'Etourdi* (*The Blunderer,* Molière), *Ce que murmure la Sumida* (*What the Sumida Murmurs,* Motokiyo); 1947: *The Doctor in Spite of Himself, Le Voyage de M. Perrichon* (Labiche); 1948: *The Wedding* (Chekhov), *The Playboy of the Western World*; 1949: *La Cagnotte* (Labiche), *Measure for Measure*; 1950: *L'Illusion* (Copeau), *La Savetière Prodigieuse* (*The Marvelous Cobbler,* Lorca), *Kagekiyo* (Chikimatsu Monzaemon); 1951: *Les Fausses confidences* (Marivaux), *Macbeth*; 1962: *Le Drame du Fukuryu-Maru* (Gabriel Cousin); 1966: *L'Homme seul* (*Man Alone,* Gatti); 1967: *Monsieur Fugue, ou le mal de terre* (*Mister Fugue, or Earthsick,* Liliane Atlan).

SELECTED BIBLIOGRAPHY: Bradby, David. *Modern French Drama, 1940–1980.* Cambridge, England: Cambridge University Press, 1984; Gontard, Denis. *La Décentralisation théâtrale en France, 1895–1952.* Paris: Société d'édition d' enseignement supérieur, 1973; Mignon, Paul-Louis. *Jean Dasté.* Paris: Presses Littéraires de France, 1953; Poirot-Delpech, Bernard. "*Le Mariage.*" *Au soir le soir.* Paris: Mercure de France, 1969: 124–26; Simon, Alfred. *Dictionnaire du théâtre français contemporain.* Paris: Larousse, 1970: s.v. "Dasté" and "décentralisation."

Cynthia Running-Johnson

GORDON DAVIDSON [b. May 7, 1933, Brooklyn, New York]. Born into an artistic family—his father, Joseph, taught theatre at Brooklyn College, and his mother, Alice, was a concert pianist—Gordon Davidson studied theatre at Cornell and Case Western Reserve universities. After working as a stage manager off-Broadway, he was invited in 1964 by John Houseman* to be assistant director for *King Lear* at the University of California at Los Angeles (UCLA). In 1965, Davidson became managing director of the Theatre Group at UCLA and then artistic director when it moved to the Mark Taper Forum in Los Angeles in 1967.

He continues in this position to the present and has fostered the Forum's preeminence as a major theatrical regional center, known especially for nurturing and introducing new plays that have gone on to achieve notable success on Broadway.

Davidson has continually championed the development of new artists through the foundation of programs like the New Theatre for Now (1967), the Lab (1972), and Taper Too (1983). These programs have provided an outlet for such playwrights as Sam Shepard, John Guare, and Lanford Wilson.

Davidson's own directing vision has led him to plays which question the status quo, often utilizing innovative staging and production techniques to help achieve this intent. Attempting to revitalize the classics by challenging audience complacency, his direction of John Whiting's *The Devils* in 1967 at the Forum shocked viewers with its erotic violence. The production was saved from foreclosure by the intervention of a wealthy patron. *In the Matter of J. Robert Oppenheimer* (1969) and *The Trial of the Catonsville Nine* (1970) dealt with issues of individual conscience in conflict with society. *The Shadow Box* (1975) and *Children of a Lesser God* (1979), both of which won Tony Awards for Best Play, centered upon human beings facing major physical challenges. Working closely with the playwrights to reshape the structure of their plays, Davidson often employs such cinematic techniques as episodic and overlapping scenes. *Children of a Lesser God,* dealing with the problems of a deaf woman and her "hearing" husband, employed dialogue in sign language and used an actress who was actually hearing impaired.

Although financial decline has lessened the Forum's ability to promote new playwrights formally, the Mark Taper Forum under Davidson's direction continues to stand in the forefront as an incubator of successful commercial productions.

ADDITIONAL PRODUCTIONS: 1966: *Candide* (Leonard Bernstein); 1972: *Mass* (Bernstein); 1977: *Savages* (Christopher Hampton); 1979: *Terra Nova*; 1986: *The Real Thing*.

SELECTED BIBLIOGRAPHY: Anderson, Douglas. "The Dream Machine: Thirty Years of New Play Development in America." *The Drama Review* 32 (Fall 1988): 55–84; Bartow, Arthur. *The Director's Voice: Twenty-One Interviews*. New York: Theatre Communications Group, 1988: 67–86; Davidson, Gordon. "Reflections on Beginnings." *Theatre 1*. New York: International Theatre Institute, 1969: 64–67; Eder, Richard. "He Doesn't Merely Direct New Plays, He Nurtures Them." *New York Times* 27 March 1971; sec. 2: 4, 26; Herbert, Ian, ed. *Who's Who in the Theatre*. New York: Gale Research Co., 1981; *Who's Who in America*. Wilmette, Illinois: Macmillan Directory Division, 1990–91; Zeigler, Joseph Wesley. *Regional Theatre: The Revolutionary Stage*. New York: Da Capo Press, 1977.

Ann Demling

HOWARD DAVIES [b. ca. 1945, Durham, England]. While working as a stage manager at the Bristol Old Vic, Howard Davies launched his directing career in its studio theatre with a range of new plays, classics, and twentieth-century standards which established a repertorial versatility that was to become a hallmark of his work. After directing in fringe theatre and repertory for three years, Davies joined the Royal Shakespeare Company (RSC) in 1974 as an assistant to John Barton*; but he soon began creating his own productions, which, in the succeeding decade with the RSC, distinguished him as one of the finest directors in the company. While remaining in touch with the demands of classical repertory with *Macbeth, Henry VIII,* and *Troilus and Cressida,* Davies staged productions of new plays by some of Britain's best emerging and established playwrights. As an RSC associate director, he founded and supervised the company's intimate Warehouse Theatre, designed specifically as a venue for high-quality productions of new plays.

At the Warehouse, and in the RSC's other theatres, Davies collaborated on productions noted for intimacy, imagination, and a strong underlying commitment to the playwright's vision. He directed the impeccably conceived, critically acclaimed productions of *Piaf* (Gems, 1978), *Good* (1981), and *Les Liaisons Dangereuses* (Christopher Hampton, 1985), which had highly successful London and New York showings, and staged works by C. P. Taylor, Edward Bond, David Edgar, Tom McGrath, Hanif Kureishi, Trevor Griffiths, Caryl Churchill, and Pam Gems. The visual inventiveness, imaginative conception, and strong ensemble performance associated with Davies's work has been more recently displayed at the Royal National Theatre, which Davies presently serves as one of the company's associate directors.

ADDITIONAL PRODUCTIONS: **Bristol Old Vic:** *Narrow Road to the Deep North, Candida, Long Day's Journey into Night, Early Morning, Woyzeck, Spring's Awakening.* **Royal Shakespeare Company, 1974–87:** *Man Is Man, The Iceman Cometh, Bandits* (C. P. Taylor), *Good, The Fool* (Edward Bond), *The Bundle, The Jail Diary of Albie Sacks* (David Edgar), *No Limits to Love* (David Mercer), *The Innocent* (Tom McGrath), *Outskirts* (Hanif Kureishi), *The Time of Your Life, Softcops* (Caryl Churchill), *The Party* (Trevor Griffiths), *Flight* (David Lan). **Royal National Theatre, 1987–90:** *Cat on a Hot Tin Roof, The Secret Rapture* (David Hare), *Hedda Gabler, The Crucible, Long Day's Journey into Night.* **Other theatres:** *The Threepenny Opera, The Caucasian Chalk Circle, Birds of Passage* (Hanif Kureishi), *After Aida* (Julian Mitchell).
SELECTED BIBLIOGRAPHY: Edwards, Christopher. "Faces behind the Spaces." *Plays and Players* 338 (November 1981): 17–19; Martin, Nick. "Once More with Feeling." *Guardian* 7 February 1989: 37; Morley, Sheridan. "Aiming to 'Demystify' Opera." *The Times* 13 March 1986: 12; Royal National Theatre Press Office, 1991.

James DePaul
Chris Flaharty

LEO DE BERARDINIS [b. January 3, 1940, Gioj, Salerno, Italy]. A leading avant-garde theatre artist, Leo De Berardinis is acclaimed as an actor, director, author, and producer of his own work. After studying at the Piccolo Teatro of Milan, De Berardinis made his acting debut in 1962 under Carlo Quartucci's direction in Samuel Beckett's *Endgame.* Three years later, he and Perla Peragallo collaborated in Rome, producing a controversial *La faticossa messinscene* *dell'Amleto di Shakespeare* (1967) and an even more controversial *Sir and Lady Macbeth* (1968).

Shortly thereafter, De Berardinis and Perla moved to the Naples area, where they established an experimental community theatre in the working-class village of Marigliano, utilizing the talents of amateur actors. In Marigliano, they produced works (e.g., *King Lacreme Lear Napulitane,* 1973) which juxtaposed classical and folkloric texts and others (e.g., *De Berardinis-Peragallo,* 1979) which were primarily autobiographical and depended upon improvised material. Their personal and artistic partnership lasted until 1981, when De Berardinis returned to Rome to perform textual interpretations and solo improvisations.

During his "third production phase," which extended from 1983 to 1987, De Berardinis worked in Bologna with the Cooperativa Nuova Scene, producing Shakespeare through collaborative, improvisational work with a company of young professionals. His final production with the Cooperativa was *Novecento e mille* (1987), a penetrating, philosophical overview of this century which utilized texts of T. S. Eliot and Antonin Artaud, Karl Marx and Antonio Gramsci, Luigi Pirandello and Samuel Beckett, Vladimir Mayakovsky and Pierre Paulo Pasolini, Toto' and Eduardo De Filippo, Franz Kafka and Charlie Chaplin.

With the establishment of his own company, De Berardinis continues an ongoing exploration of theatrical form and meaning through classical text, music, actor improvisation, company collaboration in scripting, and solo performance. *Ha da' passa' 'a nuttata* (1989) epitomizes his multifaceted approach in its reincarnation of major themes from the Eduardo De Filippo* canon.

As Marco De Marinis suggests, De Berardinis "is one of the few author-directors from the new Italian theatre of the 1960s and 1970s who has remained faithful to the spirit of experiment, and attempted consistently to renew himself and his processes in theatremaking" (De Marinis, 49). In addition, he is a leader among his contemporaries because of his visionary, twentieth-century interpretation of both classical and contemporary "master" texts as ongoing inspirational foundations for avant-garde theatre. De Berardinis's place in the long, traditional line of Italian master actor-author-directors is assured through his uncompromising pursuit (based always upon the work of the actor as the primary theatrical force) of new ways to reveal human nature and to provoke self-knowledge through theatre.

ADDITIONAL PRODUCTIONS: As Actor: 1963: *Endgame* (Ripresa Company); Scabia's *Zip Lap Lip . . .* (Teatro Studio de Genova). As Actor-Director with Perla Peragallo: 1967: *Amleto*; 1968: *Sir and Lady Macbeth*. With Carmelo Bene*: 1968: *Don Chisciotte*. With Perla at Teatro de Marigliano: *Omaggio a Charlie Parker* (film); 1972: *O' Zappatore*; 1973: *King Lacreme Lear Napulitane*; 1974: *Sudd*; 1979: *De Berardinis-Peragallo*. With La Cooperativa Nuova Scena Company of Bologna: 1983: Gelber's *The Connection*; 1985: *King Lear*; Solomon's *Il cantico dei cantici*; 1986: *The Tempest*; With Teatro di Leo: 1987: *Delirio* (coproduced with Santarcangelo dei Teatri); Also: 1981: *Leo De Berardinis Re-Incarna* (video by Simone Carella); 1988: *Macbeth* (Teatro Ateneo, Rome);

1989: *Ha da' passa' 'a nuttata* (Spoleto Festival); 1990: *Toto' Principe di Danimarca* (with Astiteatro); 1991: *L'Impero della ghisa* (Taormina Arte Festival). [All scripts adapted from classical sources by De Berardinis unless otherwise indicated.]

SELECTED BIBLIOGRAPHY: Attisani, Antonio. "Prefisso." *Teatro come differenza*. Ravenna: Edizioni Essegi, 1988; Bartolucci, Giuseppe. *Teatro Italiano*. Salerno: Discorsi/3, 1983; D'Aponte, Mimi. "Reflections on the Contemporary Italian Avant-garde." *Western European Stages* Fall 1989: 30–38; De Marinis, Marco. "From Shakespeare to Shakespeare: The Theatre Transcended" [Interview with Leo de Berardinis]. *New Theatre Quarterly* 7 (February 1991): 49–63; Quadri, Franco. *L'avanguardia teatrale in Italia*. Vol. 1. Torino: Einaudi, 1977.

Mimi Gisolfi D'Aponte

BERNARD DE COSTER [b. November 30, 1954, Brussels, Belgium; d. March 7, 1991, Brussels, Belgium]. In his brief career—directing his first play at twenty, and his first professional production at twenty-three—Bernard De Coster earned the title "Boy King" of the Belgian theatre and comparisons with Mozart and Peter Brook.* After viewing De Coster's production of *The Architect and the Emperor of Assyria* (1986), Fernando Arrabal proclaimed him the best director in the world. With prodigious energy, De Coster staged over forty-five spectacular productions of widely diverse styles in fifteen years, designing lights and sound (and sometimes sets and costumes), as well. His extraordinary visual imagery won him not only the respect of the profession, but the loyalty of the general public, who flocked to his shows.

In 1972–73, De Coster simultaneously studied acting with Claude Etienne* at the Brussels Conservatoire and scene design with Serge Creuz at la Cambre, before becoming technical director of the Théâtre de l'Esprit Frappeur. When he directed his first play, *Caligula* (1974), with a group of law students, an enthusiastic press drew the directors of the major Belgian theatres to see the work of this talented newcomer. Claude Etienne invited him to stage *The Oresteia* for the Rideau in 1977; from then on, De Coster directed and designed lights for the Rideau, the Théâtre National de Belgique, the Parc, and for Maurice Béjart at the Opera. Constantly in demand, De Coster saw no need to found his own theatre or seek work outside Belgium, although he did direct *The Abduction from the Seraglio* for the Geneva Opera (1981) and Turino's Teatro Regio (1983), and European tours of his productions were acclaimed by foreign audiences.

Although he was noted for a theatre of phantasmagoric images, underlined with musical scoring, De Coster also worked hard with his actors, exploring with them the limits of their potential. Even when he was struck by terminal illness, De Coster's devotion to his art kept him working, creating what are now considered his testaments to the theatre: *Lettre aux Acteurs* (Valère Novarina, 1989) and *Conversations avec J. L. Borges à l'occasion de son 80ème anniversaire* (texts presented by Willis Barstone, 1990). De Coster died of AIDS in 1991 and was mourned by Belgian colleagues and audiences alike.

ADDITIONAL PRODUCTIONS: 1978: *The Trial*; 1979: *Ondine, Turandot, La Balade du Grand Macabre* (Ghelderode); 1980: *Don Giovanni* with Maurice Béjart; 1981: *Le Roi se meurt, Cyrano de Bergerac, La Muette* with Béjart; 1982: *Aida Vaincue* (René Kalisky), *Caligula, Le Navire Night* (Marguerite Duras), *The Trojan Women, Sortie de l'Acteur* (Ghelderode); 1983: *Une femme Camille Claudel* (Anne Delbée), *Frankenstein*; 1984: *Fantomas* (Ernst Moerman), *L'École des femmes, La Vie Parisienne*; 1985: *Sur le Fil* (Arrabal); 1986: *A Life in the Theatre*; 1987: *Leonardo* (Pietro Pizzuti); 1988: *Phèdre*; 1990: *Le Pic du Bossu* (Mrożek), *Fin de Partie*.
SELECTED BIBLIOGRAPHY: André, Luc. *Théâtre National de Belgique, 1945–1985*. Brussels: Impresor, 1984; *En scène pour demain*. Brussels: Libres Images aux Presses de la Bellone, 1988; Etienne, Claude. *40 années du Rideau de Bruxelles*. Brussels: Rideau de Bruxelles, 1983; ''Hommage à Bernard De Coster.'' *acteurs* 90–91 (May-June 1991): 94–95.

Suzanne Burgoyne

EDUARDO DE FILIPPO [b. May 24, 1900, Naples, Italy; d. October 31, 1984, Rome, Italy]. This major Neapolitan-Italian actor, director, playwright began performing at age four in the theatre company of his natural father, Eduardo Scarpetta, and at age ten became a full member of the Vincenzo Scarpetta Company. In 1931, together with his brother Pepino and sister Titina, De Filippo founded the Teatro Umoristico, and two years later was asked by Luigi Pirandello* to stage his *Liola'* in Neapolitan. This production was followed in 1935 by Pirandello's *Il berretto a sonagli* with De Filippo playing the protagonist and in 1937, by *Il nuovo abito,* co-written by De Filippo and Pirandello. De Filippo continued acting throughout his career and approached both directing and playwriting from the performer's vantage point. In 1945, he founded Il teatro di Eduardo with his sister, debuting what was to become his signature piece, *Napoli milionaria,* at the San Carlo in Naples; and in 1954, he resurrected the San Ferdinando, a historic Neapolitan theatre which had been bombed and which he had bought following World War II.

De Filippo's reputation as a world-famous actor grew from his twentieth-century embodiment of the more disciplined aspects of the commedia dell'arte tradition. His world-weary, comi-tragic protagonists were said to be reincarnations of the Neapolitan Pulcinella-Eduardo mask, and he was often compared to Charlie Chaplin. Virtuoso character delineation through scripting and directing, rather than through company improvisation, was his forte.

De Filippo's sixty-odd plays were written between 1921 and 1973, and they have earned him ongoing comparison with Goldoni and Molière as an understated comedic critic of his society. As Eric Bentley expressed it in the 1950 essay which first introduced De Filippo to an American readership, ''In play after play he has put his finger on the black moral spot.''

De Filippo pursued his role as social critic first through a dialect theatre much beloved by the Neapolitans, and after World War II, through a nationally and internationally produced repertory whose settings often remained Neapolitan. Favorite themes included the humiliations of illegitimacy, the horrors of poverty and unemployment, the moral corruption of the individual for the sake of survival, the human ability to delude one's self and others, and the failure of communication among those most closely related. These themes were played out repeatedly against the backdrop of a family unit, often in wartime, with comedy usually dominating the first part of the dramatic action and tragedy often overwhelming humor by the final curtain. In accepting the 1973 International Feltrinelli Prize, De Filippo remarked, "At the basis of my theatre is always the conflict between man and society, a conflict based upon reaction to injustice and anger over hypocrisy."

De Filippo's best-known plays were written between 1945 and 1948 and evoke the postwar miseries of Italy generally and Naples specifically. In *Napoli milionaria, Questi fantasmi, Filumena Marturano, Le bugie con le gambe lunghe, La grande magia,* and *Le voci di dentro,* poverty, unemployment, hypocrisy, greed, jealousy, and self-delusion reign; in *Filumena Marturano* and to some degree in *Napoli milionaria,* however, the negative aspects of human existence are overcome by love. It is important to note that De Filippo's Neapolitan neorealism anticipated by two years the postwar neo-realism of leading Italian filmmakers Vittorio De Sica and Roberto Rossellini. De Filippo's own film record, which was substantial, reached its zenith with his internationally acclaimed *Marriage Italian Style* (1964), based upon *Filumena Marturano.*

Although produced unsuccessfully on Broadway three times, De Filippo achieved acclaim in Europe and in the Soviet Union, and in London, Laurence Olivier, Joan Plowright, and Ralph Richardson starred in his plays. De Filippo himself performed in successful international tours of *Questi fantasmi, Figlio di Pulcinella,* and *L'Arte della commedia,* the latter underscoring his frequent use of performance art as a vehicle for conveying social criticism.

The final act of De Filippo's career brought new initiatives—a professorship at the University of Rome which yielded 500 hours of taped theatre lectures; numerous productions of his plays for RAI-TV; his appointment as Commendatore, Cavaliere, member of the French Legion of Honor, Doctor of Letters, and finally senator in the Italian Parliament in 1981. In the same year, he read his Neapolitan poetry to a crowd of 15,000 at a peace demonstration in Rome.

As social critic, De Filippo remained vigilant to the end of his life, always tapping more universal themes. His 1940s neo-realistic view of war developed into an admonition against conflict in *Paura numero uno* (1951) and into a scornful view of militaristic patriotism in *Il Monumento* (1970). Accepting an invitation from Einaudi Press, De Filippo's final writing task, at age eighty-four, was the translation of Shakespeare's *The Tempest* into seventeenth-century Neapolitan. Why, he was asked, *The Tempest?* "It teaches tolerance and benevolence, and what better lesson can an artist give us today?" was his reply.

ADDITIONAL PRODUCTIONS: 1921: *Farmacia in turno* (Pepino Villon Company); 1929: *Sik-Sik, l'artefice magico*; 1931: *Natale in casa Cupiello* (Molinari Company); 1945: *Napoli milionaria*; 1946: *Filumena Marturano* (Eduardo Company); 1954: *Napoli milionaria* (Eduardo Company at the San Ferdinando); 1955: *Questi fantasmi* (Paris Festival);

1956: *Filumena Marturano* (as *Best House in Naples* on Broadway; in Moscow at the
Maly and Vakhtangov theatres; and in Leningrad at the Regional Theatre and Theatre of
Drama and Comedy); 1958: *Il figlio di Pulcinella* (Theatre of Nations); 1973: *Sabato,
domenica e lunedi'* (in London, Old Vic, starring the Oliviers, and on Broadway, 1974);
1975: international tour of *L'arte della commedia*; 1977: *Napoli milionaria* as opera
(Spoleto Festival), *Le voci di dentro* (Rome, Teatro Eliseo), *Filumena Marturano* (Lon-
don, Lyric Theatre, with Joan Plowright), *Gli esami non finiscono mai* (Moscow, Vakh-
tangov Theatre); 1981: *Filumena Marturano* (Broadway); 1983: *Le voci di dentro* (as
Inner Voices in London, National Theatre, with Ralph Richardson).
SELECTED BIBLIOGRAPHY: Antonucci, Giovanni. *Eduardo De Filippo*. Firenze: Le
Monnier, 1988; Bentley, Eric. "Son of Pulcinella." *In Search of Theater*. New York:
Vintage Books, 1954: 265–78; Cohn, Ruby, and Helen Krich Chinoy. "Eduardo De
Filippo." *Actors on Acting*. New York: Crown Publishers, 1959: 471–72; D'Aponte,
Mimi. "Encounters with Eduardo De Filippo." *Modern Drama* 16 (December 1973):
347–53; De Filippo, Isabella Q. *Eduardo*. Milano: Bompiani, 1985; Mignone, Mario.
Eduardo De Filippo. Boston: Twayne Publishers, 1984; Viviani, Vittorio. *Storia del
teatro Napoletano*. Napoli: Guida Editori, 1969: 880–934.

Mimi Gisolfi D'Aponte

KAZIMIERZ DEJMEK [b. May 17, 1924, Kowel, Poland]. Kazimierz Dejmek
made his debut as an actor in Rzeszów in 1944, soon after the retreat of the
German Army from the southeastern territories of Poland. He started his career
in Łódź where he met Leon Schiller,* who at that time was a director and a
professor. There, Dejmek organized a group of the young actors interested in
studying Stanislavsky's method. In 1949, with the support of the Ministry of
Culture and Art, the group formed Teatr Nowy, which inaugurated its activities
with the sociorealist play by Czech author Vaška Káňi titled *Brygada szlifierza
Karhana*. In the same year, Dejmek became administrator of the theatre, a
position equivalent to that of director and one he held until 1962, and again from
1975 to 1980. His managerial skills gained him a reputation as one of the best
theatre administrators in the country. In the years between 1962 and 1968, he
managed Teatr Narodowy in Warsaw, and since 1981 he has been in charge of
Teatr Polski.

At Teatr Nowy, Dejmek, an independent director since 1951, underwent a
significant evolution—from realism (in the spirit of Konstantin Stanislavsky*),
to the grotesque (*Łaźnia* by Mayakovsky, 1956; *Święto Winkelrida* by Andrze-
jewski and Zagórski, 1956), to poetical synthesis (*Noc listopadowa* by St. Wyspiański, 1956), and finally to a style which "resuscitated past forms." The
common denominator of Dejmek's work has been his effort to achieve a certain
social resonance. In *Łaźnia*, he attacked party bureaucracy; Święto Winkelrida
was a satire of Polish and Russian relations; while *Żywocie Józefa* (1958) dealt
with undesirable social characteristics rooted in tradition. As a result, Dejmek
came to be recognized as a director who dealt with contemporary issues using
the words of the classics, a director who claimed that the theatre should provoke
the audience to evaluate reality critically. Thus, Dejmek, who started under the

official auspices of the government, became "inconvenient," and his works were considered subversive of cultural policies. This became apparent in 1968, when *Dziady* by Adam Mickiewicz, a Polish national romantic drama, was removed from the program altogether, and Dejmek was dismissed from the directorship of the Teatr Narodowy.

Old Polish plays, known to the international audiences and whose playscripts were written by Dejmek from preserved texts, played a significant role in his work. After *Żywot Józefa* (which he repeated in 1965 and 1985), Dejmek prepared *Historia o Chwalebnym Zmartwychwstaniu Pańskim* (Łódź, 1961; Warsaw, 1962) and *Dialogus de Passione,* with staging forbidden by censors in 1969, but staged in Italy in Piccolo Teatro in 1972 and premiered in Łódź in 1975. These productions made him an heir of Leon Schiller even though his usage of Polish literature was quite different.

In his directing, Dejmek was principally interested in the layman's perspective, in the moral sense of a text, and in the particular contemporary situation. His relation to contemporary dramaturgy was thus always defined by textual, political, and moral criteria. By the end of the 1950s and in the 1960s, during the great repertoire boom in Poland when everybody was staging new Western dramas, Dejmek produced only two: *Visit of the Older Lady* (1958) and *The Deputy* (Hochhuth, 1966), which was restaged in Dusseldorf in 1970 (where he also directed *The Trial of the Catonsville Nine* by Daniel Berrigan in 1971). In 1977, he staged *The Visit* by Friedrich Dürrenmatt in Zurich, and beginning in 1975, he staged numerous plays by Sławomir Mrożek (*Garbus,* 1975; *Vatzlav,* 1979; *Ambasador,* 1981; *Letni dzień,* 1984; *Kontrakt,* 1986; *Portret,* 1987; *Tango,* 1990). *Vatzlav* and *Ambasador* are considered to be Dejmek's greatest achievements.

At the same time that Dejmek aimed to create a theatre style based on the old folk and ritualistic theatre, he was formulating his own unique idea of a universal stage architecture. For its pattern, Dejmek used a two-story stage divided into three parts which resembled a Polish Christmas crèche. In such an architectural arrangement, Dejmek, together with scenographer Andrzej Stopka, directed not only old Polish plays, but also the prologues to *Kordian* and *Dziady.*

What distinguishes Dejmek from other directors is his sensitivity to various styles and his ability to utilize historical and theatrical forms from medieval morality plays to nineteenth-century operettas, the best of which was a production of *Operatka* by Witold Gombrowicz (1975). His aesthetic consciousness and his knowledge of forms combine with his reluctance to stage "effects of the contemporary theatre" and his aversion of overvisualization and extreme physical expression. He demands from his actors solid craftsmanship, and he regards himself as a practitioner who values craftsmanship above theory. While at the beginning of his career he was viewed as a revolutionary who bravely adjusted texts to suit his intentions, during the 1980s, he came to be regarded as a director willing to fight for the rights of the author and the merits of the text while strongly opposing theatrical gimmickry.

ADDITIONAL PRODUCTIONS: 1953: *Henryk IV na łowach* (St. Bogusławski); 1958: *Measure for Measure*; 1960, *Julius Caesar*; 1962: *Słowo o Jakubie Szeli* (B. Jasieński); 1965: *Kordian* (J. Słowacki); 1968: *Uncle Vanya*; 1971: *Jeu de massacre* (Ionesco); 1972: *Historia o Chwalebnym Zmartwychwstaniu Pańskim* (at Schauspiel, Essen); 1977: *Die Frist* (Dürrenmatt); 1982: *Wyzwolenie* (St. Wyspiański); 1984: *Wesele* (St. Wyspiański); 1987: *Portret*; 1991: *Ubu Roi*.

SELECTED BIBLIOGRAPHY: Czanerle, Maria. *Teatr pokolenia*. Łódź: Wydawnictwo Łódzkie, 1964; Grodzicki, August. *Reżyserzy polskiego teatru*. Warszawa: Interpress, 1979; Raszewski, Zbigniew. "Dejmek." Pamiętnik Teatralny 3–4 (1981); *Teatr Nowy w Łodzi Praca zbiorowa pod red. St. Kaszyńskiego*. Łódź: Wydawnictwo Łódzkie, 1983.

Elzbieta Wysińska

GEORGE DEVINE [b. November 20, 1910, London, England; d. January 20, 1966, London, England]. George Devine is best remembered for his work with the English Stage Company, which he founded at the Royal Court in 1956. His directing credits range from Bertolt Brecht's *The Good Woman of Setzuan* (1956) to a Japanese-styled *King Lear* (1955) to the first production of John Arden's *Live Like Pigs* (1958) to the world premiere of the opera of *Troilus and Cressida* (1954). Influenced by Russian director Theodore Komisarzhevsky, French theorist Michel Saint-Denis,* and English actor-director John Gielgud,* Devine's work as a director reflects no real specialty nor specific style. Both a visionary and a skeptic, Devine was a man of paradox. He stimulated creativity in others, but was not always able to hone his own creative impulses. He had a regard for the classics, but understood equally well the new plays that were written during his nine-year stint as artistic director of the English Stage Company. He was successful in maintaining a long-term vision of what he wanted, while at the same time assuming the day-to-day responsibility of running a theatre.

Devine's directing career can be divided into three periods: his early work in the late thirties and forties at the Young and Old Vic theatres; a free-lance period which followed the war; and his years at the English Stage Company (1956–65). Although each period reflects a different kind of growth in Devine's career, all reflect his commitment to ensemble work and to maintaining a balance between the need for commercial success and the importance of artistic experimentation which allowed for the possibility of failure.

Devine made his directing debut with an adaptation of *Great Expectations* (1939) that demonstrated his ability to cast well and his knowledge of all areas of theatre. Such traits, along with his organizational skills and trust in his company, became Devine's trademark. His first West End hit was Daphne Du Maurier's *Rebecca* (1940). Several school productions at the Young Vic reflected Saint-Denis's influence in terms of the movement and improvisation techniques which Devine employed in *Servant of Two Masters* (1949) and *The Knight of the Burning Pestle* (1950).

After the war, Devine served as a free-lance director, working at the Shakespeare Memorial Theatre. There, he directed a variety of plays and operas including *Bartholomew Fair* (1950), which received mixed reviews; *Volpone*

(1952), which critic Kenneth Tynan praised for its pictorial qualities; and an unusual production of *King Lear* (1955), designed by American-born Japanese designer-sculptor Isamu Noguchi. *King Lear,* with John Gielgud in the title role, was a departure from Devine's previous work, as he tried to bring about a change in both acting style and staging. Devine's "essentialism theory" was developed as the result of working with Noguchi's designs, which offered "elemental shapes of the universe: egg-forms, triangular caverns, airborne prisms, a multi-faceted ramp and other mobile abstract pieces" (Wardle, 153). Although Devine was not completely successful in achieving his goals for change, the production remains a watershed for Shakespearean drama in the fifties.

Devine's years with the English Stage Company reflect more a managerial success than a directorial one. Although Devine directed a number of strong productions (including the first English production of *The Crucible* [1956]; *Rosmersholm* [1959] with Peggy Ashcroft, which was considered one of his strongest artistic and commercial successes; and *Platonov* [1960], which demonstrated his flair for directing subtle comedy), it was Devine's ability to run a theatre and to bring together the best combination of artists to realize a production that was his greatest contribution to English theatre.

Devine championed new works by John Osborne, Ann Jellicoe, and John Arden while his own work often achieved popular success without critical recognition. Still, he paved the way for the new wave of playwrights in the late sixties and made it possible for plays like Edward Bond's *Saved* to find an audience. He trusted the writer "to a fault," which may be partially responsible for his mixed critical and artistic success as a director. Ultimately, as Irving Wardle notes, Devine created a writer's theatre, but not a literary theatre (Wardle, 183).

ADDITIONAL PRODUCTIONS: 1940: *The Tempest* (co-directed with Marius Goring); 1946: *King Stag* (Gozzi); 1951: *The Wedding* (Chekhov), *Don Carlo* (opera); 1952: *Eugene Onegin* (opera); 1953: *The Taming of the Shrew, Romeo and Juliet* (opera by Heinrich Sutermeister), *King Lear, King John*; 1955: *The Magic Flute*; 1956: *The Mulberry Bush, Don Juan, Death of Satan* (both by Ronald Duncan), *The Country Wife*; 1957: *Nekrassov* (Jean-Paul Sartre, translated by Sylvia and George Lesson); 1958: *Major Barbara, Endgame, The Sport of My Mad Mother* (codirected with Ann Jellicoe); 1959: *Cock-a-Doodle-Dandy* (Sean O'Casey); 1961: *August for the People* (Dennis); 1962: *Happy Days, Twelfth Night*; 1963: *First Results* (collective creation for Sunday Night Productions without Decor, co-directed with William Gaskill* and Claude Chagrin), *Exit the King*.

SELECTED BIBLIOGRAPHY: Doty, Gresdna, and Billy J. Harbin, eds. *Inside the Royal Court Theatre, 1956–1981: Artists Talk*. Baton Rouge: Louisiana State University Press, 1990; Findlater, Richard, ed. *At the Royal Court: 25 Years of the English Stage Company*. Ambergate, England: Amber Lane, 1981; Gaskill, William. *A Sense of Direction*. London: Faber and Faber, 1981; Hayman, Ronald. "The Royal Court 1956–1972." *Drama* Summer 1972: 45–53; Taylor, John Russell. "The Devine Years." *Drama* Autumn 1978: 25–30; Tschudin, Marcus. *A Writer's Theatre: George Devine and the English Stage Company at the Royal Court 1956–1965*. Berne: Lang, 1972; Tynan, Kenneth. *Curtains*. New York: Atheneum, 1961; Wardle, Irving. *The Theatres of George Devine*. London: Jonathan Cape, 1978.

Judy Lee Oliva

JOHN DEXTER [b. August 2, 1925, Derby, England; d. March 23, 1990, London, England]. In the late 1950s, after operating a factory lathe, serving as a sergeant in World War II in North Africa, recovering from a bout with polio, and playing on a BBC radio soap opera, John Dexter made a name for himself as a director with the English Stage Company of George Devine* at the Royal Court Theatre. He served as associate director of the National Theatre under Sir Laurence Olivier from 1963 to 1966 and with Peter Hall* from 1971 to 1975, and worked in West End and on Broadway, winning two Tony Awards for direction. He staged operas, first at Covent Garden in 1966, and later in Hamburg, Paris, and New York. He served as director of production at the Metropolitan Opera from 1974 to 1981, and subsequently was production advisor there while joint artistic director of London's Mermaid Theatre. Dexter returned to Broadway to stage the Tony Award–winning *M. Butterfly* (1988) and *The Threepenny Opera* (1990).

Dexter brought to the stage an exciting combination of minimalist design and choreographic movement. Intuitive and influenced by his designers, he shifted easily between small, naturalistic plays and sweeping epics. Although he came from the generation of England's "angry young men" and remained class-conscious (he always wanted to know what a character earned), he acknowledged that he was no revolutionary. From Bertolt Brecht* he took platforms and stark lighting, not politics. Like Peter Brook,* Dexter emphasized the visual, contributing to a new acceptance of simple staging and ritualistic movement. In a thirty-year collaboration with the designer Jocelyn Herbert, Dexter propelled Brechtian austerity toward elegant abstraction. He lacked the university training of many directors of his generation, but developed a reputation as an intellectual. Influenced by Jan Kott's insight into sexual ambiguity in *As You Like It,* he proposed an all-male production. When Olivier objected, Dexter left the National.

Endlessly inventive, Dexter exemplified the director's expanding role in shaping plays. His staging became associated with Arnold Wesker's plays, just as the director Michael Blakemore was identified with Peter Nichols's plays and Lindsay Anderson with David Storey's. Dexter expanded Wesker's general stage directions into details of movement (reminiscent of the acclaimed 1933 Lee Strasberg* Group Theatre show, *Men in White*), which served the playwright's perspective as he brought workers' routine to interesting stage life while simultaneously making that routine a kind of choreographed beauty. Dexter made a virtue of limited resources, staging productions on small Royal Court budgets, using bottle caps to achieve the stunning Aztec sun in *Royal Hunt of the Sun* (1964), and recycling stock costumes at the Metropolitan Opera. Following his departure from the Royal Court to join Olivier at the new National Theatre, Dexter continued a high degree of involvement in the writer's process. He began rehearsals for Peter Shaffer's *Black Comedy* when the playwright had only the beginning of a script, heightened the ritual in Shaffer's *Royal Hunt of the Sun*, and emphasized the non-naturalistic elements of his *Equus* (1973). Dexter won his first Tony for his 1974 New York production of *Equus*.

Like Peter Hall and Jonathan Miller,* Dexter combined a stage career with opera, achieving a second international reputation. He joined the Met in the newly created position of director of productions, managing in tandem with Anthony Bliss and musical director James Levine. In his new position, Dexter exercised both his facility with new works and his management skills, controlling costs and introducing new technology. Although he proclaimed an emphasis on human feelings, many complained that his stark staging stripped pageantry from older operas and emotion from new ones.

Dexter's last project, *The Threepenny Opera* on Broadway, could have been a brilliant culmination to his career, combining grand scale with the working-class sympathy of his personal and professional beginnings. However, it was a muddle, pleasing neither those interested in politics nor those who looked for craft. Word of backstage acrimony caused more stir than the performances. The crowning touch of Dexter's career remains the earlier *M. Butterfly*, with its dazzling visual elements and movement, which won him his second Tony Award. Though acerbic, with a reputation for being difficult, Dexter nevertheless enjoyed long, creative relationships, notably with Wesker, Herbert, and Levine.

ADDITIONAL PRODUCTIONS: 1958: *Chicken Soup with Barley** (Arnold Wesker); 1959: *The Kitchen* (Wesker), *Roots** (Wesker); 1960: *I'm Talking about Jerusalem** (Wesker); 1962: *Chips with Everything* (Wesker, New York); 1963: *Saint Joan, Half a Sixpence, Chips with Everything* (New York); 1964: *Armstrong's Last Goodnight* (John Arden), *Othello* with Laurence Olivier, *Royal Hunt of the Sun* (Peter Shaffer), also New York; 1965: *Black Comedy, Do I Hear a Waltz?* (New York); 1967: *Black Comedy and White Lies* (New York); 1971: *Tyger* (musical of William Blake's life); 1972: *The Old Ones* (Wesker); 1973: *Misanthrope*; 1974: *Pygmalion*; 1975: *Phaedre Britannica*; 1980: *The Life of Galileo*; 1983: *Heartbreak House*. **Opera:** 1966: *Benevenuto Cellini* (Covent Garden); *I Vespri Siciliani* (Hamburg, Paris, and 1973, Metropolitan Opera); *Boris Godunov, Billy Budd, Un Ballo in Maschera* (Hamburg); 1976: *Aida, Dialogues of the Carmelites, Lulu*; 1977: *Rigoletto*; 1978: *Billy Budd, Mahagonny*; 1980: *Parade* trilogy, including *Les Mamelles de Tiresias*; 1981: *Oedipus Rex*.

(**Chicken Soup with Barley, Roots,* and *I'm Talking about Jerusalem* are best known as the Wesker Trilogy.)

SELECTED BIBLIOGRAPHY: Cook, Judith. "John Dexter." *Directors' Theatre*. London: Harrap, 1974: 35–41; Elsom, John, and Nicholas Tomalin. *The History of the National Theatre*. London: Cape, 1978; Hayman, Ronald. "Arnold Wesker and John Dexter." *Playback 2*. London: Davis-Poynter, 1973: 63–79; Leech, Michael. "John Dexter." *Plays and Players* 20 (October 1972): 31–33; Leeming, Glenda. *Wesker the Playwright*. London and New York: Methuen, 1983; Morowitz, Charles, ed. *Current Biography Yearbook 1976*. New York: Wilson, 1976: 121–23; Robinson, Francis. *Celebration: The Metropolitan Opera*. Garden City, NY: Doubleday, 1979; Smith, Patrick J. *A Year at the Met*. New York: Knopf, 1983.

David Carlyon

GLENDA DICKERSON [b. February 9, 1945, Houston, Texas]. An actress, folklorist, educator, and playwright, Glenda Dickerson has directed over fifty dramatic and musical productions, many of them noted for their use of a ritualistic style of performance. One of the few black women to stage a Broadway production—*Reggae* by Melvin Van Peebles, Kendrew Lascelles, and Stafford Harrison (1980)—her directing credits also include Off-Broadway, regional, and university productions throughout the nation, as well as assignments which have taken her to Kenya and Barbados.

As the daughter of a career army officer, she traveled extensively throughout the world. While a student at Howard University's Drama Department, Dickerson studied oral interpretation, Greek classical theatre, and Shakespeare under Professor Owen Dodson.* A respected writer and director in his own right, Dodson expanded Dickerson's appreciation of her ethnic heritage by exposing her to the lives and works of significant black writers and cultural leaders. In the late 1960s, disillusioned with the degradation suffered by actors participating in the "cattle call" auditioning process, Dickerson formed her own New York–based theatre company called TOBA (Tough on Black Actors) Players. At this time, she began the development of a performance style utilizing song, music, and the spoken word, similar to the form that playwright Ntozake Shange later called a "choreopoem."

After earning an M.A. in speech and theatre arts from Adelphi University in 1969 and studying with director Peter Brook,* Dickerson returned to Howard University as an assistant professor. As a director for Washington, D.C., university and regional theatres, Dickerson explored the power of the spoken word wedded with a visual statement. Seeking to reveal the continuity within the African diaspora, she often conceived of many of her productions using such sources as the Greek theatre and the folktales, oral histories, and literature of Africa and black America. As an important component of the creative process, Dickerson required actors to attend long hours of rehearsal where she fostered a sense of ensemble acting and grounded the performers in techniques of the language arts, music, and movement. In such shows as *The Unfinished Song* (Dickerson, 1969) and *Jesus Christ, Lawd Today* (Dickerson, with music by Clyde Barrett, 1972), the performance style removed the usual barriers between the actors and audience. Actors and musicians interacted with the audience by using the auditorium as well as the stage area. Through the careful orchestration of familiar secular and religious rituals, music, literature, call and response performance techniques, and symbolic visual images, the audience shared a common theatrical experience which culminated in an emotional catharsis.

Most of Dickerson's subsequent productions continued to refine this style of ritualistic theatre. In 1981, she became founding director of the Owen Dodson Lyric Theatre—a self-described "griot" preserving the history and folklore that chronicles the African-American experience. In such acclaimed works as *No* (adapted by Dickerson from the writings of Alexis De Veaux, 1981) and *Shakin' the Mess Outta Misery* (Shay Youngblood, 1988), Dickerson stages works which bridge the past and present while celebrating the dignity and beauty of African Americans.

ADDITIONAL PRODUCTIONS: 1971: *Trojan Women* (adapted by Dickerson from Euripides); 1972: *The Torture of Mothers* (adapted by Dickerson from Truman Nelson's novel); 1973: *Jump at the Sun* (adapted by Dickerson from Zora Neale Hurston's novel, *Their Eyes Were Watching God*); 1974: *Owen's Song* (adapted by Dickerson and Mike Malone from the dramatic and poetic works of Owen Dodson); 1980: *Magic and Lions* (adapted by Dickerson based on the prose and poetry of Ernestine Walker); 1982: *Rashomon* (adapted by Dickerson from the Japanese classic); 1983: *Haitian Medea* (adapted by Dickerson from Euripides), *Saffron Persephone Brown* (Dickerson); 1988: *Eel Catching in Setauket* (adapted by Dickerson from oral histories of the African-American community of Setauket, New York).

SELECTED BIBLIOGRAPHY: Boston, Taquiena, and Vera J. Katz. "Witness to a Possibility: The Black Theatre Movement in Washington." *Black American Literature Forum* 17 (Spring 1983): 22–26; Cloyd, Iris, ed. *Who's Who among Black Americans*. 6th ed. Detroit: Gale Research, 1990; Fabre, Genevieve. *Drumbeats, Masks and Metaphor: Contemporary Afro-American Theatre*. Trans. Melvin Dixon. Cambridge, MA: Harvard University Press, 1983; Hatch, James V., and Omanii Abdullah. *Black Playwrights, 1823–1977*. New York: R. R. Bowker, 1977; Peterson, Bernard L., Jr. *Contemporary Black American Playwrights and Their Plays*. Westport, CT: Greenwood Press, 1988.

Addell Austin Anderson

ALEKSEY DENISOVICH DIKY [b. February 25, 1889, Ekaterinoslav (Dnepropetrovsk), Ukraine; d. October 1, 1955, Moscow]. Diky was the brother of a popular Ukrainian actress who encouraged his early interest in acting. In 1909 he moved to Moscow to study with some of the leading members of the Moscow Art Theatre, and in 1910 he was accepted into the Art Theatre company. In 1922, Diky was invited to become part of the directorial "collective" of the new Second Moscow Art Theatre.

Although his prior directorial experience was limited to some Chekhov one-acts staged in 1912, Diky soon rose to prominence at the Second Art Theatre. His most acclaimed and controversial production was Eugeny Zamyatin's adaptation of Nikolai Leskov's satirical story *The Flea* (1925). The play was performed in the broad comic style of the vaudeville and fairground theatres, and the settings and costumes were cartoon-like stylizations of traditional Russian folk art.

Unfortunately, the Second Art Theatre's directorial collective soon deteriorated into a bitter rivalry between Diky and Michael Chekhov.* The mass resignation of Diky and his supporters in 1928 insured the theatre's ultimate demise.

For several years thereafter, Diky had no permanent post, although he was active as a guest director. Most notably, he staged a popular production of Alexei Fayko's *Man with a Briefcase* (1928), a satire on bureaucratic middlemen for the Theatre of the Revolution, and collaborated on *The Red Poppy,* the "first ever socialist ballet," at the Bolshoi Theatre in 1929. In 1931 Diky founded his own studio theatre, which staged a number of original works, including the first adaptation of Leskov's *Lady Macbeth of Mtsensk*. In 1932, he became artistic director of the Theatre of Trade Unions, which had absorbed much of the Second Art Theatre company.

Diky was a follower rather than a leader of the avant-garde, but his taste for topical satire and his association with figures such as Zamyatin and Vsevolod Meyerhold* became political liabilities in the 1930s. In 1936 his studio was closed and he lost his post at the Trade Unions' Theatre. During the 1936–37 season he was a guest director at the Bolshoi Dramatic Theatre in Leningrad, but thereafter he worked primarily as an actor, in both theatre and film.

ADDITIONAL PRODUCTIONS: 1923: *The Playboy of the Western World*; 1936: *Death of Tarelkin*; 1946: *Smug Citizens* (Gorky); 1953: *Shadows* (Saltykov-Shchedrin).

SELECTED BIBLIOGRAPHY: Litvinenko, N. G. *Aleksey Diky.* Moscow: Vseros. teatr. ob-vo, 1976; Rudnitsky, Konstantin. *Russian and Soviet Theater: 1905–1932.* Trans. Roxane Permar. New York: Abrams, 1988; Slonim, Marc. *Russian Theatre from the Empire to the Soviets.* New York: Collier, 1962.

Cheyanne Boyd

OWEN VINCENT DODSON [b. November 28, 1914, Brooklyn, New York; d. June 21, 1983, New York, New York]. Beginning as an undergraduate at Bates College in Maine with a production of Shaw's *Candida* (1936) and ending in Manhattan with the staging of his own drama *The Confession Stone* (1972), Dodson's directorial career spanned 118 productions, almost all of them in educational theatres of black colleges. For twenty-five years, he, along with Anne Cooke (later Anne Cooke Reid) and James Butcher, built the drama department at Howard University into one of the finest undergraduate departments in the nation. The Howard Players became the first college drama group in America to be invited to perform abroad; Dodson directed DuBose Heyward's *Mamba's Daughters* and Anne Cooke directed *The Wild Duck* for a tour of Norway, Denmark, Sweden, and Germany (1949).

Because in the earlier years of the twentieth century, few roles other than minstrel stereotypes were available to black actors, Dodson, a published poet, created quality roles for blacks by staging his own poetic dramas—*Divine Comedy* (1938), *Garden of Time* (1939), *Bayou Legend* (1948). The lofty style of these verse plays, with their attendant spectacle, became Dodson's forte.

Trained at the Yale Drama School (M.F.A., 1939), he insisted that his students act in world-class verse drama. His productions ranged from *Medea in Africa* (1940) and *Oedipus Rex* (1966) through Maurice Maeterlinck's *Pelléas and Mélisande* (1951), *Alcestis* (1952), *Richard III* with Toni Morrison (1953), *Julius Caesar* (1960), Federico Garcia Lorca's *Blood Wedding* (1961), *Antigone* (1961), *Dr. Faustus* with Gordon Heath (1962), and T. S. Eliot's *Family Reunion* with Earle Hyman (1952). Dodson directed three productions of *Hamlet*: the first (1945) with Gordon Heath, the second (1951) with Earle Hyman, and the third with St. Clare Christmas in celebration of Shakespeare's 500th birthday (1964).

Because of his insistence on visual beauty and impact, his budgets burst their bounds. His elaborate use of spectacle and his careful attention to minor roles and extras (each of whom he gave an individual persona) became a hallmark of his style. He had perfected his handling of crowds in the navy during World War II where he wrote and directed eleven pageants to promote morale among African-American seamen. This aspect of his career reached its climax when he wrote *New World A-Coming* (1944) and staged this pageant at Madison Square Garden

(1944). In the center of the stadium, a gigantic red star platform rested on a huge blue stage. The theatre unions had given Dodson access to the big names—Langston Hughes, Canada Lee, Abbie Mitchell, Josh White, Marie Young, and Will Geer. Pearl Primus danced and Duke Ellington's orchestra played. For his walk-ons, he used seventy-six "lesser" bodies. Gordon Heath directed the "voice crew" and James Gelb the lighting. Ray Elliott and Evelyn Araumburo wrote original music. The pageant played before an audience of 25,000 people.

Two other directorial distinctions mark Dodson's career—his use of nonconventional casting and his production of original plays. In selecting his actors, Dodson pioneered in multiethnic casting. From his earliest productions, he cast the roles using black, white, or Asian, whoever was best suited for the part; the families in Arthur Miller's *All My Sons* (1947) and in *Death of a Salesman* (1960) presented mothers, fathers, and children, from light to dark, and without self-consciousness.

Dodson staged several American premieres of contemporary European classics—Albert Camus's *Malentendu* (*Cross-Purpose*) (1951), Kaj Munk's *The Word* (1952), and Mario Fratti's *The Return* and *The Academy* (1966), as well as those of leading African-American playwrights—Countee Cullen and Floyd Barbour. His world premieres of James Baldwin's *Amen Corner* (1955) and Ted Shine's *Morning, Noon and Night* (1962) have become black theatre legends.

His direction of original plays and the classics inspired a generation of African-American artists to pursue professional theatrical careers—Gordon Heath, Earle Hyman, Roxie Roker, Zaida Cole, Graham Brown, Shauneille Perry, Debbie Allen, and many others.

ADDITIONAL PRODUCTIONS: 1939: *No More Peace*; 1941: *Cherry Orchard*; 1942: *Hedda Gabler*; 1949: *Great God Brown*; 1949: *Electra*; 1950: *No More Peace*; 1955: *Finian's Rainbow*; 1958: *Noah*; 1959: *Look Back in Anger*; 1960: *A Moon for the Misbegotten*; 1960: *Tea and Sympathy*; 1961: *Rashomon*; 1963: *Long Day's Journey into Night*; 1965: *Blues for Mr. Charlie*.

SELECTED BIBLIOGRAPHY: Colby, Vineta, ed. *World Authors 1980–1985*. New York: H. W. Wilson Company, 1991: 217–19; *Dictionary of Literary Biography*. Vol. 76. Detroit: Gale Research, 1988: 30–36; Hatch, James V. *Sorrow Is the Only Faithful One; A Biography of the Life of Owen Dodson*. Champaign: University of Illinois Press, 1993; Hatch, James, Douglas A. M. Ward, and Joe Weixlmann. "The Rungs of a Powerful Long Ladder: An Owen Dodson Bibliography." *Black American Literature Forum* 14 (Summer 1980): 60–68; Logan, Rayford W., and Michael R. Winston, eds. *Dictionary of American Negro Biography*. rev. ed. New York: W. W. Norton and Co., 1993.

James V. Hatch

DECLAN DONNELLAN [b. 1953, Manchester, England]. Although he studied law at Cambridge, Declan Donnellan chose a career in the theatre, working as a free-lance director with the Activists at the Royal Court and teaching regularly at the Arts Educational School. In 1980, he and a friend from Cambridge, designer Nick Ormerod, collaborated on a production of *'Tis Pity She's a Whore*, which launched a fertile creative partnership that generated nearly a score of lively, inventive interpretations of the classics over the next decade. In 1981, they created the theatre company Cheek by Jowl with the aim of making classics more accessible to modern audiences and confronting them "cheek by jowl" with high-energy, innovative, strongly theatrical productions performed in a contemporary context. Since staging *The Country Wife* in 1981, Donnellan has directed Shakespeare and other classics for Cheek by Jowl, many of which have been British premieres of works by Racine, Corneille, Calderón, Lessing, and other world-class dramatists. The company regularly tours abroad, and has won numerous nominations and awards, including three Olivier Awards for Donnellan's work (Most Promising Newcomer, 1985; Director of the Year, 1987; Outstanding Achievement, 1990).

In 1988, Donnellan and Ormerod were invited to work at the Royal National Theatre, where they produced a brilliant and hugely successful production of Lope de Vega's powerful *Fuente Ovejuna,* followed in 1990 by an ambitious interpretation of Henrik Ibsen's dramatic epic *Peer Gynt.* Because of these productions, Donnellan has recently been named an associate director of the National. Donnellan's dynamic, visceral directing style is marked by a ferocious energy in the pacing and the playing; imaginative staging; striking and evocative visual images; and sharp attention to the emotional center of the play. Rather than strict adherence to the formalistic structure of the language, Donnellan's style places a priority on the clear expression of the text through the creation of a specific and detailed physical life for the characters. He builds a strong working ensemble with his actors, removing boundaries on creative exploration at rehearsals, encouraging interpretive risk-taking, and allowing the actors almost limitless freedom to experiment with their character impulses. Donnellan utilizes improvisation and game playing to a large extent in rehearsal to generate expressive raw material which he ultimately shapes and "edits" into the performance. Music (often played by the actors on the stage) is used extensively and integrally in Donnellan's productions to amplify the emotional impact and resonance of the scenes, while underscoring and singing enhance the essential theatricality of his approach. As a trademark ritual of his Cheek by Jowl productions, Donnellan has the acting company stand before the audience preceding each play as a frank acknowledgment of the theatrical illusion and an invitation to the audience to join into the pretense of the performance and to experience the ultimate truth of the play.

ADDITIONAL PRODUCTIONS: Cheek by Jowl, 1981–91: Eight Shakespearean productions including *Othello, Pericles, A Midsummer Night's Dream, Twelfth Night,* and *The Tempest*; also, an adaptation of *Vanity Fair*; *Andromache* (Racine); *The Man of Mode*; *The Cid*; *A Family Affair* (Ostrovsky); *Philoctetes* (Sophocles); *The Doctor of Honour* (Calderón); *Sara* (Lessing); *Lady Betty* (Donnellan and Paddy Cunneen); *Don Giovanni* (at Scottish Opera Go Round); *Bent* (at Northcote Theatre); *Mahagonny* (at Wexford Festival); *Macbeth* (at Finnish National Theatre); *Philoctetes* (at Finnish National Theatre); *The Masked Ball* (at Opera 80), 1992: *Angels in America* (Tony Kushner; London, National Theatre).

SELECTED BIBLIOGRAPHY: Materials located at the Press Offices of Cheek by Jowl, the Royal National Theatre, and the 1991 International Theatre Festival at the State University of New York, Stony Brook.

James DePaul
Chris Flaharty

CHARLES DULLIN [b. April 15, 1885, Yenne, Savoy, France; d. December 11, 1949, Paris, France]. As an actor, director, and teacher, Charles Dullin dedicated his life to serving his idea of theatre as a necessary force for cultural and social renewal. Born into a solid middle-class family (his father was the local justice of the peace) and raised in a fairy-tale chateau in the small Savoy town of Yenne, Dullin briefly entered the seminary to study for the priesthood, but soon discovered his true vocation. At the age of eighteen in Lyons, he had his first exposure to the theatre, was smitten and henceforth devoted his life to Thespis.

In Paris in 1905, he began his theatrical training by playing a variety of roles in the "théâtres de quartier" (neighborhood theatres). In 1907–8, he worked with André Antoine* at the Odéon theatre and in 1911, joined Jacques Rouché at the Théâtre de l'Art, where he played his first memorable role as Smerdiakov in *The Brothers Karamazov,* adapted by Jacques Copeau.*

In 1913, Copeau invited Dullin to join his newly founded Vieux Colombier. There he learned the highly physical art of mime and gesture which Copeau emphasized, and in 1914, Dullin repeated his acclaimed performance as Smerdiakov to Copeau's Ivan and Jouvet's* Father Zossima. He achieved further recognition in Claudel's *The Exchange* and especially as Molière's miser, Harpagon, a role he played over 1,000 times throughout his career. Along with Louis Jouvet* and others, he followed Copeau to New York in 1917, playing numerous roles at the Garrick Theatre until he broke with Copeau and returned to Paris in 1919.

In 1921, he opened his own theatre and acting school, the Atelier, where he worked to achieve the "rebirth of the actor" through a rigorous training of body and voice similar to the process he had experienced with Copeau. Taking as his models the commedia dell'arte and Japanese theatre, he stressed intense physical exercises supplemented by improvisational games which taught the students to act with their hands, feet, muscles, and limbs. They also learned to feel, smell, handle, see, and hear invisible objects, as Antonin Artaud described his training. In protest against what he called the "amateurism, dilettantism, and histrionics" of most actors of his time who were more interested in financial gain and personal success than in the regenerative role of the theatre, Dullin demanded the actor's total dedication to the art of the theatre and required a sense of honesty and respect toward author and audience. Jean Vilar,* Jean-Louis Barrault,* Marcel Marceau, Antonin Artaud—an entire generation of theatre directors, actors, and writers learned their profession at Dullin's school.

As one of the members of the Cartel des Quatre formed in 1927, Dullin unstintingly carried out their common project to practice simplicity in staging, to "serve the playwright," to respect the audience; to reject realism in favor of poetry; and to use the great traditions of dramatic art as a solid base for "a search for new forms in keeping with the spirit of our times." Most importantly, perhaps, was the Cartel's conviction that new, broader audiences had to be created in order for the theatre to survive.

Thanks to the Popular Front government, Dullin was given the opportunity in 1937 to address this question. Commissioned to write a policy report on theatrical decentralization, Dullin urged the establishment of permanent theatrical enclaves throughout France which would be devoted to the renewal and broadening of the social base of French audiences. These "artistic prefectorates," as he called them, would house "people's theatres," which would serve not only their local communities, but surrounding areas through tours and other cultural visits. Although the report was shelved, its influence was to be felt in the important popular theatre and decentralization movements which changed theatre practices in postwar France.

In his seventeen years at the Atelier, Dullin staged some sixty-nine plays. He excelled in producing Shakespeare, Calderón, and Lope de Vega, but he was also the first to introduce Luigi Pirandello* (*The Pleasure of Honesty*, 1922) to French audiences, and he promoted the work of a number of new playwrights, especially Armand Salacrou. Dullin was an extraordinarily expressive actor. Along with his Harpagon, his portrayals of the title role in Ben Jonson's *Volpone* (1929) and Richard III in André Obey's adaptation are memorable.

In 1941, Dullin became director of the Théâtre Sarah Bernhardt, rebaptized the Théâtre de la Cité by the Germans. There, in this large house, he hoped he could gather and affect an audience other than the bourgeois elite of the commercial theatres. In 1943, he courageously staged Jean-Paul Sartre's first play, the anticollaborationist *The Flies,* during the German occupation. He presented Calderón's *Life Is a Dream* (1943) and his famous *Volpone*. He played in *King Lear* (1944) and the lead in Corneille's *Cinna* (1947), but ultimately, the enterprise was a failure financially. Debts accumulated and Dullin was severely criticized.

Disappointed and disillusioned, Dullin left the Théâtre de la Cité in 1947. During the last two years of his life, he played in films (*Quai des Orfèvres* with Jouvet and Sartre's *Les Jeux sont faits*) and toured in his original production of Salacrou's *L'Archipel Lenoir* (1948). A second tour included Molière's *The Miser* (1949) with Dullin once more as the avaricious Harpagon. It was to be his last performance. He died on December 11, 1949.

ADDITIONAL PRODUCTIONS: 1922: *Such Stuff as Dreams Are Made of* (Calderón); 1933: *Richard III* (Shakespeare); 1936: *Mercadet ou Le Faiseur* (Balzac); 1937: *Right You Are If You Think You Are* (Pirandello); 1941: *The Miser*; 1949: *La Marâtre* (Balzac).

SELECTED BIBLIOGRAPHY: Arnaud, Lucien. *Charles Dullin*. Paris: L'Arche, 1952; Arnaud, Lucien. "Charles Dullin et la mise en scène." *Théâtre populaire* 2 (1953): 27–33; Arnoux, Alexandre. *Charles Dullin, portrait brisé*. Paris: Emile-Paul, 1951; Dullin, Charles. *L'Avare*. Paris: Seuil, 1946; Dullin, Charles. *Ce Sont les dieux qu'il nous faut.*

Paris: Gallimard, 1969; Dullin, Charles. *Cinna.* Paris: Seuil, 1948; Dullin, Charles. *Souvenirs et notes de travail d'un acteur.* Paris: Lieutier, 1946; Sarment, Jean. *Charles Dullin.* Paris: Calmann-Levy, 1950.

Philippa Wehle

ELEONORA DUSE [b. October 3, 1858, Vigevano, Italy; d. April 21, 1924, Pittsburgh, Pennsylvania]. Eleonora Duse was born into an itinerant acting family; her great-grandfather, Luigi Duse, was a great interpreter of Goldoni. By the early 1880s, Duse had already become well-known in Italy. In 1886, she became an actress-manager, overseeing all artistic and administrative aspects of her own company and spending much of her life on tour. By 1893, Duse was internationally acclaimed. After an Egyptian tour in 1889–90, she went to St. Petersburg, Moscow, and Russian provincial capitals in 1891, serving as inspiration to Anton Chekhov, Konstantin Stanislavsky,* and Vladimir Nemirovich-Danchenko.* She subsequently traveled to Austria, Germany, the United States (which she toured four times), England, and France.

The repertory that brought her fame, besides classics by Goldoni and Shakespeare, consisted of plays by Dumas *fils* (*Lady of the Camellias, Dionisia, Demimonde, Francillon, Princess of Baghdad, Wife of Claude*) and Sardou (*Theodora, Fedora, Odette, Let's Get a Divorce*), but she also encouraged new Italian writers such as Giuseppe Giacosa (*Countess of Challant, Sad Loves*) and Marco Praga (*Ideal Wife, Innamorata*). She was the first to present Henrik Ibsen in Italy (*A Doll's House*, 1891) and in Russia (*A Doll's House*, 1891–92).

Throughout her career, Duse fought against the rhetorical tradition in acting. Her art, often seen as a synthesis of realism and "idealism," lacked the customary theatricality of movement, gesture, voice, and passion that typified the techniques of Sarah Bernhardt in France (with whom she was constantly compared) or Henry Irving* in England. She used little makeup and often turned her back to the audience; words were treated as the outer ripplings of inner depths and feeling; and her language was silence, gesture, movement, quietness, mood, sensations, and emotions. One of the strongest qualities of her art was a slow revelation of the truth. Her modulations, pauses, and silences were compared with music. She was lauded for the living simplicity of her characters. In directing her troupe, she concentrated on bringing out the subtleties in scenes between two or three characters, rather than on theatrical exits, entrances, and stage business. Her company was praised for its ensemble work and its realistic approach.

Later in her career, Duse turned away from her popular repertory, preferring new works by Gabriele D'Annunzio, Maurice Maeterlinck, Maxim Gorky, and Henrik Ibsen, and encouraged new ideas in scenic design such as Gordon Craig's setting for *Rosmersholm* (1906). Between 1905 and 1908, she was associated with Aurélien Lugné-Poe,* who became her company manager. In 1909, she retired from the stage, but returned in 1921 and toured Italy, England, and America. Near the end of her life, she envisioned a theatre of her own which was small, simple, with plain white-washed walls and very little scenery; where one could be heard clearly; where a communion between audience and player could be created; where she would be free to experiment with plays of high spiritual value; and where she could rid the theatre-temple of commercialism.

ADDITIONAL PRODUCTIONS: 1882: *Lady of the Camellias*; 1884: *Cavalleria rusticana* (Giovanni Verga); 1888: *Antony and Cleopatra*; 1892: *Heimat/Magda* (Hermann Sudermann); 1897: *Dream of a Spring Morning* (Gabriele D'Annunzio); 1899: *La Gioconda*; 1901: *Dead City, Francesca da Rimini*; 1903: *Hedda Gabler*; 1904: *Monna Vanna* (Maeterlinck); 1909: *The Lady from the Sea*; 1922: *Ghosts, Thy Will Be Done* (Count Tommaso Gallarati-Scotti), *Closed Door* (Praga).

SELECTED BIBLIOGRAPHY: Le Gallienne, Eva. *The Mystic in the Theatre: Eleonora Duse*. Carbondale: Southern Illinois University Press, 1965; Lugné-Poe, Aurelien. *Sous les étoiles*. Paris: Gallimard, 1933; Mapes, Victor. *Duse and the French*. New York: The Dunlap Society, 1898; Pirandello, Luigi. "The Art of Duse." *The Columbian Monthly* 1 (July 1928): 244–51; Shaw, George Bernard. "Duse and Bernhardt." *The Saturday Review* 15 June 1895: 787–89; Signorelli, Olga. *Eleonora Duse*. Roma: Casini, 1955; Symons, Arthur. *Eleonora Duse*. New York: Benjamin Blom, 1927, 1969; Weaver, William. *Duse: A Biography*. New York: Harcourt Brace Jovanovich, 1984.

Jane House

JOHANNE DYBWAD [b. August 2, 1867, Oslo (Christiania), Norway; d. March 4, 1950, Oslo, Norway]. After her debut as an actress at Den Nationale Scene in Bergen in 1887, Dybwad joined the ensemble of Christiania Theatre in Oslo the following year. In 1899, she began a tenure at the new Nationaltheatret which lasted until 1947. In her lifetime, Dybwad played more than two hundred roles and directed over forty productions.

Although she staged Bjørnstjerne Bjørnson's *Beyond Human Power* in Stockholm in 1901, Dybwad really began her directing career in 1906 at Nationaltheatret with *Pelléas and Mélisande*. She usually played a major role in productions she directed, which some thought limited her objectivity. Dybwad staged memorable productions of Ibsen plays and of works by Euripides, Shakespeare, Bjørnson, and Nordahl Grieg.

A woman with phenomenal intelligence and an iron will, Dybwad wielded power, choosing scripts, controlling productions, and casting August Oddvar, her favorite co-star. Around 1909, she began to experiment beyond the confines of realism, developing a style which might be called "exalted" or "heightened realism." Although sometimes criticized for her departure from realism, Dybwad was nevertheless praised for her originality, theatricality, and understanding of human experience. When she directed *As You Like It* (1912) with a festive atmosphere of beauty and freedom, critics credited Dybwad with genius equal to Shakespeare's. Without concern for historical authenticity, she would shape his comedies into sparkling entertainment culminating in a dance.

In 1918, Dybwad directed Euripides' *Medea,* collaborating for the first time with the designer Oliver Neerland. To unify the action, Dybwad used the chorus in a way that brought a mystical quality to the performance. Dybwad played Medea with an outpouring of passion, a thirst for revenge, and anguished mother love. Later work, especially with Ibsen, showed the influence of this encounter with Greek tragedy. Her *Rosmersholm* (1922) used a setting with Greek columns, and Dybwad's blocking was compared to the Parthenon frieze. The action of *Ghosts* (1925) had the timeless air of ritual, and every detail of the unified production, including her flame-red crocheting, supported the interpretation of Mrs. Alving as a passionate, liberated woman who would not hesitate to give Osvald morphine. With her dedication to a vision of the theatre as a temple, O'Neill's *Mourning Becomes Electra* (1933) was, of course, the perfect work for Dybwad to direct with the dimensions of Greek tragedy.

Dybwad often directed foreign classics, such as Schiller's *Maria Stuart* (1929), and frequently imported scripts and new ideas about production styles from the Continent. Dybwad was especially interested in the work of Max Reinhardt.* She used a German-inspired expressionistic style in directing the plays of Nordahl Grieg. In 1927, she directed Grieg's *Barabbas* with sculptural stage pictures and musical dialogue, and in 1935, *Our Power and Our Glory* (Grieg) with vividly contrasting episodes and an attempt at epic technical effects.

Dybwad's directing method was demanding, rehearsals were long, and blocking was exact and detailed. She would insist on ample time to prepare her productions, opening only when she considered them ready. Designed to hold audience attention, her productions were marked by energy, control, and clarity. In order to maintain a brisk tempo, she often made extensive cuts and rearranged scenes. In preparing a production, Dybwad first identified the essence of a play, then built her interpretation around that vision, developing the appropriate style which was sometimes intimate, but more often bold or monumental.

Johanne Dybwad was a forceful and brilliant individual whose productions nevertheless failed to establish a lasting tradition. Working in isolation, she established a distinctive, intense style to replace subdued, traditional realism, but directors after her searched for a style better suited for a younger generation. They could nevertheless measure their work against the universal perspective of Dybwad's Ibsen productions, the strength and complexity of her central female characters, the symphonic effect of spoken dialogue in certain plays, the perceptive analysis of human relationships, and her example of self-discipline and vitality.

ADDITIONAL PRODUCTIONS: 1910: *The Master Builder*; 1915: *Much Ado about Nothing*; 1924: *Anne Pedersdotter* (Hans Wiers-Jenssen); 1926: *Six Characters in Search of an Author, The Vikings dt Helgeland*; 1928: *Hoppla, wir leben!* (Ernst Toller); 1931: *Lady Inger of Ostraat*; 1933: *Lysistrata*; 1936: *Coriolanus*; 1937: *King Lear*.

SELECTED BIBLIOGRAPHY: Elster, Kristian, d.y. *Skuespillerinden Johanne Dybwad*. Oslo: H. Aschehoug, 1931; Marker, Frederick J., and Lise-Lone Marker. *The Scandinavian Theatre*. Totowa, NJ: Rowman and Littlefield, 1975: 174–75; Normann, Axel Otto. *Johanne Dybwad*. Oslo: Gyldendal, 1950; Rønneberg, Anton. *Nationaltheatret gjennem femti år*. Oslo: Gyldendal, 1949; Waal, Carla Rae. *Johanne Dybwad*. Oslo: Universitetsforlaget, 1967.

Carla Waal

E

ANATOLY VASILIEVICH EFROS [b. June 3, 1925, Moscow; d. January 13, 1987, Moscow]. After graduating from the Moscow Theatre Institute (GITIS) in 1950, Efros began his directing career in Ryazan and then worked as artistic director of several Moscow theatres: the Central Children's Theatre (1954–63), the Lenin Komsomol Theatre (1963–67), and, after the prominent director Yuri Lyubimov* left Russia, the Taganka Theatre (1985–87). He also directed in the United States and Japan. While Efros did not lead his own theatre between 1967 and 1985, primarily due to ideological incompatibilities with the party line, he directed his most innovative and famous productions at the Theatre on Malaya Bronnaya during that time.

In the contemporary Soviet plays *My Friend, Kolka* (A. Chmelik, 1959) and *On the Wedding Day* (Victor Rozov, 1964), Efros challenged the young to be intolerant of and rebel against pettiness and complacency, no matter how hard life may become. In *A Cabal of Hypocrites* (Bulgakov, 1967) Efros showed the relationship between an artist and tyranny. A "little" man—Molière—was pitted against an enormous man—Louis XIV—who pushed Molière away with his foot without even noticing it, thus carelessly destroying a talent. The whole bureaucratic system worked against an artist, who suffocated in the small space left for him. Efros's *The Three Sisters* (1967) was a production about the loneliness of people in hostile society, the impossibility of hopes, and the realization that dreams don't always come true. The legendary dance of a drunk Chebutikin was an embodiment of loneliness, despair, and lost hopes. *Romeo and Juliet* (with Olga Yakovleva, 1970) was a production about crushed youth, the fight between spirituality and a corrupt world. With the older characters, Efros created an image of gangsters who built a prison-like world where nothing young and rebellious could survive. In *Marriage* (Gogol, 1974) Efros used revolving scenic panels to run parallel scenes in which the characters' dreams, hopes, and thoughts were shown simultaneously with real actions and conversations. One of Efros's most memorable productions was *Brother Alyosha* (adapted from Dostoyevsky's *The Brothers Karamazov*, 1972). While in real life the notion of Christian love was replaced by the notion that Soviet people have to be treated according to their ideological beliefs, Efros—for the first time in the history of Soviet theatre—dared to remind the audience that its salvation was Christian love and forgiveness toward each other. In the last scene of the show, Alyosha asked everyone on stage to take another person's hand. Standing in a semicircle and facing the audience, the actors led by Alyosha openly addressed the audience and asked them to give each other their hands and love each other, thus surviving harsh reality. It was one of the rare occasions when the audience didn't applaud at the end of a show. Instead, every evening hundreds of people left the theatre in complete silence, hiding tears from each other.

Efros was not interested in monumental or heroic drama, nor did he stage plays which sent optimistic messages to audiences about Soviet society helping its people survive and taking complete care of people's lives. The audience of Efros's productions despaired, cried, and hopelessly hoped for a better life together with Efros's characters. The audience also was able to associate itself with Efros's characters, because it felt that it wasn't alone in its struggle with life, that other people were as miserable, and that they all shared the same problems and joys. In Efros's theatre the audience received compassion, consolation, and complete understanding.

ADDITIONAL PRODUCTIONS: 1964: *104 Pages about Love* (Edvard Radzinsky); 1965; *My Poor Marat* (Aleksei Arbuzov); 1966; *The Sea Gull* with Olga Yakovleva; 1975; *The Cherry Orchard* with Vladimir Visotsky; 1981; *Tartuffe*.

SELECTED BIBLIOGRAPHY: Efros, Anatoly. *Rehearsals Are My Love*. Moscow: Iskusstvo, 1975; Efros, Anatoly. *Profession: Director*. Moscow: Iskusstvo, 1979; Efros, Anatoly. *A Continuation of a Theatre Story*. Moscow: Iskusstvo, 1985; Shah-Avisova, T. "On the Move." *Theatre* 3 (1966): 31–40; Turovskaya, M. "Thoughts about Life." *Productions of Those Years*. Moscow: Iskusstvo, 1957.

Paulina Shur

SVEINN EINARSSON [b. September 18, 1934, Reykjavík, Iceland]. Trained in Paris and Sweden as a dramaturg, Einarsson first came to directing in 1965, two years after becoming artistic director of the Reykjavík City Theatre. While at the City Theatre, he staged works by the French and Polish absurdists and mounted his own adaptation of *Christianity at Glacier* (1969–70), written by Iceland's Nobel Laureate Halldór Laxness. He also instituted a policy of staging at least one new play by an Icelandic writer each season, and came in this way to direct works by several of the most important playwrights in his country in the 1960s, 1970s, and 1980s.

In 1972, after nine years at the City Theatre, Einarsson became artistic director at the National Theatre of Iceland, where he remained until 1983. With this larger and better-subsidized company, he directed more classics than he had at the City Theatre, where his 1969 staging of Sophocles' *Antigone* had been the first Greek tragedy produced in Iceland. His production of *The Silken Drum*, mounted originally at the National Theatre, showcased a contemporary Icelandic opera at the Caracas Festival in 1982, and he has also directed in the Faroe Islands, in Norway, and in Finland.

In addition to other operas and the classic and contemporary plays he has directed, Einarsson has staged children's plays, productions for television, and radio plays. In the late 1980s, he became head of the dramatic division of Icelandic State Television, but he continued to direct stage productions both in Iceland and abroad. He is also recognized as the foremost historian of the theatre in Iceland.

Einarsson's main contribution to the practical theatre in Iceland lies in the strong influence he commanded in his joint capacities as an artistic director and a stage director. His dramaturgical skill manifested itself not only in his own productions, with their close attention to the values of the texts and to problems of translation, but in those of other directors at the theatres with which he was associated. His stagings have been marked by simple, imagistic, and handsome designs, and he imported foreign designers like Una Collins and Baltasar as collaborators.

Einarsson brought decidedly continental tastes to a theatre scene more closely aligned previously with those in the Scandinavian countries. He helped redefine the image of stage directing in the light of his interests as a scholar and critic, removing it from its earlier association with actors and others who had grown up in the theatre. He affiliated the theatre with dramatic currents important in Europe during the 1950s and 1960s, and in doing so helped reorient the Icelandic theatre as an intellectual institution, moving it away from its earlier locus in more strictly nationalistic concerns.

ADDITIONAL PRODUCTIONS: 1965–66: *Journey to Baghdad* (J. Jakobsson); 1966–67: *Tango* (Mrożek); 1967–68: *Hedda Gabler*; 1974–75: *The Silver Moon* (Laxness; codirector Hédinsdóttir); 1975–76: *The Imaginary Invalid*; 1978–79: *If Reason Sleeps* (A. B. Vallejo; sets by Baltasar); 1979–80: *Snow* (Ragnarsson); 1982–83: *Oresteia*; 1985–86: *The Bell of Iceland* (Laxness); 1986–87: *The Miser*; 1987–88: *The Father*.

SELECTED BIBLIOGRAPHY: Programs from the National Theatre of Iceland and the City Theatres of Reykjavík and Akureyri; ''Theatre in Iceland,'' three pamphlets covering 1975–80, 1980–85, and 1985–88 (Reykjavík: Association of Icelandic Actors et al., 1982, 1985, and 1988).

Leigh Woods

SERGEI MIKHAILOVICH EISENSTEIN [b. January 23, 1898, Riga; d. February 11, 1948, Moscow]. The leading theorist of cinema technique and one of the foremost filmmakers of the silent era, Sergei Eisenstein began his artistic career as a scenic designer and stage director during the revolutionary period of Soviet theatre. Mounting only four productions in 1923 and 1924, Eisenstein established himself as one of the youngest and most innovative directors in Moscow. In addition, his critical writings gave shape and political depth to the experimental and pioneering ideas of constructivism on the living stage.

Arriving in Moscow in the fall of 1920, Eisenstein had already trained as a designer for Red Army agitprop productions. In the early months of 1921, he worked with Valeri Smishlayev at the Moscow Proletkult Theatre in an adaptation of Jack London's *The Mexican.* In the fall Eisenstein also joined the Directing Workshop of Vsevolod Meyerhold* and secured an appointment as a costume designer at the MASTFOR cabaret of Nikolai Foregger.* Disappointed by the lack of directorial opportunity at all three studios, Eisenstein started his own troupe and actor training program for the Per Tru Proletkult theatre. Incorporating Meyerhold's Biomechanics, acrobatics, boxing, fencing, and eccentric dance with Rudolf Bode's Expression-Gymnastics, Eisenstein invented his own acting program, called Expressive Movement. In the spring of 1923, Eisenstein's first production, *The Wiseman,* a wild and updated circus adaptation of Nikolai Ostrovsky's nineteenth-century comedy *Enough Simplicity for Every Wiseman,* caused a great deal of controversy and discussion in Moscow's theatre world. Substituting trick-film clips, dangerous acrobatics, and knockabout satire for the slow melodramatic unraveling of Ostrovsky's plot, Eisenstein went far beyond Meyerhold in destroying the primacy of literary text. As an explanation, Eisenstein published a manifesto, "The Montage of Attractions," in the influential journal *LEF.* Declaring the theatre's true function as the selected accumulation of powerful effects in the spectator's subconscious mind, Eisenstein justified the Soviet avant-garde's obsession with popular entertainment forms (attractions) and streamlined, industrial processes (montage technique).

After remounting *The Mexican* in an expressive, antipsychological version, Eisenstein began work with writer Sergei Tretyakov on an "agit-guignol," *Listen, Moscow!,* about a Communist uprising in a German town. Simpler in structure (but perfectly crafted) and hewing more closely to current left-wing ideology, *Listen, Moscow!* created an atmosphere of absolute audience hysteria. Caught up in the production's disturbing emotional effects, one spectator even rushed the stage, threatening to shoot a bourgeois villain. Other audience responses were equally strong. Before entering the Soviet cinema industry in 1924, Eisenstein directed *Gas Masks,* a contemporary melodrama by Tretyakov. Performed in an actual gas plant on the outskirts of Moscow, *Gas Masks* once again utilized the superphysical acting skills of Eisenstein's troupe. Yet, this time, the relationship between the environmental reality of the factory and Eisenstein's sensational theatricalities appeared unconnected and forced.

SELECTED BIBLIOGRAPHY: Eisenstein, Sergei. "Montage of Attractions." [1923] *The Drama Review* 18 (March 1974): 77–85; Gerould, Daniel. "Eisenstein's Wiseman." *The Drama Review* 18 (March 1974): 71–76; Gordon, Mel. "Program of the Minor Leftists in the Soviet Theatre." Diss. New York U., 1981; Gordon, Mel. "Eisenstein's Later Work at the Proletkult." *The Drama Review* 22 (September 1978): 107–12; Gordon,

Mel, and Alma Law. "Eisenstein's Early Work in Expressive Behavior." *Millennium Film Journal* no. 3 (Winter/Spring 1979): 25–29; Rudnitsky, Konstantin. *Russian and Soviet Theater 1905–1932*. Trans. Roxane Permar. New York: Harry N. Abrams, 1988.

Mel Gordon

ALFRED EMMET [b. March 29, 1908, Ealing, Middlesex, England]. Alfred Emmet was instrumental in creating the climate of educated interest in theatre that spawned the regional and community theatre movement in England. His professionalism in directing amateur, yet artistic, theatre productions paved the way for the foundation of national theatre companies.

Emmet founded the Questors theatre in 1929 and artistically guided the theatre through four decades of growth, artistic notice, resourceful management, and facility expansion until his retirement in 1969. The Questors was and is unique in its devotion to quality, theatrical training, and the introduction of new plays and playwrights.

As the name implies, the Questors theatre proposed a progressive production agenda that attempted to bring the new and unusual to English audiences. Prior to the era of the National Theatre and the Royal Shakespeare Company, writers had only the commercial theatre as a testing ground. Many fine plays that might not have succeeded on the commercial stage found a nurturing home in the Questors. Though few critics have written of the Questors' unique achievement, it was taken quite seriously as a contemporary and popular alternative theatre, with many of its daring productions reviewed in *The London Times* alongside West End shows.

Among Emmet's enduring achievements were the founding of an educational training program for actors, the rediscovery of many lost European classics, and the creation of a flexible theatre building with a unique open stage that could be refitted for proscenium, thrust, and arena productions. The space was influential, prompting many later prominent British companies to create something akin to it.

Another of Emmet's unique achievements was the founding and the seventeen-year existence of an international play festival which developed young actors and playwrights and provided theatrical education for London youth. An early success was James Saunders's *Next Time I'll Sing to You* (1962), and throughout its history, the festival offered notable debuts of many foreign plays and encouraged the international flavor of the English theatre scene.

As a director, Emmet's style has been described as orderly and professional. His high standards, a keen eye for new scripts, and the choice of controversial and distinguished plays separated his theatre from many lesser alternative theatres. *The London Times*, for example, praised Emmet's 1943 production of *The Dark River* for an effective performance by Peggy Ashcroft and a plot hinged on the idea that nostalgia for things past can ruin present happiness. The production employed Chekhovian techniques on the English stage.

In 1946, Emmet created a stir with the London debut of Aleksandr Ostrovsky's nineteenth-century comedy, *Diary of a Scoundrel,* a satire on class in which a young man (played by Emmet) attempts to marry wealth by stealth. Emmet's production was lauded for its high energy and its ability to make Ostrovsky's Russian ideas universal. In 1958, Emmet premiered a Labiche farce, *Everybody Loves Celimare,* which like *Diary of a Scoundrel* had suffered from inadequate English translations. Emmet chose to concentrate on frenetic pacing and a wide range of actor business to convey the comedy of a man besieged by his lovers' husbands. His 1967 production of Lydia Rogosin's *The Corruptible Crown* took a revisionist look at the reigns of Richard III and Henry VII, suggesting their actions weren't motivated by self-interest, but rather by a need to prevent civil war and to crush usurpers.

Emmet was an able administrator and popularizer of the amateur theatre movement who wrote frequently about theatre at home and abroad. He left the Questors with a professional administrative staff, and his own position was filled by a four-person directorate.

Under Emmet's leadership the Questors became one of England's leading alternative theatres, quietly and skillfully mounting numerous English premieres and setting a standard for future community theatres to rival. For his achievements in creating a national theatre community, Emmet was designated to the Order of the British Empire (OBE) in 1971.

ADDITIONAL PRODUCTIONS: 1943: *The Dark River*; 1954: *Better a Dead Hero*; 1961: *A Quiet Clap of Thunder*; 1962: *Next Time I'll Sing to You* (James Saunders); 1964: *The Other Palace*; 1965: *The Igloo.*

SELECTED BIBLIOGRAPHY: Emmet, Alfred. "The Long Prehistory of the National Theatre." *Theatre Quarterly* 6 (Spring 1976): 55–62; Hartnoll, Phyllis, ed. "The Questors Theatre." *The Oxford Companion to the Theatre.* Oxford, England: Oxford University Press, 1983; Herbert, Ian, ed. *Who's Who in the Theatre.* Vol. 1, Biography. Detroit, Michigan: Gale Research Co., 1981.

                                                                              Stuart Lenig

CLAUDE ETIENNE [b. Adrien Antoine Constant De Backer, May 22, 1917, Brussels, Belgium; d. April 21, 1992, Brussels, Belgium]. Prior to World War II, Belgian French-language theatre was dominated by touring Parisian companies and stars. Although a few predecessors established native troupes, Claude Etienne (along with Jacques Huisman*) is credited as a pioneer in the development of Belgium's now-flourishing theatrical life. In 1943, Etienne founded the Rideau de Bruxelles, a theatre devoted to promoting new talent. During Etienne's fifty years as director (1943–93), the Rideau launched the careers of numerous Belgian playwrights, actors, and directors, as well as producing French-language premieres of plays by such dramatists as Arthur Miller, Tennessee Williams, Christopher Fry, and Tom Stoppard.

After beginning his career as an actor and serving as stage director for the Théâtre du Vaudeville, Etienne studied dramatic art at the Brussels Conservatoire. He opened the Rideau on March 17, 1943, with a production of *La Matrone d'Ephèse* by Belgian author Georges Sion. The cast included Raymond Gérôme, who later directed the Rideau's French-language premieres of *A Streetcar Named Desire* and *All My Sons* before eventually becoming a Parisian star.

An adherent of the tradition of Jacques Copeau* and the Cartel, Etienne believed the director's task was to serve the author. He promoted Belgian play-writing by commissioning plays and founding Les Cahiers du Rideau to publish new Belgian drama. Etienne made his mark on Belgian letters by persuading authors such as Paul Willems and Liliane Wouters to write for the stage and by producing works by a long list of native dramatists including Sion, Charles Bertin, and Jean Sigrid. Although the Rideau also mounted a classical repertoire, it focused on contemporary premieres—world, French-language, or Belgian de-buts. Viewing the Rideau as a "house of authors," Etienne insisted on faithful translations, translating some plays himself with the aid of his wife, Denyse Périez. The Rideau also served as a cultural ambassador, sponsoring European tours, including the first Belgian tour to the USSR in 1966. Etienne's contri-butions to Belgian theatre earned him such awards as the annual Eve du Théâtre, the Medaille Beaumarchais de la Société des Auteurs, and a 1984 knighthood.

Claude Etienne's directing style was influenced by his reverence for the text and especially for actors. An acclaimed actor and acting teacher himself, he imparted to performers his intimate understanding of the spoken word, and he served as an "ideal spectator." With a capacity for active listening and his devoted searching for the style appropriate to each play, he inspired the creativity of the artists with whom he worked.

ADDITIONAL PRODUCTIONS: 1945: *La Terre est Ronde* (Armand Salacrou); 1946: *Le Malentendu* (Camus); 1947: *Les Prétendents* (Charles Bertin); 1948: *Le Bon Vin de Monsieur Nuche* (Paul Willems); 1951: *The Lady's Not for Burning*; 1953: *Henry V*; 1956: *Le Bal des voleurs*; 1958: *Hamlet, The Visit* with Mary Marquet; 1959: *Les Cavaliers* (Jean Sigrid), *Antigone* (Anouilh); 1966: *Intermezzo*; 1969: *La Guerre de Troie n'aura pas lieu*; 1970: *Crime and Punishment*; 1971: *Mon Faust* (Valéry); 1975: *Yes, peut-être* (Marguerite Duras), *This Property Is Condemned*; 1977: *Les Indifférents* (Odilon-Jean Perier); 1979: *La Leçon*; 1980: *À Memphis il y a un Homme d'une Force prodigieuse* (Jean Audureau).

SELECTED BIBLIOGRAPHY: Centre Belge de l'Institut International du Théâtre. *The Theatre in French-Speaking Belgium*. Brussels: Archives et Musée de la Littérature, 1991; *En scène pour demain*. Brussels: Libres Images aux Presses de la Bellone, 1988; Etienne, Claude. *40 années du Rideau de Bruxelles*. Brussels: Rideau de Bruxelles, 1983; *Theatre in Belgium*, special issue of *World Theatre* 9 (Spring 1960).

Suzanne Burgoyne

NIKOLAI NIKOLAEVICH EVREINOV [b. February 26, 1879, Moscow; d. February 7, 1953, Paris, France].

One of the most fascinating and enigmatic avant-garde directors of pre-revolutionary Russia, Nikolai Evreinov theorized about theatricality as a means for tapping into theatre's more vital and healing powers. His concept of "monodrama," in which the audience experiences events through the dramatized senses of a protagonist, was original if not ultimately influential. Through a series of diverse experiments, ranging from cabaret sketches to a mass spectacle, Evreinov, who was also a prolific playwright, pushed his theatre work in many directions, with varying degrees of success.

Born in Moscow, Evreinov moved to St. Petersburg in 1892 to attend the Imperial School of Jurisprudence. A theatre enthusiast since childhood, he initiated the first season of the Ancient Theatre in 1907, cofounded by Baron Nikolai Drizen. In its 1907–8 season, the Ancient Theatre presented a series of short medieval plays; their second season (1911–12) was devoted to the Spanish Golden Age. Evreinov employed the technique of "artistic reconstruction": not an antiquarian approach, but his stylized attempt to recreate the total performative experience surrounding dramas of the past. Evreinov's interest in theatre as ritual led him to pay particular attention to the role of the audience in each era, going so far as to include period spectators for each cycle of plays.

After a scandalous production of Friedrich Schiller's *The Maid of Orleans* at the Maly (with a male actor in the title role) in 1908, Vera Komissarzhevskaia hired him to replace Meyerhold at her struggling theatre. There, his highly erotic *Salomé* (1908) was banned before it opened. In 1909, he founded the Merry Theatre for Grown-Up Children, which led to his work at Zinaida Kholmskaia's and Aleksandr Kugel's Crooked Mirror Theatre. Evreinov served as artistic director from 1910 to 1917 at the Crooked Mirror, a cabaret-style venue that performed parodies, sketches, satires, and one-acts. There Evreinov wrote and directed his famous satire of directorial style, *The Inspector General* (1912). This minor parodic gem treats Gogol's work from five perspectives, including a version by Konstantin Stanislavsky*, and a version by Gordon Craig.

Although many theatre artists such as Vsevolod Meyerhold* and Vladimir Mayakovsky initially embraced the momentous changes of the revolution, Evreinov's "life as theatre" philosophy proved too aristocratic for the changing artistic world around him. He emigrated, first to Prague, and finally to Paris in 1925. Ironically, he is perhaps best remembered today for a momentous and patriotic performance: *The Storming of the Winter Palace* (1920). For this mass spectacle staged at the very site of the actual historical event (and employing some of its participants from three years earlier), Evreinov utilized a cast of 8,000.

Although he continued directing in Paris, staging several operas for the Opera Russe Prive de Paris, none of his later work could match the strikingly creative endeavors of his early experiments.

ADDITIONAL PRODUCTIONS: 1911: *Fuente Ovejuna*; 1915: *The Fourth Wall*; 1929: *Snow Maiden*; 1929: *Tsar Sultan*; 1930: *Ruslan and Liudmilla* (Glinka).

SELECTED BIBLIOGRAPHY: Carnicke, Sharon Marie. *The Theatrical Instinct: Nikolai Evreinov and the Russian Theatre of the Early Twentieth Century*. New York: Peter Lang, 1989; Evreinov, Nikolai. *The Theatre in Life*. New York: Brentano, 1927; Golub, Spencer. *Evreinov: The Theatre of Paradox and Transformation*. Ann Arbor: UMI Research Press, 1984; Moody, C. "Nikolai Nikolaevich Evreinov: 1879–1953." *Russian Literature Triquarterly* 13 (Fall 1975): 659–95; Proffer, Ellendea, ed. *Evreinov: A Pictorial Biography*. Ann Arbor: Ardis, 1981.

Lurana Donnels O'Malley

RICHARD EYRE [b. March 23, 1943, Barnstaple, Devon]. Following studies at Cambridge University (B.A.), Eyre began his directing career with a production of Ann Jellicoe's *The Knack* in 1965 for the Phoenix Theatre, Leicester. For one season (1966–67), he served as assistant director of the Phoenix Theatre, followed by six seasons (1967–72) as first the associate director and then director of productions at the Royal Lyceum Theatre, Edinburgh. In 1971–72, he directed foreign tours for the British Council and productions for the 7:84 Company and the Everyman Theatre in Liverpool. From 1973 to 1978, he served as artistic director of the Nottingham Playhouse. After several seasons working for BBC-TV and as a free-lance director, in 1981 Eyre joined the Royal National Theatre as an associate director and in 1988 succeeded Sir Peter Hall* as artistic director. In addition to his stage directing, Eyre has directed a number of well-received films, including *The Ploughman's Lunch* (1983).

Eyre's directing style is not easily pigeon-holed. He achieved national recognition mainly for his stagings of provocative new plays like Howard Brenton's *The Churchill Play* (1974). Indeed, during his tenure at Nottingham, he was responsible for about fifteen major premieres. Eyre has proven equally adept, however, at staging revivals of popular American musicals and premodern classics. He received the 1982 Society of West End Theatres (SWET) Director of the Year Award for his glittering, slick *Guys and Dolls*. His 1980 Royal Court *Hamlet*, with Jonathan Pryce doubling as Hamlet and the Ghost, was generally viewed as an exciting, if unorthodox interpretation. In contrast, his 1989 *Hamlet* with Daniel Day-Lewis in the title role, although more straightforward in approach and less daring, was praised for its avoidance of cliché and its attention to detail. Whether the play is contemporary or classical or as disparate in style as a Victorianized *Bartholomew Fair* (1988) or a *Richard III* (1990) relocated to England between the wars, Eyre often has been commended for his directorial wit and intelligence, and for his masterly management of crowd scenes, orchestration of spectacular visual effects, and casting acumen.

Since assuming leadership, Eyre has invigorated the National Theatre by appointing several young associate directors, by hosting performances by regional and foreign companies, and by increasing the number and length of National Theatre tours. He also has continued to strongly support new writing and generally has expanded the range and popularity of National Theatre presentations.

ADDITIONAL PRODUCTIONS: 1972: *The Great Exhibition* (David Hare); 1976: *Comedians* (Trevor Griffiths); 1977: *Touched* (Stephen Lowe); 1982: *Schweyk in the Second World War, The Beggar's Opera*; 1985: *The Government Inspector*; 1986: *Futurists* (Dusty Hughes); 1987: *High Society*; 1988: *The Changeling*; 1989: *The Voysey Inheritance* (Harley Granville Barker*); 1990: *Racing Demon* (Hare); 1991: *White Chameleon* (Christopher Hampton), *Napoli milionari* (Eduardo De Filippo*).

SELECTED BIBLIOGRAPHY: Reviews of Eyre's productions since 1981 are collected in issues of *London Theatre Record*. For overviews of Eyre's leadership of the National Theatre, see Michael Billington's essays in *Plays International* [''A la carte NT.'' February 1990: 28–31, and ''Thumbs Up on the South Bank.'' February 1991: 22–26]. See also George Rowell and Anthony Jackson. *The Repertory Movement: A History of Regional Theatre in Britain*. Cambridge, England: Cambridge University Press, 1984.

Daniel J. Watermeier

RONALD EYRE [b. April 13, 1929, Mapplewell, Yorkshire, England]. After four years as a teacher, Ronald Eyre accepted a position with the BBC in 1957, eventually becoming a producer-director. He wrote and directed at least a dozen television plays, but his 1974–77 series for the BBC, "The Long Search," is the best remembered. Eyre is better known as a stage director, having begun his professional career with a 1963 production of *Titus Andronicus* at the Birmingham Rep. He has directed in all of the major theatres in London as well as the Chichester and Brighton festivals. His nearly thirty years of directing include not only television and stage work, but also opera, a challenge accepted in 1982 with Verdi's *Falstaff*. Eyre's work reflects an allegiance to text, a divided interest between classic revivals and new scripts, and a record of working with many of England's most renowned actors.

Consistently well-received, Eyre's directing is regarded as technically conservative, although his interpretation is often nontraditional. His 1965 production of Shaw's *Widowers' House* at the Theatre Royal, Stratford East initiated a revival of Shaw's plays in England and led to his production of *Mrs. Warren's Profession* at the National in 1970. In both, Eyre was meticulous with pacing and in *Mrs. Warren's Profession* adhered strictly to Shaw's stage directions to achieve the appropriate rhythm and tension. Eyre directed two of John McGrath's plays, *Events While Guarding the Bofors Gun* (1966) and *Bakkes Night of Fame* (1968) which introduced the notion of colorblind casting. Both premiered at the Hampstead Theatre Club and were followed by a pivotal production of Donald Howarth's *Three Months Gone* at the Royal Court in 1970 which launched Eyre's mainstream directing career.

Unlike many directors, Eyre maintains a free-lance status, and has never been associated with any particular theatre. He dismisses the virtues of an established ensemble, but invariably casts many of the same actors in his productions, perhaps a key to his success and longevity. Donald Sinden starred in *London Assurance* (1970) and in *Othello* (1979), both at the Royal Shakespeare Company (RSC). In *Othello*, Eyre offered a rare amoral interpretation of villainy; while in *London Assurance*, he rewrote portions of the play to achieve a more modern perspective. Sir Alec Guinness starred in John Mortimer's new play *A Voyage Round My Father* (1971) and later in Alan Bennett's *Habeas Corpus* (1973). Eyre directed Sir John Gielgud* in Charles Wood's new play, *Veterans* (1972), at the Royal Court and in *Saint Joan* (1984).

In 1982, Eyre was part of an unprecedented collaboration on the opera *Falstaff*, conducted by Carlo Giulini and staged by Eyre. Presented first in Los Angeles, it subsequently opened at Covent Garden in London and closed in Florence. This signaled a new career for Eyre, but he maintained his approach of following the author's stage directions closely and insisted on weeks of uninterrupted rehearsals. Eyre excels in directing comedy, creating interesting stage pictures and clever stage movement. He rarely experiments with technical innovations, although in the 1981 production of *The Winter's Tale*, he used changes in light to punctuate the main turning points of the play. He has written for the stage

(*Something's Burning,* 1974), but has had more success with other types of writing, including an adaptation of Gogol's *The Government Inspector,* which opened in April of 1991 at London's Greenwich Theatre. Eyre's ability to reconcile star casting, nontraditional text interpretation, and an eclectic choice of both new plays and classic revivals in mainstream theatre reflects a unique approach to directing. It is this approach, and not any particular style, that defines Eyre's contribution to directing.

ADDITIONAL PRODUCTIONS: 1968: *Ghosts*; 1971: *Much Ado about Nothing*; 1972: *A Pagan Place* (adapted by Edna O'Brien); 1974: *The Marquis of Keith* (adapted by Eyre); 1975: *London Assurance* (RSC revival); 1978: *Saratoga* (Bronson Howard's 1870 American comedy); 1979: *Tishoo* (Brian Thompson); 1982: *Hobson's Choice* (Harold Brighouse); 1983: *A Patriot for Me*; 1984: *Saint Joan*; 1986: *When We Are Married* (J. B. Priestley), *A Walk in the Woods, The Chalk Garden*; 1987: *J. J. Farr* (Ronald Harwood); 1988: *The Sneeze* (Anton Chekhov, adapted by Michael Frayn); 1990: *Hidden Laughter* (Simon Gray).

SELECTED BIBLIOGRAPHY: Hayman, Ronald. "Ronald Eyre." *Playback.* London: Davis-Poynter, 1973: 110–26; Kenyon, Nicholas. "The Making of an Inter-continental *Falstaff.*" *London Sunday Times* 11 April 1982; Mullin, Michael, and Karen Morris Muriello, eds. *Theatre at Stratford-Upon-Avon.* Vol. 2, *Indexes and Calendar.* Westport, CT: Greenwood Press, 1980; Say, Rosemary. "Passion in Tatters." *Sunday Telegraph* 12 August 1979; Wardle, Irving. "Actions into Dreams." *London Times* 1 July 1981.

Judy Lee Oliva

F

ROBERT FALLS [b. March 2, 1954, Springfield, Illinois]. Robert Falls is in the vanguard of the second generation of major regional theatre directors. The Illinois native majored in playwriting and directing at the University of Illinois, where he directed his first play, Michael Weller's *Moonchildren,* in 1974. The production was picked up by Chicago's St. Nicholas Theatre, and provided the young student with his professional debut. Upon graduation, he moved to Chicago and became a member and then artistic director of the off-Loop Wisdom Bridge Theatre in 1977. He worked there continuously for nine years.

Acclaimed for his work at Wisdom Bridge and at the St. Nicholas, Falls began to gain international attention. His adaptation of Jack Henry Abbott's *In the Belly of the Beast* (1983) toured to London and Glasgow in 1985, and he was then invited to direct the premiere of *Orchards* Off-Broadway (1986). Shortly thereafter, at age thirty-one, he was named artistic director of Chicago's Goodman Theatre.

Falls is an heir to the so-called Chicago theatre style, a sprawling, performance-oriented style passed down from Viola Spolin through the Second City. He has enlarged upon that tradition by applying its robustness and freshness to the classics and musicals as well as to new plays. His interest in groups such as Mabou Mines and the Wooster Group and in choreographers such as Merce Cunningham has fed his fearless, cinematic approach, and he has tackled Shakespeare, Molière, and new plays with equal aplomb. Loving spectacle and big productions, he daringly launched his tenure at the Goodman with Brecht's *Galileo* (1987). *Pal Joey* (1988) exemplified his enthusiasm for musicals, which he treats as seriously as the classics. His playwriting background aids him in the extensive research he does for productions and his unusually keen dramaturgical ability was a major factor in the success of *In the Belly of the Beast*.

The recipient of eight Joseph Jefferson awards for outstanding direction, Falls is known as an actor's director, a midwife to performances and, consequently, one of his first changes at the Goodman was to increase rehearsal periods to four and a half weeks. He is also an audience's director, with a mission to bring the classics to Chicago. A past president of Theatre Communications Group, his vision extends beyond Chicago to the entire national regional theatre movement.

ADDITIONAL PRODUCTIONS: 1976: *Moonchildren* (Michael Weller); 1978: *Othello*; 1979: *Curse of the Starving Class*; 1981: *Bent* (Martin Sherman); 1982: *We Won't Pay! We Won't Pay!* (Dario Fo); 1985: *Hamlet*; 1986: *Orchards* (adapted from Chekhov by Wendy Wasserstein, John Guare, David Mamet, Maria Irene Fornes,* Michael Weller, Samm-Art Williams, Spalding Gray); 1987: *Road* (Jim Cartwright, American premiere); 1989: *Pravda* (Howard Brenton and David Hare, American premiere at the Guthrie Theatre, Minneapolis), *The Speed of Darkness* (Steve Tesich, world premiere at the Goodman Theatre, Chicago); 1991: *Book of the Night* (Louis Rosen and Thom Bishop, world premiere).

SELECTED BIBLIOGRAPHY: Bartow, Arthur. *The Director's Voice*. New York: Theatre Communications Group, 1988: 87–104; Christiansen, Richard. "Dramatic Developments: Goodman Theatre's Robert Falls Prepares to Open in His Biggest Role Ever." *Chicago Tribune* 28 September 1986: 10–16; Christiansen, Richard. "Feeling the '40s: *Pal Joey* Revival Takes a Moody Look at Life as a Cabaret." *Chicago Tribune* 29 May 1988: 4–5; Christiansen, Richard. "From Prison to the Wisdom Bridge: A Killer's Letters Become a Powerful Play." *Chicago Tribune* 26 September 1983: sec 12: 20; London, Todd. "Chicago Impromptu." *American Theatre* 7 (July/August 1990): 14–23, 60–64; Steele, Mike. "*Pravda* Director Hears Echoes of *Front Page*." *Minneapolis Star and Tribune* 13 January 1989; *Theatre Profiles* 9. New York: Theatre Communications Group, 1990.

Lila Wolff-Wilkinson

WILLIAM GEORGE FAY [b. November 12, 1872, Dublin, Ireland; d. October 27, 1947, London, England]. William George Fay began his theatrical career as an advance agent and touring actor. After settling in Dublin, he and his brother Frank J. began to produce and direct plays, intending to perform Irish and Gaelic plays by native dramatists using Irish actors. They sought to eliminate the stereotypical "stage Irishman" and the use of Irish accent and idiom as vehicles for laughter. In 1902, with a group of amateur actors directed by William, they produced *Deirdre* by AE (George Russell) and W. B. Yeats's *Kathleen ni Houlihan,* one of the first Irish nationalist plays.

Later that year, they formed the Irish National Dramatic Company, which merged with Yeats's Irish Literary Theatre to form the Irish National Theatre Society in 1903. Yeats, Lady Augusta Gregory, John Millington Synge, and others began to write Irish plays specifically for the new company. In 1904, Miss A. E. F. Horniman, a friend and patron of Yeats, purchased and refurbished the buildings which became the Abbey Theatre and allowed the company to use them without charge. She also provided enough financial support for

William, Frank, and a few others to be able to work for the Abbey full-time. William directed, acted, and was the general manager.

The realistic and precise style of acting identified with the early Abbey Theatre was the result of William Fay's work. He trained the actors to use as little movement and gesture as possible and, with the help of Frank, taught them to bring out the music of the language. The effect was an artlessness unspoiled by English theatrical conventions. As a director and manager, Fay was very concerned with details. Most of the plays performed during this time were "peasant plays" (those dealing with peasant life) and were produced as realistically as possible. Sets, costumes, and props were authentic; and many of the actors were from peasant families and therefore familiar with the language, movement, and habits of country people. Fay often had the actors rehearse their lines repeatedly until he felt that they had the proper interpretation. He was also convinced that the ensemble was most important; there should be no stars.

As well as being the stage manager (director) for the company, Fay also created many of the comedy parts in the Abbey's burgeoning repertory of Irish plays. Among them were Bartley Fallon in Lady Gregory's *Spreading the News* (1904), Martin Doul in *The Well of the Saints* (1905), and Christy Mahon in *The Playboy of the Western World* (1907).

In 1908 there was a disagreement between Fay and the directors of the Abbey Theatre, and both of the Fays resigned. W. G. was quickly hired by Charles Frohman to perform some Irish plays in New York and Chicago, where they were fairly well received. William Fay continued acting and directing primarily in Great Britain and worked in films.

ADDITIONAL PRODUCTIONS: 1902: *A Pot of Broth* (Yeats); 1903: *In the Shadow of the Glen* (Synge); 1904: *On Baile's Strand* (Yeats), *Riders to the Sea* (Synge); 1913: *Brand* (Ibsen); 1928: *The Workhouse Ward* (Gregory), *Birthright* (Murray), *The Adding Machine*.

SELECTED BIBLIOGRAPHY: Colum, Padraic. "The Abbey Theatre Comes of Age." *Theatre Arts* 10 (September 1926): 580–84; Fay, Gerard. *The Abbey Theatre*. New York: Macmillan, 1958; Fay, W. G., and Catherine Carswell. *The Fays of the Abbey Theatre*. New York: Harcourt, Brace and Co., 1935; Fay, William George. *Merely Players*. London: Rich and Cowan, 1932; Flannery, James W. *W. B. Yeats and the Idea of a Theatre*. Toronto: Macmillan of Canada, 1976; Horgan, Robert, and Michael J. O'Neill. *Joseph Holloway's Abbey Theatre*. Carbondale, IL: Southern Illinois University Press, 1976; Robinson, Lennox. *The Irish Theatre*. London: Macmillan, 1939.

Candice M. Coleman

JÜRGEN FEHLING [b. March 1, 1895, Lubeck, Germany; d. June 14, 1968, Hamburg, Germany]. After studing theology and law in Berlin, Fehling began his theatrical career as an actor in 1909. In 1919 he first directed at the Berliner Volksbühne, and in 1922 he became director at the Staatstheater Berlin, where he worked until 1945. In addition to his work at the Staatstheater, Fehling directed numerous plays at other theatres in Berlin, Munich, and Vienna.

Fehling's work as a director is the antithesis to both the bourgeois neo-romantic theatre of Max Reinhardt* and to the political theatre of Erwin Piscator.* As an admirer of Konstantin Stanislavsky,* Fehling continued in the tradition of Otto Brahm.* This psychological realism led him most often to plays by Shakespeare, Heinrich von Kleist, and Christian Dietrich Grabbe, whose powerful language and extreme characters could best be used to show the existential struggle of modern man. Fehling saw his theater as resistance against emerging decadence, as a fight against the "theater of thoughtless decay."

Between 1922 and 1945 Fehling worked on more than one hundred productions and established himself as one of the most productive and energetic directors of his time. One of Fehling's most celebrated productions was the 1937 performance of Shakespeare's *King Richard III*. In this five-hour show critics were taken aback by his use of the theatrical space. Black figures which emerged from a seemingly endless open space emphasized the loneliness of human existence. Only lights and thin translucent curtains were used to structure the open space in which the tragedy unfolded.

After World War II, Fehling failed to find steady employment at a Berlin stage (although he directed the successful production of Jean-Paul Sartre's *The Flies* in 1948 at the Deutsches Theater). The same was true in Munich, and his career ended in the 1950s after depression kept him from working.

ADDITIONAL PRODUCTIONS: 1923: *Das Kathchen von Heilbronn* (Kleist, designed by Caspar Neher); 1925: *Die Sundflut* (Ernst Barlach, with Heinrich George), *Romeo and Juliet*; 1927: *Three Sisters, Measure for Measure*; 1930: *Nora* (with Lucie Mannheim); 1932: *Wilhelm Tell* (with Bernhart Minetti); 1933: *Tannhauser*; 1936: *Don Juan und Faust* (Grabbe, with Gustaf Grundgens); 1938 *Maria Magdalena* (Hebbel); 1940: *Prinz Friedrich von Homburg* (Kleist); 1941: *Julius Caesar*; 1942: *Der Biberpelz* (Hauptmann).

SELECTED BIBLIOGRAPHY: Ahrens, G., ed. *Das Theater des deutschen Regisseurs Jurgen Fehling*. Berlin: Quadriga, 1985; Brauneck, Manfred. *Klassiker der Schauspielregie*. Hamburg: Rowohlt, 1988; Fehling, Jürgen. *Die Magie des Theaters*. Velber: Reihe Theater Heute 17, 1965; Mannheim, L. "Uber Jurgen Fehling." *Theatre Heute* 8.2 (1968): 14–17.

Kai Hammermeister

MAX FERRÁ [b. July 14, 1937, Camagüey, Cuba]. After emigrating to the United States in 1959, Max Ferrá took theatre classes at New York University and participated in play readings before becoming one of the cofounders of Asociacion de Arte Latinoamericano (ADAL) in 1966. ADAL became INTAR (International Arts Relations, Inc.), a theatre and art gallery dedicated to the expression of the Hispanic experience in the United States. Max Ferrá remains the artistic director of INTAR, a position he has held since its inception.

At first, INTAR produced Latin-American, European, and American plays in Spanish, with approximately one-third of these productions directed by Ferrá. In the mid–1970s, Ferrá changed the focus of INTAR to plays written in English by Americans of Hispanic descent and to English translations of Latin-American drama. To encourage young Hispanic playwrights, INTAR created the Hispanic

Playwrights-in-Residence Laboratory in 1979 under the direction of playwright-director Maria Irene Fornes.*

As a stage director, Max Ferrá looks for "kaleidoscopic scripts," plays that cinematically transform time and place in the "Boom Style" (the style of the Latin-American boom in fiction). Ferrá prefers to work with the aid of a dramaturg for at least a year on each show, refining both the script and the production style. Since 1976, he has become more interested in realism and in comedy, although fluidity, musicality, and magical realism remain important aspects of his directorial style. Max Ferrá has directed in Latin America and at the Puerto Rican Traveling Theatre as well as at INTAR.

ADDITIONAL PRODUCTIONS: 1970: *El cepillo de dientes* (*The toothbrush*, Jorge Diaz); 1972: *The House of Bernarda Alba*; 1976: *Nuestro New York!* (sketches and music by Estrella Artau); 1979: *Rice and Beans* (Hector Quintero, translated by Luis Avalos); 1981: *Crisp!* (Jacinto Benavente, adapted by Dolores Prida and Max Ferrá, music by Galt McDermott); 1984: *The Dining Room* (in Paraguay), *The Cuban Swimmer* and *Dog Lady* (Milcha Sanchez-Scott, designed by Ming Cho Lee); 1985: *Savings* (book and lyrics by Dolores Prida, music by Leon Odenz); 1986: *La Chunga* (Mario Vargas Llosa); 1987: *Our Lady of the Tortilla* (Luis Santeiro); 1990: *The Lady from Havana* (Luis Santeiro).
SELECTED BIBLIOGRAPHY: Gayle, Stephen. "Language No Barrier." *New York Post* 11 December 1972; Gent, George. "A Theatrical Haven for Spanish Art." *New York Times* 25 December 1973: 26; Nelson, Don. "Hispanic Voice of America." *New York Daily News* 21 October 1990; Prida, Dolores. "Hispanic Theatre: A Coming of Age. An Interview with Max Ferrá." *New York Theatre Review* March 1979: 21–22; Salas Rojas, Alexandra. "Max Ferrá. The Moving Force behind INTAR." *Canales* 18 (15 November 1990).

David Pasto

ZELDA DIAMOND FICHANDLER [b. September 18, 1924, Boston, Massachusetts]. Although she has served as artistic director of the Acting Company in New York and the Graduate Acting Program at New York University's Tisch School of the Arts, Zelda Fichandler is best known as the cofounder and former producing director of Washington, D.C.'s Arena Stage, a post she held from 1951 to 1991. Along with Margo Jones* of Dallas and Tyrone Guthrie,* founder of the theatre named for him in Minneapolis, Fichandler is considered one of the most important figures in the development of regional theatre in America.

Growing up in Washington, D.C., daughter of a scientist who developed the detonating device for the atomic bomb and blind-instrument flying for airplanes, Fichandler abandoned early impulses to become an actress, majoring instead in Russian language and literature at Cornell University with the intent of becoming a journalist. After graduating Phi Beta Kappa and still unsure as to what she wanted to pursue, she entered the pre-med program at George Washington University with plans of becoming a psychoanalyst. However, still interested in the stage, she soon switched departments to take a master's degree in theatre arts, a degree she received in 1950.

Encouraged to go into directing instead of acting by her husband, Washington economist Thomas Fichandler, she joined forces with one of her professors,

Edward Magnum, to found a 247-seat theatre-in-the-round in an old movie house, the Hippodrome, which they renamed the Arena Stage. During their first year, they produced seventeen plays and within five years had staged fifty-five. Magnum left in 1952 to head a theatre in Hawaii, leaving Fichandler as the Arena's sole guiding artistic force. Her husband became the theatre's business manager and later its executive director, a post he held until his retirement in 1986.

In 1955, after outgrowing the original theatre, the Fichandlers took a year's hiatus for the purpose of finding a larger space which would enable their growing company to more easily pay its bills. The Arena Stage reopened in 1956 in the former Old Heurich Brewery, dubbed "The Old Vat." Over the next five years, the theatre continued to grow and prosper. However, its future was threatened by the impending demolition of the Old Vat building for the construction of the Constitution Avenue Bridge. Securing the necessary funding from various foundations, the Fichandlers erected a permanent 827-seat arena theatre at Sixth and Maine Avenue in 1961. Ten years later, a second proscenium/thrust stage, the Kreeger, was added to the building, and in 1976, a portion of the basement was remodeled, creating the Old Vat Room for cabaret performances. Thus, it became possible for the Fichandlers to stage three productions simultaneously in extremely different stage spaces.

By the time she stepped down as producing director in 1991, Zelda Fichandler had produced over 400 plays and had directed over 50. In 1976, Arena Stage was awarded the first Tony Award given to an American regional theatre. Fichandler also received the prestigious Margo Jones Award for "significant contribution to the dramatic art through the production of new plays," and numerous other awards.

As a director, Fichandler has evolved from very specific preplanned, almost "choreographic" staging to a more organic process which relies on her actors' intuitive responses, often sparked by improvisations during rehearsals. Her preparation is extensive, including "total submersion in research, total saturation about the period and place of the play" (Sweeney, 15). She considers the *actor* the primary component in the theatre and continues to be most interested in the concept of a permanent acting *company* as the ideal artistic situation, albeit a difficult one to maintain financially.

As a producer, Fichandler has championed the development of new plays and multicultural casting. Ever aware of international theatre, she was the first to take an American troupe of actors to perform in the Soviet Union in 1973 and Hong Kong in 1980. She has constantly endeavored to produce works by European playwrights and was instrumental in bringing three prominent European directors, Liviu Ciulei,* Yuri Lyubimov,* and Lucian Pintilie,* to America. Alan Schneider,* one of the most important American directors for three decades, always considered Arena Stage his home, directing some of the most important Arena productions from 1951 to 1983.

ADDITIONAL PRODUCTIONS: **Directing**: 1950: *The Firebrand* (Edwin Justus Mayer, Fichandler's first Arena production); 1960 (and 1968): *Six Characters in Search of an Author*; 1969: *Edith Stein* (Arthur Giron, world premiere); 1973: *Inherit the Wind* (Soviet Union tour); 1974: *Death of a Salesman* (with Robert Prosky as Willy Loman); 1975:

An Enemy of the People; 1978: *Duck Hunting* (Alexander Vampilov, world premiere); 1980: *After the Fall* (Hong Kong International Arts Festival); 1987: *The Crucible*; 1991: *Born Guilty* (Ari Roth, world premiere, last production as producing director). **Producing** (all premieres): 1967: *The Great White Hope* (Howard Sackler, awarded Pulitzer Prize); 1969: *Indians* (Arthur Kopit); 1970: *Pueblo* (Stanley R. Greenberg); 1971: *Moonchildren* (Michael Weller); 1973: *Raisin* (musical); 1974: *Zalmen or The Madness of God* (Elie Wiesel); 1982: *K2* (Patrick Meyers).

SELECTED BIBLIOGRAPHY: Bartow, Arthur. *The Director's Voice*. New York: Theatre Communications Group, 1988: 105–27; Fichandler, Zelda. "The Essential Actor." *American Theatre* 2 (March 1986): 16–17 +; Fichandler, Zelda. "On Risk and Money." *American Theatre* 3 (November 1986): 26–27 +; McAnuff, Des. "The Times of Zelda Fichandler." *American Theatre* 7 (March 1991): 18–25 +; Maslon, Laurence. *The Arena Adventure: The First 40 Years*. Washington, DC: Arena Stage, 1990; Richards, David. "Passionate Arena." *Washington Post* 17 November 1985: G–1 +; Sweeney, Louise. "Zelda Fichandler Looks for 'Main Event' in Each Play She Directs." *Christian Science Monitor* 4 April 1990: 15; "Zelda Fichandler Awards Banquet Speaker." *SETC Convention News* 7–11 March 1984.

Robert Chapel

(WILLIAM) CLYDE FITCH [b. May 2, 1865, Elmira, New York; d. September 4, 1909, Châlons-sur-Marne, France]. Perhaps the most prolific and successful playwright in the United States between 1890 and 1909, Fitch was known as a pioneer realist who captured America's "leisure class" on the stage. He supervised the staging of many of his dramas, and sent copious notes to his producers when he could not be directly involved. It is clear from numerous interviews and observations that Fitch conceived his plays in their entirety as he wrote them and that he attempted in rehearsal to have his vision realized as completely as possible. He staged only his own plays. Fitch would frequently go onstage in rehearsal to show his actors exactly how to gesture in a manner consistent with the class or the intentions of their characters. Indeed, he was legendary for skills in impersonation and demonstration, particularly of women's gesture and habits. He always insisted on the creation of highly detailed scenery and costumes which reflected character, environment, and plot development. His historical dramas in particular were lavishly embellished with scenic detail. He also knew the visual and atmospheric values of nature, and his contemporaries regarded him as a director who frequently took advantage of newer stage technologies to produce natural effects.

A significant number of his plays contained a pivotal female role. Many successful Fitch female stars complimented him for his understanding of women and many more would-be stars sought his guidance. New scholarship by Kimberley Bell Marra demonstrates that Fitch's female characters were a principal element in his theatrical technique and that they helped to establish the "Gibson girl" ideal of femininity. From Marra's feminist perspective, the popular Fitch productions constituted "Broadway gender tyranny," a collective fetishism by which the image of the ideal woman was venerated and maintained.

ADDITIONAL PRODUCTIONS: 1898: *The Moth and the Flame* with Effie Shannon; 1901: *The Climbers* with Amelia Bingham, *Captain Jinks of the Horse Marines* with Ethel Barrymore, *The Stubbornness of Geraldine* with Mary Mannering; 1902: *The Girl with the Green Eyes* with Clara Bloodgood; 1903: *Her Own Way* with Maxine Elliot; 1905: *Her Great Match* with Maxine Elliot; 1907: *The Truth* with Clara Bloodgood (New York), and Marie Tempest (London).

SELECTED BIBLIOGRAPHY: Cochrane, James. ''The Development of the Professional Stage Director.'' Diss. State U of Iowa, 1958; Marra, Kimberley Bell. ''Tyranny of the Ideal Feminine in American Culture: A Study of Gender Production in the Theatre of Clyde Fitch.'' Diss. U of Wisconsin–Madison, 1990; Masters, Robert W. ''Clyde Fitch: A Playwright of His Time.'' Diss. Northwestern U, 1942; Moses, Montrose J., and Virginia Gerson, eds. *Clyde Fitch and His Letters*. Boston: Little, Brown and Company, 1924.

Maarten A. Reilingh

JÜRGEN FLIMM [b. July 17, 1941, Giessen, Federal Republic of Germany]. The student unrest which erupted in the Federal Republic of Germany (FRG) in the late 1960s shaped the social conscience of an entire postwar theatre generation. With Bertolt Brecht* as their primary critical and aesthetic model, committed young directors moved quickly from student theatre productions through apprenticeships in key professional theatres to prominence within the FRG theatre system. The reins of leadership passed rapidly from established prewar theatre makers to this group of social activists. Jürgen Flimm's career follows this scenario. Following university studies in Cologne, Flimm obtained a directing assistantship at the prestigious Munich Kammerspiele theatre. There he was influenced by the directing methodology of Hans Schweikart and Fritz Kortner as well as by his contemporary Peter Stein.* After an early directorial success with *Bremer Freiheit* (Fassbinder) in 1971, Flimm had continual access to major theatres within the FRG.

Insightful dramaturgical analysis developed with longtime collaborators such as Volker Canaris and Wolfgang Wiens has been a continuing strength in Flimm's work. The resulting directorial focus centers on the examination of the individual caught within political, social, or psychic conflicts. Flimm views the nature of the actor's performance as critical in his productions, as is the scenographic space in which the actor is placed. He prefers concentrated psychological spaces which will frame the character and the action in an evocative, associational manner. External references to specific time and place are left to verbal references or to props and costumes. Flimm has always collaborated with one of two theatre designers, Rolf Glittenberg or Erich Wonder, to achieve the desired scenographic effects. Both designers are known for the haunting beauty of their empty, existential spaces. Since scenography carries so much of the intended meaning of the conflict or dilemma in a Flimm production, its dominance provokes critical debate whenever Flimm premieres a play.

The majority of the plays Flimm chooses to stage come from German drama of the nineteenth and early twentieth centuries. Rarely does he work with a contemporary script. Flimm prefers to find meaningful references to the problems of today's world through the use of older, denser texts. The works of Heinrich von Kleist, Georg Büchner, Anton Chekhov, and Brecht have given him ample opportunity to examine the nature of the contemporary condition, often in existential terms. Even though the nature of the examination is serious, a Flimm production can sparkle with humor. As a master showman, Flimm has always provided his audience with a good show, entertaining them within a critical mode of commentary. His use of spectacle for the sake of enjoyment makes him difficult to evaluate, but easy to fault by socially committed theatre critics from the intellectual Left.

Flimm's need for extraordinary talent in all elements of theatre production has led him to seek out supervisory positions in which he can develop and keep a highly qualified artistic ensemble. His management career began at the Thalia Theater in Hamburg, as artistic manager (*Oberspielleiter*) for the 1973–74 seasons. In 1979 he accepted the position of artistic and managing director (*Schauspieldirektor*) for the city theatre of Cologne. There his dreamlike production of *Käthchen von Heilbronn* began what was to be an extraordinarily successful six years for Flimm and his theatre. Besides staging his own productions, he brought in directors whose critical and aesthetic approaches differed from his own, including Luc Bondy, Jürgen Gosch,* and Robert Wilson.* In 1985 Flimm became head (*Intendant*) of the Thalia Theatre. Most of the company he had developed in Cologne came with him to Hamburg. Although many of his own Thalia productions have not received the critical acclaim of earlier years, Flimm remains an extremely popular director and Intendant. Major directors from what was East Germany have worked at the Thalia Theater under Flimm's management, including Ruth Berghaus, Alexander Lang, and Thomas Langhoff. Flimm's production of *Platonov* in 1989 was heralded for the high quality of the performances. At present, the Thalia's company and that of Claus Peymann's Burgtheater in Vienna are regarded as the two best acting ensembles in the German-speaking theatre world.

ADDITIONAL PRODUCTIONS: 1973: *Geschichten aus dem Wiener Wald* (*Tales from the Vienna Woods* by Horváth), Thalia; 1975: *Leben Eduards des Zweiten von England* (*Edward II* by Marlowe/Brecht), Thalia; 1976: *Marya* (Babel), Munich State Theater; 1977: *The Chairs*, Thalia, *Dantons Tod* (Büchner), Thalia; 1978: *Die Wupper* (Lasker-Schüler), Deutsches Theater/Hamburg; 1980: *Uncle Vanya*, Cologne; 1981: *Baal* (Brecht), Cologne; 1982: *Leonce und Lena* (Büchner), Cologne; 1983: *Faust I*, Cologne; 1984: *Die Jungfrau von Orleans* (*Joan of Arc*), Cologne; 1989: *Platonov*, Thalia Theater/Hamburg.

SELECTED BIBLIOGRAPHY: Canaris, Volker. *Jürgen Flimm*. Frankfurt am Main: Fischer Taschenbuch Verlag, forthcoming; Kässens, Wend, and Jörg W. Gronius. "Jürgen Flimm" in *TheaterMacher*, 25–47. Frankfurt am Main: Athenäum, 1987; . . . *Zum Augenblicke sagen, verweile doch!: Bilder von Hermann und Clärchen Baus aus sechs Jahren Theaterarbeit unter der Leitung von Jürgen Flimm 1979 bis 1985*. Cologne: Schauspiel Köln and Verlag der Buchhandlung Walther König, 1985.

Marna King

DARIO FO [b. March 24, 1926, Leggiuno, Varese (Lombardy, Italy)]. From his first foray into the theatre with the satirical revue *Dito nell'occhio* (1953) which he, Franco Parenti, and Giustino Durano presented in the rented, off-season Piccolo Teatro of Milan, Dario Fo has consistently put his uniquely talented "finger in the eye" of Italian institutional bureaucracy. Trained in painting at the Brera Academy and in architecture at the Polytechnic Institute of Milan (1940–45), Fo first concentrated on set design, but then began to improvise comic monologues, satirical sketches, and fantastical narratives. He was influenced by two significant traditions—the work of French mime Jacques LeCoq, and the acclaimed professional theatre of the Rame family, whose gifted daughter, Franca Rame,* Fo married in 1954. The Rames were strolling players who performed a repertory of eighteenth-century drama in northern Italy, and Fo adapted material both from their actor and marionette texts for his first solo success at the Teatro Stabile of Torino in 1958.

On the larger canvas of theatre history, Dario Fo emerges as the quintessential twentieth-century commedia dell'arte creator and performer who not only fulfills the legacies of the Neapolitan actor Toto' and the Neapolitan playwright-actor-director Eduardo De Filippo,* but also brings his renewal of this tradition into a highly political forum. La Compagnia Dario Fo–Franca Rame of Milan (1959–68) proved popular and successful and, despite its biting, political satires, led to the couple's even more successful 1962 television series, "Canzonissima," a program ultimately censored for just such satire. In 1968, the Compagnia Fo-Rame disbanded to form the Associazione Nuova Scena under the auspices of the Italian Communist party (PCI) and performed for working-class audiences in nontraditional spaces such as labor halls and factories. By 1970, the PCI had begun to resent Fo's satire of its bureaucracy and revisionist policy, causing Fo and Rame to break ranks again, this time establishing an independent political theatre group, Il Collettivo Teatrale La Comune.

Throughout his twenty-year organizational odyssey (and up to the present time), Dario Fo's political message has remained consistently clear: beware institutional power. At first disseminated through sketches and revues, this message became the comic backbone of a half dozen Foian plays which have offered brilliant political parodies. *Accidental Death of an Anarchist* (1970), *We Won't Pay! We Won't Pay!* (1974), *About Face* (1981), *Archangels Don't Play Pinball* (1959), *Almost by Chance a Woman: Elizabeth* (1987), and *Mistero Buffo* (1969) are dramatic vehicles initially written, directed, and performed by Fo in Italy and eventually produced internationally, facts which led Tony Mitchell to write that by 1978, "Fo was already the most widely performed playwright in world theatre."

Fo's political-philosophical scenarios are generally created through the machinations of a central clown protagonist endowed with Foian mimic, linguistic, and improvisational abilities who, in trouble with the institutional bureaucracies through little fault of his own, succeeds almost inadvertently in toppling or in unnerving those in power. Madcap laughter, fantastical denouements, references (both clear and oblique) to controversial political questions and personalities (labor strikes, police brutality, corporate and governmental power, papal authority) provide food for satirical fun focused on serious issues.

Fo's enormous talent and intellectual verve is perhaps best exemplified by the one-man *Mistero Buffo,* in which he creates, in the style of medieval jugglers who roamed the marketplaces of European cities, a persona who is chatty, confiding, entertaining, and gossipy. Through his dexterous body language and amazing verbal acuity (''grammelot'' is a nonsense language invented and often employed by Fo which sounds like all, but none, of the Romance languages), this comic protagonist creates a jumble of historical and contemporary events through transformations before the audience's eyes, turning Italian peasant, royal French advisor, English lawyer, pope.

As teacher and director, Fo's political concern for the underdog is served by his commitment to the technical prowess of the performer. Whether teaching theatre workshops in London, directing in Cambridge, Massachusetts, or thinking aloud in his manual for actors, Fo consistently empowers the performer to become his own author-director. Consummate twentieth-century man of the theatre, Dario Fo sends forth his comically clad, politically barbed message—beware institutional power—via commedia dell'arte method, and both message and method continue to resound around the world.

ADDITIONAL PRODUCTIONS: 1958: *Comica finale* (Torino); 1959: establishment of La Compagnia Dario Fo–Franca Rame; 1966: *Ci Ragiono e Canto*; 1967: *La signora e' da buttare*; 1968: *Grande pantomima* (Milan); 1977: Italian TV series of Foian plays performed by Fo; Italian controversy over *Mistero Buffo*; 1978: *Mistero Buffo* (Berlin International Festival); 1979–80: *Tale of a Tiger* (Germany, Sweden, Denmark), *Accidental Death* (London); 1981: *We Won't Pay!* (Off-Broadway); 1983: *About Face* (Yale Rep); 1984: *Accidental Death* (Broadway); 1986: *Mistero Buffo* (U.S. tour and Off-Broadway); 1987: *About Face* (Off-Broadway); *Archangels* (American Repertory Theatre).

SELECTED BIBLIOGRAPHY: D'Aponte, Mimi. ''From Italian Roots to American Relevance: The Remarkable Theatre of Dario Fo.'' *Modern Drama* 32 (December 1989): 532–44; Jenkins, Ron. ''Clowns, Politics and Miracles.'' *American Theatre* 3 (June 1986): 10–16; Mitchell, Tony. *Dario Fo: People's Court Jester.* London and New York: Methuen, 1984; Schechter, Joel. ''Dario Fo: The Clown as Counter-Informer.'' *Durov's Pig.* New York: Theatre Communications Group, 1985: 142–57; Valentini, Chiari. *La Storia di Dario Fo.* Milan: Feltrinelli, 1977.

Mimi Gisolfi D'Aponte

VALERY VLADIMIROVICH FOKIN [b. February 28, 1946, Moscow]. After graduating from the Shchukin Theatre College in 1970, Fokin worked in the Contemporary theatre (Sovremennik) in Moscow. Since 1985 he has been the artistic director of the Moscow Ermolova theatre. He has also directed plays in the United States, Hungary, Poland, and Japan, and since 1976 he has been a pupil and follower of Jerzy Grotowski.*

Fokin belongs to a new generation of Soviet directors who started to work in theatre just before perestroika and changed Aesopian, indirect language to a plain and direct address to an audience.

In *Valentin and Valentina* (Roshchin, 1970) Fokin showed social and moral stratification of Soviet society. In *Provincial Anecdotes* (By Vampilov with Oleg Tababov, 1974) the absurdity of Soviet life was expressed through walls that literally staggered, chairs that fell down, or cupboard doors that opened by themselves. In the *Monument* (by Vetemaa, with Raikin, 1978) the plaster-cast figures onstage were silent witnesses of the heroes' actions. His first production at Ermolova theatre, Alexander Furavsky's *Speak . . .* (1985), was a turning point for theatre audiences toward new theatrical expression. Fokin used an ascetic, antitheatrical language to talk about the past, present, and future. With *Speak . . .* perestroika and glasnost came to the theatre. In this and the following productions, Fokin spoke about the most painful problems of the country, which were taboo for many decades. He used scenic metaphors to express the loneliness, alienation, hopelessness, or despair of people in Russia. *Sports Scenes of 1981* (by Eduard Radzinsky, with Tatyana Doronina, 1986) talked about moral corruption and the devaluation of the elite. The clothes that were frantically torn off were metaphors for human beings stripped of their dignities. Vladimir Nabokov's *Invitation to an Execution* (1989) was set as a show-booth in which masks performed their bloody murder of a human being who didn't wear a mask. The theatre audience was seated directly onstage, thus being forced to feel that it carried personal responsibility for everything cruel and absurd that happened with the main character.

Fokin's theatre is a theatre of heightened social responsibility, in which everyone shares accountability for the downfalls of Soviet life. Fokin's theatre provides new insight and asks direct questions that audiences must search deep within themselves to answer.

ADDITIONAL PRODUCTIONS: 1984: *The Inspector General*; 1985: *Who's Afraid of Virginia Woolf?* with Guft, Volchek, Neelova; 1988: *The Second Year of Freedom* (Buravsky).

SELECTED BIBLIOGRAPHY: Ovchinnikova, S. "Invitation to an Execution." *Literary Russia* 7 April 1989; Ovchinnikova, S. *Valery Fokin.* VTPO: Souztiatr, 1991; Shur, Paulina. "The Lonely People." *The New Time* 23 (1989): 46; Smelyansky, A. "How Could We Revive Our Theatre?" *Theatre* 12 (1987): 47–50.

Paulina Shur

NIKOLAI MIKHALOVICH FOREGGER [b. April 6, 1892, Moscow; d. June 8, 1939, Kuibshev, Ukraine]. Descended from Russo-Austrian aristocracy, Nikolai Foregger was considered one of the most innovative and controversial of all the Soviet directors and choreographers in the early twenties. A graduate of Kiev University, Foregger had briefly worked with Aleksandr Tairov* in 1917 before joining the Red Army as a performer. In 1920, he returned to Moscow and opened the Theatre of the Four Masks—a contemporary, Soviet commedia dell'arte. By December 1921, Foregger had perfected a novel form of entertainment that combined grotesque comedy with highly stylized movement. His *The Parody Show,* a biting attack on the theatrical pretensions of the Moscow Art Theatre and Tairov as well as the Moscow Proletkult, found an appreciative audience among Vladimir Mayakovsky's influential circle of writers and artists.

On Russian New Year's Day 1922, Foregger presented his most famous production, *Good Treatment for Horses.* Written by Vladimir Mass, *Good Treatment* uncovered the corrupt and petty bourgeois aspects of the new Soviet Russia. In the third act, vulgar capitalists from Odessa enter a slightly decadent Moscow cabaret, where they are amazed and awed at the latest Western dances and "hot" music. Combining abstract gestures (called *tea-fyz-trenage*) with steps from an American jazz dance manual, Foregger created an entirely new kind of Eccentric performance. So popular was this third act that it reappeared in *Better Treatment for Horses* and *Improved Treatment for Horses.*

Known as MASTFOR, Foregger's troupe occupied a permanent theatre space beginning in October 1922 and offered over thirty different programs of sketches and dances in Eccentric and Constructivist costuming and sets. As his popularity grew, so did Foregger's inventiveness: foxtrots, tangos, apache dances, and shimmies merged with aerial somersaults, pyramid building, folkloric leaps, and mechanical bows and swings. Wooden machines were even constructed in the foyer to teach MASTFOR'S spectators *tea-fyz-trenage.*

In February 1923, MASTFOR's Machine Dances created a sensation across the entire Soviet avant-garde. Precise human enactments of lynch-pin rotations on locomotive wheels, pistons within expanding cylinders, and turning flywheels, hand-pumps, and lathes impressed even Foregger's most bitter enemies. "Celebrating the new god of the Machine," the MASTFOR performers found a novel use for their old, comical mechanical gestures.

At the height of its fame in January 1924, the MASTFOR Cabaret was destroyed by fire. Foregger and some of his leading performers worked in other theatres but with much less success since their original work was already widely imitated. By 1927, Foregger had failed in attempts to rebuild the MASTFOR in Leningrad and once again in Moscow. Choreographing for the amateur Blue Blouse movement and other leftist theatres of satire temporarily kept his name and movement innovations alive. In 1929 Foregger returned to the Ukraine, where he worked in semi-obscurity until his death ten years later.

ADDITIONAL PRODUCTIONS: 1922: *Kidnapper of Children, The Supernatural Son, Evening of Dances*; 1923: *Dance of the Machines, Walk, Passion, Death.*

SELECTED BIBLIOGRAPHY: Carter, Huntly. *The New Theatre and Cinema of Soviet Russia.* New York: International Publishers, 1925; Foregger, Nikolai. "Experiments in the Art of the Dance" [1926]. *The Drama Review* 19 (March 1975): 74–77; Gordon, Mel. "Program of the Minor Leftists in the Soviet Theatre." Diss. New York U, 1981; Gordon, Mel. "Foregger and the Dance of the Machines." *The Drama Review* 19 (March 1975): 68–73; Rudnitsky, Konstantin. *Russian and Soviet Theater 1905–1932.* Trans. Roxane Permar. New York: Harry N. Abrams, 1988.

Mel Gordon

RICHARD FOREMAN [b. June 10, 1937, New York, New York]. Richard Foreman's work as a director cannot be separated from his work as playwright, scenographer, composer, and producer. The work of an auteur, Foreman's productions are highly controlled, formally rigorous emanations of his own thinking and writing processes.

After receiving a B.A. from Brown University in 1959 and an M.F.A. in playwriting from Yale in 1962, Richard Foreman joined the playwriting unit of the Actors' Studio, working in the style of Clifford Odets and Arthur Miller. He abandoned this style after exposure to the raw, self-conscious forms of new American underground film. In a space abandoned by New York Film-Maker Cooperative, Foreman created the "Ontological-Hysteric Theatre" in 1968, producing his groundbreaking *Angelface*.

"Ontological-Hysteric" refers to Foreman's desire to locate the essence of theatrical experience through the isolation of conflictual ("hysterical") elements into discrete phenomenological "events." In this process, Foreman combines Brecht's alienation methods with Gertrude Stein's notion of a "continuous present," fixing the audience's attention on each moment while defeating functions of memory and expectation. There is no narrative; only the persistent, self-reflexive manifestation of the composition process itself. Theatrical practice always attempts to reflect Foreman's thought processes during the writing of the play. In this "theatre of the mind," Foreman's characters are not to be seen as independent beings, but rather as fragments of his own consciousness.

The physical construction of Foreman's theatre is a vital part of his work. Equipped with a stage that is far deeper than it is wide, Foreman maintains control over audience focus through control of perspective. The opening and closing of the space pushes and pulls one's focus, playing with illogical visual relations. Strings crisscross the space producing diagrammatic "sight-lines" that unite the composition and direct the gaze. They frame the attitudes of the actors, linking the audience's visual experience with Foreman's mental projections, and inanimate objects take on a life of their own, moving through the space independently or levitating. Other devices used to direct audience attention to the particularity of the moment include loud noises or buzzers that frame a phrase or image; Foreman's taped voice commenting on the action; written comments projected on a screen; and characters' actions frozen into tableaus directed toward an awareness of the moment's composition.

Foreman's primary hope for the audience is "duo-consciousness": the capacity to watch the action while simultaneously watching oneself watching. Foreman disrupts the "seductive state of absorption," waking spectators to each new moment in all its singularity, forcing them to actively work at generating their own connections between events. He directs dialogue as a musical conductor might and meticulously blocks and choreographs all movement, but he does not provide "motivation" for the actors. Instead they perform literal, task-like actions. Perhaps for this reason, he has preferred to work with nonactors. In early performances, he sat at light and sound boards in the audience's first row directing the action. A tape-recorded score—including bits of music, sound effects, actor's lines, and Foreman's voice-over—provides the basic structure and mechanism for each play, contributing to the sense that each production is a massive thought-machine.

A turning point for Foreman was *PAIN(T)* in 1974. Prior to this, his productions moved slowly, with tableaus frozen for extended contemplation and attention directed toward a particular focus. After *PAIN(T),* actions increased in speed, and images and sounds bombarded the audience from all directions in the hopes that an unfocused attention would take in the entirety of the stage composition. Events became more homogeneous, and continuity developed between them. *Egyptology* (1983) marked a movement away from Foreman's mental hermeticism toward external experience. By the time of *Film Is Evil, Radio Is Good* (1987) and *A Symphony of Rats* (1988, with the Wooster Group), a more discursive and even political orientation became apparent, although the perceptual concerns of the early work were not abandoned, only redirected.

While Foreman's work is often classified with that of Robert Wilson* as a "Theatre of Images," its concern with the role of language in perception is vital. The overt, designative role of verbal and written text is as powerful and self-conscious an element as his visual constructs. Although he has directed more commercial productions of plays by Bertolt Brecht,* Vaclav Havel, Kathy Acker, and others, his primary importance stems from the Ontological-Hysteric Theatre, which has influenced the experimental work of the Wooster Group, Mabou Mines, and performance artists such as Stuart Sherman. Its presence can also be felt in the recent "Language Plays" of Len Jenkin and Mac Wellman.

ADDITIONAL PRODUCTIONS: 1968: *Angelface*; 1971: *Total Recall (Sophia = Wisdom): Part 2*; 1972: *HOTEL CHINA*; 1972–73: *Sophia = (Wisdom) Part 3: The Cliffs*; 1973: *Classical Therapy, or A Week under the Influence*; 1974: *Vertical Mobility (Sophia = (Wisdom) Part 4)*; 1975: *Pandering to the Masses: A Misrepresentation*; 1975–76: *Rhoda in Potatoland (Her Fall-Starts)*; 1977: *Book of Splendors: Part Two (Book of Levers)*; 1978: *Blvd. de Paris (I've Got the Shakes)*; 1981: *Penguin Touquet*; 1985: *Miss Universal Happiness*, with the Wooster Group.

SELECTED BIBLIOGRAPHY: Bartow, Arthur. *The Director's Voice: Twenty-One Interviews*. New York: Theatre Communications Group, 1988: 128–39; Cole, Susan Letzler. *Directors in Rehearsal: A Hidden World*. New York: Routledge, 1992: 125–44; Davy, Kate. *Richard Foreman and the Ontological-Hysteric Theatre*. Ann Arbor: UMI Research Press, 1979; Davy, Kate, ed. *Richard Foreman: Plays and Manifestos*. New York: New York University Press, 1976; Foreman, Richard. *Reverberation Machines: The Later Plays and Essays*. Barrytown, NY: Station Hill Press, 1985; Marranca, Bonnie. *The Theatre of Images*. New York: PAJ Publications, 1977; Schechner, Richard. "Richard Foreman on Richard Foreman." *The Drama Review* 31 (Winter 1987): 125–35.

Jon Erickson

MARIA IRENE FORNES [b. May 14, 1930, Havana, Cuba]. In 1945, Maria Irene Fornes emigrated to New York with her mother and sister. Possessing little formal schooling, Fornes spent the next several years working in a series of factory and office jobs. At the age of nineteen, she began painting, and this pursuit ultimately led her to move to Europe for several years. Upon her return to New York in the 1960s, she began writing plays, and by 1968, Fornes was directing and designing many of her own productions. Her best known plays include *Dr. Kheal* (1968), *Fefu and Her Friends* (1977), *Eyes on the Harem* (1979), and *The Conduct of Life* (1985).

Although Fornes has directed works by Calderón, Ibsen, Chekhov, and others, she is most celebrated for her direction of her own plays. Her productions are characterized by their unconventional utilization of space, striking verbal imagery, and focus on visual detail. As both director and playwright, Fornes's approach to her material has been labeled ''cinematic,'' because she deliberately manipulates the spatial relationship between performer and spectator. After the first scene of *Fefu and Her Friends,* for example, she divided the audience into four smaller groups which then moved from one room to another to witness subsequent scenes of the play. For the spectators, this novel technique fostered a greater sense of intimacy with the characters, and a richer overall involvement in the theatrical event.

As one reflection of Fornes's sensitivity to women's issues, strong, nontraditional female protagonists figure in many of her plays. Her depiction of complex friendships between female characters, examination of sexuality and conventional gender roles, innovative directorial interpretations, and adaptations of classic male-authored texts have earned Fornes a reputation as a leading voice in feminist theatre.

Between 1973 and 1979, Fornes was managing director of the New York Theatre Strategy, an organization comprised of experimental playwrights united by a desire to introduce alternative plays and staging techniques to a broad audience. Fornes was also associated with the Open Theatre, a group known for its emphasis on the primacy of the actor. In addition, Fornes's exploration of biculturalism has made her a powerful influence in the Hispanic theatre community.

Fornes has received numerous awards for her work as a director and playwright. The winner of several Obies, including one in 1982 for sustained achievement in theatre, she has been the recipient of grants from the Guggenheim Foundation, the National Endowment for the Arts, and the Rockefeller Foundation. She has also received a New York State Governor's Arts Award and an award from the American Academy and Institute of Arts and Letters. Currently, Fornes conducts playwriting workshops across the United States, and serves as playwrights lab director for INTAR in New York.

ADDITIONAL PRODUCTIONS: 1967: *The Annunciation*; 1968: *Molly's Dream*; 1974: *Aurora* (music by John FitzGibbon); 1975: *Cap-a-Pie* (music by José Raul Bernardo); 1980: *Evelyn Brown: A Diary*; 1981: *Life Is a Dream* (adapted by Maria Irene Fornes, music by George Quincy); 1981: *A Visit* (music by George Quincy); 1982: *Exiles* (Ana

Maria Simo), *The Danube*; 1983: *Mud*; 1984: *Sarita* (music by Leon Odenz); 1985: *Cold Air* (Virgilio Piñera, adapted by Maria Irene Fornes); 1987: *Abington Square, Hedda Gabler* (adapted by Maria Irene Fornes).

SELECTED BIBLIOGRAPHY: Betsko, Kathleen, and Rachel Koenig. *Interviews with Contemporary Women Playwrights*. New York: Beach Tree Books, 1987; Cohn, Ruby. *New American Dramatists, 1960–1980*. New York: Grove Press, 1982; Cole, Susan Letzler. *Directors in Rehearsal: A Hidden World*. New York: Routledge, 1992: 35–55; Fornes Maria Irene. *Promenade and Other Plays*. New York: Performing Arts Journal Publications, 1987; Keyssar, Helene. *Feminist Theatre*. New York: Grove Press, 1985; Paran, Janice. "Redressing Ibsen." *American Theatre* 4 (November 1987): 14–20; Sontag, Susan. Preface. *Plays*. New York: Performing Arts Journal Publications, 1986.

Debra Brinegar Charlton

BOB FOSSE [b. Robert Louis Fosse, June 23, 1927, Chicago, Illinois; d. September 23, 1987]. Fosse was one of the foremost director-choreographers of his time. The only director-choreographer to be honored with a Tony, an Oscar, and an Emmy in the same year, Fosse put his unmistakable stamp on such Broadway shows as *Sweet Charity* and *Chicago,* and an autobiographical film, *All That Jazz*.

The Fosse style was perhaps the most distinctive of the great director-choreographers of the 1960s through the 1980s. The conception and the choreography of his productions were often impossible to separate. Fosse always felt that he was at a disadvantage as a dancer because of his stooped shoulders and gawky frame—he was almost impossibly skinny as a young performer. He transformed these characteristics into a stoop-shouldered dancing style which emphasized the joints of the body contorted to odd postures rather than the flowing line of Gower Champion* or the head-thrown-back, free style of Michael Bennett.* Because of the peculiarity of this style, he chose as subjects the outcasts of society and the fringe elements of human existence. *Sweet Charity* (1966), perhaps his most characteristic work, is the story of a taxi dancer cum prostitute who is always searching for love but whose heart, which she wears tattooed on her upper arm, is inevitably broken. It is the story of a human spirit that refuses to be trampled, no matter what the circumstances, a theme he was to explore over and over again.

Fosse was born in Chicago to Cyril and Sadie Fosse, of Norwegian descent. His first teacher, Frederick Weaver, instilled in Fosse a fascination for vaudeville. Already at this young age, Fosse's difficulty in turning out, his slouch, and a penchant to turn his palms toward the audience with his fingers splayed were in evidence. Weaver paired Fosse with another talented student, Charles Grass, and as the Riff Brothers they began to make their first, tentative forays into show business. Because both were underage, they accepted what jobs they could find, often in sleazy strip-tease establishments. Later, Fosse maintained a fascination with, if not an affection for, the underbelly of society.

Fosse moved on to Broadway and was hired for the chorus of *Call Me Mister* in 1946. During the tour Fosse met and married his first wife, dancer Mary-Ann (née Marian) Niles. The team did make a small success on the nightclub and television revue circuit. The marriage soon broke up as Fosse began an affair with Joan McCracken, whom he eventually married. At the same time he was hired to play Joey in a touring summer stock production of *Pal Joey* (1951). However, when the show was taken to Broadway, Harold Lang was hired for the title role and Fosse reduced to understudy.

After two MGM films, *Give a Girl a Break* and *Kiss Me Kate,* in which Fosse choreographed his own numbers, he was hired to choreograph the Broadway production of *The Pajama Game* (1954). The producers had little faith in Fosse and hired Jerome Robbins* to stand by. In New Haven, the second act opener "Steam Heat" stopped the show, and director George Abbott* wanted to cut it. Robbins convinced him to keep the number, which turned out to be Fosse's first major triumph. The next Abbott show, *Damn Yankees* (1955), was also choreographed by Fosse and earned him a Tony Award and a solid reputation.

In *Damn Yankees,* Fosse met Gwen Verdon, who would become his third wife. Two successful musicals followed with Verdon, *New Girl in Town* (1957) and *Redhead* (1959), Fosse's first directing credit. By this point Verdon was a constant fixture in Fosse's life. He choreographed *How to Succeed in Business without Really Trying* in 1961 and directed *Little Me* the following year. These successes were crowned by the birth of Fosse and Verdon's daughter, Nicole Providence Fosse, in 1963.

After the success of *Sweet Charity,* he was hired to direct the film. Instead of casting Verdon, however, Hollywood opted for Shirley MacLaine, whom Verdon coached in the role. The movie was a commercial failure, and Fosse found himself at forty with no offers. The success of the film of *Cabaret* (1972), however, completely changed his reputation. It was followed in the same year by a *Concert for T.V.* by Liza Minnelli and *Pippin,* the three of which earned him his triple crown of Oscar, Emmy, and Tony awards. Fosse then made the film *Lenny* (1974), was reunited with Verdon for the musical *Chicago* (1975), and then directed his autobiographical movie, *All That Jazz* (1979).

His final works were *Dancin'* (1978), the disastrous *Star '80* (1983), and his last work, a Broadway show called *Big Deal* based on the film *Big Deal on Madonna Street* with period music totally of Fosse's choosing. The show opened in 1986 and closed after sixty-two disappointing performances.

ADDITIONAL PRODUCTIONS: 1956: *Bells Are Ringing* (co-choreographer); 1961: *The Conquering Hero* (fired as director-choreographer); 1965: *Pleasures and Palaces*; 1986: *Sweet Charity* (revival).

SELECTED BIBLIOGRAPHY: Challender, James Winston. "The Function of the Choreographer in the Development of the Conceptual Musical: An Examination of the Work of Jerome Robbins, Bob Fosse, and Michael Bennett on Broadway between 1944 and 1981." Diss. Florida State U, 1986; Gottfried, Martin. *All His Jazz.* New York: Bantam Books, 1990; Grubb, Kevin Boyd. *Razzle Dazzle: The Life and Works of Bob Fosse.* New York: St. Martin's Press, 1989; Sloan, Ronna Elaine. "Bob Fosse: An Analytic-Critical Study." Diss. City U of New York, 1983.

David Payne Carter

JIŘÍ FREJKA [b. April 6, 1904, Outěchovice, Bohemia, Czechoslovakia; d. October 27, 1952, Prague, Czechoslovakia]. Along with E. F. Burian* and Jindřich Honzl,* Frejka formed a trio of leading Czech avant-garde theatre artists whose careers often crossed during the interwar years. Of the three, Frejka was the first to organize and produce plays in the early 1920s. He was also the director whose career most successfully spanned World War II to continue productively in the postwar era; and yet the complex political pressures of the post–1948 Communist era ultimately led to Frejka's being shunted aside and to his taking his own life.

In the 1920s, in the recently independent Czechoslovak Republic, Frejka epitomized the lighthearted, playful dismissal of the remnants of bourgeois realism in theatre. Poetical and lyrical by temperament, he was equally inspired by the commedia dell'arte tradition and the new mode of constructivism. Working with conservatory students and young professionals, he organized and directed a number of lively productions in Prague's equivalent of Off-Off-Broadway. The plays were usually witty adaptations of classic and contemporary material ranging from Aristophanes to Czech writers of the Poetism movement. The settings, most often by the important young designer Antonin Heythum, were minimal, but colorful and highly inventive—ladders, ramps, slides, and lathing on which the actors ingeniously improvised.

In 1925, Frejka launched the Osvobozené Divadlo (Liberated Theatre), which became the most celebrated of the avant-garde groups. Jindřich Honzl soon joined Frejka as codirector, and E. F. Burian participated as composer, musician, and actor. Friction with Honzl led to Frejka's leaving the company in 1927 to set up his own group called Theatre Dada, and later, the Modern Studio (1928). With these new groups, Frejka continued his special mode of consciously playful dilettantism, but also added more distinctly satiric cabaret entertainment.

The great watershed for Frejka occurred in 1929 with an invitation from K. H. Hilar* to guest direct in the National Theatre. Frejka became Hilar's assistant and gradually learned how to work within the elaborate internal structure of the National Theatre and with its established stars. After Hilar's death in 1935, Frejka became one of the core directors and proceeded to mount some of his most impressive productions (*Fuente Ovejuna,* 1935; *Julius Caesar,* 1936; *Revizor,* 1936; and *Boris Godunov,* 1936) which increasingly demonstrated Frejka's shift from poetical *jeux d'esprit* to more challenging productions which responded to the threat of fascist militarism and other serious issues of the 1930s. During these years, Frejka had the good fortune to form a lifelong creative association with František Tröster, the most gifted of the generation of Czech designers after Vlastislav Hofman. Frejka's mature style of theatre was best captured by his own term, "hyperbolic realism"—staging that is based in reality but favors considerable freedom for stylized heightening in scenography and physically expressive acting—which closely resembled the "fantastic realism" of Aleksandr Tairov.* Frejka thus managed to bring to establishment theatre the freshness and lyrical sensibility that characterized his youthful work.

Unlike Honzl and Burian, Frejka was able to continue working during the war years. In successive productions at the National Theatre, he attempted to support the morale of the subjugated Czechs in productions like V. K. Klicpera's *Zlý Jelen* [*The Evil Stag*] and Plautus's *Pseudolus,* both in 1942.

Immediately after the war, the process of cultural reorganization resulted in Frejka's being shifted from the National Theatre to the leadership of the Vinohrady Theatre. This was Prague's second most important theatre, but it became more creative than the National Theatre during Frejka's tenure (1945–50). There he established an impressive ensemble of artists, including several who would become the dominant artists of the following decades. In his productions at the Vinohrady, as in those at the National Theatre, Frejka usually succeeded in balancing the criteria of artistic excellence and social and cultural relevance. Major productions included *Macbeth* (1946), *The Merry Wives of Windsor* (1949), Georges Neveux's *Theseus* (1946), Gribojedov's *Woe from Wisdom* (1947), and Beaumarchais's *The Marriage of Figaro* (1950). Concurrently, Frejka played a leading role in establishing a new drama academy, DAMU, where he functioned as dean and then rector from 1946 to 1949. The cultural fallout from the new Communist regime's coming to power included Frejka's displacement from the Vinohrady Theatre to the musical theatre in the Karlin district of Prague. Although Frejka was ill-suited to its operetta repertoire, he nevertheless tried to maintain his standards in the few productions he did there before his death in 1952.

ADDITIONAL PRODUCTIONS: 1925: *Circus Dandin* (adapted from Molière); 1926: *Depeše no Kolečkách* [*Telegram on Wheels*] (Vítězslav Nezval), *Ecclesiazusae* (Aristophanes); 1927: *The Eiffel Tower Wedding Party*; 1928: *The Infernal Machine*; 1932: *Julie, or The Dreamer* (Georges Neveux); 1934: *The Birds*; 1938: *Romeo and Juliet*; 1943: *Strakonický Dudák* [*The Bagpiper from Strakonice*] (J. K. Tyl); 1945: *The 14th of July* (Romain Rolland).

SELECTED BIBLIOGRAPHY: Burian, Jarka. "High Points of Theatre in the First Czechoslovak Republic." *Modern Drama* 27 (March 1984): 98–111; Frejka, Jiří. *Železná Doba Divadla* [*The Iron Age of Theatre*]. Prague: Melantrich, 1945; Frejka, Jiří. *Živé Divadlo* [*Living Theatre*]. Prague: E. Pleskot, 1936; Hajek, Jiří, ed. *Česlé Divadlo 3* [*Czech Theatre 3*]. Prague: Divadelní Ústav, 1980; Rutte, Miroslav, and František Bartoš. *The Modern Czech Scene.* Prague: Vladimír Zikeš, 1938; Träger, Josef, ed. *Jiří Frejka.* Prague: Dívadelní Ústav, 1964; Vočadlo, Otakar. "The Theater and Drama of Czechoslovakia." *The Theater in a Changing Europe.* Ed. T. H. Dickinson. New York: Henry Holt, 1937.

Jarka M. Burian

G

MARGARITA GALBAN [b. October 27, 1936, Havana, Cuba]. Margarita Galban is the artistic director and cofounder of the Bilingual Foundation of the Arts, a professional theatre company in Los Angeles that produces Spanish classic and contemporary Hispanic plays. All plays produced by the company are performed both in English and Spanish.

Galban began her career in the theatre as an actress. She performed on stage and radio in her native Cuba before she moved to Mexico in 1959. As a member of El Teatro Popular de Mexico, she enjoyed tremendous success and received Mexico's coveted Best Actress Award for her performance in Federico García Lorca's *The House of Bernarda Alba*. During this period, she also adapted several theatrical works for television.

Galban came to the United States in 1968 and was awarded a scholarship in directing at the Lee Strasberg* Actors' Studio West. In 1969, she founded Teatro Seis Actores, a Spanish-language theatre company in Hollywood, and began to work exclusively as a director. Her work with the company featured the *Festival de Lorca* wherein she adapted and directed scenes and excerpts from Lorca's poetry, prose, and short stories. During the 1970s, Galban also directed several programs for Spanish language television and PBS.

In 1973, Galban cofounded the Bilingual Foundation of the Arts (BFA) along with actress-producer Carmen Zapata and designer Estela Scarlata. The company, which produces in both English and Spanish, is the longest running theatre in Los Angeles devoted exclusively to Hispanic plays. Galban's work with the company has continued to focus upon the works of Lorca, along with contemporary Hispanic writers. Lorca plays Galban has directed at BFA include *Blood*

Wedding (1984), *Dona Rosita, the Spinster* (1990), *The House of Bernarda Alba* (1976), *Mariana Pineda* (1988), *The Shoemaker's Prodigious Wife* (1986), and *Yerma* (1981).

In 1980, Galban's production of *Fanlights*, by Puerto Rican playwright Rene Marquez, toured to New York's Lincoln Center to critical acclaim. The National Endowment for the Arts commissioned Galban to adapt selections from Lorca's work into a new American opera, *Lorca, Child of the Moon*, which she directed in a workshop production for BFA in 1987.

ADDITIONAL PRODUCTIONS: 1973: *Los Signos de Zodiaco* (Sergio Magana); 1976: *Rosalba y los Llaveros* (Emilio Carballido), *Uprooted* (Humberto Robles Arenas); 1982; *Fuente ovejuna* (Lope de Vega), 1983: *El cepillo de dientes* (Jorge Diaz); 1986: *Orinoco!* (Emilio Carballido); 1990: *La Nonna* (Roberto M. Cossa).

Tony Curiel

PATRICK GARLAND [b. 1936, Oxford, England]. Patrick Garland attended Oxford University where he was president of his student Thespian organization. After leaving Oxford, Garland moved to London, acting in various theatres, including the Bristol Old Vic, from 1959 to 1961. He directed his own adaptation of *Brief Lives* at Hampstead and New York and *Hair*, *Tel Aviv*, and *Cyrano* (in his own adaptation) for the National Theatre.

Garland is best known (most notably in the United States) for his productions of *A Doll's House* and *Hedda Gabler* (both 1971), which were produced by Hillard Elkins and which starred the producer's wife, Claire Bloom, in the roles of Nora and Hedda. In a letter outlining his approach to *A Doll's House*, Garland revealed some of his predilections: an emphasis on a comparatively rapid pace ("Almost all plays . . . are taken too slowly, especially Ibsen and Chekhov") and an inclination toward "getting through" the laborious exposition and to the conflicts. His work with actors supports his emphasis on a rapid tempo, and he criticizes their inability to "throw away" dialogue and their penchant for over-characterization.

During the 1970s and 1980s, Garland regularly produced and directed for British television, most notably the "Famous Gossip" series and "On the Margin." He is perhaps best known, however, for his interview with Laurence Olivier on the occasion of Sir Laurence's eightieth birthday, during which Garland was seen coaching Olivier on his oral interpretation of poet Philip Larkin's line, "They fuck you up your mum and dad."

In 1989, Garland produced a version of Thomas Hardy's *The Dynasts: An Epic-Drama of the War with Napoleon* (1903), retitled *Victory*. This adaptation of Hardy's poem, which the poet himself regarded as "more or less resembling a stage play . . . although not one" was seen by at least one observer as an "eccentric reading" of the work in a vain attempt to humanize the text. Featuring 131 scenes and 370 actors, the original has cinema-like qualities that apparently have dissuaded even the most earnest directors from attempting to restage it.

In his most recent creative effort (March 1991), Garland wrote, directed, and produced an adaptation of Virginia Woolf's *A Room of One's Own* for the New York stage. Featuring Eileen Atkins as the legendary Woolf, Garland's production received positive critical response to the "kneading and abridging" of the original. It was faulted, however, for the interwoven, tape-recorded commentary which provided the actress a momentary respite, but threatened the whole with the vagaries of electronic reproduction.

SELECTED BIBLIOGRAPHY: Gussow, Mel. "Of Women and the Ruling Class (Men?)." *New York Times* 5 March 1991: sec. C: 11, 13; Parker, John, ed. *Who's Who in the Theatre*. 15th ed. Toronto: Isaac Pitman, 1972: 813; Simon, John. "Two from the Heart, Two from Hunger." *New York* 18 March 1991: 76; Soller, Larry Steven. "Critical Reaction to Productions of *A Doll's House* on the New York Stage." Diss. U of Georgia, 1973; Taylor, Neil. "Controlling the Course of History." *Times Literary Supplement* 26 May 1989: 582; Williams, Hugo. "People Games." *New Statesman* 18 December 1987: 39.

Larry Soller

JEAN GASCON [b. December 21, 1920, Montreal, Quebec, Canada; d. April 13, 1988, Stratford, Ontario, Canada]. After earning his B.A., Jean Gascon enrolled in medical school, but abandoned his studies in 1946, shortly before finishing, to devote himself to a theatrical career. During his studies, he had performed first as an amateur actor and later with the semiprofessional troupe, Compagnons de saint Laurent, where he made his first attempt at direction, in the early 1940s, with *Noah* by André Obey.

After a stay in France (1946–51), during which he performed with Ludmilla Pitoëff (see Georges Pitoëff), the Grenier-Hussenot Company, and at the Centre dramatique de l'Ouest (Western Dramatic Center) in Rennes, Gascon returned to Montreal, where he founded, with several friends, the Théâtre du Nouveau Monde. As artistic director from 1951 to 1966, Gascon refined his enormous talents as an actor and a director. A dynamic director, he surrounded himself with devoted collaborators in whom he inspired fervor, enthusiasm, and affection, for him the perfect working climate.

At the Théâtre du Nouveau Monde, Jean Gascon mounted no less than forty productions. From the inaugural play, Molière's *L'Avare* (1951), he made his mark. With little interest in theories or purely empirical training, he was inspired above all by the great directors of the French Cartel des Quatre (in particular Louis Jouvet* and Charles Dullin*) and their successors (Jean-Louis Barrault* and Jean Vilar*). Through simplification and exaggeration, he used symbols easily deciphered by the audience. Always faithful to the work and what he perceived to be the author's intent, he never sought to become a star director, in the fashion of some of his contemporaries. For Gascon, the best direction was that which knew how to make itself invisible. He endeavored to avoid banal truths and, through a subtle aesthetic transportation, to recapture the original truth in the works he staged.

An actor himself, he had an extraordinary skill for directing his co-workers, often giving them a demonstration of what he expected from them. Gradually, he developed a marked interest in playing all types of roles, especially those which seemed most out of his range, including female roles. He directed general movements in a manner which would be the envy of more than one choreographer. Among others, the incidental ballets of *Le Malade imaginaire* (1956) and *Le Bourgeois gentilhomme* (1963, English; 1967, French) will be long remembered. It was with Molière, often in collaboration with the designer Robert Prévost, that Gascon had his most successful productions.

Although inspired by drama and tragedy, Gascon shone particularly in the direction of comedies, where he gave free rein to his imagination and his natural sense of humor. In addition to Chekhov, Claudel, and Shakespeare, his name remains permanently tied to Molière, Labiche, Feydeau, and Bertolt Brecht.* The morose was not his strength, and while respecting the social significance of those works and the profound humanity of their characters, he knew how to uncover the comedy in them, sometimes taking small liberties but never betraying the author. Audiences of the period remember fondly Diafoirus's visit with Argan, for example, or the engagement feast of Macheath and Polly, and many other fittingly delirious tableaus, where without ever harming the text, Jean Gascon created absolutely irresistible performances. On occasion, he recovered or invented "lazzi," becoming, in a sense, an heir of the greatest Italian *commedia* tradition.

In 1967, Gascon became executive artistic director of the Stratford Festival in Ontario, assisted by John Hirsch* until 1969. He then directed the company by himself until 1974. There, he found almost ideal working conditions—generous budgets and elaborate technical facilities—which he was unable to find in his native city. His productions, in order to be as sumptuous as possible, kept the clarity and the human and completely functional character, which make up their principal characteristics. Since he was not himself of British descent, he simply delivered to the public his own interpretation of Shakespeare, avoiding the mannerisms to which some directors turn. But it was again with Molière and Feydeau that he knew his greatest public and critical success, rediscovering with these familiar authors all his strength, vitality, and existential joy.

Gascon also directed *Il Barbiere de Seviglia* and *Tosca* for the Montreal Opera. During his last years, failing health caused him to lose his certainty and spiritual vigor, although his collaborators said he had recaptured his old self on his return to Stratford to direct *My Fair Lady* in 1988. He died there. Many of the more than sixty productions he staged constitute brilliant chapters in the annals of Canadian theatre.

ADDITIONAL PRODUCTIONS: **In French:** 1952: *Celimare le bien-aimé* (Labiche); 1953: *Tartuffe*; 1956: *L'échange* (Claudel); 1957: *Un chapeau de paille d'Italie* (Labiche); 1958: *Le temps des lilas* (Dubé); 1959: *Venise sauvée* (Lebesque/Otway); 1960: *Les femmes savantes* (Molière), *Le dindon* (Feydeau); 1961: *L'Opera de quat'sous* (*Threepenny Opera*); 1962: *Richard II*, *Le Médicin malgré lui* (Molière); 1964: *Danse de mort* (Strindberg); 1965: *L'École des femmes*, *Lorenzaccio* (Musset); 1966; *La dalle des morts*

(Savard); 1975: *Long voyage vers la nuit* (*Long Day's Journey into Night*, O'Neill), *Les rivaux* (Sheridan/Roux); 1978: *Le Cid*; 1982: *Amphitryon* (Molière). **In English:** 1959: *Othello*; 1963: *Comedy of Errors*; 1965: *The Rise and Fall of the City of Mahagony*; 1966: *The Dance of Death* (Strindberg); 1968: *The Sea Gull, Tartuffe*; 1969: *The Alchemist* (Jonson); 1970: *The Merchant of Venice, Cymbeline*; 1971: *The Duchess of Malfi, There's One in Every Marriage* (Feydeau); 1972: *Lorenzaccio* (Musset), *The Threepenny Opera*; 1973; *The Taming of the Shrew, Pericles*; 1974: *The Imaginary Invalid, La Vie Parisienne* (Offenbach), 1981: *The Misanthrope*.

Jean-Louis Roux

WILLIAM GASKILL [b. June 24, 1930, Shipley, Yorkshire, England]. In one year, William Gaskill's directing credits grew from a Sunday night production of N. F. Simpson's *A Resounding Tinkle* (1957), to a main stage production of John Osborne and Anthony Creighton's *Epitaph for George Dillon* (1958) that transferred to London's West End and New York. Gaskill is regarded as the preeminent interpreter of Restoration and eighteenth-century comedy but a commitment to playwrights and new plays also distinguishes his career. During his six years as artistic director at the Royal Court (1965–72), Gaskill continued George Devine's* legacy of a writer's theatre, introducing new work by Edward Bond, John Arden, and John Osborne. Influenced by Brecht's* Berliner Ensemble, Gaskill promotes writer-director-designer collaboration to achieve the maximum impact from verbal and physical images. His earliest experience with a living playwright (N. F. Simpson) was formative, as was his introduction to Bertolt Brecht. These influences, in conjunction with Devine's comedy technique and mask work and Gaskill's own beliefs in the Konstantin Stanislavsky* tradition, are the foundations for Gaskill's directing. He first implemented these ideas in John Arden's *The Happy Haven* (1960) and in *The Caucasian Chalk Circle* (1962), offering the first major Brecht productions in Britain. *The Recruiting Officer* at the National (1963) was a pivotal production as it marked Gaskill's first attempt at applying a combination of Brechtian and Stanislavskian aesthetics to a classic.

Gaskill directed Arden's *Armstrong's Last Goodnight* and Brecht's *Mother Courage* in 1965 before accepting the position as associate director of the Royal Court. His first production there was Bond's *Saved*, a play that focused on violence and that led to a three-year battle with the Lord Chamberlain. The outcome of the battle ended censorship in England in 1968 and gave impetus to the Fringe Theatre Movement. Gaskill's association with Bond was especially fruitful since Bond's plays were epic in nature and benefited from Gaskill's Brechtian approach. After *Saved* (1965), Gaskill directed Bond's *Early Morning* (1968), *Lear* (1971), and *The Sea* (1973).

The gulf between alternative experimental theatre and mainstream theatre in England prompted Gaskill's revolutionary venture, *Come Together* (1970), an attempt to reconcile equally vital but different elements in the theatre. The attempt failed and prompted Gaskill's eventual association with the Joint Stock Company. He was more successful with his Restoration comedy ventures in such productions as *The Double Dealer* (1969) and *The Beaux' Strategem* (1970) at the National with Maggie Smith. In 1972, Gaskill resigned as associate director of the Royal Court, but he continued to direct classics, including *A Fair Quarrel* (1979), *She Stoops to Conquer* (1982), *The Relapse* (1983), *The Way of the World* (1984), and *Women Beware Women* (1986). Gaskill's directing approach in these productions changed the classical acting style, encouraging a simpler, less affected presentation. Gaskill's Joint Stock association (1974–83) was his last affiliation with one particular theatre. He returned to his experimental approach of collaborating with actors, writers, and designers to create works such as David Hare's *Fanshen* (1975).

Gaskill's work at the Royal Court, first under George Devine and then as his successor, established Gaskill's reputation, shaped his "style," and provided an outlet for new writers. His fight against censorship is a watershed in contemporary British theatre, as is his method of directing Restoration and eighteenth-century comedy by combining Brechtian and Stanislavskian aesthetics. Lindsay Anderson, a colleague at the Royal Court, described Gaskill's directing approach, observing that Gaskill "directs new plays like classics and classics like new plays" (Lewis, 18).

ADDITIONAL PRODUCTIONS: 1959: *One Way Pendulum* (N. F. Simpson); 1961: *Richard III*, *Cymbeline*; 1962: *Infanticide in the House of Fred Ginger* (Fred Watson); 1963; *Baal*; 1966: *A Chaste Maid in Cheapside*, *Macbeth*; 1967: *Three Sisters*, *Dingo* (Charles Wood), *Fill the Stage with Happy Hours* (Wood); 1970: *Cheek* (Howard Barker); 1971: *Man Is Man*; 1972: *Measure for Measure*; 1975: *The Speakers* (Heathcote Williams), *The Government Inspector*; 1976: *Yesterday's News* (Joint Stock creation, codirected with Max Stafford-Clark); 1977: *A Mad World, My Masters* (Barry Keefe), *The Madras House* (Harley Granville Barker*); 1978: *The Ragged Trousered Philanthropists* (Stephen Lowe); 1979: *The Gorky Brigade* (Nicholas Wright); 1980: *An Optimistic Thrust* (Joint Stock creation); 1981, *Touched* and *Tibetan Inroads* (Lowe); 1986: *Women Beware Women*; 1987: *Infidelities* (Marivaux, translated by Gaskill); 1988: *The Marriage of Figaro* (translated by Gaskill), 1989: *Man, Beast and Virtue* (Pirandello); 1991: *Black Snow* (Keith Dewhurst), *The Rules of the Game* (Pirandello).

SELECTED BIBLIOGRAPHY: Doty, Gresdna, and Billy J. Harbin, eds. *Inside the Royal Court Theatre, 1956–1981: Artists Talk*. Baton Rouge: Louisiana State University Press, 1990; Findlater, Richard, ed. *At the Royal Court: 25 Years of the English Stage Company*. Ambergate, England: Amber Lane, 1981; Gaskill, William. "Finding a Style for Farquhar." *Theatre Quarterly* 1 (January-March 1971): 15–21; Gaskill, William. *A Sense of Direction*. London: Faber and Faber, 1981; Lewis, Peter. "The Return of Larry's Other Lieutenant." *London Times* 6 September 1989; Ritchie, Rob. *The Joint Stock Book: The Making of a Theatre Collective*. London: Methuen, 1987; Roberts, Philip, *The Royal Court Theatre 1965–1972*. London: Routledge and Kegan Paul, 1986.

Judy Lee Oliva

VITTORIO GASSMAN [b. September 1, 1922, Genova, Italy]. Vittorio Gassman's mother, Luisa Ambron, was an actress in her youth. The Italian stage and film actor's father was German. Also a director and producer, Gassman was married to and divorced from actresses Nora Ricci and Shelley Winters. He has been called "Mattatore" (Matador) which means "great showman" because of his bravado performances which are in the grand style of nineteenth-century acting.

Vittorio Gassman studied at the Accademia nazionale d'arte drammatica, but left in 1943 for a professional acting career. After working as an actor for nine years in a number of companies, Gassman joined Guido Salvini's Teatro Nazionale in 1950, debuting as director as well as starring in Henrik Ibsen's *Peer Gynt*. In 1951, he received the Saint Vincent prize for his direction of Ugo Betti's *The Gambler*. The following year, he founded the Teatro d'arte Italiano, a new national company, which he co-directed with Luigi Squarzina.* In 1954, the Compagnia Gassman started touring with Dumas-Sartre's *Kean*, Sophocles' *Oedipus Rex*, and Silvio Giovanetti's *Sangua verde*. The company performed in Rome, Syracuse, and Milan.

In 1958, Gassman opened a Theatre Club in Rome with partner Dame Peggy Ashcroft. He wrote, directed, and played the leading role in *La Pulce nell'orecchio* (*A Flea in Her Ear*). Two years later, he founded the Teatro Populare Italiano whose philosophy was to produce rarely performed Italian classics. The theatre is said to have been the equivalent of the Théâtre National Populaire of Jean Vilar,* the Barraca of Federico García Lorca, and the Theatre Workshop of Joan Littlewood.* He opened the first season with the *Adelchi* of Alessandro Manzoni.

In 1979, Gassman opened the Bottega Teatrale Vittorio Gassman, a theatre school in Florence. A number of notable guest artists and teachers visited the school which has three resident teachers: Gassman, Alvaro Picciardi, and Paolo Giuranna. Gassman continues to direct, to tour and to be involved with student productions. Among his most recent work is the adaptation of plays by Aeschylus, Sophocles, and Euripides titled *The Riddle of Oedipus* and *The Offspring of Oedipus* performed in summer 1990 at the Teatro Greco in Syracuse.

ADDITIONAL PRODUCTIONS: 1949: *Ghosts*; 1951: *Oreste* (Vittorio Alfieri); 1952: *Hamlet*, *Tre quarti di luna* (Squarzina); 1953: *The Fugitive* (Betti), *The Persians*, *Leonora* (L. Troiani); 1958: *Irma la Douce* (translated and adapted by Gassman); 1962: *Marziano a Roma* (Ennio Flaiano); 1980: *Saul* (Alfieri); 1982: *Fone', la voce e la traccia* (Pietro Pasolini); 1983–84: *I misteri di Pietroburgo* (based on the written works of Dostoyevsky, created in collaboration with Gerardo Guerrieri).

SELECTED BIBLIOGRAPHY: Gambetti, G. *Vittorio Gassman*. Bologna: Cappelli, 1962; Gassman, V., and L. Salce. "L'educazione teatrale." Archivo Gassman, unpublished manuscript; Guerrieri, Gerardo. "Vittorio Gassman." *Scenario* 2 (1949); Lane, John Francis. "Rise of the Matador." *Plays and Players* 10 (June 1963): 18–19; *Quaderni del Teatro Populare Italiano* diretti da Luciano Codignola, Vittorio Gassman, Luciano Lucignani. Torino: Einaudi, 1960; *Vittorio Gassman Intervisti sul teatro* a cura di Luciano Lucignani. Roma-Bari: Laterza, 1982.

Shirley Vendrasco Burke

[THOMAS] MICHAEL GATES [b. January 9, 1944, St. Louis, Missouri]. A perfunctory examination of Michael Gates's background shows an academic who works primarily in African-American theatre at the California State University, Sacramento. A more rigorous look reveals that Gates has been instrumental in directing one of the oldest ongoing black theatre programs at a predominantly white institution west of the Mississippi. For two decades this program, along with its resident acting troupe, the Sons/Ancestors Players, has provided the only consistent offerings in black theatre in the Central California region. The importance of such a program is twofold: the academic area of black theatre has been fully supported by its host institution with praise by the National Association of Schools of Theatre (NAST), and the program has also served as a cultural extension into an adjacent community with few other opportunities to see black theatre.

Gates took the helm of this program in 1972 after cofounder Paul Carter Harrison left to research and study further. Harrison, considered by many as the dean of contemporary black theatre critical theory, had already guided the Sons/Ancestors Players to national attention through the world premieres of two well-known ritual dramas: Melvin Van Peebles's *Ain't Supposed to Die a Natural Death* and Harrison's own *The Great MacDaddy*.

Under Gates's direction this company continued to garner national attention by becoming one of the first black theatre groups to perform at the Kennedy Center for the Performing Arts, Washington, D.C., in April 1973. Gates has continued bringing new material and regional premieres of both mainstream and experimental work to Sacramento, an area which usually languishes in the shadow of the San Francisco Bay area. Gates's direction of experimental rituals such as Aisha Rahman's *Unfinished Women Cry on No Man's Land While a Bird Dies in a Gilded Cage* (1981) and Pearl Cleage's *A Puppet's Play* as well as traditional works including *Tambourines to Glory* (1980) and *Little Ham* by Langston Hughes are such examples. These examples reflect the variety of African-American literature usually promoted in larger media centers or areas with higher densities of black population and culture. Gates holds a B.F.A. in theatre from Howard University and an M.A. in theatre from the California State University, Sacramento.

ADDITIONAL PRODUCTIONS: 1972: *The Sty of the Blind Pig* (Phillip H. Dean), Sacramento; 1975; *Hotel Happiness* (Margaret Ford Taylor), Seattle, Washington; 1976: *The River Niger*, Oakland, California; 1977: *Little Ham* (Langston Hughes), Sacramento; 1981: *Unfinished Women Cry on No Man's Land while a Bird Dies in a Gilded Cage* (Aisha Rahman), Sacramento; 1983: *Zooman and the Sign* (Charles Fuller); 1985: *A Soldier's Play* (Fuller), Sacramento.

SELECTED BIBLIOGRAPHY: Michener, Charles. "The Young Troupes." *Newsweek* 14 May 1973: 106.

Thomas-Whit Ellis

FIRMIN GÉMIER [b. February 13, 1869 or 1870, Aubervilliers, France; d. November 26, 1933, Paris, France]. Firmin Gémier, noted actor, director, and producer, was born in Aubervilliers, a working-class suburb of Paris, the son of innkeepers. He was essentially self-taught and received his early acting training playing melodramas at neighborhood theatres such as the Théâtre de Belleville in a Paris working-class district. In 1882, he joined the Théâtre-Libre of André Antoine,* where he perfected his skills in a wide variety of roles. He continued at the Odéon and the Théâtre de l'Oeuvre, playing nearly 200 roles between 1892 and 1914, and achieving his first notoriety as Père Ubu in Alfred Jarry's *Ubu roi*, staged by Aurélien Lugné-Poe* at L'Oeuvre in 1896.

Gémier's growing interest in bringing theatre to all classes of society, not just to a privileged few, led him to explore ways of creating a people's theatre through a socially relevant repertory and mass spectacle. By 1902, he directed Romain Rolland's national epic *Quatorze Juillet* at the Renaissance and Emile Fabre's social chronicle *La Vie publique* (1902) about electoral politics in a provincial town. Romain Rolland's important treatise on people's theatre, *Théâtre du peuple* published in 1903, had a profound influence on Gémier's desire to create theatre by and for the people. That same year, he staged a huge, open-air spectacular involving 2,400 actors and 18,000 spectators as part of a festival celebrating the centenary of the entry of the Pays de Vaud into the Swiss Confederation.

In 1911, Gémier took to the road with his national traveling theatre ("théâtre national ambulant") designed to bring theatre to the people of France via a 1,600-seat circus tent and fully equipped proscenium arch stage, which was loaded onto thirty-seven wagons drawn by eight traction-engines. The experiment, the first in theatrical decentralization, was short-lived due to lack of financial support, but Gémier was ever determined to reach a broad-based audience. By 1917, he had eliminated footlights because they created a barrier between audience and play, had linked audience and play together by steps leading to the stage, and had (as he phrased it) plunged the audience directly into the dramatic action by having extras surging through the house.

In 1919, he experimented further by staging *Oedipus, King of Thebes* (by Georges de Bouhélier) as mass spectacle, with some 200 high-jumpers, javelin and discus throwers, at the Cirque d'Hiver. This was followed by a Provençal nativity play, Charles Hellem and Pol d'Estoc's *La Grande Pastorale*, directed by Gaston Baty,* with dancers and animals filling the enormous circus space.

In 1920, the French National Assembly created the Théâtre National Populaire, to be housed in the old Trocadéro Palace, and Gémier was chosen as its director. His project—to create an authentic civic theatre—was doomed to failure from the outset because of insufficient funding and lack of a permanent company. When he was appointed director of the Odéon in 1922, Gémier hoped to mount productions there that he would later transfer to the Trocadéro, but again he was disappointed.

During his eight years as director of the Odéon, he played and staged a varied repertory including fifty-one revivals and premieres of forty-three "great plays," as well as modern works by Henri Lenormand and Jean-Jacques Bernard. In 1927, he visited the United States with his Odéon company and played a season at the Jolson Theatre in New York.

Gémier, as an actor, is perhaps best remembered for his burly peasant, roughly cutting bread while smoldering over the dishonor of his child, in Eugène Brieux's *Les Trois Filles de M. Dupont*; his stark Tartuffe and Harpagon; or for his barbaric Shylock, with his broad strokes of grotesque comedy which stunned New York audiences when he was chased from the stage by the indignant mob and ran up the aisles and around the theatre.

Undoubtedly, however, Gémier's greatest contribution to the theatre of his time lies in his efforts to establish a people's theatre based on a repertory of national epics which dramatized the life of the people themselves.

ADDITIONAL PRODUCTIONS: 1903: Jacques Dalcroze's "Open-Air Spectacular," Switzerland; 1917: *Les Butors et la Finette* (François Porché).

SELECTED BIBLIOGRAPHY: Blanchart, Paul. *Firmin Gémier*. Paris: L'Arche, 1954; Brown, William Langdun. "Firmin Gémier, and the 'Théâtre du Peuple.' " Diss. Cornell U, 1978; Gémier, Firmin. "Creating a Travelling Theatre for the Provinces." *Theatre Quarterly* 6 (Autumn 1976): 28–30; Gémier, Firmin. *Le Théâtre*. Paris: Grasset, 1925; Gontard, Denis. "An Example of 'Popular' Itinerant Theatre: Gémier's National Travelling Theatre (1911–12)." *Western Popular Theatre*. Ed. David Mayer and Renneth Richards. London: Methuen, 1977: 123–32.

Philippa Wehle

SIR (ARTHUR) JOHN GIELGUD [b. April 14, 1904, London, England]. Related to the famous Terry clan, which included Ellen Terry and Edward Gordon Craig, as well as to leading Polish actors, Gielgud had an early interest in theatre. With a talent for drawing, he first intended to be a designer, but later decided upon acting and enrolled at the Academy of Dramatic Art (later RADA). After finding early success as an actor, he began directing and producing, thus initiating a long and celebrated career which (in a triumvirate with Lord Laurence Olivier and Sir Ralph Richardson) dominated English theatre. Gielgud was knighted in 1953.

Gielgud immeasurably influenced the English-speaking stage, and his critically acclaimed productions helped revive popular interest in Shakespeare. Influenced by his work with Harley Granville Barker,* the reforms of William Poel,* and Terry family stories of nineteenth-century performance, Gielgud bridged the old and new, and is credited with removing encrustations from Shakespeare. Gielgud's *Hamlet* (he had a directorial hand in five versions) was acclaimed as one of the best of this century, and his staging of *Romeo and Juliet* (1935), in which he alternated the roles of Romeo and Mercutio with Olivier, created a sensation. His experience in modern comedies—his first major West End appearance was as replacement for Noel Coward—allowed him to contribute a light touch to the most solemn tragedies, cultivating Shakespeare as entertainment as well as culture.

Gielgud also fostered ensemble acting. Influenced by the teamwork he shared at Lilian Baylis's Old Vic and by his work with Michel Saint-Denis,* Gielgud produced a famous 1937–38 season at the Queen's Theatre, and another in 1944–45, during which he kept his company together from production to production and employed long rehearsal periods. Throughout his career, Gielgud surrounded himself with good actors, avoiding the self-aggrandizement of the actor-manager tradition he inherited. His popular, critical, and financial success pointed the way for the Royal National Theatre, Royal Shakespeare, and English Shakespeare Companies.

In his directing, Gielgud emphasized the spoken word. With Shakespeare, he often preferred little or no movement and referred to some passages as arias. His own traits as an actor, including his famous voice and youthful physical awkwardness, contributed to his emphasis on text, as did his work with the Russian director Theodore Komissarzhevsky, who stressed rhythm in speeches and scenes. Gielgud brought poetic sensitivity, extraordinary understanding of text, and a keen intelligence to his directing and often created some of his greatest successes when he acted in his own productions, despite his penchant for focusing on the other actors and neglecting his own acting. Although his ensembles helped cultivate a director's theatre, he avoided the common director-centered tendency of slighting the contributions of actor and playwright. Intuitive and not dogmatic, he sought the style appropriate to each play and avoided forcing a concept on it. Gielgud was regarded as a kaleidoscope of ideas, and often changed approach from rehearsal to rehearsal. While his changeability on occasion frustrated actors and his notorious habit of speaking bluntly could offend, his conviviality and lack of malice usually offset his liabilities.

In the United States, Gielgud won two Tony Awards: for his one-person Shakespeare anthology, *The Ages of Man* (1959); and for direction of *Big Fish, Little Fish* (1960). Nevertheless, he did not always rise in triumph. In the 1970s, he directed a poorly received production of Edward Albee's *All Over* (1971) and found himself stymied by the disparate elements of a Broadway musical when he was fired as director of the revival of *Irene*. Unlike Olivier, Gielgud did not adapt easily to new theatrical trends although he did direct a controversial *King Lear* in 1955 that prepared the way for the innovative 1962 production by Peter Brook.* When Gielgud ultimately began acting in newer plays, such as David Storey's *Home* in 1970, he was successful. Similarly, although he mostly avoided film and television (with some exceptions, including a silent film in the 1920s), he found popularity in electronic media late in his career, especially with the movie *Arthur*. Gielgud has written a number of books and articles, most notably *Early Stages* (1939) and *Backward Glances* (1989), which combine theatrical anecdotes with his views on acting and directing.

ADDITIONAL PRODUCTIONS: 1932: *Romeo and Juliet*; 1933: *Richard of Bordeaux*; 1934: *Hamlet*; 1937–38: *Richard II, The Merchant of Venice* at Queen's Theatre; 1939: *The Importance of Being Earnest*; 1940: *The Beggar's Opera*; 1942: *Macbeth*; 1943: *Love for Love*; 1947: *The Importance of Being Earnest*, New York, *Medea* with Judith Anderson, New York; 1948: *The Glass Menagerie*; 1949: *The Heiress, The Lady's Not for Burning, Much Ado about Nothing*; 1951: *The Lady's Not for Burning*, New York; 1952: *Macbeth*; 1953: *The Way of the World*; 1954; *Charley's Aunt, The Cherry Orchard* (Gielgud adaptation); 1955: *Twelfth Night*; 1956: *The Chalk Garden* (Enid Bagnold), *Nude with Violin* (Noel Coward); 1957: *The Trojans* (Hector Berlioz, at Covent Garden, Gielgud's opera debut), *The Ages of Man*; 1958: *The Ages of Man*, New York; 1959: *The Complaisant Lover* with Ralph Richardson, *Five Finger Exercise* (Peter Shaffer), New York; 1961: *A Midsummer Night's Dream* (Benjamin Britten, at Covent Garden),

Big Fish, Little Fish (Hugh Wheeler); 1962: *The School for Scandal*, New York; 1964: *Hamlet* with Richard Burton, New York; 1965: *Ivanov*, New York; 1968: *Don Giovanni*; 1972: *Private Lives* with Maggie Smith; 1974: *The Constant Wife* (Somerset Maugham) with Ingrid Bergman, New York; 1975: *The Gay Lord Quex* (Arthur Wing Pinero).
SELECTED BIBLIOGRAPHY: Chinoy, Helen Krich, and Toby Cole. *Directors on Directing*. New York: Macmillan, 1985; Gielgud, John. *Backward Glances*. London: Hodder and Stoughton, 1989; Gielgud, John. *Early Stages*. New York: Macmillan, 1939; Gielgud, John. *Stage Directions*. New York: Random House, 1963; Gilder, Rosamond. *John Gielgud's Hamlet: A Record of Performance*. New York: Oxford University Press, 1937; Harwood, Ronald, ed. *The Ages of Man: An Actor at Eighty*. London: Hodder and Stoughton, 1984; Hayman, Ronald. *John Gielgud*. London: Heinemann, 1971; Herbert, Ian, ed. *Who's Who in Theatre*. Detroit: Gale Research, 1981.

David Carlyon

BILL (WILLIAM G.) GLASSCO [b. August 30, 1935, Quebec City, Canada]. The son of a prominent Canadian business executive, Glassco studied English literature at Princeton (A.B., 1957), Oxford (M.A., 1959), and the University of Toronto (Ph.D., 1966). From 1967 to 1969 he studied acting and directing at New York University, an experience which proved vital to his later work. In 1970, after some productions with Canadian community groups, he and his wife, Jane Glassco, operated their own summer stock company north of Toronto, called the Red Barn Theatre. That fall, he began workshopping new scripts with the Factory Theatre Lab, a fledgling Toronto company dedicated to producing new Canadian plays. There Glassco's acclaimed production of David Freeman's *Creeps* (1971), a bitter comedy set in a sheltered workshop, helped to touch off a new nationalistic movement in Canadian theatre.

In 1971 the Glasscos founded Tarragon Theatre in Toronto, to produce and develop new Canadian scripts under circumstances more attuned to public success than those at the Factory Lab. Housed in a converted warehouse seating about 170, Tarragon opened to much acclaim with a rewritten version of *Creeps*, and soon scored an even bigger hit with David French's *Leaving Home* (1972). In the ensuing three years, Bill Glassco staged premieres of four more plays by Freeman and French, and the English-language premieres of three plays by Michel Tremblay, probably Canada's most celebrated playwright. All these achievements pushed Tarragon Theatre and Bill Glassco to the forefront of theatre in Canada.

After a one-year sabbatical, Glassco broadened the Tarragon mandate to include foreign classics, often in new translations by Canadian writers. Between 1976 and 1982 he directed nine more premieres (or English-language premieres of Quebec plays) at Tarragon Theatre, including two each by French and Tremblay. He also staged a new translation (by French) of *The Sea Gull* (1977), co-directed *A Dream Play* (1977) and *Happy End* (1981) with puppetmaster Felix Mirbt, and accepted outside assignments in Vancouver, Ottawa, and Stratford.

In 1982 Glassco left Tarragon to embark on a free-lance career. In this period he continued to direct important new Canadian plays, including Judith Thompson's *White Biting Dog* (1984), French's *Salt-Water Moon* (1984), and Tremblay's *Albertine in Five Times* (1985). He also enhanced his reputation for staging international plays with excellent productions of Henrik Ibsen's *The Master Builder* (1983) and Caryl Churchill's *Cloud Nine* (1984), and began staging opera as well.

In 1985 Glassco became artistic director of Toronto's largest theatre company, CentreStage. There he directed premieres of several important new plays, including *Better Living* (1986) and *Nothing Sacred* (1988) by George F. Walker, and *1949* (1988) by David French. In 1986 Glassco helped to engineer a merger between CentreStage and a vital alternative company, Toronto Free Theatre. With this "supercompany," as the press called it, Glassco and his co-artistic director Guy Sprung sought to create a theatre which would focus on Canadian drama yet would be important enough to rival the nearby Stratford and Shaw festivals. While the company survived into the 1990s (renamed the Canadian Stage Company), the partnership did not. Glassco left in 1989 to resume free lancing, and Sprung was dismissed the following year. Since leaving Canadian Stage, Glassco has pursued lifelong interests by directing a Francophone company and by staging several operas.

Glassco's greatest influence has been in helping to create a new body of Canadian drama. He is particularly identified with David Freeman and David French, whose scripts he has helped to develop, and with Michel Tremblay, whom he also served as co-translator. Glassco's polished productions of the work of these writers, who are now major figures in modern Canadian drama, brought them early success at Tarragon and hastened their ascension to the larger stages of Canada's regional theatres. His greatest successes have been in an evocative style which might be called poetic realism. Despite his scholarly background, Glassco's occasional forays into classical theatre have been less happy. This may be attributed in part to values learned at New York University, in particular from teachers Peter Kass and Olympia Dukakis, who brought him to appreciate truthful interaction rather than grand effects. Such interaction—with playwrights as well as among actors—lies at the heart of Glassco's finest work.

ADDITIONAL PRODUCTIONS (premieres only): 1972: *Forever Yours, Marie-Lou* (Tremblay); 1973: *Battering Ram* (Freeman), *Of the Fields, Lately* (French); 1974: *You're Gonna Be Alright, Jamie Boy* (Freeman), *Hosanna* (Tremblay); 1975: *Bonjour, là, bonjour* (Tremblay), *One Crack Out* (French); 1976: *Artichoke* (Joanna Glass), Canadian premiere; 1978: *Le Temps d'une vie* (Roland Lepage); 1979: *Jitters* (French), *Damnée Manon, Sacrée Sandra* (Tremblay); 1980: *Mother Country* (Margaret Hollingsworth), *The Impromptu of Outremont* (Tremblay); 1981: *The Riddle of the World* (French); 1982: *White Boys* (Tom Walmsley); 1988: *The Real World* (Tremblay), *Midnight Madness* (Dave Carley); 1989: *The Invention of Poetry* (Paul Quarrington); 1991: *I Had a Job I Liked Once* (Guy Vanderhaghe).

SELECTED BIBLIOGRAPHY: Conlogue, Ray. "The Glassco Era." Toronto *Globe and Mail* 3 October 1981: E7; Johnston, Denis W. "Diverting the Mainstream: Bill Glassco and the Early Years of Tarragon Theatre." *Canadian Drama* 13 (1987): 121 73; Johnston, Denis W. *Up the Mainstream: The Rise of Toronto's Alternative Theatres, 1968–1975.*

Toronto: University of Toronto Press, 1991; Thalenberg, C. Eileen, and David Mc-
Caughna. "Shaping the Word: Guy Sprung and Bill Glassco." *Canadian Theatre Review*
26 (Spring 1980): 30–43.

Denis W. Johnston

JÜRGEN GOSCH [b. 1944, Coltbus, formerly German Democratic Republic].
Jürgen Gosch, a young actor turned director, premiered his first important production, Georg Büchner's *Leonce und Lena*, at the East Berlin Volksbühne
Theater in 1978. East German officials condemned the production for its Beckett-
like aesthetic. Since the authorities had recently reenforced rigid control over
the content and form of East German theatre, Gosch was denied further work
in his homeland. He joined the exodus of similarly condemned German Democratic Republic (GDR) theatre artists to West Germany.

Because of the excellence and eccentricity of Gosch's work in the GDR, the
West German theatre community watched his productions in their country very
closely. Gosch created a bitter controversy over interpretation when he portrayed
Hamlet as a dangerous neurotic who was as afflicted as the court by the rottenness
in the society (*Hamlet*, Bremen, 1980). After staging a radical reinterpretation
of Maxim Gorky's *Lower Depths* in Cologne in which Gosch transformed the
people of Gorky's milieu into the rich but lost souls of present day, Gosch
accepted a permanent position as director for Jürgen Flimm's highly visible city
theatre of Cologne.

There, Gosch worked exclusively with dramaturg Wieland Wiens and scenographer Axel Manthey to create thought-provoking and controversial classical
productions which examined the inability of contemporary society to feel or
dream. The mannered characters were framed in highly artificial, artistic spaces
reminiscent of expressionistic New German Art. Gosch's growing fame as a
director in Cologne also included an extremely successful staging of *Oedipus
Rex* (1984), a breakthrough attempt in minimalist, anti-heroic interpretation and
staging of ancient Greek tragedy for contemporary West German society.

In 1985, Gosch moved with Jürgen Flimm* and his company to the Thalia
Theater in Hamburg, where Gosch restaged the most successful of his Cologne
productions. In 1988 Gosch accepted the artistic leadership of the prestigious
Berlin Schaubühne. Unfortunately, his talents and style did not mesh with the
long-established Schaubühne ensemble. After a disastrous first production of
Macbeth, Gosch resigned to resume a free-lance career in Germany.

ADDITIONAL PRODUCTIONS: 1982: *Woyzeck, The Misanthrope*, Cologne; 1983: *A Midsummer Night's Dream*, Cologne; 1984: *Waiting for Godot*, Cologne; 1985: *Horatio*
(Corneille), Cologne; 1991: *The Sea Gull*, Bochum.

SELECTED BIBLIOGRAPHY: Merschmeier, Michael. "Der Formkünstler als Herausfor-
derer." *Theater heute* Oct. 1988: 3–7; Rischbieter, Henning, "Nicht die DDR sondern
sich selbst erklären." *Theater 1981* (*Theater heute* yearbook): 19–27; Rühle, Gunther.
"Über Regisseure." In *Anarchie in der Regie?* Frankfurt am Main: Suhrkamp Verlag,
1982.

Marna King

ALEKSEI GRANOVSKY [b. 1890, Moscow; d. March 11, 1937, Paris, France]. The child of an assimilated Jewish family, Aleksei Granovsky founded one of the most successful theatres in the Yiddish-speaking world, the Moscow GOSET (Russian acronym for State Jewish Theatre). Educated in theatre arts at Riga, St. Petersburg, and Munich, Granovsky worked as a director under Max Reinhardt* in 1913. He returned to Russia at the beginning of World War I and continued to direct in the spectacular Reinhardt tradition, mounting epic productions of *Oedipus*, *Macbeth*, and *Faust*. His desire to create a German-language theatre was thwarted by revolutionary and demographic dictates, and he was given a small Yiddish studio in its place.

Gathering an especially talented cadre of Jewish artists, musicians, and actors, Granovsky reinvented the aesthetic and theatrical possibilities of Yiddish drama, working in a language that he had only recently mastered. Beginning with *Evening of Sholom Aleikhim*, Granovsky sought to balance the needs of a traditional Jewish audience with those of younger, Yiddish-speaking Communists. Like his first set and costume designer, the young Marc Chagall, Granovsky used the idioms and folkloric life of the *shtetl* (Jewish village) in a refracted, avant-garde theatrical presentation. Non-Yiddish speaking spectators and foreign tourists soon flocked to the GOSET for productions that blended the best of Jewish comic entertainment with grotesque movement and musicalized speech.

Under Granovsky's exacting direction, Solomon Mikhoels and Benyamin Zuskin became reigning stars in the Jewish and theatrical communities of Moscow. Imitated on street corners and at parties throughout the twenties, their ironic and original characterizations gave the GOSET an enthusiastic following that rivaled only the largest theatres in the Soviet Union. In addition, Granovsky's pictorial sense of composition—with super-expressive scenes of dancing crowds against modernist sets—was widely praised. Photographs of GOSET productions were frequently reproduced in international journals.

At the conclusion of a highly successful European tour in 1928, Granovsky defected from the Soviet Union because of political and financial pressures. He returned to Berlin, where he worked with Reinhardt and the exiled Habima Players on a number of projects. Fleeing the Nazis, he settled in Paris, where he died in 1937.

ADDITIONAL PRODUCTIONS: 1922: *Koldunya*; 1923: *200,000*; 1925: *Night in the Old Market*; 1927: *Voyage of Benjamin III*.

SELECTED BIBLIOGRAPHY: Adler, Lois. "Alexis Granovsky and Jewish State Theatre of Moscow." *The Drama Review* 24 (September 1980): 27–42; Burko, Faina. "The Soviet Yiddish Theatre in the Twenties." Diss. Southern Illinois U, 1978; Gordon, Mel. "Granovsky's Tragic Carnival: *Night in the Old Market*." *The Drama Review* 29 (Winter 1985): 91–94; Rudnitsky, Konstantin. *Russian and Soviet Theater 1905–1932*. Trans. Roxane Permar. New York: Harry N. Abrams, 1988; Sandrow Nahma, *Vagabond Stars*. New York: Harper and Row, 1977.

Mel Gordon

HARLEY GRANVILLE BARKER. *See* BARKER

PAOLO GRASSI [b. October 30, 1919, Milan, Italy; d. March 14, 1981, London, England]. Paolo Grassi was a theatrical director, dramatic critic, and the founder-director of the first Stabile Theatre in Italy (Piccolo Teatro di Milano). His career culminated with his appointment as manager of Milan's Scala Opera.

Grassi began his theatrical career in 1937, and four years later he founded the avant-garde Palcoscenico (Stage), an experimental group which included Giorgio Strehler,* with whom Grassi collaborated at the Piccolo Teatro. From 1945 to 1947, while contributing to several theatrical publications, Grassi served as the drama critic for *Avanti!*, the daily publication of the Socialist party. He returned to directing in 1946, founded in Piccolo in 1947, and in 1956 organized the Venice Theatre Company, which toured abroad with Diego Fabbri's *Between Two Crosses* during the 1955–56 season.

Grassi was Italy's leading postwar advocate of a radical renewal of the Italian theatre. He believed that municipal theatres must be created, to which all social classes, especially the masses, will be attracted, and whose repertories would be modeled on those of the most advanced European theatres. The repertories chosen by Grassi, which were brought to countries throughout Europe and South America, maintained the highest cultural level and included works by Shakespeare, Molière, Carlo Goldoni, Carlo Gozzi, Henrik Ibsen, Henry-François Becque, Anton Chekhov, Jean-Paul Sartre, Bertolt Brecht,* Luigi Pirandello,* and Diego Fabbri.

In his call for renewal of the Italian theatre, Grassi opposed the theatre of "vision" through imagery, but sought instead a theatre that appealed to man's reason. In rejecting Samuel Beckett's vision of a crumbling world, the rituals and solipsism of Jerzy Grotowski,* and the anarchistic mystification of the Living Theatre, Grassi espoused Brecht's dramaturgy and aesthetic.

ADDITIONAL PRODUCTIONS: 1941: *Gli interessi creati* (Jacinto Benavente); 1946: *Giorno d'ottobre* (Georg Kaiser); 1955: *Processo a Gesù* (Fabbri).

Mario B. Mignone

ANDRÉ GREGORY [b. 1934, Paris, France]. Following his graduation from Harvard Univerity in 1956, Gregory studied with Sanford Meisner, with choreographer Martha Graham, with the Neighborhood Playhouse, and with Lee Strasberg* in the director's unit of the Actors' Studio. Subsequently, Gregory worked as a stage manager at the New York City Center and then at the Phoenix Theatre. He later coproduced *Deirdre of the Sorrows* (1959) and *The Blacks* (1961). His directorial debut came in 1962 with *P.S. 193*, produced at the Writers' Stage. With this production, Gregory began a career marked by imagination, innovation, and controversy.

In 1963, Gregory became artistic director of the Seattle Repertory Company, which he cofounded. Two years later he moved to Philadelphia and joined the newly established Theatre of the Living Arts company as artistic director. Gregory's play selection ranged from the conventional *Time of Your Life* to the challenging *Endgame* and also included one new American play per year. In 1966, Gregory directed Rochelle Owens's *Beclch*, which precipitated the termination of his contract. Believing that the theatre should provoke, Gregory's production included an innovative musical underscore, African-American dance, and nudity. The Board of Directors of the Theatre of the Living Arts and Gregory disagreed over the controversial production, and Gregory left. He then began the Inner City Repertory Company, a federally funded project that brought theatre to minority high school students in Los Angeles. He stayed with the project one year.

In 1968, New York University (NYU) invited Gregory to teach a six-week theatre seminar, despite some concerns regarding his ability to work effectively with others. Gregory worked well with the students, forming a company (the Manhattan Project) with them. NYU supported the project, providing the company with work space while the Rockefeller Foundation contributed a small stipend for salaries. Gregory decided to work organically, allowing the group's interactions to determine the nature of its theatre, rather than simply enacting scripts. Their first production, which was based upon *Alice in Wonderland*, evolved in 1970 out of the group rehearsal process. Strongly influenced by Jerzy Grotowski,* the company emphasized physicalization in its acting style and experimented with using actors as props and set pieces. For example, in *Alice in Wonderland*, actors served as mushrooms, tables, chairs, and even the rabbit hole. As much as possible, the actors created the physical illusion of Alice's descent into the rabbit hole and the world she discovered there.

Gregory and his students experimented with *Alice in Wonderland* for two years. Finally, in a small room without stage lighting, the company performed *Alice* before an appreciative audience. This production was innovative in a number of ways. The company's organic rehearsal process, which emphasized the contributions of the actors, permitted the company to adapt and modify the story to fit their particular needs while their interactions, rather than the text, determined the actions. Gregory did not "direct"; instead, he helped bring focus to the actors' work, advised them on the process, and served as a source of inspiration and motivation.

In recent years, Gregory's creative interests have turned to acting and to film. He co-wrote his most famous filmscript. *My Dinner with André* (1981), with Wallace Shawn. This two-character film featured Gregory and Shawn in a discussion about a variety of topics, including the state of the theatre, and during the course of the film, Gregory stated his artistic philosophy: that theatre should inspire spectators and assist them in understanding life's struggles.

ADDITIONAL PRODUCTIONS: 1963: *The Firebugs*; 1965: *Galileo*; 1966: *Uncle Vanya*; 1967: *Tartuffe*; 1968: *Leda Had a Little Swan*; 1969: *The Bacchae*; 1973: *Endgame*; 1974: *Our Late Night* (Wallace Shawn); 1975: *The Sea Gull*; 1983: *The Middle Ages*; 1984: *Protocol, War on the Third Floor, All Night Long*.

SELECTED BIBLIOGRAPHY: Herbert, Ian, ed. *Who's Who in American Theatre*. 16th ed. Detroit, MI: Gale Research, 1977; Little, Stuart W. *Off Broadway*. New York: Coward, McCann and Geoghegan, 1972; The Manhattan Project. *Alice in Wonderland: The Forming of a Company and the Making of a Play*. New York: E. P. Dutton, 1973; Novick, Julius. *Beyond Broadway*. New York: Hill and Wang, 1968; Zeigler, Joseph Wesley. *Regional Theatre*. New York: Da Capo, 1977.

Geraldine Maschio
Sullivan White

ULU GROSBARD [b. January 9, 1929, Antwerp, Belgium]. Ulu Grosbard was the son of a Jewish diamond and textile merchant. In the early 1940s, his family fled Nazi-occupied Belgium, eventually settling in Cuba. In Havana, Grosbard served as a diamond cutter for five years until he emigrated to the United States in 1948. His unusual first name is the result of Grosbard's own childhood mispronunciation of Israel, his given name. The nickname was adopted by his family, and Grosbard later had it legalized.

Grosbard received a B.A. and an M.A. in English from the University of Chicago, attended Yale Drama School for one year (1952), and then served in the U.S. Army until 1955. He was introduced into directing while he was working in the film industry, serving as an assistant to such directors as Arthur Penn* (*The Miracle Worker*), Sidney Lumet (*The Pawnbroker*), and Elia Kazan* (*Splendor in the Grass*).

One of Grosbard's earliest stage directing experiences was the 1962 Off-Broadway premiere of *The Days and Nights of Beebee Fenstermaker*. The writer, William Snyder, was a former Yale friend and had asked Grosbard to direct the play. Actress Rose Gregorio, who later married Grosbard in 1965, played Beebee and a then-unknown actor named Robert Duvall played the male lead.

Grosbard made his Broadway directing debut in 1964 with Frank Gilroy's *The Subject Was Roses*, featuring a young Martin Sheen. Gilroy went on to win the Pulitzer Prize for Playwriting and the Drama Critics Circle Award for *The Subject Was Roses*. Grosbard followed *The Subject Was Roses* with a production of Arthur Miller's *A View from the Bridge* (1965), a play that eight years earlier had been Grosbard's first directing project. Grosbard had expressed a desire to direct the rewritten script in an Off-Broadway venue, and Miller eventually granted him permission. This production of *A View from the Bridge* featured Duvall and John Voight, while Dustin Hoffman served as assistant director. With this production, Grosbard began a working relationship with Miller, and he subsequently directed the premier of *The Price* in 1968.

Grosbard is equally noted for directing the Broadway premiere of David Mamet's *American Buffalo* in 1977. Once again, the director used Robert Duvall in a cast that also featured actors John Savage and Kenneth McMillan. Although not known for directing comedies, Grosbard enjoyed a pleasant collaboration with Woody Allen in the 1981 premiere of Allen's *The Floating Light Bulb*.

In the early 1970s, Grosbard began directing films. He worked with Dustin

Hoffman on *Who Is Harry Kellerman . . . ?* in 1971 and *Straight Time* in 1978, directed Duvall and Robert De Niro in *True Confessions*, and De Niro and Meryl Streep in *Falling in Love*.

As evidenced by his frequent collaborations with Duvall, Grosbard enjoys working repeatedly with certain actors. He has been known to bide his time on a project until a specific actor becomes available. He is known as a detailed, exacting director, one who provides strong, yet unobtrusive guidance to his actors. Grosbard studied with Lee Strasberg* and admires the Method system of acting, a system that influences his work with actors.

Grosbard is as selective about the projects he undertakes as the actors he casts. From 1962 through 1982, he directed only ten plays and four films. He chooses to work only on projects in which he has a strong interest; however, once committed to a script, Grosbard meticulously nurses the play through production. His careful, thorough directing style lends itself to new play work, and consequently Grosbard has focused on contemporary playwrights.

Grosbard has received Tony nominations for directing *The Subject Was Roses* and *American Buffalo*. He received an Obie Award and the Clarence Derwent Award for Directing for the 1965 production of *A View from the Bridge*. Grosbard rarely works in regional theatres, choosing instead to work in New York City and in the film and television industries.

ADDITIONAL PRODUCTIONS: 1957: *A View from the Bridge*; 1966: *The Investigation*; 1967: *That Summer—That Fall*; 1968: *The Subject Was Roses* (Film); 1979: *The Woods*; 1981: *True Confessions* (Film); 1982: *The Wake of Jamey Foster*, *Weekends Like Other People*; 1990: *The Tenth Man*.

SELECTED BIBLIOGRAPHY: Cohen, Ron. "Ulu Grosbard: From Tears to Laughter." *Women's Wear Daily* 12 October 1982: 24; Mathews, James. "The Subject Is Ulu." *WPAT Gaslight Revue* July 1965: 43–60; Shewey, Don. "A Director with an Eye for the Telling Detail." *New York Times* 10 October 1982: 28, 37.

Andrea Urice

JAN GROSSMAN [b. 1925, Prague, Czechoslovakia]. Along with Otomar Krejča* and Alfred Radok* Jan Grossman was one of the most significant directors in postwar Czech theatre. Originally a literary critic, theorist, and editor, he entered the theatre shortly after World War II as a reader at the National Theatre in Prague. In the late 1940s, he moved to Brno, where he served as a dramaturg at the State Theatre and had his first experience as a director, staging Heinrich von Kleist's *The Broken Jug* in 1952. A significant association with E. F. Burian* in his Prague D Theatre followed in the 1950s, when Grossman became Burian's dramaturg and participated in the direction of several more plays. In the early 1960s, Grossman directed in a provincial theatre in Kladno, a short distance from Prague, and then began his most significant theatrical activity, serving first as dramaturg and then as director and head of drama at the Divadlo na Zábradlí [Theatre on the Balustrades] in Prague from 1962 to 1968, years when the nation moved from the restrictions of a rigid Communist system to the enlightened Prague Spring of 1968 and its motif of socialism with a human face.

The intimate Zábradlí theatre had been founded in 1958 as an outlet for many of the social frustrations of the day. Grossman brought a sense of literary and theatrical discipline and structure to the theatre, formulating a program or artistic policy that gave a special identity to the theatre and brought it sustained successes at home, international attention, and tours abroad. In this, he had the good fortune of being aided by Václav Havel, who became Grossman's associate, dramaturg, and resident playwright.

Grossman followed E. F. Burian's advice that the crucial thing in developing a theatre's program is not a matter of titles but of themes. Grossman's themes involved the concept of a theatre of conscious "appeal" to its spectators; that is, its plays would present carefully conceptualized and theatrically inventive models of social, political, psychological behavior that confronted audiences with implicit questions regarding the society in which they lived. During his tenure, the plays, which tended toward absurdist satires, were mostly original works like Havel's first three full-length plays, *The Garden Party* (1963), *The Memorandum* (1965), and *The Increasing Difficulty of Concentration* (1968) or adaptations of plays like Alfred Jarry's *Ubu Roi* (1964) and Kafka's *The Trial* (1966), both extensively revised and directed by Grossman.

Both Grossman and Havel resigned from the Zábradlí theatre for nonpolitical reasons even before the Soviet-led invasion and occupation of August 1968. For the next six years, Grossman directed abroad, principally in Holland and Switzerland, before returning to regular directing in Czechoslovakia (first at Cheb from 1974 to 1979; then in Hradec Králové, from 1980 to 1982; and eventually in Prague at a suburban theatre, the S. K. Neumann, from 1982 to 1988). The circle became nearly complete in 1988 when Grossman was able to accept an invitation to direct at the Zábradlí once again, in this case a highly admired staging of Molière's *Don Juan* in his own adaptation. Fact became more dramatic than fiction when, after the Velvet Revolution swept the previously jailed dissident Václav Havel to the presidency of Czechoslovakia at the end of 1989, Grossman staged Havel's previously banned *Largo Desolato* at the Zábradlí in April 1990. Later that same year, Grossman was once again named head of drama at the theatre, and in the summer of 1991, he was named artistic director of the theatre.

ADDITIONAL PRODUCTIONS: 1954: *Hagenbek* (F. Sramek); 1961: *Mother Courage*; 1973: *The Sea Gull*, *The Inspector General*; 1974: *Dobrý Voják Švejk* [*The Good Soldier Schweik*] (J. Hašek); 1975: *School for Wives*; 1979: *The Cherry Orchard*; 1981: *Herr Puntilla and His Servant Matti*; 1984: *Oedipus the King*, *The Duchess of Malfi*; 1987: *Who's Afraid of Virginia Woolf?*, *Measure for Measure*; 1991: *Hǒre, Hǒre, Strach, Oprátka a Jámá* [*Woe, Woe, Fear, the Noose and the Pit*] (K. Steigerwald).

SELECTED BIBLIOGRAPHY: Burian, Jarka. "Art and Relevance: The Small Theatres of Prague, 1958–1970." *Educational Theatre Journal* 23 (October 1971): 229–57; "Divadelní Bibliografie Jana Grossmana." *Divadelní Revue* 3 (1990): 97–99; Šormová, Eva. "Divadlo na Zábradlí." *Divadelní Revue* 2 (1990): 65–72; Tynan, Kenneth. "The Theatre Abroad." *The New Yorker* 1 April 1967: 99ff.

Jarka M. Burian

JERZY GROTOWSKI [b. August 11, 1933, Rzeszów, Poland]. Jerzy Grotowski spent his childhood in Rzeszów and Przemyśl, and spent the war period with his mother and brother in the village of Nienadówka near Rzeszów (later to become an important center of creativity). Grotowski's father, Marian, a forestry engineer and painter, was interned in a POW camp in Hungary, and his mother, a teacher, raised Grotowski and his older brother, Kazimierz. Grotowski was schooled in Nienadówka, Rzeszów, and Cracow, where he lived from 1950. After completing his studies at the drama department in Cracow (1951–55), the acting department, and directing department at Moscow GITIS (1955–56), Grotowski traveled throughout Central Asia during the summer of 1956, and after a short but incredibly intense political experience connected with Polish October 1956, he made his debut as a director at Stary Teatr in Kraków, staging Eugène Ionesco's *The Chairs* (1957). During the same period, he took "study trips" to the Jean Vilar* theatre in France and the Emil František Burian* theatre in Czechoslovakia, published articles about theatre in *Współczesność*, *Teart*, and other magazines, and gave a series of lectures on Oriental philosophical thought as Cracow's Student Club *Pod Jaszczurami* between December 1957 and June 1958. Beginning in 1959, he taught in the Drama Department at Państwowa Wyższa Szkoła Teatralna im. L. Solskiego in Kraków, while at the same time completing his studies and obtaining his diploma in October 1960.

After staging several of his own plays in Stary Teatr in Kraków, Teatr 13 Rzędów in Opole, and Teatr Polskiego Radia, Grotowski became artistic director of Teatr 13 Rzędów, and together with one of his closest collaborators, Ludwik Flaszen, from September of 1959 onward, he turned this institution into an avant-garde theatre, renaming it Teatr Laboratorium. Between 1965 and 1984, Wrocław was its home, and its name changed several times. From 1975 until its dissolution in 1984 it was called Instytut Laboratorium.

On August 12, 1982, during Martial Law in Poland, Grotowski left his native country and after a short stay in Italy and Haiti, he emigrated to the United States. He first worked at Columbia University as a drama professor, and in 1983, he became a professor at the School of Fine Arts, University of California at Irvine. In 1985, Centro di Lavoro di Jerzy Grotowski, founded by Centro per la Sperimentazione e la Ricerca Teatrale di Pontedera, was established.

There are four distinct periods in Grotowski's thirty-year career: the Theatre of Performance, from Grotowski's debut in 1957 (or 1959, the beginning of Teatr 13 Rzędów) to 1969; the Theatre of Participation, Active Culture, or Paratheatre (1969–78); the Theatre of Sources (1976–82); and Ritual Arts, which describes works conducted from 1985 in Italy. In addition, there was a short transitional period after Theatre of Sources while Grotowski was working in California (1983–85), which he called Objective Drama.

The best known of these is the first period, the Theatre of Performance. During this period, Grotowski actively sought what is most basic for the theatre, and he discovered this in the actor-spectator relationship. Beginning in 1960, he worked closely with architect Jerzy Gurawski to create different spatial compositions for each performance. Their "extreme reductiveness" became known as Poor Theater and assumed full shape in the final performances of *Książę Niezłomny* (Calderón-Słowacki, 1965), *Apocalipsis cum Figuris* (1968), and in his methodical, long-term work with actors.

Polish works and foreign classics formed the core of Grotowski's work during this period. These included *Kain* (Byron, 1960); Goethe's *Faust* at Polski Teatr in Poznan (1960); *Misterium buffo* (Mayakovski, 1960); *Siakuntala* (Kalidasa, 1960); *Dziady* (A. Mickiewicz, 1961); *Kordian* (J. Słowacki, 1962); Marlowe's *Dr. Faustus* (1963); and *Studium o Hamlecie* (Shakespeare-Wyspiański, 1964) as well as *Akropolis* (St. Wyspiański, 1962), *Książę Niezłomny*, and *Apocalipsis cum Figuris*.

During such productions, the audience was not supposed to view the performance but was to *witness* it, the performance progressing not *for* but *in relation to* the spectators. Grotowski expressed his theories for this type of theatre in *Towards a Poor Theater* (1968), a book which was widely distributed during the 1960s and became a bible for theatre experimentalists internationally. The book is regarded as one of the most important works about theatre written in the twentieth century.

Grotowski's work with the actor led him out of the Theatre of Performance into the domain of cultural studies. During the Theatre of Participation period, there were no "performances," since the boundaries between actors and audience ceased to exist, and the active participation of all present was assumed. Projects during this stage of Grotowski's career included *Święto* (1972); "Special Project," Uniwersytet Poszukiwań Teatru Narodów (summer 1975); and the so-called complex research program which included *Otwarcia—miasto* (Wrocłwa, 1976), *Nocne czuwanie*, and *Czuwanie* (1976–77), *Droga* (1977), *Przedsięwzięcie Góra* (Project: *The Mountain of Flame*) (1977), and *Drzewo ludzi* (1979).

Grotowski's third creative stage, the Theatre of Sources, was conceived as a transcultural experience. Grotowski conducted his work mainly in Brzezinka and Ostrowina near Oleśnica, but he also undertook research expeditions to places throughout the world where ancient customs were still alive. Between 1976 and 1982, he traveled to Haiti to study voodoo, to Bengal to explore traditions of Baul, to Nigeria to gather information on the Yoruba tribe, and to Mexico to examine the Huichol tribe.

Grotowski is one of a handful of international artists who truly changed the course of the twentieth-century theatre and, in this regard, may justifiably be compared with Konstantin Stanislavsky.* It was Grotowski who created (worked out) a new paradigm of acting and of thinking about acting. It was also Grotowski who defined a new hierarchy of theatrical needs and who opened completely different and heretofore unexplored and unrealized perspectives for artists. Grotowski's paradigm is based upon two principles. The first, changeability or constant existence in "in statut nascendi," involves the artist in permanent creative polemics with himself and results in his perpetual development; while the second, faithfulness to one's creative path, is complementary to the first and encourages consistency in one's explorations.

Since gaining international recognition for his work and his theories, Grotowski has conducted classes at drama schools worldwide. He has published (and still is publishing) texts which are significant, not only in theatre circles, but for their reflections on the state of contemporary culture and the place of a man in it. For his work, Grotowski has received numerous awards and recognitions, especially in France and the United States. He has received honorary doctorates from the University of Pittsburgh (1973), DePaul (1985), and Wrocław University (1991). In 1973, the American Institute for the Research and Study of the Work of Jerzy Grotowski was established in New York to disseminate Grotowski's discoveries and ideas, and beginning in 1990, the Center of Studies on Jerzy Grotowski's Work and of the Cultural and Theatrical Research has conducted activities in the former headquarters of Teatr Laboratorium.

SELECTED BIBLIOGRAPHY: Barba, Eugenio. *Alla ricerca del teatro perduto. Una proposta dell'avanguardia pollaca*. Padova: Marsilio Editori, 1965; Brook, Peter. *The Empty Space*. New York: Atheneum, 1968; Brook, Peter. *The Shifting Point 1946–1987*. Berlin: Alexander Verlag Gmbh, 1987; Burzylnski, Tadeusz, and Zbigniew Osiński. *Grotowski's Laboratory*. Trans. Bolesław Taborski. Warsaw: Interpress Publishers, 1979; Grotowski, Jerzy. "Around Theatre: The Orient—The Occident." Trans. Maureen Schaeffer Price. *Asian Theatre Journal* 6 (Spring 1989): 1–11; Grotowski, Jerzy. "Holiday." *The Drama Review* 17 (June 1973): 113–35; Grotowski, Jerzy. "*Jour saint*" *et autres textes*. Trans. Jerzy Grotowski and George Lisowski. Paris: Gallimard, 1974; Grotowski, Jerzy. *Towards a Poor Theatre*. New York: Simon and Schuster, 1968; Grotowski, Jerzy. "Tu es le fils de quelqu'un" (You Are Someone's Son). *The Drama Review* 31 (Fall 1987): 30–41; Kumiega, Jennifer. *The Theatre of Grotowski*. London: Methuen, 1986; *On the Road to Active Culture. The Activities of Grotowski's Theatre Laboratory Institute in the Years 1970–1977*. Editorial arrangement and press documentation by Leszek Kolankiewicz. Trans. Bolesław Taborski. Wrocław, 1979; Osiński, Zbigniew. *Grotowski and His Laboratory*. Trans. Lilian Vale and Robert Findlay. New York: PAJ Publications, 1986; Puzyna, Konstanty. "Grotowski's *Apocalypse*." *The Drama Review* 15 (Fall 1971): 36–46; Temkine, Raymonde. *Grotowski*. Trans. Alex Szogy. New York: Avon Books, 1972.

Zbigniew Osiński

JERZY GRZEGORZEWSKI [b. July 22, 1939, Łódź, Poland]. After graduating from Państwowa Wyższa Szkoła Sztuk Plastycznych in Łódź, and while finishing studies at the department of directing at Panstwowa Szkoła Teatralna in Warsaw, Jerzy Grzegorzewski began a career as a director and a stage designer with productions of *Kałkaskie koło kredowe* (1966) and *Biała diablica* (1967) in Łódź. Grzegorzewski belongs to the generation which made its debut during the period of rapid growth of alternative theatre and search for new theatrical forms in Poland, a period characterized by the work of Jerzy Grotowski,* Tadeusz Kantor,* and Józef Szajna.* Unlike artists like Szajna, however, Grzegorzewski did not form his own company, but worked instead with various theatres, thus preserving an artistic independence which manifested itself in the choice of repertoire he selected and the choice of methods he employed.

Grzegorzewski practices what has been called the Theatre of the Author, and he designs settings for most of his productions, his visual compositions being created and based on his own screenplays and dramaturgic elaborations. Literature (both drama and prose) forms a starting point and context for the performance, which manifests the individual expression of its creator. With the production of *Dziady* by A. Mickiewicz, a significant work in Polish classical literature, Grzegorzewski used the term ''Dziady-improvisations,'' which can be applied to many of his productions, but applies especially to those works derived from the novels *Ameryka*, *Ulisses*, and *Pod wulkanem*.

In Grzegorzewski's productions, the word is dominated by an image or coexists with it. This image does not have the features of a painting, however. Grzegorzewski creates spatial compositions that include the movement of the characters which are carefully timed with the movement of the real objects. Decorations are often constructed using musical instruments (i.e., stringed instruments, an open concert piano, or various mechanical objects such as pantographs, mangles, or electronic timetables). Grzegorzewski detaches these objects from their natural functions and transforms them with lighting. He treats space in a similar manner.

In the seventies, Grzegorzewski conducted a series of experiments in Teatr im. Jaracza in Łódź, Warsaw Ateneum Theatre, and Wrocław Polish Theatre aimed at expanding the stage area. *The Balcony* by Jean Genet (1972) was staged on both levels of the theatre, while for *Ameryka* by F. Kafka (1973) the cloakrooms, foyer, and the smoking room became the stage of Teatr Ateneum after the removal of the dividing wall. For *Śmierć w starych dekoracjach* by St. Różewicz (1978), the huge theatre hall of Teatr Wrocławski became the stage, and seating was moved to the stage, while the second part of ''Bloomusalem'' from *Ulisses*, staged at Ateneum Theatre in 1974, achieved the proportions of a happening. Its action took place in the several parts of the building, causing the audience to move in relation to the actors. At Centrum Sztuki Studio, where Grzegorzewski has been working as artistic director since 1982, he has returned twice (in *Dziady* and in a parody collage of Franz Lehar's and Emmerich Kalman's operettas *Usta milczą dusza śpiewa*, 1986) to his experiments with moving the audience.

Grzegorzewski's stage reality is obtained through similar visual elements, although each one creates a different system of associations. His directorial style is readily recognizable because of its ahistorical character and the poetic nature of his dream visions. Viewing his productions requires a similar theatrical sensitivity and literary preparation from spectators. Grzegorzewski's greatest success was his production of Wyspiański's *Wesele*, a drama that is close to his sense of aesthetics, staged in Stary Teatr in Kraków in 1977. The play to which he continuously returns, however, is Chekhov's *The Sea Gull*, which he produced in 1971, 1979, and 1990 and which led him from psychological motives to issues of creativity and the condition of the artist. Grzegorzewski has also had success with staging of two musical productions (*Opera za trzy grosze* by Teresa Budzisz-

Krzyżanowska, 1986, and *Usta milczą dusza śpiewa*), both exhibiting the clash of Grzegorzewski's style with the rigidity of the conventional.
ADDITIONAL PRODUCTIONS: 1976: *Ślub*; 1979: *Dziesięć portretów z czajką w tle* (Teresa Budzisz-Krzyżanowska); 1982: *Parawany*; 1984: *Pułapka* (Różewicz); 1987: *Tak zwana ludzkość w obłędzie* (based upon *na motywach sztuk* by S. I. Witkiewicz).
SELECTED BIBLIOGRAPHY: "Bloomusalem—Próby zapisu spektaklu." *Dialog* 12 (1974); Grodzicki, August. *Reżyserzy polskiego teatru*. Warszawa: Interpress, 1979; Sugiera, Małgorzata. "Poetyka teatre Grzegorzewskiego." *Dialog* 90.

Elzbieta Wysińska

SIR WILLIAM TYRONE GUTHRIE [b. July 2, 1900, Tunbridge Wells, England; d. May 15, 1971, Annagh-ma-Kerrig, Ireland]. A charismatic and beloved genius whose eclectic contributions to the English-speaking theatre were unparalleled, the peripatetic Tyrone Guthrie greatly influenced the direction of twentieth-century theatrical practice. Guthrie was largely responsible for the contemporary popularity of the thrust stage as an alternative to the proscenium arch, and he was the guiding force behind the creation and construction of two of the most significant noncommercial theatres in North America—the Stratford Festival Theatre in Ontario, Canada, in 1953, and the celebrated Guthrie Theatre in Minneapolis, Minnesota, in 1963.

A dedicated advocate of the repertory tradition, Guthrie was also influential during the early years of the Edinburgh Festival of Music and Art, reviving David Lyndsay's Scottish epic, *The Satire of the Three Estates*, in 1948. As one of the leading artistic lights at London's hitherto conservative Old Vic in the 1930s and 1940s, Guthrie also nurtured a progressive repertory company that was later to blossom into the Royal National Theatre of Great Britain.

Although he is perhaps best known for his often maverick contemporary interpretations of Shakespeare's classics, Guthrie's creative directorial hand also frequently touched the commercial theatre on both sides of the Atlantic, bringing noted productions of *The Matchmaker* (1955) and *The Tenth Man* (1959) to Broadway. His classic and contemporary work could also be seen, at various times, in Scotland, Finland, Germany, Israel, Australia, Poland, and elsewhere. A frequent director of opera at Sadler's Wells, Guthrie was also an actor, play-wright, and prolific author of books about theatre, and he had a considerable understanding of theatre management and architecture. He directed over 400 productions in a career which lasted almost fifty years.

The grandson of Irish actor Tyrone Power, Guthrie acted at Oxford University under the direction of James B. Fagan. After working for the BBC in Belfast, Guthrie became artistic director of the Festival Theatre, Cambridge, opening his tenure with a production of *Six Characters in Search of an Author* (1929). His production of James Bridie's *The Anatomist* (1931) opened London's West-minster Theatre, but his most celebrated work was to follow at the Old Vic, a theatre with which Guthrie was associated on and off from 1933 through 1967.

Following the death of Lilian Baylis, Guthrie served as the Old Vic's influential administrator from 1937 to 1945.

Guthrie's thirty-eight productions at the Old Vic rejected the theatre's stuffy propensity for pictorial realism, and included a sophisticated version of *Measure for Measure* (1933) which starred Charles Laughton and Flora Robson. Guthrie directed Laurence Olivier in *Hamlet* (1937), a romantic production which was later mounted at Elsinore, Denmark. He repeated that play in 1938, this time employing Alec Guinness in the uncut title role and a then-radical modern-dress concept. Ralph Richardson starred in Guthrie's extravagant and highly successful Old Vic version of *Peer Gynt* in 1945.

After an invitation from Tom Patterson, Guthrie headed for Stratford, Ontario, in 1952, initially to offer advice on starting a new repertory theatre. By the following summer, Guthrie's production of *Richard III* with Alec Guinness had opened the newly created Festival in a huge tent designed by close Guthrie collaborator Tanya Moiseiwitsch. A permanent building followed in 1957, and Guthrie directed at the increasingly influential Stratford Festival throughout the late 1950s.

After beginning what he hoped would become Canada's National Theatre, the constantly traveling Guthrie increasingly turned his attention to the American repertory theatre movement. Peter Zeisler convinced Guthrie that the New York theatre was in a hopeless state of decline due to financial paranoia, and the two men spread the word that they would establish a repertory stage free from commercial pressure in whatever city submitted the highest bid. Minneapolis provided ample funds and the Guthrie Theatre was the result in 1963. Like Stratford, the Guthrie was designed by Moiseiwitsch with an intimate open stage, and planned under Guthrie's close direction. Guthrie's modern-dress *Hamlet* starring George Grizzard was the successful first production, and Guthrie also directed Hume Cronyn in *Richard III* (1965).

Prior to his death in 1971, Guthrie returned home to direct the National Theatre Company at the Old Vic in *Tartuffe* (1967), starring John Gielgud.* His last production was the *Barber of Seville* (1971) at Brighton's Theatre Royal.

Most commentators agree that Guthrie was at his best when choreographing vividly theatrical Shakespearean epics in his typically experimental manner. He was particularly adept at handling large crowd scenes on the open stage, and he loved movement, pageantry, and flamboyant action. As John Gielgud noted, "he had a marvelous talent for filling the stage one moment and emptying it the next" (Rossi, 65). Guthrie was a master of pacing and tension, and his general conception of theatre was that it should be bold, broadly stated, and larger than life. The consummate showman, Guthrie's direction was always lively, and he frequently could not resist inserting special effects or clever bits of stage business into his productions, often to the chagrin of theatrical purists. He was known to rearrange Shakespearean texts to suit his directorial ends, and he would often compose ad-libs for participants in Shakespearean crowd scenes. He was one of the first directors to update classic texts to promote contemporary relevance; he directed *The Taming of the Shrew* (1954) at Stratford as a Wild West farce and gave the Old Vic's *Troilus and Cressida* (1956) a setting just prior to World War I. A down-to-earth pragmatist when it came to acting, Guthrie was generally critical of what he understood as the American method, mainly because he felt that it failed to teach good speech. He was not an advocate of theatre that was consciously moral or political, and preferred transporting his audience into some openly artificial theatrical world; he frequently likened directing to conducting an orchestral symphony. Guthrie hated the picture-frame limitations of the proscenium and claimed to have "abandoned the idea of illusion as the aim of theatrical performance," choosing to conceptualize theatre as the "direct descendent" of sacred ritual (Guthrie, *A Life in the Theatre*, 338, 350).

Perhaps more than any other single individual, Tyrone Guthrie established the twentieth century as the age of the director—a creative artist newly freed to explore the text without worrying about the cloying effects of tradition.

ADDITIONAL PRODUCTIONS: 1924: *The Triumph of Death*; 1929: *All for Love*, *The Rivals*; 1932: *Love's Labour's Lost*, *Follow Me* (Guthrie); 1933: *Richard II*, *Twelfth Night*; 1936: *Call It a Day* (Dodie Smith); 1937: *Henry V* (with Laurence Olivier), *School for Scandal*; 1938: *Othello*; 1941: *King John* (codirected with Lewis Casson), *The Cherry Orchard*; 1946: *Cyrano de Bergerac*; 1948: *Oedipus Rex*, *The Beggar's Opera*; 1950: *The Miser*; 1953: *Henry VIII*; 1956: *Tamburlaine the Great* (with Anthony Quayle); 1960: *H.M.S. Pinafore*; 1962: *The Alchemist*; 1963: *Hamlet*; 1967: *The House of Atreus*; 1968: *Volpone*; 1969: *Uncle Vanya*; 1970: *All's Well That Ends Well*.

SELECTED BIBLIOGRAPHY: Forsyth, James. Tyrone Guthrie, A Bibliography. London: Hamish Hamilton, 1976; Guthrie, Sir Tyrone. *A Life in the Theatre*. New York: McGraw-Hill, 1959; Guthrie, Sir Tyrone. *A New Theatre*. New York: McGraw-Hill, 1964; Guthrie, Sir Tyrone. *In Various Directions: A View of the Theatre*. New York: Macmillan, 1965; Guthrie, Sir Tyrone. *Tyrone Guthrie on Acting*. New York: Viking, 1971; Joseph, Steven, ed. *Actor and Architect*. Manchester, England: Manchester University Press, 1964; Leiter, Samuel L. *From Belasco to Brook*. Westport, CT: Greenwood Press, 1991; Rossi, Alfred. *Astonish Us in the Morning: Tyrone Guthrie Remembered*. Detroit: Wayne State University Press, 1980.

Chris Jones

H

ADRIAN HALL [b. December 3, 1928, Van, Texas]. Since the 1960s, the American resident theatre movement not only has produced an interesting and diverse repertory but has also developed much of the best directorial talent of the present generation. While the commercial theatre grew more conservative, these resident theatre directors presented a challenging mix of new and classical drama by employing the latest innovations and techniques in staging. Although sharing a commitment to the production of drama of quality, these new directors, including Gordon Davidson,* Mark Lamos,* Gary Sinise, and, notably, Adrian Hall, embrace a wide range of artistic sensibilities.

After graduating from college in 1948, Hall left his native Texas, where Margo Jones* had been an early mentor, to study theatre, first at the Pasadena Playhouse in 1951 and later in New York City with the director's unit of Lee Strasberg's Actors' Studio from 1961 to 1963. At the same time, he began directing at summer theatres around Houston and New York as well as at Off-Broadway houses such as Equity Library Theatre (Lillian Hellman's *Another Part of the Forest*, 1956; William Saroyan's *The Time of Your Life*, 1957; and Horton Foote's *The Trip to Bountiful*, 1959), the Maidman Theatre (Tennessee Williams's *Orpheus Descending*, 1959), and the Greenwich Mews Theatre (Sean O'Casey's *Red Roses for Me*, 1961), and for regional companies including the Barter Theatre, Abingdon, Virginia (Williams's *The Milk Train Doesn't Stop Here Anymore*, 1963) and at the Fred Miller Theatre, Milwaukee (Brendan Behan's *The Hostage*, 1964).

In 1965, Hall accepted the artistic directorship of the Trinity Square Repertory Company in Providence, Rhode Island, which propelled his rise to national prominence. Never shy about using unconventional staging methods or about presenting controversial subjects—e.g., James Purdy's *Eustace Chisolm and the Works*, 1974, which dealt openly with the issues of abortion and homosexuality long before it became common or accepted theatrical material—Hall quickly provoked great excitement, and occasionally dismay, with his local audiences by mixing techniques from vaudeville and the circus with some of the latest methodologies from experimental theatres in Europe. With the close collaboration of resident designer Eugene Lee, Hall presented an interesting array of environmental stagings often employing the architecture of real spaces, such as Friedrich Dürrenmatt's *The Visit* (1986), which was staged inside Providence's old Union Train Station. Hall has also adapted and directed the work of contemporary novelists, journalists, and diarists with notable success in productions which include Robert Lowell's *The Old Glory* (1967); Robert Penn Warren's *Brothers to Dragons* (1972); *A New Play: Jonestown* by James Reston, Jr. (1984); Richard Wright's *Native Son* (1985); and Jack Henry Abbott's *In the Belly of the Beast* (1986).

For all the unconventionality of his stagings, Hall insists that production values be kept at a sophisticated but simple level: unit settings, white lighting, contemporary costuming, and an ensemble effort of actors and technicians working in close and continuous collaboration from the choice of the work to the end of its run. Many of Hall's productions have been transferred to Broadway, presented internationally, or adapted for television. Under Hall's direction the Trinity Rep was the first American company to be invited to the Edinburgh Festival (1968). The company also received an Antoinette Perry (Tony) Award in 1981 as a noteworthy American repertory company. In addition to his artistic acumen, Hall is an energetic and indefatigable organizer who has built and maintained a large ensemble of full-time performers who have remained together for most of their professional careers.

Hall returned to Texas in 1983–89 to lead the Dallas Theatre Center while at the same time retaining his leadership of Trinity Rep until 1989 when he was replaced by Anne Bogart,* who was dismissed in 1990. Hall continues to maintain an intimate association with the Providence company while accepting directorial assignments around the country and abroad.

ADDITIONAL PRODUCTIONS: 1971: *Son of Man and the Family* (by Hall and Richard Cumming about Charles Manson); 1973; *Feasting with Panthers*, from the works of Oscar Wilde, 1979: *Buried Child* (Shepard), premiere, Yale Rep; 1982: *The Hot House* (Pinter); 1983: *The Tempest, Fool for Love* (Shepard); 1990: *Timon of Athens*, New York Shakespeare Festival; 1991: *King Lear*, American Repertory Theatre, Boston.

SELECTED BIBLIOGRAPHY: Bartow, Arthur. *The Director's Voice.* New York: Theatre Communications Group, 1988: 140–57; Bartow, Arthur. "Double Jeopardy." *American Theatre* 2 (February 1986): 10–17; Block, Carolyn, "Adrian Hall" (interview). *Theater* 15 (Spring 1984): 14–19; Sommers, Michael. "Adrian Hall: 25 Years at Trinity Rep." *Theatre Crafts* (November 1988: 59–63, 76–81.

Thomas Leff

SIR PETER HALL [b. November 22, 1930, Bury St. Edmunds, Suffolk, England]. While he was still an undergraduate of English and drama at Cambridge University, Peter Hall directed his first professional play, Luigi Pirandello's *Enrico IV* (1953), at the London Arts Theatre. Within two years, as the new director of the Arts Theatre, he staged the English-language premiere of Samuel Beckett's *Waiting for Godot*, and in 1957, he founded his own short-lived company, the International Playwrights Theatre. By 1959, Hall had directed his landmark production of *A Midsummer Night's Dream* with Charles Laughton, Vanessa Redgrave, Albert Finney, and Ian Holm for the Royal Shakespeare Theatre in Stratford. The play was staged as a marriage ceremony in a permanent setting designed by Lila de Nobili to resemble an Elizabethan courtyard. The production was televised in America; revived in 1962, 1963, and 1967; and filmed in 1968. Thus began Hall's multifaceted career as artistic administrator, producer, and director that has spanned four decades during which his output has been enormous. He is credited with having produced over 700 shows, directed over 150 scripts, mounted at least 15 operas, and made 7 films.

As managing director of the Royal Shakespeare Company (RSC) from 1960 until 1968, Hall turned the former summer stock company into a permanent ensemble with a winter home at the Aldwych Theatre in London and a summer home in Stratford. Besides bringing in such notable directors as Michel Saint-Denis,* Peter Brook,* Paul Scofield, and John Barton* and producing more than 100 productions during his tenure, Hall established a studio company and a training school. His important Shakespearean interpretations for the company included *Troilus and Cressida* (1960, 1961) set in a huge sandbox designed by Leslie Hurry; *The Wars of the Roses* (1963), an adaptation of the *Henry VI* plays and *Richard III*, which was expanded in 1964 to include *Richard II*, *Henry IV, Part I and Part II*, *Henry V*, and *Edward IV*; *Hamlet* with David Warner as the young college student in rebellion against the establishment; and *Macbeth* (1967), which starred Paul Scofield and utilized the symbolic device of blood-red carpeting that revealed a bleached white floor underneath.

Of particular note was Hall's directorial approach to *A Cycle of Seven History Plays*. Experimenting with the idea of joint direction, Hall oversaw the shared directorial responsibility of a company of directors composed of John Barton,* Clifford Williams,* Peter Wood, and Frank Evans. Each of the RSC Shakespeare productions reflected Hall's symbolic realistic style. His interpretations emphasized the contemporary political and social relevance of each play and used imagistic settings, often designed by John Bury, to symbolically reflect a central theme of the text. The stage space thus became a key element in revealing the playwright's intentions.

Hall began his two-decade collaboration with Harold Pinter by codirecting *The Collection* with the playwright in 1961. Productions of *The Homecoming* (1965, revived in New York in 1967), were followed by *Landscape* and *Silence* (1969), *Old Times* (1971), *No Man's Land* (1975), *Betrayal* (1978 and 1980), and *Other Places* (1983). Hall's approach to directing Pinter developed from his concept that the playwright's text was sacrosanct. His interpretation would surface during a rigorous and systematic rehearsal process. First, he would "expose the melodrama" and explore the emotional intensity underlying each play. Then, each actor would "construct a mask" to disguise these emotions of the characters. From this point, rehearsals proceeded with the precise execution of Pinter's language, stage directions, pauses, and silences. In final stages, Hall shaped and tightened the scenes which had emerged in rehearsal, and "orchestrated" the play. The productions which resulted from this process won Hall the reputation as Harold Pinter's definitive interpreter.

Hall's subsequent career included serving as the codirector of the Royal Opera House, Covent Garden, in 1971; becoming the artistic director of the National Theatre in 1972; and serving as artistic director of the Glyndebourne Festival Opera in 1984. Upon leaving the National Theatre in 1988, Hall founded the Peter Hall Company, whose most notable productions were *Orpheus Descending* (1988) with Vanessa Redgrave and *The Merchant of Venice* (1989) with Dustin Hoffman and Judi Dench. In his various roles as artistic director and as an associate professor of drama for the University of Warwick since 1966, Peter Hall has had an enormous impact on English theatre. His emphases on researching a play's meaning and background, on actors speaking Shakespearean verse or Beckett's and Pinter's poetic drama with complete understanding of its meaning and rhythms, and on simple symbolic staging in which the text is of primary importance is reflected in current theatrical training across Great Britain and the United States. Under his tutelage, an entire generation of designers, directors, and actors have honed their craft.

For over thirty-nine years, Peter Hall has done exactly what he has enjoyed most, directing plays and running his own theatre. As he has said, "It's a huge privilege, trying to spend your life getting inside the head of Shakespeare, or Chekhov, or Wagner and working out how they really wanted to see their work interpreted on the stage" (Clipping, Theatre Collection, New York Public Library). In recognition of his influence and contributions to the art of theatre, Peter Hall was knighted in 1977 and awarded the Critics Circle Award in 1988.

ADDITIONAL PRODUCTIONS: 1954: *Blood Wedding* (Federico García Lorca), *The Immoralist* (André Gide), *The Lesson* (Eugène Ionesco), *South*; 1955: *Mourning Becomes Electra*, *Burnt Flower-Bed* (Ugo Betti), *Listen to the Wind*; 1956; *The Waltz of the Toreadors*, *Gigi*, *Love's Labour's Lost*; 1957; *Camino Real*, *Cymbeline*; 1958: *Cat on a Hot Tin Roof*, *Twelfth Night*, *Brouhaha*, *Shadow of Heroes*; 1959: *Madame De . . .*, *A Traveler without Luggage* (Jean Anouilh), *Coriolanus*, *The Wrong Side of the Park*, 1960: *Two Gentlemen of Verona*; 1961: *Ondine* (Jean Giraudoux), *Becket* (Jean Anouilh, with Eric Porter and Christopher Plummer), *Romeo and Juliet*; 1964: *Eh?* (Henry Livings); 1965: *The Government Inspector*; 1966: *The Staircase*(Charles Dryer); 1969: *A Delicate Balance*, *Dutch Uncle*; 1970: *The Battle of Shrivings*; 1972: *All Over* (Edward Albee), *Via Galactica*; 1973: *The Tempest* (revived 1988); 1974: *John Gabriel Borkman*, *Happy Days*; 1975: *Judgement*; 1977: *Tamburlaine the Great*, *Bedroom Farce* (Alan Ayckbourn); 1978: *Volpone*, *The Country Wife*, *The Cherry Orchard*; 1979: *Amadeus* (revived in 1980 in New York); 1980: *Othello*; 1981: *Family Voices*; 1982: *The Importance of Being*

Earnest, The Oresteia; 1983: *Jean Seberg* (Marvin Hamlisch); 1984: *Coriolanus, Animal Farm*; 1985: *Yonadab* (Peter Shaffer); 1986: *The Petition*; 1987: *Antony and Cleopatra*; 1988: *The Winter's Tale, Cymbeline, Twelfth Night*; 1989: *The Trojan Women*; 1990: *The Rose Tattoo, Born Again* (Eugène Ionesco), *The Wild Duck*.

SELECTED BIBLIOGRAPHY: Addenbrooke, David. *The Royal Shakespeare Company: The Peter Hall Years*. London: William Kimber and Co., 1974; Goodwin, John, ed. *Peter Hall's Diaries*. London: Hamish Hamilton, 1983; Goodwin, John, ed. *Royal Shakespeare Company, 1960–1963*. London: Reinhardt, 1964; Gow, Gordon. "In Search of a Revolution." *Films and Filming* 14 (September 1969): 40–46; Hall, Peter. "Avoiding a Method." *Theatre Arts* August–September 1963: 24–25; Hall, Peter. "*Gambit* Interview: Chris Barlas Talks to Peter Hall." *Gambit: International Theatre Review* 7:28 (1976): 19–39; Hall, Peter. "Shakespeare and the Modern Director." *Performing Arts* January 1968: 19–20; Itzin, Catherine, and Simon Trussler. "Peter Hall: Directing Pinter." *Theatre Quarterly* 4 (November 1974–January 1975): 4–17; Lustig, Vera. "Born Again?" *Plays and Players* 444 (November 1990): 10–13.

Andrea J. Nouryeh

JED HARRIS [b. Jacob Hirsch Horowitz, February 25, 1900, Lemburg, Austria; d. November 15, 1979, New York, New York]. After a childhood in an unloving household and a disillusioning fling with academia at Yale, Harris began his show business career in 1921 as a reporter for *Billboard*. His name first appeared in a theatre program for A. A. Milne's *The Romantic Age* in 1922, but as an associate producer, Harris was allowed no creative contribution. Somewhat disillusioned by his experience, he turned to press agentry, working first for the Shubert organization and then the successful Chicago run of the comedy *Applesauce*.

His first full production credit was *Weak Sisters* in 1925, followed shortly by *Love 'Em and Leave 'Em* (with George Abbott* directing) in 1926. Both were successful enough to establish Harris as an important Broadway producer. It was during the 1926, 1927, and 1928 seasons, in fact, that Harris earned the nickname "The Meteor" and appeared on the cover of *Time* magazine. During these two seasons, he produced and helped (sometimes intrusively) write and direct four of Broadway's biggest hits: *Broadway* (1926); *Coquette* (1927); *The Royal Family* (1927); and *The Front Page* (1928). Each production exhibited what became Harris trademarks: quick-paced dialogue and movement; an emphasis on physical humor when possible; a questioning of middle-class values; and close attention to scenic detail.

Harris announced his retirement from the theatre at the end of the 1928 season, but he returned in 1930 to produce and direct *Uncle Vanya* (featuring Lillian Gish). This seemingly out-of-character choice demonstrated an hitherto undiscovered Harris skill—the ability to communicate with and inspire actors. Conversely, Harris could also be monstrously egotistical and extremely cruel to those around him. Over the course of his career, he managed to anger and alienate some of the most prestigious, talented people in the theatre. While nearly everyone who worked with him agreed that he was a gifted producer and director, few wished to work with him twice. After the success of *Uncle Vanya*, Harris had complete artistic and financial control of all his productions. Because he usually created a box-office success, actors, writers, and designers usually deferred to his demands.

Harris subscribed to no particular artistic movement or theory. He was a product of the commercial theatre, and consequently his first concern was audience appeal. This, however, does not mean that Harris never took chances. A gambler in temperament, Harris was self-confident enough to believe that he could make an audience like a play, and as a result, the chances he took were daring ones. In 1937, his production of *The Green Bay Tree* explored homosexuality; in the same year, he successfully presented what was considered box-office poison, an Ibsen play (*A Doll's House*); and in 1947, he revamped a recently failed adaptation of a Henry James novel into the Broadway success *The Heiress*. His biggest gamble, however, was *Our Town* (1938). The quiet simplicity of this production demonstrated another Harris quality, the ability to adapt his skills to the demands of a particular script.

Even successes such as *Our Town*, however, couldn't compensate for the difficulties that Harris himself presented. His irascibility eventually created financial hardships, so much so that Harris was forced to hire out as a director for other producers. He even "demeaned" himself by producing a television series ("The Billy Rose Show," 1950). Although he did not die until 1979, the last major stage production he directed was *The Crucible* in 1953.

ADDITIONAL PRODUCTIONS: 1933: produced and directed *The Lake* (Dorothy Massingham and Murray MacDonald) with Katharine Hepburn.

SELECTED BIBLIOGRAPHY: Behrman, S. N. *People in a Diary*. Boston: Little, Brown, 1972; Gordon, Ruth. *My Side*. New York: D. I. Fine, 1986; Gottfried, Martin. *Jed Harris: The Curse of Genius*. Boston: Little, Brown, 1984; Harris, Jed. *A Dance on a High Wire*. New York: Crown, 1979; Harris, Jed. *Watchman, What of the Night?* New York: Doubleday, 1963.

Alan Kreizenbeck

KAREL HUGO HILAR (BAKULE) [b. November 1, 1885, Sudoměřice, Bohemia, Czechoslovakia; d. March 6, 1935, Prague, Czechoslovakia]. Like several other twentieth-century directors, Jacques Copeau* for example, Hilar came to theatre by way of literature. At first a poet, critic, and essayist strongly influenced by the French symbolists, he subsequently earned a Ph.D. in classical philology and became an editor as well as theatre reviewer before becoming directly involved with theatre operations. In 1910, he became a secretary and reader at the Vinohrady municipal theatre, which was second in Prague only to the National Theatre. Within a few years, his activities began to embrace directing, and by 1914 he was chief of drama at the Vinohrady. During the next twenty years (six at the Vinohrady and fourteen at the National Theatre), Hilar dominated Czech theatre with bold, large-scale productions of classics as well as contemporary Czech and foreign drama that brought international attention to Czech theatre.

A colorful, dynamic personality, Hilar seemed instinctively attracted to the concentration, intensity, and aggressiveness of the expressionistic mode, to which he brought his own sophisticated literary sense as well as a Dionysian sense of theatre as celebration and rite. Not satisfied with the subtleties of an Anton Chekhov, the intellectual wit of a Bernard Shaw, or the discursive social problem play, Hilar was instead attracted to the Greeks (*Medea*, 1921; *Oedipus*, 1932), Shakespeare (*Antony and Cleopatra*, 1917; *Coriolanus*, 1921), August Strindberg (*Dance of Death*, 1917; *Queen Christina*, 1922), and Eugene O'Neill (*Strange Interlude*, 1930; *Mourning Becomes Electra*, 1934), as well as to other works such as Molière's *Le Malade Imaginaire*, 1921; Sheridan's *School for Scandal*, 1916; and the Čapek brothers' *Insect Comedy*, 1922, which contained elements of the satiric, grotesque, and baroque. Essentially apolitical, Hilar was rarely drawn to plays with an ideological message; it was as if he, like his productions, were larger than life, not to be limited by matters of sociopolitical concern.

Hilar always worked in large theatres, and he seemed to have an intuitive feel for expressive staging that exploited time, space, and movement, often staging large-cast productions that challenged his mastery of crowd composition and movement. Although Hilar embodied Gordon Craig's vision of the director as all-controlling master artist of the theatre, he knew that his creativity required strong contributions from designers and actors. Most of his productions were done in close collaboration with Vlastislav Hofman, the first great Czech stage and costume designer, although Hilar also worked productively with other Czech designers (e.g., Bedrich Feuerstein and Antonin Heythum) who became internationally known.

Hilar's work with actors was more stormy and problematical. Shaping and planning a production in great detail, Hilar insisted that his actors subordinate their individual creativity to his overall vision. Above all, Hilar was concerned with the dynamics, large strokes, and total orchestration of a production; therefore, he had little patience with actors who insisted on their individual interpretations, just as he never revealed much interest in a Stanislavskian concern with internal truth in acting. Nevertheless, some of Czechoslovakia's greatest actors, Ladislav Pešek among them, swore by his directorial inspiration and support.

It was at the Vinohrady theatre that Hilar did his most striking, expressionistically charged productions. His reputation became such that he was the logical choice to replace Jaroslav Kvapil* in 1921 as head of drama at the National Theatre, which had drifted aimlessly after Kvapil's departure in 1918. Almost a generation younger than Kvapil, Hilar represented the nervous drama of the new century, whereas Kvapil was more nearly identified with turn-of-the-century impressionistic harmony. Hilar's first great creative period culminated with the production of *Romeo and Juliet* in 1924, by which time his expressionistic staging had become modulated and enriched by his greater interest in human psychology.

Shortly thereafter, Hilar suffered a major stroke which incapacitated him for more than a year, after which his work became more restrained, more thoughtful, more focused on inner complexities, but without losing its mastery of large-scale, expressive stage mounting. *Hamlet, Oedipus the King*, and *Mourning Becomes Electra* were the most outstanding productions of his last phase, which ended with a second and fatal stroke in 1935. Hilar's greatest legacy was perhaps his influence on younger directors, whom he encouraged and nurtured. Jiří Frejka* was the most outstanding of these, and Frejka in turn became a significant influence on the following generation, exemplified in such leading postwar directors as Jaromír Pleskot and Otomar Krejča.*

ADDITIONAL PRODUCTIONS: 1914: *Penthesilea* (Kleist); 1915: *The Snob* (Sternheim); 1916: *The School for Scandal*; 1917: *Antony and Cleopatra*; 1919: *The Hussites* (Arnost Dvorak), *The Cid*; 1920: *The Dawns* (Emile Verhaeren); 1922: *Edward II* (Marlowe); 1926: *Hamlet*; 1931: *Elizabeth of England* (F. Bruckner); 1932: *Marriage* (N. Gogol); 1933: *Midsummer Night's Dream*.

SELECTED BIBLIOGRAPHY: Burian, Jarka. "High Points of Theatre in the First Czechoslovak Republic." *Modern Drama* 27 (March 1984): 98–111; Burian, Jarka. "K. H. Hilar and the Early Twentieth-Century Czech Theatre." *Theatre Journal* 34 (March 1982): 55–76; Hilar, K. H. *Boje Froti Včerejšku 1915–1925* [*Battles against the Past*]. Prague: Fr. Borový, 1925; Hilar, K. H. *Pražská Dramaturgie* [*Prague Dramaturgy*]. Prague: Sfinx Janda, 1930; Rutte, Miroslav, and František Bartoš. *The Modern Czech Scene.* Prague: Vladimír Zikeš, 1938; Vočadlo, Otakar. "The Theatre and Drama of Czechoslovakia." *The Theater in a Changing Europe.* Ed. T. H. Dickinson. New York: Henry Holt, 1937.

Jarka M. Burian

JOHN S. HIRSCH [b. May 1, 1930, Siofók, Hungary; d. August 1, 1989, Toronto, Canada]. When John Hirsch emigrated to Winnipeg in 1947, he was surprised to find no professional theatre; indeed, there was very little in all of Canada. This artist would become a figure second to none in the development of world-class theatre in his adoptive country. Though his theatrical enthusiasms included puppet shows, children's theatre, musical comedy, and burlesque, Hirsch achieved his greatest distinction as a director of classics: Shakespeare was his predominant passion. His dedication to his art was so absolute and so eloquent that he came to be seen as a "theatre rabbi," important also to the growth of nonprofit theatre in the United States.

Born into a highly cultured upper-middle-class family, János Hirsch was not yet fourteen when the Nazis invaded Hungary. The boy was sent to Budapest, where he attended school, ahead of the roundup of Siofók Jews which led to the extermination of his immediate family: father, mother, and younger brother. Hirsch remained in the city's ghetto with his beloved grandfather; the old man died near the war's end, and the teenaged survivor eventually became part of the first boatload of war orphans sent to Canada. For the rest of his life John Hirsch would deal with his memories of atrocity through his work. Many of his best productions were grounded in his intimate knowledge of war, death, and evil.

From childhood Hirsch knew he wanted a life in the theatre, and it took him just ten productive years in Winnipeg to educate himself and to found, with Tom Hendry, his own Theatre 77; the next year it became the Manitoba Theatre Centre (MTC). During Hirsch's eight years as artistic director (1958–66), MTC grew into one of North America's leading nonprofit theatres. His most memorable production from this era is a legendary *Mother Courage* (1964), among the earliest on this continent, featuring Zoe Caldwell and a cast of brilliant young Canadians. It was staged by an artist who had survived his own Thirty Years' War.

John Hirsch often created his own opportunities. *The Dybbuk* (1974–75), seen across Canada and in Los Angeles, is a particularly successful example: his adaptation of S. Ansky's Yiddish classic made it more Shakespearean and incorporated horror he had witnessed; his staging overflowed with feeling for the lost civilization of his childhood. Yet it is also true that much of Hirsch's best work was done at North America's leading classical theatre, the Stratford Festival, already a major institution when Michael Langham hired him to direct *The Cherry Orchard* in 1965. Hirsch had an affinity for Anton Chekhov, seeing in the plays a world he had known; later he would stage at Stratford a rapturously received *Three Sisters* (1976), with Maggie Smith.

Hirsch's notable productions of Shakespeare also began at Stratford in the 1960s. In his brilliantly original *Richard III*, starring Alan Bates (1967), he created a world so evil and so dead—again drawing on his past—that Richard was morally the best person in it. His 1968 *A Midsummer Night's Dream* was marked by images of decadence and dark sensuality; his 1984 *Dream*, also at Stratford, made it high romance. Hirsch found himself increasingly drawn to the fairy-tale side of Shakespeare: he knew miraculous resurrection in his own life. His 1983 *As You Like It* was likewise a romance, moving from a court whose brutality reflected Nazi terror to a forest in which four generations could live in the light. His wonderful Stratford *Tempest* (with Len Cariou, 1982) was both spectacular and wise.

Stratford's associate artistic director in 1968 and 1969, Hirsch was persuaded, late in 1980, to return as artistic director, to save a theatre on the verge of collapse. Restoring the Festival to former glory was impossible—the institution was badly damaged, and other theatres had sprung up to challenge its preeminence—but when Hirsch left after the 1985 season the theatre's survival for the foreseeable future was assured. The flamboyant Hirsch never felt comfortable in proper-British Stratford; his 1969 departure coincided with his *Satyricon*, created with Tom Hendry and Stanley Silverman, a burlesque-based—and finally highly moral—depiction of hedonism which outraged many. The Ontario theatre was nonetheless his primary artistic home.

Marking the start of Hirsch's U.S. career, *Yerma*, starring Gloria Foster (1966), was the first of seven plays he directed at Lincoln Center. Others ranged from *Galileo* (1967) and *Saint Joan* (with Diana Sands, 1968) to *The Time of Your Life* (1969) and *Beggar on Horseback* (1970). He won an Obie for his Chelsea Theatre Center production of Heathcote Williams's *AC/DC* (1971), giving this visionary piece about the insidiousness of electronic media a multi-media staging long before the trend evolved. Hirsch had worked in television from its earliest days in Winnipeg; he was head of CBC Drama from 1974 to 1977. His concern about media power was evident in his last acclaimed production, the Oliver North–influenced *Coriolanus* he did for California's Old Globe Theatre in 1988. Another theatre important to Hirsch was the Seattle Repertory Theatre; he was consulting artistic director for two seasons (1979–80).

Involved with the training of young artists all his professional life, the charismatic Hirsch spent much of his last years teaching in places like Yale School of Drama and Southern Methodist University, passionately insisting on theatre's high calling. He put it this way in *The Director's Voice*: "If your emotions, mind and spirit, as well as your senses, are not fed in the theatre, if you are not nurtured by some great vision clearly important to your existence, what the hell is theatre for?" (173–74).

ADDITIONAL PRODUCTIONS: 1967: *Colours in the Dark* (James Reaney); 1968: *The Three Musketeers* (Peter Raby adapt.) with Douglas Rain, *We Bombed in New Haven* (Joseph Heller) with Jason Robards; 1969: *Hamlet*; 1970: *The Sea Gull*; 1971: *Antigone*; 1973: *Guys and Dolls*; 1979: *The Tempest* with Anthony Hopkins; 1980: *Pal Joey*, *American Dreams Lost and Found* (Hirsch, adapt. from Studs Terkel); 1983–84: *Tartuffe* with Brian Bedford; 1984: *A Streetcar Named Desire*; 1985: *King Lear* with Douglas Campbell, *The Glass Menagerie*; 1987: *Three Men on a Horse*.

SELECTED BIBLIOGRAPHY: Bartow, Arthur. *The Director's Voice: Twenty-One Interviews*. New York: Theatre Communications Group, 1988: 158–74; "A Classic Debate." *Theatre Communications* (now *American Theatre*) (6 January 1984): 14–19 (Richard Foreman and Hirsch debate approaches to the classic repertoire); Knelman, Martin. *A Stratford Tempest*. Toronto: McClelland and Stewart, 1982; O'Neal, Cecil. "Directing Shakespeare." *Canadian Theatre Review* 54 (Spring 1988): 46–51; Osborn, M. Elizabeth. "Vision and Purpose: John Hirsch, David Bassuk, and Novel Stages." *Dramatics* April 1991: 14–19; Osborn, M. Elizabeth, ed. and introd. "John Hirsch at Yale." *Theater* 22 (Winter/Spring 1990): 120–23; Raby, Peter, ed. *The Stratford Scene: 1958–1968*. Toronto: Clarke, Irwin and Company, 1968; Shakespeare, William. *As You Like It, A Midsummer Night's Dream, The Tempest*. Ed. Elliott Hayes and Michal Schonberg, Stratford Festival Editions, Toronto: CBC Enterprises, 1983 and 1984.

M. Elizabeth Osborn

JINDŘICH HONZL [b. May 14, 1894, Humpolec, Bohemia, Czechoslovakia; d. April 20, 1953, Prague, Czechoslovakia]. Honzl's career had several distinct, contrasting phases. A dedicated Marxist-Leninist, he devoted his early theatre activities in the 1920s to organizing proletarian mass spectacles and to propaganda performances by labor groups known as the Blue Shirts. Overlapping this activity and extending beyond it into the 1930s, however, was his involvement with the Osvobozená Divadlo (Liberated Theatre), the most significant of the many avant-garde theatre groups in the new Czechoslovak Republic in the 1920s. Inspired by French and particularly Soviet models, Honzl mounted a score of essentially apolitical futuristic, dadaistic, or surrealistic works by contemporary French and Czech writers who were more concerned with the poetry of theatre than with ideology. The common thread was perhaps Honzl's rejection of inherited systems, conventions, and values, artistic as well as political. He elaborated his carefully reasoned critical, theoretical views on art and society in many publications.

A more moderate path was evident in his long-lasting association with the comic duo of Jiří Voskovec and Jan Werich, uniquely gifted satirists in a form halfway between political cabaret and musical revue. Honzl was the director of some twenty of their productions, which took on an increasingly serious sociopolitical slant as the threat of fascism increased during the 1930s. His work with Voskovec and Werich was interrupted between 1929 and 1931 when Honzl worked for two years in the large State Theatre in Brno, Moravia, where he staged more conventional works for a broad public.

During the German occupation of World War II, Honzl kept a low profile and limited his theatre work to small staged readings and dramatizations supportive of Czech cultural identity. Immediately after the war, Honzl became a resident director and advisor in the National Theatre, and for two years its head of drama, as well as the founder of a studio theatre designed to encourage new talent and more experimental productions within the framework of the National Theatre. In the National Theatre itself he directed a number of classics of both world and Czech drama, again in a more conservative vein, but without sacrificing his sense of theatre's profound responsibility to reflect and examine issues relevant to its society. Chronic ill-health forced his resignation in 1950, after which he pursued his critical and theoretical work and lectured on drama and theatre.

As a director, Honzl was especially noted for the precision and methodical detail of his work, his tendency to strip away accumulated conventions and start fresh with a clear conceptual basis, and carefully planned staging that placed great faith in the contributions of the actors.

ADDITIONAL PRODUCTIONS: 1926: *The Mute Canary* (G. Ribemont Dessaignes), *The Breasts of Tiresias* (G. Apollinaire); 1927: *Methusalem* (I. Goll); 1928: *Orfeus* (Cocteau), *Ubu Roi*; 1929: *Volpone*; 1932: *Caesar* (Jiří Voskovec and Jan Werich); 1935: *The Treasury of the Jesuits* (Louis Aragon and André Breton), 1937: *Těská Barbora* [*Big Barbara*] (Voskovec and Werich); 1938: *Pěst na Oko* [*A Fist in the Eye*] (Voskovec and Werich), *Julietta* (opera by Bohuslav Martinu); 1946: *The Insect Comedy* (designed by Josef Svoboda); 1948: *The Revizor* (Gogol, designed by Svoboda).

SELECTED BIBLIOGRAPHY: Burian, Jarka. "High Points of Theatre in the First Czechoslavok Republic." *Modern Drama* 27 (March 1984): 98–111; Honzl, Jindřich. *Základy a Praxe Moderniho Divadla* [*The Foundations and Practice of Modern Theatre*]. Prague: Orbis: 1963; Obst, Milan, and Adolf Scherl. *K Dějinám Česke Divadelní Avantgardy* [*The Czech Theatrical Avant Garde*]. Prague: Československá Akademie Věd, 1962; Rutte, Miroslav, and Frantisek Bartoš. *The Modern Czech Scene*. Prague: Vladimír Zikeš, 1938; Vočadlo, Otakar. "The Theater and Drama of Czechoslovakia." *The Theater in a Changing Europe*. Ed. T. H. Dickinson. New York: Henry Holt, 1937.

Jarka M. Burian

ARTHUR M. HOPKINS [b. October 4, 1878, Cleveland, Ohio; d. March 22, 1950, New York, New York]. In 1913, after working as a journalist, a vaudeville press agent, and a nickelodeon operator, Arthur Hopkins began a thirty-three year career that resulted in his directing and producing some of the most notable American productions of the 1920s and 1930s. These included *Anna Christie* (1921), the John Barrymore *Hamlet* (1922), *What Price Glory?* (1924), *Paris Bound* (1927), *Holiday* (1928), and *The Petrified Forest* (1935). During the 1930s and 1940s, Hopkins expanded his show-business endeavors to encompass filmmaking—*His Double Life* (1934), *Swing High, Swing Low* (1937)—and producing a radio series, "Arthur Hopkins Presents."

Hopkins, who produced most of the plays he directed, thus maintaining a degree of artistic autonomy unequalled on Broadway, was regarded as an experimentalist throughout his career. In 1918, his direction of Nazimova in *The Wild Duck*, *Hedda Gabler*, and *A Doll's House* reintroduced Americans to the dramaturgy of Henrik Ibsen well in advance of the Ibsen epidemic that would sweep through New York in the mid-twenties. Hopkins employed symbolist techniques resembling those used in European productions of Maurice Maeterlinck's *Blue Bird* for his staging of the poetic fantasy *The Poor Little Rich Girl* (1913); his direction of Elmer Rice's *On Trial* (1914) introduced the use of the jack-knife stage and the cinematic flashback technique on the Broadway stage; his controversial *Macbeth* (1922), created in collaboration with Robert Edmond Jones, was one of the boldest examples of expressionism ever seen in America; and productions like *Macbeth* and Sophie Treadwell's *Machinal* (1928) earned him a reputation as a pioneer in the theatrical exploration of Freudian and Jungian psychologies.

At a time when realism was gaining ascendancy on the American stage and few were eager to embrace what was then called the New Theatre, Hopkins actively championed an anti-illusionistic, synthetic theatre. Like others of his generation who were adherents of the New Theatre—Winthrop Ames,* Maurice Browne,* Samuel Hume,* and Robert Edmond Jones—Hopkins had immersed himself in the theories of Richard Wagner, Adolphe Appia, Gordon Craig, and Georg Fuchs and had traveled to Europe to see these new methods as practiced by Max Reinhardt* and others. The theatre he brought back to America could trace its lineage, through Appia and Craig, to the symbolists of the 1880s and 1890s and was a direct repudiation of Belascoesque naturalism and the "Facsimile Realism" then popular on Broadway.

In addition to his directing, Hopkins authored three plays, an autobiography titled *To a Lonely Boy*, and two theoretical works (*Reference Point, How's Your Second Act?*) in which he discussed his views on the theatre and outlined his theories of directing. In *How's Your Second Act?*, Hopkins stipulated that the director's highest goal was "capturing the unconscious mind of the audience—the deep, subliminal self that resides beneath and beyond the reaches of consciousness." Consequently, in order to discourage an audience from consciously assessing a production while it was in progress, he encouraged his actors and designers to remove any unnecessary, material details that might interfere with the unconscious communication between performer and spectator. This desire to "still the conscious mind" of the spectator and to communicate on a sub-conscious level, which Hopkins termed "Unconscious Projection," led him to advocate minimalism in scenic practices, a simplified acting style that avoided calling attention to itself and a performance in which the hand of the director remained invisible.

Hopkins also applied his Theory of Unconscious Projection to his work with actors. Firmly believing that all communication with actors should likewise be on the unconscious level, Hopkins steadfastly refused to "intrude" on rehearsals and maintained a laissez-faire directing style. Such innovative theories and prac-tices, which reflected the influence of the rebellious European originators of the New Theatre, earned Hopkins the honorary title of "The Gordon Craig of Broad-way."

ADDITIONAL PRODUCTIONS: 1913: *Poor Little Rich Girl*; 1914: Rice's *On Trial*; 1916: *The Devil's Garden*; 1917: *The Deluge*; 1918: *The Wild Duck*, *A Doll's House*, *Hedda Gabler* with Nazimova, Tolstoy's *Redemption*; 1919: Gorky's *Night Lodging* (*The Lower Depths*), *The Jest* with John and Lionel Barrymore; 1920: *Richard III* with John Bar-rymore; 1921: *Anna Christie* with Pauline Lord; 1922: Expressionistic *Macbeth* with Lionel Barrymore, *The Hairy Ape* (in collaboration with James Light), *Hamlet* with John Barrymore (designed by R. E. Jones), *Romeo and Juliet* with Ethel Barrymore; 1924: *Second Mrs. Tanqueray* with Ethel Barrymore, *What Price Glory?*; 1927: *Paris Bound*; 1928: *Machinal* with Clark Gable, *Holiday*; 1935: *Petrified Forest* with Leslie Howard and Humphrey Bogart; 1946: *The Magnificent Yankee*.

SELECTED BIBLIOGRAPHY: Chinoy, Helen Krich. "The Profession and the Art (Di-recting: 1862–1920)." *The American Theatre: A Sum of Its Parts*. New York: Samuel French, 1971: 125–52; Cole, Toby, and Helen Krich Chinoy. *Directors on Directing*. Indianapolis: Bobbs-Merrill Company, 1963; Gorelik, Mordecai. *New Theatres for Old*. New York: E. P. Dutton, 1962; Hopkins, Arthur. *How's Your Second Act?* New York: S. French, 1931; Hopkins, Arthur. *Reference Point*. New York: S. French, 1948; Mac-gowan, Kenneth. *The Theatre of Tomorrow*. New York: Boni and Liveright, 1921; Parent, Jennifer. "Arthur Hopkins' Production of Sophie Treadwell's *Machinal*." *The Drama Review* 26 (Spring 1982): 87–100; Sievers, W. David. *Freud on Broadway*. New York: Hermitage House, 1955.

John W. Frick

JOHN HOUSEMAN [b. Jacques Haussmann, September 22, 1902, Bucharest, Romania; d. October 31, 1988, New York, New York]. From the 1930s until his death in 1988, John Houseman contributed his talents to the American theatre as well as to film and subsequently television. He started six major theatre companies, produced at least eighteen major Hollywood movies, and acted in film and on television. Houseman's theatrical career flourished as a result of the Great Depression. During this time, the federal government formed the Federal Theatre Project (FTP), a part of the Works Progress Administration. FTP's executive director Hallie Flanagan hired Houseman to run the Negro Theatre

Project in Harlem. Under his direction, 750 women and men produced *Walk Together Chillum!* (1936) at the Lafayette Theatre, the first FTP production in the country.

The Negro Theatre Project's most famous production, however, was the 'Voodoo'' *Macbeth* (1936), a Haitian adaptation of Shakespeare's *Macbeth*. Orson Welles* directed the show, beginning a fruitful period of collaboration with Houseman. *Macbeth* toured the country, bringing acclaim to the Negro Theatre Project as well as to Houseman and Welles. Under Houseman's guidance, the Negro Theatre Project became one of the best run and most prestigious programs of the entire Federal Theatre Project. In 1937, Houseman and Welles founded the Mercury Theatre. During its two-year history, the Mercury Theatre company produced classical plays with contemporary concepts. The most important of these productions was a modern-dress version of *Julius Caesar* (1939) in which the conspirators represented German and Italian fascists. Despite artistic success, financial constraints forced the closing of the Mercury in 1939.

Subsequently, Houseman headed the American Shakespeare Festival. He changed the focus of the Festival, making it a permanent classical repertory company, and expanded its operations. He also directed the University of California's Professional Theatre Group. Houseman spent the last twenty-five years of his career pursuing a variety of projects in theatre, film, and television. Most significantly, he headed Juilliard's Drama Department, a new division in the Juilliard School. In collaboration with Michel Saint-Denis,* Houseman planned the curriculum which emphasized classical training. Houseman also formed the Acting Company, a repertory touring company, in which Juilliard graduates performed.

As an artistic director, Houseman influenced the development of classical theatre and the repertory system in America. Arguably, his most lasting theatrical contribution was his work with students.

ADDITIONAL PRODUCTIONS: 1934: *Four Saints in Three Acts, Lady from the Sea, Valley Forge*; 1935: *Panic* (Archibald MacLeish); 1936: *Conjur Man Dies, Hamlet, Horse Eats Hat*; 1937: *Doctor Faustus, The Cradle Will Rock, The Shoemaker's Holiday*; 1938: *Heartbreak House, Danton's Death, Hello Out There*; 1939: *The Devil and Daniel Webster*; 1941: *Native Son*; 1946: *Lute Song*; 1950: *King Lear*; 1954: *Coriolanus*; 1956–59: *King John, Othello, Much Ado about Nothing, A Winter's Tale, Measure for Measure, Hamlet, Merry Wives of Windsor*; 1960: *The Three Sisters*; 1961: *Six Characters in Search of an Author*; 1962: *Antigone*; 1964: *The Sea Gull*; 1971: *The Losers*; 1972: *The School for Scandal, Women Beware Women, Lower Depths, The Hostage*; 1972: *The Country Girl*.

SELECTED BIBLIOGRAPHY: Banham, Martin, ed. *The Cambridge Guide to World Theatre*. Cambridge: Cambridge University Press, 1988; Herbert, Ian, ed. *Who's Who in American Theatre*. 16th ed. Detroit, MI: Gale Research, 1977; Houseman, John. *Final Dress*. New York: Simon and Schuster, 1983; Houseman, John. *Front and Center*. New York: Simon and Schuster, 1980; Houseman, John. *Run-Through*. New York: Simon and Schuster, 1972; Houseman, John. *Unfinished Business*. New York: Applause Theatre Books, 1989; McGill, Raymond D., ed. *Notable Names In the American Theatre*. Clifton, New Jersey: James T. White and Company, 1976.

Geraldine Maschio
Sullivan White

JORGE HUERTA [b. November 20, 1942, East Los Angeles, California]. At an early age, Jorge Huerta, a first-generation Mexican-American, appeared on television shows and in movies as a Chicano child actor, playing "Mexican kid" and "refugee" roles. While teaching high school in Riverside, California, in 1966, Huerta was strongly influenced by Luis Valdez* and the Chicano theatre group, El Teatro Campesino. Thereafter, Huerta became actively involved in Latino theatre, and while a doctoral student at the University of California at Santa Barbara, he formed El Teatro de la Esperanza in 1971. First experimenting with "actos," the troupe then progressed to the form of docudrama exhibited in their groundbreaking 1974 production of *Guadalupe*, which toured Mexico and generated national interest in Chicano theatre.

In 1974, Huerta became the first Hispanic in the United States to receive a doctoral degree in theatre. A professor in theatre at the University of California at San Diego (UCSD) since 1975, Huerta has toured Europe three times in productions with Chicano theatre students. His *Chicano Theatre: Theme and Forms*, published in 1982, remains the primary text for university Chicano theatre courses. In 1987, Huerta initiated the country's first graduate program in Hispanic American theatre at UCSD. In addition to directing university productions, Huerto directs for such theatres as Puerto Rican Traveling Theatre in New York, Seattle Group Theatre, San Diego Group Theatre, Old Globe, La Compania de Teatro de Albuquerque, San Diego Repertory Theatre, and Gala Hispanic Theatre in Washington, D.C. Huerta co-founded Teatro Meta at San Diego's Old Globe Theatre, a venue which provides opportunities for Latino actors and brings Latino plays to English-speaking audiences. He serves as artistic director for Mascara Magica, San Diego's first professional Latino theatre, which he cofounded with William Virchis.

During his career, Huerta has received grants from the Ford Foundation, the National Endowment for the Arts, the California Arts Council, and the California Council for the Humanities. In 1988, Dr. Huerta was honored as a "Distinguished Artist" by the California State University System. In June 1990, Nosotros, the national organization of Hispanics in film and television, awarded Huerta a special citation for his contributions to Hispanic theatre.

Huerta's thrust as a director lies in a desire to find creative ways to bring Latino scripts—Chicano, Puerto Rican, Cuban, Latin American—to English-speaking audiences. While Chicano theatre often employs a combination of English and Spanish within a text, Huerto also directs bilingual productions of Latino scripts, alternating a Spanish and an English staging with the same (bilingual) cast. As an educator, Huerta continues to encourage and foster the talent of Latino actors, directors, and playwrights.

ADDITIONAL PRODUCTIONS: 1974: *Guadalupe*; 1984: *The Fanlights* (Rene Marquez); 1985: *I am Celso* (adapted by Huerta and Ruben Sierra from the poems of Leo Romero), *Quente Negro* (Estela Protillo); 1987: *Who Killed Don Jose?* (Rudolfo Anaya); 1988: *El Jardin* (Carlos Morton); 1988 and 1991: *Ardiente paciencia/Burning Patience* (Antonio Skarmeta); 1989: *Orinoco* (Emilio Carballido); 1991: *Man of the Flesh* (Octavio Solis, co-directed with Sam Woodhouse).

SELECTED BIBLIOGRAPHY: Beel, Susan. "From Chicano Child Actor to National Figure." *San Diego Business Journal* 10 December 1990: 10–11; Huerta, Jorge. *Chicano Theatre: Themes and Forms.* Ypsilanti, MI: Bilingual Press, 1982; Huerta, Jorge. "El Teatro Esperanza: Keeping in Touch with the People." *The Drama Review* 21 (March 1977): 37–46; Huerta, Jorge. "The Influences of Latin America on Teatro Chicano." *Theatre Quarterly* 2 (Spring 1983): 68–77; Huerta, Jorge. *Necessary Theatre: Six Plays about the Chicano Experience.* Houston: Arte Publico Press, 1990: Kanellos, Nicolas, and Jorge Huerta. *Nuevos Pasos: Chicano and Puerto Rican Drama.* Houston: Arte Publico Press, 1990; Stein, Pat. "Huerta Is in Touch with Latino Theatre." *Blade-Citizen Preview* [Oceanside, CA] 28 September 1990: 18–19.

Sherry Engle Johnson

JACQUES HUISMAN [b. August 4, 1910, Brussels, Belgium]. During his forty-one years as director of the Théâtre National de Belgique (1945–86), Jacques Huisman played a key role in expanding Belgian theatre audiences through extensive tours, the establishment of Belgium's first theatre festival (at Spa), and aggressive promotion to unions and schools. Inspired by Léon Chancerel, Huisman's oft-repeated goal was to bring into the theatre people who had never attended before.

An electrical engineer by trade, Huisman studied with Moscow children's theatre specialist Natalia Sats* while serving an apprenticeship in a Soviet factory. In 1935, he and his brother Maurice founded Les Comédiens Routiers Belges, an amateur troupe allied to Scouting, which performed improvised children's plays in *commedia dell'arte* style. In 1940, Herman Closson wrote for the company *Les Quatre Fils Aymon*, a Resistance play based on Belgian legend, which Les Routiers toured throughout Wallonia, changing the title when Occupation forces banned the play.

In 1945, the Huisman brothers were asked to found the Théâtre National de Belgique (TNB), arousing protest that such an enterprise should be entrusted to "amateurs." A superb organizer, Jacques Huisman ran the TNB and its ever-growing staff like a factory. During the TNB's early years, Jacques Huisman staged most of the plays himself, later sharing that task with guest directors. In 1950, Maurice left the TNB, eventually becoming director of the Opera (1959–81) and cofounder with Maurice Béjart of the Ballet du XXième Siècle.

An advocate of popular theatre, Jacques Huisman did not seek primarily a workers' audience, although he initiated programs to develop audience contact, both in his Brussels headquarters and the provinces to which he toured. His repertoire, though eclectic, reflected his own predilection for serious drama which treated social themes. His staff actively sought the best of contemporary international drama and the TNB archives, supervised by multilingual Danielle De Boeck, consequently remain an excellent research resource. Dramatists introduced to the French-speaking world by the TNB include Dario Fo* and Peter Nichols. Huisman directed highly acclaimed French-language premieres of *Death of a Salesman* and *The Crucible*, the latter the occasion for the U.S. State Department's rejection of Arthur Miller's passport application. One of the first Belgian directors to produce Bertolt Brecht,* Huisman nonetheless remained skeptical of Brechtians and of theorists in general. For Huisman, the director's task was to facilitate the encounter between audience and text. A strong sense of stage composition and an intimate knowledge of technical possibilities characterized his direction. With his engineer's fondness for statistics, Huisman noted on retirement that the TNB had in forty-one years produced 22,000 performances of 271 plays for an audience of 12 million, traveling 100,000 kilometers to fulfill its missions of decentralization and cultural ambassadorship.

ADDITIONAL PRODUCTIONS: 1946: *Romeo and Juliet, Ondine*; 1948: *Our Town*; 1949: *Pelléas et Mélisande*; 1951: *Death of a Salesman* with production supervision by Peter Brook,* *Peau d'ours* (Paul Willems); 1954: *The Crucible, Barabbas* (Ghelderode); 1956: *The Good Woman of Setzuan*; 1958: *Uncle Vanya*; 1961: *A Man for All Seasons*; 1962: *The Resistible Rise of Arturo Ui*; 1964: *Threepenny Opera*; 1965: *Mother Courage* (with Suzy Falk); 1968: *The Price*; 1972: *Public Health*; 1981: *Amadeus*; 1982: *Educating Rita*; 1984: *A Doll's House*.

SELECTED BIBLIOGRAPHY: André, Luc. *Théâtre National de Belgique, 1945–1985*. Brussels: Impresor, 1984; Centre Belge de l'Institut International du Théâtre. *The Theatre in French-Speaking Belgium since 1945*. Brussels: Archives et Musée de la Littérature, 1991; *En scène pour demain*. Brussels: Libres Images aux Presses de la Bellone, 1988; *Theatre in Belgium*, special issue of *World Theatre* 9 (Spring 1960); *Théâtre National de Belgique, 1945–1975*. Brussels: Impresor, n.d.

Suzanne Burgoyne

SAMUEL HUME [b. June 14, 1885, Berkeley, California; d. September 1, 1962, Berkeley, California]. After attending the University of California, Hume traveled to Europe, where he studied theatre and met famed modern theatrical theorist and director Edward Gordon Craig. He returned to the United States and, after graduating, earned his master's degree at Harvard, studying under Professor George Pierce Baker.

One of his earliest triumphs was to organize "The New Stagecraft Exhibition," in 1914, which featured his own work as well as that of Robert Edmond Jones. The exhibition was shown in Cambridge, New York, Chicago, and Detroit. As a result of this exhibition, Hume was hired as the director of the Detroit Arts and Crafts Theatre, where he could put many of his newly acquired theories into practice. His duties included directing, designing, and acting in the productions.

He soon built and experimented with a neo-Craigian permanent adaptable setting that was comprised of three-dimensional pieces that could serve as walls,

194

NICHOLAS HYTNER

fences, doorways, or buildings. This system of flats, platforms, and pylons could be used for many plays, or many scenes within a play. With this type of setting for his plays, Hume could adhere to the principles of the New Stagecraft of simplification, suggestion, and synthesis, which were opposed to the realistic-naturalistic impulses of design in the early part of the century.

As a teacher, Hume went on to become professor at the University of California and was director of its Greek Theatre project. Eventually, he helped to found the drama department there. Hume's second book, *Theatre and School*, published in 1932, demonstrated his lifelong commitment to educational theatre.

ADDITIONAL PRODUCTIONS: Hume directed, designed, acted in, or produced the following productions: At the Detroit Arts and Crafts Theatre—1916: *Sham, The Tents of Arabs, The Wonder Hat*; 1917: *The Chinese Lantern, Helena's Husband, Suppressed Desires, The Romance of the Rose, The Doctor in Spite of Himself*; 1918: *The Tragical History of Doctor Faustus, The Golden Doom, Riders to the Sea*; At the University of California—1920: *Henry the IV, Parts I and II*; 1921: *The Pillars of Society*; 1922: *Arms and the Man*; 1923: *If*; 1924: *Major Barbara*.

SELECTED BIBLIOGRAPHY: Bolin, John Seelye. "Samuel Hume: Artist and Exponent of American Art Theatre." Diss. U of Michigan, 1970; Cheney, Sheldon. "Sam Hume's Adaptable Settings." *Theatre Arts Magazine* 1 (Aug. 1917): 149; Feinsod, Arthur. *The Simple Stage: Its Origins in the Modern American Theater.* Westport, CT: Greenwood Press, 1992; Hume, Samuel, and Lois M. Foster. *Theatre and School.* New York: Samuel French, 1932; Hume, Samuel, and Walter Réne Fuerst. *Twentieth-Century Stage Decoration.* London: Alfred A. Knopf, 1928. repr. New York: Benjamin Blom, 1967.

Tom Mikotowicz

NICHOLAS HYTNER [b. May 7, 1956, Manchester, England]. A dynamic director whose reputation rests principally on his massive, dramatic productions, the youthful Nicholas Hytner has enjoyed a rapid rise to fame. Although he is best known in America for the musical *Miss Saigon*, Hytner has worked at the Royal Shakespeare Company (RSC) and the National Theatre (NT), and has directed extensively for major British opera companies. His fascination with broad visual strokes has given him a natural affinity for opera, and his successes have usually occurred in tandem with an acclaimed designer.

Much of Hytner's work has been in huge theatres like the Royal Opera House, Covent Garden, and the 2,358-seat London Coliseum. Although he denies being obsessed with spectacle, Hytner remains a director who places a premium on stylization and extensive visual interpretation. His productions are never over-awed by the massive auditoria they fill.

An admirer of the visual style of continental European directors, Hytner has rarely directed a production without an extensive concept in mind. Unlike many of his contemporaries, Hytner has typically avoided comment on political issues. He told *The Times* that he is more at home working on pieces that embody a search for spiritual, emotional, and intellectual fulfillment, and express the joys and miseries that result from that search. He has often said that he dislikes the director's "corrupt position" and the pressure to "make something new," instead of investing that responsibility in the playwright or composer.

Born and educated in Manchester, Hytner studied and directed at Cambridge. After graduation, he directed Benjamin Britten's *Turn of the Screw* at the Kent Opera, and worked at Exeter's Northcott Theatre and the Leeds Playhouse. He also served as associate director at Manchester's Royal Exchange Theatre.

His English National Opera (ENO) production of *The Magic Flute*, which featured a mirror-floored white set and sliding screens, emphasized the theme of a spiritual quest for wisdom; while his production of the contemporary Finnish piece, *The King Goes Forth to France* (1987), caught the opera's enigmatic ambiguity. Although Hytner had a colossal cast, the production was praised for avoiding pomposity and evoking great comic irony. Hytner's NT version of *Ghetto*, a musical play about Lithuanian Jews on their way to the death camps in 1963, was dignified and compelling, although it was, as usual, spectacular. Critics used descriptive terms like "masterful sweep," "magnificently staged," and "blazingly theatrical."

Measure for Measure (1988), Hytner's RSC debut, was performed on a set designed by Mark Thompson that was dominated by two pillars encrusted with gold. The stylized production was set in a timeless no-man's land, and the director was praised for his rapid pacing and brisk revelation of the play's moral truths. Sheridan Morley described Hytner's debut as having "flamboyant, operatic confidence," indicative of the need for new blood in RSC halls. Hytner's successful RSC *Tempest* was regarded as one of the most beautiful productions of the 1989 season. Although the directorial concept was cool and lucid—Prospero's island was merely a white, tilted disc—Hytner enchanted his audiences by concentrating on spoken eloquence and the warmth of his Prospero (John Wood). Many considered it the best *Tempest* in decades.

When *Miss Saigon* opened in London in 1989, it was hailed as a stunning feat of visual spectacle, meticulously controlled by Hytner. Among the highlights were a helicopter descending from the flies and a giant statue of Ho Chi Minh. Hytner was praised for his lean staging, his filmic evocation of powerfully resonant images, and his ability to hold the audience in an emotional vise. The production was a popular hit, testimony to Hytner's ability to emphasize narrative clarity as well as spectacle. The 1991 Broadway opening was less critically successful, after the production had been sullied by a dispute between Actors Equity and producer Cameron Mackintosh over the casting of Jonathan Pryce as a Eurasian. Many New York critics considered the production strangled by its own spectacle.

Hytner has already carved out a reputation as a spectacular, high-budget director, nonetheless able to pull truth from artificiality.

ADDITIONAL PRODUCTIONS: 1985: *The Scarlet Pimpernel*; 1987: *Mumbo Jumbo* (Robin Glendinning), *Xerxes*, *The Magic Flute*, *The Knot Garden* (Tippett); 1989: *Ghetto* (Joshua Sobol), *Julius Caesar* (Handel); 1990: *Volpone*; 1991: *Clemenza di Tito*; 1992: *Carousel*.

SELECTED BIBLIOGRAPHY: "Conjuring with the Spiritual on a Grand Scale." *The Times*

29 June 1987; "Enigmatic Quest." *The Times* 31 August 1987; "On Stage, the British Field a New Line-Up." *New York Times* 27 August 1989; Reviews of *Miss Saigon* reprinted in *London Theatre Record* 10–23 September 1989.

Chris Jones

I

SIR HENRY IRVING [b. John Henry Brodribb, February 6, 1838, Kenton Manderville, England; d. October 13, 1905, Bradford, England]. First as an actor and later as an actor-manager, Henry Irving brought a unique and dominating artistic presence to the late nineteenth-century London stage. His extraordinary imagination and meticulous discipline won him a popular following even as he sparked controversy and left many critics dissatisfied. Irving was particularly noted for his attention to the "telling" detail, which was most apparent by way of his unconventional technique as an actor. Not blessed with a powerful voice—he stuttered as a youth—nor a graceful gait, Irving turned his physical shortcomings into theatrical assets. But these were more than pragmatic choices; they developed out of Irving's desire to probe the deeper psychological motivations of the character through distinctive, and often unexpected, use of movement, voice, and visual means (costume, makeup, props, setting), this in opposition to the typical method of his day which relied principally upon a beautiful and rhetorical delivery of speeches to carry the expressive import of the drama. As a result, Irving was remembered more for the tattered hat and muffler of his Dubosc than the ringing declamation of a Henry V. The playwright's language, however, remained but one tool in his bag of theatrical effects. As Irving later wrote, "plays are made for the theatre and not theatre for plays"; and throughout his career he brought the intelligent and forceful sensibility of a character actor into the playing of tragic roles.

This comprehensive approach carried over into staging. Historically sensitive to dress and architecture, Irving's productions reflected his diligent research, a quality modeled to some extent on the Saxe-Meiningen* troupe that had visited

London in 1881. Irving always employed the latest scenic technology and was admired for his subtle use of gaslight. He also collaborated with the most prominent actors of his day, including Johnston Forbes-Robertson, William Terriss, John Martin-Harvey, Edwin Booth, and for many years Ellen Terry. Under Irving's artistic leadership from 1878 to 1899, the Lyceum Theatre significantly influenced and raised standards of production from the mediocrity into which the theatre had declined since William Charles Macready's retirement in 1851.

Nevertheless, it must be remembered that Irving's theatre was fundamentally a commercial enterprise that depended upon popular appeal. When not playing Shakespeare, Irving preferred melodramatic material and star vehicles, prompting critics like Bernard Shaw and Max Beerbohm to complain that he lacked both artistic merit and social conscience. To the end of his life Irving refused to play a single role of Henrik Ibsen, Bernard Shaw, Gerhart Hauptmann, Maurice Maeterlinck, Henri Becque, or Leo Tolstoy.

Irving's work provided continuous fodder for vigorous critical debate about a wide range of theatrical issues, among them the proper mien for an actor's expressiveness, the fidelity owed an author's text, and management's responsibility to produce new works. These issues usually arose due to Irving's controversial acting technique. William Archer wrote his famous essay "Masks or Faces" in 1888, reacting to the dispute involving Irving and the French actor Coquelin over Diderot's doctrine extolling the "controlled" actor. While Irving promoted the trend toward realism, including emotionalism and idiosyncratic acting methods, Coquelin's work emphasized cool restraint and stylized methods. Irving, it must be added, was also guilty of the common practice of "adapting" scenes, or introducing new material into established texts in order to facilitate the staging of a play, something rejected by his immediate successors (J. T. Grein, Granville Barker,* Bernard Shaw, and William Poel*), who wanted to reassert the authority of the playwright. Moreover, Irving's protégé and "adopted" son Gordon Craig also came to reject the tyranny and personal whimsy of the actor-manager, but for different reasons and toward a different end: Craig proposed the establishment of a supreme artist of the theatre, the modern director.

ADDITIONAL PRODUCTIONS: 1871: *The Bells* (Leopold Lewis); 1872: *Eugene Aram*; 1874: *Hamlet, Richelieu*; 1879: *The Merchant of Venice*; 1880: *The Corsican Brothers*; 1882: *Romeo and Juliet, Much Ado about Nothing*; 1884: *Twelfth Night*; 1892: *King Lear*; 1893: *Becket*; 1895: *King Arthur, Don Quixote*; 1898: *Peter the Great*.

SELECTED BIBLIOGRAPHY: Bingham, Madelaine. *Henry Irving and the Victorian Theatre*. Boston: Allen and Unwin, 1978; Craig, Edward Gordon. *Henry Irving*. London: J. M. Dent and Sons, 1930; Irving, Lawrence H. F. *Henry Irving: The Actor and His World*. New York: Macmillan, 1952; Taylor, George. *Henry Irving at the Lyceum*. London: Cambridge University Press, 1980; Terry, Ellen. *The Story of My Life*. New York: Schocken, 1982.

Thomas Leff

J

BARRY JACKSON [b. September 6, 1889, Birmingham, England; d. April 3, 1961, Birmingham, England]. In 1907, following five years work in an architect's office, Barry Jackson formed the Pilgrim Players, an amateur theatrical group that in 1913 became the Birmingham Repertory, a company that forever changed the landscape of English theatre. While offering early opportunities for Laurence Olivier, Ralph Richardson, Paul Scofield, and Peter Brook,* Jackson and the Birmingham Repertory promoted an ideal of entertainment based on the classics along with selected modern works and some pieces of original work. His theatre focused on the text, avoided excessive scenery, and promoted a comparatively rapid pace of performance.

In 1903, Jackson's attendance at the Gordon Craig production of *Much Ado about Nothing* prompted him to publicly note the impressive simplicity of Craig's scenic design which featured proscenium-high panels of cloth and an early experiment using projected scenery. As a result of Craig's production, as well as the 1908 production of *Measure for Measure* directed by William Poel* and produced by Miss Horniman at the Stratford Memorial Theatre, Jackson formulated his personal approach to directing which was suffused with ''a direct and amiable candor and always possessed the sense of a friendly game.'' He decried the tedious nineteenth-century productions of Charles Kean with their interminable scene changes, which frequently required ''one hundred and forty operatives each night'' and their singular lack of focus on Shakespeare's language.

Although Jackson wrote very little concerning his own directorial approach, he did appear to influence his other colleague-directors' work at the Birmingham

Repertory, resulting in a "Jackson style" which was characterized by a lack of all "gallimaufry," by absolute insistence on the rapidity of the text, by quickly paced action featuring no extraneous music and no long waits between the acts, and by little raising and lowering of the tableau curtain.

In addition to directing, Sir Barry assumed the difficult task of keeping the Birmingham Repertory solvent. His managerial and producing skills were unique, considering that besides the numerous seasons at "The Rep," he founded the Malvern Festival, which served as a showplace for Bernard Shaw's plays from 1929 to 1937; led the Stratford Festival in 1947–48; and rounded out his career with invitations to manage performances at the Old Vic between 1952 and 1956. Jackson was so prolific as a manager that in 1932 alone, he produced six productions in Canada, seven in London, seven in Malvern, and thirteen in Birmingham.

By virtue of his selection of plays for each season, Jackson was instrumental in a healthy revitalization of Shakespeare, and produced as well numerous works of George Bernard Shaw. In 1923, when Jackson approached the then fabled writer about producing *Back to Methuselah* for only the second time, Shaw's only response was "Is your family well provided for . . . ?" Jackson nevertheless produced Shaw throughout his years at Malvern and Birmingham and always had an aversion to the more popular drawing room comedies. He did not always serve as artistic director, often leaving that responsibility in the early years to others, including John Drinkwater (sixty-three plays between spring of 1913 and autumn of 1918) and H. K. Ayliff. Following Anthony Quayle's assumption of the directorship of Stratford in the autumn of 1948, Sir Barry presented a tour throughout Holland of the Michael Langham* production of *The Importance of Being Earnest* featuring John Neville as Worthing. From 1952 to 1956, the Birmingham Rep launched a series of productions featuring the three parts of *King Henry the Sixth* and Shaw's *Caesar and Cleopatra*.

Following a triumphal production of *Caesar and Cleopatra* at the International Theatre Festival in 1956, Jackson participated briefly in the Edinburgh Theatre Festival before returning to his hometown theatre where he continued to participate at a less rigorous pace until he died on Easter Monday, April 3, 1961, regarded by many to have been "a golden torch in a foggy world."

ADDITIONAL PRODUCTIONS: 1913: Premier Birmingham Repertory production of *Twelfth Night* (also designed by Jackson); 1925: *Hamlet* (modern dress); 1926: *Rosmersholm*, *The Marvelous History of Saint Bernard* (Henri Ghéon, adapted by Jackson); 1927: *All's Well That Ends Well* (modern dress); 1928: *Back to Methuselah*, *The Adding Machine*; 1929: *Macbeth* (modern dress); 1950: *The Importance of Being Earnest* (Old Vic); 1952–53: *King Henry the Sixth, Parts One, Two and Three* (Old Vic); 1956: *Caesar and Cleopatra* (Old Vic).

SELECTED BIBLIOGRAPHY: Banham, Martin, ed. *Cambridge Guide to the Theatre*. London: Cambridge University Press, 1988; Bishop, G. W. *Barry Jackson and the London Theatre*. 1933. repr. New York: Benjamin Blom, 1963: 507; Hartnoll, Phyllis, ed. *Oxford Companion to the Theatre*. 4th ed. London: Oxford University Press, 1983: 431; Kemp,

Thomas C. *The Birmingham Repertory Theatre: The Playhouse and the Man.* Birmingham: Cornish Brothers Limited, 1948; Oxbury, H. F. *Great Britons: 20th Century Lives.* London: Oxford University Press, 1985: 81–82. Trewin, J. C. *The Birmingham Repertory Theatre: 1913–1963.* London: Barrie and Rockcliff, 1963.

Larry Soller

BRIGITTE JAQUES [b. August 19, 1946, Vevey, Switzerland]. Brigitte Jaques began her theatrical career in 1969 as an actress under the tutelage of Antoine Vitez.* He called on her often until 1974 when she made her stunning directorial debut with Frank Wedekind's *Spring's Awakening* for Paris's prestigious Festival d'Automne. Like her mentor's, Jaques's stance is both passionately intellectual and wrenchingly physical. She has thus been able to grapple with the changing registers of authors such as Paul Claudel (*Break of Noon*, 1990) or Tennessee Williams (*The Night of the Iguana*, 1991) and maintain, in her staging, the tension between grotesque caricature and powerful emotional changes.

In the same vein, her preferred scenic aesthetic, often created by Emmanuel or Olivier Peduzzi, blends a self-conscious, theatricalized space with weighted realistic touches, like the slightly outgrown coat worn by "the actress" in Jaques's 1986 production of *Elvire-Jouvet 40.* This prize-winning and multifaceted piece, which she adapted from the Conservatory lessons of Louis Jouvet* on performing Elvire in Molière's *Don Juan*, confirmed her as a director with a gift for taut choreography and energetic silences. She imparted these skills, as well as an ability to take on and reinterpret complex foreign texts, to her acting students during her tenure at the Rue Blanche School (1980–88).

In 1991, Jaques was named to head with François Regnault, her longtime collaborator, Le Théâtre d'Aubervilliers. This appointment—to one of the first subsidized theatres in Paris's working-class suburbs—will permit her to pursue her interest in how classics can speak to contemporary audiences in contemporary terms. She intends to stage all five of Corneille's neglected Roman tragedies in order to address the agonizing effects of decolonization.

ADDITIONAL PRODUCTIONS: 1985: *La Mort de Pompée* (Corneille); 1988: *Sophonisbe* (Corneille); 1989: *L'Imposture* (adaptation of Bernanos), *Horace* (Corneille); 1992: *La Place Royale* (Corneille), *Suréna* (Corneille).

SELECTED BIBLIOGRAPHY: Makward, Christiane P., and Judith G. Miller. *Out of Bounds: Women's Theater from the French.* Ann Arbor: University of Michigan Press, 1993; Marcabru, Pierre. "Quand les femmes s'en mêlent." *Le Point* 27 October 1990: 10–11; Temkine, Raymonde. *Le Théâtre au Présent.* Paris: Bouffoneries/Contrastes, 1987.

Judith G. Miller

JERZY JAROCKI [b. May 11, 1929, Warsaw, Poland]. A graduate of the Department of Acting at Państwowa Wyższa Szkola Teatralna in Crakow (1952) and the Department of Directing at GITIS at Moscow (1957) where he studied under N. M. Gorchakov, Jarocki made his debut in Katowice with the play *Bal manekinów* by the futurist poet Bruno Jasieński. This play, which represents the repertoire of the Polish avant-garde of the period between the wars, signalled

Jarocki's interests, and resulted later in his staging of the most interesting plays by St. Witkacy, Gombrowicz, St. Różewicz, and S. Mrożek, all writers in the vanguard of Polish drama of that period. The most prominent of all was Jarocki's production of Gombrowicz's *Ślub*, staged five times in its entirety. The world premiere took place in Gliwice (with sets designed by Krystyna Zachwatowicz) in 1960, and it was restaged in Zurich (1972), Warsaw (1974), Nowy Sad (1981), and Cracow (1991).

The first years of Jarocki's professional work fall within the period when theatres were exploring previously forbidden regions of dramaturgy, and were involved in an intensive search for new, oftentimes extreme forms of expression. During this period, Jarocki opted to stay with contemporary Polish and foreign drama (John Osborne, Friedrich Dürrenmatt, Mrożek) and was generally recognized for his realistic staging and his ability to work with actors in productions like *A View from the Bridge* (1960) and *Long Day's Journey into Night* (1961). Of equal interest, however, were those productions (e.g., *Tango* by Mrożek, 1965) which afforded Jarocki the opportunity to abandon uniform formulas, to "counter-argue" realism, to propose grotesque solutions, and to produce splendid effects. Thus, although his professionalism and perfectionist tendencies contributed to the fact that he was never perceived as an experimenter, he did, in fact, at different times of his career, experiment in the sphere of acting, visualization of metaphor, and organization of space; and most significantly, he staged some of the most unconventional dramas of the era (e.g., the surreal, poetic dramas *Stara kobieta wysiaduje*, 1969, and *Na czworakach*, 1974, both by St. Różewicz). In these productions, Jarocki's theatrical vision expressed the poetic vision contained in the word.

From 1962, working with Stary Teatr in Kraków, Jarocki played a significant role in developing the abilities of the actors of this theatre. Together with them he created extraordinary performances using purely formal methods (as he did in *Matka*, 1964, and *Szewcy*, 1971, by St. Witkiewicz); evoked a Proustian mood in *The Cherry Orchard* (1975); and created reality out of dreams (or more precisely surreal nightmares) in *Proces* by Kafka (1973), *Życie snem* by Calderon (1983), and *Ślub*. At Stary Teatr he also exhibited talent as a playwright and adaptor, adapting Kafka's *Proces*, creating screenplays for *Moja córeczka* by St. Różewicz and *Sen o Bezgrzesznej*, and giving stage form to *Słuchaj Izraelu*, a play by Sito.

During the 1970s, Jarocki worked with Teatr Dramatyczny in Warsaw where he directed *Na czworakach*, *Ślub*, and such important works as Mrożek's *Rzeźnia* (1975). At Teatr Dramatyczny he also started to experiment with moving the audience and expanding the stage space, and staged *King Lear*, which was one of the few classical plays directed at that time. He closed this period of his career with a production of *Murder in the Cathedral* by T. S. Eliot, which was staged at Bazylika Św. Jana during Martial Law in 1982. Jarocki also directed in the Netherlands, Switzerland, Yugoslavia, Germany, and the Soviet Union. According to the Yugoslavian critics, Jarocki's staging of *Zmierzch* in 1979, which had been expanded since its Cracow production, was filled with a poetry and a spirit that opened new perspectives for theatre directors of that country.

Jarocki's theatre is "expansionistic," with a richness of forms (which includes the stage setting, music, composition of movement, gestures, costumes, and the use of props) that coalesce with mathematical precision. For Jarocki, the inspiration for this type of theatre lies in contemporary dramatic literature, not in the "systems" proposed by reformers of the theatre. Thus, in spite of the abundance of symbols in his theatre, themes play the leading role for Jarocki, and he remains fascinated by Gombrowicz's "humanly human church" while at the same time expressing his fears concerning the direction of the development of our civilization and the fate of the individual in society.

ADDITIONAL PRODUCTIONS: 1967: *Zmierzch*; 1968: *Moja córeczka*; 1969: *Trzy siostry*; 1970: *Paternoster* (Kajzar); 1975: *Garbus* (Mrożek); 1979: *Sen o Bezgrzesznej*; 1981: *Pieszo* (Mrożek); 1987: *Portret* (Mrożek).

SELECTED BIBLIOGRAPHY: Grodzicki, August. *Reżyserzy polskiego teatru*. Warszawa: Interpress, 1979: 97–112; Jarocki, Jerzy. "Potyczkio 'Ślub.' " *Dialog* 2/1991; Morawiec, Elzbieta. "Jerzy Jarocki: w trybach losu." *Dialog* 6/1979; Wirth, Andreas. "Teatr Jerzego Jarockiego." *pierwodruk Politik und Kultur* 5/1988 and *Dialog* 2/1991.

Elzbieta Wysińska

LEOPOLD JESSNER [b. March 3, 1878, Königsberg, Germany (today Kaliningrad in Lithuania); d. December 13, 1945, Hollywood, California]. After an acting debut in 1897, Jessner assumed his first important directorial position as head director of the Thalia Theatre in Hamburg, where from 1904 to 1915 he specialized in the staging of contemporary dramas by Henrik Ibsen, Gerhart Hauptmann, Frank Wedekind, Anton Chekhov, Bernard Shaw, and Maurice Maeterlinck, gradually exploring what would later become his signature principles: simplification of the dramatic text and stage set, and concentration of the language and acting. In 1911, he also became the manager of the labor-union-supported Hamburg People's Theatre (Volksschauspiele) in a step that was characteristic of his social democratic politics and his Schillerian ideal of the theatre as an institution of moral education.

In 1915, Jessner took over as managing director of the New Theatre in Königsberg, where he added classical dramas to his repertoire (Schiller, Shakespeare, Kleist, Goethe). The reason for Jessner's appointment in 1919 as the manager of the State Theatre in Berlin is generally regarded to have been his administrative skills rather than his aesthetic vision. Nonetheless, the prestigious position (later he became general manager of all the Berlin State theatres as well as director of the State Theatre School) launched his reputation as one of the most important directors of the twenties and, next to Max Reinhardt,* as one of the founders of modern directorial theatre in Germany.

That an outsider and avowed liberal was chosen to direct the former royal theatre marked a crucial hiatus in the cultural politics of the new Weimar Republic. Moreover, Jessner's conviction that the theatre was a political forum, coupled with his innovative style, influenced the entire German theatre scene during the twenties. It also reaped him constant criticism from the rightist press and political parties leading ultimately to his resignation from the managerial post in 1930. Jessner remained at the State Theatre as a director, however, until the spring of 1933, when Nazi racial discrimination against Jews forced him to emigrate, first to London and finally in 1939 to Hollywood after sojourns in Rotterdam, Jerusalem (productions at Habima), and Vienna.

Jessner developed his dramaturgical model in reaction to the dominant stage naturalism as well as to Reinhardt's synthetic model with its emphasis on refined psychological and atmospheric detail. His first three productions in Berlin summarized his strongly visual, abstractionist approach which defined a drama's idea and then focused on one motif that controlled the staging. His *Wilhelm Tell* (1919), for example, eliminated all ornamental and Swiss folkloric decoration by universalizing the dramatic conflict to a struggle between forces of power and freedom situated against a symbolically austere backdrop. The denial of the play's traditional, classical idyll in favor of a topical interpretation led to the first theatre scandal of the Weimar Republic when the premiere was interrupted during the third act. Jessner went even further with *The Marquis of Keith* (1920), conceived as a critique of middle-class philistinism that stressed the circus-like elements in Wedekind's play. Symbolic color-coding of the set and costumes, the grotesque play of shadows, the calculated use of tempo and rhythm in movement and in the delivery of lines point to Jessner's conviction that a production must consist of a clearly comprehensible plot with equally simple stage architecture against which the word and the actor's body convey the text's meaning. *Richard III* (1920) picked up all these elements and perfected the use of vertical stage space that became synonymous with the director's name in the "Jessner stairs." Concentrating on the idea of the dangerous tyrant, he symbolically constructed the action around the huge staircase dominating the stage. This, together with architectonic lighting, became a means of space delineation that also reinforced the political message through the play's dramaturgy.

Jessner continued to refine his staging style as the art of variation and repetition of a drama's theme, although by the mid–1920s his productions were becoming less visually stylized. Yet, with an ensemble of talented actors (Fritz Kortner, Werner Krauss, Gustav Gründgens) and designers (Emil Pirchan, Caspar Neher) and with a commitment to balancing the repertoire by introducing younger dramatists (e.g., Ernst Barlach, Bertolt Brecht,* Arnold Bronner, Else Lasker-Schüler, Carl Zuckmayer) and directors (Jürgen Fehling,* Erich Engel, Erwin Piscator*), he transformed the Staatliches Schauspielhaus Berlin into the leading German theatre of the twenties. Although his impact in postwar Germany has been less direct or pronounced than that of Reinhardt or Piscator, his legacy has lived on in the shape of the modern repertory and in the training of the political actor.

ADDITIONAL PRODUCTIONS: 1906: *Earth Spirit* (Wedekind); 1910: *Danton's Death* (Büchner); 1911: *The Marquis of Keith* (Wedekind), staged again in 1920; 1914: *Officers* (Fritz von Unruh); 1921: *Fiesco* (Schiller); 1924: *Wallenstein* (Schiller); 1926: *Hamlet*, *East Pole Train* (Arnolt Bronnen), *Herodes and Mariamne* (Hebbel); 1928: *The Weavers* (Hauptmann), *Oedipus Rex*, and *Oedipus at Colonus*.

SELECTED BIBLIOGRAPHY: Jessner, Leopold. *Schriften*. Berlin: Henschelverlag, 1979, includes complete list of stagings: 306–16; Patterson, Michael. *Revolution in German Theatre 1900–1933*. Boston: Routledge and Kegan Paul, 1981; Rühle, Günther. *Theater für die Republik im Spiegel der Kritik*. 2 vols. Berlin: Henschelverlag, 1988, contemporary theatre reviews of all major Jessner productions in Berlin; Willett, John. *The Theatre of the Weimar Republic*. New York and London: Holmes and Meier, 1988.

Marc Silberman

DAVID HUGH JONES [b. February 19, 1934, Poole, England]. Best known as a straightforward, self-effacing director of classical and contemporary drama, with a penchant for minute detail and a distaste for obtrusive directorial concepts, David Jones directed frequently for the Royal Shakespeare Company (RSC) of which he is an associate artist, since 1962. His prolific career also includes extensive directorial work in the English regional theatre; productions at Stratford, Ontario; the 1983 film of Harold Pinter's *Betrayal*; and time at the BBC as head of the arts program "Monitor" and then the "Play of the Month" series. From 1979, Jones directed the ambitious but ultimately short-lived classical repertory company at the Brooklyn Academy of Music.

A year after making his London directing debut at the Mermaid, Jones, the son of a Welsh minister, joined the RSC in 1962. Along with Trevor Nunn,* John Barton,* and Terry Hands, Jones was influential in the development and direction of the RSC over the next twenty years. Jones soon became director of the RSC's Aldwych, where he was heralded as a reliable administrator who brought stability to the theatre. Artistically, he changed the theatre's emphasis to one of large-cast, infrequently performed classic plays, and included in the repertory his own 1971 production of Gorky's *Enemies*. Attracted by the play's energy and exuberance, Jones went on to direct several other Gorky pieces, including the Obie-winning *Summerfolk* (1974).

Although 1973 included one of Jones's most-praised RSC productions (*Love's Labour's Lost*), Jones became embroiled in a controversy during rehearsals of John Arden's four-hour epic, *The Island of the Mighty*. The playwright alleged the director refused him permission to talk to the cast, and accused Jones of intransigence and subversion of the play's anti-imperialist message.

In 1976, Jones's production of Chekhov's infrequently revived *Ivanov* emphasized the play's satirical capacity, and had a highly physical and boldly comic style, a considerable departure from previous productions. His Warehouse production of *Baal* (1979) was celebrated as a perfect model for small theatres because he crammed the play's twenty-two scenes and fifty characters into the RSC's Warehouse, with the set restricted to one wall.

When Jones arrived to lead the Brooklyn Academy of Music's classical troupe, he was expected to use his RSC experience to form an American company, partially funded by the Ford Foundation, of a similarly large scale. The first season, opening with Jones's production of *The Winter's Tale* and including Gorky's obscure *Barbarians*, surprised commentators by its ambitious choice of plays and was a critical success. The troupe's second year was less favorably received, and funding was lost before year three began.

Since returning to England, Jones has directed frequently in the West End, including a critically praised production of Ronald Harwood's *Tramways* (1984) and a 1985 revival of *Old Times*, seen by some as superior to the original production by Peter Hall.*

ADDITIONAL PRODUCTIONS: 1961: *Krapp's Last Tape*; 1962: *The Investigation* (with Peter Brook*); 1967: *As You Like It*; 1968: *Diary of a Scoundrel, The Tempest, As You Like It*; 1969: *The Silver Tassie*; 1972: *The Lower Depths*; 1975: *Twelfth Night*; 1976: *Zykovs*; 1977: *All's Well That Ends Well*; 1979: *Cymbeline*; 1981: *A Midsummer Night's Dream*; 1983: *The Custom of the Country* (Nicholas Wright).

SELECTED BIBLIOGRAPHY: Allen, David. "David Jones Directs Chekhov's *Ivanov*." *New Theatre Quarterly* 14 (1988): 232–46; Beauman, Sally. *The Royal Shakespeare Company: A History of Ten Decades*. Oxford: Oxford University Press, 1982; Gems, Pam. "The Island of the Ardens." *The Best of Plays and Players*. Vol. 2. London: Methuen, 1988: 80–85; Gussow, Mel. "Straightforward Director." *New York Times* 15 February 1980.

Chris Jones

MARGARET VIRGINIA (MARGO) JONES [b. December 12, 1911, Livingston, Texas; d. July 24, 1955, Dallas, Texas].

Director-producer Margo Jones pioneered the American resident theatre movement, established the first professional theatre-in-the-round in the United States, and nurtured the work of budding playwrights, including Tennessee Williams, William Inge, Joseph Hayes, and Jerome Lawrence and Robert E. Lee. When Jones established her theatre in Dallas in 1947, the first permanent nonprofit professional resident theatre, she helped inspire the development of a national network of resident theatre companies.

After receiving an M.A. from Texas Woman's University, she worked and studied at the Southwestern School of the Theatre in Dallas and with Gilmor Brown at the Pasadena Playhouse. In 1935, she traveled around the world seeing theatre and then returned to Texas and became assistant director of the Houston Federal Theatre Project. In 1936, she attended the Moscow Art Theatre Festival where she met Brooks Atkinson, the influential *New York Times* theatre critic who would later champion her direction of new plays and her efforts to decentralize the American theatre. In 1936, Jones also founded the Houston Community Players, which she directed until 1942. She earned national attention as a member of the National Theatre Conference and in 1939 was named by *Stage* magazine as one of twelve outstanding theatre directors outside of New York, the only woman selected.

From 1942 until 1944, Margo Jones taught theatre and directed plays at the University of Texas. In early 1942, she met playwright Tennessee Williams, and they began their personal and professional association. She directed his play *You Touched Me* (co-written with Donald Windham) at the Pasadena Playhouse and at the Cleveland Playhouse in 1943, bringing Williams to the attention of national theatre critics, and in 1944 she directed Williams's *The Purification* at the Pasadena Playhouse. During this time she formulated an idea which would change the shape of theatre in America. She wanted to establish a network of nonprofit professional resident theatres outside of New York. Dallas theatre critic John Rosenfield encouraged her to apply for a Rockefeller Fellowship and to establish her prototype theatre in Dallas. She began her fellowship in 1944 studying theatre around the country, but interrupted the fellowship to codirect *The Glass Menagerie* (with Eddie Dowling). With the commercial success of *The Glass Menagerie*, Margo Jones had the impetus she needed to found her theatre.

Incorporated in 1945 as Dallas Civic Theatre, her theatre did not open until the summer of 1947. In the interim, Jones raised money, looked for a suitable theatre space, and directed *On Whitman Avenue* by Maxine Wood and *Joan of Lorraine* (starring Ingrid Bergman) by Maxwell Anderson on Broadway. In June of 1947, the theatre opened, now called Theatre '47, the name to change with the year. It was the first professional arena theatre in the country and the first modern nonprofit professional resident theatre. From its conception, the theatre's resident company performed only new plays and classics of world theatre. The inaugural season introduced the first play of William Inge, *Farther Off from Heaven*, later revised as *The Dark at the Top of the Stairs*, and *Summer and Smoke* by Tennessee Williams. Later seasons included classics by Shakespeare, Ibsen, and Chekhov and new works by Dorothy Parker, Sean O'Casey, George Sessions Perry, and Joseph Hayes.

With her personal and professional partner, Manning Gurian, Jones took new plays from her Dallas season and produced them, with varying degrees of success, on Broadway and on tour, including Williams's *Summer and Smoke*. While running the Dallas theatre, she worked to establish resident theatres like hers around the country. She lectured widely and in 1951 published *Theatre in the Round*, which inspired other theatre leaders to follow her lead.

In 1955, after it had been turned down by many Broadway producers as too controversial, Jerome Lawrence and Robert E. Lee's play, *Inherit the Wind*, was produced by Theatre '55 in Dallas, then moved to Broadway. During Jones's management of her Dallas theatre, from 1947 to 1955, 70 percent of the plays she produced were world premieres.

Although Margo Jones is primarily noted for her pioneering efforts, she was a gifted director who believed that the playwright's text was primary. When she codirected the world premiere of *The Glass Menagerie*, she fought to keep the play's original ending and coordinated all the technical aspects of the production in addition to collaborating in the staging. Her directing strengths lay in good casting and the creation of a warm, nurturing atmosphere for both actors and playwrights. She tended to concentrate more on a play's overall shape and flow from scene to scene and on character groupings and stage pictures than on the specifics of actors' performances. She preferred not to coach actors, but liked to work improvisationally with them, giving free rein to their creative impulses. On the intimate space of her arena stage, using minimal sets, but making intricate use of flexible, imaginative sound and lighting, she was successful at giving a fluid, seamless quality to productions, especially in the plays of Tennessee Williams, Shakespeare, and Ibsen.

Margo Jones's work focused attention on playwrights and the development of new plays, but more importantly her efforts at decentralization transformed the theatre map. Today, Broadway is no longer the only center of theatrical activity; over 300 resident theatres flourish from coast to coast, a national theatre for America.

ADDITIONAL PRODUCTIONS: 1947: *Hedda Gabler*; 1948: *Twelfth Night, Leaf and Bough* (Joseph Hayes); 1949: *The Coast of Illyria* (Dorothy Parker and Ross Evans); 1950: *Cock-a-Doodle Dandy* (Sean O'Casey).

SELECTED BIBLIOGRAPHY: Jones, Margo. *Theatre in the Round*. New York: Rinehart and Company, Inc., 1951; Sheehy, Helen. *Margo: The Life and Theatre of Margo Jones*. Dallas, Texas: Southern Methodist University Press, 1989.

Helen Sheehy

LOUIS JOUVET [b. December 24, 1887, Crozin, Finistère, France; d. August 16, 1951, Paris, France]. Louis Jouvet was one of France's most celebrated actors and directors between the two world wars. His hallmark performances as Jules Romains's Dr. Knock, Molière's Don Juan, Tartuffe, and Arnolphe in *L'École des femmes* are legendary. He is equally well remembered for his numerous film portrayals (in Renoir's *Les Bas-Fonds* and Carné's *Hôtel du Nord*, for example). As a director, his conviction that great drama is first and foremost great writing led to his scrupulous respect for the written text. For Jouvet, the director's principal role was to serve the playwright.

It is said that Jouvet became a pharmacist to please his family and an actor to please himself. Soon after he passed his pharmacological exams, he began training himself as an actor by attending lectures by experienced men of the theatre and by playing any role he could find (as Father Zossima in *The Brothers Karamazov* with Charles Dullin* at Jacques Rouché's Théâtre des Arts in 1911, for example). He also managed various theatres and briefly formed his own acting company with a group of friends. Even though he failed the entrance exams at the Paris Conservatory of Dramatic Art three times, he remained undaunted in his determination to dedicate himself totally to the theatre.

In 1913, Jacques Copeau* recruited Jouvet for his new Vieux Colombier Theatre where, as stagehand, mechanic, painter, stage manager, and actor, he received the rigorous training and respect for his craft which were the hallmarks of Copeau's experiment in theatre reform. He accompanied Copeau to America in 1917 where for two years, they performed a varied repertory at New York's Garrick Theatre before returning to Paris in 1920.

Jouvet left the Vieux Colombier in 1922 to become director of the Comédie des Champs-Elysées, the smaller of the two auditoriums which formed the Théâtre des Champs-Elysées. In 1927, with Gaston Baty,* Dullin, and Georges Pitoeff,* he formed the Cartel des Quatre, an informal alliance dedicated to theatrical reform and renewal.

That same year, Jouvet's encounter with author-diplomat Jean Giraudoux marked the beginning of one of France's great theatre partnerships. Their first production together, a dramatization of Giraudoux's novel *Siegfried et le limousin*, opened May 3, 1928, and played for an unprecedented 302 performances. This was only the beginning of a remarkable sixteen-year collaboration between the director-actor and the author. Equally fruitful was Jouvet's work with Christian Bérard, who became his set designer.

In 1934, the year Jouvet opened his new 450-seat theatre, the Athénée (now known as the Athénée-Louis Jouvet), he also became a professor at the Paris Conservatory of Dramatic Art, where he taught until the German occupation. As a teacher and director, Jouvet sought to challenge his students' preconceived notions about acting through a Socratic process of probing, questioning, and commenting. Teaching them to "breathe the text," to inhabit a role, to persevere through difficult and painful trial and error, he relentlessly urged them toward a new awareness and understanding of the characters they played, as well as a heightened awareness of themselves.

In the early war years Jouvet was invited to tour his Athénée repertory in South America. He left France in May 1941 and did not return until February 1945. He devoted his final years to productions of Molière and Giraudoux, his two favorite authors, as well as to new work (he is the first to have staged Genet's *The Maids* in 1947). That same year, he realized his lifelong dream of staging Molière's *Don Juan ou le Festin de Pierre*. His highly original interpretation of Don Juan as frightened believer rather than sensuous seducer was one of the highlights of his career.

Like Molière, Jouvet died in the theatre (in August 1951) preparing for a new role in an adaptation of Graham Greene's *The Power and the Glory*.

ADDITIONAL PRODUCTIONS: 1923: *Knock* (Jules Romains, with sketches for decor by Jouvet), *Monsieur Le Trouhadec saisi par la débauche* (Romains, sets designed by Jouvet); 1933: *Intermezzo* (Giraudoux, decor and costumes by L. Leyritz); 1935: *Tiger at the Gates* (sets by Mariano Andreu, costumes by Alix); 1936: *L'École des femmes* (Molière, set by Christian Bérard); 1937: *Electre* (Giraudoux, sets by G. Monin, costumes by D. Bouchène); 1939: *Ondine* (Giraudoux, sets by Pavel Tchelitchew); 1945: *The Madwoman of Chaillot* (Giraudoux, sets by Christian Bérard); 1950: *Tartuffe* (sets by Georges Braque); 1951: *Le Diable et le Bon Dieu* (Sartre, sets by Félix Labissse).

SELECTED BIBLIOGRAPHY: Cézan, Claude. *Louis Jouvet et le théâtre d'aujourd'hui.* Paris: Editions Emile-Paul Frères, 1948; Jouvet, Louis. *Le comédien désincarné.* Paris: Flammarion, 1954; Jouvet, Louis. *Réflexions du comédien.* Paris: la Nouvelle Critique, 1938; Jouvet, Louis. *Témoignages sur le théâtre.* Paris: Flammarion, 1952; Kérien,

Wanda. *Louis Jouvet, notre patron*. Paris: Editeurs Français Réunis, 1963; Knapp, Bettina. *Louis Jouvet, Man of the Theater*. New York: Columbia University Press, 1957; Mutert, Ruth Pauline Joerling. "Louis Jouvet's 'Le Comédien désincarné,' Translation and Critical Introduction." Diss. U of Missouri–Columbia, 1970; *Revue d'Histoire du Théâtre* 4:1–2 (1952); Simon, Charles Edwin. "Louis Jouvet, Teacher of Dramatic Art." Diss. Case Western Reserve U, 1975; Van Meyer, John Edward "The Theater of Louis Jouvet." Diss. U of Florida, 1959.

Philippa Wehle

K

MICHAEL KAHN [b. September 9, 1940, Brooklyn, New York]. After graduation from New York's High School of Performing Arts, Michael Kahn attended Columbia University and trained with Michael Howard and the Actors' Studio before launching his prolific career in 1962 as producer of *P.S. 193* on the Writer's Stage. He has directed in many Off-Broadway theatres, including La Mama ETC, where his original production of van Itallie's *America Hurrah* appeared. In 1966, his program of three Thornton Wilder plays at the Cherry Lane under the auspices of Edward Albee, and *Measure for Measure* in Central Park for Joseph Papp's New York Shakespeare Festival, were both nominated for the Vernon Rice Award.

In 1967, Kahn was asked to direct *Merchant of Venice* at the American Shakespeare Festival Theatre in Stratford, Connecticut. For nine years, he served as the Festival's artistic director, staging some twenty productions, including *Three Sisters* (1969), *Othello* (1970), and an antiwar *Henry V* (1969), all of which moved to Broadway. His *Mourning Becomes Electra* (1971) revival was recorded by Caedmon. *Measure for Measure* (1973) and *Romeo and Juliet* (1974) were produced at Washington's Kennedy Center, where *Cat on a Hot Tin Roof* with Elizabeth Ashley (1974) also moved before its successful New York run.

While at Stratford, Kahn developed a reputation for fine work in regional theatre. Nominated for a Jefferson Award for *Tooth of Crime* 1974) at the Goodman in Chicago, he has also directed at Cincinnati's Playhouse in the Park, at the Guthrie in Minneapolis, in Los Angeles, and in Washington. *Show Boat* with Donald O'Connor, staged for the Houston Grand Opera in

1989, went on to Broadway to win a Tony nomination. Kahn later took it to Cairo, Egypt, to represent the United States in the inaugural season of the National Cultural Center Opera House. Kahn's other opera credits include the Texas Opera Theatre, and the Houston Grand, Washington, San Francisco Spring, and Greater Miami Operas.

In 1974, Kahn became artistic director of the McCarter Theatre in Princeton, New Jersey, where he combined classical repertory with thought-provoking modern pieces, and American and world premieres. His *Beyond the Horizon* (1974) was filmed for the PBS "Theatre in America" series. Before his 1979 resignation from McCarter, Kahn directed world premieres of *The Night of the Tribades* and Sam Shepard's *Angel City* (1975).

Kahn maintains an active teaching schedule at New York University and at the Juilliard School where, while serving as chairman of the Acting Department, he became an artistic director of the Acting Company from 1978 to 1990. Among his celebrated Acting Company productions was a program of ten short plays by Tennessee Williams (reprised as *Five by Tenn*) which toured throughout the Soviet Union and Eastern Europe in 1990.

In 1986, Kahn was named artistic director of the newly reformed Shakespeare Theatre at the Folger in Washington, directing its inaugural production of *Romeo and Juliet* (1986), which focused on the contemporary crisis of teenage suicide. In 1989, *Twelfth Night* with Kelly McGillis won the Helen Hayes Award, and *Merry Wives of Windsor* featured Pat Carroll as the first actress to play Falstaff. The latter was restaged at the outdoor Carter Barron Amphitheatre with Paul Winfield as Falstaff.

As a result of Kahn's leadership, the Folger company has enjoyed an artistic and financial renaissance. His classical productions place strong emphasis on language, rhythms, meaning, and stress. Emphasizing Shakespeare's texts themselves, Kahn strives to tell clear and lively stories and to bring audiences the surprise and immediacy of contemporary plays.

ADDITIONAL PRODUCTIONS: 1965: *Funnyhouse of a Negro* (Adrienne Kennedy); 1967: *Merchant of Venice*; 1970: *All's Well That Ends Well, Othello* (Stratford); 1975: *A Streetcar Named Desire* (McCarter, with Glenn Close and Shirley Knight); 1988: *Macbeth* (Folger), *'Tis Pity She's a Whore* (American Repertory Theatre, Cambridge); 1990: *Richard III* (with Stacy Keach); 1991: *King Lear*.

SELECTED BIBLIOGRAPHY: Berry, Ralph. *On Directing Shakespeare: Interviews with Contemporary Directors*. New York: Barnes and Noble, 1977: 74–91; Cooper, Roberta K. *The American Shakespeare Theatre: Stratford, 1955 to 1985*. Washington: Folger Books, 1987; Haddad, Miranda Johnson. "The Shakespeare Theatre at the Folger." *The Shakespeare Quarterly* 41 (Winter 1990): 507–20; Henry, Gerrit. "Kahn Plays Shakespeare Straight." *New York Times* 22 August 1976: sec. 2: 1, 5; Rosenfeld, Megan. "Michael Kahn's Star Turn." *Washington Post* 21 April 1991: G1, 4; Rothstein, Mervyn. "Shakespeare on the Potomac: A Reappearing Act." *New York Times* 16 September 1990: sec. 2: 7.

William H. Rough

TADEUSZ KANTOR [b. April 6, 1915, Wielopole, Poland; d. December 8, 1990, Kraków, Poland]. In 1955, after working as a theatre director and a stage designer, Kantor, together with Maria Jarema, established the Cricot 2 company in Kraków. The aim of the theatre was to continue the tradition of Cricot, Kraków's prewar theatre of visual artists, and to seek new and radical methods of acting and staging in its contacts with the contemporary avant-garde poets and artists. Outside of Poland, the most widely known productions of Kantor's Cricot 2 theatre were *The Dead Class* (1975), *Wielopole, Wielopole* (1980), *Let the Artists Die* (1985), *I Shall Never Return* (1988), and *Today Is My Birthday* (1990).

Kantor, a visual artist, theatre director, and theoretician, was perceived as an experimentalist of nontraditional theatre. On the one hand, he was grounded in constructivism, surrealism, and Bauhaus; on the other hand, he created his own individual aesthetics whose contradictory elements constituted the *modus vivendi* of his artistic endeavors. Accordingly, art and theatre were, for Kantor, an answer *to*, rather than a representation *of*, reality. They were autonomous structures constantly acquiring new thought dimensions in the process of questioning and suppressing illusionistic effects of traditional theatre. In Kantor's theatre, a bombed room, a cafe, a wardrobe, a cloakroom, and a poorhouse were regarded as real places of the "lowest rank"; that is, as "poor" places manifesting Kantor's insistence that theatre be a real place (rather than a conventional building) where the vision of the ever-present artist "onstage" is executed. *The Return of Odysseus* (1944), for example, was not staged in a theatre building (nearly all the theaters in Kraków were destroyed), but in a room of a house damaged by war. This method of breaking theatrical illusion, however, was not limited to the external aspects of representation. In his *Zero Theatre* (1963), Kantor evoked negative emotions such as apathy, melancholy, and depression by emphasizing "non-acting," "surreptitious acting," "erasing," "automation," and "acting under duress" onstage in order to question patterns of traditional plot development and acting.

The *Theory of a Theatre of Real Space/Theatre Happening* (1967), *The Impossible Theatre* (1969–73), the *Theatre of Death* (1975), the *Room of Memory* (1980), the *Theory of Negatives* (1985), the *Theory of Hyperspace* (1986), the *Inn of Memory* (1988), and the *Theory of the Found Reality* (1990) mark subsequent stages in what Jan Kott has called Kantor's "theatre of essence." All of these theories indicate a rupture between the traditional theatre and Kantor's theatre, and were the extension, the elaboration, or often the rejection of previously accepted tenets concerning theatrical illusion of space, text, character, and time. The *Theatre of Real Space* postulated that, during a performance, the actors ought to perform activities and characters in a way which agreed with the reality of the performance space and its characteristics. In the *Theatre of Death*, Kantor reintroduced the impassable barrier, which had been erased in *The Return of Odysseus*, between the auditorium and the performance space, in order to suggest that the present time of performance was only a self-consistent point of convergence of the past (life) and the future (death). The *Room of Memory* presented the audience with the artist's immaterial memory enacted by the actors onstage. In the *Theory of Negatives*, events onstage brought forth and joined other "memories," that is, characters, from different past events. These "memories" were interimposed as if they had been the frames of a film negative stacked one atop another. The *Theory of Hyperspace* focused on the attributes of space—tension, rhythm, density, speed, and direction—and their execution onstage. The *Inn of Memory* created a meeting ground for Kantor and his memories/actors. The *Found Reality* explored the ambiguity contained in representation positioned in the liminal space between reality and illusion.

In recognition of Kantor's achievements, the French Ministry of Culture organized an international symposium in June of 1989, "Tadeusz Kantor: peintre, auteur, homme de théâtre: ses résonances á la fin du XXe siècle," to honor the Polish director's contribution to visual arts in this century.

ADDITIONAL PRODUCTIONS: 1938: *The Death of Tintagiles* (Maeterlinck); 1942: *Balladyna* (Juliusz Słowacki); 1944: *The Return of Odysseus* (Stanisław Wyspiański); 1957: *The Cuttlefish* (Stanisław Witkiewicz); 1961: *The Country House* (Stanisław Witkiewicz); 1963: *The Madman and the Nun* (Stanisław Witkiewicz); 1967: *The Water-Hen* (Stanisław Witkiewicz); 1973: *Dainty Shapes and Hairy Apes* (Stanisław Witkiewicz); 1979: *Where Are the Snows of Yesteryear* (cricotage); 1986: *The Wedding* (cricotage); 1987: *The Machine of Love and Death* (cricotage); 1988: *I Shall Never Return, A Very Short Lesson* (cricotage); 1990: *The Silent Night* (cricotage).

SELECTED BIBLIOGRAPHY: Bablet, D., and B. Eruli. *T. Kantor: Textes de Tadeusz Kantor.* Vol. 11. *Les Voies de la Création Théâtrale.* Paris: Centre National de la Recherche Scientifique (CNRS), 1990; Kantor, Tadeusz. "The Milano Lessons: Lesson XII." *The Drama Review* 35 (Winter 1991): 136–47; Kantor, Tadeusz. "The Writings of Tadeusz Kantor, 1956–1985." Trans. Michal Kobialka. *The Drama Review* 30 (Fall 1986): 114–76; Kłossowicz, J. *Tadeusz Kantor: Teatr.* Warszawa: Państwowy Instytut Wydawniczy, 1991; Nawrocki, P., and H. Neidel. *Kantor. Ein Reisender—seine Texte und Manifeste.* Nurnberg: Institut fur Moderne Kunst, 1988; Plesniarowicz, K. *Teatr Smierci Kantora.* Chotomów, Poland: Verba, 1990; *Wielopole, Wielopole.* Trans. M. Tchorek and G. Hyde. London: Marion Boyars, 1990.

Michal Kobialka

ELIA KAZAN [b. September 7, 1909, Istanbul, Turkey]. Kazan immigrated to New York with his Greek family in 1913. As a result of a strict and isolated childhood, he rebelled against wealth, privilege, and social status, but retained his ethnic pride and an obsession with obtaining the American dream. These attitudes are reflected most clearly in his film *America America* (1963).

The most important influences in shaping his artistic sensibilities, however, were his two-year exposure to Alexander Dean's directorial methods at the Yale Drama School (1930–32), and his association with the Group Theatre under Harold Clurman,* Cheryl Crawford, and Lee Strasberg* (from 1932 until the end of the decade). The Group provided him his first theatrically committed experience and introduced him to the acting system of Konstantin Stanislavsky* and to the leftist theatre of social change. Kazan's ability to do many odd jobs soon earned him the nickname "Gadget" or "Gadge," and he was always heavily involved with the planning of all production facets—sound, lights, costumes, and scenery.

Kazan's first commercial hit was Thornton Wilder's *The Skin of Our Teeth* (1942). His most significant and seminal theatre work, however, was done in collaboration with Arthur Miller and Tennessee Williams, often with vital input from designer Jo Mielziner. He directed Miller's *All My Sons* (1947), *Death of a Salesman* (1949), and *After the Fall* (1964). Kazan's first production of a Williams script was *A Streetcar Named Desire* (1947), followed by *Camino Real* (1953), *Cat on a Hot Tin Roof* (1955), and *Sweet Bird of Youth* (1959). These six productions (of thirty major assignments) best exemplify his directorial style and made him America's most respected serious director of the 1940s and 1950s, one who was able to get poetry from the common things of life.

Kazan's directing style, drawn from the Method which he had begun to learn from Strasberg, was perfect for its time, even if anathema to modernist tastes and unsuccessful when applied to the classics. Kazan, later in his career, admitted his shortcomings in this regard, quitting the stage after a disastrous production of Middleton and Rowley's *The Changeling* (1964), which he directed while he was codirector of the fledgling Repertory Theatre of Lincoln Center.

During the 1940s and 1950s, however, Kazan's sensibilities, compromising temperament, even his idiosyncracies, matched the psychological themes of Miller, Williams, and even the clichés of William Inge (*The Dark at the Top of the Stairs*, 1957). In his notebook for *Streetcar*, which he regards as a "poetic tragedy," and in those for other plays, Kazan thoroughly analyzed characters whose lives were frequently overpowered by lies, illusions, or buried secrets. Kazan's unique talent was manipulating actors in such a way as to extract large, ambivalent emotions from them and to find workable associations for the roles. Ultimately, he was most concerned with staging these emotions (rarely with humor) and the conflicts between characters. "Direction," he has stated, "finally consists of turning psychology into behavior."

Kazan productions were often frenzied, overwrought, and even sensational. In his preparation, he focused upon characters' actions and intentions, with copious and vivid descriptions (utilizing active verbs) in the margins of texts where he divided scenes into "beats." Extraordinarily extensive notes accompany most of his working scripts. For *After the Fall*, for example, there are 100 pages of detailed, typed commentary, and Kazan's production books at the Wesleyan University Cinema Archives offer further evidence that he found some rationale in Dean's emphasis on picturization in staging. Ironically, Kazan placed little emphasis on preplanned blocking.

In the late 1950s, although still in demand in the theatre, Kazan turned more to film. Growing ever more impatient with other people's work, he resorted more to autobiographical touches in his films. Ultimately he found the greatest satisfaction writing fiction.

Kazan has had four discrete careers: first, as apprentice actor, stage manager, and general assistant with the Group Theatre; next, as theatre director; then, as director of such films as *A Tree Grows in Brooklyn* (1945), *A Streetcar Named Desire* (1951), and Kazan's only film based on a stage production, *Viva Zapata!* (1952), *On the Waterfront* (1954), *East of Eden* (1955), *Baby Doll* (1956), *The Arrangement* (1969), and *The Last Tycoon* (1976); and finally, as writer of six novels—*America America* (1962), *The Arrangement* (1967), *The Assassins* (1971), *The Understudy* (1974), *Acts of Love* (1978), and *The Anatolian* (1982). His autobiography, which appeared in 1988, provides a less than flattering portrait of Kazan the artist and man, arrogant and egotistical, though surprisingly short on vanity.

ADDITIONAL PRODUCTIONS: 1938: *The Gentle People* (Irwin Shaw); 1939: *Thunder Rock* (Robert Ardrey); 1943: *Harriet* (Florence Ryerson and Colin Clements) with Helen Hayes, *One Touch of Venus* (S. J. Perelman and Ogden Nash); 1944: *Jacobowsky and the Colonel* (adapted by S. N. Behrman); 1953: *Tea and Sympathy* (designed by Mielziner); 1958: *J. B.* (designed by Boris Aronson); nineteen films.

SELECTED BIBLIOGRAPHY: Basinger, Jeanine, John Frazer, and Joseph W. Reed, Jr., eds. *Working with Kazan*. Middletown, CT: Wesleyan Film Program, 1973; Ciment, Michel, ed. *Elia Kazan: An American Odyssey*. London: Bloomsbury, 1988 [includes "Notebook for *A Streetcar Named Desire*"]; Ciment, Michel. *Kazan on Kazan*. New York: Viking Press, 1974; Clark, Leroy Watson. "The Directing Practices and Principles of Elia Kazan." Diss. Kent State U, 1976; Kazan, Elia. *Elia Kazan: As Life*. New York: Alfred A. Knopf, 1988; Michaels, Lloyd. *Elia Kazan: A Guide to References and Resources*. Boston: G. K. Hall, 1985; Murphy, Brenda. *Tennessee Williams and Elia Kazan: A Collaboration*. New York: Cambridge University Press, 1992; Pauly, Thomas H. *An American Odyssey: Elia Kazan and American Culture*. Philadelphia: Temple University Press, 1983.

Don B. Wilmeth

WOODIE KING, JR. [b. July 27, 1937, Mobile, Alabama]. One of the most important figures in contemporary black theatre, Woodie King is an accomplished director, producer, actor, editor, educator, and filmmaker.

Raised in Detroit, King began acting while still a child. He earned an undergraduate degree in theatre from the Will-O-Way School in 1961, and continued his studies at Detroit's Wayne State University, where his teachers included Harold Clurman,* Tyrone Guthrie,* Guthrie McClintic,* and Basil Rathbone.

In 1962, King and a group of his fellow students, feeling they were the victims of discrimination in casting at Wayne State, converted a tavern into a 100-seat performance space called the Concept East Theatre. Associated with the National Association for the Advancement of Colored People (NAACP), the group performed five or six plays a season, primarily works by young black playwrights such as Amiri Baraka (then LeRoi Jones), Ed Bullins, and Ron Milner, but also occasional pieces by white writers, including Edward Albee and Jack Gelber. While at Concept East, King learned to produce powerful, stylized productions on shoestring budgets; at the same time, he directed, acted, learned theatrical management, toured several productions, and wrote theatrical criticism for a Detroit newspaper.

In 1964, King came to New York to participate in the black theatre movement. He studied directing with Lloyd Richards* (whom he considers his greatest influence) and theatre administration with Wynn Handman at the American Place Theatre (where he staged several shows including a workshop reading of Ron Milner's *Who's Got His Own*), and co-founded an Off-Off-Broadway company, Theatre Genesis. He acted Off-Broadway in *A Study in Color* (1964) and *Day of Absence* (1966) at St. Marks Playhouse, in *Who's Got His Own* (1966) and *The Displaced Person* (1966–67) at the American Place Theatre, and on Broadway in *The Great White Hope* (1968).

In 1965, with federal funding, King created and ran a pioneering cultural training program for young blacks and Latinos at Mobilization for Youth, an antipoverty program on New York's Lower East Side. There he produced plays by J. E. Franklin, Lonnie Elder, and Douglas Turner Ward,* and supervised a number of award-winning short films created by program participants.

As an outgrowth of the Mobilization for Youth program, King founded the New Federal Theatre in 1970, at New York's Henry Street Settlement House, his longest-lived theatrical venture. Inspired by the Negro units of the original Works Progress Administration (WPA) Federal Theatre Project, the New Federal Theatre created productions (as W.E.B. DuBois had once urged) about, by, for, and near its audience. It had an "open-door" policy: government subsidies allowed the theatre to charge no admission fees until 1976, and audience members were free to come and go as they pleased. An early New Federal Theatre production was *Right On!* (1970), a dramatic work about Harlem poets, which King later made into a film documentary.

Throughout the 1970s, King grew increasingly busy as a director and producer working both at the New Federal Theatre and with other theatre groups around the country. His work in this period included Milner's *What the Winesellers Buy* (1973), Athol Fugard's *Sizwe Banzi Is Dead* (1976), a revival of the Federal Theatre Project's "Voodoo" *Macbeth* (1976), Milner's *Season's Reasons* (1976), Bullins's *Daddy* (1977), Elaine Jackson's *Cockfight* (1977), and Lorraine Hansberry's *A Raisin in the Sun* (1978). As a producer, King's work included *The Taking of Miss Janie* (1975), and (as coproducer with Joseph Papp) Ntozake Shange's *For Colored Girls Who Have Considered Suicide When the Rainbow Is Enuf* (1978). King also produced and directed a dramatic film, *The Long Night* (1976), two documentaries, *The Black Theatre Movement* (1978) and *The Torture of Mothers* (1980), and a docudrama, *Death of a Prophet* (1982).

In 1980, King was named producer of the National Black Touring Circuit, which was organized with funding from the Ford Foundation and the National Endowment for the Arts, and directed the Circuit's first production, Shange's *Boogie Woogie Landscapes* (1980). In the early 1980s he began to direct more interracial plays, such as Stephen Taylor's *Appear and Show Cause* (1982, Cleveland; 1985, New York), for which he won the 1986 Audelco Award. His Broadway production of Milner's *Checkmates* (1987), starring Ossie Davis and Ruby Dee, received mixed reviews, but earned him the NAACP's 1987–88 Image Award for Best Director. In 1989, he produced and directed an adaptation of James Weldon Johnson's *God's Trombones*, and in 1990 directed the first of a series of productions of Rob Penny's *Good Black* (1990). For the future, he is hoping to direct black casts in plays traditionally performed by white actors, such as Oscar Wilde's *The Importance of Being Earnest* and Nikos Kazantzakis's *Christopher Columbus*.

King has edited several anthologies of black literature, including *Black Drama Anthology* (co-edited with Milner, 1972); published a volume of his own essays, *Black Theatre, Present Condition* (1981); and edited *New Plays for the Black Theatre* (1989). He has also taught at Yale, Columbia, Penn State, New York University, Oberlin, and Hunter.

Hard-working, creative, and politically committed, King has made a career of doing ambitious productions with little funding. "I just don't stop working because I don't have a million dollars to work with," he has said, adding wryly, "there's no question if I had a million I could do twenty times better."

ADDITIONAL PRODUCTIONS: 1977: *First Breeze of Summer*; 1978: *Love to All*; 1982, 1983: *Home* (Samm-Art Williams); 1984: *Dinah, Queen of the Blues* (Sasha Dalton and Ernest McCarty); 1985: *Love to All*, *Ameri/Cain Gothic* (Paul Carter Harrison); 1986: *Boesman and Lena* (Fugard), *I Have a Dream*; 1987: *Lady Day at Emerson's Bar and Grill*, *'night, Mother* (Marsha Norman); 1988: *Splendid Mummer*, 1990: *Joe Turner's Come and Gone* (August Wilson), *The Member of the Wedding* (Carson McCullers); 1991: *Harvest the Frost* (1991).

SELECTED BIBLIOGRAPHY: Bailey, Peter. "Woodie King, Jr.: Renaissance Man of Black Theatre." *Black World* April 1975: 4–10; King, Woodie. *Black Theatre, Present Condition*. New York: National Black Theatre Touring Circuit, 1981; Lewis, Barbara. "Rapping With Woodie King." *The Black Theatre Alliance Newsletter* November, 1977; Lewis, Barbara. "The King of Black Theatre Producers." *New York Amsterdam News* 27 January 1979; Nadler, Paul. Personal Interview with Woodie King. 6 January 1993; Marquis *Who's Who*. Vol. 8, *Contemporary Theatre, Film, and Television*. 45th ed. Detroit: Gale, 1984; Clippings file on Woodie King, Jr., The Billy Rose Collection, The New York Public Library.

Paul Nadler

OTOMAR KREJČA [b. November 11, 1921, Skryšov, Czechoslovakia]. Along with Alfred Radok,* Krejča was Czechoslovakia's leading postwar director. His career, like that of Radok, was significantly affected by political circumstances, including exile. Not formally schooled in theatre, Krejča was first a successful actor, ultimately performing some 130 roles in theatre and film. After gaining practical experience during the war years in provincial theatres, Krejča joined the D46 Theatre of E. F. Burian* in the first postwar season, playing Prometheus and Cyrano. He then worked for another significant Czech director, Jiří Frejka,* at the Vinohrady Theatre from 1946 to 1951, playing some twenty roles and taking his first steps toward directing.

From 1951 to 1964, Krejča was a member of the National Theatre, where he acted in several plays directed by Radok and where he served as head of drama from 1956 to 1961. During this period, his work shifted from acting to directing as he focused on working with new playwrights (František Hrubín, *A Sunday in August*, 1958; Josef Topol, *Their Day*, 1959; and, Milan Kundera, *Owners of the Keys*, 1962). Krejča's other outstanding productions at the National Theatre included *The Sea Gull* (1960) and *Romeo and Juliet* (1963), both designed by Josef Svoboda (as were most of Krejča's productions during this period). Other notable Krejča-Svoboda collaborations occurred abroad: *Hamlet* (1965) in Brussels and later, *Waiting for Godot* (1970) in Salzburg.

In 1965, seeking greater freedom than the institutionalized National Theatre provided, Krejča launched his own studio theatre, Divadlo za Branou [Theatre Beyond the Gate], where he and his creative team (dramaturg Karel Kraus, designer Svoboda, and resident playwright Josef Topol) from the National Theatre attracted international attention with new works and classic revivals. Actors were contracted for one season at a time rather than given indefinite tenure, and no fixed number of new productions was determined for each season, thereby allowing adequate rehearsal time. In his stagings of Anton Chekhov's *The Three Sisters* (1966), *Ivanov* (1970), and *The Sea Gull* (1972), Alfred de Musset's *Lorenzaccio* (1969), and a conflation of Sophocles' *Oedipus* and *Antigone* (1971), Krejča revealed mature directorial methods: exhaustive study and conceptualization of the text with an eye to current social and ethical issues; an elaborately prepared promptbook and staging plan to which actors were expected to adjust; a lengthy rehearsal period with great attention to detail; and the creative integration of scenography with the rest of the production. Although Krejča was sometimes criticized for his exhaustive, overly analytical approach to directing, his productions were notable not only for their multiple levels of meaning, but also for their vivid, physicalized imagery frequently embodied in masks and highly expressive patterns of movement (e.g., the elaborate system of masks in *Lorenzaccio* or the desperately agitated movement (resembling birds trapped in a cage) of Chekhov's three sisters at the end of the play.

Despite the August 1968 military invasion of Czechoslovakia, the Gate Theatre survived until 1972, by which time it was one of the few remaining symbols of the liberal, creative era prior to the invasion. In 1972, however, the theatre was administratively closed, and Krejča (whose productions had often implied a critical, though not overtly accusatory, view of Czech socialist society) was out of work. From 1974 to 1976, he was allowed to direct in a suburban Prague theatre, but his future seemed bleak until diplomatic negotiations resulted in his being able to direct in West Germany and elsewhere outside Czechoslovakia. From 1976 to 1990, Krejča directed some thirty productions in various parts of Europe, working only occasionally with the same theatre more than once or twice. Twelve of these productions were of Chekhov, clearly his favorite playwright. With the toppling of the Communist regime in Czechoslovakia in 1989, Krejča, who had been gradually reestablishing contacts in Prague for almost a year, was able to revive the Gate Theatre with direct sponsorship by the new Ministry of Culture. Back in his former quarters, he set about reestablishing his company, now known as Theatre Beyond the Gate II, with many of his former actors. For his first production in Prague after eighteen years he chose *The Cherry Orchard*, a play which he had staged four times during his years abroad, but had never before directed in Czechoslovakia. Opening in January 1991, the finely tuned, serious, conservative production stressed the seemingly fated, tragic plight of its protagonist, Ranevskaya. The mixed critical reception of the production was less significant than the resurrection of a company under a director whose work had helped make Prague a theatre center of Europe in the 1960s.

ADDITIONAL PRODUCTIONS: 1954: *An Ideal Husband* (Wilde); 1963: *Zahradní Slavnost* [*The Garden Party*] (Václav Havel); 1964: *Konec Masøpustu* [*End of Carnival*] (Josef Topol); 1975: *Platonov*; 1978: *Measure for Measure*; 1982: *The Father*; 1985: *Uncle Vanya*; 1986: *Miss Julie*; 1989: *Twelfth Night*.

SELECTED BIBLIOGRAPHY: Burian, Jarka. "Art and Relevance: The Small Theatres of Prague." *Educational Theatre Journal* 23 (October 1971): 229–57; Burian, Jarka. "Krejča's Voice Is Heard Again in Prague." *American Theatre* 8 (June 1991): 36–37; Burian, Jarka. "Otomar Krejča's Use of the Mask." *The Drama Review* 16 (September 1972): 48–56; Černý, Jindřich. *Who Is Otomar Krejča?* Prague: Orbis, 1968.

Jarka M. Burian

LES KURBAS [b. December 12, 1887, Stary Scalat, Ukraine; d. October 15, 1942, in one of Stalin's camps]. After graduating from the Vienna University, Kurbas returned to the Ukraine, where he created experimental "Young Theatre" in Kiev in 1916. Kurbas tried to break the traditions of the national theatre, which was realistic, relied on melodramas or light comedies, and included folk singing and dancing for entertaining an audience. In 1918 Kurbas staged (and performed in) Sophocles' *Oedipus Rex* in which he followed Max Reinhardt* in his sense of pageantry, poetry of form, and ideas of theatre as magic. Tragic tension was created by the Chorus's synchronized movements and the monumentality of the sculptural expression. In plays of Molière, Carlo Goldoni, Franz Grillparzer, and contemporary Ukrainian dramatists, Kurbas continued to establish new theatrical forms and acting style.

In his best works, Kurbas did something new in Ukrainian theatre: his actors combined emotions with grotesque eccentricities; he also included close-ups of the actors' faces on the cinema screen. The most distinctive characteristic of his directorial style was the graphic quality of mise-en-scènes, simplicity of groupings, a spareness of his sets, and dynamic rhythm. One of his major achievements was making traditional songs and dances integral parts of the tragic action, which he demonstrated in *Haydamaks* (1920), a play by Taras Shevchenko about the uprising of rebellious Cossacks.

In 1922 Kurbas's theatre was renamed "March" and moved from Kiev to Kharkov, the capital of the Ukraine at that time. Kurbas retained his position as artistic director until 1933. In 1923 he directed *Gas* by Georg Kaiser and *Jimmy Higgins* after Upton Sinclair. These productions, designed by Vadim Meller, had distinctive expressionistic style. Like most directors of his time, Kurbas was also influenced by constructivism. In many productions, he illuminated the mass crowd scenes and urbanized sets from below, above, and the side; had many intersections and stairs onstage; and used the synchronous movements of actors to imitate different mechanisms. In *Macbeth* (1924), Kurbas combined the principles of the Elizabethan theatre with those of the propaganda theatre (all characters wore the same militarized uniform). In *The People's Malakhy* by Mikola Kulish (1928) Kurbas achieved unprecedented, for the Ukrainian stage, authenticity, poignancy, and veracity of the characters. He also wrote and directed the films *Vendetta* (1924), *MacDonald* (1924), and *Arcenalczi* (1925).

ADDITIONAL PRODUCTIONS: 1930: *Dictatorship* (Mikitenko); 1933: *Maklena Grasa* (Kulish).

SELECTED BIBLIOGRAPHY: Kurbas, Les. *Spogady Cuchasnikiv*. Kiev: Misteztvo, 1969; Rudnitsky, Konstantin. *Russian and Soviet Theater, 1905–1932*. Trans. Roxane Permar. New York: Harry N. Abrams, 1988; *Stanovlenie Ukrainskoi Sovetskoi Rezhissury*. Leningrad, 1984: 23–24.

Paulina Shur

JAROSLAV KVAPIL [b. September 25, 1868, Chudenice, Bohemia, Czechoslovakia; d. January 10, 1950, Prague, Czechoslovakia]. Kvapil is generally regarded as the father of twentieth-century Czech stage direction, but it is also true that his work represents a culmination and refinement of symbolist-inspired *fin de siècle* theatre. His roots were in literature; he wrote poetry, essays, criticism, plays, and librettos (including the libretto for Dvořák's opera *Rusalka*). Kvapil had the unusual good fortune of never having been forced to work for theatres other than Prague's two largest, the National Theatre and the Vinohrady Theatre. He joined the National Theatre as a literary advisor in 1900, but soon began directing successfully, and by 1911 was head of drama at what the Czechs call their "little golden chapel on the Moldau."

Kvapil's directing career had two main periods: eighteen years at the National Theatre; and, starting in 1921, seven years at the Vinohrady Theatre. After 1928, he functioned productively in a number of cultural and educational positions, while occasionally guest directing. He returned to the National Theatre after World War II as a consultant, and also supervised revivals of a few of his prewar successes at the Vinohrady Theatre. His career, during which he directed some two hundred productions, was formally capped by his being declared a National Artist in 1946.

Kvapil's most significant achievements were concentrated in the first two decades of the century. He brought to Czech theatre—an actors' theatre dominated at the time by vestiges of romanticism and genre realism—a respect for theatre as an art that is unified and shaped by the interpretation and vision of a single artist, the director. In this, he reflected the approach of Adolphe Appia and Gordon Craig, as well as the practices of Max Reinhardt* and the leaders of the Munich Artists' Theatre.

Kvapil also had enormous respect for the playwright and the actor. He favored the classics, above all Shakespeare and Molière, and contemporary playwrights, both native and foreign, much of whose work appeared on Czech stages for the first time under his direction. Eclectic in the best sense, Kvapil also greatly admired Konstantin Stanislavsky,* translating the Russian master's concern with psychological subtlety and realism to his own work on plays by Henrik Ibsen, Anton Chekhov, Paul Claudel, Maxim Gorky, and their Czech counterparts, and to Shakespeare as well.

His staging was rooted in tendencies associated with the symbolists and impressionists. He inclined more toward a graceful, harmonious blending of elements— toward a pictorial, painterly scene of mood and atmosphere—rather than to a dynamic, intense confrontation of clashing forces occurring in an architecturally delineated stage space. Lighting and music also became significant components of a Kvapil production, reinforcing the tone and mood of his work with the actors, which was marked by his adopting a supportive approach with them, relying more on their creativity than on his own imposed concepts.

Although Kvapil was primarily oriented toward a *l'art pour l'art* approach, he nevertheless strongly felt, in his fashion, the social responsibility of theatre. In 1916, in the midst of World War I, while the Czechs were still under Austro-Hungarian rule and ostensibly fighting the English and other Allied forces, he mounted a cycle of fifteen Shakespeare plays; in 1918, still before the end of the war, he presented another cycle, of forty-five Czech plays, as a sign of the Czechs' craving for independence.

ADDITIONAL PRODUCTIONS: 1902: *The Petty Bourgeois* (Gorky); 1904: *The Wild Duck*; 1905: *Hamlet* with Eduard Vojan; 1907: *The Three Sisters*, *Oresteia*; 1909: *Ghosts*, *The Merchant of Venice*; 1912: *The Master Builder*, *The Blue Bird*; 1917: *A Revolutionary Trilogy* (Viktor Dyk); 1921: *Troilus and Cressida*; 1925: *Perifery* (František Langer).

SELECTED BIBLIOGRAPHY: Kvapil, Jaroslav. *Souborné Dílo J. K.* [Collected Works]. 4 vols. Prague, 1945–48; Rutte, Miroslav, and František Bartoš. *The Modern Czech Scene*. Prague: Vladimír Zikeš, 1938; Vočadlo, Otakar. "The Theater and Drama of Czechoslovakia." *The Theater in a Changing Europe*. Ed. T. H. Dickinson. New York: Henry Holt, 1937.

Jarka M. Burian

L

MARK LAMOS [b. March 10, 1946, Chicago, Illinois]. In 1980, Mark Lamos became the artistic director of the Hartford Stage Company of Connecticut. There, he has emerged as one of America's most daring and imaginative interpreters of the classics, especially Shakespeare.

Born and raised in Chicago, Lamos attended Northwestern University on a scholarship, preparing for a musical career as a violinist. But, pursuing his interest in the classics, he transferred to theatre, and after graduation he began an acting career at the Guthrie Theatre, Minneapolis. In the 1970s, Lamos performed in regional theatres and on Broadway in plays ranging from *King Lear* (Lamos portrayed Edgar) and *Hamlet* to *The Caretaker* and the musical *Cyrano*.

Directing was not an early career choice for Lamos. His professional debut occurred at the Guthrie Theatre's second stage, Guthrie II. In 1976, under the mentorship of Michael Langham,* Lamos staged Athol Fugard's *Hello and Goodbye* and Jerome Kilty's *Dear Liar* on this experimental stage. Then, in 1979, Langham hired Lamos as associate director of the California Shakespearean Festival. Over the next two seasons Lamos directed *The Taming of the Shrew*, *Romeo and Juliet*, *Hamlet*, and *A Midsummer Night's Dream*. During those same years, he became artistic director of the Arizona Theatre Company, staging *A Flea in Her Ear*, George Kelly's *The Showoff*, *The Sea Gull*, and *Twelfth Night*.

Lamos assumed the artistic helm of the Hartford Stage in 1980 where he began to develop his radical interpretations of classical plays. His Hartford productions were designed to dispel the audience's preconceptions of classic plays in performance. He seldom rewrites scripts, preferring to alter mood or setting to illuminate the work. His use of provocative visual images makes a classic text accessible and relevant. For example, his 1987 production of *Hamlet* (with Richard Thomas in the title role) was conceived as a reenactment of the events in a politically unstable banana republic, reproduced on a movie set.

His process employs the free use of painting, sculpture, and music as reference points. *Pericles* (1987) was set in a Magritte-like landscape that included a floating rocking chair. These eccentric visual worlds are the end product of several long-standing collaborations with designers, most notably John Conklin and Michael Yeargan.

The 1986 Lamos-Yeargan production of *Twelfth Night* began with an exploration of ideas on gender and the formal visual aspects of Oriental theatre. As the concept evolved, these germinal ideas were abandoned, and the thematic focus that emerged was centered on the end of youthful celebration and the initiation of responsibility. The mise-en-scène became what Lamos referred to as a "cosmic Roseland," a 1930s ballroom complete with piano, mirror ball, and Cole Porter melodies.

Lamos's work with actors has garnered him the reputation as a major innovator of a unique American style of Shakespearean performance. His personal and highly specific approach to directing actors attempts to release the performer's impulses through the text. Lamos credits his background in music as a valuable asset for his understanding of complex scripts. It enables him to assist actors in their discovery of the musicality of the verse.

His penchant for elaborate staging has been realized in exceptional productions of *The Greeks* (1982), a nine-play, seven-hour marathon, and *Peer Gynt* (1989), with Richard Thomas, designed by John Conklin. He mounted international productions of *Desire under the Elms* at the Pushkin Theatre, Leningrad (1988), and the opera *The Voyage of Edgar Allan Poe* at the Storan Theatre in Sweden (1986). He also directed *Don Giovanni* for the St. Louis Opera and *Arabella* for the Santa Fe Opera.

ADDITIONAL PRODUCTIONS: (productions at Hartford Stage Company, Connecticut, unless listed otherwise) 1981: *Cymbeline, Undiscovered Country* (adapted by Tom Stoppard); 1984: *Anatol* (Arthur Schnitzler); 1985: *The Tempest*; 1988: *A Midsummer Night's Dream*; 1990, *The Illusion* (Corneille, adapted by Tony Kushner); 1991, *Master Builder* (adapted by Irene Berman, Gerry Baumman) with Sam Waterston.

SELECTED BIBLIOGRAPHY: Bartow, Arthur. "Mark Lamos." *The Director's Voice.* New York: Theatre Communications Group, 1988: 175–93; deVries, Hilary. "A Shakespeare Wallah Expands His Stage." *New York Times* 5 March 1989: sec. 2: 5, 39; Gussow, Mel. "The Greeks, Nine Classics Condensed." *New York Times* 28 February 1982: 50; Holmberg, Arthur. "Erotic 'Dreams.' " *American Theatre* 6 (April 1989): 12–17; Powers, Kim. "Mark Lamos" (interview). *Theater* 15 (Spring 1984): 20–26; Powers, Kim. "Mark Lamos Conquers the Classics." *TheaterWeek* 10 December 1990: 23–31; Sheehy, Helen. "Mary Layne: The Lamos Connection." *American Theatre* 7 (July/August 1990): 45–46; Steele, Mike. "Peer Today." *American Theatre* 6 (July/August 1989): 22–29.

Richard Warner

RALF RUNAR LÅNGBACKA [b. November 20, 1932, Narpio, Finland]. Nationally renowned as an expert in both Brecht's theatre and Chekhov's dramaturgy, Ralf Långbacka is a reformer of traditional performance and of Finnish theatre direction. As a drama professor and a visiting director in various theatres in Finland and other Scandinavian countries (the Det Norska Teatre [the Norwegian Theatre] in Oslo, the Göteburg City Theatre, the Dramastiska Teatre [the Art Theatre] in Stockholm, and the Suomen Kansallisooppera [the National Opera of Finland]), Långbacka has had a strong influence on theatre. At these theatres and others, Långbacka has repeatedly returned to Brecht's and Chekhov's dramas. His direction of these plays is somewhat of a cross between the playwright's dialogue and the director's critical examination of how the play would be interpreted in another era.

In directing Bertolt Brecht,* Långbacka has used the playwright's dialectic to move the audience smoothly and consciously back to the society of that period and to examine and comprehend people and their environment as only the theatre is able. Realism, to Långbacka, has meant expressing in an aesthetic way an ideological attitude concerning the theatre's connection with society and the performance's connection with its audience. Each period, according to the director, has to discover its own realism.

In *The Life of Galileo* (1973), Långbacka examined the conscience of a scientist, and the researcher's ethics, morality, and responsibilities were exposed to the changing circumstances of the period. In directing the nationalist play *Herr Puntila and His Servant Matti* (1970), Långbacka achieved a serious interpretation of the work by employing *Gestus* instead of naturalism and psychological realism to express the intense feelings of the script.

Långbacka has also subjected Chekhov's dramaturgy to the Brechtian critical method and has examined the conflict of Chekhov's people within the context of their time period. Långbacka has concluded that Chekhov's comedy can be directed without a poetic spirit and style, and he believes that an intellectual, dispassionate, critical social analysis can replace empathy and sentimentality.

Långbacka's reputation has flourished with his analytical interpretations of Georg Büchner's, Henrik Ibsen's, and Eugene O'Neill's plays. For *Danton's Death* (1976), the presentation was slanted toward the author's own writings, historical view, and the revolutionary manifesto "The Messenger of Hessen"; while *Peer Gynt*'s (1981) powerful humanism was rendered vital by means of the director's ability to unite intense, sentimental acting with precise Brechtian analysis.

ADDITIONAL PRODUCTIONS: 1961: *Uncle Vanya*; 1962: *The Three Sisters*; 1965: *Marat/Sade*; 1966: *The Sea Gull, Uncle Vanya, The Cherry Orchard*; 1971: *The Rise and Fall of the City of Mahagonny* (Brecht-Weill), *The Three Sisters*; 1975: *The Good Woman of Setzuan*; 1978: *The Cherry Orchard*; 1979: *Macbeth* (Verdi), *Herr Puntila and His Servant Matti* (film); 1986: *Platonov* (Chekhov); 1987: *The Life of Galileo*; 1989: *Don Giovanni* (Mozart).

SELECTED BIBLIOGRAPHY: Fischer-Lichte, Erika. "All the World's a Stage: The Theatrical Metaphor in the Baroque and Postmodernism." *Nordic Theatre Studies*. Special
International Issue. Proceedings of the XIth FIRT/IFTR (International Federation for
Theatre Research) Congress. Denmark: Munksgaard, 1990; *Haavesta vai pakosta. Nä-
kökulmia teatteriohjaajan työhön* (*Fantasy or Necessity. Visual Angles to the Theatre
Director's Work*). Helsinki: State printing, Theatre college, 1986; Långbacka, Ralf. *Bland
annat om Brecht. Texter om teater* (*Something Else About Brecht. Articles about Theatre*).
Ekenäs: Söderströms, 1981; Långbacka, Ralf. *Möten med Tsehov* (*Meeting with Chekhov*).
Ekenäs: Söderströms, 1986; *Teatterikirja, Ralf Långbacka, Kalle Holmberg* (*Theatre
Book, Ralf Långbacka, Kalle Holmberg*). Helsinki: Love, 1977.

Hanna-Leena Helavuori

MICHAEL LANGHAM ([b. August 22, 1919, Somerset, England]. When Michael
Langham left law school in September 1939 to join the British armed services,
he did not realize that he was embarking on a career in the arts. He became
interested in theatre while a prisoner of war from 1940 to 1945, continued his
theatrical activity after the war, and by 1948, was employed by the Birmingham
Repertory Company as its artistic director, a position he also held at the Glasgow
Citizens' Theatre (1953–54). During the 1950s, he directed for the Royal Shakespeare Company, the Old Vic, and National Theatres, in Holland, Belgium,
Germany, and Australia, as well as at Sadler's Wells.

Langham will most likely be remembered, however, for his work on this side
of the Atlantic. As artistic director and general manager from 1955 to 1967, he
presided over the establishment of the Stratford (Ontario) Shakespeare Festival
as a production company of international renown and as a leading institution in
the cultural life of Canada. He assumed the position of artistic director at the
Guthrie Theatre in Minneapolis, in 1971 when the theatre was on the brink of
financial and artistic ruin, and resuscitated that company before he left in 1977.
In 1978, Langham became the director of the Juilliard School's Drama Division,
a position he held until his retirement in 1992.

Langham assumed control of the Stratford Festival during a time of rising
nationalism. He was determined to give the theatre a distinctly Canadian identity,
and yet create a solid ensemble of well-trained, adaptable, and responsive actors.
Based on a humanist interpretation and his beliefs that an artist must remain
conscious of the parallels between real life and the world created on the stage,
that the internal struggle of the protagonist is of primary concern, and that the
text of Shakespeare's plays must be treated as musical scores, his productions
often challenged his actors and audiences alike.

By the time he took over at the Guthrie, Langham had become masterful at
using the thrust stage, and was a fine administrator as well. He worked to create
a sense of community ownership of the Guthrie, to develop an ensemble, and
to produce theatre that was relevant (rather than merely up-to-date) and capable
of being understood by all audiences. Nevertheless, his productions frequently
captured the poetry and grandeur of Shakespeare often absent in American productions of the period.

Langham carried his commitment to well-trained actors to his work as an educator at Juilliard and, since 1986, at Balliol College at Oxford under the auspices of the British American Drama Academy. He resigned the Juilliard post to concentrate on directing in Great Britain. Langham has been influential in the careers of many artists, including Christopher Plummer, whom he directed in *Hamlet* (the first production on the Stratford Festival thrust stage, 1957), in *Cyrano de Bergerac* (which he adapted with Anthony Burgess, 1962), and most recently in Garson Kanin's *Peccadillo* (1986); Zoe Caldwell, in *Love's Labour's Lost* (1961), which remains one of the Festival's greatest successes, and *The Prime of Miss Jean Brodie* on Broadway (1967); and Brian Bedford, in many productions, most recently the critically praised *Merchant of Venice* at the Folger (1988) and Stratford (1989).

ADDITIONAL PRODUCTIONS: 1951: *Othello* (at Old Vic and Berlin tour); 1954: *The Beggar's Opera* (Sadler's Wells); 1956: *Hamlet* (Stratford-on-Avon), *Henry V* (Christopher Plummer and actors from Montreal's Théâtre du Nouveau Monde, designed to reflect an optimistic Canadian nationalism); 1963: *Andorra* (Max Frisch) on Broadway, *Troilus and Cressida* and *Timon of Athens* (both dark productions to reflect changing Canadian political tendencies); 1966: *Henry V* (designed to make a statement against violence); 1969: *The Way of the World* (National Theatre, London); 1970: world premiere of *A Play* by Aleksandr Solzhenitsyn (at the Guthrie); 1980: *Arms and the Man* (Guthrie); 1982: *Arms and the Man* (Stratford); 1988: *No Time for Comedy*, with Michael Learned and Brian Bedford; 1992: *Timon of Athens* (Stratford). **Stratford Festival, 1957–67:** *Coriolanus* with Paul Scofield, *Taming of the Shrew*, *Love's Labour's Lost* (established the company's international reputation when performed in Chichester), *The Country Wife*, *The Government Inspector*, *School for Scandal*. **Guthrie Theatre, 1971–77:** *Diary of a Scoundrel*, *Oedipus*, *King Lear*, *The Winter's Tale*, *Measure for Measure*. **Juilliard, 1980–92:** *Much Ado about Nothing*, *Ring Round the Moon*, *The Beggar's Opera*.

SELECTED BIBLIOGRAPHY: Campbell, Nora R. "The Stratford Shakespeare Festival of Canada: Evolution of an Artistic Policy (1953–1980) as a Basis for Its Success." Diss. U of Wisconsin–Madison, 1982; Dallin, Howard Vincent. "The Theatrical Concepts and Directorial Approaches of Michael Langham." Diss. U of Minnesota, 1979; Langham, Michael. Introduction. *The Stratford Scene 1958–1968*. Ed. Peter Raby. Toronto: Clarke Irwin, 1968; Russo, Peggy Anne. "The Great Stage of Fools: The Stratford Festival's King Lear 1964." Diss. U of Michigan, 1988.

Mark S. Weinberg

PIERRE LAROCHE [b. August 2, 1931, Brussels, Belgium]. After graduating from the Brussels Conservatory, Pierre Laroche joined the Rideau de Bruxelles of Claude Etienne* in 1957. As a director, Laroche (like Jean Vilar*) was drawn to the great poetic works; however, he also revealed an instinctive gift for Belgian surrealism. Since Etienne wanted to promote Belgian playwriting, Laroche proved a valuable collaborator. Named associate director of the Rideau (1961–68), Laroche directed premieres of plays by Charles Bertin, Jean Sigrid, and especially Paul Willems. His production of Willems's *It's Raining in My House* (1962) became one of the Rideau's perennial successes, with numerous revivals and European tours, including to the USSR (1966) and to the Montreal World

Exposition (1967). It was awarded the grand prize at the Barcelona Festival, and Laroche directed a film version of the play in 1969.

Laroche's directorial work is marked, not only by vivid visual imagery and a strong musical sensibility, but by concern for the actor's creative process. He studied Method acting at the Actors' Studio in New York and in Belgium with Harry Friehback-Brown. During rehearsals for Laroche's *Babel* (a collective creation), the Living Theatre gave workshops for the cast. In 1959, Laroche cofounded the Belgian theatre/media institute l'I.A.D., and he has taught at the Brussels Conservatory, the University of Kansas, and the Toneelacademie in Holland.

Laroche has directed for Belgian theatres including the Parc and the National as well as for Dutch companies, and from 1980 to 1981 he served as co-artistic director of the Haagse Comedie in The Hague. In recent years, he has developed a second career as a leading actor, winning a 1989 Adam de la poésie for his performances of contemporary Belgian authors. Laroche's poetic sensibility is complemented by an unerring instinct for theatrical possibilities. His successful stage adaptations include Apollinaire's surrealist text *L'Enchanteur pourrisante* (*The Rotting Magician*), which represented Belgium at the Spoleto Festival and the London World Theatre Festival in 1973, and *Blaise Pascal* (Pierre Laroche, 1976). Being drawn to the dreamworld of surrealism, however, does not for Laroche imply an evasion of contemporary life; he seeks works which shed light on our era, and his staging of Dante's *Purgatory* (with costumes by Elena Mannini) for the Théâtre National in 1992 reflected his belief that while we may not know heaven or hell, purgatory is an accurate reflection of our lives.

ADDITIONAL PRODUCTIONS: 1961: *A Bashful Man at Court* (Tirso de Molina, Belgian Eve du Théâtre for direction); 1962: *The Possessed* (Dostoyevsky/Camus); 1963: *Warna* (Paul Willems), *The Green Bird* (Gozzi); 1965: *A View from the Bridge*; 1966: *Le Marché des petites heures* (Paul Willems); 1967: *The Investigation*; 1968: *The Idiot*, *The Tale of Tobie and Sara* (Claudel, with original music by Darius Milhaud); 1969: *Royal Hunt of the Sun*; 1971: *Break of Noon* (Claudel); 1974: *The Brothers Karamazov*; 1975: *Blood Wedding*; 1979: *Tartuffe*; 1982: *Don Juan*; 1983: *The Tempest*, *The Marriage of Figaro*; 1984: *Struggle of the Dogs and the Black* (Bernard-Marie Koltès).

SELECTED BIBLIOGRAPHY: Etienne, Claude. *40 années du Rideau de Bruxelles*. Brussels: Rideau de Bruxelles, 1983; Laroche, Pierre. "A Belgian Surrealist: Pierre Laroche Talks to P & P." *Plays and Players* May 1973: 28–29; Laroche, Pierre. *Blaise Pascal*. 3rd ed. Brussels: Cahiers du Rideau, 1979; Saada, Serge. "Le grand théâtre ment beaucoup moins que la vie: Entretien avec Pierre Laroche." *Alternatives Théâtrales* June 1990: 113–14.

Suzanne Burgoyne

LAURETTE LAROCQUE-AUGER (JEAN DESPREZ) [b. September 1, 1906, Hull, Quebec, Canada; d. January 27, 1965, Montreal, Canada]. In 1923, Laurette Larocque-Augier, then working in her father's bookstore in Hull, began working with the Beaulne Group (Groupe Beaulne), directed by Leonard Beaulne. She stayed with that company until 1929.

In 1927, she participated with Jacques Auger in the foundation of the Academic Circle (Cercle Academique), and in 1929, she went to Paris for theatrical studies with Auger, now her husband. In Paris she specialized in phonetics. When she returned to Canada, she became director of the theatre department at the School of Music and Speech of the University of Ottawa (École de musique et de déclamation de l'Université d'Ottawa). Under the auspices of the school she directed the following plays:

L'Innocente (one act) by H. R. Lenormand, which won the Bassborough Trophy and the Canadian Festival of Dramatic Art in 1935;

Othello by Shakespeare in 1936;

L'Indienne, of which she was the author and which won first prize in the regional dramatic art competition in 1936; revived in 1939;

La Fleur Merveilleuse by Michel Zamacols in 1936;

Carnaval au bord de la Mer, a sketch of which she was the author and which was presented on the occasion of the 1937 French Language Congress;

Les Boules de Neige by Louvigny de Montigny in 1937;

Under the auspices of the Ottawa Canadian-French Institute, in 1938, *Les Patriotes*, a play in verse in three acts and a prologue by Fulgence Charpentier.

She wrote for the Quebec Eucharistic Congress in 1938, *Le Dernier Miracle du Frère André*, which was performed there by the Jacques Auger Troup.

Then settling in Montreal, she pursued a career as a director and dramatist. She became one of the most popular authors of radio and television series, until her death in 1965.

For the theatre she wrote and directed:

1938—*Toto*, one act, French MRT prize;

1941—*La Guerre des Croix*, for the Comedie de Montreal, at the Stadium;

1941—*Les Corbeaux Nazis*;

1942—*La Tragédie de Mayerling*, in ten scenes, for the Comedie de Montreal, at the National Monument;

1949—*La Cathédrale*, in three acts, eighteen scenes and epilogue, at the National Monument;

1951—*Anne de Boleyn*, one act for the French MRT, at Gesu;

1951—*Le Mal*, one act;

1954—*Un Amant Viendra ce Soir*, one act.

For the cinema she wrote the screenplay for *Père Chopin*, the first French language film made in Canada (Fedor Ozep and George Freedland), a production of Renaissance-Films, in 1945.

Her first radio series, "C'est la Vie," ran from 1940 to 1943 and was followed by "La Marmaille" (1940–42); "Jeunesse Doree" (1942–65); "Yvan L'Intrépide" (1945–54); "Docteur Claudine" (1952–64); "Carré Saint-Louis" (1954);

"Père Alexandre" (1954); "L'Aube du Bonheur" (1955). For television she wrote "Je Me Souviens" (1955–56); "Prise de Bec" (1956–58); "Joie de Vivre" (1959–63). She also had columns in *Metro-Express, Tele-Radiomonde*, and *La Patrie* and had an important influence on Montreal's theatre world.

Larocque-Auger used the pseudonym Jean Desprez. She used the male name "Jean" (John) to protest against the domination of male directors in the theatre of the time. She said that if only men could succeed as directors, she had no choice but to take a man's name.

Laurette Larocque-Auger fought for a French-language Canadian theatre on the stage and on Quebec radio. She had an exceptional sense of spectacle, of the audience's point of view, the balances of staging, the contrasts of rhythms and tones, as well as those of lighting techniques. However, her impetuous character brought her unforgettable quarrels with the critics.

SELECTED BIBLIOGRAPHY: Béraud, Jean. *350 ans de théâtre au Canada français.* Montreal: Le Cercle du livre de France, 1958; Bergeron, Raymond, and Marcelle Ouellette. *Voice, visage et légendes, Radio-Canada 1936–1986*; Bourassa, André-G., and Jean-Marc Larrue. *Les Nuits de la "Main," cent ans de spectacles sur le boulevard Saint-Laurent (1891–1991).* Montreal: VLB éditeur, 1993; Fortin, Marcel. "Le théâtre d'expression française dans l'Outaouais des origines à 1967." Diss. U. of Ottawa, 1985; Legris, Renée. *Dictionnaire des auteurs de radio-feuilletons québécois.* Montreal: Fides, 1981; Rinfret, Edouard G. *Le théâtre canadien d'expression française (repertoire analytique des origines à nos jours).* 2 vols. Montreal: Leméac, 1976. Montreal: Les enterprises Radio-Canada, 1986.

Guy Beaulne

JO (GEORGES) LAVAUDANT [b. February 18, 1947, Grenoble, France]. In the wake of the political and cultural upheavals of May 1968, Lavaudant joined the Théâtre Partisan, a student theatre group in Grenoble. He quickly assumed the position as stage director, although he continued to act in smaller roles for many years. The Théâtre Partisan's collective productions, including textual collages by Lavaudant himself (*Les Tueurs, La Mémoire de l'iceberg*) set the course for his later work. The troupe also experimented with the classics. *Lorenzaccio* (1973) drew critical acclaim, and in 1975 the Théâtre Partisan left its small theatre to produce it again in Grenoble's Maison de la Culture.

In 1976, Lavaudant became codirector of Grenoble's Centre Dramatique National des Alpes (CDNA) where he developed a distinct style that subordinated the text to the mise-en-scène, often dissolving character and narrative into a juxtaposition of musical numbers, modern dance, and bits of discourse drawn from a wide range of sources. This fragmentation, along with the spectacular visual images afforded by monumental sets, striking lighting effects, and lavish costumes, led critics (both sympathetic and hostile) to label his productions "aesthetic," "decadent," and Lavaudant's preferred term, "baroque." Although Lavaudant brought this style to known texts by Bertolt Brecht,* Luigi Pirandello,* and Jean Genet, it is best typified by his own textual collages *L'Education Sentimentale* (1976) and *Les Cannibales* (1979), and especially his landmark productions of Pierre Bourgeade's *Palazzo mentale* (1976 and 1986; winner of the Grand prix de la critique dramatique of 1977).

More recently, Lavaudant has pursued new interests, experimenting with opera and working abroad, in Mexico (1986 and 1988), and directing *Phèdre* in Bhopal, India (1990). In 1986, he was named director at the Théâtre Nationale Populaire (TNP) in Villeurbanne, but it is as yet difficult to gauge how his position in a major national theatre (with substantial national subsidies) will affect his work. Brecht's *Baal* and *In the Jungle of Cities* (1988), Lavaudant's own *Veracruz* (1988), and Michel Deutsch's *Féroé la nuit* . . . (1989), while still employing epic fragmentation, were more contemplative, pondering rather than reveling in the dispersal of subjectivity and fixed meaning. In the program notes to *Platonov* (1990), he identified with Chekhov's attempt "to describe incoherence to the most minute detail without seeking to reinstate an order based on false values," echoing the preoccupations of his time much as his early collective theatre and the celebratory deconstructions of the 1970s did. Lavaudant is one of the most prominent and well-subsidized directors working in France today.

ADDITIONAL PRODUCTIONS: 1976: *Louve basse* (Denis Roche), *King Lear*; 1978: *Herr Puntila and His Servant Matti*; 1981 and 1982: *Géants de la montagne* (Pirandello); 1982, 1987, and 1988: *L'Enlèvement du sérail* (Mozart); 1983: *Les Céphaides* (Jean-Christophe Bailly); 1984: *Richard III*, *The Balcony*; 1988: *Pawana* (Jean-Marie Le Clezio); 1991–92: *Le Retour de Pandora* (Jean-Christophe Bailly).

SELECTED BIBLIOGRAPHY: Belleret, Robert, ed. *Les Acteurs de la Région Rhône-Alpes*. Paris: Le Monde Editions, 1991: 159–71; Lavaudant, Georges. "Une Perspective sur la décennie." *Europe* 648 (April 1983): 13–20; Poulet, Jacques. "Chapitre suivant: Revoltes. . . . Entretien avec Georges Lavaudant." *France Nouvelle* 1738 (5 March 1979): 43–50; Sandier, Gilles. *Le Théâtre en crise*. Grenoble: La Pensée Sauvage, 1982: 46, 273–74, 305–6.

Timothy Scheie

JORGE LAVELLI [b. 1931, Buenos Aires, Argentina]. Jorge Lavelli, a naturalized French citizen, has directed over fifty productions in Europe, the United States, and South America. A principal member of the mid-sixties' "new avant-garde," Lavelli directed controversial stagings of both contemporary dramatic scripts and a classic repertoire, including Fernando Arrabal's *L'Architecte et l'empereur d'Assyrie* (1967), *Much Ado about Nothing* (1969), Eugène Ionesco's *Jeux de massacre* (1970), *Old Times* by Harold Pinter (1973), and *The Sea Gull* (1974). He began to produce experimental interpretations of traditional operatic texts with Mozart's *Idomeneo* in 1975. In 1988, he was appointed first director of the Théâtre National de la Colline in Paris.

A former student of economics and then drama in Buenos Aires and Paris, Lavelli made a startling entry onto the French theatre scene in 1963 with his staging of Witold Gombrowicz's *Le Mariage*. The production won that year's Prix du Concours des Jeunes Compagnies. His subsequent work as part of the group labeled the "Théâtre panique," which included Jérome Savary,* Victor Garcia, and Fernando Arrabal, continued in this experimental vein. Through the late sixties and the seventies, Lavelli produced numerous plays influenced by the repopularized ideas of Antonin Artaud on the theatre of cruelty, psychodrama, and the happening.

Involved in opera as well as theatre since 1975, Lavelli has directed ambitious lyric productions in France, Italy, and the United States, such as Charles François Gounod's *Faust* (1975–76 in Paris, New York, and Washington), *Madame Butterfly* (1978, Milan), and *The Marriage of Figaro* (1979, Aix-en-Provence). As head of the Théâtre de la Colline, he has continued to direct both dramatic and lyric pieces. In all of his work, Lavelli has been concerned with avoiding the anecdotal and emphasizing the play of natural and psychological forces onstage. He strives to reduce narrative line, characters, set, and costume to their essential, mythic elements. Preferring that the production begin and end "in liberty," Lavelli first discusses and refines his basic ideas with the play's designers and then, during rehearsals, works to suggest, rather than prescribe, solutions to the actors.

ADDITIONAL PRODUCTIONS: 1966: *L'Échange* (Claudel); 1969: *Le Concile d'amour* (*The Council of Love*, Oskar Panizza); 1971–72: revival of *L'Architecte et l'empereur d'Assyrie* in Cologne and Nuremberg; 1974: *Les quatre jumelles* (*The Four Twins*, Copi); 1976: *Exit the King*, *Faust* in New York and Washington, D.C.; 1977: *Pelléas et Mélisande* (Debussy), *La Mante Polaire* (*The Polar Mantle*, Serge Rezvani); 1980: *Doña Rosita la soltera* (Lorca); 1982: *Magdalena* (Prokoviev); 1985: La Nuit de Madame Lucienne (Copi); 1987: *Polyeucte* (Corneille); 1988: *Réveille-toi, Philadelphie!* (Billetdoux); 1989: *Opérette* (Gombrowicz); 1990: *Greek* (Steven Berkoff), *La Nonna* (Roberto Cossa); 1991: *Comédies Barbares* (Ramón Maria Valle-Inclán); 1992: *Kvetch* (Berkoff).

SELECTED BIBLIOGRAPHY: Kerr, Cynthia B. "*Polyeucte*, ou le Triomphe de l'irrationnel." *Papers on French Seventeenth Century Literature* 16 (1989): 29–44; Norès, Philippe, and Colette Godard. *Lavelli*. Paris: Christian Bourgeois, 1970; Obregón, Osvaldo. "Entretien avec Jorge Lavelli." *Cahiers du Monde Hispanique et Luso-Brésilien* 40 (1983): 137–48; Satgee, Alain, and Jorge Lavelli. *Lavelli: Opéra et mise à mort*. Paris: Fayard, 1979; Simon, Alfred. *Dictionnaire du théâtre français contemporain*. Paris: Larousse, 1970: s.v. "Arrabal" and "Lavelli"; Whitton, David. *Stage Directors in Modern France*. Manchester: Manchester University Press, 1989.

Cynthia Running-Johnson

WILFORD (CARSON) LEACH [b. August 26, 1929, Petersburg, Virginia; d. June 21, 1988, New York, New York]. Known as an educator, playwright, and director, Leach earned an M.A. (1954) and a Ph.D. (1957) from the University of Illinois. He taught theatre at Sarah Lawrence from 1958 to 1981 and at Yale from 1978 to 1979. His association with experimental professional theatre began when he met Ellen Stewart, head of La Mama ETC, and subsequently became La Mama's artistic director in 1970. His productions with this company were marked by a playful ingenuity and by his "twisting" audience expectations. He won an Obie Award in 1972 for his work with La Mama.

Leach's success at La Mama brought him to the notice of Joseph Papp, with whom he had a long association. Directing over twenty-one productions at the

New York Shakespeare Festival, he is best known for the Tony Award–winning productions of *The Pirates of Penzance* (1980) and *The Mystery of Edwin Drood* (1985). Critics praised *Pirates of Penzance* for its exuberant sense of farce, and audiences enjoyed its unusual casting of rock singers Rex Smith and Linda Ronstadt as the romantic leads. The production incorporated a variety of techniques to free it from preconceived notions of Gilbert and Sullivan, including the use of electronic music, a Keystone Kops–like chorus, and an eclectic mixture of choreographic styles. Leach encouraged improvisation in rehearsals and often incorporated these explorations (such as the Pirate King's fencing match with the orchestra leader) into the production. The success of this production, transferred to Broadway in 1981, helped bring Papp's Public Theatre out of debt. It also won an Obie and a Drama Desk Award (1981) in addition to the Tony.

The Mystery of Edwin Drood, a musical adaptation by Rupert Holmes of Dickens's unfinished novel, was a parody of Victorian music-hall and melodramatic styles. The production used audience participation and good-natured camp to create a spirited farce. It was awarded a Tony in 1986. *Pirates of Penzance* and *The Mystery of Edwin Drood*, as well as classics directed by Leach, demonstrated his insistence that masterpieces be freed from conventional trappings in order to restore the original spirit of the work, and thus revitalize them for modern audiences.

ADDITIONAL PRODUCTIONS: 1970: *Carmilla* (Wilford Leach); 1974: *C.O.R.F.A.X. (Don't Ask)* (Wilford Leach); 1978: *The Taming of the Shrew*; 1979: *The Mandrake* (Wallace Shawn).

SELECTED BIBLIOGRAPHY: Barron, James. "Wilford Leach, Theatre Director and Papp Associate, Dies at 59." *New York Times* 21 June 1988: sec. 1: 22; Kroll, Jack. Review of *The Pirates of Penzance*. *Newsweek* 19 January 1981: 87; Rigdon, Walter, ed. *The Biographical Encyclopedia and Who's Who of the American Theatre*. New York: James H. Heineman, 1966; Sauvage, Leo. Review of *The Mystery of Edwin Drood*. *New Leader* 4–18 November 1985: 18–19; Simon, John. Review of *The Pirates of Penzance*. *New York* 11 August 1980: 41; *Who's Who in America*. 1988–89 ed. Wilmette, Illinois: Macmillan Directory Division, 1989.

Ann Demling

ELIZABETH ALICE LECOMPTE [b. April 28, 1944, New Jersey]. Elizabeth LeCompte graduated from Skidmore College in applied art and art history, having worked summers at Off-Off-Broadway's Café Lena. She joined the Richard Schechner* Performance Group in 1970, where she acted and served as assistant director.

In 1975, LeCompte, Spalding Gray, and other members of the Performance Group began to explore a different kind of work from Schechner's—a less psychological, less ritualistic, less narrative theatre. Their early work centered on Gray's examining himself as object and subject, performer and observer, and they worked improvisationally with "found" objects: toys; clothing; preexisting dramatic material; music; video; film; and pieces of set from previous work. LeCompte took notes and reported what she liked.

In 1980, Schechner left the Performance Group, but the new company retained the Performing Garage and the corporate status, renaming itself the Wooster Group after the New York street on which the Garage is located. LeCompte became artistic director. The group's first pieces were *Sakonnet Point* (1975), *Rumstick Road* (1977, 1980), and *Nayatt School* (1978), the trilogy known as *Three Places in Rhode Island*. The works were based on the actors' individual responses to Gray and his biographical artifacts. *Rumstick Road* dealt specifically with the suicide of Gray's mother and reactions to it by Gray family members, his mother's psychiatrist, and the actors. Since *Rumstick Road* used taped interviews with Gray's family against their will and with the mother's psychiatrist without his knowledge, it became the subject of critical attack on ethical grounds. *Nayatt School* dealt with the nature of the performer as subject, and with loss. This marked the first collaboration with filmmaker Ken Kobland. *Point Judith* (1979–80) evolved as an epilogue to the trilogy.

Route 1 & 9 (1981) was their next and perhaps most controversial work. Because of a blackface routine in it, the Wooster Group lost New York State Arts Council funding on grounds of racism. Ironically, the routine was meant to confront the performers' and audience's racism through an unmediated, outrageous portrayal of the worst racial stereotyping.

L.S.D. (1983) continued the Wooster Group's practice of appropriating preexisting dramatic texts, and then deconstructing and absorbing them into a new structure. Arthur Miller's *The Crucible* was used in *L.S.D.* during its initial development, but Miller refused permission to use his text, threatening legal action. Ultimately, a new text was substituted. *St. Anthony* (1987), the final part of a second trilogy, *The Road to Immortality*, was built around Flaubert's text and was developed with director Peter Sellars.* The piece theatricalized the Wooster Group's history.

The size of the group's oeuvre is small, because each piece evolves over a long period of experimentation and is revived and revised. The works continue to evolve with each presentation. Besides open-endedness, long-term collaborative development, and the use of found objects, characteristics of the group's work are wild theatricality, "pornography," and intellectual rigor. LeCompte describes the work as "multiplex," celebrating multiple perspectives and interpretations. She consistently refuses to impose a moral and is not bound by conventions of cause and effect. She uses set design, film sequences, tape recordings, and television monitors to play cinematically with perspective, moving back and forth between close-up and panoramic foci, thus allowing the spectator many visual choices.

The work of the Wooster Group is mediated through each member of the company and finally through LeCompte. Stanislavskian acting is rejected, and actors approach the material as themselves, maintaining their subjectivity. As David Savran writes in *Breaking the Rules*, "They do not attempt to represent, but to explore what it means to represent . . . , to submit to the diagnostic gaze"

(Savran, 81). Each piece is densely layered visually, kinetically, and aurally, creating performance rather than literary texts.

LeCompte has acknowledged Schechner, Richard Foreman,* and Robert Wilson* to be among those who have significantly influenced her work, especially Foreman's use of nonrepresentational gesture and Wilson's musical rather than logical structure. Filtered through her, these influences merge with the material introduced by her company. Theatre works emerge from the process; they are not predetermined. The result is a LeCompte/Wooster Group signature style that has as much to do with the process of its creation as with performance.

The Group received a 1991 Obie for Sustained Achievement. The unusual longevity (sixteen years) of the collective aside, LeCompte has led it to become arguably American's most important experimental group.

ADDITIONAL PRODUCTIONS: 1983: *L.S.D.: (. . . Just the High Points . . .)*; 1984: *North Atlantic, L.S.D.: (. . . Just the High Points . . .)* in Boston, Washington, New York; 1985: *Miss Universal Happiness* (with Richard Foreman); 1986; *L.S.D.: (. . . Just the High Points . . .)* in Edinburgh, Wales, London, Brussels, Amsterdam, Frankfurt, Milan; 1991: *Brace Up.*

SELECTED BIBLIOGRAPHY: Bierman, James. "Three Places in Rhode Island." *The Drama Review* 81 (March 1979): 13–30; Calhoun, John. *"The Road to Immortality* and Europe: The Wooster Group tours *L.S.D.: (. . . Just the High Points . . .)." Theatre Crafts* May 1989: 69–75; Cole, Susan Letzler. *Directors in Rehearsal: A Hidden World.* New York: Routledge, 1992: 91–124; LeCompte, Elizabeth. "The Making of a Trilogy: Introduction." *Performing Arts Journal* 3 (Fall 1978): 80–86; Robinson, Alice M., Vera Mowry Roberts, and Milly Barranger, eds. *Notable Women in the American Theatre: A Biographical Dictionary.* Westport, CT: Greenwood Press, 1989: 528–31; Savran, David. "Adaptation as Clairvoyance: The Wooster Group's *Saint Anthony." Theater* 18 (Fall-Winter 1986): 36–41; Savran, David. *Breaking the Rules: The Wooster Group.* New York: Theatre Communications Group, 1988: Savran, David. "Terrorists of the Text." *American Theatre* 3 (December 1986): 18–24, 45; Schmitt, Natalie Crohn. *Actors and Onlookers: Theater and Twentieth-Century Views of Nature.* Evanston, IL: Northwestern University Press, 1990: chs. 1–2.

Lila Wolff-Wilkinson

EVA LE GALLIENNE [b. January 11, 1899, London, England; d. June 3, 1991, Westport, Connecticut]. In a career that spanned the twentieth century, Eva Le Gallienne was a consummate theatre artist; acclaimed stage actress at twenty and well into her eighties, director, producer, teacher, and translator of the plays of Ibsen. The daughter of English poet Richard Le Gallienne and Danish journalist Julie Norregaard, Eva Le Gallienne learned her craft while working in the theatre, embarking on a full-time acting career while still in her teens. A Broadway star before she was twenty-five, Le Gallienne turned her back on the commercial theatre in the 1920s.

She founded the Civic Repertory Theatre in New York City in 1926, modeling her theatre on the national theatres of Europe, and functioned as leading actress, director, and producer. She directed Chekhov and Ibsen; revived Shakespeare and Molière, Dumas and Barrie; and premiered new American work. She also adapted *Alice in Wonderland* (1932), bringing Lewis Carroll's book to marvelous theatrical life. With these and other productions she created a library of living plays in rotating repertory, among the very few true repertory theatres in America. After seven successful years, the Civic closed, a victim of the depression. Le Gallienne returned to Broadway stardom, but continued her work toward a national repertory theatre. The example of the Civic Repertory Theatre lived on, however, foreshadowing and laying the groundwork for Off-Broadway and the regional theatre movement.

Le Gallienne was an accomplished, thoughtful director who approached the art of directing through critical analysis of the script and through her understanding of acting and actors. She believed that only a director who had been an actor could understand how to handle players. Adept at coaching actors, she changed her directing technique to fit the individual. In her autobiography, *With a Quiet Heart*, she summarized her philosophy, writing, "No two actors can be treated alike. Some need to be flattered, some cajoled; some even bullied. Some like to be told precisely how to read a line or execute a piece of business, while others must be left strictly alone. . . . A great director . . . must be . . . an artist and a craftsman [and] . . . a psychologist'' (99).

Although Le Gallienne began her directing career with productions of Ibsen's *The Master Builder* and *John Gabriel Borkman*, it was her Civic Repertory production of *The Three Sisters* in 1926 (among the first professional productions of Chekhov in the United States) that first earned her critical accolades as a director. To prepare *The Three Sisters*, she took her new company to Weston, Connecticut, for several weeks of preliminary work. They did not rehearse formally, but tried through improvisational work to become the characters, thinking and speaking as the characters. At first Le Gallienne made no attempt to shape the performances, but used the time to get to know the actors, allowing them to explore the characters with no sense of pressure.

Le Gallienne was noted for her ability to create an ensemble, especially in Ibsen's plays. She shaped the performances, paying particular attention to actors' interplay and the spaces between lines—infusing the silences with active thought. Le Gallienne also had a thorough knowledge of the technical areas of the theatre. Often, to prepare a production she would first design and build a model of the set creating a complete production plan, including blocking, set changes, lighting, and properties.

Eva Le Gallienne, a recipient of numerous honors including a special Tony Award and the National Medal of Arts, like her actor-manager predecessors Mrs. Fiske, Eleonora Duse,* and Sarah Bernhardt, has influenced generations of theatre people through the example of her work and her writing.

ADDITIONAL PRODUCTIONS: 1926: *Twelfth Night*; 1928, 1933–34, 1939–40, 1948, 1964: *Hedda Gabler*; 1928, 1933, 1944, 1968: *The Cherry Orchard*; 1928: *Peter Pan*; 1929; *The Sea Gull*; 1930, 1933: *Romeo and Juliet*; 1930: *Alison's House* (Susan Glaspell, won Pulitzer Prize); 1932: *Liliom*; 1932, 1933, 1947, 1982: *Alice in Wonderland*; 1933–

34, 1975: *A Doll's House*; 1934–35: *L'Aiglon* (with Ethel Barrymore); 1937: *Hamlet* (Le Gallienne as Hamlet, Uta Hagen in her acting debut played Ophelia); 1963: *The Sea Gull*; 1964: *Liliom*.

SELECTED BIBLIOGRAPHY: Le Gallienne, Eva. *At 33*. New York: Longman's, Green and Co., 1934; Le Gallienne. "The Story of the Civic Repertory." Unpublished Mss. in the Papers of Eva Le Gallienne (currently held by Helen Sheehy); Le Gallienne, Eva. *With a Quiet Heart.* New York: Viking Press, 1953; Schanke, Robert A. *Eva Le Gallienne: A Bio-Bibliography*. Westport, CT: Greenwood Press, 1989.

Helen Sheehy

ÉMILE LEGAULT [b. March 29, 1906, Ville Saint-Laurent, Quebec, Canada; d. August 28, 1983, Montreal, Canada]. A dramatist, director, and essayist, Father Émile Legault was ordained a priest on June 29, 1930, and shortly thereafter became a professor at the College Saint-Laurent, in a suburb of Montreal. A year later, he was appointed director of the college theatre, a position he held until 1936. In his first attempts at direction, he tried to counter the facile conventions of bourgeois French realist theatre then popular in Quebec, and he advocated a return to authentic theatrical forms. His productions of classical and modern works, such as *Athalie* (1933), *Polyeucte* (1934), *Noé* (André Obey, 1935 and 1942) and *Le Comédien et la grâce* (1936), provided the tone for a movement toward the purification and rehabilitation of French-Canadian theatre which he began during those years. Influenced from 1932 on by the theatre of Henri Ghéon, and involved in the Catholic Action movement in 1935, Legault found in the motto "Faith through dramatic art" his own aesthetic doctrine which he sought to spread through a stylized mystical-poetic repertoire. In order to accomplish this theatrical renewal, in September 1937, he founded the Companions of Saint Laurent (Compagnons de saint Laurent), an amateur company which he directed until 1952.

During his fifteen years with the Compagnons, Father Legault directed most of the several hundred works in the troupe's repertoire. His productions between 1937 and 1939, taken from the religious plays of Louis Barjon S. J. and Henri Ghéon (*Celle qui la porte fit s'ouvrir*, 1937; *Le Noël sur la place*, 1937; *Le Mystère de la messe*, 1938; and *Le jeu de saint Laurent du fleuve*, 1938) form a sort of rough sketch of his revolutionary undertaking. On his return from an educational trip in Europe, at the end of 1939, he widened his scope and shaped the broad outline of his program in terms of both ethical and aesthetic principles, strongly influenced by Jacques Copeau* and his disciples. Choosing a theatre of art which synthesized poetics, presentation, and convention, he constructed a repertoire of varied dramatic forms at first, which wavered between Christian theatre and traditional classic theatre. He began by reviving the masterpieces of Molière, Racine, and Corneille: *Les Fourberies de Scapin* (1944), *Les Femmes savantes* (1940), *Athalie* (1941), and *L'Illusion comique* (1949). To these slightly modernized works, he added those of Shakespeare and the romantic poets Beaumarchais, Musset, and Marivaux, proposed as production and direction models.

From 1945 on, at the Gésu theatre and then the Théâtre des Compagnons, Legault produced contemporary texts by dramatists as varied as Paul Claudel, Jean Anouilh, Jean Giraudoux, Federico García Lorca, Carlo Goldoni, and Luigi Pirandello.* He also staged works by American dramatists such as Tennessee Williams, Thornton Wilder, and Emmet Lavery, and in 1956, he presented the world premiere of *L'Honneur de Dieu* by Pierre Emmanuel.

The choice of this extensive and original repertoire reveals the changing spirit of a director seeking to blend genres, evolving from poetic humor (*Apollon de Bellac*, 1947) to satire (Anouilh's *Le Bal des voleurs*, 1946 and 1951) and to exaggerated farce (*Les Gueux au paradix*, 1951 and *L'Impromptu de Barbe Bleue*, 1949). With such comedies, presented alternately with dramas and tragedies like Claudel's *L'Échange* (1947) and Cocteau's *Oedipe-Roi* (1944), he assured a balance within the repertoire and unveiled the secret to the strength of a director concerned with winning public approval while guaranteeing the immortality of his troupe.

This strength is even more apparent in the pedagogic strategies adopted by Father Legault in realizing another aspect of his program: that of the actor's reform. In order to change the public image of the performer and allow him to recapture his prestige and dignity, the young director drew on knowledge acquired in London and Paris in 1938–39. At the heart of the troupe, he put to the test the lessons of the Parisian Cartel (Jacques Copeau, Louis Jouvet,* Charles Dullin,* Gaston Baty*) and the methods in use at that time by the Parisian troupes (les Compagnons de Notre Dame, les Compagnons de Jeux ou les Commédiens routiers [traveling players]). He also drew inspiration from the experience of the Théophiliens directed by Gustave Cohen in the training of the actor through the use of empirical procedures or similar approaches. Thus, the "purist" approach adapted by the Compagnons emanated, for the most part, from the principles and staging of the École du Vieux-Colombier and the Centre Kellerman de Paris. From 1946 on, following the example of these theatrical artisans, he trained his students in a veritable laboratory of dramatic studies, insisting on the merits of experimentation and improvisation. His Atelier des Compagnons (Compagnon's Studio), founded in 1949, furnished the essential resources for the construction of a new theatre and established the development of a French-Canadian theatre. Thus, in 1953, when he formed the Compagnie des Jongleurs de la Montagne (The Mountain Jugglers Company) at the Oratoire Saint-Joseph, several former Compagnons committed themselves to this new venture. Legault wrote and produced *Premiers Gestes* (1953), *Le Grand Attentif* (1956), and *Kermesse des Anges et des Hommes* (1960) for this company. Thus Émile Legault takes his place as the force behind Quebec's first theatre movement and its first professional director.

ADDITIONAL PRODUCTIONS: 1937: *La Bergère au pays des loups* (Ghéon); 1939: *Le Misanthrope*; 1940: *Brittanicus* (Racine); 1941: *La Tour* (Léon Chancerel), *Le Jeu de Nostre Dame* (Barjon); 1942: *Le Jeu d'Adam et Ève* (Gustave Cohen), *L'Annonce faite à Marie* (Claudel); 1943: *Le Mariage forcé* (Molière), *Le Comedien et la Grâce* (Ghéon);

Le Barbier de Séville (Beaumarchais); 1945: *Le Pauvre sous l'escalier* (Ghéon), *On ne badine pas avec l'amour* (Musset), *Le Jeu de l'amour et du hasard* (Marivaux); 1946: *La Nuit des rois* (*Twelfth Night*), *Antigone* (Anouilh), *Les Romanesques* (Rostand); 1947: *Le Jeu des deux mondes* (Roger Varin); 1948: *Le viol de Lucrèce* (Obey), *La Ménagerie de verre* (*The Glass Menagerie*, Williams); 1949: *Le Malade imaginaire*; 1950: *Le Chemin de la croix* (Ghéon); *Roméo et Juliette*, *La Passion de Notre-Seigneur* (André Legault), *Le Voyage de Monsieur Perrichon* (Eugène Labiche); 1951: *Notre petite ville* (*Own Town*, Wilder), *Henri VI* (Pirandello), *Un Caprice* (Musset); 1952: *Les Noces de sang* (Lorca). SELECTED BIBLIOGRAPHY: Benson, Eugene, and L. W. Conolly. *The Oxford Companion to Canadian Theatre*. New York: Oxford University Press, 1989: 109–10, 297; *Cahiers des Compagnons* 1.1–2 (September–December 1944), 2.1–6 (May 1945–December 1946); Caron, Anne, *La Père Émile Legault et le théâtre au Québec*. Montreal: Fides, 1978; Gagnon, Gilles. ''Le Théâtre des Compagnons de Saint-Laurent.'' *Culture* 30.2 (June 1969): 129–45; Hamelin, Jean. ''Des initiaterus: Les Compagnons (1940–1948)'' and ''Les Compagnons chez eux (1948–1952).'' *Le Renouveau de théâtre au Canada français*. Montreal: Editions du Jour, 1961: 7–30, 52–62; Jasmin-Bélisle, Helene. *Le père Émile Legault et ses compagnons de saint Laurent. Une petite histoire*. Montreal: Leméac, 1986; LaFlamme, Jean, and Rémi Tourangeau. ''La Realisation du fondateur des Compagnons de saint Laurent.'' *L'Église et le Théâtre au Québec*. Montreal: Fides, 1979: 315–17, 332–38; Lefebvre, Paul. ''Le Père Émile Legault et le Théâtre au Québec.'' *Jeu* 11 (Spring 1979): 102–4; Legault, Émile. *Confidences*. Montreal: Fides, 1955; Nadeau, Jean-Marie. ''Présentation du R. P. Émile Legault.'' *Société royale du Canada* 12 (1957–58): 73–77.

Rémi Tourangeau

ROBERT LEPAGE [b. December 12, 1957, Quebec]. Robert Lepage studied at the Conservatoire d'art dramatique in Quebec from 1975 to 1978. In the summer of 1978, he began an apprenticeship in Paris with Alain Knapp, who approached performance, direction, and writing from a perspective that emphasizes creative work above all. On his return to Quebec, Lepage joined with Jacques Lessard, who had just founded the Théâtre Repère. Lepage's theatrical work would henceforth follow the processes of the REPERE Cycles, which recommend approaching creation through the slant of sensory REsources (objects, sounds, texts, music, etc.) explored through scores (Partitions). The results of these free explorations are summarized in an Evaluation before being brought out in REpresentation. The performance created becomes, in its turn, a sensory resource. This creative approach was fundamental for Robert Lepage, and he has remained faithful to it.

His first four years in professional production gave him the opportunity to explore sound, image, poetry, and space. As in a real laboratory, Lepage experimented with multiple facets of the actor's performance, objects, and scenic techniques, with the attribution of masculine characters to the players and vice versa. In creating *Circulations* (coauthor, 1984), he presented his own stage vocabulary, which included both realistic and bizarre elements. The presence of objects is a constant, miniatures invested with a personal, and sometimes spiritual or even magic, sense. Electro-acoustic music and the regular use of sound manipulation equipment contribute to the creation of spellbinding atmospheres (by Bernard Bonnier and Robert Caux). Image projections on various backdrops, the use of photographs, printed matter, charts, and the lighting treatment are always outstanding. (Lepage usually designed his own lighting, sometimes working with Lucie Bazzo.) The visual and the auditory are omnipresent in Lepage's theatrical creations.

Creator and set designer, actor and director, Robert Lepage prefers themes which also mark dramatic and theatrical writing: the voyage, travel, exile; the creative state, not as anguish but as a moment of forming answers to questions; identity, always ambiguous; lies, illusion, dreams, fantasy; reflections of reality and the reverse of concrete reality. These themes are tied to fables with a recurring emphasis (lost love, the quest for a father, the police investigation, psychological drama) or to fabulous adventures (recognition of genius, continental drift, the meeting of East and West). The very contemporary, formal techniques and components of his theatre articulate stories of romantic love or melodrama as much as philosophical reflections.

Enumerating the different elements that enter into the creation of Lepage's spectacles does not explain the magic released in them, magic that is also tied to the presence of Lepage as actor and that values the command of time and space. It is there that the strength of his work is found. His mastery of theatrical time is manifested through a slow performance rhythm conferring a real amplitude to the proceedings. Time in his productions seems immobile, as though in suspension. Lepage plunges us into a fascinating universe. His mastery of space allows him to play on/with points of view: submerged, in flight, on a diagonal, turned inside out and back. Beginning with light, water, and plane surfaces, Lepage places the audience in full view of themselves and at the heart of the visual illusion to which they agree in the theatre. He juggles these elements in an empty space where the magic of the chosen objects operates in a theatrical time which is itself an entity.

ADDITIONAL PRODUCTIONS: 1980: *L'École, c'est secondaire* (co-creator); 1982: *En attendant* (co-creator); 1983: *Coriolan et la monstre aux mille têtes* (after Shakespeare); 1985: À propos de la demoiselle qui pleurait (André Jean), *Point de fuite* (coauthor), *La Trilogie des dragons* (coauthor); 1986: *Vinci* (conceived by Lepage), *Le Bord extrême* (based on Bergman's *The Seventh Seal*); 1987: *Pour en finir une fois pour toutes avec Carmen* (coauthor), *Le Polygraphe* (coauthor); 1988: *Les Plaques Tectoniques* (co-creator), *Le songe d'une nuit d'été* (Shakespeare); 1989: *La Vie de Gallilée* (Brecht), *Roméo et Juliette* (Shakespeare), *Echo* (based on *A Nun's Diary* by Ann Diamond); 1991: *Les Aiguilles et l'Opium* (conceived by Lepage); 1992: *Alanienouidet* (Marianne Ackermann and Lepage), *A Midsummer Night's Dream, Macbeth, The Tempest, Coriolanus* (translated by Michel Garneau); 1993: *Le Château de Barbe-Bleue* (Bartok), *Erwartung* (Schönberg).

SELECTED BIBLIOGRAPHY: "Les dix ans de Repère." Special issue of *L'Annuaire théâtral* (revue de la Société d'histoire du théâtre du Québec) 8 (1990); Hunt, Nigel. "The Global Voyage of Robert Lepage." *The Drama Review* Summer 1989: 104–18; Lafon, Dominique. "*Les Aiguilles et l'Opium.*" *Jeu, Cahiers de théâtre* 62 (1992): 85–

90; Lefebvre, Paul. "New Filters for Creation." *Canadian Theatre Review* 52 (Autumn 1987): 30–35; Lévesque, Solange. "Plaques tectoniques." *Jeu, Cahiers de théâtre* 54 (1990): 155–58; Report on *La Trilogie des dragons* in *Jeu, Cahiers de théâtre* 45 (1985): 40–210; Report on *Vinci* in *Jeu, Cahiers de théâtre* 42 (1987): 85, 126; Sidnell, Michael J. "*Polygraph*: Somatic Truth and an Art of Presence," followed by the script of *Polygraph* by Marie Brassard and Lepage, translated by Gyllian Raby. *Canadian Theatre Review* 64 (Summer 1990): 45–65.

Hélène Beauchamp

ROBERT (BOBBY) LEWIS [b. March 16, 1909, Brooklyn, New York]. Broadway director, theatre educator for six decades, and advocate of the fusion of style and substance, Robert Lewis began his artistic career studying music. He studied at the Institute of Musical Art before turning to theatre in 1929. He joined the Civic Repertory Theatre of Eva Le Gallienne* that year and performed in five productions. On the strength of his 1931 performance in the Actor's Workshop production of Maxwell Anderson's *Gods of the Lightning*, Harold Clurman* and Lee Strasberg* invited Lewis to become an original member of the Group Theatre. Lewis's memorable performances in this company included a comic intern in *Men in White* (1933), a labor spy in *Waiting for Lefty* (1935), and the pyromaniac Mr. May in Clifford Odets's *Paradise Lost* (1935). For this role, Lewis dyed his hair red, combed it to suggest tongues of fire, and wore a black leather finger guard, a visible reminder of a past arson attempt. These audacious and specific external character choices illustrate the theatrical style that distinguished Lewis in a company known for its dedication to psychological realism.

His directing career began with the Group Theatre production of William Saroyan's *My Heart's in the Highlands* in 1939. Lewis's ability and interest in fantasy and lyrical form made him the logical choice to direct this play. His approach to the poetic nature of the script revealed the inner moments with carefully orchestrated staging and underscoring.

After pursuing a film acting career in Hollywood (1942–46), Lewis returned to Broadway with his production of *Brigadoon*, which established his reputation as a skillful director of heightened realism in musical theatre. That same year (1947) also marked the inception of the Actors' Studio. Lewis, Elia Kazan,* and Cheryl Crawford developed this laboratory to continue the noncommercial, experimental work begun by the Group Theatre. During the first year, Lewis taught classes emphasizing external characterization and the use of intentions by asking actors to solve tasks fusing internal choices with external craft solutions. His students included Marlon Brando, Montgomery Clift, Maureen Stapleton, Eli Wallach, Jerome Robbins,* Anne Jackson, Sidney Lumet, and Karl Malden.

The 1950s became Lewis's most productive decade. His staging of John Patrick's *The Teahouse of the August Moon* (1953; 1954, in London) earned the New York Drama Critics' Circle Award for Best Director, and the play won the Pulitzer Prize. Other successes ranged from Arthur Miller's adaptation of *Enemy of the People* (1950) to Truman Capote's first play, *The Glass Harp* (1952). He staged a mystery, *Witness for the Prosecution* (1954), and a David Merrick musical, *Jamaica* (1957), featuring Lena Horne.

As one of America's leading teachers, Lewis has had far-reaching influence on the philosophy and methodology of actor training. His classroom career began in 1936 at Sarah Lawrence College; he co-directed the Group Theatre Studio (1938); and he established the Robert Lewis Theatre Workshop in 1952. He directed the Lincoln Center Training Program (1962), and his association with the Yale School of Drama extended over thirty-five years (1941–76). He became the chair of Yale's Acting/Directing Department in 1974 with a prospectus calling for a holistic approach to directorial interpretation with form and content fused and derived from the script.

Perhaps Lewis's greatest influence came from a series of lectures he delivered on "The Method" in New York City in 1957. These in-depth discussions of the Konstantin Stanislavsky* system and its subsequent American interpretation became his text, *Method or Madness?* This book has served as authoritative source material, helping to refute the growing misconceptions about this specialized approach to actor training. Lewis also wrote *Advice to the Players*, an acting text, and *Slings and Arrows*, an autobiography.

ADDITIONAL PRODUCTIONS: 1949: *Regina* (Blitzstein); 1950: *The Happy Time* (Samuel Taylor); 1959: *Candide* (L. Hellman, music by L. Bernstein); 1965: *On a Clear Day You Can See Forever* (Lerner); 1978: *The Club Champion's Widow* (Noonan) with Maureen Stapleton.

SELECTED BIBLIOGRAPHY: Clurman, Harold. *The Fervent Years*. New York: Hill and Wang, 1958; Cole, Toby, and Helen Krich Chinoy, ed. "Robert Lewis." *Actors on Acting*. New York: Crown Publishers, 1970: 629–34; Garfield, David. *A Player's Place: The Story of the Actors Studio*. New York: Macmillan Publishers, 1980; Lewis, Robert. *Advice to the Players*. New York: Harper and Row, 1980; Lewis, Robert. "Discovering the 'Life of Our Times.' " *American Theatre* 3 (April 1986): 12–17, 48; Lewis, Robert. *Method or Madness?* New York: Samuel French, 1958; Lewis, Robert. "A Point of View and a Place to Practice." *Theatre Arts Monthly* April 1960: 62–64; Lewis, Robert. *Slings and Arrows*. New York: Stein and Day Publishers, 1984.

Richard Warner

[MAUDE] JOAN LITTLEWOOD [b. October 6, 1914, Clapham, London, England]. At sixteen, Joan Littlewood was offered a scholarship to the Royal Academy of Dramatic Art, and despite not graduating, by the time she was twenty-five she was co-founder of Theatre of Action (1934) and Theatre Union in Manchester (1936). Her working-class upbringing and early left-wing theatrical endeavors laid the foundation for her directing career under the auspices of the Theatre Workshop, founded in 1945 with Ewan MacColl. In the same year, she was first able to bring together her ideas of light and sound, voice and movement in a production of MacColl's ballad opera, *Johnny Noble*. Influenced by Rudolf Laban, dance and movement were to become a significant aspect of what Littlewood called "dance theatre."

Littlewood's directing methods were formulated in early productions written by MacColl; further developed via a permanent company of actors, artists, and playwrights; and formalized in her collectively created production of *Oh What a Lovely War* (1963). Though this play clearly reflects Littlewood's style, approach, and polemics, it often overshadows earlier productions pivotal to Littlewood's success as one of Britain's few postwar female directors of nontraditional theatre.

From 1945 to 1953, Theatre Workshop was an itinerant company largely sustained by school productions and foreign tours. During this period, it attempted new plays such as MacColl's *Uranium 235* (1946) with fifteen scenes and fifty-seven characters, played by twelve actors, or classics such as Molière's *The Flying Doctor* (1945). Every play was based on social and political issues, and improvisation became the primary directing tool for Littlewood, who incorporated commedia techniques and music hall antics similar to those of the early San Francisco Mime Troupe.

In 1953, the Theatre Workshop found a permanent home at the Theatre Royal, Stratford East. Littlewood directed eight productions in her first season ranging from her version of *A Christmas Carol* (1953), to a new play by Anthony Nicholson, *Van Call* (1954), to *Richard II* (1954). Improvisation was used in the development of all types of text, as in *Richard II* where Littlewood guided the cast in improvisational explorations of subtext before giving actors the script. From 1953 to 1955, thirty-six new pieces were presented by the Theatre Workshop under the guidance of Littlewood, who espoused a new style of acting which was more lifelike, a "casualness in classics."

At the Paris International Theatre Festival in 1955, Littlewood directed a modern-dress production of *Volpone* which received more recognition in Europe than in England, but the notoriety drew attention to future productions. That same year, Littlewood directed the first English production of *Mother Courage* which, while not a critical success, did reflect the experimental risks that Littlewood took to explore a theatre geared for working-class audiences. By 1958, Littlewood's emphasis had switched from classics and revivals to contemporary plays. She attracted new writers to the Theatre Workshop including Brendan Behan and Shelagh Delaney. Littlewood directed Behan's *The Quare Fellow* (1956) and *The Hostage* (1958) and Delaney's *A Taste of Honey* (1958), as well as Frank Norman's musical *Fings Ain't Wot They Used T'Be* (1959). She continued to use improvisation as a developmental tool for new scripts, with or without the approval of the playwright. Her collaboration with Behan was the most significant, although her work with John Wells on *Mrs. Wilson's Diary* (1967) proved to be an asset evidenced by over 250 performances as a West End transfer.

Overall, Littlewood's directing methods contributed to a change in acting style; eliminated the curtain and the proscenium arch; and emphasized the importance of process over product, changing the way plays were produced and the sort of plays presented. She never realized her goal of achieving a working-class audience, but did pave the way for other artists to work toward that goal in the Fringe Movement. She left England to retire in France in 1975 and has not directed since.

ADDITIONAL PRODUCTIONS: Note: Many of these plays remained in the repertory. 1934–35: *Waiting for Lefty*; 1936: *Las Edition* (MacColl), *Miracle at Verdun* (Hans Chlumberg), *Fuente Ovejuna*; 1937: *Lysistrata*; 1938: *The Good Soldier Schweik* (adapted from Jaroslav Hašek); 1945: *Don Perlimplin*; 1947: *Operation Olive Branch* (MacColl's version of *Lysistrata*); 1948: *The Other Animals* (MacColl), *The Gentle People* (Irwin Shaw); 1949: *As You Like It*; 1950: *Alice in Wonderland*; 1952: *Henry IV*; 1953: *Treasure Island*; 1954: *The Dutch Courtesan*, *The Cruel Daughters* (adpated by Littlewood from Balzac); 1955: *Arden of Faversham*; 1956: *Edward II*; 1957: *Macbeth*, *You Won't Always Be on Top* (Henry Chapman); 1958: *Celestina* (adapted from Fernando de Rojas); 1959: *Make Me an Offer* (Wolf Mankowitz); 1960: *Sparrers Can't Sing* (Stephen Lewis); 1964: *A Kayf Up West*, *Henry IV* (adapted by Littlewood from Parts I and II); 1966: *The Marie Lloyd Story* (Daniel Farson and Harry Moore); 1970: *The Projector* (John Wells), *Forward Up Your End* (Ken Hill); 1972: *Costa Packet* (Frank Norman); 1973: *So You Want to Be in Pictures* (Peter Rankin).

SELECTED BIBLIOGRAPHY: Coren, Michael. *Theatre Royal: 100 Years of Stratford East*. London: Quartet Books, 1984; Goodman, Judith Lea. "Joan Littlewood and Her Theatre Workshop." Diss. New York U, 1975; Goorney, Howard. *The Theatre Workshop Story*. London: Methuen, 1981; Leiter, Samuel L. *From Belasco to Brook*. Westport, CT: Greenwood Press, 1991; McCarthy, Sean, and Hillary Norris. " 'Revenons A Nos Moutons. . . . ' " *Theatrephile* 4 (Sept. 1984): 57–61; MacColl, Ewan. "Grass Roots of Theatre Workshop." *Theatre Quarterly* 3 (Jan.–March 1973): 58–68; Norman, Frank. *Why Fings Went West*. London: Lemon Tree Press, 1975; Reynolds, Stanley. "Oh What a Lovely War." *The Guardian* 25 (June 1984).

Judy Lee Oliva

JOSHUA LOGAN [b. October 5, 1908, Texarkana, Texas; d. July 12, 1988, New York, New York]. The name Josh Logan—director, producer, playwright, adapter, and lyricist—is synonymous with lavish Broadway productions as well as spectacular Hollywood musicals of the 1950s and 1960s. Logan's theatrical career began at Princeton University in 1928 as a founder of the University Players, and in 1931 he traveled to the Soviet Union to study with Konstantin Stanislavsky.* He made his New York directorial debut with *To See Ourselves* by E. M. Delafield in 1935 and directed his first Broadway musical, *I Married an Angel* by Rodgers and Hart, in 1938. Throughout his career he was known as a director who could harness the creative energies of scores of individuals to produce extravagant productions which, if not intellectually daunting, were still some of the best examples of the genres in which he worked.

So significant was his impact that he can easily be included among the giants of American popular theatre. He collaborated with luminaries such as Richard Rodgers, Lorenz Hart, Oscar Hammerstein, David Merrick, William Inge, Irving Berlin, Paddy Chayefsky, Alan J. Lerner, and Mel Brooks. He directed perhaps the most impressive array of performers ever assembled for the American stage and screen including Mary Martin, Kim Stanley, Paul Newman, Joanne Woodward, William Holden, Marlon Brando, Henry Fonda, Cliff Robertson, Anthony Perkins, Leslie Caron, and Charles Boyer.

Logan had an uncanny ability to flesh out weak or ambiguous characters, transforming them into memorable theatrical figures. Nowhere was this skill more evident than in his 1948 stage adaptation of Tom Heggen's novel, *Mister Roberts*. He felt that the original was compelling but lacked dramatic intensity. He sequestered himself with Heggen and transformed Roberts from a shadowy figure into a formidable character, while creating sharply focused theatrical conflict out of the author's anecdotal narrative.

He also gained a reputation for combining masterful directorial skills with sensitivity and understanding. In 1951, Logan restaged his production of *South Pacific* (New York, 1949) for London. Although the majority of the cast was new, the preliminary blocking, at Rodgers's insistence, slavishly followed the New York staging. Logan found the production lifeless, but the company was convinced that there was no time for new staging. Even the normally even-tempered Mary Martin was afraid to submit to new direction. With tact and ingenuity, Logan altered some business and modified various physical relation-ships, but primarily concentrated on reviving the cast's confidence. All of this he managed by changing a single cross. The play went on to become one of the great successes of the London season.

Logan was also capable of engaging in brutal struggles with temperamental stars to maintain the artistic integrity of a project. While Logan was directing Marlon Brando in the 1957 film *Sayonara*, the two became involved in an argument when the actor refused to follow one of Logan's directions for an entrance. The disagreement grew so heated that they withdrew to Brando's dressing room. There tempers continued to rage with personal insults and re-criminations hurled back and forth. In the midst of this fury, Logan still managed to communicate the motivation for this entrance. Brando then recognized the validity of Logan's reasoning, returned to the set, and gave an electrifying performance.

During his illustrious career he won four Tony Awards (two for *Mister Roberts* and one each for *South Pacific* and *Picnic*), a Golden Globe Award for Best Director (*Picnic*), and was nominated for two Academy Awards (*Picnic* and *Sayonara*). Although many of Josh Logan's theatre productions are deemed too simplistic for contemporary tastes and his films are criticized for lack of subtlety, his ability to create colorful, exciting, sensual presentations is uncontested. Moreover, his innovative theatrical techniques and his talent to elicit consistently dynamic and moving performances from a wide variety of performers are a tribute to his competence and commitment.

ADDITIONAL PRODUCTIONS: 1938: *Knickerbocker Holiday* (Kurt Weill and Maxwell Anderson); 1940: *Charley's Aunt* (Brandon Thomas); 1942: *By Jupiter* (Rodgers and Hart); 1946: *Annie Get Your Gun* (Herbert and Dorothy Fields and Irving Berlin); 1952: *Wish You Were Here* (Logan, Arthur Kober, and Harold Rome); 1953: *Picnic* (William Inge); 1954: *Fanny* (Logan, Rome, and S. N. Behrman); 1956: *Picnic* (film), *Bus Stop* (film); 1958: *South Pacific* (film), *The World of Suzie Wong* (film); 1962: *All American* (Charles Strouse, Lee Adams, and Mel Brooks), *Mr. President* (Berlin, Howard Lindsay, and Russel Crouse); 1967: *Camelot* (film); 1969: *Paint Your Wagon* (film); 1970: *Look to the Lilies* (Jule Styne, Sammy Cahn, and Leonard Spigelgass).

SELECTED BIBLIOGRAPHY: Boroff, Phil Dean. "Josh Logan's Directorial Approach to the Theatre and Motion Pictures: A Historical Analysis." Diss. Southern Illinois U, 1976; Logan, Joshua. *Josh.* New York: Delacorte Press, 1976; Logan, Joshua, *Movie Stars, Real People and Me.* New York: Delacorte Press, 1978.

John H. Houchin

CHARLES LUDLAM [b. April 12, 1943, Floral Park, New York; d. May 28, 1987, New York, New York]. Charles Ludlam was the leading practitioner of Ridiculous Theatre. In a 1978 interview, he said Ridiculous Theatre had "to do with humor and unhinging the pretensions of serious art. . . . It takes what is considered worthless and transforms it into high art. The Ridiculous Theatre . . . draws its authority from popular art, an art that doesn't need any justification beyond its power to provide pleasure" (*Performing Arts Journal*, 69). Ludlam put that definition into practice in the comically broad, energetic productions that parodied classic art forms and current social standards that he wrote, staged, and performed with the Ridiculous Theatrical Company, the company he ran from 1967 until his death.

Growing up on Long Island, Ludlam saw a Punch and Judy show at a local fair at age six that, along with the movies he saw almost weekly, kindled his interest in theatre. He soon set up a puppet theatre in his basement and entertained his mother and younger brother. He also appeared in school plays and apprenticed at a summer stock theatre in 1958. The following year, a performance by the Living Theatre made a great impression on him. With several high school classmates, Ludlam formed his own Students' Repertory Theatre in Northport, which performed modern and avant-garde works.

In 1961, Ludlam entered Hofstra University on an acting scholarship, where he studied, acted in, and directed the classics. Realizing that Ludlam's flamboyant, excessive performances were unsuited for the commercial theatre, his teachers encouraged him to write and direct, rather than act. Ludlam, however, found a more hospitable outlet for his talents—New York's experimental theatre of the mid–1960s.

When he moved to New York's Lower East Side in 1965, Ludlam started working with director John Vaccaro's Playhouse of the Ridiculous, which got its name from a friend's description of one of Vaccaro's productions. Ludlam's first New York stage role was Peeping Tom in Ronald Tavel's *The Life of Lady Godiva* in 1966. In *Screen Test*, Tavel's next play, Ludlam appeared in drag as Norma Desmond, Gloria Swanson's character in the film *Sunset Boulevard*. Improvising brilliantly, Ludlam soon expanded the play from thirty minutes to two hours and became the star of the company.

When Tavel left the company in a dispute over his next play, *Gorilla Queen*, the director produced a play Ludlam was writing, *Big Hotel*. During the rehearsals for their next play, Ludlam's *Conquest of the Universe*, Ludlam and Vaccaro quarreled, and Ludlam left Vaccaro's company, along with seven other actors who had been performing in *Big Hotel*.

Ludlam and his fellow performers formed a company which they called the Ridiculous Theatrical Company, and Ludlam staged his own production of *Conquest of the Universe*, entitled *When Queens Collide*, which competed with Vaccaro's production. Ludlam's early plays were collages, collections of quotations, scenes from films, books, and other plays. The productions were epic, energetic, and shapeless, almost chaotic, and gave the actors the opportunity to improvise. The production style was broad and extravagant, like Ludlam's own style. According to Steven Samuels's biographical essay in *The Complete Plays of Charles Ludlam*, "He was simultaneously devoted to the virtuosic use of language and the sheer physicality of stage presentation, energized by the clash of opposing philosophies and divergent acting styles. Tawdry, flamboyant sets and costumes, nudity and simulated sex were juxtaposed with the words of Wilde, Joyce, Shakespeare, and Baudelaire" (xiii).

Bluebeard, which he staged in 1970, was the Ridiculous Theatrical Company's first popular success. The play, a parody of the horror film *The Island of Lost Souls*, featured Ludlam as Baron Khanazar von Bluebeard, a mad scientist trying to create a third sex. The show's success helped keep the company together and enabled it to tour Europe. The company also received several small grants around that time which allowed Ludlam to continue producing his work.

After several other productions, Ludlam's next popular success was *Camille*, his parody of the play by Dumas *fils*, in which he played the title role. He did not play Camille as an exaggerated drag queen, but instead tried, as a man, to portray a woman honestly. Cross-gender casting remained a characteristic of Ludlam's productions.

During the 1970s, Ludlam continued to parody other genres in his productions, including *Hot Ice*, a 1974 takeoff on gangster films; and *Der Ring Gott Farblonjet*, a 1977 epic parody of Wagner's *Ring of the Nibelung*. In the 1980s, Ludlam changed direction and wrote contemporary farces. In these fast-paced comedies, including *Reverse Psychology* in 1980 and *Secret Lives of the Sexists* in 1982, he used contemporary situations and characters, rather than parodies of classic dramas, but the exaggerated, comic staging, which never hesitated to interrupt the plot for a joke, remained the same.

Perhaps Ludlam's most successful production was *The Mystery of Irma Vep* in 1984, "a penny dreadful" in which Ludlam and fellow actor Everett Quinton played eight parts with dizzyingly quick costume changes.

Ludlam received several Obie awards, including one for distinguished achievement shortly before his death in 1987. He also won the Rosamund Gilder Award for distinguished achievement in 1986. He taught drama, playwriting, and commedia dell'arte at New York University, Carnegie-Mellon, Yale, and Connecticut College for Women. Since Ludlam's death of AIDS on May 28, 1987, the

Ridiculous Theatrical Company has been directed by Everett Quinton, a company member since 1976 and Ludlam's lover.

ADDITIONAL PRODUCTIONS: All plays written by Charles Ludlam unless otherwise noted: 1967: *When Queens Collide*; 1968: *Big Hotel, Whores of Babylon* (Bill Vehr), *Turds in Hell* (Ludlam and Vehr); 1969: *The Grand Tarot*; 1971: *Eunuchs of the Forbidden City*; 1972: *Corn*; 1975: *Stage Blood*; 1976: *Caprice*; 1978: *The Ventriloquist's Wife, Utopia, Inc.*; 1979: *The Enchanted Pig, A Christmas Carol*; 1980: *The Country Wife* (Wycherly, at Carnegie-Mellon University); 1981: *Love's Tangled Web*; 1982: *Exquisite Torture*; 1983: *Le Bourgeois Avant-Garde, Galas*; 1985: *Salammbô, The English Cat* (opera by Werner Henze, Santa Fe Opera); 1986: *Die Fledermaus* (Santa Fe Opera), *The Artificial Jungle*; 1987: *The Sorrows of Delores* (film).

SELECTED BIBLIOGRAPHY: "Charles Ludlam." *Current Biography Yearbook* 1986: 315–18; Dasgupta, Gautam. "Interview: Charles Ludlam." *Performing Arts Journal* 3 (Spring/Summer 1978): 69–80; Ludlam, Charles. *The Complete Plays of Charles Ludlam*. Ed. Steven Samuels and Everett Quinton. New York: Harper and Row, 1989; Ludlam, Charles. *Ridiculous Theater: Scourge of Human Folly: The Essays and Opinions of Charles Ludlam*. Ed. Steven Samuels. New York: Theatre Communications Group, 1992; Tomkins, Calvin. "Ridiculous." *The New Yorker* 15 November 1976: 55–98; Wharton, Robert Thomas III. 'The Working Dynamics of the Ridiculous Theatrical Company: An Analysis of Charles Ludlam's Relationship with His Ensemble from 1967 through 1981." Diss. Florida State U, 1985.

Stephen M. Vallillo

AURÉLIEN-FRANÇOIS LUGNÉ-POE [b. December 27, 1869, Paris, France; d. June 19, 1940, Villeneuve-les-Avignons, France]. While still in a Paris lycée, Aurélien Lugné and several friends founded the Cercle des Escholiers, a unique experimental theatre. He adopted the name Lugné-Poe in honor of symbolist idol Edgar Allan Poe, to whom he believed he was distantly related. Attracted to experimental radicalism, he became an actor with Théâtre Libre in 1888. Quickly rejecting Antoine's naturalistic approach, he allied himself with symbolists Maurice Denis and Paul Fort, the young poet who founded the Théâtre d'Art. In 1893, Fort turned over responsibility for the landmark production of Maurice Maeterlinck's *Pélleas and Mélisande* to Lugné-Poe, who intoned his role of Golaud in a slow, ritualized, hallucinatory style that earned him the lifelong nickname, *le clergyman somnambule*.

With Camille Mauclair, Louis Malaquin, and Edouard Vuillard, Lugné-Poe opened the Théâtre de l'Oeuvre, designed to challenge intellectual inertia and create controversy. Its symbolist productions of Henrik Ibsen and others (both foreign and French) caused near riots, inspired a bomb attack on the Chamber of Deputies, and served to label the director as politically radical and dangerous. In 1896, Lugné-Poe's production of Alfred Jarry's *Ubu Roi*, a mocking, grotesque play that virtually assaulted its infuriated audience, signified the dawn of radical absurdism in the theatre, and made Théâtre de l'Oeuvre the most talked-about theatre in Europe.

In 1897, Lugné-Poe replaced symbolism with a no less experimental eclecticism in his theatre, publicly rejecting the symbolist manifesto with the charge that its writers had produced almost nothing of merit. Headstrong subscribers, friends, and critics alike deserted him, and his career fell into relative obscurity. Nonetheless, Théâtre de l'Oeuvre survived as a public theatre, and for another thirty-years Lugné-Poe presented there some of Europe's finest actors, including Eleonora Duse,* Isadora Duncan, Antonin Artaud, and Jean-Louis Barrault.* Lugné-Poe continued to direct, act, tour the Orient and the Americas, and write his memoirs. He received the Livre d'Or in 1938.

ADDITIONAL PRODUCTIONS: 1893: *Rosmersholm, Enemy of the People*; 1894: *Terra Cotta Cart* (scenery by Toulouse-Lautrec); 1895: *Salomé* (Wilde), *Peer Gynt*; 1897: *Les Loups* (Romain Rolland); 1898: *Measure for Measure* (at the Cirque d'Eté); 1901: *Le Roi Candaule* (André Gide); 1914: *L'Otage* (Paul Claudel); 1925: *Tour à Terre* (Armand Salacrou).

SELECTED BIBLIOGRAPHY: Braun, Edward. *The Director and the Stage*. London: Butler and Tanner, 1982; Jasper, Gertrude R. *Adventure in the Theatre: Lugné-Poe and the Théâtre de l'Oeuvre to 1899*. New Brunswick, NJ: Rutgers University Press, 1947; Lugné-Poe, Aurelien. *La Parade*. Vols. 1–4. Paris: Librairie Gallimard, 1931–46; Robichez, Jacques. *Le Symbolisme au Théâtre: Lugné-Poe et les Debuts de l'Oeuvre*. Paris: L'Arche, 1957; Whitten, David. *Stage Directors in Modern France*. Manchester: Manchester University Press, 1987.

William H. Rough

GEORGE LUSCOMBE [b. November 17, 1926, Toronto, Ontario, Canada]. One of the seminal figures in modern Canadian theatre, George Luscombe has focused almost exclusively on Toronto Workshop Productions, the left-wing ensemble he founded in 1958 and directed until 1988.

Growing up in a working-class district of Toronto in the early days of World War II, Luscombe first studied commercial art, but his increasing interest in socialism led him to join the Co-operative Commonwealth Federation (CCF), the social-democratic party that played an important role in Canadian politics through the 1940s. His first theatrical efforts were agitprops for the CCF Youth Club, including a song-and-dance troupe that performed for striking workers on picket lines.

After the war, Luscombe played some touring repertory roles in Ontario, but the condition of Canadian theatre was such that he had to travel to Britain for further training as an actor. For two seasons he played juvenile leads in a "fit-up" company in Wales, which left him with a love of melodramatic theatricality that would frequently surface in his later work. It was a chance encounter with Joan Littlewood* that set him on his future course. From 1952 to 1957, he worked as an actor in Littlewood's Theatre Workshop at Stratford East, where he was introduced to the techniques of Konstantin Stanislavsky* and Laban. Luscombe's own method, which developed over the next three decades, drew upon Littlewood, Stanislavsky, and Rudolf Laban in equal measures.

Luscombe returned to Canada in 1957 at a time of considerable artistic ferment, encouraged in large part by the founding of the Canada Council in that same year. In 1958 he founded his own Workshop Theatre (renamed Toronto Work-shop Productions [TWP] when it began full-time operations in 1963) with the intention of building an ensemble in the Littlewood mode. Like his mentor, Luscombe preferred to write his plays in rehearsal with group theatre techniques, using mime, actor-generated sound effects, and presentational performance to renew classical texts, or more commonly, to adapt nondramatic works. His first production, *Hey Rube!* (1960; revived 1966; 1984), was an acrobatic, backstage look at circus performers under assault by a philistine society; although less political than most of his productions, it was his favorite, and he revived it periodically throughout his career.

Although he directed dozens of ensemble plays, Luscombe's reputation rests upon a handful of productions that helped redefine Canadian theatre at a crucial stage of development in the 1960s and 1970s. His first international hit was perhaps his most political: *Chicago '70* (1979) was a living newspaper about the trial of the Chicago Seven, with an *Alice in Wonderland* motif, developed and performed while the trial was in progress. It ran for over a year in Toronto, played for three months in New York, and toured in Europe.

Luscombe's greatest achievement was a trilogy of documentary dramas on working-class history that began in 1974 with his most celebrated production, *Ten Lost Years*, written with Jack Winter, his longtime dramaturg, and musician Cedric Smith. In this adaptation of Barry Broadfoot's collection of oral history about the Great Depression in Canada, Luscombe's ensemble theatricality jux-taposed storytelling, dialogue, music, and a complex collage structure. The original production ran for three months, followed by a three-month national tour in 1974; it was revived in 1975, and again for three months in 1981. The following productions in the trilogy, *The Mac Paps* (1979), about the Canadian Mackenzie-Papineau Battalion in the Spanish Civil War, and *The Wobbly* (1983), about the International Workers of the World, used similar techniques but failed to recapture the immense popularity of *Ten Lost Years*.

Throughout his career, Luscombe preferred to adapt nondramatic sources, either oral history or novels (*The Good Soldier Schweik*, Mark Twain's *Letters from the Earth*). He believed firmly that his plays were never finished and insisted that the playwright was part of the collaborative ensemble. In 1986, he stepped down as artistic director of TWP, and two years later he terminated his affiliation with TWP in an acrimonious dispute with his board of directors. Since that time he has dedicated his efforts to teaching in universities. In 1978 he was awarded an LL.D. by York University, and was inducted as a Member of the Order of Canada in 1981.

ADDITIONAL PRODUCTIONS: 1963: *Before Compeigne* (Winter) 1965: *The Mechanic* (Winter); 1967: *Gentlemen Be Seated* (Jan Carew); 1968: *Che Guevara* (Fratti); 1969: *Mr. Bones, The Good Soldier Schweik*; 1972: *Fanshen* (Salutin); 1972: *Letters from the Earth*; 1974: *You Can't Get There from Here, Mr. Pickwick*; 1975: *The Captain of Kopenick, Summer '76*; 1976: *The Golem of Venice* (Winter); 1980: *Ain't Looking*; 1984: *The Last Hero.*

SELECTED BIBLIOGRAPHY: Filewod, Alan. *Collective Encounters: Documentary Theatre in English Canada.* Toronto: University of Toronto Press, 1987; Filewod, Alan. "George Luscombe." *"Ten Lost Years,"* "Toronto Workshop Productions." In Eugene Benson and L. W. Conolly, eds., *The Oxford Companion to Canadian Theatre.* Toronto: Oxford University Press, 1989; Friedlander, Mira. "Survivor: George Luscombe at Toronto Workshop Productions." *Canadian Theatre Review* 38 (1983): 44–52; Winter, Jack. "An Experience of Group Theatre."*Toronto Star* 27 January 1962.

Alan Filewod

YURI PETROVICH LYUBIMOV (Iurii Liubimov) [b. September 30, 1917, Yaroslavl]. A longtime fixture of the Moscow theatre scene, Yuri Lyubimov has risen to international prominence since the mid–1980s as a result of a forced exile from the USSR. Born in the Yaroslavl district, Lyubimov grew up in Moscow and studied at the Shchukin Drama School, graduating in 1939. In 1946, he joined the Vakhtangov Theatre as an actor. It was at the Shchukin Drama School that Lyubimov, using student actors, mounted a production of Bertolt Brecht's *The Good Woman of Setzuan*: this 1964 production would become the cornerstone of the new Moscow Theatre of Drama and Comedy at Taganka.

In the ensuing decades, the Taganka Theatre's experimental production style and courageous (though veiled) criticism of the Soviet system and its mindset brought the theatre a wide and devoted following: in the USSR's pre-glasnost years when citizens had little faith in official news and culture, the Taganka provided an underground source of hope and community.

Lyubimov's directorial style synthesizes elements from the work of both Bertolt Brecht* and Vsevolod Meyerhold.* His *mise-en-scène* derives much of its grotesque power from Meyerhold's experiments, but the centrality of political commentary in the Taganka productions shows the influences of Brecht. Like Brecht, Lyubimov employs fragmentation, multiple media, multiple focus, printed materials, song, poetry, and presentational acting—all in the service of exposing social ills. A prime example of this circus/cabaret approach is *Ten Days That Shook the World* (1965), a piece of satirical patriotism that runs to this day in Moscow.

The production of *Ten Days* was based on a novel by John Reed; over the years, Lyubimov has adapted and directed several novels or groups of poems for stage presentation: *Listen!* (1967, based on Mayakovsky); *Under the Skin of the Statue of Liberty* (1972, based on the poems of Evgeny Evtushenko); *Crime and Punishment* by Dostoyevsky (1979, Moscow; 1983, London; 1987, Washington, D.C.); *The Master and Margarita* by Bulgakov (1977). Lyubimov's staging of drama classics, such as *Tartuffe* (1968) or *Hamlet* (1971, with Vladimir Vysotsky), is inventive and relevant, as in the former play when actors representing Molière's company must alter their play to suit the ideology of the official censor. The Taganka's attention to the classics is a shrewd means of avoiding censorial intervention; the resulting lack of attention to dramatic work by contemporary playwrights is also symptomatic of Lyubimov's quest for total artistic control.

Like Meyerhold before him, the fiesty and brilliant Lyubimov constructs and conducts every detail of his productions. Every aspect of the actors' performances is rigidly prescribed, leading to complaints (especially from actors outside the USSR) of directorial despotism. Lighting and shadow are particularly prominent elements of the staging, almost functioning as independent characters in the action. Another Lyubimov hallmark is an emphasis on audience involvement: ushering spectators past the victims' bodies for *Crime and Punishment*, handing them red ribbons as they arrive for *Ten Days*.

Almost as important as these stylistic devices is the spirit of the Taganka, engendered by Lyubimov during the oppressive atmosphere of the 1960s and 1970s, as a vivacious theatre devoted to free expression; if Lyubimov was the head of this unofficial phenomenon, poet and performer Vladimir Vysotsky (1938–80) was its heart.

Much of the Taganka's work has been born out of the particular restrictions of the Soviet system, and Lyubimov and his company have endured much criticism and censorship from the Soviet authorities. As recently as 1982, *Boris Godunov* was banned before opening; in Lyubimov's hands, Pushkin's drama became volatile and current: an indictment of oppression in general and Stalinism in particular. On a 1983 visit to England, Lyubimov gave interviews criticizing Soviet interference with his work. As a result, in March 1984, he was dismissed as head of the Taganka, and in July was stripped of his citizenship. As the Taganka struggled on under varying leadership, Lyubimov settled in Israel and gained an international reputation, particularly as a director of opera. Gorbachev's *glasnost* policy ultimately led to the restoration of Lyubimov's full citizenship in the USSR and has enabled the director to return to the Taganka where he continues to create new productions.

ADDITIONAL PRODUCTIONS: 1968: *Alive!* (Boris Mozhaev, production banned); 1969: *Rush Hour* (Ezni Stavinsky); 1971: What Is to Be Done? (Nikolai Chernyshevsky), *The Dawns Are Quiet Here* (Boris Vasiliev); 1981: *Three Sisters*; 1986: *Jenufa* (London); 1987: *Lulu* (Chicago); 1987: *The Feast in Time of Plague* (Purchase, New York).

SELECTED BIBLIOGRAPHY: Batchelder, Vernita Mallard. "The Theatre Theory and Theatre Practice of Jurlj Ljubimov: 1964–1971." Diss. U of Georgia, 1978; Gershkovich, Alexander. *The Theatre of Yuri Lyubimov: Art and Politics at the Taganka Theatre in Moscow.* Trans. Michael Yurieff. New York: Paragon House, 1989; Law, Alma. "Lyubimov's Return Is Soviet Sign." *American Theatre* 5 (November 1988): 46–47; Lyubimov, Yuri. *Le feu sacré: Souvenirs d'une vie de théâtre.* Paris: Fayard, 1985; Pera, Pia. "Russian Interpreter Pia Pera Talks to Yurii Lyubimov." *Drama* 157 (1985): 24–27; Yurieff, Michael. "Lyubimov's Theatrical Synthesis: Directing *The Master and Margarita* and *Crime and Punishment* in the US and USSR." Diss. New York U, 1989.

Lurana Donnels O'Malley

M

DES McANUFF [b. June 19, 1952, Princeton, Illinois]. In the 1970s, Des McAnuff founded Dodger Productions and directed its *Gimme Shelter* (1978) at the Brooklyn Academy of Music, for which he won a Soho Arts Award in 1979. As a playwright, composer, and director, he intermixes elements of rock culture with theatrical performance.

McAnuff attracted Joseph Papp's notice and subsequently directed his own musical plays, *Leave It to Beaver Is Dead* (1979) and *The Death of von Richtofen as Witnessed from Earth* (1981), at the Public Theatre. The latter, which received a Villager Award, focused on Hitler's rise to power in Germany, examining reasons for the failure to prevent Nazi supremacy. As well as his own plays, he has directed such classics as *The Sea Gull* (1985) at the La Jolla Playhouse and *Macbeth* (1983) at the Stratford Festival in Canada.

In 1982, McAnuff became artistic director of the La Jolla Playhouse in San Diego, making that theatre a prominent arena for innovative approaches to classical plays and a major launching center for new plays. Many of the latter moved to Broadway. Most significant of these were *Big River* (1984) and *A Walk in the Woods* (1988), both directed by McAnuff and both Tony Award winners. *Big River*, a musical adaptation by William Hauptman of the novel *Huckleberry Finn*, was first produced at Yale by the American Repertory Theatre and then at the La Jolla Playhouse. Acclaimed for its tuneful score, written by country artist Roger Miller, and for its ensemble performances, it received a Tony Award in 1985 for best musical.

A Walk in the Woods, also produced at Yale Repertory Theatre and the La Jolla Playhouse, emphasized McAnuff's interest in explorations of the political and individual conscience. Based on actual arms control negotiations between the United States and the Soviet Union at Geneva in 1982, the play is a series of dialogues between a stuffy American diplomat and an urbane Russian negotiator. Although political differences are never resolved, the two individuals develop a personal relationship that transcends this schism. Stressing the woods in which the talks occur as an important psychological factor, McAnuff wrote musical accompaniment that subtly underscored both seasonal and emotional moderations in background and character relationships.

McAnuff's partnership with Lee Blessing, the author of *A Walk in the Woods*, continued with the production of *Fortinbras* (1991), another cynical examination of politics, in which Blessing comically explores what happens in Shakespeare's Elsinore when Fortinbras takes over after Hamlet's death.

McAnuff's collaboration with Dodger Productions, which has developed productions such as *Pump Boys and Dinettes* on Broadway, and his leadership of the La Jolla Playhouse demonstrate a commitment to and involvement in all aspects of production. His ability to integrate elements of pop music and culture into classical formats and his willingness to explore contemporary political and ethical questions have put McAnuff into the forefront of a new generation of theatrical directors.

ADDITIONAL PRODUCTIONS: 1976: *The Bacchae* (Euripides); 1979: *Holeville* (Jeff Wanshel, Des McAnuff); 1981: *Mary Stuart* (Wolfgang Hildescheimer); 1988: *Two Rooms* (Lee Blessing); 1993: *Tommy* (Pete Townshend, 1993 Tony Award, Best Director).

SELECTED BIBLIOGRAPHY: Bartow, Arthur. *The Director's Voice: Twenty-One Interviews*. New York: Theatre Communications Group, 1988: 212–31; Breslauer, Jan. "Des McAnuff" (interview). *Theater* 15 (Spring 1984): 33–38; Brustein, Robert. Review of *A Walk in the Woods*. *New Republic* 4 April 1988: 25–26; Henry, William A. III. Review of *Fortinbras*. *Time* 15 July 1991: 66; Oliver, Edith. Review of *A Walk in the Woods*. *The New Yorker* 14 March 1988: 80; Simon, John. Review of *A Walk in the Woods*. *New York* 14 March 1988: 70–72; *Who's Who in America*. 1900–91 ed. Wilmette, Illinois: Macmillan, 1991; Winer, Laurie. "The Nuclear Age and Its Problems Come to the Stage." *New York Times* 21 February 1988; sec. 2: 5, 13.

Ann Demling

GUTHRIE MCCLINTIC [b. August 6, 1893, Seattle, Washington; d. October 29, 1961, Sneden's Landing, New York]. Guthrie McClintic, one of the most distinguished and prolific American directors of his generation, lived continually in the shadow of his wife, Katharine Cornell, whom he directed in twenty-eight productions. Ninety-four productions in over four decades of directing included the Pulitzer Prize–winning *The Old Maid* (1935), and the Critics' Circle Prize–winning *Winterset* (1935) and *High Tor* (1937).

Born in Seattle, McClintic was a stagestruck youngster, who received his theatrical education at New York's American Academy of Dramatic Art. Although he performed in stock and on Broadway, he never achieved stardom as an actor. His career as a director began when he got a job stage managing for Winthrop Ames,* a popular American producer and director of the 1910s and

1920s. With Ames, the youthful McClintic not only developed the skills and artistry for which he later became famous, but gained an offer to direct, through Ames's office, a Broadway venture. Not wanting to make his Broadway debut with an inferior property, McClintic spent a season as the resident director of Jessie Bonstelle's Repertory Company in Detroit. There he met Cornell, who was the leading lady. (When he had first seen Cornell perform in 1917, he noted, "Interesting, monotonous, watch.") Upon returning to New York in 1921, he found a script he wanted to direct, A. A. Milne's *The Dover Road*, which started him on his distinguished career.

McClintic first directed Cornell in 1925, in Michael Arlen's adaptation of his best-selling novel, *The Green Hat*. There followed a number of similar vehicles in which McClintic developed his skills as a director, and largely through his tutelage, Cornell developed a considerable following. He persuaded her to produce the play which provided her most famous role, Elizabeth Barrett Browning in *The Barretts of Wimpole Street* in 1931.

The production was an artistic as well as commercial success and is emblematic of the contributions McClintic made to the American theatre. His directorial style was gentle and thorough. Rather than lay a concept on an existing vehicle, he allowed each play he directed to fulfill its potential as a stage experience. In a typical example of his taste and thoroughness, McClintic portrayed the relationship between Miss Barrett and her father, the overbearing and terminally Victorian Edward Moulton-Barrett, so that its incipient incestuousness not only was perceived but also added to the piquancy of the heroine's escape from home into the arms of Robert Browning. It was the sort of directorial detail which McClintic made popular, finding fascinating actions with which to delineate the characterizations in his impeccably cast productions.

Perhaps the heart of McClintic's art lay in his conceptual abilities. He claimed that as he read a play he could see how each element would contribute to all others and, indeed, it was his scenic designers whom he hired first. His productions were integrated wholes, despite the fact that his wife was the jewel at the center of the composition. His 1942 production of Chekhov's *Three Sisters*, for instance, with Cornell, Judith Anderson, and Ruth Gordon, was praised as surpassing the Moscow Art Theatre in terms of ensemble and insight.

McClintic helped to establish a respect for the American theatre. Emerging from a tradition of popular entertainment, McClintic took the Broadway stage to newfound heights of artistic achievement which were also successful at the box office. His faith in Maxwell Anderson, for instance, a playwright who treated complicated and idiomatically American stories in verse, gave that playwright respectable and competent productions. McClintic produced five of Anderson's plays including *Saturday's Children* (1928), *Winterset* (1935), *Wingless Victory* (1936), *High Tor* (1937), *Star-Wagon* (1937), and *Key Largo* (1939). McClintic more than once stretched his audience too far with plays of high artistic goals but little dramatic interest. His productions were often obvious but rarely ineffective. At his best, as in *The Barretts of Wimpole Street* or his production of

Romeo and Juliet (1933) with Cornell and Basil Rathbone (and later Maurice Evans, whom McClintic introduced on the American stage), McClintic was a director who was able to combine artistic integrity, novelty of interpretation, and the show business élan necessary to sell a solid property to Broadway.

ADDITIONAL PRODUCTIONS: 1926: *The Shanghai Gesture* (John Colton); 1928: *The Age of Innocence*; 1933: *Alien Corn* (Sidney Howard), *Jezebel* (Owen Davis); 1934: *Yellow Jack* (Howard); 1935: *The Old Maid* (Zoë Akins); 1936: *Ethan Frome* (Davis), *Hamlet*; 1937: *Candida*; 1939: *No Time for Comedy* (S. N. Behrman); 1941: *The Doctor's Dilemma*; 1945: *You Touched Me* (Tennessee Williams); 1946: *The Playboy of the Western World*, *Antigone*; 1948: *Life with Mother* (Lindsay and Crouse); 1949: *Medea*; 1951: *The Constant Wife* (Maugham); 1957: *Four Winds*.

SELECTED BIBLIOGRAPHY: Cornell, Katharine. *I Wanted to Be an Actress: The Autobiography of Katharine Cornell as Told to Ruth Woodbury Sedgwick*. New York: Random House, 1939; Malvern, Gladys. *Curtain Going Up!* New York: J. Messner, 1943; McClintic, Guthrie. *Me and Kit*. Boston: Little, Brown and Co., 1955; Mosel, Tad. *Leading Lady: The World and Theatre of Katharine Cornell*. Boston: Little, Brown, and Co., 1978.

David Payne Carter

(JAMES MORRISON) STEELE MacKAYE [b. June 6, 1842, Buffalo, New York; d. February 25, 1894, Timpas, Colorado]. MacKaye was one of the early régisseurs who helped to establish the director's role in the United States. He was an actor and lecturer who promulgated the techniques of François Delsarte and opened the Lyceum Theatre School for Acting (1884), which later became the American Academy of Dramatic Arts. He was also a playwright whose *Hazel Kirke* (1880) nudged American playwriting toward realism. Today, he is remembered chiefly as a theatre inventor and architect who conceived whole theatres and left improvements which are still in use.

Educated in the arts in Paris, MacKaye made a return trip (1869) to study with Delsarte before he embarked on a series of lectures on Delsarte and aesthetics. An independent producer in the following years, he also acted in New York in *Mondaldi* (1872) and in London as Hamlet (1873). MacKaye opened his Madison Square Theatre with *Hazel Kirke* (1880), where he installed his unprecedented elevator double-stage in order to minimize the disruptive effect of scene changes. Other innovations in this theatre included a form of air-conditioning and folding seats. Forced out of Madison Square, MacKaye supervised the building of the Lyceum Theatre, which opened in 1885 with lighting installed by his friend, Thomas Edison. Through these ventures, MacKaye hoped to foster a stable acting company and production values similar to those he had witnessed in France.

MacKaye's directing practice was compared to that of Augustin Daly.* Both were known for their insistence that actors carry out their instructions completely. MacKaye frequently resorted to his Delsarte-based understanding of human expression when directing his actors. His realistic and detailed crowd scenes in his own *Paul Kauvar* (1887) drew the praise of David Belasco.*

MacKaye's most ambitious scheme was for the Chicago World's Fair of 1893, where he planned to build a "Spectatorium" that housed twenty-five stages. Because of a nationwide financial panic, a smaller "Scenitorium" was produced instead (1894). Besides the two structures themselves, over fifty inventions for this project include a light curtain, cloud machine, proscenium adjustor, wave maker, and three different moving stages.

ADDITIONAL PRODUCTIONS (all plays by MacKaye): 1875: *Rose Michel* (translated from Ernest Blum) with Rose Eytinge; 1877: *Won at Last*; 1880: *Hazel Kirke* (originally *Will of Iron*, 1878); 1886: *The Drama of Civilization*, a spectacle for "Buffalo Bill" Cody; 1894: *The World Finder*, a "spectatorio."

SELECTED BIBLIOGRAPHY: Guthrie, David Gordon. "The Innovations of Steele MacKaye in Scenic Design and Stage Practice as Contributions to the American Theatre." Diss. New York U, 1974; Hannon, Daniel Leroy. "The MacKaye Spectatorium: A Reconstruction and Analysis of a Theatrical Spectacle Planned for the World's Columbian Exposition of 1893, with a History of the Producing Organization." Diss. Tulane U, 1970; MacKaye, Percy. *Epoch: The Life of Steele MacKaye*. New York: Boni and Liverwright, 1927; Schaal, David. "Rehearsal-Direction Practices and Actor-Director Relationships in the American Theatre from the Hallams to Actor's Equity." Diss. U of Illinois, 1956.

Maarten A. Reilingh

GILLES MAHEU [b. May 2, 1948, Montreal, Quebec]. An actor, director, dramatist, choreographer, and designer, Gilles Maheu studied mime with Michel Poletti, with whom he founded the Théâtre Antonin Artaud in Switzerland in 1967. From 1969 to 1975, he continued his training in Europe, most notably at Etienne Decroux's School of Physical Mime in Paris and with Yves Lebreton at the Odin Teater in Denmark, under the auspices of Eugenio Barba.* During the years he studied physical expression, he participated in a number of theatrical productions in Quebec and in Europe. In 1972, he acted in and created, with Yves Lebreton, *Possession*, which toured Europe and North America for three years.

In 1975, Maheu turned to street theatre and founded the Children of Paradise (Les Enfants du Paradise), a Montreal mime troupe formed to create productions through improvisation. From 1977 to 1980, the young group presented its first theatrical productions, including *La Famille Rodriguez—Le voyage immobile*, which were warmly welcomed by Montreal's critics and public. In 1980, the group became Carbone 14 (Carbon 14), and took up residence at the Free Space Theater, a Montreal theatre dedicated to research and experimentation. In this permanent location, rich in theatrical possibilities, Maheu produced his most creative work.

Maheu's working methods and the productions of Carbone 14 are rooted in improvisation and the aesthetic renewal that dominated Quebec's theatre scene in the 1980s. Strongly grounded in the European mime tradition and influenced by American postmodern trends, the productions of Carbone 14 in the 1980s demonstrate rigorous creative work and research on the actor's craft and affirmation of an original theatrical style of writing. Maheu's use of innovative theatrical and technological methods indicates bold aesthetic choices; his multidisciplinary approach borders on the transgression of theatrical codes.

Driven to create a true "abstract popular theatre" and to revive, like Antonin Artaud, a theatre of emotion in which lively and dangerous forces confront each other, Maheu positions his artistic work between contemporary theatre and performance. Appropriating the different languages of dance, music, the visual arts, and cinema, his productions attain a high degree of formal perfection in which the poetry of the word and the image always triumph.

Maheu's productions between 1981 and 1992 also question the sociopolitical and ideological transformations of the millennium's end. In *Pain Blanc* (1981), the first Carbone 14 creation, the director and his team indulge in a grotesque parody of the consumer society; with *L'Homme Rouge* (1982) a one-man show played by Maheu, he explores the limits of solitude and the discomfort of living. With the vivid production of *Rail* (1983–84), which received first prize for set design at the 1985 Theater Festival of the Americas (Festival de Theatre des Ameriques, FTA) in Montreal, he vehemently denounces physical and moral violence. His participation in the creation of *Le Titanic* (1985), in coproduction with the FTA, takes an allegorical look at the tragic outcome of great collective destinies. His staging of *Hamletmachine* by Heiner Müller,* which received first prize for scenic design at the 1987 FTA, offers a troubling vision of the confrontation of ideologies. But Maheu earned his greatest fame with *Le Dortoir* (1988), coproduced with the Ottawa National Arts Center. Successfully presented in twenty countries between 1988 and 1992, this poetic chronicle of childhood and memory won, among other honors, first prize for choreography in 1990 at the eleventh Dora Manor Moore Award in Toronto. The same year, Maheu received the special prize of the Theater Critics Association of Quebec for the "experimental trajectory that most influenced the 1980s."

Still fascinated by the work of the German dramatist Heiner Müller, Maheu drew from his work the archetypes that nourish the mythic and poetic voyage of *Rivage à l'abandon* (1990). This "surprising oratorio," revived in 1991 in coproduction with the City Theater of Liege, Belgium, prefigured *Peau, chair et os*, a contemporary "opera" freely inspired by Müller's *Paysage sous surveillance* and Euripides' *Alceste*, in which the director explores in allegorical form the eternal conflict between the sexes. In the summer of 1992, he presented *Le Café des aveugles*, first staged at the Toronto World Stage Festival, then revived successively in Seville, Mexico, and Montreal. A mingling of all languages in order to splinter theatrical form, this production, Carbone 14's most complete, took the form of a powerful "live video clip."

In addition to directing the company, Maheu also performed in several Carbone 14 productions while continuing his training as an actor. Guest professor in Canadian universities where he taught mime and acting, he had also directed theatre workshops in the United States and in Europe. His reputation also extended to the film world. In 1988, his commanding appearance in the film *Un zoo la nuit* by Jean-Claude Lauzon, won him a place among the finalists for the best actor Genie-Award in Toronto. Two years later, his theatrical work *Le Dortoir* was made into a film produced by François Giraud and won numerous international awards, among them best artistic performance at the International Emmy Awards in New York.

SELECTED BIBLIOGRAPHY: *Cahiers de théâtre JEU* (Montreal), nos. 28, 36, 38, 52, 63; Pavlovic, Diane. "Gilles Maheu Corps à Corps." *Canadian Theatre Review* 52 (Fall 1987): 22–29. Trans. Roger E. Gannon and Rosaline Gill.

Marcel Fortin

JUDITH MALINA See JULIAN BECK

EMILY MANN [b. April 12, 1952, Boston, Massachusetts]. Growing up amidst the turbulence of the late 1960s and early 1970s gave Emily Mann both an abhorrence of violence and a strong belief in the theatre's moral obligations. She first became recognized as a playwright, particularly for *Still Life* (1980), about the aftershocks of the Vietnam War, and *Execution of Justice* (1984), about the trial of Dan White. While writing, she also worked consistently as a director at major regional theatres, directing her own works, but more often working with classical or other texts.

Both as a playwright and as a director, Mann stresses authenticity. Her writing reflects her use of documented material, such as interviews and trial transcripts, for the text of her plays, and she often rearranges sequences, fuses others together, and makes rapid cuts, much like a film director. Her "theatre of testimony" is a subjective form of docudrama which allows the writer the freedom to create both the strongest moral statement and the deepest catharsis.

As a director, Mann attempts to free the actor and the audience from preconceived stereotypical judgments about a play's characters. She strives to let each character tell his or her story with as much integrity as possible. Her directing methodology is Stanislavsky-based, and she works from moment to moment, exploring the emotional and intellectual range of each character and discovering how that character's actions relate to the play's main idea.

Mann became interested in theatre at the University of Chicago Lab School. She later studied with Tony Richardson in London, and completed her training at the Guthrie Theatre, where she began her professional career as an assistant director. She became artistic director of the Guthrie II (1977–79) and later served as resident director for the Brooklyn Academy of Music (1981–82). In 1990, she assumed the artistic directorship of the McCarter Theatre.

ADDITIONAL PRODUCTIONS: 1977: *Annulla Allen: The Autobiography of a Survivor* (Mann); 1979: *The Glass Menagerie*; 1980: *Still Life* (Mann); 1982: *A Doll's House*; 1986: *Execution of Justice* (Mann); 1987: *Hedda Gabler*; 1989: *Betsey Brown* (coauthored with Ntozake Shange).

SELECTED BIBLIOGRAPHY: Betsko, Kathleen, and Koenig, Rachel. "An Interview with Emily Mann." *Interviews with Contemporary Women Playwrights*. New York: Morrow, 1987: 274–87; Breslauer, Jan, and Susan Mason. "Emily Mann" (interview). *Theater* 15 (Spring 1984): 27–32; Chinoy, Helen Krich, and Linda Walsh Jenkins. *Women in American Theatre*. Revised ed. New York: Theatre Communications Group, 1987: 329, 344–45, 350, 352; Cole, Susan Letzler. *Directors in Rehearsal: A Hidden World*. New York: Routledge, 1992: 56–74; Kolin, Philip C., and LaNelle Daniel. "Emily Mann: A Classified Bibliography." *Studies in American Drama, 1945–Present* 4 (1989): 223–66; Parks, Suzan-Lori. "In Search of 'Betsey Brown.'" *American Theatre* 8 (April 1991): 20–24; Shteir, Rachel. "New Artistic Directors: Emily Mann." *Theater* 21 (Winter 1990–91): 20–26.

Alan Kreizenbeck

MARCEL LOUIS-NOEL MARÉCHAL [b. December 25, 1937, Lyons, France]. A significant presence in southern France, Maréchal is an actor and director of extraordinary charisma. The atmosphere of his native Lyons permeates his work, and he has gained a reputation for a politicized yet flamboyantly entertaining staging style. As founder of the Théâtre du Cothurne and, later, the Théâtre du Huitième, Maréchal has, along with Roger Planchon,* turned Lyons into a celebrated theatre town. In 1975, he moved to Marseilles where he founded (and is currently the director of) Le Théâtre de la Criée. He also founded the Festival du Sail-sous-Cazon, participated in regional festivals (including Avignon), and toured widely abroad.

For Maréchal, the text is the essential component of theatre, and he prefers those that address fundamental human dilemmas with powerful psychological appeal for audiences. Often, he heightens the contemporary appeal of older plays by situating them in a modern economic or psychological context. For Maréchal, however, revolutionary theatre is not characterized by political didacticism; rather, political message is a by-product of the kind of deep-seated theatrical engagement he attempts to make inescapable. His is a "poetic realism," a theatre strongly anchored in reality, but always aesthetically charged and entertaining.

Maréchal's flair for flamboyant staging led him to experiment with a multistage format ("théâtre éclaté"), as seen in *La Moscheta*, a poetic homage to the oppressed of the world (1962, 1968); in *L'Homme aux sandales de caoutchouc*, a play by Kateb Yacine about the Vietnamese revolution, staged in a noisy, circus-like atmosphere with the comical accentuated by masks and papier-mâché heads (1971); and in his own play, *Une Anémone pour Guignol*, where he explores the vagaries of life through Guignol's rich Lyonnais patois (1975).

With his vigorous stagings, Maréchal relies on his troupe's inventiveness and energy to make the text come alive. An actor himself, Maréchal, who prefers a grand gestural style to achieve what he calls a "theater of paroxysm," has been called an athlete onstage. Unsurpassed in performing Molière, Maréchal's repertoire is extensive, including award-winning performances in *Don Juan*, *Danton's Death*, and *La Moscheta*. Maréchal is also the author of *La Mise en Théâtre* (1974), a series of reflections on his career, and of *L'Arbre de mai* (1984).

ADDITIONAL PRODUCTIONS: 1963, 1965, 1974: *Le Cavalier Seul* (Jacques Audiberti); 1964: *Endgame*; 1966, 1986: *Capitaine Bada* (Jean Vauthier); 1978: *The Imaginary Invalid*; 1984: *King Lear*; 1988: *The School for Wives*.
SELECTED BIBLIOGRAPHY: Maréchal, Marcel. *La Mise en théâtre*. Paris: Union Generale d'Editions (UGE), 1974; Pierron, Agnès. *Maréchal, sa carrière lyonnaise*. Dole-du-Jura: Presses Jurassiennes, 1977; Sandier, Gilles. *Le Théâtre en crise*. Grenoble: Pensée sauvage, 1982: 131–59, 191, 351–52.

June Miyasaki

FILIPPO TOMMASO MARINETTI [b. December 22, 1876, Alexandria, Egypt; d. December 2, 1944, Bellagio (Como), Italy]. When Filippo Tommaso Marinetti founded the Futurist movement in Paris in 1909, he had already achieved a degree of literary and theatrical notoriety as a poet, novelist, and playwright; as a declaimer of poetry in France and Italy; and as a contributing co-founder of the Italian journal *Poesia*. A tireless and peripatetic visionary and chief proponent of the Italian Futurists, Marinetti wrote manifestos as well as plays, poetry, and novels; directed evenings of Futurist readings; and staged tours of the brief Futurist dramas known as *sintesi*. As a movement, Futurism celebrated modernity through principles such as "dynamism," "simultaneity," and "novelty," and condemned traditional life and art as static and outmoded. These ideas, incorporated by Futurist writers and artists into various media, soon reached an international audience as Marinetti and other Futurists traveled to publicize and promote their revolutionary movement.

As principal theorist and practitioner, impresario, publicist, poet, playwright, director, and performer, Marinetti exhorted his fellow Futurists to perform their poetry or music as well as to design, write, and act in one another's plays together with professional actors. Marinetti's talents as a performer, his genius for promotion and collaboration, and his penchant for dynamic rhetorical exchanges with a live audience became the driving forces of Futurist events.

Through four manifestoes on theatre, published between 1911 and 1912, Marinetti and his cohorts announced their intention to revolutionize theatre, drama, and stage practices. They planned to bring the dynamism of modern life to the stage by using models (such as the variety theatre) traditionally ignored, by challenging the audience to become active participants in the theatrical event, and by insisting upon collaboration between artists from different areas of expertise and upon the simultaneous relevance and contribution of the scenic and performing arts as well as the dramatic text. In 1915, 1916, and in the 1921 Theatre of Surprise Tour, Futurists, together with two professional acting companies, offered a repertory of *sintesi* which aimed at incorporating Futurist theories into brief, anticonventional dramas and at achieving the kind of interactive actor-audience atmosphere found in popular entertainment events.

Though persuasive and charismatic, Marinetti was often unable to convince professional theatre artists and technicians of the viability of his ideas for revising theatre practice, and he was often disappointed by their unwillingness or inability to translate his theories into practice. Though contemporary critics praised some of his innovations, the lighting effects in *Vengono* (*They Are Coming*, 1915), for example, they deplored the long wait between plays due to set changes and acting techniques which were described as being better suited to nineteenth-century dramas. Nevertheless, Marinetti's achievements as theorist, founder, and leader of the Futurist movement and theatre are considerable, and Futurism's continuing influence can be seen in virtually all post–World War II experimental theatre.

SELECTED BIBLIOGRAPHY: Antonucci, Giovanni. *Lo Spettacolo Futurista in Italia*. Rome: Vita Nova, 1974; Appollonio, Umbro, ed. *Futurist Manifestos: Documents of Twentieth-Century Art*. New York: Viking Press, 1970; Carruso, Luciano, and Giuliano Longone, eds. *Il teatro futurista a sorpresa: documenti*. Florence: Salimbeni, 1979; Flint, R. W., ed. *Marinetti*. New York: Farrar, Straus and Giroux, 1971; Gordon, R. S. "The Italian Futurist Theatre: A Reappraisal." *The Modern Language Review* 85 (April 1990): 249–61; "Il teatro futurista italiano." *Sipario* 260 (December 1967). Special Futurist issue; Kirby, Michael. *Futurist Performance*. New York: E. P. Dutton, 1971; Verdone, Mario. *Teatro del Tempo Futurista*. Rome: Lerici, 1969.

Jana O'Keefe Bazzoni

ALBERT MARRE [b. Albert Moshinski, September 20, 1925, New York, New York]. A graduate of Oberlin College and Harvard University, Albert Marre staged two of the most successful musicals in the history of Broadway: *Kismet* (1953) and *Man of La Mancha* (1966), for which he won the Tony Award for Best Director of a Musical.

Though Marre is known primarily for his work on large-scale Broadway musicals, his work spans a number of genres and venues. In 1946, he became director of the Allied Repertory Theatre in Berlin, Germany, and from 1948 to 1952, he was managing director of the Brattle Theatre Company in Cambridge, Massachusetts. In 1952, he began a two-year tenure as artistic director of the New York City Center Drama Company, where he directed critically acclaimed productions of *Love's Labour's Lost* (1953), *Misalliance* (1953), and *The Merchant of Venice* (1953). Marre's *Love's Labour's Lost*, which was set in Edwardian England and featured bicycles, croquet, a phonograph, and motorcars, established his reputation as a highly inventive director who was especially adept at handling large groups of actors with finesse and style.

Marre's musical staging was characterized by opulence and innovation. In *Kismet*, which featured his wife, Joan Diener, he collaborated with choreographer Jack Cole to create a lavish extravaganza which set the standard for Broadway spectacle. According to Walter Kerr in the *New York Herald-Tribune*, Marre "staged the whole jeweled bazaar with a swirling and flamboyant gusto." In *Man of La Mancha*, he divided the orchestra in two, placing the musicians in the wings at either side of a raked stage, creating stereophonic sound.

Other noteworthy productions directed by Marre include Enid Bagnold's *The Chalk Garden* (1955), featuring the Irish actress Siobhan McKenna; the musical *Cry for Us All* (1970), to which he contributed the libretto in collaboration with

William Alfred; and Jean Anouilh's *Time Remembered* (1957) with Helen Hayes and Richard Burton, of which Brooks Atkinson wrote in the *New York Times*: "Albert Marre has ingeniously combined loveliness and drollery, piling magnificence so high that it becomes funny" (41).

Albert Marre is first and foremost a practitioner of his craft, rather than a theorist or scholar. When Twyla Tharp's *Singin' in the Rain* ran into trouble in 1985, it was Marre who was called in to stage the nonmusical scenes. His work has appeared on Broadway stages for almost four decades, and he has collaborated with the leading performers of twentieth-century American theatre.

ADDITIONAL PRODUCTIONS: 1955: *Kismet* (London production); 1956: *Saint Joan* with Siobhan McKenna; 1957: *Good as Gold* (John Patrick) with Roddy McDowell and Zero Mostel; 1963: *Too True to Be Good* (Shaw) with Lillian Gish, Eileen Heckart, Glynis Johns, and Robert Preston; 1968: *Man of La Mancha* (London production); 1975: *Home Sweet Homer* (music by Mitch Leigh, book by Roland Kibbee and Marre, lyrics by Charles Burr and Forman Brown) with Yul Brynner; 1980: *An April Song* (musical by Mitch Leigh based on Anouilh's *Leocadia*) with Glynis Johns; 1989: *Chu Chem* (book by Ted Allen, music by Mitch Leigh, lyrics by Jim Haines and Jack Wohl).

SELECTED BIBLIOGRAPHY: Atkinson, Brooks. "Theatre: Ideal Blend." *New York Times* 13 November 1957: 41; Coffin, Rachel W., ed. *New York Theatre Critics' Reviews 1953*. New York: Critics' Theatre Reviews, 1953; Green, Stanley. *Encyclopedia of the Musical Theatre*. New York: Da Capo Press, 1976; Laufe, Abe. *Broadway's Greatest Musicals*. New York: Funk and Wagnalls, 1977; Lerner, Alan Jay. *The Musical Theatre: A Celebration*. London: William Collins' Sons and Co., 1986.

Pamela Myers-Morgan

MARSHALL W. MASON [b. February 24, 1940, Amarillo, Texas]. In 1961, Mason graduated from Northwestern University, where he worked with Alvina Krause and directed several productions. Within a year, he arrived in New York and began working in Off-Off-Broadway theatres, as well as studying at the Actors' Studio. There, studying under Lee Strasberg* and Harold Clurman,* he learned the Americanized Stanislavksy system of acting, which is the foundation of his directing style.

Mason joined forces with former Northwestern graduates Rob Thirkield, Claris Nelson, and Dennis Parichy to form the theatre group named Northwestern Productions. After a series of productions at the Caffé Cino and the Cafe La Mama, including Nelson's *The Rue Garden* (1962), the group moved to Off-Broadway. However, after Mason directed *Little Eyolf* and *Arms and the Man* at the Actors' Playhouse in 1964, the group disbanded.

At the Caffé Cino, Mason met playwright Lanford Wilson. Soon afterward, Mason directed Wilson's full-length play, *Balm in Gilead* (1965), at La Mama ETC. This successful production marked the beginning of a collaboration between the playwright and the director that has lasted until the present. Mason also directed Wilson's one-act *Home Free!* (1965) at the Cherry Lane Theatre and a series of plays by other playwrights such as Samuel Beckett's *Krapp's Last Tape* (1965) and Tennessee Williams's *The Mutilated* (1966).

Having worked together since 1965, Mason, Wilson, Thirkield, and Tanya Berezin in 1969 formed the Circle Company, which eventually became the Circle Repertory Theatre. Mason became the first artistic director, a position he held until his resignation in 1987. The ensemble was dedicated to developing a company of classically trained performers that would have a common style and means of communication, and a knowledge of all of the production elements, encompassing playwriting, acting, directing, and design.

Most significant in the work of this company was the production style that Mason developed with playwright Wilson: "lyric realism." Reacting against the popularity of antirealist and absurdist drama of the early 1960s, Mason focused on plays that dealt with human emotions and relationships. "Lyric realism" stressed the rhythm and music of the dialogue and went beyond realism into an ultranaturalistic mode. As director, Mason emphasized the need for minutely detailed settings and the exploration into the psychological aspects of the characters. In all, he directed eighteen plays by Wilson, twelve of which were done at the Circle Repertory Theatre. He directed the premieres of such plays as *The Hot l Baltimore* (1973), *Serenading Louie* (1976), *The Fifth of July* (1978), *Talley's Folly* (1979); *Angels Fall* (1983), and *Burn This* (1987). Many of these productions were developed at the Circle Repertory Theatre and then moved on to successful runs on Broadway.

Mason also directed the premieres of works by other writers, some of whom were playwrights-in-residence at the Circle Repertory Theatre. His Broadway debut came with his Obie Award–winning Circle Rep production of Jules Feiffer's *Knock, Knock* (1976), and his production of William Hoffman's *As Is* (1985), one of the first plays dealing with AIDS, earned the Drama Desk Award and a Tony nomination. Mason codirected Albert Innaurato's *Gemini* on Broadway (1977) and directed *The Mound Builders* (1975) for PBS TV. In 1979, Mason earned a Theatre World Award, and in 1983 he won an Obie Award for Sustained Achievement in the Theatre.

Mason also directs frequently at other American regional theatres, including the Mark Taper Forum and the Center Theatre Group at the Ahmanson Theatre in Los Angeles; the Academy Festival Theatre in Lakewood, Illinois; and the South Coast Repertory Theatre in Costa Mesa, California.

ADDITIONAL PRODUCTIONS: 1960: *Cat on a Hot Tin Roof*; 1968: *The Madness of the Lady Bright* (Wilson); 1974: *Battle of Angels*, *The Sea Horse* (Edward J. Moore): *The Mound Builders* (Wilson); 1978: *Ulysses in Traction* (Innaurato); 1979: *Hamlet*, *Mary Stuart*; 1981: *Foxfire*; 1985: *Talley and Son* (Wilson); 1988: *Summer and Smoke*, *V & V Only*; 1990: *Sunshine*.

SELECTED BIBLIOGRAPHY: Bartow, Arthur. *The Director's Voice: Twenty-One Interviews*. New York: Theatre Communications Group, 1988: 194–211; Ryzuk, Mary S. *The Circle Repertory Company: The First Fifteen Years*. Ames: Iowa State University Press, 1989.

Tom Mikotowicz

LYNNE (CAROLYN) MEADOW [b. November 12, 1946, New Haven, Connecticut]. Lynne Meadow is first and foremost a professional stage director—a position in theatre not traditionally available to women. After earning her B.A. from Bryn Mawr in 1968, she overcame a bias against women in the directing program at Yale Drama School and trained there until 1970. While looking for directing work in New York City, she became artistic director of the Manhattan Theatre Club. She has held that position continuously since 1972. Her work as a producer has been recognized with prestigious awards.

Meadow's work as a producer was fueled by her desires as a director, and so she developed a theatre of quality in which she could direct regularly. Under her active and powerful leadership, Manhattan Theatre Club grew from a maze of theatre spaces for rent into a productive, respected Off-Broadway theatre complex which has won many esteemed awards. Significant Manhattan Theatre Club productions include Broadway transfers of *Crimes of the Heart, Mass Appeal, Ain't Misbehavin'*, and *Loot*. Meadow produces and directs literate plays by living playwrights. If a play is not finished, she helps shape the script by suggesting rewrites. With a completed play, it is her stated directorial style not to reinterpret a work, but to get as close as possible to understanding the playwright's intentions and to fulfill those intentions as faithfully as possible. Her directorial hand seems very subtle, although her productions are careful and highly orchestrated pieces of work. Her rehearsal method is straightforward; she makes suggestions and asks actors guiding questions about their characters. Cast members often receive excellent reviews and awards for their performances under her direction.

Meadow first gained widespread recognition as a talented director in 1976–77 for David Rudkin's *Ashes*, which was co-produced by Joseph Papp. Since then, to avoid being characterized as a director of women's issues, she has directed plays dealing with a wide range of subject matter. Although the collaborative artists she selects usually differ for each production, she has worked on repeated occasions with designer John Lee Beatty, actor Brian Murray, and playwright Alan Ayckbourn. In 1992, after sixteen years of critical and popular praise, Meadow overcame the resistance to women as directors on Broadway when she staged Ayckbourn's *A Small Family Business* with Brian Murray, Jane Carr, Anthony Heald, and Caroline Lagerfelt.

ADDITIONAL PRODUCTIONS: 1982: *Sally and Marsha* (Sybille Pearson) with Bernadette Peters and Christine Baranski; 1983: *The Three Sisters* with Dianne Wiest, Sam Waterston, Jeff Daniels, and Jack Gilford; 1988: *Woman in Mind* (Alan Ayckbourn) with Stockard Channing; 1989: *Eleemosynary* (Lee Blessing) with Eileen Heckart and Joanna Gleason; 1991: *Absent Friends* (Ayckbourn).

SELECTED BIBLIOGRAPHY: Masson, Linda J. K. "Lynne Meadow. Director." Diss. New York U, 1987; Pereira, John. "The History of the Manhattan Theatre Club." Diss. City U of New York, 1986; Raymond, Gerard. "An Interview with Lynne Meadow." *Theater Week* 11 May 1992: 18–23.

Linda J. K. Masson

VSEVOLOD EMILEVICH MEYERHOLD (Karl Theodore Kasimir) [b. January 28, 1874, Penza; d. February 2, 1940, Moscow]. Vsevolod Meyerhold began his career as an acting student of Vladimir Nemirovich-Danchenko* and was an original member of the Moscow Art Theatre company in 1898, where he created the roles of Treplev in *The Sea Gull* and Tusenbach in *Three Sisters* (1901).

Heavily influenced by Anton Chekhov, Meyerhold was determined to create a theatre capable of dealing with the symbolic element that he saw at the center of Chekhov's work. Resigning from the Moscow Art Theatre in 1902, he worked as an actor-director in the provinces, experimenting with stylization until 1905 when Konstantin Stanislavsky* placed him in charge of the experimental Theatre-Studio. He prepared Maurice Maeterlinck's *The Death of Tintagiles* and Gerhart Hauptmann's *Schluck and Jau*, but neither production was ever staged for the public, and Meyerhold left at the end of 1905.

Meyerhold was hired by actress-manager Vera Komissarzhevskaya to direct her theatre in Saint Petersburg. His production of *The Fairground Booth* by Aleksandr Blok (1906) had a major influence on his later work as he began experimenting with *commedia dell'arte* and other nonliterary theatrical forms. Komissarzhevskaya dismissed him, believing, as had Stanislavsky, that Meyerhold placed too much emphasis on the director at the expense of the actor.

Meyerhold was almost immediately appointed a director for the Imperial Theatres in Saint Petersburg, where he remained until the Revolution. Among his productions, *Tristan and Isolde* (1909) and Molière's *Don Juan* (1910) were notable for his use of the grotesque. At the Imperial Theatres, Meyerhold did little experimenting, applying his creative talents to a series of small theatre-studios where he directed and acted under the name Dr. Dapertutto. Before the Revolution, Meyerhold directed *Columbine's Scarf* by Arthur Schnitzler (1910), began to train actors to his requirements at his own theatre-studio (1913–17), published a journal, *The Love of Three Oranges* (1914–16), and directed two films (now lost). The culmination of this period came with his monumental production of Mikhail Lermontov's *Masquerade* (1917) at the Alexandrinsky Theatre. In *Masquerade*, Meyerhold applied all that he had discovered to create a vivid picture of decadent Saint Petersburg society on the eve of the Revolution.

The Russian Revolution gave a political focus to Meyerhold's experiments. He staged the first Soviet play, *Mystery-Bouffe* (1918), beginning a collaboration with Vladimir Mayakovsky that lasted until the poet's suicide in 1930. In 1920–21, Meyerhold was head of the Theatre Department of the Ministry of Enlightenment, and declared a revolution in the theatre to replace the outmoded, naturalistic style with a ''scientific-based,'' agitprop style. Called biomechanics and based on a series of études, it attempted to substitute physical movement for psychology as the determinant of an actor's performance. Meyerhold opened both a school and a theatre in which to apply this technique (1922). Among his students were film director Sergei Eisenstein* and actor Igor Illinsky. Meyerhold used his students to stage Fernand Crommelynck's *The Magnanimous Cuckold*

(1922). The set, by artist Lyubov Popova, was a machine for acting based on constructivism, which became another major influence on Meyerhold. In 1923, Meyerhold became the first theatre director to be awarded the title "People's Artist of the Republic," but was criticized for his production style. Refusing to back down, Meyerhold staged a daring, constructivist production of Alexander Ostrovsky's *The Forest* (1924), which was universally condemned as formalistic.

Meyerhold considered the director the ultimate author of a production, leading him to take many liberties in staging. This belief reached its peak in his masterwork, Gogol's *The Inspector General* (1926). Meyerhold rewrote the script, adding elements from earlier versions and from Gogol's other writings. This production, while heavily criticized, ran successfully as part of Meyerhold's repertory until 1938. Meyerhold staged no major contemporary works because of a lack of acceptable scripts until Mayakovsky's *The Bedbug* (1929) and *The Bathhouse* (1930).

In 1930, Meyerhold's Theatre toured Germany and France where it excited tremendous interest. Returning to the Soviet Union, Meyerhold worked almost exclusively with the classics during the 1930s, staging a straightforward version of Dumas *fils' The Lady of the Camellias* (1934), *Tchaikovsky's The Queen of Spades* (1935) for the Leningrad Maly Opera, and three Chekhov one-acts, titled *33 Swoons* (1935). With the promulgation of socialist realism as a state doctrine in 1934, Meyerhold's artistic position became increasingly untenable. Ostracized by the government, Meyerhold was unable to receive permission to stage Nikolai Ostrovsky's socialist-realist work, *How Steel Was Tempered*, and in early 1938 his theatre was closed.

All but abandoned, Stanislavsky offered Meyerhold a position at the Moscow Opera Theatre, where he completed the staging for *Rigoletto* after Stanislavsky's death. In June 1939, he was arrested, and on February 2, 1940, Meyerhold was executed.

ADDITIONAL PRODUCTIONS: 1906: *Hedda Gabler*, *Sister Beatrice* (Maeterlinck); 1907: *Life of Man* (Andreev); 1911: *Orpheus and Eurydice* (Gluck); 1917: *Death of Tarelkin* (Sukhovo-Kobylin); 1920: *The Dawns* (Verhaeren); 1923: *Earth Rampant* (Tretyakov), *D. E.* (Ehrenburg); 1925: *Bubus the Teacher* (Faiko), *The Mandate* (Erdman); 1926: *Roar, China!* (Tretyakov); 1928: *Woe from Wit* (Griboyedov); 1929: *Commander of the Second Army* (Selvinsky).

SELECTED BIBLIOGRAPHY: Braun, Edward. *Meyerhold on Theatre*. New York: Hill and Wang, 1969; Braun, Edward. *The Theatre of Meyerhold*. New York: Drama Book Specialists, 1979: Hoover, Marjorie. "International Workshop Honoring 110th Anniversary of Meyerhold's Birth." *Soviet and East European Performance* 9 (Summer 1989): 13–22; Hoover, Marjorie. *Meyerhold: The Art of Conscious Theater*. Amherst: University of Massachusetts Press, 1974; Leach, Robert. *Vsevolod Meyerhold*. Cambridge: Cambridge University Press, 1989; Rudnitsky, Konstantin. *Meyerhold the Director*. Ed. Sydney Schultze. Trans. George Petrov. Ann Arbor: Ardis, 1981; Schmidt, Paul. *Meyerhold at Work*. Austin: University of Texas Press, 1980; Slonim, Marc. *Russian Theater*. New York: Collier Books, 1962.

Edward Dee

JONATHAN WOLFE MILLER [b. July 21, 1934, London, England]. Jonathan Miller is a director of insight and originality who is known for often taking iconoclastic stands on the direction of venerable works and generating renewed enthusiasm for classics by reinterpreting them in novel ways. Although trained as a physician at Cambridge, Miller fell into directing through his activities with the Cambridge Footlights drama club. In 1960, he was invited to join the satirical revue, *Beyond the Fringe*, a progenitor of other zany British comedy troupes. *Beyond the Fringe* played to filled houses in London and New York and toured frequently, securing a theatrical reputation for all its performer-creators. In 1963, Miller left the revue to write for television, but returned to the stage to direct poet Robert Lowell's *Benito Cereno* at the Yale Repertory Theatre (1964–65).

In 1970, he staged a vigorous *Merchant of Venice* translated to nineteenth-century Trieste, which restored the work's undercurrent of anti-Semitism. The production featured a famous offstage howl from Shylock (Laurence Olivier) which aroused great tragic feelings about the character. In 1973, Miller was appointed an associate director at Britain's National Theatre, but found the bureaucracy stifling and left in 1975. In the 1970s, he found fulfillment in directing opera, particularly for small companies where he was free to inject ideas on the setting and contextualizing of the productions. For the Glynbourne Opera, he directed Leoš Janáček's *The Cunning Little Vixen* (1975), and in 1978, he was appointed an associate director of the English National Opera, a position he retains to the present. There, he staged a successful but controversial ''Mafia'' *Rigoletto* set in New York's Little Italy in the 1950s.

In 1980, he narrated and wrote ''The Body in Question,'' an educational television series exploring the human body with one episode featuring a televised autopsy. This led to a turn as producer of the BBC's ''Shakespeare Plays'' (1981–82), a series of the Bard's entire canon. He personally directed six of the works including *Anthony and Cleopatra*, *Taming of the Shrew*, *Othello*, and *The Merchant of Venice*, each using unusual casting to obtain special impact. For *Merchant of Venice*, he cast Warren Mitchell, an actor known to British television audiences for playing an Archie Bunker–style bigot. For the libidinous Petruchio, he cast comedian John Cleese, and for the fiery Othello, he cast the subdued and reserved Anthony Hopkins. In 1982, he directed a ''cool'' *Hamlet* and made his American opera debut with a production of *Cosi Fan Tutti*. The following year, he directed a production of Mozart's *The Magic Flute* and announced his first retirement from the stage.

In 1986, however, Miller returned to create another tempest with a new production of *Long Day's Journey into Night* starring Jack Lemmon. He described the American classic as ''a fairly fast-moving, rattling, conversation piece,'' and directed it at a jaunty pace, cutting an hour off the running time and overlapping the dialogue (*American Theatre*, 4). Some critics felt he had deprived O'Neill of his mythic power, while others claimed he had made O'Neill accessible to a new generation.

In 1987, Miller was appointed artistic director of the Old Vic Theatre and crusaded to bring the venerable old house back to popular prominence. In his first season, he directed five productions, including a revival of Bernstein's *Candide* for which he won an Olivier Award for best direction. In 1990, after directing sixteen productions in three years, he announced his retirement from the Old Vic at the end of the 1991 season.

Miller's technique is perhaps blessed by a lack of formal dramatic training, affording him an outsider's perspective on theatre convention. His direction is distinguished by a cool, intellectual approach that favors research as a means of informing productions. The texts are often illuminated and dominated by anthropological investigations into the actual conditions and conventions of the time. The sets for his BBC "Shakespeare Plays" series were strongly influenced by his examinations of North European Renaissance paintings. Art, period social mores, and the era's *zeitgeist* infuse his spectacle with life beyond the script. Robert Brustein described his work on Sheridan's *School for Scandal* (1968), for example, as having created "an absolutely realistic eighteenth century, where the servants were pregnant and women didn't wash" (*Horizon*, 64).

At times, critics have found Miller's work all research and lacking in essential passion, as if Miller was theorizing on the work rather than confronting the work itself. He has often been cast as something of a theatrical gadfly, a professor lecturing actors, but he has managed to have a profound effect on American and European opera and play production, outlasting many of his detractors. In 1983, he was made a Commander of the Order of the British Empire.

ADDITIONAL PRODUCTIONS: 1978: *The Marriage of Figaro*; 1980: *Falstaff*; 1981: *Otello*; 1985: *Don Giovanni*; 1987: *Tristan and Isolde*; 1988: *Andromache*; 1991: *Katya Kabanova* (Leoš Janáček).

SELECTED BIBLIOGRAPHY: Berry, Ralph. *On Directing Shakespeare*. London: Hamish Hamilton, 1989; Engstrom, John. "Starting Over." *Horizon* June 1983: 62–64; Gilliatt, Penelope. "The Doctor in Spite of Himself." *New Yorker* 17 April 1989: 52; Levene, Ellen. "Directors on Design: Jonathan Miller." *Theatre Crafts* April 1985: 18–23; Miller, Jonathan. *Subsequent Performances*. New York: Viking Books, 1986; Romain, Michael, ed. *A Profile of Jonathan Miller*. Cambridge, England: Cambridge University Press, 1992; Sherlock, Ceri. "An Enlightened View." *Opera News* June 1982: 10–14; Wetzsteon, Ross. "The Director in Spite of Himself." *American Theatre* 2 (November 1985): 4–9+.

Stuart Lenig

JULIAN MITCHELL [b. 1854, possibly in New York, New York; d. June 24, 1926, Long Branch, New Jersey]. As a director and "ensemble" director, Mitchell staged the Amazon marches of spectacles and the pony choruses of intimate revues. Like his rivals R. H. Burnside* and Ned Wayburn,* he worked on over 200 shows in rapid succession through long-term associations with producers and performers. He began his career as a performer in a production of *The Black Crook* at Niblo's Garden and became known as an eccentric comic in the farces of Charles H. Hoyt, among them *A Hole in the Ground*.

Mitchell worked for many decades as general stage director for Joe Weber and Lew Fields's revues and musical parodies, such as *Cyranose de Bric-a-Brac* (1898), and for both the Joe Weber Travesty Company and Lew Fields after the celebrated pair's feud and breakup. Mitchell brought his fondness for spectacle to a series of musical comedies based on fantasies, including the original *Wizard of Oz* (1903) and Victor Herbert's operetta *Babes in Toyland* (1903). Married on and off for many years to dancer Bessie Clayton, he specialized in romantic star vehicles for her and other soubrettes. He became associated with the "advanced vaudeville" circuit of Klaw and Erlanger in 1907 with a feature act based on *The Last of the Mohicans* and followed them into Broadway revues for Anna Held. Their *Follies* at the Jardin de Danse was the first of his ten editions of the *Ziegfeld Follies* (1907–15, 1924, 1925). In the 1910s, his growing deafness led Mitchell to abandon stage direction for choreography in most of his assignments, such as *The Count of Luxemburg* in 1912. He remained a popular dance director for operettas and romantic musicals, despite his disability and his feuds with both Florenz Ziegfeld, Jr., and the Shubert Brothers. Mitchell was reunited with Ziegfeld for the *Follies of 1924* and *1925* and the Marilyn Miller musical *Sunny* (1925). Julian Mitchell is generally believed to be the model for the dying director Julian Marsh in the Warner Brothers backstage film *42nd Street*, based on a novel by one-time Mitchell chorus dancer Bradford Ropes.

ADDITIONAL PRODUCTIONS: 1902: *Twirly Whirly* (William T. Francis, Edgar Smith, starring Weber and Fields); 1906: *The Parisian Model* (Max Hoffman and Harry B. Smith); 1907: *The Girl behind the Counter* (Howard Talbot, Arthur Anderson, and Edgar Smith); 1908: *The Soul Kiss* (Maurice Levi and Harry B. Smith); 1917: *Hitchy-Koo of 1917* (E. Ray Goetz and Glen MacDonough, starring Raymond Hitchcock); 1981: *The Kiss Burglar* (Raymond Hubbell and Glen MacDonough); 1920: *Mary* (Louis A. Hirsch, Otto Harbach, and Frank Mandel); 1921: *The Perfect Fool* (written by and starring Ed Wynn).

BIBLIOGRAPHY: There are no lengthy studies of Mitchell as director or choreographer. Material on his work can be found in scholarly studies of his collaborators Lew Fields and Florenz Ziegfeld, Jr., his rivals, such as Ned Wayburn, and his wife. See: Camille Hardy. "Bessie Clayton: An American Genee." *Dance Chronicle* 2.4 (1979): 251–78.

Barbara Cohen-Stratyner

ARIANE MNOUCHKINE [b. 1939, Paris, France]. Ariane Mnouchkine, founder and artistic director of one of France's most original theatre companies, the Théâtre du Soleil, was born in Paris in 1939 of a Russian father and an English mother. Since 1964, when Mnouchkine first created the Théâtre du Soleil as an offshoot of a university theatre group which she had formed with fellow students in 1959, she has dedicated her life to the creation of an authentic popular theatre, resolutely engaged in the political and social issues of contemporary society and exuberantly theatrical. From the start, the Soleil was organized as a cooperative: important decisions were made by majority vote and tasks and responsibilities were equally shared. By 1968, the company agreed to the principle of equal salaries and began collectively creating original texts.

The first Soleil productions (*Les Petits Bourgeois*, Arthur Adamov's adaptation of Maxim Gorky's *The Smug Citizens*, 1964–65, and *Le Capitaine Fracasse*, 1965–66, adapted from Théophile Gautier's novel by Phillipe Léotard), performed in Paris in 1964 and 1965 respectively, went unnoticed for the most part. Their version of Arnold Wesker's *The Kitchen* in 1967–68, performed in the abandoned Cirque Medrano, however, was a major critical and public success (63,400 spectators). To create *The Kitchen*, the Soleil developed their now familiar working methods: painstaking research and documentation; long periods of improvisational work to find character and costume; constant editing and self-criticism; and intensive work on gesture, voice, and physical skills. Mnouchkine and her company achieve their ends through a thorough grounding in traditional performance styles, from Kabuki to Kathakali, from commedia dell'arte to improvisation and Western circus techniques, which they transform and reinvent.

In 1968, along with other young theatre companies, the Soleil responded to the "events of May" as artists and "workers," and actively reexamined the real function of theatre. For strikers in occupied factories, they appropriately performed *The Kitchen*, a protest play which effectively equated the alienating conditions of workers in a huge restaurant kitchen with those of factory workers. Their participation in the May events convinced the Soleil that theatre can and must be politically effective, but raised the question, what kind of theatre? Abandoning the literary text, they chose instead to construct their own texts through a process of "collective creation." Their first attempt, *Les Clowns* (1969), in which each company member sought to discover his or her own personal "clown" as a means of exploring the relationship of the artist to society, was not successful, but it served as the necessary groundwork for future Soleil productions.

In 1970, the Théâtre du Soleil moved to its permanent headquarters, the Cartoucherie, a nineteenth-century munitions warehouse in the Vincennes woods just outside of Paris. They transformed the huge space (some 36,000 square feet) into a large black-box theatre and a lobby where audiences gather in advance of performances; browse among books, maps, and genealogical charts which provide background history for Soleil productions; and sample delicacies from the country of current productions (Mediterranean delicacies during the *Atrides*, for example).

At the Cartoucherie, the Soleil pioneered its epic narrative theatre style, beginning with its ground-breaking production, *1789* in 1970. Like *Les Clowns*, *1789* was a "collaborative creation" (as were the next two Soleil productions, *1793* and *L'Age d'or, première ébauche*) which took place simultaneously on a number of connected platforms. Spectators were free to move from one playing area to another to watch the Third Estate being swindled by the nobility and the clergy in the form of a Punch and Judy show; to applaud the women of Paris bringing the king back to Versailles; or to sit on bleachers, harangued by "revolutionaries" who recounted the events of the first year of the French Revolution. The experience was exhilarating. Bombarded by the Revolution from all sides without a minute's letup, audiences experienced the mounting tension as the action moved toward the taking of the Bastille and culminated in a joyful, carnival-style celebration of the overthrow of tyranny. The piece was highly successful, attracting more than 250,000 spectators from 1970 to 1973.

Equally popular was *1793*, which followed in 1974, but Mnouchkine, ever intent on realizing her dream of dramatizing contemporary reality in contemporary terms, soon turned to the more current issues of the plight of poor immigrant workers in France and the exploitation of land developers in *L'Age d'or* (*The Golden Age*, 1975) and the artist's responsibility to speak out in a totalitarian regime in *Mephisto, the Novel of a Career* (1979). With *Mephisto*, Mnouchkine had come to the realization that to make effective political theatre, the company needed the support of a strong poetic text. Consequently, she adapted Klaus Mann's novel herself.

In 1981, Mnouchkine went even further. For her next project, the presentation of six Shakespeare plays (ultimately only three were produced—*Richard II*, *Twelfth Night*, and *Henry IV, Part I*), the Oxford-educated Mnouchkine did her own translations. She also directed the plays using an Oriental conception in style, costume, and staging. Inspired by Noh, Kabuki, and Kathakali techniques, the Shakespeare plays, as they were called, offered audiences a rare experience of total theatre. Here at last was a perfect blend of movement, voice, sound, and a defining environment composed of original music by resident composer Jean-Jacques Lemêtre, "performing" on his wide array of instruments from around the world, and a stylized set of jute flooring and black curtains. Elaborate costumes from Elizabethan ruffs to Noh battle dress suggested a mix of East and West. For over three years, the Soleil performed its spectacular Shakespeare trilogy at home and abroad, playing to packed houses during its first visit to the United States for the Los Angeles Olympic Arts Festival in 1984.

By 1985, Mnouchkine was finally able to realize her desire to theatricalize the modern world, thanks to noted feminist author Hélène Cixous, who wrote two modern epics for the Théâtre du Soleil. Her *L'Histoire terrible mais inachevée de Norodom Sihanouk, Roi du Cambodge* (*The terrible but unfinished history of Norodom Sihanouk, King of Cambodia*) was a nine-hour chronicle of Cambodia's struggle to remain independent, while *L'Indiade ou L'Inde de Leurs Rêves* (*Indiade or the India of Their Dreams*) related the tale of the bloody founding of Pakistan, from the ashes of the dreams of Gandhi, Nehru, and Mohammed Ali Jinnah.

In 1990, the Soleil returned to the past—ancient Greece, this time—to create *Les Atrides* (*The House of Atreus*). In four parts, *Les Atrides* was composed of Euripides' *Iphigenia in Aulis* and Aeschylus' *Oresteia* (*Agamemnon*, first presented in November 1990; *The Libation Bearers*, January 1991; and *The Furies*, May 1992, completed just before going on a lengthy international tour). Danced rather than acted, *Les Atrides* featured a sumptuously attired chorus (more Indian than Greek) which reigned over the fates of the principal characters. Springing onto the stage from nowhere, they whirled around, perched on walls, peered from behind them, or mourned in black robes, palms painted deep red, ever present, ever intent on following the tale of unchained violence and brutality.

Although the Soleil has been a collective since its inception, Ariane Mnouchkine is unquestionably in charge. Hers is the vision that informs; hers the voice that is heard. Under her superb direction, the Théâtre du Soleil has truly become what its name suggests—a theatre of great power, warmth, and luminosity.

ADDITIONAL PRODUCTIONS: 1968: *A Midsummer Night's Dream* (adapted by Phillipe Léotard); 1974: *1789* (film adaptation of the play); 1976–77: *Molière* (film written and directed by Mnouchkine).

SELECTED BIBLIOGRAPHY: Bablet, Denis, and Marie-Louise Bablet. *Le Théâtre du Soleil, Diapolivre* (84 slides, text and sound track of *1789*). Paris: Centre National de Recherche Scientifique (CNRS), 1979; Champagne, Lenore. *French Theatre Experiment since 1968*. Ann Arbor: UMI Research Press, 1984; Miller, Judith. "Le Théâtre du Soleil." *Theatre and Revolution in France since 1968*. Lexington, KY: French Forum, 1977; Mounier, Catherine. "Deux créations collectives du Théâtre du Soleil: *1793. L'Age d'or.*" *Les Voies de la création théâtrale V*. Paris: C.N.R.S., 1977; Nes Kirby, Victoria. "*1789.*" *The Drama Review* 15 (Fall 1971): 73–91; Thompson, Julie Ann. "Ariane Mnouchkine and the Théâtre du Soleil." Diss. U of Washington, 1986; *Travail Théâtral: Le Théâtre du Soleil*. Lausanne: La Cité, 1976; Richardson, Helen Elizabeth. "The Théâtre du Soleil and the Quest for Popular Theatre in the Twentieth Century." Diss. U of California, Berkeley, 1990.

Philippa Wehle

PHILIP MOELLER [b. August 26, 1880, New York, New York; d. April 26, 1958, New York, New York]. As a founding member of the Theatre Guild, which evolved from New York's Washington Square Players in 1919, Philip Moeller directed a number of landmark productions of the American theatre. These included Eugene O'Neill's *Strange Interlude* (1928), *Mourning Becomes Electra* (1931), and *Ah, Wilderness!* (1933); Elmer Rice's *The Adding Machine* (1922); and the American premieres of George Bernard Shaw's *Saint Joan* (1923), *Arms and the Man* (1925), and *Major Barbara* (1928).

A graduate of Columbia University, Moeller had no formal training as a director; his early theatrical experience was in playwriting. Among his plays are *Molière, Sophie, Helena's Husband*, and the highly praised biographical comedy, *Madame Sand*. Moeller's background in playwriting contributed to a directing style which had as its goal the illumination and elucidation of the playwright's ideas through the medium of theatrical presentation. He worked improvisationally, suiting his methods to the requirements of each new script. Moeller's most noteworthy work was on Eugene O'Neill's *Strange Interlude*, which opened January 30, 1928. To handle the play's asides, in which characters reveal their innermost thoughts through lengthy monologues, he developed the innovative technique of freezing the primary action while speeches were delivered directly to the audience. Though widely used since, this technique was revolutionary in 1928. O'Neill was so pleased that, in a letter to Guild Board member Theresa Helburn, he referred to Moeller's work as "the most imaginative directing I've ever known,'' and subsequently Moeller became one of the foremost interpreters of O'Neill's work.

Moeller was also adept at working with designers. His most frequent collaborator was fellow Guild Board member, Lee Simonson, although he also worked with Robert Edmond Jones, Cleon Throckmorton, Jo Mielziner, and other leading designers of the period. Simonson designed the settings for twenty-seven of Moeller's fifty-six productions, including the expressionistic sets for Rice's *The Adding Machine* and O'Neill's *Dynamo* (1929).

If a dominating motif can be identified in the work of Philip Moeller, it is music. He composed the incidental music for several Guild productions, found the rhythms of his staging for many plays in the structure of musical composition, and it was the musicality of the language which most drew Moeller to the plays of Eugene O'Neill.

In the early thirties, Moeller was signed to direct three films for RKO-Radio, among them *Break of Hearts* (1935) with Charles Boyer and Katharine Hepburn. For the last twenty years of his life, he lived in New York, in virtual retirement.

Philip Moeller's contribution to American theatre and his place in the history of twentieth-century directing are often overshadowed by the stature and character of the Theatre Guild itself. For twenty years, Moeller submerged his personal ego and worked as a member of a team whose aim was to produce works of artistic merit. Yet, in this environment of collaboration, Moeller nevertheless forged a directing style which helped to define the role of the modern director as a theatre artist, as distinct from the producer.

ADDITIONAL PRODUCTIONS: 1919: *Bonds of Interest* (Jacinto Benavente); 1922: *R.U.R.* (Čapek); 1923: *The Devil's Disciple*; 1924: *They Knew What They Wanted* (Sidney Howard), the Guild's first Pulitzer Prize winner; 1925: *Caesar and Cleopatra* (Shaw) with Helen Hayes; 1927: *Right You Are If You Think You Are* (Pirandello) with Edward G. Robinson; 1929: *The Camel through the Needle's Eye* (František Langer, adapted by Moeller); 1930: *Elizabeth the Queen* (Maxwell Anderson) with Alfred Lunt and Lynne Fontanne, *Hotel Universe* (Philip Barry) with Ruth Gordon.

SELECTED BIBLIOGRAPHY: Barnes, Howard. "Moeller of the Theatre Guild." *New York Herald-Tribune* 10 February 1929: 2, 5; Bogard, Travis, and Jackson R. Bryer, eds. *Selected Letters of Eugene O'Neill*. New York: Arno Press, 1973; Eaton, Walter Prichard. *The Theatre Guild: The First Ten Years*. New York: Brentano's, 1929; Helburn, Theresa. *A Wayward Quest*. Boston: Little, Brown and Company, 1960; Langner, Lawrence. *The Magic Curtain*. New York: E. P. Dutton and Company, 1951; Nadel, Norman. *A Pictorial History of the Theatre Guild*. New York: Crown Publishers, 1969; Wainscott, Ronald H. *Staging O'Neill: The Experimental Years, 1920–1934*. New Haven: Yale University Press, 1988; Waldau, Roy S. *Vintage Years of the Theatre Guild: 1928–1939*. Cleveland: The Press of Case Western Reserve University, 1972.

Pamela Myers-Morgan

LÁSZLÓ MOHOLY-NAGY [b. July 20, 1895, Bacsbaro, Hungary; d. November 24, 1946, Chicago, Illinois]. Though Moholy-Nagy's practical work for the theatre was limited to some scenic design in the late 1920s, his writings about theatre and his reflections on the interaction between the stage and other media and fields of science and art are nonetheless an important contribution to the development of the German and European theatre and stage directing in this century.

After publishing drawings and poems in Hungarian avant-garde magazines before World War I, Moholy-Nagy came into contact with the Dada movement in Berlin after the war. During these years he developed a radical constructivism, in which he emphasized the independence of form, color, and movement and the dynamism of interaction of these elements. In 1922 he wrote: "Constructivism is the socialism of vision!" In Moholy-Nagy's socialist view, the mechanization of society creates fundamentally new forms of art and communal living. His whole work focuses on the analysis of changing perception in the new media. In his work as a photographer and experimental filmmaker he laid the foundations for his stage designs which used the interaction of light and movement.

So Moholy-Nagy's work tied in with the general project of the Bauhaus, which he joined as a teacher in 1923. The Bauhaus at Weimar was an educational institution with classes in all areas of visual perception, from architecture to design, from theatre to film and photography. The stage workshop at the Bauhaus was mainly interested in the *architectural* definition of space: space is something that is created, not naturally found. The central purpose of the stage workshop thus became research on the relationship between the human figure and surrounding space. Moholy-Nagy's special project was the mechanization of theatre. In *The Theatre of the Bauhaus* (1925) he wrote: "Nothing stands in the way of making use of complex apparatus such as film, automobile, elevator, airplane and other machinery" (67). This leads also to a breakdown of the spatial separation between spectator and actors: Moholy-Nagy proposed a multiplicity of stages and bridges all through the theatre. In 1928 and the following years he created some stage sets and other scenic elements for the Kroll-Oper and the Piscator-Buhne in Berlin. But his important contributions to the theatre were in the theoretical realm: here he helped to redefine the space of the theatre and to emancipate theatrical elements such as light, set, and costumes from the human figure.

SELECTED BIBLIOGRAPHY: Caton, Joseph Harris. *The Utopian Vison of Moholy-Nagy*. Ann Arbor: UMI Research Press, 1984; Moholy-Nagy, László. *The New Vision and Abstract of an Artist*. 1928. 3rd rev. ed. New York: Wittenborn and Co, 1946; Moholy-Nagy, László. *Vision in Motion*. Chicago: P. Theobald, 1947; Moholy-Nagy, Sibyl. *László Moholy-Nagy: An Experiment in Totality*. Cambridge, MA: MIT Press, 1950; Schlemmer, Oskar, Farkas Molnar, and László Moholy-Nagy. *The Theatre of the Bauhaus*. Middletown, CT: Wesleyan University Press, 1961.

Kai Hammermeister

OLOF MOLANDER [b. 1892, Helsinki, Finland; d. May 1966]. Considered by many the first important Swedish director, Olof Molander began his fifty-one year career in the theatre as an acting student in the School of Drama of the Royal Dramatic Theatre in 1911. His acting debut (Freddy in *Pygmalion*) took place at the Royal Dramatic Theatre in 1914. In the years between 1914 and

1918, Molander acted in over fifty productions, gaining special recognition for his performance in the title role in Molière's *George Dandin*.

In 1918, Molander suffered a partial paralysis which jeopardized his acting career. During his absence from the stage, he began to study directing, became especially intrigued by Gordon Craig's theories of the theatre, and wrote several articles about Craig. He made his directing debut at the Royal Dramatic Theatre in 1919 with a highly successful interpretation of *The Merchant of Venice*.

Throughout his career, Molander was well-known for directing August Strindberg and Eugene O'Neill. His first attempt at directing Strindberg (*The Pelican*, 1922), while generally considered successful, attracted relatively little attention; but his direction of *A Dream Play* in 1935 was hailed as the work of a genius. Molander's innovative staging set the play in the Stockholm of Strindberg's era, and the style exhibited in this production was described as a merger of "traditional" views of directing, New Realism, and symbolism. Shortly before he began directing *A Dream Play*, Molander had begun preparation for conversion to Catholicism, which some critics maintain contributed to the warm religiosity of his new directing style.

Molander's unique style and "modern" view of directing had actually been demonstrated two years earlier in his production of O'Neill's *Mourning Becomes Electra* in Stockholm. This landmark production was the European premiere of the play and was instrumental in O'Neill's receiving the Nobel Prize in 1936.

In 1934, Molander was appointed artistic director of the Royal Dramatic Theatre, a tenure which was marked by difficulties and tensions. Molander's regime was opposed from within by a group of actors and from without by various government ministers. Five years after he accepted the position, Molander left the Royal Dramatic Theatre and, until 1942, worked as a free-lance director in Stockholm and throughout Scandinavia.

In 1942, Molander returned to the Royal Dramatic Theatre to mount Strindberg's *The Ghost Sonata*, a production which ranked in scale and quality with his earlier production of *A Dream Play*. In the twenty-one years that followed, Molander directed thirty-eight plays by some of the most notable playwrights in the Western canon. Among these were the world premiere of *A Touch of the Poet*, the European premieres of *The Iceman Cometh* and *A Moon for the Misbegotten*, Strindberg's *Damascus I* and *II*, and a new version of *A Dream Play*.

In his later years, Molander returned to acting and remained active as a director of radio plays. He ended his career at the Municipal Theatre in Stockholm where he staged all three parts of *Damascus* (1965). His directing, which included radio, film, and 118 separate productions at the Royal Dramatic Theatre, is best remembered for its unique style which blended "living realism" with religious symbolism.

SELECTED BIBLIOGRAPHY: Engel, P. G., and L. Janzon. *Sju Decennier*. Stockholm: Stockholm Forum, 1974; Molander, Olof. *Detta ar jag*. Stockholm: Stockholm Forum, 1961; Molander, Olof. *Harald Molander—The Man and the Artist*. Stockholm: Stockholm Forum, 1950; Molander, Olof. *Harriet Bosse*. Stockholm: Stockholm Forum, 1920; Olsson, Tom J. A. *O'Neill och Dramaten*. Diss. U Stockholm, 1977.

                                                                              Tom J. A. Olsson

MEREDITH MONK [b. November 20, 1942, New York, New York]. Only two years after she graduated from Sarah Lawrence College in 1964, where she studied voice and piano, Meredith Monk captured the attention of the dance world with *16 Millimeter Earrings*. During this work, she wore a white globe over her head on which were projected images of her own face. By 1991, when her commissioned, full-scale opera *Atlas* opened at the Houston Grand Opera, she had examined the creation of the self; the identity of the person in place, time, and culture; and modes of representing ideas and subjects through an astounding array of media and combinations.

Monk is a composer, singer, playwright, actor, and filmmaker, as well as a dancer and choreographer. Her work with her company, "The House," has earned her three Obies, first prize at the Venice Biennale, a CINE (Council on International Nontheatrical Events) Golden Eagle, two German Critics Prizes for record of the year, and various fellowships. She is considered by many to be a leading postmodern performer whose works not only use a variety of conventions and styles to present meaning, but also to reveal the meaning of the (re)presenting.

Heir to the examination of sound, movement, and syntax fostered by pioneers like John Cage and Merce Cunningham, Monk has established the importance of exploration, expression, and the creation of meaning and idea through sound and movement, while continuing to reveal ways of sounding and moving as being filled with implications themselves. Her nonlinear performances use movements that often alternate between the mundane, the ritualistic, the human, and the mechanistic, and various vocal techniques (including glottal effects, animal sounds, vocal gymnastics, yodeling, hocketing, and ululation, but rarely words) that give the sense of the voice as choreographed rather than scored. Many critics have commented upon the impact of her inextricably meshed techniques and images, as well as the striking sense of invitation to the audience to collaborate in the creation of the meaning of the piece itself.

Monk's works often examine themes such as the importance of ancestral heritage; the petrifying effect of actions ritualized without human and emotional context; the education and destiny of women; the meaning of ecology and geography; and the religious mysteries of the East.

Monk has worked in a variety of styles: *Juice*, a 1969 "theatre cantata" in three parts, began with a cast of eighty-five in the corridors of the Guggenheim and, after intermissions of a week or more, diminished to presentation on a video screen; *Quarry*, a 1976 Obie Award winner, was an "excavation" into the horror of the holocaust and its relation to the present, featuring ten actor-dancers, a chorus of thirty, and three instrumentalists, which used actions that were described as mundane, ritualistic, and processional; *The Games* (1985), a five-person dance set in a high-tech future that remembers only the formal rules of the twentieth-century actions it performs, was developed in collaboration with Ping Chong; while *Facing North*, a 1991 two-person piece, featured Monk and Robert Een moving in a white cloth-covered space, first as gods in masks setting up miniatures of an arctic world, and then with masks removed to signify their participating in that world. Her search for form and meaning in performance pieces, intellectually dense and profoundly evocative, continues to this day to expand the boundaries of performance and challenge audiences to expand their perceptions as well.

ADDITIONAL PRODUCTIONS: 1968: *Co-op*; 1970: *Needle Brain Lloyd and the Systems Kid*; 1972: *Vessel* (Obie citation); 1973: *Education of the Girlchild*; 1979: *Recent Ruins*; 1986: *Turtle Dreams* (Cabaret), *Acts from Under and Above*; 1987: *Duet Behavior* (with Bobby McFarrin); 1989: *Book of Days* (film).

SELECTED BIBLIOGRAPHY: Forte, Jeanie Kay. "Women in Performance Art: Feminism and Postmodernism." Diss. U of Washington, 1986; Foster, Susan. "The Signifying Body: Reaction and Resistance in Postmodern Dance." *Theatre Journal* 37 (March 1985): 45–64; Marranca, Bonnie. "Meredith Monk's Atlas of Sound." *Performing Arts Journal* 40 (January 1992): 16–29. Also, Jack Anderson has published many reviews and short articles on Monk in the *New York Times* which add up to an excellent chronicle and description of her work.

Mark S. Weinberg

GREGORY DEAN MOSHER [b. January 15, 1949, New York, New York]. Former artistic director of Lincoln Center Theatre (1986–92) and the Goodman Theatre in Chicago (1978–85), Gregory Mosher has made his mark as a director *and* producer during his short but highly successful career. He is most closely identified with directing the premiere productions of David Mamet's plays.

Growing up in New York City, he directed his first play, Edward Albee's *The American Dream*, for a community theatre while still a high school student. After attending both Oberlin and Ithaca colleges, he returned to New York and Juilliard in 1971. When one of his teachers, William Woodman, left the school in 1974 to become artistic director of the Goodman, he invited the twenty-five year old Mosher to supervise a second stage which was formed to develop new plays. Woodman returned to New York in 1978, and Mosher became the Goodman's artistic director.

During his years at the Goodman, Mosher directed or produced over eighty plays, half of which were American premieres of writers such as Edward Albee, Spalding Gray, John Guare, Wole Soyinka, Michael Weller, David Rabe, Emily Mann, Tennessee Williams, and David Mamet. In his final year in Chicago, Mosher formed a second theatre on Briar Street, the New Theatre, which was to be devoted to fostering new works by American writers.

Mosher's six years as artistic head of the previously ill-fated Lincoln Center theatres were truly remarkable. In fact, so successful were he and Bernard Gersten (executive producer) that at times they were accused of creating "theatre for profit" in a not-for-profit theatre. The truth, however, was that in order to keep their popular shows running, they would invariably need to move them to a Broadway theatre in order to produce additional plays at Lincoln Center.

Mosher's directorial work has been described as specific, simple, straightforward, and dedicated to the sanctity of the playwright's words. He routinely gravitates toward small-cast plays with minimal production values in which language is paramount. In his effort to honor the playwright's intentions, he does not attempt to impose a personal directorial stamp on the production. His rehearsal process is described as patient and low key, as he attempts "to create an atmosphere where real chances can be taken, where risk will be supported" (Morrow and Pike, 111).

Being intensely work-oriented, Mosher has numerous accomplishments. He successfully changed the fortunes of two theatres with checkered histories, and as one of the leaders in the American theatre to foster new plays, he has refused to tax playwrights for royalties from future productions of plays first directed by him, a common practice at many institutional theatres. He was also one of the first American directors to promote interracial casting and to further the cause of South African playwrights.

In 1992, Mosher stepped down as artistic director of Lincoln Center in order to devote more time to do what he enjoys most—directing plays. He believes that one ultimately should concentrate on "a play, not an institution. There's something invigorating about devoting oneself to one project at a time" (Coe 51).

ADDITIONAL PRODUCTIONS: **Directing:** 1976: *American Buffalo* (premiere); 1977: *A Life in the Theatre* (Mamet, premiere); 1978: *Native Son*; 1982: *Edmund* (Mamet, premiere), *A House Not Meant to Stand* (Tennessee Williams's last play); 1984: *Glengarry Glen Ross* (premiere, Pulitzer Prize, Tony Award nomination); 1985: *The Cherry Orchard* (Mamet adaptation at the New Theatre); 1988: *Speed the Plow* (premiere, Tony Award nomination), *Our Town* (Lyceum Theatre, New York, Tony Award nomination), *Boy's Life* (Mitzi Newhouse Theatre); 1992: *A Streetcar Named Desire* (with Jessica Lange and Alec Baldwin at Ethel Barrymore Theatre, New York). **Producing:** 1983: *The Comedy of Errors* (with the Flying Karamazov Brothers); 1986: *The House of Blue Leaves* (Lincoln Center); 1987: *The Front Page, Anything Goes, Sarafina* (from South Africa); 1988: *Waiting for Godot* (with Robin Williams and Steve Martin); 1990: *Six Degrees of Separation* (John Guare, premiere).

SELECTED BIBLIOGRAPHY: Bartow, Arthur. *The Director's Voice*. New York: Theatre Communications Group, 1988: 231–40; Christiansen, Richard. "Mosher's New Role a Challenge." *Chicago Tribune* 1 May 1985: 1–2; Coe, Robert. "The Last Temptation of Lincoln Center." *American Theatre* 5 (November 1988): 14–23 + ; Kissel, Howard. "The B-Team." *New York Daily News* 16 November 1986: 14–16 + ; Mamet, David. "Our Best Director." *Theatre Week* 20 April 1992: 29–32; Morrow, Lee Alan, and Frank Pike. *Creating Theatre*. New York: Vintage, 1986: 85–136; Ross, Laura. "Beginning Again at 60." *American Theatre* 1 (February 1985): 16–17; Rothstein, Mervyn. "Lincoln Center's Theater Team Looks Back." *New York Times* 6 March 1990: C17 + .

Robert Chapel

HEINER MÜLLER [b. January 9, 1929, Eppendorf (Saxony), Germany]. Harassed in East Germany because of his anti-Stalinism—excluded from the Writers' Union in 1961, publicly criticized by the Socialist party in 1965, and practically unpublished in the East from 1961 to 1973—and largely misunderstood in West Germany as an anti-Communist dissident, by the 1980s Heiner Müller was recognized as a leading intellectual voice in both Germanies, and major theatre

festivals focused on his plays (1983: The Holland Festival; 1986: Müller Factory
in Dortmund; 1988: Müller Werkschau in West Berlin; 1990: Experimenta 6 in
Frankfurt). One of the most prolific dramatists writing in German and among
the most frequently staged German playwrights since Bertolt Brecht,* Müller
also became in the 1980s a challenging stage director of his own texts. Even
before his time, however, he was directly involved with the theatre in East Berlin
as dramaturg at the Maxim Gorky Theatre from 1958 to 1960, the Berlin Ensemble from 1970 to 1976, and the Volksbühne after 1976. Moreover, he worked
closely with directors who staged his plays, including B. K. Tragelehn, Manfred
Karge and Matthias Longhoff, Fritz Marquardt, and Robert Wilson.*

Without having established a system, Müller has nonetheless formulated over
the years—largely in a critical appropriation of Brechtian notions—his ideas on
dramaturgy in essays, program notes, and interviews. Central to his approach
is the notion of the "synthetic fragment," a nonmimetic structural concept
referring to a collage of apparently independent scenes which characterizes both
his dramatic texts and his staging techniques. Underlying this notion is Müller's
resistance to obvious meaning and his rejection of closure. For him the theatre
is a "laboratory of social fantasy," and the audience interacts with the stage to
produce a text. This utopian, democratic motivation refunctionalizes the relationship between text, stage, and audience by creating complex signifying strategies which emphasize the *work* of art as an active, nonconsumerist process.

Müller's early stagings already revealed basic features of this approach: de-
dramatization of plot, causality, and character with a corresponding revaluation
of other theatrical elements (e.g., masks, ritualized movements, music); the
integration of the grotesque, exaggeration, and black humor in order to shock
or bewilder the audience; as well as the collaborative effort of director and
designers to comment on each other's interpretations. After several encounters
with Robert Wilson (*CIVIL warS*, 1984; *Hamletmachine*, 1986; *Quartett*, 1987;
The Forest, 1990), Müller's political theatre of discourse is even more radically
characterized by the power of visual and linguistic image. *The Scab* (1988) and
Hamlet/Machine (1990) became operatic, multimedia productions in which the
original texts were cut, reordered, and augmented with other texts while the
expressive quality of the stage and the staging (color, voices, noise, music,
images, and movement) increasingly represented subjectively structured psychic
spaces.

ADDITIONAL PRODUCTIONS: 1981: *The Mission* (together with Ginka Czolakova); 1982:
The Mission, Macbeth (together with Ginka Czolakova); 1991: *Mauser*.

SELECTED BIBLIOGRAPHY: Eke, Norbert Otto. *Heiner Müller. Apokalypse und Utopie*.
Paderborn: Schöningh, 1989 (includes an extensive international bibliography through
1987 and a chronological listing of Müller's texts); Müller, Heiner. *The Battle*. Trans.
Carl Weber. New York: PAJ Publications, 1989; Müller, Heiner. *Explosion of a Memory*.
Trans. Carl Weber. New York: Performing Arts Journal Publications, 1989; Müller,
Heiner. *Germania*. Trans. Bernard and Caroline Schütze. New York: Semiotexte, 1990;

Müller, Heiner. *Hamletmachine and Other Texts for the Stage*. Trans. Carl Weber. New York: Performing Arts Journal Publications, 1984; Silberman, Marc. ''Heiner Müller's *Der Lohndrücker*, 1988.'' *Theater* 19 (Summer/Fall 1988): 22–34; Teraoka, Arlene. *The Silence of Entropy or Universal Discourse: The Postmodernist Poetics of Heiner Müller*. New York: Peter Lang Publishing, 1985.

Marc Silberman

N

BETTY NANSEN (née Müller) [b. March 19, 1873; d. March 15, 1943, Copenhagen, Denmark]. Danish actress, director and theatre manager, Betty Nansen belonged to a family of touring actors and at age nineteen, made her debut at the Casino Theatre in Copenhagen. While there, Nansen attracted the attention of the author Herman Bang, who was also a prominent director. Bang directed her in several plays, and until his death in 1912, he privately rehearsed all her major parts with her. Through her marriage in 1896 to the writer, journalist, and publisher Peter Nansen, she was admitted to a cultural and literary environment which was to have a significant influence upon her development. Following her marriage, she turned her interest from the typical star repertory (French comedy and melodrama) to the classics and the modern drama, especially Henrik Ibsen, Bjørn Bjørnson,* and August Strindberg.

As an actress, Nansen demonstrated a paradoxical mix of cold calculation and passionate expressiveness which sometimes bordered on self-exposure. She specialized in women with strong passions who relentlessly followed their own dictates despite middle-class conventions, and her interpretations seemed so stunningly modern that before she was thirty, she was hailed by the critics as the woman of a new era.

Nansen was attached to the Royal Theatre and several private theatres in Copenhagen, toured the provinces, and traveled to other Scandinavian countries. After her divorce from Peter Nansen, she made films in the United States during World War I, but returned disillusioned and fully determined to become mistress in her own house. In 1917, she bought an old theatre and gave it her own name, which was set in brightly illuminated letters above the entrance.

The Betty Nansen Theatre was a "star" theatre in the sense that Nansen was the indisputable ruler of the theatre. She chose the repertory, played the main female parts, and directed most of the performances; but behind the image of the conceited prima donna was a person with a strong sense of duty and an almost inhuman capacity for work. Within a few years, Nansen made her small theatre the leading literary stage in Copenhagen.

Stylistically, Nansen was firmly rooted in the naturalistic directing tradition of William Bloch,* a tradition she shared with Herman Bang, her old master. Like Bloch and Bang, Nansen possessed the capacity to penetrate the psychology of the characters and hence to enter imaginatively into the spirit of a play. Nansen's demand for plasticity (she often compared the art of the actor with that of a sculptor) onstage, however, gave her productions a firmness of structure and her characters a one-sidedness which led stylistically away from sheer naturalism toward a more stylized theatre. This tendency was perhaps most evident in her productions of the classics and in comedy where she showed a preference for the burlesque.

Although the plays of Ibsen and Strindberg continued to occupy an important place in her theatre's repertory, beginning in the late 1920s, Nansen's interest shifted to social issues. With her production of Ernst Toller's *Yippee. We're Alive* (1928), which was inspired by the Erwin Piscator* Berlin production the year before, she introduced documentary theatre into Denmark.

Through her efforts, Nansen made her "theatre of humble means" a serious competitor to the Royal Theatre, from whom she ultimately "stole" Ibsen and Strindberg. She also contributed measurably to the Danish theatre by producing European and Scandinavian drama (Schiller, Shakespeare, Adam Oehlenschlä-ger) in interesting interpretations, by introducing important foreign dramatists (e.g., Maurice Maeterlinck, Eugene O'Neill, Luigi Pirandello,* Romain Rolland) and by encouraging new Danish dramatists (especially Kaj Munk).

ADDITIONAL PRODUCTIONS: 1917: *Hedda Gabler, The Father*; 1921: *Hamlet*; 1924: *The Last Journey* (Sutton Vane), *Six Characters in Search of an Author*; 1925: *Ghosts* (also shown in Paris at the Théâtre de l'Oeuvre); 1932: *The Word* (Kaj Munk); 1933: *Mourning Becomes Electra, The Green Pastures*; 1939: *Johnson over Jordan* (Priestley); 1940: *You Can't Take It with You, The Mother* (Karel Čapek).

SELECTED BIBLIOGRAPHY: Kvam, Kela. "Betty Nansen. A Unique Figure in Danish Theatre." *Nordic Theatre Studies: Yearbook for Theatre Research in Scandinavia*. Vol. 1. Munksgaard Copenhagen, 1988.

Kela Kvam

VLADIMIR IVANOVICH NEMIROVICH-DANCHENKO [b. December 11, 1858, the Caucasus; d. April 25, 1943, Moscow]. Vladimir Nemirovich-Danchenko cofounded and codirected the Moscow Art Theatre (MAT), a company which had a major influence on twentieth-century theatre. Although most often recognized as the literary and business manager of the Art Theatre, he was a talented director in his own right.

Nemirovich-Danchenko became interested in the theatre early. As a child, he lived across from a summer theatre, and he acted and wrote plays while growing up. After graduating from the University of Moscow, he wrote dramatic criticism, short stories, and novels as well as eleven plays, mostly comedies or melodramas. *The Wild Rose*, staged at Moscow's Maly Theatre in 1882, was his first play to be produced. *A New Affair* won the Griboyedov Prize as the season's best play in 1890, as did *The Worth of Life* in 1896. In 1891, he began teaching dramatic courses at the Moscow Philharmonic's school, where his students included Olga Knipper, Ivan Moskvin, and Vsevelod Meyerhold.*

Nemirovich-Danchenko grew dissatisfied with the Russian theatres where his students worked after graduation and began seeking ways to create a more artistic theatre company. In June 1897, he and Konstantin Stanislavsky,* then an amateur actor and director who had staged semiprofessional productions with the Society of Art and Literature, forged a plan for the future in a meeting that lasted eighteen hours, during which they mapped out their dreams for what became the Moscow Art Theatre.

In their initial discussions, the two agreed to split the responsibility of running the company into two parts, literary and production. Nemirovich-Danchenko had veto power over questions concerning literary matters, and Stanislavsky controlled production questions. Nevertheless, both men staged productions, often hand in hand.

As a writer himself, Nemirovich-Danchenko was sensitive to the playwright's intentions and always tried to realize those intentions in his work. As literary manager, he chose the plays that the MAT would produce. For the first season, among other titles, he proposed that the MAT produce Anton Chekhov's *The Sea Gull*, which Stanislavsky did not initially understand but came to appreciate as he talked with Nemirovich-Danchenko and worked on the production. Both men worked on staging the play. Nemirovich-Danchenko worked with actors on the play's ideas and interpretation for several weeks before Stanislavsky sent detailed staging instructions which Nemirovich-Danchenko implemented. Stanislavsky joined the company for the final rehearsals. *The Sea Gull* was a great success, establishing both the MAT as an important theatre and Chekhov as a significant dramatist.

Nemirovich-Danchenko continued to co-direct with Stanislavsky in addition to staging his own productions. As in the rehearsals for *The Sea Gull*, Stanislavsky prepared a detailed mise-en-scène, while Nemirovich-Danchenko spent more time working with the performers. Among other productions, the two directors staged *The Cherry Orchard* (1904), Maxim Gorky's *The Lower Depths* (1902), Alexander Griboyedov's *Woe from Wit* (1906), Nikolai Gogol's *The Inspector General* (1908), and *The Living Corpse* (an adaptation of Tolstoy's *Redemption* in 1911). Nemirovich-Danchenko also took over the last three weeks of rehearsal from Stanislavsky for *The Three Sisters* in 1901.

Nemirovich-Danchenko championed both Henrik Ibsen and Anton Chekhov for the MAT, and he directed productions of their plays, including *When We*

Dead Awaken (1900), *Pillars of Society* (1903), *Rosmersholm* (1908), and *Ivanov* (1904). He also directed Shakespeare's *Julius Caesar* in 1903 with Stanislavsky as Brutus, a production noted for the detailed, realistic performances of the crowds, and dramatized and directed two Dostoyevsky novels, *The Brothers Karamazov* (1910) and *Nikolai Stavrogin* (1912, based on *The Devils*).

His later productions were noteworthy as well, especially his staging of Tolstoy's *Resurrection*. In his 1931 dramatization of the novel, Nemirovich-Danchenko cast an actor as the "Character on the Author's Behalf," who narrated the production and provided some of Tolstoy's description. This character walked among the actors and through the audience, unseen by the other performers, giving voice to the character's thoughts and giving the author's commentary.

Nemirovich-Danchenko also founded a Musical Studio at the MAT in 1919 (renamed the Nemirovich-Danchenko Musical Theatre in 1926), where he developed a musical production style showing that the MAT's methods could work in musicals and operettas as well as nonmusical productions. He wanted to find the musical ideas in every theatrical element of the production, including the performers, the scenery, and the costumes, and he trained performers to be "singing actors." Productions by the Nemirovich-Danchenko Musical Theatre included *The Daughter of Madame Angot* (Lecoque, 1920), *Carmen*, Offenbach's *La Perichole*, and *Lysistrata* with music by Glière (all 1922–24).

Nemirovich-Danchenko remained at the head of the MAT until his death in 1943.

ADDITIONAL PRODUCTIONS: 1905: *Children of the Sun* (Gorky); 1906: *Brand*; 1907: *Boris Godunov*; 1909: *Anathema* (Andreev); 1912: *Peer Gynt, Ekaterina Ivanovna* (Andreev); 1914: *Thought* (Andreev); 1916: *There Will Be Joy* (Dmitry Merezhkovsky); 1929: *Uncle's Dream* (adapted from Dostoyevsky); 1931: *Three Fat Men* (Soviet propaganda play by Olesha); 1934: *Lady Macbeth of Mtsensk District* (Dmitry Shostakovich), *The Storm* (Ostrovsky); 1937: *Anna Karenina*.

SELECTED BIBLIOGRAPHY: Benedetti, Jean, ed. *The Moscow Art Theatre Letters*. New York: Routledge, 1991; Houghton, Norris. *Moscow Rehearsals*. New York: Harcourt Brace, 1936; Markov, P. A. *The Soviet Theatre*. New York: Benjamin Blom, 1972; Morgan, Joyce Vining. *Stanislavski's Encounter with Shakespeare*. Ann Arbor: UMI Research Press, 1984 (includes extensive description of Nemirovich-Danchenko's production of *Julius Caesar*); Nemirovitch-Dantchenko, Vladimir. *My Life in the Russian Theatre*. New York: Theatre Arts Books, 1936; Saylor, Oliver M. *Inside the Moscow Art Theatre* New York: Brentano's, 1925.

Stephen M. Vallillo

MIKE NICHOLS [b. Michael Igor Peschkowsky, November 6, 1931, Berlin, Germany]. From a shy emigré of seven, arriving in the United States in 1939 with but two English sentences at his disposal ("I do not speak English." "Please do not kiss me."), Nichols became one of the preeminent comic performers in America by the time he was thirty. He began performing as a student at the University of Chicago in 1949 and there met his longtime partner and collaborator Elaine May. Nichols began his professional career as a comedian in 1957, writing and performing droll comic dialogues for radio, television, and nightclubs with May. The two soon achieved national prominence and amicably dissolved their partnership after a successful Broadway run in 1961. (They were reunited in the 1980 Long Wharf Theatre production of *Who's Afraid of Virginia Woolf?* in the roles of George and Martha.)

In the early 1960s, Nichols turned to directing and had a string of successes with the plays of Neil Simon, beginning with *Barefoot in the Park* in 1963. He has also directed a number of David Rabe's plays, including *Streamers* (1976) and *Hurlyburly* (1984). Although he often stages mainstream stage comedies, Nichols lately has worked in other genres, including the 1988 Lincoln Center production of *Waiting for Godot* with Steve Martin and Robin Williams. He has also proved adept as a film director, with such hits as *Who's Afraid of Virginia Woolf?* (1966), *The Graduate* (1967), *Catch–22* (1970), *Carnal Knowledge* (1971), and *Postcards from the Edge* (1990). Nichols occasionally directs for television including the ABC series "Family."

Nichols developed his penchant for lightness, spontaneity, and timing as a comic, and an appreciation for craft under the tutelage of Lee Strasberg.* Nichols uses events from his own life to encourage the actors to pour their own experience into the role. He seeks a central moment ("event" in his terminology) in each scene that will physically convey the essence of what the playwright is saying. Deeply affected by the work of Elia Kazan,* Nicholas always pushes actors to evolve their characters in terms of specific behavior. His skill as a satirist helped him evolve a keen eye and ear for the minute physical, vocal, and gestural details of each scene and a refined instinct for the subtle rhythms and precise timing of brisk comic dialogue.

He approaches each moment in the play as a discrete problem to be solved, each in its own turn. He has been known to carry his obsession for detail to great lengths: he had *The Odd Couple* (1967) set repainted less than twenty-four hours before the opening, and he insisted on a real cabdriver for the role of the telephone man in *Barefoot in the Park*. Although noted for his clarity and precision onstage, Nichols eschews any set methodology. With characteristically self-effacing humor, he analogizes directing and sex: "You never see anybody else doing it, so you're never sure you're doing it right" (Gelb, 20).

ADDITIONAL PRODUCTIONS: 1964: *Luv*; 1967: *The Little Foxes*; 1968: *Plaza Suite*; 1971: *The Prisoner of Second Avenue*; 1973: *Uncle Vanya*; 1977: *The Gin Game*; 1984: *The Real Thing* (Tom Stoppard); 1986: *Social Security*; 1992: *Death and the Maiden* (Dorfman).

SELECTED BIBLIOGRAPHY: Gelb, Barbara. "Mike Nichols: The Director's Art." *New York Times Magazine* 27 May 1984; sec. 6: 20; Gussow, Mel. "Mike Nichols for the Fun of It." *New York Times* 26 November 1976: C1, C4; Hellman, Lillian. "And Now—An Evening with Nichols and Hellman." *New York Times* 9 August 1970: 9, Kanfer, Stefan. "Some Are More Yossarian Than Others." *Time* 15 June 1970: 66–74; Nichols, Mike. *Life and Other Ways to Kill Time.* Seacaucus, NJ: L. Stuart, 1988; "Playboy

Interview: Mike Nichols.'' *Playboy* June 1966: 63–74; Rothstein, Mervyn. ''Nichols Tries to Put the Fun Back in 'Godot.' '' *New York Times* 13 September 1988: C13; Schuth, Wayne H. *Mike Nichols*. Boston: Twayne, 1978.

Stephen Nelson

HANS JACOB NILSEN [b. November 8, 1897, Fredrikstad, Norway; d. March 6, 1957, Oslo, Norway]. Eclectic, experimental, and imaginative, Nilsen introduced expressionism to the Norwegian stage, and was also one of Norway's finest actors. He is best known for his emphasis on the social satire in Ludvig Holberg's comedies, for his reinterpretations of Ibsen and Shakespeare, and for his anti-Nazi productions both before and during the German occupation.

Nilsen began introducing elements of German expressionism in 1933, with a production of Johann Sigurjonsson's *Dangerous Powers*, and that same year achieved a huge popular success with an expressionist production of Holberg's *Jeppe of the Hill*. In the 1930s, Nilsen's directing became increasingly experimental and politically charged, and he was dismissed as artistic director at Den National Scene for pursuing an anti-Nazi repertoire. After the German occupation, Nilsen continued, more guardedly, to direct productions critical of the Quisling regime, including Holberg's *Jean de France* (1942) and *Brand* (1942) at the National Theatre.

In the fall of 1942, Nilsen fled to Sweden. There he helped found a company of Norwegian actors in exile called Den Frie Norske Scene (The Free Norwegian Stage). After the war, Nilsen alternated experimental plays (*Green Pastures*, 1947; *The Lives of Insects*, Čapek, 1947) with patriotic productions, portraying Hamlet and Brand as heroic Resistance fighters. Nilsen served as artistic director of several of the more important Norwegian theatres, including Det Norske Theatret (The Norwegian Theatre) in Oslo (1933–34, 1946–50), Den Nationale Scene (The National Stage) in Bergen (1934–40), and Folketeatret (The Folk Theatre) in Oslo (1950–57). These theatres were continually underfinanced, and Nilsen became known for combining administrative acumen and artistic accomplishment under trying circumstances.

For all his imaginative restlessness, Nilsen was, above all, a practical man of the theatre. His antiromantic *Peer Gynt* (with Nilsen as Peer) in 1948, for example, became a popular as well as critical success because of his careful handling of the public reaction. Nilsen took an essentially optimistic approach to his art. As he once put it, ''Hopelessness is the spirit of our age. But faith must be the spirit of our theatre'' (Nygaard and Eide, 57).

ADDITIONAL PRODUCTIONS: 1930: *The Pickwick Club* (František Langer); 1934: *Girls in Uniform* (Christa Winsloe); 1936: *Our Honor and Our Power* (Nordahl-Grieg); 1940: *Henrik and Pernille* (Holberg); 1945: *The Moon Is Down* (John Steinbeck); 1946 *Hamlet* with Nilsen as Hamlet; 1948: *Playboy of the Western World*, *Viking* (Johan Borgen); 1950: *The Madwoman of Chaillot*; 1953: *Brand*.

SELECTED BIBLIOGRAPHY: Nygaard, Knut, and Eiliv Eide. *Den Nationale Scene: 1931– 1976*. Oslo: Gyldendal, 1977; Rønneberg, Anton. *Nationaltheatret qiennom femti år*.

Oslo: Gyldendal, 1949; Skavlan, Einar. *Norsk Teater 1930–1953*. Oslo: Aschehoug, 1960; Sletbak, Nils. *Det Norske Teatret Femti År: 1913–1963*. Oslo: Det Norske Samlaget, 1963.

Eric Samuelsen

ADRIAN NOBLE [b. 1950, Chichester, England]. Strongly influenced by childhood theatregoing, Adrian Noble, the son of a Chichester undertaker, contemplated a theatrical career from age twelve. He eventually realized his ambition when, as a student at Bristol University, he became aware of his talent for visualizing a production and expressing ideas through the medium of theatre. Noble trained professionally as a director at the Drama Centre, "a school he gratefully remembers for its emphasis on the imaginative potency of the theatre, especially the classical theatre" (Nightingale, 20). Joining the Bristol Old Vic in 1976, Noble was offered the rare opportunity for a young director of creating new productions of classics—Shakespeare, Middleton, and Restoration comedies. His predilection for this repertory and its challenges shaped his major work of the past decade.

In 1980–81, Noble directed a hallmark production of *The Duchess of Malfi* at the Manchester Royal Exchange, which subsequently moved to London, bringing to the capital Noble's signature style—bold, imaginative conception, narrative clarity, inventive visual texture, and richly theatrical effects. Moving almost immediately to the directorial ranks of the Royal Shakespeare Company (RSC), Noble created *A Doll's House* for the company, receiving wide acclaim. He also received both the *Plays and Players* London Drama Critics Award and the *Drama* Award (which were granted jointly to *A Doll's House* and *The Duchess of Malfi*).

The same qualities of style, penetrating emotional and intellectual insight, contrasting intimacy and spectacle that distinguished these productions have marked most of Noble's subsequent works. For the RSC, he has created distinctive interpretations of *Henry V*, *As You Like It*, *Measure for Measure*, *The Winter's Tale*, *Macbeth*, Alexander Ostrovsky's *The Forest*, Henrik Ibsen's *The Master Builder*, and a stunning Shakespearean epic, *The Plantagenets*, among others. Noble has been praised by critics and colleagues for his brilliant compositional skill and his effective use of light and darkness for dramatic statement. His approach to the classic repertory stresses textual rigor, a thorough exploration of a play and its resonances for a contemporary audience. These are expressed in a dynamic and imaginative style, the point of which, Noble says, is "to speak to the spirit and the heart. To create *mighty* experiences."

The dynamism found in Noble's productions seems paradoxical compared to his subtle leadership in the rehearsal process. Tentative, sometimes anguished, Noble's mild manner in rehearsal allows the process to be actor-oriented, nonconfrontational, open to suggestion and debate, and freely and generously creative. Yet his politic, unpretentious working approach is balanced by an underlying firmness of purpose that ultimately allows him to control the formation of a production's distinctive vision.

Beginning with the 1990–91 season, Noble assumed the artistic directorship of the RSC, with intentions of returning it to its mission of performing classic works. With the establishment of an in-house actor training program and summer workshops for young directors, Noble seems ready to reaffirm the RSC's commitment to its classical roots and the unique demands of presenting complex texts. While not eschewing new plays (Noble has directed several notable productions), his own working philosophy bears directly upon his artistic scheme for the company. Noble maintains that it is necessary to produce new plays, not simply because they are new, but because they excite and amaze people— because, in his own words, they make them "emotionally more literate, because they open mental doors." He further asserts that we do the classics because they deal with "the very frontiers of human experience" and because contained within them are the "spiritual, intellectual and emotional history of the nation."

ADDITIONAL PRODUCTIONS: *Doctor Faustus* (Royal Exchange). RSC, 1981–91: *A New Way to Pay Old Debts* (Massinger), *Comedy of Errors, Lear, Antony and Cleopatra, The Desert Air, As You Like It, The Art of Success* (Nick Dear), *Kiss Me, Kate*. Other theatres: *Don Giovanni* (Kent Opera), *Three Sisters* (Royal Court and Dublin's Gate Theatre), *The Fairy Queen* (Purcell, Aix-en-Provence Festival), *Twelfth Night* (Japan).

SELECTED BIBLIOGRAPHY: Hiley, Jim. "The Verse That Could Happen." *The Times* 20 March 1991: 25; Hill, George. "Making Dramas Out of a Crisis." *The Times* 15 February 1990: 13; Nightingale, Benedict. "Noble Thoughts, Now for the Deeds."*The Times Supplement* 12 January 1991: 20; Rea, Kenneth. "Peter Brook and Adrian Noble on the Physical Life of the Actor." *Drama* 153 (Autumn 1984): 13–17; Roper, David. "New Blood for the Ensembles." *Plays and Players* 346 (July 1982): 13–14, 16; Royal Shakespeare Company Press Office, 1991.

James DePaul
Chris Flaharty

TREVOR NUNN [b. January 14, 1940, Ipswich, England]. While a student at Cambridge, Trevor Nunn staged Elizabethan classics for the Marlowe Society and zany musical sketches for the Footlights Revue. For one who would soon become the youngest artistic director of the Royal Shakespeare Company and later one of the best known (and richest) directors of large-scale commercial musicals, this combination seems most apt. It also partially explains how a man who spent years in the subsidized British theatre devoted to the classics distinguished himself during the 1980s with such extravagant Broadway productions as *Cats* (1981), *Starlight Express* (1984), and *Les Misérables* (1985).

Born in Ipswich, where his father worked as a cabinetmaker, Nunn made the decision to follow a theatrical career when he was still at grammar school. By the time he started his career at Downing College, Cambridge, he was convinced he wanted to be a performer. He organized and played in a rock-and-roll band known as the Trackers for two years and also performed in sketches that once included a drag act.

An especially formative part of his Cambridge experience was study with critic

F. R. Leavis who believed that art should not only entertain, but should focus society's attention on itself. Of equal importance, Nunn's experience there brought him into contact with talented peers ranging from Derek Jacobi and Ian McKellen to comedic actor-writer Peter Cook to Monty Python's John Cleese and Graham Chapman.

In 1962, Nunn was awarded an ABC-TV Director's Scholarship to the Belgrade Theatre, Coventry, where he served as an assistant director, an experience he disliked until he was allowed to actually direct. In 1964, he was invited to join the Royal Shakespeare Company (RSC) by artistic director Peter Hall,* who had seen his work at Coventry. Nunn's first year and a half at the RSC was undistinguished to the point that experienced actors rejected offers to work with him. The turning point in Nunn's early career occurred in 1965 with his staging of *The Revenger's Tragedy*. This production, which signaled the beginnings of a powerful and effective directorial style, was a Jacobean black comedy and featured a riveting central performance by unknown Alan Howard. (The production was revived in 1969 and won the London Theatre Critics Best Director Award.) After the success of *The Revenger's Tragedy*, other triumphs followed—*The Taming of the Shrew* (1967, with Janet Suzman, who later married Nunn) and *The Relapse* (1967)—through which Nunn further defined his style as a classical stage director.

When Peter Hall asked him to become artistic director of the Royal Shakespeare Company in 1968, Nunn became, at twenty-eight, the youngest person ever to hold that post. He met the new challenge with characteristic energy, making the establishment of a third performance space a priority, an effort that eventually resulted in the creation of the Other Place. At the time, the RSC was performing in Stratford and at the Aldwych Theatre in London.

By the 1970s, Nunn was leaving his mark on the classical repertoire. In 1965, Nunn brought his friend, designer Christopher Morley, from Coventry to design *The Revenger's Tragedy*. Subsequently, after years of collaboration, Morley's elegant, spare sets helped fix Nunn's vision of Shakespeare by focusing on the private person rather than the public issues. If Peter Hall's epic *Wars of the Roses* seemed influenced by Jan Kott's symbols of ladders leading to power, Nunn responded to the images of Christopher Morley's simplified sets with man at the center, and to the subtle, allegorical use of color in costume design. The team scored again in 1972 with *The Romans*, a Shakespeare tetralogy consisting of *Titus Andronicus*, *Coriolanus*, *Julius Caesar*, and *Antony and Cleopatra*, for which Nunn worked with Morley to redesign the Stratford stage itself. Their desired goal was to minimize the impression of the proscenium arch and to bring the audience closer to the stage so that the audience seemed to wrap around the playing space.

Nunn has consistently enjoyed a reputation as a director who inspires confidence in actors. From the outset, he demonstrated the difference of his management style from that of Peter Hall by making himself accessible, and performers like Judi Dench and Peggy Ashcroft have commented upon his openness and clarity of vision. Perhaps nowhere was this more evident than in the hypnotic 1976 *Macbeth* (with Dench and Ian McKellen) in the RSC's Other Place, a small ramshackle building envisioned by Nunn and director Buzz Goodbody as a performance space. Making a virtue of the limitations of the tiny theatre, Nunn focused upon the simple ritual and upon the emotional landscape of the play, eschewing broad scenic effects. He built the production upon the actors' abilities to create the play's spiritual and emotional environment and his own ability to transmute their sensitivities into a powerful theatrical statement about intense personal guilt.

In 1978, Nunn was joined by Terry Hands in the joint directorship of the company. During his first ten years as artistic director with the RSC, Nunn had been in rehearsals virtually all that time, but he had directed only one non-Shakespeare play, *Hedda Gabler* (1975). His subsequent non-Shakespeare production, *Nicholas Nickleby* (directed by Nunn with John Caird*), was an unlikely popular success for the RSC in 1980. Running eight and a half hours over two evenings, the production was a dazzling demonstration of what a disciplined ensemble can create. As he had been earlier with Christopher Morley, Nunn seemed perfectly in tune with his designer, John Napier. The production was imaginative, spare, involving, and clearly focused on the human element in David Edgar's script. *Nickleby* became the RSC's most popular production, moving successfully to Broadway where a record ticket price of $100 for the two-part production did little to dampen audience enthusiasm for the event. The success of *Nickleby* accomplished something else; it established Trevor Nunn as a potential force in the commercial theatre.

Nunn's next commercial undertaking, Andrew Lloyd Webber's *Cats*, took place outside the confines of the RSC. Nunn envisioned the work as a kind of "chamber piece," but the composer insisted that the musical interpretation of the T. S. Eliot book be on a much grander scale. Nunn opened the show in 1981 in London, where it proved enormously popular, before taking it to Broadway, a move that involved far more than simply rehearsing a new cast. Not only was it necessary to adapt the play to meet the Broadway audience's demand for overstatement, but the move was complicated by the choice of the mammoth Winter Garden Theatre. In the end, the show was given a radical reworking which was most evident in John Napier's extravagant "environmental" setting. The "chamber piece" had become a massive spectacle. Audiences loved it, and Trevor Nunn became a hot commercial property.

In 1985, the RSC opened *Les Misérables*. Nunn had been offered the opportunity to direct the show by commercial producer Cameron Mackintosh, and the subsidized RSC seemed a likely choice for such a risky project. It was Nunn's first directorial effort for the RSC since his staging of *Henry IV, Parts I and II* for the 1982 opening of the Barbican Theatre, the RSC's new home. The Macintosh project also marked the first time the theatre had undertaken a project that was conceived and negotiated as a clearly commercial venture. The worldwide success of *Les Misérables* and that of the Lloyd Webber musicals *Cats*,

Starlight Express, and *Aspects of Love* (1990) made Trevor Nunn the world's most successful director of musicals and, according to David Edgar, who wrote the *Nickleby* script, an artist who was able "to take a popular form and inject nobility of purpose into its execution."

In 1986, Nunn directed *The Fair Maid of the West* for the new Swan Theatre in Stratford-upon-Avon. In June of that year, he and Peter Hall were accused in a *Times of London* article of using their positions with leading theatres to amass fortunes while their theatres remained recipients of large government subsidies. After a good deal of public debate, Nunn resigned as artistic director.

In 1991, Nunn returned to his aesthetic and professional roots to direct the first two plays (*Measure for Measure* and a new adaptation of *The Blue Angel*) in the rebuilt Other Place in Stratford. Both productions were greeted by critical acclaim and popular success.

ADDITIONAL PRODUCTIONS: **Belgrade Theatre, Coventry (1962–65)**: *The Caucasian Chalk Circle, Peer Gynt, Around the World in 80 Days.* **The Royal Shakespeare Company (1965–92)**: *The Alchemist, Henry V, King Lear, Much Ado about Nothing, The Winter's Tale, Henry VIII, Hamlet, Romeo and Juliet, The Comedy of Errors, As You Like It, All's Well That Ends Well, Once in a Lifetime, The Three Sisters, Juno and the Paycock, Othello, Peter Pan.*

SELECTED BIBLIOGRAPHY: Barnes, Philip. *A Companion to Post-war British Theatre*. London: Croom Helm, 1986: 167–81; Beauman, Sally. *The Royal Shakespeare Company: A History of Ten Decades*. New York: Oxford University Press, 1982; Cook, Judith. *Director's Theatre*. London: Harrap, 1974: 111–24; Elsom, John. *Post-war British Theatre*. London: Routledge and Kegan Paul, 1976; Kroll, Jack. "All the Stages Are His World." *Newsweek* 10 Feb. 1986: 71; "Nunn Easing Up on Pedal at RSC." *Variety* 4 Feb. 1987: 166; *RSC News*. Stratford-upon-Avon: Royal Shakespeare Company, 1984–89; Rubin, Leon. *The Nicholas Nickleby Story*. New York: Penguin Books, 1981.

George Black

$$O$$

NIKOLAI PAVLOVICH OKHLOPKOV [b. May 15, 1900, Irkutsk; d. January 7, 1967, Moscow]. Nikolai Okhlopkov was the only major avant-garde director from the Russian theatre to continue working unabated through the period of Stalinist repression into the early sixties. Chiefly for that reason, he represented different facets of the socialist realist period to Soviet and Western theatre historians. An energetic and politically committed artist in the Mayakovsky mode, Okhlopkov produced many Communist plays that sometimes defended unpopular policies of the totalitarian system. In the West, however, Okhlopkov was often heralded as the foremost practitioner of environmental theatre and the leading scenic innovator during the difficult period of the thirties and forties.

The son of a Siberian army colonel, Okhlopkov left military school to pursue a career in the theatre. His first project in 1921, a huge May Day spectacle in Irkutsk entitled *The Struggle of Labor and Capital*, was among his most successful creations. Sent to GITIS, a Moscow directing academy, Okhlopkov quickly gained a reputation as an experimental actor at the Vsevolod Meyerhold* theatre. By the end of the twenties, he had appeared in six films, half of which he directed himself.

In 1931, Okhlopkov was invited to direct at the Krasnaya Presnaya Theatre (later called the Realistic Theatre), located at the edge of a working-class neighborhood in Moscow. Attempting to creatively justify the scenic limitation of the tiny stage and auditorium of 325 seats, he invented the theory of environmental production. To engage the new spectator at the deepest social level, Okhlopkov declared, the theatre must envelop its audience in action that takes place on every level—under, over, behind, and beside it. The old proscenium stage, a

180-degree peephole, only replicated the pre-revolutionary mold of pedagogical artist and passive observer.

Between 1932 and 1937, Okhlopkov mounted six productions, each staged according to an entirely novel actor-audience arrangement. Glorifying the struggle to collectivize a peasant farming region, *The Start* (by V. P. Stavsky, 1932) unfolded in eighty-three short scenes, many of them overlapping in sequence or simultaneously enacted in different places on the multilayered set. The auditorium was reorganized so two blocks of spectators on either end faced a square platform at the center of the theatre and a circular ramp on a higher level over it. Mixing divergent theatrical conventions, such as naturalistic scenography (e.g., real cut sunflowers and fruit-tree branches), stylized Asian gestures, and broad fairbooth comedy, and then adding them to a contemporary propaganda melodrama resulted in a unique offering and long-lasting notoriety for Okhlopkov's troupe.

In 1933, an environmental adaptation of Maxim Gorky's novel *Mother* once again wedded Okhlopkov's witty ultra-realism—as actors naturally treated nearby spectators as trusting assistants—to traditional mimic pretense, with performers hanging their actual garments on imaginary hooks affixed to invisible walls. The heyday of Okhlopkov's eclectic approach came the following year with productions of *The Iron Flood* and *Aristocrats*.

Based on a Civil War novel by A. Serafimovich, *The Iron Flood* (1934) recreated the life of an isolated cossack unit as it attempted to fight its way back to the Red Army lines. Covered in a tent-like fixture and subject to imaginary attacks across three Kabuki ramps in their midst, the audience experienced the fears, love complications, vulgar amusements, constant bickering, and deprivations of the soldiers and their families. After the finale when the Red Army broke through the White enclosure, Okhlopkov's performers jumped off the stage and applauded the spectators for bringing revolution to Russia. More popular still was Nikolai Pogodin's *Aristocrats* (1934), the first Soviet play about life in a gulag. Chinese and Japanese techniques that utilized "invisible" stage servants and symbolic properties provided a special irony that accompanied the anti-Soviet sentiments of the unrepentant prisoners, the Aristocrats. And by the edges of the curious S-shaped stage platform, actresses playing prostitutes propositioned smiling male spectators.

The entire Soviet avant-garde, including Okhlopkov's troupe, underwent severe restructuring in the middle thirties. In 1937, the Realistic Theatre merged with the Aleksandr Tairov* Kamerny Theatre. The following year it separated and then disappeared. Okhlopkov himself joined the Vakhtangov Theatre, where he directed Vladimir Solovyov's patriotic play *Fieldmarshal Kutuzov* in 1940 on a wide, triptych stage that could display three simultaneous actions. Other wartime spectacles followed, all with Okhlopkov's signature decoration: oversized symbolic objects as set pieces, such as guitars and Komsomol badges.

Around 1950, Okhlopkov drew up designs for the development of an outdoor "future theatre." Although the plans for the amphitheatre were never approved, aspects of it were integrated into Okhlopkov's remaining productions, especially in his 1961 *Medea*. Equally controversial was Okhlopkov's radical interpretation of *Hamlet* (1954), where the set consisted of twelve grid-like boxes and a curtain of iron bars, a physical manifestation of the Hamlet's Danish prison. Both classical productions were viewed as Okhlopkov's final protests against Stalinist despotism.

ADDITIONAL PRODUCTIONS: 1922: *Mystery-Bouffe* (Mayakovsky); 1936: *Othello*; 1937: *Colas Breugnon* (adaptation of Romain Rolland's novel); 1942: *Cyrano de Bergerac*; 1943: *Sons of Three Rivers* (Victor Gusev); 1944: *The Ferry Girl* (Pogodin); 1947: *The Young Guard* (adaptation of Konstantin Fadeyev's novel); 1953: *The Thunderstorm* (Ostrovsky); 1960: *Irkutsk Story* (Alexei Arbuzov); 1964: *Between the Floods* (Alexander Shtein).

SELECTED BIBLIOGRAPHY: *The Drama Review* 17 (March 1973) [Russian Issue]; van Gyseghem, Andre. *Theatre in Soviet Russia*. London: Faber and Faber, 1943; Houghton, Norris. *Moscow Rehearsals*. New York: Harcourt, Brace, and Co., 1936; Houghton, Norris. *Return Engagement*. New York: Holt, Rinehart, and Winston, 1962; Worrall, Nick. *Modernism to Realism on the Soviet Stage*. Cambridge: Cambridge University Press, 1989.

Mel Gordon

JULIUSZ OSTERWA [b. Julian Maluszek, June 23, 1885, Kraków, Poland; d. May 10, 1947, Warsaw, Poland]. Born into a poor family, Juliusz Osterwa never finished high school. Instead, he went to Teatr Ludowy, Kraków, where he made his acting debut in 1904, beginning a long and glamorous career. Handsome, endowed with a melodious voice and great personal charm, Osterwa possessed the ability to play a variety of roles, although his forte was at first comedy. Later, he became a great heroic actor. After his debut, he worked at theatres in Kraków, Poznań, Wilno, and Warsaw; was engaged with Teatr Rozmaitości, which was the National Theatre (although the name was prohibited by Russian invaders); and between 1907 and 1909, traveled extensively throughout Western Europe, observing the greatest actors and learning new theatre trends.

Osterwa made his formal directorial debut in 1907 with a production of *Horsztyński* by Słowacki in Poznań. In 1915, he first directed in Warsaw, staging Wyspiański's *The Wedding* (*Wesele*), which was a huge success and opened for him the artistic directorship of Teatr Rozmaitości. The same year, however, just before assuming the position of artistic director of Teatr Rozmaitości, he was interned in Russia during World War I. In exile, Osterwa organized Polish productions in Samara and Moscow, where he met Konstantin Stanislavsky.* In 1918, Osterwa created a ''theatre-community'' in Kiev, and after the war, he returned to Warsaw where, in 1919, he established Reduta (Redoubt), an experimental theatre-laboratory for new acting and playwriting. Three years later, he opened Reduta's ''Institute'' (acting school) which became known for its demanding training program, communal life, and new theatre ethics based on the notion of service to public and country.

Reduta was based in Warsaw from 1919 to 1925, spent six seasons (1925–31) in Wilno as a traveling company, and resided again in Warsaw between

1931 and 1939 as an Institute, or experimental theatre and school. While with Reduta, Osterwa also served as artistic director of the National Theatre in Warsaw from 1923 to 1925, and of Teatr Słowackiego in Kraków between 1932 and 1935. During this period, he directed and appeared as a guest artist throughout Poland.

At the beginning of World War II in 1939, Osterwa's home and Reduta in Warsaw were bombed, and he moved to Kraków. Unemployed, he taught acting and speech, and was connected with the underground theatre movement. Meanwhile, in his abundant writings, he formulated and outlined "theatre-religious" projects.

Following World War II Osterwa directed and acted in Kraków, Łódź, and Warsaw. He was never trusted by the Communist regime in Poland, but thanks to his enormous popularity, he was appointed head of Teatr Słowackiego and a school of drama in Kraków in the final years of his life.

Osterwa's achievements were fourfold: he was an actor, a director, a teacher, and a reformer. Truth, in Osterwa's view, was the foundation for all theatre work, having both theatrical and moral aspects, and acting was therefore a process of revealing the truth of the character through the revelation of the actor's own truth. Osterwa treated acting as a "sacrifice," as an "act of redemption," and consequently the performance was for him a "sacerdotal sacrifice for the congregation." In this context, he referred to spectators as "witnesses" and spoke of the "communion" between the actors/priests and the public/congregation. This communion was his stated goal, and the "actor-saint" was his ideal. Osterwa put moral, spiritual, and social values at the core of theatre creation.

Osterwa thus hoped to break the barriers between the actors and the spectators. During the tours with *Constant Prince* (a play he first staged in 1917 and produced many times during his career) in 1926–28, he invited people from local communities to play as extras. In directing *Outward Bound* by Sutton Vane (1932), which takes place on a boat, Osterwa staged the play on a real riverboat which sailed on the Vistula River, and actors merged with the public. Osterwa enjoyed utilizing natural spaces and architecture for open-air productions and often used live fire as lighting.

Osterwa influenced Polish theatre enormously, and is considered one of the greatest theatre artists in its history. In Poland, his stature has been compared to that of Stanislavsky in Russia. Some of his ideas resembled Appia's, and some of his staging methods were similar to those of Jacques Copeau.* Officially forgotten immediately following his death because of his opposition to communism, since the 1960s, Osterwa has once again become an inspiration for Polish directors, actors, pedagogues, and reformers.

ADDITIONAL PRODUCTIONS: 1916: *Fircyk w zalotach* (*Dandy in Love*, Franciszek Zablocki), *Fantazy* (Słowacki); 1917: *Constant Prince* (Calderón/Słowacki), *Kordian* (Słowacki); 1918: *Wyzwolenie* (*The Deliverance*, Stanisław Wyspiański); 1924: *Uciekła mi przepióreczka* (*My Little Quail's Gone*, Stefan Żeromski). *All of these productions were restaged and repeated many times by Osterwa.*

SELECTED BIBLIOGRAPHY: Guszpit, Ireneusz. *Przez teatr Poza teatr*. Wrocław: Els, 1989; Osiński, Zbigniew, ed. *Juliusz Osterwa. Reduta i teatr. Artykuły, wywiady, wspomnienia*. Wrocław: Wydawnictwo Wiedza o Kulturze, 1990; Osiński, Zbigniew, ed. *Listy Mieczysław Limanowski-Juliusz Osterwa*. Warszawa: Panstowy Instytut Wydawniczy (PIW), 1987; Osterwianka, Elżbieta, ed. *Listy Juliusza Osterwy*. Warszawa: Panstowy Instytut Wydawniczy (PIW), 1968; Śmigielski, Bogdan. *Reduta w Wilnie*. Warszawa: Pax, 1989; Szczublewski, Józef. *Pierwsza Reduta Osterwy*. Warszawa: Panstowy Instytut Wydawniczy (PIW), 1965; Szczublewski, Józef. *Żywot Osterwy*. Warszawa: Panstowy Instytut Wydawniczy (PIW), 1971; *O Zespole Reduty 1919–1939, Wspomnienia*. Warszawa: Czytelnik, 1970.

Kazimierz Braun

P

LÁRUS PÁLSSON [b. February 12, 1914, Reykjavík, Iceland; d. March 12, 1968, Reykjavík, Iceland]. Among the first Icelandic actors to train outside his native land, Pálsson attended the school at the Royal Theatre in Copenhagen, Denmark, in the late 1930s. He brought back to Iceland a polish and urbanity that distinguished his career as a leading actor and director over the next quarter century. Upon his return to Iceland in 1940, Pálsson secured his first professional directing engagement with the Reykjavík City Theatre Company, where he joined Indridi Waage and Haraldur Bjørnsson as a resident director. His work with Waage and Bjørnsson—like him actor-directors—and with a strong semiprofessional company at the City Theatre had, by the 1940s, helped establish the groundwork for the founding in 1950 of the National Theatre, Iceland's first fully professional company.

Pálsson again collaborated with Waage and Bjørnsson to form a triumvirate of resident directors that began work at the National. He also acted occasionally in his own stagings as he did in *The Bell of Iceland* (1949–50), the most successful of the three productions that opened the National Theatre's first season. In addition to his acting and directing in this production, he also adapted the novel for the stage in collaboration with author Halldór Laxness, who later became Iceland's first Nobel Laureate in literature. Pálsson's touch with actors was sure, and he was able to impart to his casts something of his own rhetorical skill and plasticity as an actor.

Strongest in the vein of poetic realism, his directing seems to have owed much to the inspiration of the French Cartel in its respect for the text and its attempts to discover style through qualities he saw as inherent in the script at hand. His single most successful production was the premiere of fellow-Icelander David Stefánsson's *The Golden Gate*, which he staged first at the Reykjavík City Theatre in 1941–42, saw revived at that theatre during 1948–49, later restaged for production at the National in 1954–55, and revived there again in 1966. The play is a seriocomic work about divine judgment, and Pálsson played the Devil with a wit and grace that typified the production as a whole.

Pálsson also showed an affinity for American drama, with notable successes with plays by Maxwell Anderson, Thornton Wilder, and Arthur Miller. Later in his career, he staged two of August Strindberg's works with distinction. Settings and costumes for his early productions were more elegant and detailed than had been the case in Iceland previously, although he was more "a force" this way at the beginning of his career than he was by the 1960s.

In 1940, when he began his career, directing was often called "actor coaching" in the theatre programs. Pálsson's example, first at the City Theatre and later in his twenty-five productions at the National, was crucial in establishing the standing of directing as an independent and far-reaching artistic function in the Icelandic theatre.

ADDITIONAL PRODUCTIONS: 1940–41: *High Tor*; 1944–45: *The Merchant of Venice*; 1946–47: *Our Town*; 1947–48: *The Inspector General*; 1948–49: *Volpone*; 1951–52: *As You Like It*; 1952–53: *Juno and the Paycock*; 1954–55: *The Silver Moon* (Laxness); 1955–56: *The Crucible*; 1956–57: *The Magic Flute*; 1957–58: *A View from the Bridge*, *The Father*; 1962–63: *The Physicists*; 1963–64: *Creditors*.

SELECTED BIBLIOGRAPHY: The only sources in English are available at the Archive of the National Theatre of Iceland, Reykjavík, Iceland.

Leigh Woods

GIUSEPPE PATRONI-GRIFFI [b.February 27, 1921, Naples, Italy]. Patroni-Griffi began to write for both the stage and screen almost immediately upon moving to Rome after World War II. Since the 1960s, while continuing to write, he also directed in both media, and since 1978, he has served as artistic director of Rome's Eliseo Theatre.

Patroni-Griffi made his directing debut in 1965 with Vitaliano Brancati's *La governante* (*The Governess*, 1952) and has since directed plays by Luigi Pirandello,* Carlo Goldoni, Bertolt Brecht,* Raffaele Viviani, Vittorio Alfieri, T. S. Eliot, Anton Chekhov, Jean Cocteau, Jean-Paul Sartre, Alberto Moravia, and his own *Anima nera* (*Black Soul*, 1981) and *Gli amanti dei amanti sono miei amanti* (*My Lovers' Lovers Are My Lovers*, 1982). Two directing projects are especially important in Patroni-Griffi's career: his revival in 1972 and 1975 of two plays by Neopolitan Raffaele Viviani* (*Napoli notte e giorno* [*Naples Night and Day*] and *Napoli: chi resta e chi parte* [*Naples: Who Stays and Who Goes*]); and his 1987–88 staging of Pirandello's theatre trilogy—*Six Characters in Search of an Author*, *Right You Are (If You Think You Are)*, and *Tonight We*

Improvise. The Viviani revival renewed interest in this important Neopolitan dialect playwright; while the production of the Pirandello trilogy, featuring the same actors and a unified directorial vision, provided a unique opportunity to theatregoers to see the three plays in relationship to one another.

Patroni-Griffi is known for careful interpretation of the text, although in his later work he has paid particular attention to scenic elements, as exemplified in his rendering of the Pirandello trilogy, designed by Aldo Terlizzi. Terlizzi is a frequent collaborator who recently directed Patroni-Griffi's *Prima del silenzio* (December 1990).

Patroni-Griffi directed his first film, *Il Mare*, in 1962 and collaborated on a screenplay of his play *Anima nera* with director Roberto Rossellini. In 1969, he directed a screen version of his play *Metti, una sera a cena* with Jean-Louis Trintignant and Tony Musante. During the 1970s, he directed *Addio, fratello crudele*, based on John Ford's *'Tis Pity She's a Whore* with Charlotte Rampling (1971); *Identikit* featuring Elizabeth Taylor (1973); and *Divina creatura* with Terence Stamp, Laura Antonelli, and Marcello Mastroianni (1975). In 1985, after a decade's absence, Patroni-Griffi resumed his film career, directing *La gabbia* with Tony Musante and Laura Antonelli.

As a playwright, Patroni-Griffi's best-known works include *D'amore si muore (One Dies of Love*, 1957), *Anima nera* (1958), *In memoria di una signora amica (In Memory of a Lady Friend*, 1963), *Metti una sera a cena (What If One Night at Dinner*, 1967), *Persone naturali e strafottenti (Natural and Exaggerated People,*1974), *Prima del silenzio (Before Silence*, 1980), *Gli amanti dei miei amanti sono miei amanti* (1982). The DeLullo-Falk-Guarnieri-Valli-Albani Company productions of some of Patroni-Griffi's plays were of particular importance. Under Giorgio DeLullo's direction, the company presented *D'amore si muore* at the 1958 Venice Biennial and at the Spoleto Festival and produced *Anima Nera* the following season. In 1967, the company produced an extraordinarily successful *Metti una sera a cena*, which enjoyed a two-year national tour. Director DeLullo and actor Romolo Valli collaborated in the memorable *Prima del silenzio* (1980).

ADDITIONAL PRODUCTIONS: 1960s: *Luv, Clothe the Naked* (Pirandello); 1970s: *Mahagonny*: 1980s: *Orestes* (Vittorio Alfieri), *Murder in the Cathedral, Uncle Vanya, La Romana (The Roman Woman*, Alberto Moravia).

SELECTED BIBLIOGRAPHY: Brandolin, Mario, ed. "A Proposito dei *Sei personaggi* e della trilogia del teatro nel teatro." *Quaderno n.38: Sei personaggi in cerca d'autore.* Trieste: Teatro Stabile del Fiuli-Venezia Giulia, 1988: 54–55; Canziani, Roberto. "E sempre processo." *Il Piccolo* 26 April 1988; Galimberti, Carlo. "Camorra in versi con Mastelloni." *Corriere della Sera* 9 July 1983; Groli, Antonio. "Peppino, Napoli a via Veneto." *Il Mattino* 19 February 1984; Quadri, Franco. "Ecco dietro il lenzuolo l'illusione del teatro." *La Repubblica* 7 May 1988; Raboni, Giovanni. "I personaggi di Pirandello sul filo della tradizione." *Corriere della Sera* 18 November 1988; Sala, Rita. "Patroni-Griffi e Parenti meta a meta." *Il Messaggero* 7 May 1980: 8; Serra, Umberto. "Patroni-Griffi interviene nel dibattito sull spettacolo." *Il Mattino* 22 July 1980.

Jana O'Keefe Bazzoni

BROCK PEMBERTON [b. December 14, 1885, Leavenworth, Kansas; d. March 11, 1950, New York, New York]. Brock Pemberton is best known as a theatrical producer who assisted Arthur Hopkins* before beginning his own producing career. However, he also directed his own productions until 1928.

Pemberton graduated from the University of Kansas in 1908 and worked as a reporter in Kansas until he went to New York in 1910. He wrote for various papers and was the assistant dramatic editor for the *New York Times* under Alexander Woollcott. Between 1917 and 1920, Pemberton apprenticed himself to Arthur Hopkins and learned virtually every job in the theatre. Although he did not direct during this period, he closely observed Hopkins's laissez-faire style. In 1920 he ventured out on his own to produce and direct the very successful *Enter Madame* (by Gilda Varesi and Dolly Byrne). His second production won the Pulitzer Prize for drama in 1921: Zona Gale's adaptation of her novel *Miss Lulu Bett*.

As a director, Pemberton felt he had a keen sense of which scripts would play, if not necessarily sell. He often produced new works by unknown authors and was willing to experiment with various dramatic constructions. He produced and directed Sidney Howard's first play *Swords* (1921), which used a poetic form, and Maxwell Anderson's *White Desert* (1923), which was written in the rhythmic prose for which he would become well-known. Pemberton also brought the work of Luigi Pirandello* to American audiences. He believed that in production a director should have complete supervision of the script and should ensure that the author was willing to rewrite as necessary.

In 1928, Pemberton turned his directing duties over to Antoinette Perry with the play *Strictly Dishonorable*, which was Preston Sturges's first Broadway success and Pemberton's first big money-maker. After this, he worked almost exclusively as a producer. He presented another Pulitzer Prize winner in 1945, Mary Chase's *Harvey*.

Pemberton had strong feelings about many theatrical issues including critics, censorship, and ticket brokering. Although he began his career as dramatic editor, Pemberton felt that too often critics used their own standards for judging a play rather than the standards of the public. His fight against ticket speculators resulted in the formation of the League of New York Theatres. He expressed some of his ideas in interviews as well as in numerous articles he wrote for magazines and newspapers. For many years he wrote the annual summary of Broadway theatre for *The New York Times*.

During his career, Pemberton was involved in many theatrical organizations. He was the president of the League of New York Theatres, vice-chair and treasurer of the Stage Relief Fund, a member of the board of governors of the American Theatre Council, and a member of the Board of Directors of the American Theatre Wing. He was also one of the founders of the USO Camp Shows.

ADDITIONAL PRODUCTIONS: 1922: *Six Characters in Search of an Author*; 1924: *The Living Mask* (Pirandello's *Henry IV*); 1934: *Personal Appearance*; 1935: *Ceiling Zero*; 1938: *Kiss the Boys Goodbye* (Clare Boothe); 1942: *Janie*; 1944: *Harvey*.

SELECTED BIBLIOGRAPHY: "Brock Pemberton, Producer, 64, Dies." *New York Times* 12 March 1950; Pemberton, Brock. "The Director." *Our Theatre Today*. New York: Samuel French, 1936: 185–95; Pemberton, Brock. "The Making of a Play-Producer." *Theatre Magazine* 49 (March 1929): 13; Saylor, Oliver M. *Our American Theatre*. New York: Brentano's, 1923.

Candice M. Coleman

ARTHUR PENN [b. September 27, 1922, Philadelphia, Pennsylvania]. A child of the Great Depression and divorced parents, Penn gained his first theatre experiences by crewing at Philadelphia's Olney High School. Drafted into the army in 1944 and stationed at Fort Jackson, South Carolina, he spent off-duty time at the Civic Theatre in nearby Columbia. Near the war's end, Penn gained further experience with the Soldiers Show Company in Paris.

Penn's first directing experience came at Black Mountain College in North Carolina, where as a student, he taught an acting class and helped initiate a performing arts department. His first professional job was in television as a floor manager for "The Colgate Comedy Hour." Two years later (1953), Fred Coe, whom Penn had met in Columbia, hired him to direct several episodes of "Gulf Playhouse: First Person." Penn directed live television dramas for the next five years, and it was in this medium that he developed the fluid, probing style that marked his later stage and film direction.

In 1956, Penn took over the Broadway production of *The Lovers*, but waited two more years for his first success, *Two for the Seesaw*. In the following seasons, he directed *The Miracle Worker* (with Coe producing, 1959), *Toys in the Attic* (1960), *An Evening with Mike Nichols and Elaine May* (1960), and *All the Way Home* (1960). His hits were more sporadic after 1960, but the musical version of *Golden Boy* (1964), *Wait until Dark* (1966), and *Sly Fox* (1976), maintained his reputation as a thoughtful and versatile director.

Penn's film career began in 1958 with the Coe-produced *The Left-handed Gun*. The experience, however, soured Penn on Hollywood, and he did not return until five years later with the screen version of *The Miracle Worker* which, again, Coe produced. Penn is best known for three films that defined America in the late 1960s and early 1970s: *Bonnie and Clyde* (1967), *Alice's Restaurant* (1969), and *Little Big Man* (1970). Each film contains themes dominant in Penn's stage work as well: familial relationships, societal outcasts, purgative violence, and conflicts between personal myths and prevalent social standards. Penn is indebted to Konstantin Stanislavsky* and Lee Strasberg* and his directorial work is focused primarily on the actor. He is noted for the expressive range he is able to obtain from his performers and for his insightful readings of the text. He is firmly a realist, but often emphasizes symbolic elements in staging, costuming, and lighting.

ADDITIONAL PRODUCTIONS: Numerous episodes for the television programs "The Philco Television Playhouse" and "Playhouse 90."

SELECTED BIBLIOGRAPHY: Adams, Cindy. "At Home with Arthur Penn." *Theatre* July 1960:16–17; Fox, Terry Curtis. "The Director as a Divided Man." *New York Sunday News* 23 January 1977; Henry, Gerrit. "Now Is the Ideal Time for Theatre." *New York Times* 12 December 1976:1, 3, 4(sec.Z); Sherman, Eric, and Martin Rubin. *The Director's Event.* New York: Atheneum, 1970; Wood, Robin. *Arthur Penn.* New York: Praeger, 1969; Zucker, Joel. *Arthur Penn: A Guide to References and Resources.* Boston: G. K. Hall and Company, 1980.

Alan Kreizenbeck

MEMÉ PERLINI [b. 1940, Montecchio, Romagna region, Italy]. Memé Perlini's grandparents were gypsies, Spanish on his mother's side and Slavic on his father's. His mother was a factory worker; his father worked in construction. As a young man, Perlini went to Rome, penniless, where he worked as a cartoonist. There, the composer Silvano Bussotti presented him to the young director Giancarlo Nanni, who offered him a job as an actor in his company at the Teatro La Fede, where his first appearances were in *L'imperatore della Cina, A come Alice* and Wedekind's *Spring's Awakening (Risveglio di Primavera)*. In 1973, he and lighting artist Lionello Aglioti founded the group *La Maschera.* With his production of *Pirandello Chi? (Pirandello Who?)* in 1973, which was loosely inspired by Pirandello's *Six Characters in Search of an Author*, Perlini established himself as an important figure on the Italian experimental scene.

Perlini's provocative and innovative productions were to the Italian avant-garde theatre of the 1970s what those of Carmelo Bene* had been to the previous decade. In Perlini's works, texts (often classical) are used fragmentarily and merely as indications; the actors are not used as characters, but as material— not as "personified situations," but as "transparencies." Finally, the scene is used simultaneously for different complementary actions; it is invaded and segmented by light-darkness, and details of frescoes are framed and revealed. In *Pirandello Chi?* the actors moved across a dark stage, revealed only by occasional flashes of light. Standing in front of the stage, Perlini, working with small projectors, cut out rectangular pieces of light which captured details—parts of bodies, parts of objects. Fragments of dialogue from *Six Characters* were added to the visual fragments, the whole accompanied by a thunderous musical score by Philip Glass, to which bits of Pink Floyd were added at intervals. The score was described as a "musical continuum that [gave] the spectator a connected structure to refer to, thus easing the tension caused by the visual lacerations" (Mele, "The Theater of Memé Perlini," p. 250). Perlini was also one of the first to use nudes on the Italian stage, although he attempted to light them in a way that robbed them of their physicality.

"The aim of our theatre," Perlini has stated, "is to destroy, not to preserve. Our blackboard of light serves first to color, to make the actors and scenery as vivid as possible, and then to erase everything and present new forms and meanings. Our aim is to stimulate the audience, to liberate them and to make them think. What's the point of spending millions for scenery and costumes?

It's too easy to please the public by showing them beautiful things. And we're not in the least interested in merely pleasing them'' (Bartolucci and Rimoldi, 118).

In 1976, Perlini presented *Locus Solus*, adapted from the novel by Raymond Roussel. In a large rectangular box, its floor covered with sand, a series of violent images of anger, madness, and sexual fury was revealed. The following year, Ellen Stewart, the director of La Mama ETC, invited the troupe to perform the work in New York. After viewing a few scenes, Stewart, hardly a prude, hastily cancelled the performances.

At present, Perlini is the director of the Teatro La Piramide in Rome.

ADDITIONAL PRODUCTIONS: 1974: *Tarzan* (Perlini); 1976: *La partenza dell'Argonauta (The Sailing of the Argonaut*, Alberto Savinio), *The Merchant of Venice*, *Grand Hotel des Palmes* (Leonardo Sciascia–Perlini); 1988: *All'uscita (At the Exit*, Perlini); 1989: *Lazzaro* (Pirandello), *Giovanna d'Arco (Joan of Arc*, Perlini), *Storia di ordinaria follia (Story of Ordinary Madness*, Perlini).

SELECTED BIBLIOGRAPHY: Bartolucci, Giuseppe, and Donatella Rimoldi, eds. *Immagine-immaginario: Il lavoro del Teatro La Maschera di Memé Perlini e Antonello Aglioti*. Torino: Studio Forma, 1978; Davy, Kate. "Perlini's *Othello*." *The Drama Review* 68 (December 1975):19–26; Mele, Rino. *La casa dello specchio. Modelli di sperimentazione nel teatro italiano degli anni Settanta*. Salerno-Roma: Ripostes, 1984; Mele, Rino. "Memé Perlini's *Yellow Whiteness*." *The Drama Review* 68 (December 1975): 9–18; Mele, Rino. "The Theater of Memé Perlini." *The Drama Review: Thirty Years of Commentary on the Avant-Garde*. Ed. Brooks McNamara and Jill Dolan. Ann Arbor: UMI Research Press, 1986: 249–54.

Robert Connolly

ROBIN PHILLIPS [b. February 28, 1942, Haslemere, Surrey, England]. Canada's preeminent classical director, Phillips is renowned for his extraordinarily prolific output and his fluid, sensitive stagings. He began his career in England, acting in Laurence Olivier's first Chichester season in 1962, and later joining the directing team at the Royal Shakespeare Company (RSC). He made his reputation as a director in the early 1970s at the Chichester Festival, and in 1973 he became artistic director of the Greenwich Theatre.

In 1973 Phillips was invited to head the Stratford Festival Theatre in Stratford, Ontario. His appointment incited a fierce controversy; Phillips was little known in Canada, and many felt that the theatre should have chosen a Canadian director to lead what was the de-facto national theatre. Phillips himself was deeply stung by the uproar.

Phillips's six seasons at Stratford were among the most exciting and were certainly the most frenetic in the company's history. His brilliance surfaced in the performances he elicited from actors and in the way he integrated stars like Maggie Smith (whom he lured to Stratford for two seasons) and William Hutt with younger actors into a smoothly functioning ensemble. In his understanding of the dynamics of the Festival's thrust stage he equalled, and at his best surpassed, Michael Langham.*

Phillips's creative record at Stratford was astonishing; in six years he directed or co-directed no less than twenty-nine productions as well as several revivals. In addition to Shakespeare, he demonstrated a flair for period comedy, especially in his 1975 *The Importance of Being Earnest*, in which William Hutt played Lady Bracknell with audacious brilliance. Under Phillips's direction, the already-celebrated Hutt revealed himself to be the finest classical actor in Canada. Another fruitful collaboration was with Calgary playwright John Murrell; in all Phillips would direct five of Murrell's plays at Stratford and elsewhere in Canada. His enormous efforts at Stratford were repaid by critical acclaim and intense loyalty on the part of his actors.

In rehearsal, Phillips approached the text in a spirit of adventure, frequently using improvisation and games to enhance the actors' creativity. At the same time he placed great stress on poetic values, especially in Shakespeare, and his productions were remarkable for the clarity of their verse. In design, Phillips favored eclecticism in Shakespeare, often setting the plays in carefully researched historical periods as diverse as a cowboy *Comedy of Errors* in 1975, a Georgian *As You Like It* in 1977, and a World War II *Cymbeline* in 1986.

Phillips departed Stratford in 1980 in the midst of a scandal even greater than that which greeted him when he began. His awareness of Canadian cultural sentiment and his commitment to his adopted country led him to propose a four-person directorate to succeed him. The theatre's board of governors accepted this proposal, only to renege on contractual agreements and offer the job instead to John Dexter.* The controversy was resolved only when the Canadian government refused Dexter a work permit, and the theatre hired John Hirsch* instead.

In 1983 Phillips took on the artistic directorship of the Grand Theatre in London, Ontario, attracted by the proximity to Stratford and by the impeccably restored Edwardian playhouse. His single season at the Grand, in which he directed seven productions, left the theatre with a massive deficit but an artistic record rarely matched. In consequence, Phillips earned a reputation as a director of genius but one that no theatre could afford to hire.

In 1987 he returned to Stratford for a brief period as director of the Young Company, where he staged a luminescent *King Lear*, in which William Hutt gave one of his finest performances. The following year, Phillips returned to England, where he had been offered the artistic directorship at the Chichester Festival, but in 1989, shortly before taking up his duties, he resigned and made a surprise return to Canada. In 1990, he accepted the position of director general at the Citadel Theatre in Edmonton, Alberta, where the constraints of a regional theatre have led him to emphasize a more popular repertoire, including *The Mousetrap* (1991), which he undertook with the same commitment and stylishness that typify all of his work.

ADDITIONAL PRODUCTIONS: 1970: *Tiny Alice* (RSC), *Abelard and Heloise* (Millar, London and Broadway); 1971: *Two Gentlemen of Verona* (RSC), *Caesar and Cleopatra* (Chichester Festival, with John Gielgud), *Dear Antoine* (Chichester, with Edith Evans); 1975: *Two Gentlemen of Verona*, *Measure for Measure*; 1976: *Antony and Cleopatra*, *A*

Midsummer Night's Dream (with Maggie Smith), *The Way of the World*; 1977: *Richard III, Hay Fever*; 1978: *As You Like It, The Devils, Judgement, Macbeth, The Winter's Tale, Uncle Vanya* (adapt. Murrell), *Private Lives*; 1979: *King Lear* (with Peter Ustinov), *Love's Labour's Lost*; 1980: *Twelfth Night, Virginia* (Edna O'Brien, Haymarket Theatre, London), *Much Ado about Nothing, Long Day's Journey into Night, The Sea Gull* (adapt. John Murrell); 1982: *The Jeweller's Shop* (Westminster Theatre, London), *Farther West* (Murrell, Theatre Calgary); 1983: *Waiting for the Parade* (Murrell), *Timon of Athens, The Doctor's Dilemma, The Club, The Prisoner of Zenda, Farther West* (Murrell, Theatre Calgary), *Arsenic and Old Lace* (with William Hutt); 1984: *New World* (Murrell); 1985: *Antony and Cleopatra* (Chichester); 1989: *A Midsummer Night's Dream, The Philadelphia Story*; 1991: *Aspects of Love* (Andrew Lloyd Webber).

SELECTED BIBLIOGRAPHY: Garebian, Keith. "The Unfinished Hero: Why Stratford (and Canada) Lost Robin Phillips." *Theatrum* 14 (1989); Good, Maurice. *Every Inch a King: A Rehearsal Journal of King Lear*. Victoria, BC: Sono Nis Press, 1982; Knowles, Richard Paul. "Robin Phillips's Strange and Wondrous Dream." *Theatre History in Canada* 9.1 (1988); Knowles, Richard Paul. "Robin Phillips: Text and Context." *Canadian Theatre Review* 52 (1987): 50–57; Knowles, Richard Paul. "Shakespeare at Stratford: The Legacy of the Festival Stage." *Canadian Theatre Review* 54 (1988): 39–45.

Alan Filewod

LORRAINE PINTAL [b.September 24, 1951, Plessisville, Quebec, Canada]. After completing her training in acting at the Academy of Dramatic Arts in Montreal in 1973, Lorraine Pintal began an active career as an actress, director, and author, often on the same production. Beginning in 1988, she was also a television producer ("Le Grand Remous," 1988; "Montreal P.Q.," 1991), and in 1992, she was named general and artistic director of the Théâtre du Nouveau Monde (New World Theater), becoming the first woman to hold the position at this prestigious Montreal institution.

After graduating from the Academy, Pintal, with seven other young actors, founded the Théâtre de la Rallonge, a company whose collective work was representative of Quebec's "young theatre" movement. The members of La Rallonge were interested not only in the actor's technique, but also in the creation of plays through improvisation with an author. Between 1974 and 1980, Pintal centered on writing, and her stage productions closely followed the author's ideas. Lorraine Pintal presented shows that were played on small stages and experimental stages, as well as on tour. As an actress, she worked with directors Gilles Pelletier, Olivier Reichenbach, and Andre Brassard.*

In 1981, she continued her interest in Québecois authors, including Marie Laberge, Francine Ruel, Suzanne Lebeau, Marco Micone, Anne Legault, and Normand Canac-Marquis, and her productions of their work contributed greatly to the development of the scripts. Her attitude toward the production of new works is one of respect: her direction serves the play to clarify the writing and the meaning. Pintal also tackled the classical and contemporary repertoire, with the production of full-scale texts on large stages for established companies with popular audiences. Her distinctive style appeared at that time. She paid particular attention to the dramatic situations, the psychological realism of the characters living them, and the emotions imparted to the audience. Her productions are thus very accessible, and it is at this level that Lorraine Pintal places her use of the celebration (*La Noce*), the sporting event (*Tanzi*) and, in a general manner, the spectacular. Her special understanding of the actor's craft leads her to respect the meeting of the actor and the character: her direction of the actor thus leads toward an intimate performance, even on a grand scale; it is a realistic performance that manages to place the characters on the outskirts of the dream and the imagination. Lorraine Pintal always works on two levels: that of the visible and the invisible, the brief reality and the forces and aspirations of the spirit.

Although Lorraine Pintal's productions are primarily realist, they do contain important experimental and provocative aspects. She has maintained ties with contemporary work, often through musical compositions and stage designs produced by contemporary artists. For sound environments, she has worked successively with Pierre Moreau, Vincent Dionne, and Philippe Menard, eclectic composers of electro-acoustic music who wrote musical responses complementing the meaning of the play. Since 1987, Pintal has worked closely on set design with Daniele Levesque, who has created theatrical spaces that infuse the productions with their tragic, and even mythic, dimension, while giving actors the dynamic lines that echo their physical movements.

In her productions of both classical texts or Québecois plays in the repertoire, Pintal presents a powerful, original point of view: resolutely urban (*Dans la jungle des villes*), feminist (*Les Femmes savantes*), social (*Ha Ha!* . . . and *Ines Peree et Inat Tendu*), political (*Les Beaux Dimanches*). Furthermore, she received much praise for *Madame Louis XIV*, a one-woman show which she premiered (1986).

ADDITIONAL PRODUCTIONS: 1986–87: *Le Syndrome de Cézanne* (Theatre Critics Association of Quebec award for best direction); 1989–90: *Ha Ha!* . . . (award for best direction and best production); 1990–91: *Hosanna* (award for best direction and best production).

SELECTED BIBLIOGRAPHY: Armstrong, Lise, and Diane Miljours. "Décoller du réalisme." Interview with Lorraine Pintal. *Jeu, Cahiers de théâtre* 25 (1982): 173–85; Pintal, Lorraine. *Madame Louis XIV*. Montreal: Centre des auteurs dramatiques, 1988; Vigeant, Louise. "*Madame Louis XIV*: solo périlleux," *Jeu, Cahiers de théâtre* 53 (1989): 72–82.

Hélène Beauchamp

LUCIAN PINTILIE [b. 1933, Tarutino, Moldavian SSR]. Pintilie was born in a Romanian village annexed by the Soviet Union in 1939. His father was an English teacher. Pintilie completed the directing program at the Institute of Theatre and Cinematography in Bucharest in 1954, although controversy about his final project delayed the granting of his diploma. From 1954 to 1957 Pintilie worked as a director for Romanian State Television. Between 1957 and 1961, he directed in Romanian provincial theatres and for the Army Theatre (later the C. I. Nottara Theatre) in Bucharest. Applying knowledge gained from both television and the theatre, in 1961 Pintilie directed a film, *Sundays at Six*, which won nine international prizes. In 1962, Liviu Ciulei* invited him to direct at the Bulandra Theatre in Bucharest, where he continued to work for the next ten years.

His Bulandra productions included Gorky's *Children of the Sun*, *Caesar and Cleopatra, Raisin in the Sun*, and *The Cherry Orchard*, as well as several plays by Romania's national playwright, I. L. Caragiale. Like most of Romania's major directors, Pintilie was more attracted to classical plays than to contemporary ones. The Romanian theatre of the 1950s and early 1960s was marked by the Stalinism that pervaded Romanian culture; it was stylistically conservative, rigidly doctrinaire, and almost wholly conventional. There was little experimentation, and new Romanian plays stayed close to the Communist party line. Only in classical plays could directors and designers mount productions that sometimes managed to circumvent state censorship by suggesting criticism of Romanian society or ideas that were counter to Party principles. Romanian audiences developed an ability to understand a production's subtext which allowed directors to address their public in a kind of secret code. Pintilie was the master at reinterpreting, and sometimes even redesigning, classical texts to make often bold political statements.

His 1966 Bulandra production of Caragiale's *Carnival Scenes* was one of his first genuinely daring reinterpretations. Avoiding the naturalism that had marked Romanian productions of Caragiale, Pintilie created a wildly anarchic comic rampage that infuriated at large portion of the cultural and political establishment but delighted audiences who saw in it not only vigorous and hilarious physical and verbal comedy, but a satiric depiction of Romanian society. In 1967 Pintilie repeated his success with another radical reinterpretation, this time of the most venerated classic of Russian realism, *The Cherry Orchard*. A loosening of cultural controls and censorship during the late 1960s and early 1970s created the opportunity for more experimentation than had been seen in the postwar theatre. During that time, however, Pintilie did no theatre, turning his attention to the making of his film *The Reconstruction*. Approved and shot during a period of cultural liberalization, a reversion to Stalinism by the Ceausescu government delayed the release of the film. Although much lauded, it was never released in a version that Pintilie approved. In 1972, Pintilie returned to theatre with a radically redesigned and reinterpreted version of Nikolai Gogol's *The Inspector General*, revised to portray two simpletons who have survived a mass murder. Even the censors saw the satiric intentions and closed the play after three performances, firing Bulandra artistic director Liviu Ciulei in the process.

Since 1972 Pintilie has worked primarily in France and the United States. Invited to do a production in France, Pintilie directed Carlo Gozzi's *Turandot*. Using taped fragments of Puccini's opera, he gathered a cast of eighteen dwarfs who danced suggestively around 225-pound Andrea Ferreol. In 1974 he began a long association with Jean Mercure's Théâtre de la Ville in Paris, where he has mounted more than fifteen productions including *The Sea Gull*, *The Three Sisters*, Eugène Ionesco's *Jack or the Submission*, and *The Future Is in Eggs*.

He has also staged operas in Avignon, Aix-en-Provence, and for the Welsh National Opera.

In 1983 he made his American debut at the Guthrie Theatre in Minneapolis with *The Sea Gull*. Designed by Radu and Miruna Boruzescu, who have worked on many of Pintilie's French productions, the text was dissected and rearranged, becoming a play about the illusory nature of memory with the action filtered through Konstantine's feverish imagination. His *Tartuffe* at the Guthrie in 1984 and later at Washington's Arena Theatre was done in an all-out farcical style with sight-gags, pratfalls, double entendres, sexual innuendo, and such stylistic extremes and accelerated energy that it became "transcendently outrageous." *The Wild Duck* at the Arena in 1988 included feathers floating from the ceiling of Ekdal's studio and a life-sized dummy of Hedwig crashing to the floor at her suicide. Pintilie's most controversial and also most admired American production has been his *Cherry Orchard* at the Arena in 1988, in which a wheat field appears in Act II and Lyubov's dead son is a character.

Of his radical reinterpretations and revisions, Liviu Ciulei has said, "Pintilie does autopsies on the world, without pity" (Steele, 9). Although he has not worked in Romania since 1972, Pintilie still lives there.

Increasingly he has talked of leaving the theatre and spending his time in Romania writing.

SELECTED BIBLIOGRAPHY: Brustein, Robert. "The Limits of the Auteur." *New Republic* 194 (27 June 1988): 26–27; Selznick, Daniel. "Lucian Pintilie Tends 'The Cherry Orchard.' " *New York Times* 29 May 1988: H:3 + ; Steele, Mike. "The Romanian Connection." *American Theatre* 2 (July/August 1985): 4–11.

Miles Coiner

LUIGI PIRANDELLO [b. June 28, 1867, Girgenti (later Agrigento), Sicily, Italy; d. December 10, 1936, Rome, Italy]. Beginning in 1916, Pirandello, then nearly fifty and an accomplished writer of short stories and novels, turned increasingly to drama. Over the next two decades as a playwright, Pirandello achieved international recognition with such works as *Right You Are (If You Think You Are)* (1917), *The Rules of the Game* (1918), *Six Characters in Search of an Author* (1921), *Henry IV* (1922), *The Man with the Flower in His Mouth* (1923), *Each in His Own Way* (1924), *Tonight We Improvise* (1929), *As You Desire Me* (1930), and *The Mountain Giants* (1931–36).

In 1924, thanks to the international success of *Six Characters* (produced in England, the United States, France, and Germany between 1922 and 1924), Pirandello won approval and financial backing from Mussolini to found the Teatro d'Arte, of which he became producer and artistic director. The theatre's principals included Pirandello's son, Stefano, Orio Vergani, and Massimo Bontempelli (writers); Lamberto Picasso (actor); and Guido Salvini (Max Reinhardt* trained designer). The theatre's leading actress was Marta Abba, for whom Pirandello wrote many roles in his later plays.

From its opening in 1925 until its demise in 1928, the Teatro d'Arte presented an international repertory of modern plays, including many by Pirandello. Pirandello and his co-founders hoped that their theatre would introduce new works, both realistic and experimental, and that the acting ensemble would grow in skill, achievement, and recognition, utilizing more rigorous study and rehearsal techniques. The opening production of Pirandello's *Festival of Our Lord of the Ship* (1925) demonstrated careful preparation of both acting and technical effects and utilized one of the innovative features of the renovated Odescalchi Theatre, designed by futurist Virgilio Marchi—movable stairs which linked the stage to the theatre house and allowed actors to enter and exit through the audience. Although poorly financed, the fledgling company struggled through its first season and was invited to appear in London, Paris, and Germany.

Pirandello, inspired by the efficiency and technical innovations of the German State Theatre, attempted to organize a similar system in Italy, to be based in Milan, Rome, and Turin. The effort, which was to feature permanent acting companies based in those cities, joined periodically by leading actors on tour, was not granted government support. In 1927, the Teatro d'Arte toured South America, offering new and known works by Pirandello. A futurist pantomime, *The Salamander*, by Pirandello with music by Massimo Bontempelli, was produced in Paris (1927) and later in Italy in cooperation with Enrico Prampolini's Futurist Pantomime Theatre. The Teatro d'Arte's second and subsequent seasons lost money, much of it Pirandello's own, and disbanded in 1928. This initial Italian experiment offered a carefully chosen and thoroughly rehearsed permanent ensemble, overseen by a unifying artistic vision and supported by scrupulous albeit rudimentary attention to the technical effects of lighting, sets, and costume.

As a director, Pirandello contributed to Italian stage history by exploring new European methods of acting and production techniques, by offering an international repertory of new plays, and by providing an Italian model on which the post-Fascist, state-supported theatres could be built. His brief career as a director ended with the demise of the Teatro d'Arte, but the influence of Pirandello's directorial experiences can be demonstrated in virtually everything written after 1925. Although he remained impatient and dissatisfied with the complex and time-consuming technical apparatus of the theatre, in the later plays, Pirandello built upon his new awareness of production values and demonstrated a new determination to utilize all elements of the theatre. In lengthy stage directions included in his post–1925 plays, Pirandello attempted to influence design elements and actors' interpretations, giving very specific indications for sets, lighting, costume, movement, and characterization. In the later plays, from *Festival of Our Lord of the Ship* and the revised version of *Six Characters in Search of an Author* (1925) to the myth plays *The New Colony* (1928), *Lazarus* (1929), and *The Mountain Giants*, Pirandello utilized his experiences as a director to become a dramatist in full command of all elements of the stage.

ADDITIONAL PRODUCTIONS: 1925: *The Mountain Gods* (Dunsany), *Our Goddess* (Massimo Bontempelli), *A Merry Death* (Nikolai Evreinov*) *The Girlfriend* (Schnitzler), *Story of a Soldier* (Charles-Ferdinand Ramuz, with music by Stravinsky), *Henry IV* (Pirandello), *Six Characters in Search of an Author*, *To Clothe the Naked* (European Tour); 1926:

Vulcan (Marinetti), *Marionettes What Passion!* (Rosso Di San Secundo), *The Lady from the Sea, The Death of Niobe* (Alberto Savinio, with sets by Giorgio De Chirico), *The Man with the Flower in his Mouth, Cap with Bells*; 1927: *The Romantic Bourgeoisie* (Roger Planchon*), *Justice* (Galsworthy), *Diane and Tuda* (Pirandello), *The Rules of the Game*; 1928: *A Real Man* (Miguel de Unamuno), *Hedda Gabler, The Virgins* (Marco Praga), *The Others' Reasoning* (Pirandello).

SELECTED BIBLIOGRAPHY: *Alberti, A. C., ed. Il teatro nel fascismo: Pirandello e Bragaglia: documenti inediti negili archivi italiani.* Rome: Bulzoni, 1981; Bassnett, Susan. "Pirandello's Debut as a Director: The Opening of the Teatro d'arte." *New Theatre Quarterly* 12 (1987): 349–51; Corrigan, Beatrice. "Pirandello as a Director." *Theatre Research* 12 (1972): 155–63; D'Amico, Alessandro, and Alessandro Tinterri. *Pirandello Capocomico.* Palermo: Salerio, 1987; Guidice, Gaspare. *Pirandello: A Biography.* Trans. A. Hamilton. London: Oxford University Press, 1975; O'Keefe Bazzoni, Jana. "Reluctant Pilgrim: Pirandello's Journey toward the Modern Stage." In *Pirandello Studies.* Ed. John DiGaetani. New York: Greenwood Press, 1991; Ragusa, Olga. "Pirandello's Teatro d'arte and a New Look at His Fascism." *Italica* Summer 1978; Sogiuzzo, A. Richard. *The Playwright in the Theatre.* Metuchen, NJ: Scarecrow Press, 1982.

Jana O'Keefe Bazzoni

ERWIN FRIEDRICH PISCATOR [b. December 17, 1893, Ulm, Germany; d. March 20, 1966, Starnberg, Bavaria]. Passionately committed to the creation of a theatre which addressed contemporary political issues, Erwin Piscator was one of the most innovative stage directors of the twentieth century. Like many of his fellow artists, he served in World War I and was profoundly influenced by the immense carnage. Believing that communism would defeat the capitalist forces which caused the war, he joined the KPD (Communist party of Germany) shortly after the armistice was signed. In 1920 he founded the Proletarian Theatre, which used amateur actors and toured agitprop sketches to beer halls and worker clubs. Although deliberately simplistic, these productions allowed Piscator to fashion a theatre which would serve as a catalyst for social change. As such, all production elements, including the script, had to be subordinated to this mission.

From the beginning of his career he altered texts drastically in order to convey effective revolutionary messages. In 1926 he encountered his first serious conflict with conservative audiences when he staged his version of *The Robbers* (Schiller) at the Prussian State Theatre. He radically rewrote the script, making Spiegelberg a proletarian hero, costumed him to resemble Trotsky and had the "Internationale" played at his death. He telescoped long, rambling scenes by staging them simultaneously and had several actors sing their speeches. Opposition was so clamorous that the production had to be withdrawn after a few performances. The first script performed at the Piscator-Buehne in 1927, Ernst Toller's *Hoppla, Such Is Life!*, was substantially altered. Lengthy documentary film sequences were added and the original ending was rewritten. On opening night of Theodore Plivier's *The Kaiser's Coolies* (1930), a new ending was written and given to the actors during intermission. Such practices, however, were not the antics of an egotistical director. Piscator viewed theatre as a process and a social laboratory, not a fixed immutable possession of bourgeois society.

His approach to acting was equally iconoclastic. He believed that a realistic acting style diluted historical truth. Moreover, such acting, with its emphasis on individual characterizations, could not convey the feelings and attitudes of the masses. In order to train his new performers, he formed an acting collective—itself a political statement—at the Piscator-Buehne. Here he hoped to prepare actors physically and psychologically to perform in an unsentimental, objective theatre.

The desire to depict broad historical epochs also led Piscator to experiment with a vast array of stage machinery. For *Rasputin* by Alexei Tolstoy and Pavel Shchegolev (1927), Traugott Mueller designed a giant hemisphere which rested on a revolve. Its massive flap-like doors opened and closed to reveal action. In addition, dates and titles were projected on downstage screens. In *The Good Soldier Schweik* (based on Jaroslav Hašek's novel, 1928), he used an arrangement of flats, conveyor belts, and screens to create an infinite variety of scenic combinations.

It was film, however, which occupied an increasingly important role in each subsequent production. In *Flags* (Alfons Paquet, 1924) he revealed portraits of characters on a backdrop during the prologue and used sidescreens for projections of posters, slogans, and news clippings. He also used film to telescope time. In Ehm Welk's *Storm over Gottland* (1927), set in the fifteenth century, shots of contemporary Moscow and Shanghai emphasized historical similarities among workers separated by 500 years. Film eventually became his fourth dimension, a piece of living scenery. Piscator was not interested in machinery and film for their own sakes. He employed these devices to facilitate the temporal and spatial demands of ''epic theatre,'' a term he coined in 1924 to describe the social, political, and historical conditions which made the dramatic action of the plays inevitable. Whereas traditional theatre only discussed this process, epic theatre portrayed the process.

In 1931 Piscator left Germany for the Soviet Union to film *The Revolt of the Fishermen*. Released in October 1934, the film had only limited success. He departed Moscow in 1936 for Paris and was warned not to return. For three years he neither wrote, directed, nor organized any projects. On New Year's Day, 1939, he arrived in New York, where he began the Dramatic Workshop, an actor training program sponsored by the New School. He softened his revolutionary rhetoric and rarely directed outside of the workshop. He returned to Germany in 1951 where political uncertainties and previous rivalries forced him into free lancing at lower echelon provincial theatres. In the spring of 1962 he was appointed *Intendant* of the Free Volksbuehne in West Berlin. Here he unveiled a more thoughtful, less belligerent version of his political theatre, focusing on issues and events that transpired just prior to and during the war. Moreover, a new generation of playwrights inspired by his theories of the epic theatre gravitated to him almost spontaneously. Among these were Rolf Hochhuth, Peter Weiss, and Heiner Kipphardt. In 1966, while producing his best work, he died of complications from a gall bladder ailment.

ADDITIONAL PRODUCTIONS: 1920: Proletarian Theatre; 1924: *The Red Revue*, commissioned by KPD for Reichstag election campaign; 1925: *In Spite of Everything*, commissioned by KPD for party congress; 1926: *Tidal Wave* (Alfons Paquet); 1929: *The Merchant of Berlin* (Walter Mehring), publication of *The Political Theatre*; 1931: *Tai Yang Awakes* (Friedrich Wolf); 1940: *St. Joan* (Shaw); 1942: *War and Peace* (adapted by Piscator and Alfred Neumann); 1948: *All the King's Men* (adapted by Piscator and Robert Penn Warren); 1952: *Danton's Death*; 1955: *Requiem for a Nun*, based on a novella by Faulkner; 1960: *Mother Courage*; 1961: *Death of a Salesman*; 1963: *The Deputy* (Rolf Hochhuth); 1964: *In the Case of J. Robert Oppenheimer* (Heinar Kipphardt); 1965: *The Investigation* (Peter Weiss).

SELECTED BIBLIOGRAPHY: Braun, Edward. *The Director and the Stage*. New York: Holmes and Meier, 1982; Innes, C. D. *Erwin Piscator's Political Theatre*. London: Cambridge University Press, 1972; Ley-Piscator, Maria. *The Piscator Experiment: The Political Theatre*. New York: James H. Heineman, 1967; Piscator, Erwin. *The Political Theatre*. Trans. Hugh Robinson. New York: Avon Books, 1978; Willett, John. *The Theatre of Erwin Piscator*. New York: Holmes and Meier, 1979.

John H. Houchin

GEORGES PITOËFF [b. September 17, 1884, Tiflis, Georgia (Russia); d. September 17, 1939, Geneva, Switzerland]. One of the most influential and prolific directors in France between the first and second world wars, Pitoëff introduced significant contemporary foreign playwrights to the French stage. He and his wife, the superb actress Ludmilla Pitoëff, were the first to produce Anton Chekhov in France, assured the success of Luigi Pirandello* in that country with their staging of *Six Characters in Search of an Author* (1923), reinterpreted Henrik Ibsen's major works, and made George Bernard Shaw's *Saint Joan* (1925) a classic of modern French theatre. Pitoëff also brought the French playwright Jean Anouilh to the attention of the public and was the major director of works by Henri-René Lenormand.

The son of a theatre director in Russia, where he was exposed to the work of Konstantin Stanislavsky* and Vsevolod Meyerhold,* Pitoëff also studied mathematics, architecture, and law in Paris from 1905 to 1911. He returned to Russia for two years to lead a traveling drama troupe, Our Theater, before ultimately moving to Western Europe. From 1915 to 1921, he and his wife lived in Geneva, where they formed a theatre company that produced plays by modern Russian and European authors. Pitoëff went with most of his troupe to Paris in 1921 at the invitation of Jacques Hébertot, director of the Théâtre des Champs-Elysées, and worked in the French capital for the rest of his life.

From 1925 onward, Pitoëff and his company were without a fixed theatre, in spite of their critical and popular acclaim. Often working under difficult conditions and undertaking a number of European tours, they nevertheless managed to produce an astounding number and variety of plays: 200 works by 114 authors during Pitoëff's eighteen years in Paris.

Pitoëff, along with directors Charles Dullin,* Louis Jouvet,* and Gaston Baty,* constituted the "Cartel des quatre," a group that exerted a strong influence on theatre between the mid-twenties and the beginning of World War II. Created in 1926 in reaction to the increasing commercialization of the theatre, it followed the lead of Jacques Copeau* in staging well-crafted, stylized productions and introducing important foreign authors of the time. Pitoëff, who often acted in his shows, placed great emphasis upon the script, believing that the goal of the director was to translate the poetic "spirit" of the play. His search for the artistic essence of the works that he chose led to inventive scenic solutions, such as his use of an elevator bathed in an unearthly light to bring Pirandello's six characters onstage. Pitoëff strived for simplicity in set, lighting, and blocking and, similarly, exacted a style of acting that was free of artifice and based upon the actor's careful and intensive analysis of the character.

ADDITIONAL PRODUCTIONS: 1917: *The Power of Darkness* (Tolstoy), *L'Échange* (Claudel); 1919: *Le Temps est un songe* (*Time Is a Dream*, Lenormand); 1920: *Les Ratés* (*The Failures*, Lenormand); 1921: *Macbeth, Uncle Vanya*; 1922: *The Sea Gull*; 1925: *Henri IV* (Pirandello); 1926: *Hamlet, Comme ci, ou comme ça* (Pirandello); 1929: *Les Criminels* (Ferdinand Bruckner), *The Three Sisters*; 1930: *A Doll's House*; 1932: *Oedipe* (Gide); 1934: *The Wild Duck*; 1935: *Tonight, We Improvise* (Pirandello); 1937: *Le Voyageur sans bagage* (*Traveler without Luggage*, Anouilh), *Romeo and Juliet*; 1938: *La Sauvage* (Anouilh); 1939: *Enemy of the People*.

SELECTED BIBLIOGRAPHY:Borgal, Clément. *Metteurs en Scène*. Paris: Fernand Lanore, 1963; Jomaron, Jacqueline. *Pitoëff, metteur en scène*. Lausanne: l'Age d'homme, 1979; Lenormand, Henri-René. *Les Pitoëff, souvenirs*. Paris: Odette Lieutier, 1943; Lorch, Jennifer. "The 1925 Text of *Sei peronaggi in cerca d'autore* and Pitoëff's Production of 1923." *The Yearbook of the British Pirandello Society* 2 (1982): 32–47; Pitoëff, Georges. *Notre théâtre*. Paris: Messages, 1949; Simon, Alfred. *Dictionnaire du théâtre français contemporain*. Paris: Larousse, 1970: s.v."Cartel" and "Pitoëff"; Surer, Paul. *Le Théâtre français contemporain*. Paris: Société d'edition et d'enseignement supérieur, 1964; Whitton, David. *Stage Directors in Modern France*. Manchester: Manchester University Press, 1989.

Cynthia Running-Johnson

ROGER PLANCHON [b. September 12, 1931, Saint Chamond, France]. Although his family moved to Lyon soon after his birth, Roger Planchon never lost his ties to his native Ardèche and depicted them in his plays dealing with rustic peasant life. Leaving school at a relatively early age, he completed his education with self-study and occasional courses. With a group of friends, he formed an amateur company which turned professional in 1949. After playing in parish halls and other makeshift houses, they converted an old Lyon shop into the small Théâtre de la Comédie in 1952. This company gradually established such a solid reputation for quality that the city of Villeurbanne (a working-class suburb of Lyon) offered the use of its large but substandard theatre, and the company took the name of the Théâtre de la Cité de Villeurbanne.

When Minister of Culture André Malraux began expanding France's network of decentralized state-subsidized theatres in 1959, Planchon's troupe was designated as the first "permanent company." In 1963, the Théâtre de la Cité became a "national dramatic center," and only a disagreement with the municipality kept Planchon from being named head of a "Maison de la Culture" (the highest echelon in Malraux's scheme). However, after Jean Vilar* and his successor Georges Wilson had both left the Théâtre National Populaire in Paris, that title and most of the accompanying status was transferred to the Théâtre de la Cité in 1972. Even the obligations that accompanied the new status have not, however, overcome Planchon's aversion to touring; he insists on extended stays in each city to approximate the long relationship he has maintained with his Lyon audience.

Working as the leader of a dedicated permanent ensemble company, some of whose members (Jean Bouise, Robert Gilbert, Claude Lochy, and Isabelle Sadoyan) went back to the original group of amateurs, Planchon has frequently produced plays that were the fruit of improvisational methods and collaboration by practically all the members of the organization. The most noteworthy of these efforts include musical satires filled with slapstick and parody: *Cartouche* (1952), *The Three Musketeers* (1958), *O M'man Chicago* (1963), *La Langue au chat* (1972), *Folies bourgeoises* (1975), and *La Mise en pièces du "Cid"* (1969, the shortened version of an interminable title that is an obvious parody of the full title of *Marat/Sade*). The same improvisational and collaborative techniques are evident in the productions of plays fully written by Planchon and other authors.

Considered the most Brechtian of French directors, Planchon uses various stage effects to place his productions in a historical context, emphasizing the effect of concurrent events on the lives of characters who, at best, only partially understand their importance. When directing classic plays, he follows the ideas of Jan Kott's *Shakespeare Our Contemporary* in drawing attention to the significance of the action for the contemporary public. In fact, these ideas are probably responsible, more than his perfectionism, for Planchon's tendency to revive the same plays in different productions over a period of years, even decades.

His productions of his own and others' plays, however, are never truly didactic; he presents many questions, but insists that he does not offer the answers. Furthermore, the Brechtian influence has been somewhat lessened over time and has almost always been modified somewhat by two other strong influences: the cinema and the French surrealist tradition. Planchon shows his love for the movies not only by dividing the action of a play into short sequences, but also by his imaginative use of staging and especially lighting to produce theatrical approximations of the cinema's shifting camera angles and framing to emphasize dramatic elements. The surrealists provided the impetus for many dreamlike elements, such as the tuxedo-clad man with a rabbit's head who reappears throughout *Folies bourgeoises*.

His direction, however, always has a strong basis in real life, though eschewing old-fashioned naturalism. Most evident in his "peasant" plays, *La Remise*

(1962), *L'Infame* (1969), and *Le Cochon noir* (1973), this *everyday reality* is also present in his productions of the classics, where both major characters and a host of extras are constantly occupied at the mundane tasks of daily life, such as farm work, eating, cleaning, and doing the laundry.

Although, since the events of May 1968, Planchon has lost the youthful idealism that led him to think he could bring vast numbers of workers to see his plays, he has never abandoned the dream of a popular theatre firmly rooted in a particular region. Of all the provincial directors, he has enjoyed the greatest national prestige. Planchon's career has epitomized the history of the dual movement of decentralized popular theatre in France since the mid-century.

ADDITIONAL PRODUCTIONS: 1953: *Le Sens de la marche* (Arthur Adamov); 1954: *The Good Woman of Setzuan*; 1957: *Paolo Paoli* (Adamov); 1962: *Tartuffe*; 1963: *Georges Dandin*; 1966: *Richard III*; 1973: *Par-dessous bord* (Michel Vinaver); 1976: *Gilles de Rais* (Planchon); 1979: *No Man's Land*.

SELECTED BIBLIOGRAPHY: Bradby, David. *The Theatre of Roger Planchon*. Cambridge: Chadwyck-Healey, 1984; Burgess, John, ed. and trans. "Taking on the TNP: Theatre as Social and Artistic Adventure." *Theatre Quarterly* 25 (Spring 1977): 25–33; Copfermann, Emile. *Théâtres de Roger Planchon*. Paris: Union Générale d'Editions, 1977; Daoust, Yvette. *Roger Planchon, Director and Playwright*. Cambridge: Cambridge University Press, 1981; Duvignaud, Jean, et al., *Itinéraire de Roger Planchon*. Paris: L'Arche, 1970; Kustow, Michael, "Roger Planchon: Actor, Director, Playwright." *Theatre Quarterly* 5 (January-March 1972): 42–57; Planchon, Roger. "I'm a Museum Guard." *Performing Arts Journal* 16 (1981): 97–109.

Dan M. Church

NIGEL R. PLAYFAIR [b. July 1, 1874, London, England; d. August 19, 1934, London, England]. An English actor-manager-director with a stylish flair for contemporary satire and English high comedy, Sir Nigel Playfair established London's Lyric Theatre, Hammersmith, as one of the most exciting, innovative, and fashionable playhouses of its era. His production of *The Way of the World* (1924) brought to prominence the work of actress Edith Evans, while his stylish 1930 black-and-white revival of *The Importance of Being Earnest* (1930) featured a young John Gielgud.* In between, he also directed *The Rivals* (1925), in which he sought to make Mrs. Malaprop "a natural personage," A. P. Herbert's revue *Riverside Nights* (1926), *The Beaux's Stratagem* (1927), *She Stoops to Conquer* (1928), and *The Critic* (1928). His 1927 production, *When Crummles Played*, was a celebrated burlesque of George Lillo's *The London Merchant*, set against the unlikely theatrical background of Charles Dickens's *Nicholas Nickleby*.

Playfair is best known, however, for his celebrated squeaky-clean production of *The Beggar's Opera* (1920), which single-handedly rekindled interest in John Gay and other hitherto ignored eighteenth-century drama. Colorfully designed by Claude Lovat Fraser, the production ran for 1,463 consecutive performances over almost three years. Its unit set and general, simplified realism influenced the development of non-naturalistic English scene design and promoted increased aesthetic unity between the work of director and designer. The Lyric *Beggar's*

Opera went through several cast changes and attracted large, enthusiastic audiences. A quietly produced New York version, with the same creative team, however, was a complete flop.

The Oxford-educated Playfair's contributions to the English theatre were numerous. As an actor, he toured the West Indies with F. R. Benson's Shakespeare Company, and he also appeared in the original productions of George Bernard Shaw's *John Bull's Other Island* (1904) and *Fanny's First Play* (1911). He also acted under Sir Herbert Tree at His Majesty's Theatre, and in 1914, Playfair appeared as Bottom in the Granville Barker* Savoy Theatre production of *A Midsummer Night's Dream*. Along with Lesley Howard and Aubrey Smith, Playfair also founded the short-lived Minerva Films company at Bushey in 1920. He directed Gielgud in the role of the Poet Butterfly in Karel Čapek's *The Insect Play*, the English translation of which Playfair was part author, at the Regent Theatre in 1923.

The Lyric Theatre, Hammersmith, an old music-hall house located in West London well away from the West End, was run down and remote when Playfair, along with Arnold Bennett and Alistair Taylor, took it over for about £2,000 in 1918. The first season, which began with a children's pantomime by A. A. Milne, included the acclaimed Birmingham Repertory Theatre production by Barry Jackson* of *Abraham Lincoln*. Yet it was Playfair's own productions—sometimes featuring his own acting—that put the soon fashionable Lyric, Hammersmith, on London's cultural map, and established the theatre as, in Peggy Ashcroft's words, "a mecca for young actors."

The celebrated productions of Restoration and eighteenth-century comedy were interspersed with reviews like *Riverside Nights* (the poster noted it was "full of delights"). When the piece played the West-End Metropole, away from Playfair's bohemian followers, it flopped disastrously thanks to its "rococo element."

Lyric regulars, however, loved Playfair's highbrow touches such as costumed musicians, elegant footmen, and open acknowledgment of the urbane audience. As one critic noted to Playfair's chagrin, the Lyric was "a theatre with a pose."

Although he was inclined toward caricature, Playfair's directorial work became known for its flair, gaiety, neatness, and fashionable decoration. He was a genial, social man who ran his theatre like a family party, evoking a sense of relaxed spontaneity in all of his productions. He either played down or avoided altogether any sexual ribaldry or general unpleasantness in the plays he chose to direct. Although Playfair kept a tight rein on his theatre, much of the actual staging of productions was done by his stage manager and righthand man, Stephen Thomas.

Known as an elegant, zestful individualist, Playfair was successful in combining scholarship with an upper-class style. His knighthood in 1928 confirmed the director's ascendent position in the social hierarchy of his day, and his promotion of stylized acting and directing was to have a pervasive influence on the British theatre of the next two decades. Yet by 1932, the party at the Lyric was over. Audiences had become tired of the limited Playfair formula, and the company was disbanded after producing *Derby Day* (1932). Two years later, Playfair (who was married to May Martin) died after a short illness.

ADDITIONAL PRODUCTIONS: 1918: *Make Believe* (A. A. Milne); 1920: *As You Like It, The Knight of the Burning Pestle*; 1922: *Polly* (with Lilian Davies); 1925: *The Duennal!*; 1929: *La Vie Parisienne*; 1933: *Beau Brummell*.

SELECTED BIBLIOGRAPHY: Playfair, Sir Nigel. *Hammersmith Hoy*. London: Faber and Faber, 1930; Playfair, Sir Nigel. *The Story of the Lyric Theatre, Hammersmith*. New York: Benjamin Blom, 1925; Short, Ernest. *Sixty Years of Theatre*. London: Eyre and Spottiswoode, 1951; Trewin, J. C. *The Gay Twenties: A Decade of the Theatre*. London: Macdonald, 1958; Wickham-Legg, L. G. *The Dictionary of National Biography 1931–40*. Oxford: Oxford University Press, 1949: 201–2.

Chris Jones

WILLIAM POEL [b. William Pole, July 22, 1852, London, England; d. December 13, 1934, London, England]. In 1875, William Poel left his job as a clerk to become an actor in the theatre company of his idol, Charles James Mathews. His theatrical apprenticeship with Mathews was supplemented by his employment (1881) by Emma Cons as manager of the Royal Victoria Coffee Hall (later the Old Vic) and a six-month stint in 1883 as stage manager for F. R. Benson.

Poel is best remembered today for initiating the theatrical reforms that rescued Shakespeare and his contemporaries from the restrictions of the picture-frame stage and replaced the spectacular, pictorial Shakespearean productions of the Victorian and Edwardian theatre with a simplified style reminiscent of Elizabethan staging. Poel's reforms were first exhibited in a generally unrecognized 1881 *Hamlet*, mounted on a bare platform in London's St. George's Hall, and later refined in productions like his 1893 staging of *Measure for Measure* at the Royalty Theatre on a reconstructed, two-level Elizabethan stage and featuring an onstage audience, and his 1897 revival of *Twelfth Night* in the hall of the Middle Temple, for which Poel constructed a stage that was clearly based upon Johannes De Witt's 1596 drawing of the Swan which had been published in 1888.

Poel's reforms were not limited, however, to his attempts to reconstruct the Elizabethan public stage. He advocated a return to the primacy of the playtext and consequently opposed the then-common tradition of editing scenes so that performers might receive applause on their entrances and exits, a practice Poel felt distorted the play and impeded its progress; he stressed the importance of ensemble acting and worked to abolish the star system; and he was obsessed with recovering the secret of Elizabethan speech, of how Shakespeare was meant to sound. The latter led Poel to propose the ill-conceived notions of "exaggerated naturalness" (the way he supposed Elizabethan actors spoke) and "tuned tones" (by which he meant that any speech which was to have significance must be inflected) and to actually "orchestrate" the voices in *Twelfth Night* (1897) with Viola played by a mezzo soprano, Olivia by a contralto, Malvolio by a baritone, Sir Toby by a bass, Sir Andrew by a falsetto, Antonio by a basso profundo, and Orsino by a tenor.

Poel served as an instructor to the Shakespeare Reading Society (many of his early "stagings" were, in fact, staged readings), and he was associated with the Elizabethan Stage Society from 1895 until 1905. His methods and theories were exported to the United States by Ben Greet and to France by Aurélien Lugné-Poe.* His productions are also considered to have been influential on the work of Harley Granville Barker* and, through him, the twentieth century.

ADDITIONAL PRODUCTIONS: 1892: *Duchess of Malfi, The Two Gentlemen of Verona*; 1895: *A Comedy of Errors, Twelfth Night*; 1896: *Two Gentlemen of Verona, Doctor Faustus*; 1897: *Arden of Faversham*; 1899: *Don Juan* (Molière); 1901: *Everyman*; 1902: *The Alchemist* (Jonson); 1905: *Romeo and Juliet*; 1908: *Samson Agonistes* (Milton); 1911: *Jacob and Esau* (sixteenth-century interlude); 1921: *Fratricide Punished*; 1932: *David and Bethsabe* (David Peele, first time produced since 1599).

SELECTED BIBLIOGRAPHY: Hutson, William. "Elizabethan Stagings of *Hamlet*: George Pierce Baker and William Poel." *Theatre Research International* 12 (Autumn 1987): 253–60; "A New Way with Shakespeare." *The Times* (London) 30 May 1913; Poel, William. *Shakespeare in the Theatre*. New York: Benjamin Blom, 1913; Speaight, Robert. *William Poel and the Elizabethan Revival*. Melbourne: William Heinemann, 1954; Sprague, A. C. "Shakespeare and William Poel." *University of Toronto Quarterly* 17 (October 1947): 29–37.

John W. Frick

ALEKSEY DMITRIVICH POPOV [b. March 24, 1892, Nikolayevsk (Pugachev); d. August 18, 1961, Moscow]. Popov was one of several gifted directors who emerged from the Moscow Art Theatre's First Studio, where he was an actor from 1912 to 1918. He became director of a studio in Kostrom in 1918, but returned to Moscow in 1923 to assume the artistic directorship of the Vakhtangov Theatre.

During his tenure at the Vakhtangov (1923–30) and subsequently as artistic director of the Theatre of the Revolution (1930–35), Popov forged a style which blended psychological realism with the heroic tone demanded by the propagandist dramas of the era. In acting, Popov advocated a synthesis of the teachings of Konstantin Stanislavsky,* Evgeni Vakhtangov,* and Vsevolod Meyerhold* to achieve carefully designed, yet psychologically credible performances.

It was, however, staging and visual design which distinguished Popov's best productions. Working with some of the leading designers of the era, including Nikolai Akimov* and Ilya Shlepyanov, Popov achieved an effective compromise between constructivism and realism. Large, bare ramps and movable platforms were adorned with realistic props and backed by huge painted or photomontage drops to evoke the industrial and agricultural workplaces so important to socialist-realist dramas of the 1930s. Skillful area lighting helped to isolate action in these spaces, with quick shifts of focus reminiscent of the cinema. Popov's work with Akimov on Boris Lavrenev's *The Break-up* (1927) and his collaboration with Shlepyanov on Pogodin's *Poem of the Axe* (1931) and *My Friend* (1932) were particularly successful examples of this "constructivist realism."

From 1936 to 1960, Popov directed the Theatre of the Soviet Army, where he gradually turned toward a more romantic style and a more classical repertory. Occasionally, he achieved striking visual effects, as in his 1937 *Taming of the Shrew*, which included horseback scenes on carousel ponies. Increasingly, however, he was constrained by the rigid socialist realism of the 1940s and 1950s.

Popov was not a great innovator or theoretician, but he absorbed and synthesized some of the most important experiments of his contemporaries. As a professor at GITIS (the State Institute of Theatre Art) from 1940 until his death, he also influenced the training of later Soviet directors.

ADDITIONAL PRODUCTIONS: 1935, 1948: *Romeo and Juliet*; 1944: *Stalingraders* (Chepurin); 1946: *Ivan the Terrible* (A. Tolstoy); 1950: *The Admiral's Flag* (Shtein); 1951: *Inspector General* (Gogol).

SELECTED BIBLIOGRAPHY: Popov, Aleksey. *Khudozhestvennaya tselostnost' spektaklya*. Moscow: Vseroc. teatr. ob-vo., 1959; Rudnitsky, Konstantin. *Russian and Soviet Theater 1905–1932*. Trans. Roxane Permar. New York: Abrams, 1988; Zolotnitsky, D. I. *Budni i prazdniki teatral'nogo oktyabrya*. Leningrad: Iskusstvo, 1978; Zorkaya, N. *Aleksey Popov*. Moscow: Iskusstvo, 1983.

Cheyanne Boyd

EUGENE WYLEY PRESBREY [b. March 13, 1853, Williamsburg, Massachusetts; d. September 9, 1931, Hollywood, California]. Eugene Presbrey began his theatrical career in Boston as a part-time actor while also working as a painter. When ill health forced him to give up painting, he switched to theatre full-time. In 1879 he moved to New York and between 1884 and 1896 served as the stage manager (director) of the Madison Square Theatre under A. M. Palmer.

As a director, Presbrey felt that the stage picture should have a fidelity to truth, or "atmosphere." In other words, every scenic detail was to be so accurately represented that the audience would believe that what it was seeing was real. This atmosphere including falling leaves, twinkling stars, real flowers (or at least the smell of them), and edible props. Presbrey also believed that the theatre should present things as they should be, not as they are, and that this could happen when the various elements of theatre came together under "skillful direction." He is described as an authoritarian director who worked more with the intellect than with emotion. According to Presbrey, the director's job was to understand the playwright so well that he could bring out the writer's ideas in every detail. Because most playwrights had little experience with the technical elements of the stage, the director was necessary to bring out the "real stuff" of the play. Presbrey's ideas about characterization differed from the old stock company traditions. He believed that it was important to find actors who were the "living prototypes" of the characters in terms of age, size, shape, personality, and so forth. These actors should have good physical and mental health; good taste, habits, and judgment; and a thorough knowledge of the world around them.

Presbrey was also a playwright who usually directed his own plays. Some of his scripts include *Marcelle* (1900), *Raffles* (1904), *Mary, Mary, Quite Contrary*

(1905), *The Adventures of Gerard* (1905), *Susan in Search of a Husband* (1906), and *The Barrier* (1908). Many of these were adaptations of other works.

Presbrey spent the last twelve years of his life in Hollywood as a screenwriter for Paramount and MGM.

ADDITIONAL PRODUCTIONS: 1884–96: Madison Square Theatre: *Alabama* (Augustus Thomas), *Elaine, Trilby, Jim the Penman* (Charles T. Young), *Broken Hearts, Sealed Instructions, Captain Swift, Aunt Jack*; 1903: *Personal*; 1909: *Joan of Arc* (with Maude Adams).

SELECTED BIBLIOGRAPHY: Coward, Edward Fales. "The Men Who Direct the Destinies of the Stage." *Theatre Magazine* July 1906: 186 + ; "Eugene W. Presbrey, Dramatist, Dies at 78." *New York Times* 10 September 1931; Henderson, Mary C. *Theatre in America*. New York: Harry N. Abrams, 1986: 104–5; Presbrey, Eugene. "The Use of the Word 'Atmosphere' Applied to the Stage." *Theatre Magazine* January 1907: 10 + .

Candice M. Coleman

HAROLD PRINCE [b. January 30, 1928, New York, New York]. Commercial musical theatre has few directors who are consistently committed to experimentation. Harold Prince, throughout thirty years as a producer and director, has pushed the limits of this frequently conservative medium. Unlike most American directors, he began his career as a producer, apprenticing himself to the legendary comedy and musical master George Abbott.* After stints as a stage manager and casting director, he teamed with Robert Griffith to produce *The Pajama Game* (1954), a modern-dress labor musical staged by Abbott and choreographed by Bob Fosse.* As a producer, Prince presented the landmark "concept" musicals *West Side Story* (1957) and *Fiddler on the Roof* (1964), directed by Jerome Robbins.* His own contributions to the development of the "concept" musical, in which all plot, visual, musical, and production elements are fully integrated to present an emotional/social state to the audience, was first recognized with *Cabaret* (1966). In this musical of Berlin in the early Hitler era, he contrasted romance plots with cabaret songs and material that were entertaining but offensively anti-Semitic. By forcing the theatre audience to act as the nonreactive cabaret audience, Prince made the musical into a political statement on apathy without undermining the performers and composers.

As a director, Prince is best known for the "concept" musicals created in collaboration with composer-lyricist Stephen Sondheim—*Company* (1970), *Follies* (1971), *Pacific Overtures* (1976), *A Little Night Music* (1973), and *Sweeney Todd* (1979), in which the collaborative team, also including designers Boris Aronson and Florence Klotz and arranger Jonathan Tunick, created highly theatrical presentations of unusual plot material—city apartment life, memories, the opening of Japan to Western trade, Swedish romance, and nineteenth-century British melodrama. Both the scores and the visual impact of these shows are legendary, but while individual elements were memorable (the ghosts in *Follies*, the sliding screens in *Night Music*, the factory whistle in *Sweeney Todd*), Prince's greatest accomplishment is the integration of the elements. Prince and Sondheim also collaborated on the environmental production of Leonard Bernstein's opera

Candide (1973), which set the travels of Candide and Cunegonde in performance sites scattered around the stage and the audience of an otherwise traditional proscenium theatre. The team split after the unsuccessful reversed-chronology musical *Merrily We Roll Along* (1981), although they have worked together since on revivals of their shows for opera companies. He has also served as director for hugely successful multiple productions of two musicals by Andrew Lloyd Webber, *Evita* (1978, London; 1979, New York) and *The Phantom of the Opera* (1986, London; 1988, New York).

Prince's involvement with the "concept" musical and theatre as a collaborative venture led him to stage operas. His premiere stagings of new works, such as *Ashmedai* (1976, New York City Opera) and *Willie Stark* (1981, Houston Grand Opera), were successful at bringing the highly articulate performance styles and designs of Broadway "concept" shows to even the largest opera houses. Prince's productions of the standard opera repertory have been highly praised, most notably his *Madama Butterfly* (Chicago Lyric Opera) and *Turandot* (Vienna State Opera), both of which are widely available on video.

ADDITIONAL PRODUCTIONS: 1962: *A Funny Thing Happened on the Way to the Forum* (prod.), *A Family Affair*; 1963: *She Loves Me*; 1965: *Baker Street*; 1966: *It's a Bird... It's a Plane... It's Superman*; 1968: *Zorba*; 1978: *On The Twentieth Century*; 1984: *Play Memory* (Joanna Glass), *The End of the World* (Kopit); 1985: *Grind*; 1987: *Roza*; 1990: *Kiss of the Spider Woman* (Purchase, New York, 1993, New York City).

BIBLIOGRAPHY: Bartow, Arthur. *The Director's Voice: Twenty-One Interviews.* New York: Theatre Communications Group, 1988: 241–54; Hirsch, Foster. *Harold Prince and the American Musical Theatre.* New York: Cambridge University Press, 1989; Ilson, Carol. *Harold Prince: From Pajama Game to Phantom of the Opera.* Ann Arbor, MI: UMI Research Press, 1989; Prince, Harold. *Contradictions: On Twenty-Six Years in the Theatre.* New York: Dodd, Mead, 1974. In 1989, the Harold Prince Collection of scrapbooks, production files, and financial records was donated to the Billy Rose Theatre Collection, The New York Public Library for the Performing Arts.

Barbara Cohen-Stratyner

CLAUDE E. PURDY [b. May 11, 1940, Lake Charles, Louisiana]. In recent years, increased awareness and sensitivity has been directed toward the field of cultural diversity via African-American drama by many prominent mainstream regional theatres. One of the major benefits of this new interest is the emergence of the journeyman specialist in black theatre, usually called upon to direct the theatre's seasonal offering(s) in this field. Perhaps one of the more important directors working in this capacity is Claude Purdy. Purdy's background includes strong credits as a nonresident director at many American theatres as well as having directed in France, Senegal, and Nigeria.

His connection to playwright August Wilson deserves special note. Purdy has distinguished himself as one of the only directors besides Lloyd Richards* to guide early drafts of *Mill Hands Lunch Bucket*, now known as *Joe Turner's Come and Gone*, and *Jitney!*, one of Wilson's earliest works. Purdy has also directed *Fences* at several leading theatres in the United States including the

Pittsburgh Public Theatre, the American Conservatory Theatre, the Los Angeles Theatre Center, and *Ma Rainey's Black Bottom* at the GeVa Theatre, Rochester, New York, the Milwaukee Repertory Theatre and Houston's Alley Theatre in 1989, the Arizona Theatre Company in 1990, and the Missouri Repertory Theatre, Kansas City in 1991.

Purdy's commitment to the direction of African-American plays is varied and includes early works of what could now be termed contemporary black theatre including Amiri Baraka's *Dutchman* and *The Slave* (American Theatre of Paris, 1966), Lonnie Elder III's *Ceremonies in Dark Old Men* and Melvin Van Peebles's searing ritual *Ain't Supposed to Die a Natural Death* (Pittsburgh Playhouse, 1971).

As is the case with other African-American directors who could be called contemporaries of Purdy, such as Ivan Dixon, Oz Scott, and Michael Shultz, Purdy's background also reflects training and work in the motion picture industry. In addition to holding a B.A. in theatre arts from Southern University, Purdy also holds an A.A. in cinema arts from Columbia College as well as additional training through the German School of Photography (New York).

ADDITIONAL PRODUCTIONS: 1967: *No Exit*, National Theatre of Senegal; 1968: *The Merchant of Venice*, University of Ibadan, Nigeria; 1969: *Mojo*, Inner City Cultural Center of Los Angeles; 1970: *Deadwood Dick Legend of the West*, Birmingham, Alabama; 1974: *Jitney!* (August Wilson), Penumbra Theatre, St. Paul, Minnesota; 1989: *Joe Turner's Come and Gone*, American Conservatory Theatre, San Francisco; Los Angeles Theatre Center, 1989; Tricycle Theatre, London, 1990.

Thomas-Whit Ellis

Q

JOSÉ QUINTERO [b.October 15, 1924, Panama City, Panama]. José Quintero, the son of the governor of Panama, graduated from the University of Southern California in 1948. He attended the Goodman Theatre School from 1948 to 1949, but he got his first theatre job when a friend asked him to join a summer stock theatre company she had formed in Woodstock, New York. The group of students had little or no practical experience; the theatre had no seats, and its stage was constructed of enormous boxes that creaked noisily if anyone took more than two steps. Yet during this summer and the next Quintero forged the alliances which would result in the formation of the Circle in the Square Theatre.

Quintero and Ted Mann, who had joined the Woodstock group during the second summer, located an abandoned nightclub at 5 Sheridan Square in Greenwich Village. They subsequently convinced their fellow board members that the space would make an ideal theatre, signed a $1,000 per month lease, appealed to several parents to loan or donate start-up money, and began to produce plays in 1950. The first company was promised sleeping accommodations in the club, use of the communal kitchen, and $10 per week. Because the theatre was originally denied a license from the city, it was unable to charge admission. Instead tickets were distributed in Washington Square Park, and anyone who attended the performance was asked to make a donation. In early spring 1952, Quintero staged a revival of Tennessee Williams's *Summer and Smoke* with his former classmate Geraldine Page. This production made an overnight sensation of Page and catapulted the Circle in the Square into the forefront of the Off-Broadway movement.

Throughout his career Quintero became known for his penetrating, passionate style and was acclaimed a significant interpreter of such playwrights as Brendan

Behan, Tennessee Williams, and Thornton Wilder. His most significant contribution to American theatre, however, lay in his direction of the works of Eugene
O'Neill. In 1956 he decided to direct a revival of *The Iceman Cometh*, but
learned that O'Neill's plays were being withheld from production. He appealed
directly to O'Neill's widow, Carlotta Monterey, who gave her permission because Quintero reminded her of her deceased husband. The revival was arguably
more successful than the original production. Quintero chose an assortment of
actors and nonactors for his cast, but selected Jason Robards to play the pivotal
role of Hickey. Robards became an immediate star, as did Quintero. Praise came
from every quarter, and Mrs. O'Neill subsequently requested that he direct the
American premiere of her husband's most illustrious play, *Long Day's Journey
into Night* (1956). Quintero cast Fredric March and his wife, Florence Eldridge,
as the elder Tyrones, and Jason Robards and Bradford Dillman as Jamie and
Edmund, respectively. Quintero was admonished by some for being too faithful
to O'Neill's directions, thereby depriving the production of his own unique
perspective.

He further enhanced his reputation by establishing Colleen Dewhurst as per-
haps the preeminent O'Neill heroine. They first worked together, along with
George C. Scott, in *Children of Darkness* in 1958. That summer he directed her
and Richard Kiley in *A Moon for the Misbegotten* for the Festival of the Two
Worlds in Spoleto, Italy. In 1974 she won a Tony Award as best actress in his
Broadway revival of *Moon* with Jason Robards.

Not all of Quintero's experiences with O'Neill were critical successes. His
1964 production of *Marco Millions* at Lincoln Center was considered flat and
lifeless. He received his most caustic upbraiding, however, for his direction of
More Stately Mansions in 1967. O'Neill did not want the play produced and
burned what he thought to be all of the drafts and notes, but one draft survived.
Quintero, according to Clive Barnes, adapted the overly long manuscript, but
this fact was not acknowledged in the program and the play was advertised as
"another O'Neill play." Barnes was incensed at this turn of events. He insisted
that the playwright's wishes should have been respected and chastised Quintero
for not claiming responsibility for the unwieldy script.

Throughout his career Quintero's uniqueness as a director stemmed from his
intuitive grasp of characters and situations. In the case of O'Neill he tells of a
spiritual bond with the playwright which transcended understanding and empathy.
During rehearsals he felt that he experienced O'Neill's own personal agony and
that his direction stemmed from this kinship of pain. He also worked very closely
with his actors, encouraging them to make their own discoveries about movement, vocal interpretation, props, and business rather than insisting that they
execute a set of predesigned instructions.

ADDITIONAL PRODUCTIONS: 1954: *Girl on the Via Flaminia* (based on the novel by
Alfred Hayes); 1959: *Camino Real* (Williams), *Our Town*; 1961: *Under Milk Wood*
(Thomas); 1963: *Desire Under the Elms* (O'Neill), *Strange Interlude* (O'Neill); 1964:
Hughie (O'Neill); 1967: *More Stately Mansions* (O'Neill); 1976: *The Skin of Our Teeth*
(Wilder).

SELECTED BIBLIOGRAPHY: Hart, Doris. ''An Historical Analysis of Three New York Productions of Eugene O'Neill's 'Long Day's Journey into Night.' '' Diss. New York U, 1982; McDonough, Edwin J. *Quintero Directs O'Neill*. Chicago: A. Cappella, 1991; Quintero, José. *If You Don't Dance They Beat You*. Boston: Little, Brown and Company, 1974; Rigdon, Walter, ed. *The Biographical Encyclopedia and Who's Who of the American Theatre*. New York: James A. Heineman, 1966.

John H. Houchin

R

SERGEI RADLOV [b. July 18, 1892, Riga; d. October 27, 1958, Riga]. Sergei Radlov's theatrical career was one of the most varied of any Soviet director. Nearly every trend of the modern Russian stage found an expression in his work. At the age of nineteen, Radlov composed poetic dialogues for Nikolai Evreinov* in St. Petersburg. During World War I, he attended classes in commedia at the studio of Vsevolod Meyerhold.* In June 1918, eight months after the Revolution, Radlov organized a mobile troupe that entertained workers and Red Army units. With the backing of the new government, he mounted comic recreations of ancient Greek and Russian farces. In addition, Radlov co-directed several mass spectacles celebrating the Bolshevik victory.

In November 1919, Radlov announced the formation of a new group, the Theatre of Popular Comedy, a company of circus performers, cabaret artists, and actors. It sought to ''Americanize'' old European classics and melodramas from the seventeenth and nineteenth centuries by updating the original dramatic material. Radlov combined the popular entertainment techniques of British music hall, American circus, minstrel shows, vaudeville, and comic film acting into a single, slapstick performance style. Radlov declared that there was a special ''Anglo-American genius'' for the production of a mass culture that unmasked the absurdity and the hectic pace of modern life.

The plot and technique of the Popular Comedy's *The Foster Child* was typical. On the main street of an unnamed Western city, the adopted son of a rich capitalist was handed some crucial documents by a wounded revolutionary. Chased by legions of police across the urban landscape, the boy tumbled over cul-de-sacs and rooftops. In the finale, the cornered young man was pulled up by a rope ladder from a Soviet airplane hidden in the clouds.

In 1922 after disbanding the Popular Comedy, Radlov created a laboratory studio for abstract theatre. His interest in pure movement led him into ballet and opera, where he became Leningrad's leading directorial practitioner at the end of the twenties. While other Soviet directors were adjusting their stylistic approaches to the canons of socialist realism, Radlov's versatility increased, as he became known for his realistic versions of Shakespeare as well as his circus-spectacles and extravagant operas.

In 1930, Radlov began an association with the Moscow GOSET, replacing Aleksei Granovsky* as the artist director of the Yiddish-speaking company. His initial productions that contrasted the wretched lot of pre-revolutionary Jews with their fulfilled lives in Soviet society proved unpopular. Only in 1935 with his celebrated *King Lear* did Radlov find his niche. Starring Solomon Mikhoels, Radlov's *Lear* challenged all the normative interpretations Russian audiences had grown to expect. Short and unattractive, this Lear became brighter in each scene as he learned the "dialectic materialism" of life. Gordon Craig praised Radlov's *Lear* as one of the greatest productions of the twentieth century.

At the Maly Theatre, and his own Leningrad studios, the Young Theatre and the Radlov-State Theatre, Radlov continued producing dynamic versions of *Othello* (1927), *Romeo and Juliet* (1936), and *Hamlet* (1938). An attempt at historical propaganda in 1938, *Key to Berlin*, about the Russian victory over the German King Frederick II, however, was ill-timed, and Radlov soon fell out of favor with the authorities. From 1953 until his death in 1958, Radlov worked in obscurity at two Russian-language theatres in Latvia.

ADDITIONAL PRODUCTIONS: 1920: *The Corpse's Bride*, *Adopted Son*; 1923: *Hinkemann*; 1927: *Othello*; 1934, 1936: *Romeo and Juliet*.

SELECTED BIBLIOGRAPHY: Gordon, Mel. "Program of the Minor Leftists in the Soviet Theatre." Diss. New York U, 1981; Gordon, Mel. "Radlov's Theatre of Popular Comedy." *The Drama Review* 19 (December 1975): 113–16; Macleod, Joseph. *The New Soviet Theatre*. London: George Allen and Unwin, 1943; Radlov, Sergei. "On the Pure Elements of the Actor's Art" (1923). *The Drama Review* 19 (December 1975): 117–23.

Mel Gordon

ALFRED RADOK [b. December 17, 1914, Koloděje nad Lužnici, Bohemia, Czechoslovakia; d. April 22, 1976, Vienna, Austria]. Considered by many to have been Czechoslovakia's most imaginative, innately talented postwar director, Radok had a varied career marked by several periods of exile as well as notable success. With no formal theatre training or even university education, Radok had the good fortune to work as the assistant of E. F. Burian* from 1939 until the wartime close of Burian's theatre in 1941. After some theatre work in the provinces and internment at a labor camp until the end of the war, Radok became part of a youthful group (which included designer Josef Svoboda and composer-director Vaclav Kašlík) that took over the large, well-equipped former German theatre in Prague.

For almost three years, their new company produced a series of dramas and operas that began to outshine the work of the National Theatre itself, with Radok's untraditional staging of *The Merry Widow* (1945), *The Tales of Hoffmann* (1946), and *Rigoletto* (1947), all designed by Svoboda, providing some of the most provocative productions. All revealed Radok's sense of theatre as conscious ceremony and his instinctive flair for *total* staging that relied heavily on a metaphoric, unconventional juxtaposition of production elements. For *The Tales of Hoffmann*, traditional painted scenery was placed in relation to modernistic skeletal structures; while for *Rigoletto*, a theatre in a theatre was reproduced by erecting a nineteenth-century proscenium stage and rotating it to reveal its backstage areas and personnel during the course of the opera itself.

In 1948, the theatre was absorbed by the National Theatre, and Radok experienced the first of his three tenures there. Although he had a major success with *The Little Foxes* (1948), his essentially apolitical nature and his tactical ineptness in the heavily politicized environment of the new socialist regime led to his being fired, and for some four years (1950–54) he worked in provincial and touring theatres. His most important production during this period was *The Eleventh Commandment* (1950), his heavily edited adaptation of a nineteenth-century farce by F. Samberk which became the prototype of the subsequent *laterna magika* form of staging. In the meantime, Radok also directed several full-length films.

A new management took Radok back into the National Theatre in 1954, where he remained until 1959. During these years he did some of his most striking work, most notably in *The Entertainer* (1957), *Today the Sun Still Sets on Atlantida* (1956), and *The Golden Carriage* (1957), all revealing not only his maturing talents, but also his concern with indirectly reflecting relevant social and ethical issues. During this time, still working closely with Svoboda, Radok also developed the *laterna magika* production form, a technically complex, artistically striking integration of live stage action with filmed images, frequently of performers who interacted with filmed images of themselves. Although it had its roots in E. F. Burian's Theatergraph system, *laterna magika* was essentially a sophisticated extension of Radok's penchant for the mutual interplay of realistic, but startlingly contrasting elements, which created a new theatrical reality and provided disturbing insights into human, social behavior. *Laterna magika* became the hit of the Czechoslovak exposition at the Brussels Expo '58, and Radok's future seemed secure. Political and economic considerations, however, led to *laterna magika*'s becoming primarily a public relations entertainment for Czech tourism, and Radok was again out of the National Theatre.

From 1962 to 1964, Radok worked with Prague's Municipal Theatres, where he staged perhaps his most memorable production, *The Game of Love* (R. Rolland, 1964, designed by Ladislav Vychodil). In it, Radok underscored the social clash between aristocracy and the masses by placing all the action in a bear pit, the rough earth of which contained the aristocrats, with the "people" contemptuously observing and harassing them from the benches rising behind the walled enclosure.

Radok's third tenure in the National Theatre began in 1965. Among his final works at the National Theatre was his own dramatization of Maxim Gorky's novel *The Last Ones* (1966), in which he innovatively employed the basic *laterna magika* techniques to heighten the inner ambiguities and ironic implications inherent in Gorky's work. In 1968, Radok was named National Artist, and it was rumored that he was to become the next head of drama at the National Theatre. This phase of his career ended abruptly in August 1968, when he fled the country immediately after the Warsaw pact invasion, thus becoming cut off from his creative roots. He found welcome in Sweden's Göteborg theatre, where he worked until his death.

ADDITIONAL PRODUCTIONS: 1943: *Before Sunset* (G. Hauptmann); 1963: *Marriage* (N. Gogol); 1967: *The House of Bernarda Alba*; 1968: *The Misanthrope* (in Göteborg, Sweden); 1970: *The Clown* (H. Boll, in Dusseldorf; 1972: *Biedermann and the Firebugs* (in Göteborg); 1974: *Heartbreak House* (in Göteborg); 1976: *The Emigrants* (S. Mrożek, in Bergan, Norway).

SELECTED BIBLIOGRAPHY: Burian, Jarka. "Alfred Radok's Contribution to Post-War Czech Theatre." *Theatre Survey* 22 (November 1981): 213–28; Havel, Václav. "Radokova Práce S Herci" [Radok's Work with the Actor]. *Divadlo* (May 1963): 56ff.; Liehm, Antonin. "Alfred Radok." *International Journal of Politics* 3 (Summer 1973): 23–39; Radok, Alfred. "Divadelní Novověk" [The New Age of Theatre]. *Divadlo* November 1962: 27–33.

Jarka M. Burian

FRANCA RAME [b. July 18, 1929, Parablago, Milan, Italy]. A member of a famous northern Italian family of strolling players whose specialty was eighteenth-century drama, and married in 1954 to Dario Fo,* Franca Rame has nonetheless established her own brand of Italian theatre. She is known throughout Italy and internationally as the leading dramatic actress and comedienne of the Fo-Rame production team during its various turbulent stages. To theatre *cognoscenti*, however, she is also known, not only as Fo's co-director and often, co-author, but also as the feminist voice in their socially and politically oriented theatre. Rame's often monologistic parodies reveal contemporary, yet universal situations in which powerless, individually compelling female characters are trapped either in domestic prisons or in violent situations with overpowering male aggressors. Although many of her protagonists do not succeed in escaping either the domestic treadmill or actual physical assault, Rame's theatrical voice is directed toward eliminating, through clear-eyed and graphic awareness, such traps for women in the future.

ADDITIONAL PRODUCTIONS: **Representative Acting Roles**: 1959: *Archangels Don't Play Pinball*; 1963: *Isabella*; 1974: *We Won't Pay! We Won't Pay!* **Representative Fo-Rame Productions:** 1981: *Female Parts* (London, British version of *Tutta casa, letto e chiesa*); 1986: *Tutta casa, letto e chiesa* (Off-Broadway); 1987: *Open Couple* (San Francisco).

SELECTED BIBLIOGRAPHY: *Dario Fo and Franca Rame Theatre Workshops at Riverside Studios* (Including texts of *Waking Up*, *I Don't Move*, *I Don't Scream*, *My Voice Is Gone* and *The Mother*). London: Red Notes, 1983; Rame, Franca, and Dario Fo. *Orgasmo Adulto Escapes from the Zoo*. New York: Broadway Play Publishing, 1985.

Mimi Gisolfi D'Aponte

MAX REINHARDT [b. Max Goldmann, September 9, 1873, Baden, Austria; d. October 31, 1943, New York, New York]. Few directors in the history of the theatre have aroused more public debate than Max Reinhardt. To some, he was little more than a set decorator; a director so eclectic in his staging and choice of scripts that he was accused of having no directorial style whatsoever; an artist who paled in significance when compared to the younger, more politically active generation of Germans that followed. To others, however, Reinhardt was a pivotal figure in the evolution of the modern concept of a theatrical director; an artist who inspired a new generation of actors, directors, and designers; and a champion of new theatrical currents in Europe at the beginning of the twentieth century.

Internationally renowned for his highly "visual" directing style and for mounting massive spectacles like Karl Vollmoeller's *The Miracle* (1911) and Hugo von Hofmannsthal's adaptation of *Everyman* (1911, 1920), Reinhardt was equally recognized by his own profession as an innovator in the minimalist staging of symbolist and expressionist scripts, and as an "actor's director" who believed that the theatre was primarily an actor's medium and who respected the individuality of each actor who worked with him.

Reinhardt, however, may be best remembered for his experimentation with theatrical space and his commitment to finding the "right" theatre for each play he directed. As early as 1901, Reinhardt postulated that the serious director should have three distinct theatres at his disposal: an intimate house for "chamber plays"; a second space for classical works; and a festival theatre for "great art of monumental effects" (*Reinhardt: Schriften*, 67). In the same year that he wrote this manifesto, Reinhardt acquired his first theatres—the cabarets Die Brille (The Spectacles) and Schall und Rauch (Sound and Smoke)—and began his directing career in space not much larger than a hotel room. In these theatres and his famous Kammerspiele (Chamber Theatre) Reinhardt produced controversial works such as Oscar Wilde's *Salomé* (1903) and Frank Wedekind's *Spring's Awakening* (1906), experimented with a directing style that transcended naturalism, and produced an expressionistic version of Henrik Ibsen's *Ghosts* (1906) which critics described as having created a world of "nightmare and depth psychology." Working in the rebuilt Schall und Rauch, which had been renamed the Kleines Theater (Little Theatre) in 1902, and the Kammerspiele, Reinhardt experienced the vitality of an actor-audience relationship created in an intimate space and became convinced of the need to maintain this relationship, even when working on a large scale.

In his work in the so-called classical proscenium theatres, the Neues Theater am Schiffbauerdamm (1903–5) and Berlin's prestigious Deutsches Theater, Reinhardt created many of the technical innovations that contributed to his fame. During this phase of his career, he experimented with the use of the revolving stage, both as a device to change scenery quickly and as a strong theatrical effect in itself; the creation of atmosphere through color; the employment of the sky-dome to create the illusion of infinite depth; and the replacement of flat scenery by three-dimensional set pieces. These and other scenic innovations were utilized in *A Midsummer Night's Dream* (1905), *The Merchant of Venice* (1905), *The Robbers* (1908), and *Faust, Part I* (1909), productions which critics regard as having been among the best of Reinhardt's career.

Much of Reinhardt's international reputation in his own time, however, resulted from the massive spectacles which involved hundreds of performers and were mounted in spaces measured, not in terms of square feet, but in acres. Beginning with *Oedipus Rex* in 1910, Reinhardt moved productions into vast arenas: his austere, minimalist *Oedipus* was staged in a Munich exhibition hall and later transferred to Berlin's Zirkus Schumann; *Everyman* opened at the Zirkus Schumann in December 1911; and the most spectacular production of all, *The Miracle*, was mounted in London's mammoth Olympia Exhibition Hall (which was transformed into a cathedral), where it was witnessed by 30,000 spectators at each performance. Inspired by these attempts, in 1919 Reinhardt converted the Zirkus Schumann into the Grosses Schauspielhaus, or the Great Spectacle House, and the following year he further enlarged the scope of theatre by staging an open-air *Everyman* in Cathedral Square in Salzburg. The August 22, 1920, opening of *Everyman* inaugurated the Salzburg Festival, which was expanded in 1922 with the addition of Reinhardt's staging of *The Great Theatre of the World*, an adaptation of Calderón's *El gran teatro del mundo* by Hugo von Hofmannsthal.

In addition to his technical innovations and his experiments with theatrical space, Reinhardt's contributions to the theatre include championing the expressionist August Strindberg, the neo-romantic Hugo von Hofmannsthal, the impressionist Anton Chekhov, the symbolist Maurice Maeterlinck, the proto-expressionists Frank Wedekind and Georg Büchner, and the international rebels Bernard Shaw and Oscar Wilde; reinterpretation of the classics of Gotthold Lessing, Johann von Goethe, and Friedrich Schiller, which considerably strengthened the German tradition of theatre; and the affirmation of the theories of Richard Wagner, Adolphe Appia, and Gordon Craig. A complete man of the theatre, Reinhardt directed opera, operetta, and movies, the most notable of his films being *A Midsummer Night's Dream* (1935) featuring Olivia de Havilland as Hermia, Mickey Rooney as Puck, and James Cagney as Bottom the Weaver.

Unable to return to Germany during World War II, Reinhardt attempted to establish an "artistic" theatre in America, but his few attempts (*Rosalinda*, 1942, and *Sons and Soldiers*, 1943) were critical and commercial failures. Reinhardt died in New York in 1943, aged seventy.

ADDITIONAL PRODUCTIONS: 1900: *Love's Comedy* (Ibsen); 1902: *Earth Spirit* (Wedekind); 1903: *The Lower Depths, Pelléas and Mélisande*; 1904: *Miss Julie, Sister Beatrice* (Maeterlinck), *Electra* (von Hofmannsthal); 1905: *Rosmersholm*; 1906: *Man and Superman, Caesar and Cleopatra*; 1910: *Sumurun* (Freksa); 1911: *Der Rosenkavalier* (Strauss), the *Oresteia*; 1912: *The Dance of Death, Venetian Night* (Vollmoeller); 1913–14: Shakespeare Cycle: *A Midsummer Night's Dream, Much Ado about Nothing, The Merchant of Venice, Hamlet, King Lear, Romeo and Juliet, Henry IV, Twelfth Night, Othello*; 1916: *Macbeth, The Ghost Sonata, Danton's Death*; 1917: *The Beggar* (Sorge), *From Morn to Midnight*; 1918: *The Son* (Hasenclever); 1921: *A Dream Play, Woyzeck*; 1924: *Six Characters in Search of an Author, Servant of Two Masters*; 1935: *The Merchant of Yonkers*.

SELECTED BIBLIOGRAPHY: Braun, Edward. "Max Reinhardt in Germany and Austria." *The Director and the Stage: From Naturalism to Grotowski*. New York: Holmes and Meier, 1982; Carter, Huntly. *The Theatre of Max Reinhardt*. New York: Mitchell Kennerley, 1914; Esslin, Martin. "Max Reinhardt, High Priest of Theatricality." *The Drama Review* 21 (June 1977): 3–24; Fetting, Hugo, ed. *Max Reinhardt Schriften: Briefe, Reden, Aufsatze, Interviews, Gesprache, Auszuge aus Regiebuchern*. Berlin: Henschelverlag, 1974; Reinhardt, Gottfried. *The Genius: A Memoir of Max Reinhardt*. New York: Knopf, 1979; Sayler, Oliver M., ed. *Max Reinhardt and His Theatre*. New York: Brentano's, 1924; Styan, J. L. *Max Reinhardt*. Cambridge: Cambridge University Press, 1982; Volbach, Walther R. "Memoirs of Max Reinhardt's Theatres 1920–1922." *Theatre Survey* 13 (Fall 1972): 1–83; Wellwarth, George E., and Alfred G. Brooks, eds.; *Max Reinhardt 1873–1973: A Centennial Festschrift*. Binghampton, NY: Max Reinhardt Archive, 1973.

John W. Frick

LLOYD (GEORGE) RICHARDS [b. circa 1922, Toronto, Canada]. To Lloyd Richards, creation and education go hand in hand. Best known for directing realistic commercial plays dealing with social issues of concern to black Americans, Richards is also a prominent theatre educator who has directed and taught at several important universities.

The son of a follower of the black nationalist leader Marcus Garvey, Richards was raised and educated in Detroit. After serving in the air force during World War II and studying theatre at Wayne University (now Wayne State), he became an announcer and disk jockey on Detroit radio. He came to New York in 1948, and began acting on radio, television, Off-Broadway, and occasionally on Broadway. His acting received consistently strong reviews, but probably because he is black, he acted only sporadically, and often had to support himself with odd jobs.

Beginning in the early 1950s, Richards spent ten years as the assistant director of the Paul Mann Actor's Studio. Mann and Richards encouraged their students to combine the internal, emotional approach of Konstantin Stanislavsky* (in his early career) and Lee Strasberg* with the external, intellectual approach adopted by the older Stanislavsky and Stella Adler. Richards's emphasis on actors has been a notable feature of his work ever since.

In the mid–1950s, Richards began to concentrate on directing. In 1959, he directed his first Broadway play, the original production of Lorraine Hansberry's *A Raisin in the Sun*, starring Sidney Poitier and Claudia McNeil. Almost immediately acclaimed as a classic by both critics and audiences, the play won the New York Drama Critics Circle Award, and ran for over a year. Richards directed a second production in London, where it was greeted with equal enthusiasm.

Richards worked steadily after *Raisin*. With Joseph Stefano's *The Committeeman* (1960) on CBS, he became the first black director of a television drama, and has worked frequently in television ever since. On Broadway, he directed the Cheryl Crawford production of *The Long Dream* (Ketti Fring's adaptation of Richard Wright's novel, 1962), Cyril Schocken's *The Moon Besieged* (1963), *I Had a Ball* (book by Jerome Chodorov, music and lyrics by Jack Lawrence and Stan Freeman, 1964), and a musical version of Marjorie Kinnan Rawlings's *The Yearling* (1965). Off-Broadway, he directed John O. Killens's *Lower Than Angels* (1965), Ronald Milner's *Who's Got His Own* (1966), and Rene Marques's *The Ox Cart* (1966). In 1966, he began directing plays in development at the Eugene O'Neill Theatre Center.

Richards stopped teaching with Paul Mann in 1962, but in the mid–1960s he began teaching for the fine arts programs of New York University and Boston University, where he also directed, and in the late 1960s, he taught at the Negro Ensemble Company. In 1968, he was elected president of the Theatre Development Fund, and the Eugene O'Neill Theatre Center named him artistic director of the National Playwright's Conference, a position he still holds.

In the 1970s, Richards's only Broadway production was *Paul Robeson* (by Phillip Hayes Dean, 1978), with James Earl Jones. Off-Broadway, his productions included *The Past Is the Past* and *Going Through Changes* (Richard Wesley, 1973), and *The Lion and the Jewel* (1977). During this period, he also taught and directed at Hunter College's Department of Theatre and Film, and was the head of actor training at New York University's School of the Arts. In the late 1970s, he became co-chair of the Theatre Panel for the National Endowment for the Arts.

In 1979, Richards was selected to succeed Robert Brustein as dean of the Yale School of Drama and artistic director of the Yale Repertory Theatre. At the time, some complained that his appointment was an attempt to "deprofessionalize" Yale's program, though in 1990 Brustein himself would accuse Richards of having sold the program out to commercial producers. Beginning in the early 1980s, Richards worked with commercial producers to bring to Broadway his Yale Rep productions of August Wilson's *Ma Rainey's Black Bottom* (1984), *Fences* (1987), *Joe Turner's Come and Gone* (1988), *The Piano Lesson* (1991), and *Two Trains Running* (1992). Richards won the 1987 Tony Award as Best Director for *Fences*.

Richards retired from Yale in 1991, but remains active as a director and teacher. "One may learn by sitting down and copying the masters," he once told the *New York Times* (11 January 1981), "but unless one develops one's own way of seeing, and unless one can transmit that to others, one hasn't attained the status of an artist, as distinct from a craftsman."

ADDITIONAL PRODUCTIONS: 1962: *The Crucible*; 1965: *The Amen Corner* (Baldwin); 1965: *The Desperate Hours* (Hayes), 1967: *That's the Game Jack*. **O'Neill Theatre Center**: 1966–68: *Rainless Sky*, *Bedford Forest*, *A Man around the House*, *Just before Morning*, *Valentine's Day*; 1973: *Richard III*, *The Rose Tattoo*; 1976: *The Sign in Sidney Brustein's Window* (Hansberry); 1978: *Night Must Fall* (Emlyn Williams). **Yale Repertory Theatre**: 1980: *Timon of Athens*; 1981: *Uncle Vanya*, *Hedda Gabler*; 1982: *A Doll's House*, *Johnny Bull* (Kathleen Betsko); 1983: *A Touch of the Poet*. **Television:** "Miss Black America" (1960–70); selected episodes of "You Are There" (1970–72), "ABC Wide World of Entertainment" (1973), "Visions" (1976), "Vision" (1977), "Roots: The Next Generation" (1979), and "Bill Moyers' Journal" (1979), "Paul Robeson" (1979), "Medal of Honor Rag" (1982).

SELECTED BIBLIOGRAPHY: Bartow, Arthur. *The Director's Voice: Twenty-One Interviews*. New York: Theatre Communications Group, 1988: 255–68; *Contemporary Theatre, Film, and Television*. Vol. 1. Detroit, MI: Gale Research Press, 1984; Freedman, Samuel G. "Leaving His Imprint on Broadway." *New York Times Magazine* 22 November 1987; *Marquis Who's Who*. 45th ed.; Pace, Eric. "Lloyd Richards Is Launching New Playwrights with a Winterfest at Yale." *New York Times* 11 January 1981: 5, 20; Clippings file on Lloyd Richards, The Billy Rose Theatre Collection, The New York Public Library for the Performing Arts.

Paul Nadler

JEROME ROBBINS [b. Jerome Rabinowitz, October 11, 1918, New York, New York]. Although interested in dance while growing up, Robbins did not seriously pursue a career in the performing arts until 1937, when he left New York University to study at the Sandor-Sorel School. He subsequently spent his summers performing and choreographing at a Poconos resort and eventually obtained Broadway chorus jobs. It was after working on *Keep Off the Grass* with choreographer George Balanchine that Robbins abandoned Broadway to perform classical works with Ballet Theatre (now American Ballet Theatre [ABT]).

Robbins's early style was described as being clear and disciplined with a flair for "character," and drew the attention of choreographers such as Balanchine, Agnes de Mille, and Mikhail Fokine. Although Robbins was often a featured performer, he was uncomfortable with the Ballet Russe style that dominated the company. His first choreographic piece for ABT broke from this artistic vein and set a new precedent for American classical dance. Performed to a score by Leonard Bernstein, *Fancy Free* (1944) was a timely ballet about three American sailors on leave in New York City. It was so well received that within a few months the half-hour ballet had opened on Broadway as the full-length musical *On the Town* (1944) with book by Comden and Green. The dance element of the show remained the focus, and for the first time, a program contained the credit, "Conceived and Choreographed by. . . . "

Robbins remained active and was equally respected by both the Broadway and classical dance communities. Between 1947 and 1949, he was invited by Balanchine to serve as associate artistic director of the New York City Ballet, joined George Abbott* as co-director of *Look Ma, I'm Dancing*, and won a Tony Award for the choreography of *High Button Shoes* (1947), which included the legendary Mack Sennett–Keystone Kop number "On a Sunday by the Sea." He was truly an inhabitant of two artistic worlds and, as such, was often given free rein on projects. He insisted on perfection, even at the expense of entire companies being brought to tears, and his manner was harsh, but his genius was never questioned.

Robbins worked at a time when, thanks to the pioneer work of Agnes de Mille, the artistic quality of musical theatre dance was being viewed with a new credibility. Through Robbins's influence, dance numbers became more closely tied to the book, often evolving into scenes of their own and serving to introduce characters and reveal plot. "The March of the Siamese Children" and "The Small House of Uncle Thomas," for example, were significant in the dramatic development of *The King and I* (1951). In order that dance numbers tell a story, Robbins required composers to create original themes for the dances, rather than simply arranging variations on song melodies.

Robbins usually maintained artistic *freedom* on his projects, but beginning with *Peter Pan* in 1954, he would have artistic *control*, as Robbins was credited with both the show's direction and choreography. By 1957, the program for *West Side Story* stated that the show had been "Conceived, Directed and Choreographed by" Robbins.

West Side Story, which was based on *Romeo and Juliet* and drew attention to unrest in the Puerto Rican community, is considered the progenitor of the *concept musical*, and *style* was its through-line. Choreography tied the show together, and the physical characterizations present in the nonmusical scenes were emotionally heightened during the dances. Transitions from one scene to another were staged as part of the dramatic action. The program did not list a chorus of singers or dancers, but rather identified each cast member by character name. *West Side Story* is hailed as Robbins's greatest contribution to musical theatre. He won a Tony Award for choreography, but *The Music Man*, not *West Side Story*, was chosen the best show of the season.

Between 1965 and 1968 Robbins worked on a project called the American Theatre Laboratory that was supported by a grant from the National Endowment for the Arts. He continued working in theatre (*Gypsy* in 1959; *Fiddler on the Roof* in 1964) and ran his own dance company, Ballets: USA, for a short period. In 1989, *Jerome Robbins' Broadway* opened at the Imperial Theatre in New York. The show was a presentation of selected, reconstructed pieces from his Broadway shows. While this alone would seem tribute enough to his legacy, a year later the New York City Ballet staged a two-week festival featuring thirty of his ballets.

ADDITIONAL PRODUCTIONS: 1945: *Million Dollar Baby* (choreographer); 1950: *Call Me Madam* (choreographer); 1956: *Bells Are Ringing*.

SELECTED BIBLIOGRAPHY: Challender, James Winston. "The Function of the Choreographer in the Development of the Conceptual Musical: An Examination of the Work
of Jerome Robbins, Bob Fosse, and Michael Bennett on Broadway between 1944 and
1981." Diss. Florida State U, 1986; Gottfried, Martin. *Broadway Musicals.* New York:
Harry N. Abrams, 1979; Hering, Doris. *"Jerome Robbins' Broadway*: Jerry's Legacy."
Dance Magazine August 1990: 44–51; Kisselgoff, Anna. "Jerome Robbins, a Creator
from Head to Foot." *New York Times Bibliographical Service* June 1990: 531–33; Kroll,
Jack." Dancing through Life," *Newsweek* 6 March 1989: 56; Mandelbaum, Ken. "Jerome
Robbins: A Life in the Theater." *Theater Week* 27 February–5 March, 1989: 11–29;
Schlundt, Christine. "Dance in the Musical Theater: Jerome Robbins and His Peers,
1934–1965." *Garland Reference Library of the Humanities.* Vol. 1213 (1989).

Colleen Kelly

LUCA RONCONI [b. March 8, 1933, Sousse, Tunisia]. After a decade as an
actor, Ronconi turned to directing in 1963 and has become one of Italy's most
innovative and controversial directors of drama and opera. In Ronconi's unique
and influential career in the theatre, his work has been consistently distinguished
by an emphasis on spectacle, nonrealistic acting styles, audience participation,
and interpretive and unconventional use of text, space, and scene design. Ronconi
makes a careful study of the text in order to discover a literary work's essence,
a subtext which is then brought to life through the design of the performing
space and scenic elements. Often he uses only certain scenes and characters from
the original text or combines and reinvents texts. Each of his impressionistic
and iconoclastic readings of often little-known or infrequently produced classic
dramas and operas offers singular demonstrations of the breadth of Ronconi's
artistic imagination.

Ronconi quickly established an international reputation for his bold approach
to the classics with *Orlando Furioso* (Ariosto, adapted by E. Sanguinetti, 1969;
tour of Europe and the United States, 1970; television version, 1975). *Orlando*
featured a cast of fifty-five performers, sheet metal horses and other scenic
machines, movable platform stages, and two fixed stages at either end of a huge
playing field. Simultaneously festival and spectacle, *Orlando Furioso* relied upon
the carefully choreographed movements of its actors and multiple stages in the
specially structured playing space to elicit audience participation and surprise,
elements and effects Ronconi has continued to emphasize. In *Orlando* and later
dramatic and operatic productions, spectators mingled with actors in outdoor,
specially designed or "found" spaces and were forced to choose which characters
and scenes to follow, thus structuring their own playgoing experience in direct
interaction with text and actors.

Ronconi has taught acting at his alma mater, Rome's National Academy of
Dramatic Art, at Denmark's Odin Theatre, and at the Theatre Laboratory he
founded in Prato in 1976. Since 1971, Ronconi has headed the theatre and music
divisions of the Venice Biennial and in 1989 became artistic director of Turin's
resident theatre.

ADDITIONAL PRODUCTIONS: 1963: *The Good Wife* (Goldoni); 1966: *The Changeling* (Middleton); 1970: *The Revenger's Tragedy* (Tourneur); 1971: *XX* (Rodolfo Juan Wilcock); 1972: *The Oresteia*; 1973: *The Wild Duck, Medea*; 1975: *Utopia*, (Aristophanes); 1977–79: *The Bacchants, The Tower* (von Hofmannsthal), *Calderón* (Pier Paolo Pasolini, while director of the Prato Theatre Laboratory); 1983: *A Dream Play*; 1984: *St. Joan, La due commedie in commedia* (Giovan Battista Andreini); 1985: *Phèdre* (Racine); 1986: *La serva amorosa* (Goldoni); 1987: *The Merchant of Venice*; 1988: *Mirra* (Vittorio Alfieri); 1989–90: *The Three Sisters, Strange Interlude, The Last Days of Mankind* (Karl Kraus). **Opera**: Forty productions in Italy, France, and Germany, including works by Wagner, Verdi, Rossini, Gluck, Mozart, and Puccini; 1974: *Die Walküre*; 1975: *Faust, Il barbiere di Siviglia*; 1977: *Nabucco, Don Carlo, Trovatore*; 1979: *Das Rheingold*; 1980: *Macbeth*; 1982: *Manon Lescaut, Les Troyens, Ernani*; 1984: *Un ballo in maschera*; 1985: *L'Orfeo, Il viaggio a Reims, Aida*; 1986: *I vespri siciliani*; 1991: *Ricciardo a Zoraida* (Rossini). SELECTED BIBLIOGRAPHY: Dossena, Angelo, ed. *Luca Ronconi: inventare l'opera; L'Orfeo, Il viaggio a Reims, Aida, tre opere d'occasione alla Scala*. Milan: Ubulibri, 1986; Giammusso, Maurizio. *La fabbrica degli attori-L'accademia nazionale d'arte drammatica storia di cinquant'anni*. Rome: Presidenza de Consigio dei Ministri, 1990; Milanese, Cesare. *Luca Ronconi e la realta del teatro*. Milan: Feltrinelli, 1973; Quadri, Franco. *I rito perduto*. Turin: Einaudi, 1972; Quadri, Franco. "Luca Ronconi." *The Drama Review* 21 (June 1977): 103–18; Quadri, Franco. "Luca Ronconi's *XX*." *The Drama Review* 15 (Fall 1971): 9–28; Quadri, Franco. "Le moment du Bilan." *Theatre en europe* 15 (October 1987): 3–10; Quadri, Franco. "Orlando Furioso." *The Drama Review* 14 (Fall 1970): 116–24.

Jana O'Keefe Bazzoni

JEAN-PIERRE RONFARD [b. 1929, France]. Actor, director, company leader, author, and professor, Jean-Pierre Ronfard is one of the most important men in Quebec's theatre. Before settling there in 1960, he traveled in Algeria, Greece, Portugal, and Austria. In Montreal, he chaired the French department at the École national de théâtre du Canada (National Theater School of Canada) (1960–65), was secretary general of the Théâtre du Nouveau Monde (1967–70), and cofounded the Théâtre Expérimental de Montréal in 1975 with Robert Claing, Robert Gravel, and Pol Pelletier. In 1979, this group split to form the Théâtre Expérimental des Femmes (Women's Experimental Theater) and the Nouveau Théâtre Expérimental (New Experimental Theater). From 1981 on, the latter occupied an old firehouse converted into a theatrical space, L'Espace Libre (Free Space), with the Gilles Maheu* troupe Carbone 14 and Jean Asselin's Omnibus.

Ronfard wrote plays for the Nouveau Théâtre Expérimental, but he also directed and performed in numerous self-run productions that questioned the whole of theatrical language: they questioned the supremacy of the dramatic text, with its linear plot, well-constructed characters, and dialogue; they explored space (*Le Titanic* was performed in a junkyard, 1985); they probed the symbolic power of objects, sometimes to the point of reconsidering the necessity of the actor. In *Les Objets parlent* (1986), there were no actors and the audience—"objects" themselves moving within the space—observed tableaus where, thanks to light and a soundtrack, the objects began to "narrate" something. In 1993, Ronfard proposed *Corps à corps* and *Violoncelle et voix*, two "dialogues" between theatre and the martial arts in the former, and between theater, voice and music in the latter. Ronfard's greatest desire is to push theatre to its limits, to study all its rules, and to take nothing for granted. Without pretension, his productions always succeed in surprising the audience while providing the intrinsic pleasures of the theatre, those of the heart, the spirit, and the senses.

An enormously cultured man, convinced of the importance of understanding the past, while not sinking into ritual, Ronfard has frequently staged classic texts. In addition to performing classical authors including Euripides (*Le Cyclope*, 1985, *Médée*, in a translation by Marie Cardinal, 1986), he also presented adaptations: Machiavelli's *La Mandragore* (1982), *Les Mille et une nuits* (1984), and Cervantes' *Don Quichotte* (1977); he rewrote, in a grotesque style, a *Lear*, from Shakespeare (1977), and composed a production based on the character of *Falstaff* (1990). He created *Le Grand Théâtre du monde*, a play about the Spanish Golden Age, in 1989. Inviting the public to what he sometimes called "ateliers" (studios), Ronfard offered them finished productions, often subtly accented, rich in meaning, purely styled, and with a probing presentation: *Autour de Phèdre* (1989), and *La Voix d'Orphée* (1990).

As a director, Ronfard has also worked in institutional settings, always choosing to challenge the public, sometimes more conservative than that of the Théâtre Expérimental, with plays by Jarry, Ionesco, Schéhadé, and some baroque Quebec authors including Réjean Ducharme (*Ha ha!...*) and Claude Gauvreau (*Les Oranges sont vertes*).

But Ronfard's name is above all associated with the famous epic lasting fifteen hours, *Vie et mort du Roi Boiteux*, which he wrote and directed in 1982. Inspired by Shakespeare and Racine as well as Quebec authors, by mythology as well as popular culture, this extended fresco explores human passions. Love, betrayal, power, envy, and other universal themes are found here in a multilevel tale in which children, in the courtyard of their lodgings in Montreal, amuse themselves by playing the roles of great heroes, brought to life in the court of a cruel king. The carnival-like writing and aesthetic of this production were highly effective in questioning Western values, exploring desires and follies, while developing a healthy humor. Entirely constructed around the image of division, this parody-parable juxtaposes that which is usually excluded: the popular and the noble, the everyday and the marvelous, the comic and the serious.

ADDITIONAL PRODUCTIONS: 1979: *Inceste*; 1984: *La Californie*; 1989: *Mao Tsé Toung ou Soirée de musique au consultat*.

SELECTED BIBLIOGRAPHY: Plays by Ronfard, published by Editions Leméac (Montreal): *Vie et morte du Roi Boiteux*. 2 vols. 1981; *La Mandragore*, 1982; *Les Mille et une nuits*, 1985; *Le Titanic*, 1986; for information on *Vie et morte du Roi Boiteux*, see LaPointe, Gilles. "*Vie et Mort du Roi Boiteux* de Jean-Pierre Ronfard." *Canadian Drama* 9 (Fall 1983): 220–25; "A la question: Jean-Pierre Ronfard." *Cahiers du théâtre Jeu* 3 (1976): 62–69; "Le démon et le cuisinier/notes en vrac." *Cahiers du théâtre Jeu* 25 (1982): 25–39; "Vous dites expérimental?" and "Les mots s'usent. Usage. Usure." *Cahiers du théâtre Jeu* 52 (1989):45–50, 113–15; Leblanc, Alonzo. "Ronfard: dérive organisée et conflit des cultures." *Etudes litteraires—Tendances actuelles de théâtre québecois* 18:3 (1985): 123–141; Vigeant, Louise. *La Lecture de spectacle théâtral.* Laval; Mondia, 1989; In English: Vigeant, Louise. "Jean Pierre Ronfard: (Im)Pure Theatre." *Canadian Theatre Review* 50 (1987): 14–19.

Louise Vigeant

HENRI RONSE [b. May 10, 1946, Brussels, Belgium]. With an extensive knowledge of literature and the arts as well as theatre, Henri Ronse created, first at his Théâtre Oblique in Paris (1971–80) then at Le Nouveau Théâtre de Belgique in Brussels (1980 on), a cultural center housing not only plays but art exhibitions, dance and musical performances, and critical seminars. Although he has directed for major companies in France, Switzerland, and Belgium, Ronse prefers to maintain his own theatre, where he can study authors (August Strindberg; Franz Kafka; contemporary Greek poets; and Thomas Bernhard, whom he introduced to the French-speaking theatre) in depth through mounting cycles of their work. An antirealist, Ronse translates his subtle and profound insights into a text into sumptuous, neo-baroque stage imagery. His productions of Belgian authors—tinged with mystery, anguish, and a fascination with death—proved the contemporary stageworthiness of Maurice Maeterlinck, Fernand Crommelynck, and Paul Willems.

At his grandmother's home in Ostend, filled with the grotesque carnival imagery of James Ensor, Ronse was initiated into Belgian art. He studied philosophy and literature at Brussels University, and became friends with Belgian surrealists Marcel Lecomte and René Magritte, who submitted Ronse's critical writings to *La Nouvelle Revue Française.* In 1966, Ronse moved to Paris, where he worked as a literary journalist, radio director, and editor for Gallimard. He founded the literary review *Obliques* (1970), followed by Le Théâtre Oblique (1971). Attracting the attention of Pierre Dux, director of the Comédie Française, Ronse staged *The Pelican* (1973), *The Ghost Sonata* (1975), and *Rodogone* (1975) for the Odéon. *Rodogone* also earned Ronse admiring New York reviews at the American Place Theatre (1976). Ronse made his debut at the Théâtre National de Belgique with *Pélleas et Mélisande* (1976), and at the Paris Opera with Jean Philippe Rameau's *Platée* (1977) and the Comédie de Genève with Frank Wedekind's *Lulu* (1977). Named director of the Festival d'Anjou in 1978, Ronse made it a multidisciplinary event, created the parallel Festival de la Tragédie Française, and tripled the audience in three years. In spite of his critical successes, however, Ronse was plagued with subsidy problems. In 1980, he resigned from the Festival and moved his operations to Brussels, founding the Nouveau Théâtre de Belgique.

As a director, Ronse is noted for reanimating texts "strangled" by naturalistic treatment. Due to his keen musical sense and taste for lavish visualization, his spectacles are often called "operas." His designers include contemporary painters, but his most frequent collaborators have been Italian designer Beni Montresor and Greek composer Thanos Mikroutsikos. Ronse himself designs ''mystical'' lighting, helping to weave the theatrical ''magic'' for which he is renowned.

ADDITIONAL PRODUCTIONS: 1977: *The Maids*; 1978: *L'Ignorant et le Fou* (Thomas Bernhard), *Athalie, Bajazet, Les Miroirs d'Ostende* (Paul Willems); 1979: *Nabucco* (Verdi), *Esther, Les Amants Puerils* (Crommelynck); 1980: *La Ville à voile* (Paul Willems); 1982: *Hélène* (Yannis Ritsos), *Une Musique de Cuivre aux Fenêtres des Incurables* (adapted from Maeterlinck by Ronse); 1983: *The Dance of Death, Le Président* (Thomas Bernhard), *The Penal Colony*; 1986: *Portrait de l'Artiste en Saltimbanque* (Pierre Bourgeade and Ronse); 1987: *Le Cocu Magnifique* (Crommelynck); 1988: *Le Bourgeois Gentilhomme*; 1990: *La Société de Chasse* (Thomas Bernhard); 1991: *La Vita breve* (Paul Willems).

SELECTED BIBLIOGRAPHY: Centre Belge de l'Institut International du Théâtre. *The Theatre in French-Speaking Belgium since 1945*. Brussels: Archives et Musée de la Littérature, 1991; *En scène pour demain*. Brussels: Libres Images aux Presses de la Bellone, 1988; Temkine, Raymonde. *Mettre en scène au présent*. Vol. 1. Lausanne: L'Age d'Homme—La Cité, 1977; Temkine, Raymonde. *Le théâtre au présent*. Paris: Patrick Pezin, 1987.

Suzanne Burgoyne

JAMES ROOSE-EVANS [b. November 11, 1927, London, England]. James Roose-Evans was a teacher at New York's Juilliard School and London's Royal Academy of Dramatic Art in the late fifties before he founded the Hampstead Theatre Club in 1959, which he served as the artistic director for ten years. At the Hampstead, Roose-Evans explored various directing techniques in a wide variety of productions ranging from Dylan Thomas's radio play *Under Milk Wood* (1961), to *The Little Clay Cart* (1964), an Indian morality play translated from Sanskrit, to more traditional English comedy like Jack Pullman's *The Happy Apple* (1967). In 1969, he founded Stage Two Theatre Workshop to explore more experimental approaches to theatre, primarily of adaptations of classical plays. His 1972 production, *Oedipus Now*, was a collectively created piece that attempted to relate the Sophoclean myth to modern issues. In *The Taming of the Shrew* (1974) and *Romeo and Juliet* (1976) he also attempted to adapt the text for a wider audience.

Much of Roose-Evans's early career was spent directing what critics called ''efficient'' productions of comedy including Oscar Wilde's *An Ideal Husband* (1966) and Colin Spencer's *Spitting Image* (1968). It was his production of *84 Charing Cross Road* (1981) that he adapted from Helen Hanff's book that brought him transatlantic acclaim. The London production won Roose-Evans *Drama* magazine's Best Director Award, and the production was transferred to New York in late 1982 where it starred Ellen Burstyn. The style for both productions was similar to Reader's Theatre, which some critics found to be nondramatic or ''anti-theatre.'' However, this style, seen earlier in the production of *Under Milk Wood* (1974), was to become his trademark.

Roose-Evans's particular brand of theatre also entailed his adapting personal accounts of British life and dramatizing those accounts using minimal, suggestive props and settings, and sometimes symbolic action. Although Roose-Evans is a well-respected director and educator, his primary contribution may, in fact, lie in staging his own adaptations. In 1984, he directed his adaptation of *Cider with Rosie*, based on Laurie Lee's autobiographical sketches, and in 1988 he enjoyed a similar success with his adaptation of Joyce Grenfell's letters to her mother. Based on Grenfel's *Darling Ma*, Roose-Evans's adaptation, *Re:Joyce*, became a hit in London, playing for several years and ultimately transferring to the Long Wharf in Connecticut. Although Alan Strachan directed the production in London's West End, Roose-Evans directed the early stages of the play while he made changes in the adaptation. With the success of these adaptation-productions and plays like A. R. Gurney's *Love Letters*, Roose-Evans reinforced his unique style of directing, and he continues to work in this style in productions like Hugh Whitemore's *The Best of Friends* (1989), based on Sydney Cockerell's book.

Roose-Evans continues to teach in both England and America and has written a number of theatre books: *Experimental Theatre*, *Directing a Play*, *London Theatre*; children's books: *The Adventures of Odd and Elsewhere*; and spiritual accounts: *The Inner Stage: Finding a Center in Prayer and Ritual*.

ADDITIONAL PRODUCTIONS: 1960: *The Dumb Waiter*; 1962: *The Sea Gull*; 1963: *Private Lives*; 1964: *The Corn is Green* (Emlyn Williams), *He Who Gets Slapped* (Leonid Andreyev); 1966: *Adventures in the Skin Trade* (based on book by Dylan Thomas); 1967: *Nathan and Tabileth* and *Oldenburg* (Barry Bermange), *The Two Character Play* (Tennessee Williams); 1973: *The Chester Mystery Plays*; 1978: *An Inspector Calls* (J. B. Priestley); 1987: *84 Charing Cross Road* (film adaptation); 1990: *Temptation* (Vaclav Havel).

SELECTED BIBLIOGRAPHY: Duder, Lewis. "Spreading the Words." *London Times* 1 April 1987; Itzen, Catherine, ed. *Directory of Playwrights, Directors, Designers*. Eastbourne, England: John Offord, 1983; Miles-Brown, John. *Directing Drama*. London: Peter Owen, 1980; Roose-Evans, James. "*84 Charing Cross Road*—'The Most Sought After Address on Broadway.' " *Drama* Summer 1983: 9–11; Wardle, Irving. "End of Fable." *London Times* 27 November 1981; Wardle, Irving. "Sophoclean Carve-up." *London Times* 10 October 1972.

Judy Lee Oliva

RICHARD ROSE [b. 1955, Maracaibo, Venezuela]. In just over a decade of professional work, Richard Rose has won recognition as the most innovative and ambitious of the current generation of young English-Canadian directors. He was raised in the northern Ontario mining town of Sudbury, and arrived in Toronto in 1971 to study theatre at York University. There he began his enduring collaboration with playwright John Krizanc, with whom he had gone to school in Sudbury. Together they founded Necessary Angel Theatre in 1978.

Rose's first major hit was also his most celebrated. In 1980 he suggested that Krizanc write a play in which the audience could exit with the characters. The result was Krizanc's *Tamara* (1981), a reflection on art and fascism set in the country home of Gabriele d'Annunzio. Staged in a nineteenth-century mansion,

Tamara was developed as an environmental performance with nine intersecting but separate narratives. The audience was invited to follow any one of the characters through the house; this fragmented structure meant that one would have to see the play nine times to see it all. Although *Tamara* ran only briefly in Toronto, it was picked up by commercial producer Moses Znaimer and opened in Los Angeles in 1984, where it was still playing in 1991. It also ran in New York at the Park Avenue Armory from 1987 to 1990, again under Rose's direction.

Rose's collaboration with Krizanc continued over the next decade and resulted in several notable successes, including *Prague* (produced in 1983 at Tarragon Theatre), about a Czech acrobatic troupe struggling against state censorship, and *The Half of It* (Canadian Stage Company, 1989).

Although the success of *Tamara* could easily have led Rose to a career in the United States, he was committed to developing an ensemble in Toronto. Necessary Angel has continued as a producing company drawing on a regular pool of actors, with whom Rose created a number of experimental collective creations. The most successful of these, *Mein* (produced at Toronto Free Theatre in 1983), was a clinical dissection of the corporate business mentality in which five actors played different aspects of one mind.

Instead of investing in a theatre space of its own, Necessary Angel sought innovative performance venues for its experiments. The most adventurous of these was an ice hockey rink in downtown Toronto which was transformed into a multimedia arena for *Newhouse*, written by Rose and D. D. Kugler in 1989. Surrounded by banks of television monitors, *Newhouse* rewrites Tirso de Molina's *Don Juan* and Sophocles' *Oedipus* to examine public policy response to a lethal sexual plague that is an analogy of AIDS: a liberal prime minister faces and loses an election over his refusal to legislate mandatory testing while the Don Juan title character spreads the virus. In performance the audience was free to move about in a manner that calls to mind medieval mansion staging; many of the scenes were simultaneously shown on the monitors by live-feed video representing the mass media.

Rose continued his explorations of nontraditional venues with his adaptation of Michael Ondaatje's *Coming through Slaughter* (1989), about New Orleans jazz great Buddy Bolden, staged in an inner-city tavern, and his workshop adaptation of another novel, Timothy Findley's *Not Wanted on the Voyage* (1991), on a ship in Toronto harbor. At the same time he directed on more conventional stages. He was the first Canadian director to stage the works of British playwright Howard Barker, with Canadian premieres of *The Castle* in 1987 and *The Possibilities* in 1989. In the following year he scored a major coup with the world premiere of Barker's *The Europeans*. Rose's fascination with epic staging and political morality perfectly complemented Barker's harshly intellectual historical fables. So too did his characteristic production style, which elicits performances of an often brutal intensity from the actors.

More recently Rose has begun to explore other media, including opera and

film; in 1990–91 he was an invited director at Norman Jewison's Canadian Centre
for Advanced Film Studies.

ADDITIONAL PRODUCTIONS: 1979: *The Uterine Knights* (Krizanc); 1979: *Electra*; 1980:
Boom; 1982: *Passchendaele* (Richard Wolfe); 1983: *Censored* (adapted from Bulgakov's
A Cabal of Hypocrites); 1985: *Desire* (collective); 1985: *Lily, Alta* (Dyba); 1988: *Dog
and Crow* (Springate); 1989: *The Glass Menagerie* (Manitoba Theatre Centre); 1991: *Don
Giovanni* (Hamilton Opera Company); 1992: *Not Wanted on the Voyage* (Canadian Stage
Company), *World of Wonders* (Stratford Shakespeare Festival).

SELECTED BIBLIOGRAPHY: Bannerman, Guy. "Hitting the Wall: Richard Rose, Howard
Barker and *The Europeans*." *Canadian Theatre Review* 65 (1990): 52–57; Filewod, Alan.
"The Words Are Too Important: An Interview with Richard Rose and D. D. Kugler."
Canadian Theatre Review 61 (1989): 33–39; Krizanc, John. *Tamara*. Toronto: Stoddart,
1989; Rewa, Natalie. "All News *Newhouse*." *Canadian Theatre Review* 61 (1989): 40–
42; Sidnell, Michael. "Ambivalences of Representation." *Canadian Theatre Review* 61
(1989): 43–44.

Alan Filewod

S

MICHEL SAINT-DENIS [b.September 13, 1897, Beauvais, France; d. July 31, 1971, London, England]. Michel Saint-Denis was an actor, director, lecturer, and above all an outstanding educator in the field of professional theatre training. He founded the London Theatre Studio (1935–39) with financial backing from Tyrone Guthrie.* In 1946, with Glen Byam Shaw and George Devine* (and the support of Laurence Olivier), he established the Old Vic School, assuming in 1949 the combined direction of the School and the Old Vic Theatre Centre, and from 1950 to 1952, the direction of the Old Vic Theatre itself. From 1952 to 1957, Saint-Denis directed the Centre Nationale Dramatique de l'Est in Strasbourg, and as part of the Center, he founded the Ecole Supérieure d'Art Dramatique. From 1952 until 1960, when the co-lingual National Theatre School of Canada opened, Saint-Denis served as consultant and advisor to the project. In 1957, he founded (with John Houseman*) the theatre school in New York City that was to become the Drama Division of the Juilliard School of Music. In 1962, he joined Peter Hall* and Peter Brook* as codirector of the Royal Shakespeare Company.

Saint-Denis began his work in the theatre with his uncle, Jacques Copeau,* as actor, manager, and secretary of the Théâtre du Vieux-Colombier (1919–24). In 1931, he took over direction of Copeau's Compagnie des Quinze, playing in Burgundy, Paris, and London. In collaboration with the troupe's playwright André Obey, Saint-Denis brought to fruition Copeau's lifelong work toward a true ensemble company. Of all who worked with Copeau, Saint-Denis remained the most true to Copeau's ideas and ideals; yet in his work in England, Canada, and the United States, Saint-Denis consciously became his own person. He embraced realism in the theatre, but with the mediation of *style*, as opposed to photographic naturalism. For him, theatre was not life; it was revelation by means of theatrical artistry.

Saint-Denis's schools, which have subsequently served as models for university and private programs, shared a similar structure and curriculum. During a period of three or four years, the *whole* actor was trained, and a unity of mind, body, and spirit was stressed. Study focused on classic dramatic works to give actors a sense of period, and disciplined experimentation and improvisation helped to create the spirit of the ensemble. Finally, the school-laboratory had to be intimately linked to an active theatre to allow students to perform regularly. Hundreds of actors who trained in Saint-Denis's schools today ensure that his influence is yet very much in evidence in Western theatre.

ADDITIONAL PRODUCTIONS: 1931: *Noah* (Obey), *The Rape of Lucrece* (Obey), *La Mauvaise Conduite* (Variot), *A Rosy Life* (Salacrou), *The Battle of the Marne* (Obey); 1934: *Don Juan* (Obey); 1935: *Noah* (for John Gielgud); 1937–38: *Macbeth*, *The Witch of Edmonton* (Dekker, Rowley, and Ford for Guthrie); 1938–39: *Twelfth Night*, *Electra* (Sophocles), *Three Sisters* (for Gielgud), *The White Guard* (Bulgakov), *The Cherry Orchard*, *The Wild Duck*; 1945: *Oedipus*; 1951: *Oedipus Rex*.

SELECTED BIBLIOGRAPHY: Alder, Henry. "The Method of Michel Saint-Denis." *The London Mercury* 39 (Nov. 1938): 47–55; Berberich, George. "The Theatre Schools of Michel Saint-Denis: A Quest for Style." Diss.U. of Southern California, 1985; "He That Directs the King." *Times Literary Supplement* 15 July 1960: 441–42; Russell, Robert. "The National Theatre School." *Tamarack Review* Spring 1963: 71–79; Saint-Denis, Michel. "The English Theatre in Gallic Eyes." *Texas Quarterly* 4 (Autumn 1961): 26–45; Saint-Denis, Michel. "A School of Dramatic Art." *World Theatre* 4 (1954–55): 37–49; Saint-Denis, Michel. *Theatre: The Rediscovery of Style*. New York: Theatre Arts Books, 1960; Saint-Denis, Michel. *Training for the Theatre*. Ed. Suria Saint-Denis. New York: Theatre Arts Books, 1982; Worsley, T. C. "Interview with Michel Saint-Denis, 'The Old Vic.' " *The New Statesman and Nation* 41 (2 June 1951): 616–17.

M. Clare Mather

GENE SAKS [b. November 8, 1921, New York, New York]. Saks began his theatre career in the late 1940s, appearing in *South Pacific* and a national tour of *Mister Roberts* with Henry Fonda. He studied with Lee Strasberg* and Sanford Meisner and played to great acclaim as the rabbi in Paddy Chayevsky's *The Tenth Man* and the overbearing children's television show host Chuckles the Chipmunk in Herb Gardner's *A Thousand Clowns*.

Impressed by a scene Saks directed at the Actors' Studio, producer Martin Gottlieb hired him to stage Joseph Stein's *Enter Laughing* in 1963, which was successfully received. That same season he directed another hit, Ronald Alexander's *Nobody Loves an Albatross*, a satire of the television industry. He turned to musicals in 1966 with *Mame*, which included his wife, Beatrice Arthur, in the cast.

Sak's association with Neil Simon has been particularly fruitful. Since 1976 he has directed eight of Simon's plays, including *Lost in Yonkers*, winner of the

1991 Pulitzer Prize and Tony Award for best play. Both men have spoken of the special rapport and shared sensibilities that have enabled their ongoing professional association to flourish.

In discussing his directorial approaches to comedy, Saks stresses the need to ground comic business and character in a tangible sense of reality, a tendency he learned from his study with Lee Strasberg. Acting under the direction of Joshua Logan* in *South Pacific* and *Mister Roberts*, he developed an appreciation for Logan's ability to compose both a compelling stage picture and a viable physical life for each performer. Perhaps owing to his lengthy career as an actor, Saks tries to give as much responsibility to the performers as possible, and speaks of not wishing to put his personal stamp on a show.

Saks has been active in film, directing four of Neil Simon's plays for the screen. His other motion picture directing credits include *Mame* and *Cactus Flower*. Saks is currently president of the Society of Stage Directors and Choreographers.

ADDITIONAL PRODUCTIONS: 1965: *Half a Sixpence*; 1968: *A Mother's Kisses* (musical); 1971: *How the Other Half Loves* (Ayckbourn); 1975: *Same Time Next Year* (Bernard Slade); 1976: *California Suite* (Simon); 1977: *I Love My Wife* (musical); 1983: *Brighton Beach Memoirs* (Simon); 1985: *Biloxi Blues* (Simon); 1986: *Broadway Bound* (Simon); 1988: *Rumors* (Simon); 1992: *Jake's Women* (Simon).

SELECTED BIBLIOGRAPHY: Barbour, David. "Gene Saks: *Enter Laughing.*" *Theater Week* 21 November 1988: 12–21; Fein, Esther B. "Two Vintage Shows Are Reshaped for a New Life on Broadway." *New York Times* 9 June 1985; sec. 2: 1, 6; Gerard, Jeremy. "From Brighton to Biloxi to Broadway." *New York Times* 30 November 1986; sec. 2: 1, 28; Gow, Gordon. "Comedy Must Spring from Truth." *Plays International* July 1989: 12–13; Saks, Gene. "Bring an Apple in the Morning." *Equity News* August/September 1988: 42–43.

Stephen Nelson

NATALIA ILINICHINA SATS [b. August 14, 1903, Irkutsk]. As the daughter of Ilya Sats, the composer for the Moscow Art Theatre, Natalia Sats was trained to be a musician, but became interested in theatre under the tutelage of Evgeni Vakhtangov.* In 1918, at age fifteen, Sats became head of the Children's Department of the Theatrical and Musical Section of the Moscow Soviet and founded the Children's Theatre of the Moscow Soviet, the world's first professional children's theatre. She was the director and artistic director of the Moscow Theatre for Children from 1920 to 1937 (renamed the Central Children's Theatre in 1936).

Working with child psychologists, Sats developed an educational theatre with programming aimed at specific age groups. Sats believed that a successful director must be musically trained in order to subordinate the various rhythms to the theme of the production. Sats began directing in 1925 but did not receive general recognition until 1927 with her production of *The Black Boy and the Monkey*, a pantomime she wrote herself. This production was the first experiment in combining live action, synchronized music, and animation. Sats was contracted

348   JÉRÔME SAVARY

to direct *Falstaff* (1931), conducted by Otto Klemperer at the Kroll Opera in Berlin. Later that year, she staged *The Marriage of Figaro* at the Teatro Colón in Buenos Aires, again with Klemperer. Offered opportunities to direct opera, Sats instead returned to Moscow. Due to a lack of suitable material for children, Sats was often forced to write her own plays, or to convince major writers to develop pieces. In 1936, Alexei Tolstoy dramatized his tale *The Golden Key*, which Sats directed later that year. Also in 1936, Sats narrated the premiere of *Peter and the Wolf*, written for her.

In 1937, Sats was arrested and sent to a Siberian labor camp. Released in 1941, Sats became a director at the Alma-Ata Opera and Ballet Theatre, where in 1945 she opened the Kazakh Children's Theatre. In 1953, Sats returned to Moscow where, after a term with the All-Union Touring Company, she resumed her previous duties at the Central Children's Theatre. Achieving her goal of introducing music to children, Sats became artistic director of the Moscow Children's Musical Theatre (opened in 1965), where she continues to stage children's operas. She has received the title "Hero of Socialist Labor."

SELECTED BIBLIOGRAPHY: Houghton, Norris. *Moscow Rehearsals*. New York: Harcourt, Brace and Company, 1936; Morton, Miriam, ed. and trans. *Through the Magic Curtain: Theatre for Children, Adolescents and Young Adults in the U.S.S.R.* New Orleans: Anchorage Press, 1979; Sats, Natalia. *Sketches from My Life*. Trans. Sergei Syrovatkin. Moscow: Raduga Publishers, 1985; Sats, Natalia, narrator. *Peter and the Wolf*. Prod. William Snyder. Hightstown, NJ: Proscenium Entertainment (videotape), 1990.

Edward Dee

JÉRÔME SAVARY [b. June 27, 1942, Buenos Aires, Argentina]. Jérôme Savary is the founder and director of the Grand Magic Circus (GMC), one of the most popular and enduring of the theatrical collectives that emerged in France during the late 1960s. His work as a director, however, represents only one facet of his career. Savary is also an accomplished actor, cartoonist, composer, dramatist, musician, photographer, and writer. In addition, his autobiography, *La Vie Privée d'un magicien ordinaire*, details his accomplishments as band leader, *bon vivant*, farmer, mechanic, and theatrical producer.

Savary's parents left France to escape Hitler's invasion. As a result, he led a peripatetic life, growing up in the pampas of Argentina, the French countryside, Paris, and New York. By his own account, he received little formal education. On the other hand, his family was well-connected with many avant-garde artists and intellectuals, and from an early age, Savary had access to those milieus.

Savary's work in the theatre bears witness to his vagabond and bohemian early life and gives voice to his disdain for conservative politics and traditional aesthetics. Grounded in a profound appreciation for the forms and themes of popular culture, his productions present a kaleidoscope of extravagant acting, sets (often designed by Savary himself), costumes (or nudity), music, and dramatic forms (Savary enjoys playing with genre boundaries). A self-proclaimed "showman," Savary provides a genuinely spectacular theatre.

When Savary was a teenager, his artistic impulses first led him toward music, particularly jazz, and music has remained a key element of all his subsequent work. His creations with the GMC relied heavily on music to establish and sustain the tempo of the performance as well as to provide a continuity linking the often disparate materials of the various scenes. Savary composed much of the music for these productions and often conducted the orchestra from the stage while acting as narrator. In his persona of Ring Master, Savary appeared simultaneously as principal actor, conductor, director, and narrator. Even in his work outside the GMC, musicality stands out as one of the defining characteristics of a Savary *mise-en-scène*, which may account for his success in directing opera.

Savary established his reputation with the iconoclastic, ribald works he created with the GMC. Beginning with a production of *Leonce and Lena* at the Hamburg Shauspielhaus in 1977, he began to stage plays written by others and quickly acquired a substantial reputation in the German and Italian theatres. His first staging of an established play in France was his landmark production of Molière's *Le Bourgeois Gentilhomme* with the GMC in 1980–81, which he revived during the 1988–89 season as the signature production of his artistic directorship of Théâtre National de Chaillot (Paris). Before his appointment to Chaillot, Savary served as artistic director of the Nouveau Théâtre Populaire de Montpellier (1982–85) and of the Centre Dramatique de Lyon (1985–88).

ADDITIONAL PRODUCTIONS: 1966–68: *The Labyrinth* (Fernando Arrabal); 1970: *Zartan, le frère mal-aimé de Tarzan* (GMC); 1972: *Les derniers jours de solitude de Robinson Crusoé* (GMC); 1973: *De Moise à Mao* (GMC); 1974: *Good-Bye Mister Freud* (GMC); 1977: *The Three Musketeers* (adaptation Savary); 1978: *Les Mille et Une Nuits* (GMC), *Around the World in 80 Days* (adaptation Savary); 1980: *'Tis Pity She's a Whore*; 1982: *L'Histoire du soldat* (C. F. Ramuz/Igor Stravinsky); 1983: *Cyrano de Bergerac* (Prix Dominique for best *mise-en-scène*); 1984: *Don Giovanni, Bye Bye Show Biz* (GMC); 1985: *Les Aventures inédites du cochon en Amazonie* (GMC); 1988: *Astérix* (adaptation Savary), *D'Artagnan* (adaptation Savary); 1990: *Zazou* (Savary).

SELECTED BIBLIOGRAPHY: Savary, Jérôme. *Album du Grand Magic Circus*. Paris: Belfond, 1974; Savary, Jérôme. *De Moise à Mao*. Paris: Editions de l'Avant-Scène, 1974; Savary, Jérôme. *La Vie Privée d'un magicien ordinaire*. Paris: Ramsay, 1985; Whitton, David. *Stage Directors in Modern France*. Manchester: Manchester University Press, 1987: 180–90.

James Carmody

GEORG II, DUKE OF SAXE-MEININGEN [b. April 2, 1826, Meiningen; d. June 25, 1914, Bad Wildungen, Germany]. Georg's popular title of the "Theatre Duke" is not to be taken lightly. He was a respected member of German royalty, related to both Wilhelm I, the king of Prussia whom he helped elevate to Kaiser, and to the British royal family. Commonly addressed as "Your Majesty," he was also a military commander who saw action in the Franco-Prussian War. He became head of state of the small German duchy of Saxe-Meiningen in 1866, following the forced abdication of his father, Duke Bernhard. A shrewd politician with a democratic love for his subjects, he also had a keen talent for drawing, a strong appreciation of the visual arts, and a love for theatre inherited from his grandfather. Already he had remodeled the Hoftheater (Court Theatre) in Meiningen, originally established in 1776. Impressed in his youth by the work of Charles Kean and Ira Aldridge among others, and by the color and passion of circus spectacle, he was incensed at the frivolity of contemporary German Shakespearean productions. Eager to use his prestige to restore classical theatre to its rightful place as high art, he assembled the company that became known throughout the world as the Meininger.

Foremost among the actors were Ludwig Chronegk (1837–95), a portly Jewish comic actor, and Ellen Franz (1839–1923), a schoolmaster's daughter. Chronegk played Rosencrantz in the Duke's very first production of *Hamlet* (1866). In 1873, he was promoted to *régisseur* of the company: its authoritative director, subject to the dictates of his patron. At home, he conducted most rehearsals as the Duke watched from the rear, interrupting at will, but on tours he was in complete charge of the company.

Following the death of his second wife, Georg married Ellen Franz in 1873, despite initial popular disapproval, and over the strenuous objections of his father. He granted the commoner-actress a royal title, and as the Baroness Helene, she became acting coach and elocutionist, helping to choose both actors and repertoire.

Helene completed the triumvirate who ruled the Meininger in its influential years. Defining the specific creative contributions of each is difficult, but undoubtedly Georg was the absolute ruler. However often Chronegk and Helene succeeded in persuading the Duke to their points of view, they remained loyal to his vision.

Georg designed costumes and sets, insisting on realistic detail and historical accuracy, and commissioned the Brückner brothers, Max and Gotthold, to paint his backdrops. He believed theatre should be passionate, not indifferent or static, and for dynamic quality he favored an asymmetrical, multilevelled set with three-dimensional pieces and realistic props. Nothing onstage could be symmetrical or parallel, and nothing important could happen at center stage.

The Duke demanded strict discipline from his casts. New plays received extensive rehearsal, and actors were not allowed to disrupt the audience's belief in the playwright's world by acknowledging applause during a scene. He permitted no stars in his ensemble and required even major players to take walk-on roles. Georg was masterful with realistic crowd scenes, taking special care in the training of extras.

Many of these ideas were not original, but none had gained much public attention before the Meininger debuted on tour in Berlin with *Julius Caesar* on May 1, 1874. Georg's cultivated friendship with leading theatre critic Karl Frenzel assured a full house, and the troupe quickly became the talk of the town. From 1874 until 1890, when Chronegk retired because of ill health, the Meininger gave 2,591 performances in thirty-six cities, in fourteen countries. Of forty-one plays, six were by Shakespeare and nine by Schiller; other authors included Ibsen, Molière, Goethe, and Bjørnson.

During the tours, the Meininger developed into an enormously influential force in nineteenth-century theatre. In Belgium, for instance, they made strong impressions on André Antoine,* in Russia on both Konstantin Stanislavsky* and Vladimir Nemirovich-Danchenko,* and in Berlin on Otto Brahm.* Their work was an inspiration to Max Reinhardt,* Gerhart Hauptmann, and countless others who set the stage for the modern theatre.

Following the end of the touring period, performances continued in Meiningen under a succession of directors. When the Hoftheater burned down in 1908, Georg immediately had it rebuilt. Whenever affairs of state and deteriorating health permitted, he maintained interest in the theatre until his death at age eighty-eight, on the eve of the royal assassination in Sarajevo.

The Meininger tours elevated the art of theatre to a new status at the center of popular debate. Critics either loved or hated the crowd scenes and historical details, and often denounced puppet-like acting and excessive attention paid to the externals of theatre at the expense of the play. But no one before Georg II of Saxe-Meiningen had made such a concerted drive to unify all the various elements of theatrical production under the leadership of a single authoritative artist. He inspired many who followed and earned the title of father of modern directing.

ADDITIONAL PRODUCTIONS: 1874: *Twelfth Night, Imaginary Invalid*; 1876: *Wilhelm Tell*; 1877: *The Pretenders* (Ibsen), *The Robbers* (Schiller); 1878: *Prince Friedrich von Homburg* (Kleist), *The Winter's Tale*; 1881: *Iphigenia* (Goethe), *Wallenstein* (Schiller); 1886: *Ghosts*; 1887: *Die Jungfrau von Orleans*; 1898: *The Merchant of Venice, The Sunken Bell* (Hauptmann), *The Wild Duck, John Gabriel Borkman*; 1907: *Egmont* (Goethe).

SELECTED BIBLIOGRAPHY: DeHart, Steven. *The Meininger Theater 1776–1926*. Ann Arbor, MI: UMI Research Press, 1981; Grube, Max. *The Story of the Meininger*. Trans. Ann Marie Koller. Coral Gables: University of Miami Press, 1963; Koller, Ann Marie. *The Theater Duke: Georg II of Saxe-Meiningen and the German Stage*. Stanford, CA: Stanford University Press, 1984; Osborne, John. *The Meiningen Court Theatre 1866–1890*. Cambridge: Cambridge University Press, 1988.

William H. Rough

RICHARD SCHECHNER [b. August 23, 1934, Newark, New Jersey]. Richard Schechner received his Ph.D. in 1962 from Tulane University. In 1964, the Free Southern Theatre hired him to serve as producing director. Between 1966 and 1967, he codirected the New Orleans Group. Schechner then moved to New York City and founded the Performance Group, which he directed from 1967 to 1980.

During the course of his career, Schechner has combined theatre practice and theatre scholarship, directing innovative productions as he developed and tested his theories of performance. The Performance Group provided him with the opportunity to formulate his theories of environmental theatre. The company performed in a Wooster Street garage (renamed the Performing Garage), an open space bearing no resemblance to a traditional theatre. There, Schechner explored the relationship of space to performance and developed the theory that the text, action, and environment of the play develop together, each element impacting the other in the creation of theatre. Using scaffolding and platforms designed by Jerry Rojo, Schechner created a series of playing-viewing spaces rather than illusionistic set designs that recreated specific time and place. The way in which performer, text, and audience interacted determined the nature of the space. This style of production focused attention upon the actor. In Schechner's productions, the actors were free to explore their own ideas as they related to the text and to contribute on equal footing with the text in the creation of theatre. In *Dionysus in 69* (1969), the Performance Group's most famous production, Schechner led the actors to develop their own physical and verbal text, a provocative celebration and birth ritual. Initially, the production did not involve nudity, but within a short period of time, all but two performers performed nude. This led Schechner to explore the theoretical and practical implications of nudity in performance.

The next year the Performance Group produced *Commune* (1970). During the performance, actors asked fifteen spectators to stand in the center of the playing space. The play continued only if the spectators participated. If a spectator refused, he or she could elect someone else or could leave the theatre. The demand for audience participation caused controversy, and one performance was stopped for three hours as a result. Because of the emphasis on audience participation and actor freedom, the Performance Group's performances continually changed from one performance to the next.

Despite the contribution of actor and audience, Schechner believes that the director is the primary theatre artist, the person who must control the production. Therefore, he takes performers through three stages. First, he initiates the production process, acting as a parent, teacher, friend, enemy, and "savior" to the actors; then, as the performers develop into a cohesive unit, Schechner shifts the focus to the group and their creative abilities. In the final stage of the process, he shapes the work. In this way, Schechner allows for actor input while assuming responsibility for the creation of the theatrical event.

Although inextricably linked to the work of the Performance Group, Schechner's greatest contributions are his theoretical writings, especially his theories of theatre and ritual. Schechner believes that theatre and ritual are interrelated, existing on a continuum of performance, which also includes sports and other forms of entertainment. In his recent book *Between Theatre and Anthropology* (1985), Schechner investigates theatre and ritual from an anthropological viewpoint and examines the way in which theatricality underlies virtually all human activity. Schechner promotes the avant-garde, and as both director and scholar, he challenges existing definitions of theatre and performance.

ADDITIONAL PRODUCTIONS: 1969–70: *Makcbeth*; 1970: *Government Anarchy* (The Performance Group); 1971–72: *Concert* (Paul Epstein); 1972: *Healing Piece, The Tooth of Crime*; 1975: *Mother Courage, The Marilyn Project*; 1977: *Oedipus* (Seneca); 1978: *Cops*; 1979: *The Balcony*; 1981: *Richard's Lear*; 1983: *The Cherry Orchard*; 1985: *Prometheus Project*; 1987: *Don Juan*; 1989: *Tomorrow He'll Be Out of the Mountains*.

SELECTED BIBLIOGRAPHY: McNamara, Brooks, Jerry Rojo, and Richard Schechner. *Theatres, Spaces, Environments: Eighteen Projects*. New York: Drama Book Specialists, 1975; Schechner, Richard. *Between Theatre and Anthropology*. Philadelphia: University of Pennsylvania Press, 1985; Schechner, Richard. *The End of Humanism: Writings on Performance*. New York: Performing Arts Journal Publications, 1982; Schechner, Richard. *Environmental Theatre*. New York: Hawthorn Books, 1973; Schechner, Richard. *Essays on Performance Theory, 1970–1976*. New York: Drama Book Specialists, 1977; Schechner, Richard. *Public Domain: Essays on the Theatre*. Indianapolis: Bobbs-Merrill, 1969; The Performance Group. *Dionysus in 69*. Ed.Richard Schechner. New York: Farrar, Straus and Giroux, 1970.

Geraldine Maschio
Sullivan White

LEON SCHILLER [b.Schiller de Schildenfeld, March 14, 1887, Kraków, Poland; d. March 25, 1954, Warsaw, Poland]. From 1906 to 1916, Leon Schiller studied theatre in Kraków and Paris, and musical composition in Vienna. During the same period, he served as a theatre critic and organized expositions of modern stage design. Between 1917 and 1920, he was literary advisor at Teatr Polski in Warsaw, where in 1917 he made his directing debut with *Królewna Lelijka* (*Princess Lelijka*). From 1924 to 1926, Schiller was artistic director of Teatr Bogusławskiego in Warsaw, and during the years between 1926 and 1939, he directed in theatres in Warsaw, Lwów, Wilno, Łødź, Sofia, and Paris where he staged ballet. In 1933, he founded and became the dean of the Department of Directing (the first program of directing in the world on the university level) at the National Institute of Theatre Arts in Warsaw.

Schiller was inspired by the Polish romantic tradition of poetic theatre, as well as the European movement to reform the theatre. In his youth, he was influenced by Stanisław Wyspiański, Polish playwright and theatre visionary at the turn of the century. Schiller also corresponded and collaborated with Gordon Craig, for whose periodical *The Mask* he wrote, and he followed in the directorial footsteps of Max Reinhardt.* Later, he was compared to Vsevolod Meyerhold* and Erwin Piscator.* Schiller expressed himself with great artistic power in three major styles: "monumental theatre," "neo-realistic theatre," and a form of music theatre called "Song-plays."

Schiller's "monumental theatre," or "theatre greater than life" (in Polish, "teatr ogromny," a term introduced by Stanisław Wyspiański), was based on an essentially romantic vision of the universe. One of Schiller's major contributions was his staging of romantic, poetic dramas using modern, anti-illusionistic means of expression.

His "monumental" productions were grand-scale, rich spectacles. They utilized modern stage design (e.g., cubism), and used elaborate light plots. With an abundance of music, their most important component was rhythm created mainly by the movement of protagonists and crowds. In his "neo-realistic theatre," Schiller, following the example of German "Zeittheater," explored contemporary political and social problems. His "neo-realism" was thus a com-

bination of real issues and real stage elements combined with expressive, sometimes expressionistic, theatrical techniques. "Song-plays" were Schiller's original invention. He scripted them, provided musical setting, and directed several
productions based on old Polish songs (folk, religious, love, military, "Bohemia," etc.) as well as Medieval and Renaissance religious dramas.

In his teaching of directing, Schiller stressed the necessity of a director's
humanistic education, the artist's professional preparation in all major areas of
theatre, and the belief in theatre as an art. He wanted to train directors as "theatre
artists" and he contributed significantly to the birth of the distinctly "poetic"
Polish directorial style.

In 1941, after the German and Soviet invasion of Poland, Schiller was imprisoned and sent to Auschwitz. Following his release the same year, he returned
to Warsaw and became active in the underground theatre. After the end of the
war, he was appointed artistic director of theatres in Łódź and Warsaw and also
became rector of schools of drama. He joined the Communist party in 1946,
served as a Communist deputy to Parliament, and was awarded several official
prizes. In 1950, he was disgraced by the Communists and was fired from his
important positions, retaining only secondary ones and working occasionally as
a guest-director.

Both artistically and personally, Schiller was a "man of renaissance" (according to Bohdan Korzeniewski), as well as a man of sharp contradictions. An
intellectual from the upper class, he became involved with communism. In his
youth, he was a militant of the avant-garde, but in 1949, he accepted the imposed
dogmatic "social-realism." He oscillated between Catholicism and Marxism,
and between mysticism and materialism. In spite of all the contradictions, he
nevertheless had a great impact on theatrical life in Poland from the 1920s to
the 1950s. In the history of Polish theatre, he remains one of its greatest artists.

ADDITIONAL PRODUCTIONS: Between 1917 and 1953, Schiller directed approximately
150 theatre productions. During his "preparatory phase" (1917–24), he directed mostly
his own scenarios of old religious dramas and "song-plays": 1922: *Pastorałka* (*Christmas
Carol*); 1923: *Wielkanoc* (*Easter*). During his most creative period (1924–39), he directed
productions of the plays/poems of the great nineteenth-century Polish romantic poets:
1926: *Nie-Boska komedia* (*The Un-Divine Comedy*, by Zygmunt Krasínski, restaged
1938); 1930: *Kordian* (Juliusz Słowacki, restaged 1935, 1939); 1932: *Dziady* (Forefather's
Eve, by Adam Mickiewicz, restaged 1933, 1934, 1937). **Twentieth-Century Polish
Writers**: 1925: *Kniaź Patiomkin* (*Prince Patiomkin*, Tadeusz Miciński), *Achilleis* (Stan-
isław Wyspiański); 1926: *Róża* (*The Rose*, Stefan Żeromski). **Other Productions**: 1924:
The Winter's Tale; 1925: *As You Like It*; 1928: *Julius Caesar*; 1929: *Brave Soldier Shveyk*
(Hašek); 1932: *Cry China* (Tretyakov); 1935: *King Lear*; 1947: *The Tempest*. Following
World War II, because of censorship, Schiller was not able to direct his favorite repertory.
He repeated his old scenarios and directed only a few large productions and some operas.

SELECTED BIBLIOGRAPHY: **Collections of Texts by Schiller**: Raszewski, Zbigniew, ed.
Teatr ogromny. Warszawa: Czytelnik, 1961; Series: Timoszewicz, Jerzy, ed. Warszawa:
Panstow Instytut Wydawniczy (PIW). Vol. 1, *Na progu nowego teatru*, 1978; Vol. 2,
Droga przez teatr, 1983; Vol. 3, *Theatrum militans*, 1987. **About Schiller**: Csato,

Edward. *Leon Schiller*. Warszawa: Panstowy Instytut Wydawniczy (PIW), 1968; Kra-
siński, Edward, ed. *Leon Schiller w Teatrze Polskim 1917–1952*. Warszawa: Teatr Polski,
1987; Kuchtówna, Lidia, and Barbara Lasocka. *Leon Schiller. W stulecie urodzin 1887–
1987*. Warszawa: Państwowe Wydawnictwo Naukowe, 1990; *Pamiętnik Teatralny* 3–4
(1955); 4 (1968); Timoszewicz, Jerzy. *Dziady w inscenizacji Leona Schillera*. Warszawa:
Panstowy Instytut Wydawniczy (PIW), 1970. Timoszewicz, Jerzy, ed. *Ostatni romantyk
sceny polskiej. Wspomnienia o Leonie Schillerze*. Krakow: Wydawnictwo Literackie,
1990.

Kazimierz Braun

OSKAR SCHLEMMER [b. September 4, 1888, Stuttgart, Germany; d. April 13,
1943, Baden-Baden, Germany]. In today's era of performance art and postmodern dance, the work of Oskar Schlemmer—German painter, sculptor, choreographer, director, and theatre visionary—has merited a new wave of attention.
Hired in 1921 to head the sculpture workshop of the Bauhaus, a teaching institute
which embraced the entire range of visual arts, Schlemmer by 1923 had expanded
the workshop into the Bauhaus Stage Shop, the first performance training sponsored by an art school.

The son of a stagestruck father, Schlemmer studied to become a painter at
the Akademie der Bildenden Künst in Stuttgart and, following four years of
military service, he accepted Walter Gropius's invitation to join the Bauhaus.
There, between 1921 and 1929, he experimented with moving the performer in
space and translated his painterly talents into movement. His most notable production was *Triadic Ballet* (1922, with music by Paul Hindemith), a performance
piece with highly stylized, imaginative costumes and movement and a nonplotted
structure.

Schlemmer's most significant contributions, however, were theoretical. He
conceived of the theatre as a medium for the transformation of the human form,
redefined theatrical space as *Raumempfindung* ("felt" volume, space occupied
by a soft pliable substance) and visualized performers who could be mechanized,
softly animated marionettes. Schlemmer's mechanical-technological view of the
performer was a fusion of Heinrich von Kleist's puppet theatre with constructivist
devices, and gained form in early versions of *Triadic Ballet* and a production
of Franz Blei's *Nuschi-Nuschi* (1920). In all of his work with the Bauhaus,
according to Roselee Goldberg, Schlemmer's "essential investigation was of
space: [his] paintings delineated the two-dimensional elements of space, while
theatre provided a place in which to 'experience' space" (Goldberg, 103).
ADDITIONAL PRODUCTIONS: 1916: *Untitled Duet*; 1921: *Mörder Hoffnung der Frauen*;
1922: *Figural Cabinet I*; 1924: *Meta or the Pantomime of Places*; 1926–27: *Treppenwitz*;
1926–29: *Dances for the Experimental Stage* (*Space Dance, Form Dance, Glass Dance,
Block Dance, Stick Dance*).
SELECTED BIBLIOGRAPHY: Goldberg, Roselee. *Performance: Live Art 1909 to the Pres-
ent*. New York: Harry N. Abrams, 1979: 63–78; "Man in Space: From Bauhaus to
Moonwalk." *Theatre Crafts* May-June 1970: 14–17, 39; Moynihan, D. S., with Leigh
George Odom. "Oscar Schlemmer's *Bauhaus Dances*: Debra McCall's Reconstructions."

The Drama Review 28 (Fall 1984): 46–58; Scheyer, Ernst. "The Shapes of Space: The Art of Mary Wigman and Oskar Schlemmer." *Dance Perspectives* 41 (Spring 1970): 28–48; Schlemmer, Oskar, László Moholy-Nagy, and Farkas Molnar. *The Theater of the Bauhaus*. Middletown, CT: Wesleyan University Press, 1961.

John W. Frick

ALAN SCHNEIDER [b. December 12, 1917, Kharkov, Russia; d. May 5, 1984, London, England]. Having directed over 200 plays, Alan Schneider was regarded as one of America's most prolific and "ecumenical" directors, staging both smash Broadway hits and radiant productions of Samuel Beckett's masterpieces.

Schneider's family immigrated to the United States in 1923. He grew up in the Baltimore area and attended Johns Hopkins for one year. He graduated from the University of Wisconsin–Madison in 1939 with a degree in political science and journalism. After earning an M.A. in theatre from Cornell in 1941, he began his directing career at Catholic University, teaching there 1941–47 and 1949–52. Schneider maintained educational ties throughout his professional life, directing at many universities. He headed the Juilliard Drama School (1976–79), and directed the graduate directing program at the University of California, San Diego (1979–84).

Schneider first gained fame as a Broadway director with the productions of *The Remarkable Mr. Pennypacker* (1953) and *Anastasia* (1954). He worked occasionally on Broadway, his biggest commercial success being *You Know I Can't Hear You When the Water's Running* (1967). His first Off-Broadway work was *Endgame* (1958). While he directed at many regional theatres, he was long associated with the Arena Stage in Washington, where he directed forty-one plays between 1951 and 1978.

Among Schneider's productions abroad were *My Heart's in the Highlands* and *Pullman Car Hiawatha* at Dartington Hall, England (1949); *The Trip to Bountiful*, Dublin and London (1956); *The Deserters* (1958), England tour; and *The Cherry Orchard*, Israel (1956). His Arena Stage production of *Our Town* toured Russia in 1973.

Of greater significance, Schneider was instrumental in popularizing several prominent avant-garde playwrights. As Edward Albee's principal director in the 1960s, he staged *The American Dream* (1961), *Who's Afraid of Virginia Woolf?* (1962), *Ballad of the Sad Cafe* (1963), *Tiny Alice* (1964), *Malcolm* (1966), *A Delicate Balance* (1966), and *Box Mao Box* (1968). These plays established Albee as a major playwright. Schneider staged the first Harold Pinter productions in America (*The Dumb Waiter* and *The Collection*) in 1962; directed *The Birthday Party* in 1967; and Pinter's *Victoria Station*, *One for the Road*, and *A Kind of Alaska* in 1984. He also championed the works of Bertolt Brecht* in the 1960s, directing the first professional production of *The Caucasian Chalk Circle* in the United States (1961); *A Man's a Man* (1962) and *The Threepenny Opera* (1963).

Schneider's most enduring relationship, however, was with Samuel Beckett. Schneider directed all of the American premieres of Beckett's plays. Schneider's

Waiting for Godot (1956) failed in Miami, but he had outstanding success with other Beckett plays. He staged *Endgame, Waiting for Godot, Krapp's Last Tape, Happy Days*, and other Beckett works many times over a 28-year period. A crusader for Beckett's plays, Schneider reached the height of his genius as director of them. Schneider proved his talent with nearly all styles of theatre, but he always had a special appreciation for the poetically theatrical. Nevertheless, in his concern for external reality, he routinely paid great attention to blocking, gesture, and physical characterization. His study with Lee Strasberg* at the American Theatre Wing in 1948 provided him a knowledge of motivation, subtext, and the given circumstances. Over the years he combined his own sense of imaginative, poetic, theatrical drama with what he called the "local situation"—the who, what, when, and where of a text—to develop a directing perspective uniquely his own.

Ultimately, he approached dramatic works as self-contained expressions of reality. His main concern was to allow the form of the play to evolve of itself. He thereby expanded the traditional American psychological perspective of directing to incorporate a subjective reality, the private vision of the playwright. In searching for each play's particular tone and style, its texture and basic structure, Schneider avoided imposing his own virtuosity on a play; rather, he sought to serve the playwright. As artist, educator, champion of new plays, and promoter of the avant-garde, Schneider infused vitality into the American stage. His pioneering stagings of Albee, Pinter, Beckett, and others changed the nature of the contemporary theatre.

ADDITIONAL PRODUCTIONS: 1941: *Jim Dandy* (Saroyan); 1948: *A Long Way from Home* (Maxim Gorky, adapted by Randolph Goodman and Walter Carroll); 1950: *Oedipus the King*; 1951: *The Glass Menagerie, The Cherry Orchard*; 1960: *Krapp's Last Tape*; 1961: *Happy Days*; 1964: *Play* (Beckett); 1971: *Waiting for Godot*; 1972: *Moonchildren, Not I, Happy Days, Krapp's Last Tape, Act without Words II*; 1976: *Texas Trilogy, Play, Footfalls, That Time* (Beckett); 1979: *Ohio Impromptu, Catastrophe, What Where* (Beckett); 1984; *Victoria Station,One for the Road, A Kind of Alaska* (Pinter).

SELECTED BIBLIOGRAPHY: Greenberger, Howard. *The Off-Broadway Experience*. Englewood Cliffs, NJ: Prentice-Hall, 1971: 63–79; Kellman, Barnet. "Alan Schneider: The Director's Career." *Theatre Quarterly* 3 (July-September 1973): 23–37; Schneider, Alan. " 'Any Way You Like It, Alan': Working with Beckett." *Theatre Quarterly* 19 (September-November 1975): 27–38; Schneider, Alan. *Entrances: An American Director's Journey*. New York: Viking, 1985; Shelton, Lewis E. "Alan Schneider's Direction of *Who's Afraid of Virginia Woolf?*" *Journal of American Drama and Theatre* 3 (Fall 1991): 39–50.

                                                                        Lewis E. Shelton

PETER SCHUMANN [b. June 11, 1934, Breslau, Germany (now Poland)]. The Bread and Puppet Theatre was so named because its director, Peter Schumann, believes that art must be cheap, nourishing, and readily available, as essential to the everyday life of ordinary people as bread. As a part of every performance, audience members habitually share a ritual meal of Schumann's own fresh, home-baked bread.

After a childhood under Nazi rule in a small Silesian village, where he was forced to run from the Russians and dodge Allied air raids, Schumann migrated to Munich, where in the 1950s he worked as a choreographer and was influenced by the work of the Bauhaus, Oskar Schlemmer,* and John Cage. Exposure to the Sicilian story-theatre puppets and to the more compositional work of Bunraku convinced him of the power of puppets to "tell truth" without any of the confusion generated by actors struggling to be realistic.

In 1961, he and his wife Elka moved to New York, where he worked with Yvonne Rainer at Merce Cunningham's studio, with the Living Theatre's Julian Beck* and Judith Malina, and with graphic artist Richard Tyler, among others. Schumann's first American production, *Totentanz* (*Dance of Death*, 1961) established his reputation for sharply political themes, attacking the establishment with simplicity, passion, and humor. Schumann's company, the Bread and Puppet Theatre, participated actively in civil rights and antiwar movements, and its grotesque, giant puppets were easily spotted at the head of peace and protest parades.

Schumann found New York politics offensive and the theatre scene to be elitist and artificial; so in 1970, at an invitation from Goddard College to become resident artists, he and his family of puppeteers left New York for Plainfield, Vermont. There, they found a more honest audience of farmers and small-town parade-watchers, and a close-to-the earth communal lifestyle which deliberately rejected both the city and the world of corporate art. After the Goddard experience, they established a permanent home base on a 160-acre farm in Vermont. Since the 1970s, they have sustained themselves with appearances and workshops on American college campuses, and have toured extensively throughout the Americas and both Eastern and Western Europe, where tours begun in 1968 and 1969 had created a fanatical following. In 1978, Schumann received Amsterdam's Erasmus Prize for outstanding cultural contributions.

Schumann continues to present shows in New York and other major cities, but since 1970, Bread and Puppet's major annual event is "Our Domestic Resurrection Circus," staged in a naturally formed amphitheatre on the Glover farm. This two-day outdoor extravaganza attracts hundreds of enthusiastic volunteer puppeteers, and up to 20,000 spectators, rain or shine. More event than theatre, it is an original, multimedia parody of circus which deals with life, death, and resurrection. Ritualistic and "basic" theatricality created in a natural setting takes the place of complicated plot structures and individual characterizations. Skits and sideshows related to a unifying idea are laced with themes of plain living, war and resistance, poverty, despair and hope. Recent subjects have focused on Central American and Middle Eastern politics, the "new world order," and the "triumph of capitalism."

ADDITIONAL PRODUCTIONS: 1962: *The Christmas Story, A Man Says Goodbye to His Mother*; 1966: *Fire*; 1969: *Cry of the People for Meat*; 1970: *Grey Lady Cantatas, The Difficult Life of Uncle Fatso*; 1971: *The 14 Stations of the Cross, The White Washing of the Dirty Sheets of Attica*; 1970–present: *Our Domestic Resurrection Circus*; 1972: *That*

Simple Light May Rise Out of Complicated Darkness; 1977: *Joan of Arc, White Horse Butcher*; 1978: *St. Francis Preaches to the Birds*; 1983: *The Fight against the End of the World*; 1984: *The Crucifixion and Resurrection of Archbishop Romero*; 1988: *Passion Play for a Young Tree, Icarus*; 1989: *Insurrection Opera & Oratorio, Uprising of the Beast*, 1991: *Columbus: The New World Order.*

SELECTED BIBLIOGRAPHY: Bell, John. "The Bread and Puppet Theatre in Nicaragua, 1987 (with text of the Nicaraguan Passion Play)." *New Theatre Quarterly* 5 (February 1989); Brecht, Stefan. *Peter Schumann's Bread and Puppet Theatre.* 2 vols. New York: Routledge, 1988; Green, Susan. *Bread & Puppet: Stories of Struggle & Faith in South America.* Burlington, VT: Green Valley, 1985; Hager, Steven. "The Power of Puppets." *Horizon* May 1980: 49–55; Kourilsky, Francoise. *Le Bread and Puppet Theatre.* Lausanne: L'Age d'Homme, 1971; Roose-Evans, James. *Experimental Theatre from Stanislavsky to Today.* New York: Universe, 1970; Rough, William. "The Bread & Puppet Theatre, An Interview with Peter Schumann." *Dramatics* 45 (December 1973): 24–29; Sainer, Arthur. *The Radical Theatre Notebook.* New York: Avon, 1975; *The Drama Review* 14 (September 1970), Special Issue devoted to the Bread and Puppet Theatre.

William H. Rough

MAURICE (AVROM-MOYSHE) SCHWARTZ [b. June 18, 1890, Sidelkov, Ukraine; d. May 10, 1960, Tel Aviv, Israel]. When Schwartz was eleven, his father left Ukraine for America in search of economic opportunity. He soon sent ship tickets for the rest of the family to join him, but Maurice had to stay alone in Liverpool due to a problem with the ticket. He worked at various jobs in London, sang in a cantor's choir, and started going to the Yiddish theatre. Schwartz spent two years in London before his father located him and brought him to the United States.

After arriving in New York, Schwartz attended school for a short time, worked in a factory, and studied at night with a German teacher who read him the German classics and Shakespeare. He then started performing with a Yiddish theatre company in New York for a short time before working two-year stints in Baltimore and Chicago as both actor and stage manager. When he took on unofficial directorial duties, he did his job so well that he was soon made the official director. Schwartz said that he spent his first thirty dollars earned as a director on ten projectors, with which he started experimenting with stage lighting.

Schwartz's epoch as a major theatre director began in 1918 when he took over the Irving Place Theatre, which had previously housed a German theatre company. Schwartz's troupe would come to be called the Yiddish Art Theatre, and would depart from the style and repertoire of earlier Yiddish theatre by emulating the practice of troupes such as the Moscow Art Theatre. However, Schwartz did not completely throw off the mantle of his melodramatic Yiddish precursors; rather, he fashioned a new coat of many colors, striking a balance between old-fashioned Yiddish theatre and the Stanislavskian approach of the new art theatre movement. Thus, the company's productions featured Schwartz in strong starring roles, but he surrounded himself with talented actors such as Celia Adler, Jacob

Ben-Ami, Bertha Gersten, and Muni Weisenfreund (who would later change his name to Paul Muni). Schwartz also drew upon the artistic talents of such scene designers as Boris Aronson, Mordecai Gorelik, and Sam Leve.

The Yiddish Art Theatre's first production was Zalmen Libin's *Man and His Shadow* (1918), a conventional melodrama. Much of the rest of the season featured plays by major European writers: for example, Bernard Shaw's *Mrs. Warren's Profession*, Henrik Ibsen's *A Doll's House* (under the title *Nora*) and *Ghosts*, and Leo Tolstoy's *Resurrection*. But the real breakthrough in the repertory came via the influence of Ben-Ami, who pushed for the presentation of new Yiddish drama. With Schwartz's grudging permission, Ben-Ami selected Peretz Hirschbein's *Farvorfn Vinkl* (*A Secluded Nook*, 1918), whose understated climaxes veered away from the grandiose effects typical of earlier Yiddish plays. Critics and intellectuals lauded the play, but Ben-Ami soon left Schwartz's company to found the short-lived Jewish Art Theatre.

One of the major achievements of the Yiddish Art Theatre was its longevity. Schwartz kept the theatre going, in a number of venues around New York City, until 1950. One secret to the company's success was the adaptation of Yiddish novels for the stage, a practice Schwartz initiated in 1922 with his version of Sholom Asch's *Motke ganef* (*Motke the Thief*). A decade later, the enormous success of *Yoshe Kalb*, adapted from I. J. Singer's novel, led Schwartz to shift the company's emphasis away from the repertory system and toward long runs. *Yoshe Kalb* ran for the entire 1932–33 season, a feat repeated by *The Brothers Ashkenazi* (1937–38), adapted from I. J. Singer's novel by Singer and Schwartz; Singer's *The Family Carnovsky* (1943–44); and AriIbn-Zahav's *Shylock and His Daughter* (1947–48).

In addition to his live theatre work, Schwartz made a number of films, directing and starring in three of them: *Broken Hearts* (1926), *Uncle Moses* (1930), and *Tevye der milkhiker* (*Tevye the Dairyman*, 1930). He acted until the very end of his life, and died in Israel while on a theatrical tour.

ADDITIONAL PRODUCTIONS: 1918: *Uriel Acosta*; *The Robbers*; 1919: *Professor Bernhardi*; *Der yidisher kenig Lear* (*The Jewish King Lear*) and *Mirele Efros* (Jacob Gordin); *The Treasure* (David Pinski); *The Father, Tevye der milkhiker* (Sholom Aleichem, adapted by Schwartz); *Got, mentsh, un tayvl* (*God, Man, and Devil*, by Gordin); *The Lower Depths*; 1920: *Di goldene keyt* (*The Golden Chain*, by I. L. Peretz); *Shver tsu zayn a yid* (*Hard to Be a Jew*, by Aleichem); 1921: *Der vilder mensch* (*The Wild Man*, by Gordin); *The Dybbuk* (Ansky); *Shmates* (*Rags*, by H. Leivick); 1922: *Dembes* (*Oaks*, by Fishl Bimko); *Uncle Vanya*; *The Inspector General, Dos groise gevins* (*The Jackpot*, by Aleichem); 1923: *Shnorers* (*Beggars*, by H. Leivick); 1924: *Wolves* (Rolland); 1925: *Yankl Boyle* (Leon Kobrin); 1927: *The Gardener's Dog* (Lope de Vega); 1928: *Kiddush hashem* (Asch, adapted by Schwartz); 1931: *Riverside Drive* (Kobrin); 1933: *The Wise Men of Chelm* (adapted by Schwartz).

SELECTED BIBLIOGRAPHY: Adler, Celia. *Tsili Adler Dertsevlt* [*Celia Adler Recounts*]. 2 vols. New York: Tsili Adler Foundation un BuchKomitet, 1959; Bialin, A. H. *Maurice Schwartz un der Yidisher Kunst Teater* [*Maurice Schwartz and the Yiddish Art Theatre*]. New York: Farlag Biderman, 1934; Durham, Weldon, ed. *American Theatre Companies,*

1888–1930. Westport, CT: Greenwood Press, 1987: 489–92; Gorin, B. *Di geshikhte fun Yidishn teater* [*The History of Yiddish Theatre*]. Vol. 2. New York: Max N. Mayzel, 1923; Lifson, David S. *The Yiddish Theatre in America.* Cranbury, NJ: A. S. Barnes, 1965; Perlmutter, Sholem. *Yidishe dramaturgn un teater-compozitors* [*Yiddish Dramatists and Theatre Composers*]. New York: Yiddisher Kultur Farband (YKUF), 1952: 277–84; Sandrow, Nahma. *Vagabond Stars.* New York: Limelight Editions, 1986; Zylbercweig, Zalmen. *Leksikon fun Yidishn teater* [*Lexicon of Yiddish Theatre*]. Vol. 3. New York: Hebrew Actors Union of America, Farlag Elisheva, 1963: 2327–68.

Joel Berkowitz

HAROLD R. SCOTT [b. September 6, 1935, Morristown, New Jersey]. A director of a wide range of dramas, Harold Scott is best known for his revivals of American plays. The son of a physician, he received his undergraduate education at Harvard and appeared in over fifty productions as a professional actor before turning his attentions to directing. From 1970 to 1976, Scott spent his summers as staff director of the Eugene O'Neill Theatre Center. In 1972, Scott became the first black hired as artistic director of a primarily white theatre institution, the Cincinnati Playhouse in the Park. Currently, he heads the graduate directing program at the Mason Gross School of the Arts, Rutgers University.

Scott's philosophy of directing has been profoundly shaped by his work as an actor with directors Elia Kazan,* Harold Clurman,* José Quintero,* and Robert Lewis.* According to Scott, the director is the unifying factor in the collaborative process. Casting is the director's most important decision, wherein the director chooses the actor who best fits his image of each character. During the rehearsal process, Scott nurtures the development of ensemble acting while aiding the actor in shedding barriers which inhibit a sincere portrayal of emotions. To guide the actor to an understanding of a role, Scott feels that the director must be able to empathize with the actor's creative process. As the actor develops his role, the director edits the performance. For Scott, this approach is enhanced as one grows older and more experienced.

The revivals of Lorraine Hansberry's *A Raisin in the Sun* (1986) and *Paul Robeson* (1988) represent Scott's most renowned productions to date. For *Raisin*, he restored passages cut from the original Broadway production and inspired critically acclaimed performances from such cast members as Olivia Cole and Starletta DuPois. A revised version of Phillip Hayes Dean's play, *Robeson*, became a tour de force for actor Avery Brooks under Scott's sensitive and imaginative direction.

ADDITIONAL PRODUCTIONS: 1971: *Terra Nova* (Ted Tally); 1974: *Waltz of the Toreadors* (Jean Anouilh); 1974: *Monkey, Monkey, Bottle of Beer, How Many Monkeys Have We Here?* (Marsha Sheiness), *The Past Is a Pest* (Richard Wesley), *He's Got a Jones* (G. Tito Shaw); 1978: *The Mighty Gents* (Richard Wesley); 1980: *Arms and the Man*; 1982: *Child of the Sun* (Damien Leake); 1988: *Les Blancs* (Hansberry); 1989: *The Member of the Wedding* (Carson McCullers).

SELECTED BIBLIOGRAPHY: Cloyd, Iris, ed. *Who's Who among Black Americans.* 6th ed. Detroit: Gale Research, 1990; Scott, Ruth. "His World's a Stage." *Rutgers Magazine*

November/December 1987: 14–17; Shirley, Don. *"He's Got a Jones*: Making and Look-ing at History." *Washington Post* 11 February 1975: B9.

Addell Austin Anderson

PETER SELLARS [b. 1957, Pittsburgh, Pennsylvania]. Labeled an iconoclastic director for his contemporized productions of classic plays and operas, Sellars was considered a major American director by the time he was twenty-seven years old. While an undergraduate at Harvard, Sellars directed more than forty experimental productions, opening a classic play or opera every two weeks at the Explosives B Cabaret. During this period, his staging of *King Lear* featured a black street musician, who drove onstage in a Lincoln Continental.

While still a student, he was invited by Robert Brustein, director of American Repertory Theatre (ART), to direct Gogol's *The Inspector General* (1980). After this success at a major American theatre, Sellars became director of the Boston Shakespeare Company. In his production of *Pericles* (1982), the lead character became homeless, lost his family, grew dreadlocks, and slept in a refrigerator box. Many of Sellar's productions for the company used strong intercultural themes and non-Western performance techniques.

Sellar's tenure, from 1983 to 1984, ended when he could not solve the financial problems of the company. Around the same time, he helped to create *My One and Only* (1982), a Broadway musical from which he was fired before it opened in New York. In the same week that he was dismissed, Sellars received a MacArthur Foundation Award of $136,000 to sustain him as an artist.

In 1984, Sellars was named the new director of the American National Theatre at the Kennedy Center for the Performing Arts. Unfortunately, Sellars left after only one season because he failed to build support for the theatre, despite his solid productions of Anton Chekhov's *A Seagull* (1985, Sellars renamed it from *The Sea Gull*); Alexander Dumas's *The Count of Monte Cristo* (1985); and Sophocles' *Ajax* (1986).

During the late 1980s, Sellars concentrated on directing operas. His most famous were the Mozart/Da Ponte operas: *Le Nozze di Figaro*, *Don Giovanni*, and *Cosi fan Tutte*. These were performed at the Pepsico Summerfare, Purchase, New York, in 1989, after previous individual productions there and elsewhere. To reveal these operas' social and political messages, each one was presented with contemporary settings and costumes, but with the original text and music intact. *Le Nozze di Figaro* was set in the posh Manhattan condominium, Trump Tower, *Don Giovanni* in the dilapidated slums of the Bronx, and *Cosi fan tutte* in a 1950s style diner. In 1990, the three operas were televised in Austria and subsequently shown on public television in the United States, thus introducing Sellar's work to an international audience.

In 1990, Sellars became an advisor to the Boston Opera Theatre, which will produce some of his earlier works as well as some new ones. He, together with his collaborators John Adams and Alice Goodman, may be credited with revi-talizing twentieth-century opera by introducing new works such as *Nixon in*

China (1988), and *The Death of Klinghoffer* (1991), about the real-life hijacking of a luxury ship and the killing of a hostage by terrorists.

In 1987, Sellars was named director of the biennial Los Angeles Festival, originated as the Olympic Arts Festival in 1984. In 1991, Sellars showcased plays from the Pacific Rim, the avant-garde, and Latin America, as well as local works. Focusing on a multicultural approach to the selection process, Sellars hoped to break through cultural barriers with these diverse theatrical presentations.

Sellar's work has been labeled "postmodern" because of his disinterest in historical reproduction, his mixed time frames, his use of a visual text different from the literal one, and his layering of imagery in any given moment of the work. His work, however, is rooted in the theories of such modern theorists as Richard Wagner, Vsevolod Meyerhold,* and Bertolt Brecht.* What he has accomplished so far in his directing career is to extend the theories of the moderns with a multicultural approach. Thus, he has helped to break down the ethnocentricity of the Western classic canon and has created a postmodern vision of theatre.

ADDITIONAL PRODUCTIONS: 1971–75 at Phillips Academy: *Portrait of a Madonna* (Tennessee Williams), *The Lesson*, *The Tempest*; 1976–80 at Harvard University: *Lulu* (Wedekind), *King Lear*, *When We Dead Awaken*; 1981: *Kabuki Western* (National Theatre for the Deaf), *Orlando* (Handel, ART); 1982: *Play/MacBeth* (Boston Shakespeare Company); *Mikado* (Chicago Lyric Opera); *The Visions of Simone Machard* (by Brecht: La Jolla Playhouse), *The Lighthouse* (Peter Maxwell Davies); 1984: *Hang on to Me* (Gorky's *Summerfolk* adapted using Gershwin's music); 1985: *Giulio Cesare in Egitto* (Handel); 1986: *Zangesi*; 1987: *Cosi fan tutte* and *Don Giovanni* (Mozart/Da Ponte operas at Pepsico Summerfare); 1988: *Le Nozze di Figaro* (Mozart/DaPonte opera at Pepsico); 1991: *The Cabinet of Dr. Ramirez* (film).

SELECTED BIBLIOGRAPHY: Bartow, Arthur. *The Director's Voice: Twenty-One Interviews*. New York: Theatre Communications Group, 1988:268–85; Coe, Robert. "What Makes Sellars Run?" *American Theatre* 4 (Dec. 1987): 12–19, 46–49; Cole, Susan Letzler. *Directors in Rehearsal: A Hidden World*. New York: Routledge, 1992: 187–96; Jenkins, Ron. "Peter Sellars" (interview). *Theater* 15 (Spring 1984): 46–52; Mikotowicz, Tom. "Director Peter Sellars: Bridging the Modern and Postmodern Theatre." *Theatre Topics* 1 (March 1991): 87–96; Shewey, Don. "I Hate Decoration Onstage: Director Peter Sellars Talks about Design." *Theatre Crafts* Jan. 1984: 24–27, 44–45.

Tom Mikotowicz

ANDREI SERBAN [b. June 21, 1943, Bucharest, Romania]. Even before completing the directing program at the Romanian Institute of Theatre and Cinematography in Bucharest in 1968, Andrei Serban created the controversy that has always marked his work. His student production of *Julius Caesar* (1965), staged as a Kabuki play with stylized singing and dancing, created a scandal, which was aggravated by his final student project, a bloody, Artaudian version of *Arden of Faversham* (1965). Any doubts about his talents were resolved, however, with his Asian-inspired, masked version of *The Good Woman of Setzuan* (1968), performed by the Young People's Theatre of Piatra Neampt. The work was a triumph in Bucharest, and the cultural press hailed Serban as the preeminent member of a talented generation of young Romanian directors. Clearly, two of Serban's major commitments as a director were evident in his early work: reinvigorating the classics and creating a fusion between Eastern and Western theatrical styles.

On seeing *The Good Woman* during an international theatre conference, Ellen Stewart of New York's La Mama Experimental Theatre Club invited Serban to come to the United States. Before leaving Romania in 1969, however, Serban directed Marin Sorescu's *Jonah* at Bucharest's Little Theatre. It was the last time Serban worked in his native language, a fact that undoubtedly helped form his complex and often ambivalent attitude toward theatrical language.

His New York directing debut at La Mama in 1970 was a reconceived and shortened production of *Arden of Faversham*. After Peter Brook* saw the production, he invited Serban to come to his International Center for Theatre Research in Paris. In 1971 Serban worked as Brook's assistant on the production of *Orghast* in Iran. Under Brook's influence, Serban began to develop the distinctive ideas that mark his form of theatre, specifically the emphasis on raw sound and physical movement, which actors use, not to represent emotions, but to create and transmit them to audiences. His experience in Iran, particularly his investigations of the Ruhozi village traditions, also gave him his first direct contact with Eastern culture. Since then Serban has visited Bali, studying its village theatres, and has worked with the Noh and Kabuki masters of Japan. Probably no other director working in America has gone so far in incorporating Asian styles and aesthetic values into his work.

Soon after returning to New York, Serban began work at La Mama on a two-year project exploring the Greek tragedies *Medea*, *Electra*, and *The Trojan Woman*, which were produced in 1974 and revived in 1987 under the title *Fragments of a Trilogy*. For *Fragments of a Trilogy*, he boldly sacrificed a *literal* understanding of the language of the plays to an entirely emotional one. By using ancient Greek together with a variety of often obscure languages, Serban assured that language could no longer be used as a medium for expressing ideas; instead, words were used for their sounds and resonances and for the emotion that they produced. To Serban the human voice itself has the capacity to transmit vibrations—"energies that go beyond cultural and geographical differences."

Together with *Fragments of a Trilogy*, Serban's other work at La Mama received a great deal of critical attention. At La Mama he formed the Great Jones Repertory Company, and between 1974 and 1976 he produced *The Good Woman of Setzuan* with Priscilla Smith, and an experimental version of *As You Like It* (1976).

In 1976 Joseph Papp invited Serban to direct *The Cherry Orchard* at the Vivian Beaumont Theatre. The text was a new version by Jean-Claude van Itallie, and the production was a major cultural event of the year, both hailed and reviled by the New York critics. Since then Serban has directed six productions for the New York Shakespeare Festival including his own version of

Mikhail Bulgakov's *The Master and Margarita* (1978) and an uncharacteristic stage adaptation of Jacques Demy's film musical *The Umbrellas of Cherbourg* (1979), which had a brief commercial engagement in London.

In 1977 Serban began a long and productive artistic relationship with Robert Brustein, then dean of the Yale Drama School and artistic director of the Yale Repertory Theatre. As associate director of the Yale Repertory Theatre in 1977, Serban directed *The Ghost Sonata* and *Sganarelle: An Evening of Molière Farces*. When Brustein moved to Harvard, founding the American Repertory Theatre (ART) there in 1979, Serban followed, directing nine productions at the ART between 1980 and 1989. Much of Serban's work is collaborative, both with actors and other artists. Two of his important collaborators are the composer Elizabeth Swados and lighting designer Jennifer Tipton. Since 1980, Serban has staged many operas both in the United States and abroad. In 1990 Serban rejected an offer to return to Romania as director of the National Theatre.

ADDITIONAL PRODUCTIONS: 1968, 1975, 1986: *The Good Woman of Setzuan*; 1972–74: *Arden of Faversham*; 1980: *The Sea Gull*; 1982: *The Three Sisters*; 1984: *The King Stag* (Gozzi); 1985: *The Marriage of Figaro*; 1986: *The Juniper Tree* (Phillip Glass, Robert Moran, Arthur Yorinks); 1989: *Twelfth Night*, *The Serpent Woman* (Gozzi).

SELECTED BIBLIOGRAPHY: Bartow, Arthur. *The Director's Voice: Twenty-One Interviews*. New York: Theatre Communications Group, 1988: 286–99; Blumenthal, Eileen. "Interview with Andrei Serban." *Yale Theatre* 8 (Spring 1977): 66–77; Coldstream, John. "Matters of the Heart." *Plays and Players* 27 (April 1980): 16–17; Steele, Mike. "The Romanian Connection." *American Theatre* 2 (July/Aug. 1985): 4–11.

Miles Coiner

JEAN-MARIE SERREAU [b. April 28, 1915, Poitiers, France; d. ca. June 1, 1973, Paris, France]. The name of Jean-Marie Serreau is often associated with those of Jacques Mauclair and Roger Blin,* the three directors well-known for their work with the avant-garde theatre. Like Jean Vilar* and Jean-Louis Barrault,* they were trained by Charles Dullin,* himself a well-known pupil of Jacques Copeau.* Although their styles differed, they all shared the sense of integrity and pioneering spirit which typified Copeau's work.

Jean-Marie Serreau was greatly responsible for the discovery and success of the theatre of the absurd, directing plays by Arthur Adamov, Eugene Ionesco, and Samuel Beckett and bringing plays by Ionesco to London. From 1952 to 1955, he directed and managed the small left-bank Théâtre de Babylone, which quickly became a focal point for the avant-garde. It was hoped that his theatre would become the postwar equivalent of Copeau's Vieux-Colombier, but like many other small theatres, Serreau's venture went bankrupt and the Théâtre de Babylone had to close its doors. During those few years, however, the audience was presented with the most important productions of the avant-garde. In 1954, during a festival called *Estivales du théâtre*, Serreau invited the main producers of the avant-garde theatre to present their most characteristic productions, providing an unforgettable event for theatre lovers who saw some of the best productions of Luigi Pirandello,* August Strindberg, Jean Genet, Adamov, and

Ionesco. Serreau offered the hospitality of his theatre to Roger Blin when the latter was searching for a place to stage the very first production of Beckett's *Waiting for Godot*.

Serreau befriended Bertolt Brecht* and was the first director in France to produce his work (*The Exception and the Rule*, 1947). In the 1960s, he produced third-world political works by Aimé Césaire and Kaleb Yacine, one of the most notable being *La Femme sauvage* (Yacine, 1964), one of the rare tragedies inspired by the Algerian war and written by an Arab author. Serreau also assembled casts including black and Arab actors and took them to Africa to perform Brecht's plays. He employed styles including non-European rhythms and gestures which contrasted with the usual European stage conventions, and he was one of the first directors to experiment with multimedia performances in an attempt to link technology, science, and poetry.

Experiment and innovation were Serreau's keywords; yet his style, which was characterized by simple but intelligent interpretation, was respectful of the text and author's intent. Like Copeau, he relied on his actors' talents and preferred plain though imaginative stage designs. From his actors, he demanded integrity and sobriety (in full accord with Brecht's distancing techniques).

In 1972–73, he managed the Théâtre de la Tempête, which joined the Théâtre du Soleil of Ariane Mnouchkine* and other experimental groups in the Cartoucherie de Vincennes. Jean-Marie Serreau was married to Geneviève Serreau, director, theatre producer, and writer of *Histoire du Nouveau Théâtre*.

ADDITIONAL PRODUCTIONS: 1950: *La grande et la petite manoeuvre* (Adamov); 1952: *La Parodie*, *Les Retrouvailles* (Adamov); 1953: *Le Ping Pong*, *Tous contre tous* (Adamov); 1954: *Amédée* (Ionesco); 1957: *Paolo-Paoli* (Adamov); 1964: *Comédie* (Beckett); 1965: *La Tragédie du Roi Christophe* (Césaire); 1966: *La Soif et la faim* (Ionesco); *Pique-nique en campagne* (Arrabal).

SELECTED BIBLIOGRAPHY: de Baecque, André. *Le théâtre d'aujourd'hui*. Paris: Seghers, 1964; Serreau, Geneviève. *Histoire du Nouveau théâtre*. Paris: Gallimard, 1966; Surer, P. *Le théâtre français contemporain*. Paris: Société d'édition et d'enseignement supérieur, 1964.

Liliane Papin

RUBEN SIERRA [b. December 6, 1946, San Antonio, Texas]. Ruben Sierra received a B.A. in drama and sociology from St. Mary's University in 1971 and an M.A. in directing and criticism from the University of Washington in 1974. Along with his directing, Sierra is a highly respected playwright, actor, producer, teacher, and administrator. He served as the producing director of the Shoestring Players (1968–69), artistic coordinator of Creative Arts of San Antonio (1972), artistic director of Teatro del Piojo (1972–75), artistic director of Teatro Quetzalcoatl (1974–76), and the founding artistic director of the Seattle Group Theatre Company (1978).

Sierra's early days with Teatro del Piojo focused on the development of *actos*, brief satirical agitprop pieces developed through improvisation. Actos developed under his direction include *La Capirotada de los Esoejos*, *School Days*, *La*

Huelga, and *El Tecato*. He also directed *The Shrunken Head of Pancho Villa* (1973) by Luis Valdez,* for the company. As artistic director of Teatro Quetzalcoatl he wrote and directed *Manolo*, a play about a Chicano who survives Vietnam only to succumb to the tentacles of drug addiction. *Manolo* toured extensively throughout the Southwest (1974–75).

Distinguishing features of Sierra's directing career are his commitment to multiethnic plays and his development of the Seattle Group Theatre into a professional theatre company dedicated to producing culturally diverse material. West Coast premieres directed by Sierra include John Klein's *T-Bone and Weasel* (1989), Manuel Puig's *Kiss of the Spider Woman (1988),* Athol Fugard's *A Lesson from Aloes* (1982), Derek Walcott's *Pantomime* (1981), Emilio Carballido's *Orinoco!* (1984), and Tom Cole's *Medal of Honor Rag* (1980). Sierra has worked extensively on new plays, and as artistic director of the Seattle Group Theatre, he created the American multiethnic Playwrights' Festival. Some of the writers with whom he has worked closely include William Mastrosimone, Derek Walcott, Emilio Carballido, Silvia Gonzales Scherer, William S. Yellow Robe, Jr., and Garry Trudeau.

Among his many other activities, Sierra has served as editor of *Metamorfosis* (1976–77); head of playwriting, School of Theatre, University of Washington (1975–78); and head of Multi-Ethnic Theatre Program (1974–78) and dean, School of Theatre, California Institute of the Arts (1989–91). He has been a consultant to the Ford Foundation and the Rockefeller Foundation. Plays written by Sierra that have been produced include *Manolo*, *Articus and the Angel*, *The Millionaire y El Pobrecito*, and *Say, Can You See?* As an actor, he has performed throughout the United States in his one-man show *I Am Celso* (adapted from the poems of New Mexican writer Leo Romero), which was presented by Joseph Papp at the Public Theatre in New York in 1985. Other roles include "Romero" in *The Fifth Sun*, "Megs" in the West Coast premiere of *Strange Snow*, "La Patumiera" in *Primary English Class*, "The Historical Event" in Amlin Gray's *How I Got That Story*, and "Black Bart" in *Deadwood Dick*. Sierra is a member of the Dramatists Guild, Screen Actors Guild, Actors Equity Association, and American Federation of Television and Radio Artists.

ADDITIONAL PRODUCTIONS: 1979: *Short Eyes* (Miguel Pinero); 1983: *The Last Carnival* (Derek Walcott); 1987: *Tamer of Horses* (William Mastrosimone), *Idioglossia* (Mark Handley); 1989: *Extremities* (William Mastrosimone); 1990: *Zone D* (Ed and Millie Lewis).

Tony Curiel

PAUL SILLS [b. November 18, 1927, Chicago, Illinois]. Son of Viola Spolin, the creator of improvisational theatre games, Sills is known as one of the originators of the Second City, a Chicago-based improvisational theatre company. Sills has employed Spolin's games in staging ensemble productions that emphasize physical freedom and split-second reactions, spontaneity and creativity.

As a student at the University of Chicago, Sills joined David Shepherd and

Eugene Troobnick in 1953 to form the Playwrights Theatre Club. Two years and twenty-five plays later, he began the Compass, the first professional improvisational acting troupe. The actors spontaneously created pieces from brief written scenarios. Although the Compass disbanded in 1957, Sills initiated a style that would foster the talents of many comedians and influence virtually all improvisational performance.

In 1959, Sills, Bernard Sahlins, and ex-Compass player Howard Alk founded the Second City. Reappropriating the condescending name that New York critics had attached to Chicago, the Second City performed short, often satirical scenes developed from rehearsed improvisation and audience suggestions. The company was extremely successful, and included, among others, Mike Nichols,* Elaine May, Ed Asner, and Joan Rivers. The Second City continues to perform today.

Sills directed the Second City's productions in Chicago, Los Angeles, and New York until 1967, when he left the company to work with Spolin on *The Game Theatre*, a production which involved audience participation. From there, Sills created and staged *Story Theatre*, a highly acclaimed ensemble performance of adaptations of Grimms' fairy tales. Opening at the Yale Repertory Theatre, *Story Theatre* then played at the Mark Taper Forum in Los Angeles, on Broadway, and became a television series, which Sills also directed. *Story Theatre* was noted for speed of presentation, cleverness, and anachronistic but relevant political and social commentary. It featured actors who wore bright colors, created "cartoonish" characters, and both narrated and "acted out" myths and fairy tales in a broad acting style.

Sills directed versions of "the best of" the Second City improvisations, including *Sills and Company* in 1986, which brought together both first and second-generation Second City actors. Like the work at the Second City, this production relied on audience suggestions.

In 1988, Sills directed *Talking to Myself* (which he adapted from Studs Terkel's novel) at the Northlight Theatre in Chicago. That same year, in conjunction with Mike Nichols and George Morrison, he founded the New Actors workshop, which provides a double focus on both Spolin's theatre games and refinements of the Stanislavsky-based "method" techniques. He currently teaches improvisation at the New York City workshop.

ADDITIONAL PRODUCTIONS: 1961: *From the Second City*; 1963: *To the Water Tower*; 1964: *Open Season at Second City, Dynamite Tonight* (Arnold Weinstein and William Bolcom); 1967: revival of *Dynamite Tonight*; 1968: *Greatshot* (Arnold Weinstein), *The American Revolution:Part I* (co-written with Arnold Weinstein); 1970: *Paul Sills's Story Theatre*; 1971: *Metamorphoses* and revival of *Story Theatre*.

SELECTED BIBLIOGRAPHY: Coleman, Janet. *The Compass*. New York: Knopf, 1990; Durham, Weldon, ed. "Yale Rep." *American Theatre Companies, 1931–1986*. Westport, CT: Greenwood Press, 1989: 535; London, Todd. "Chicago Impromptu." *American Theatre* 7 (July-August 1990):14–23, 60–64; Loney, Glenn. *20th Century Theatre*. Vol. 2. New York: Facts on File, 1983; McCrohan, Donna. *The Second City*. New York: Putnam, 1987; *New York Times* 27 September 1961; 23 January 1964; 16 March 1964; 16 March 1967; 27 October 1970; 8 November 1970; 23 April 1971; 16 December 1984;

2 May 1986; 8 June 1986; 10 June 1986; 20 July 1986; Sweet, Jeffrey. *Something Wonderful Right Away*. New York: Avon Books, 1978; *Variety* 25 June 1986, 28 September 1988.

Stacy Wolf

RUBEN NIKOLAEVICH SIMONOV [b. April 1, 1899, Moscow; d. December 5, 1968, Moscow]. Ruben Simonov had a long and distinguished career on the Soviet stage from the 1920s to the 1960s, and the diverse assortment of productions in which he participated as an actor or director mirrors the varied approaches and tastes of post-revolutionary Russia.

Simonov studied law at Moscow University before entering the Chaliapin Drama Studio in 1919. In 1921 and 1922, he worked as an actor under the direction of Evgeni Vakhtangov* at the historic Third Studio of the Moscow Art Theatre (called the Vakhtangov Theatre after 1926). There, he became a disciple of Vakhtangov and his particular blend of psychological realism and theatricality. For Vakhtangov, who considered him a favorite student, Simonov portrayed Joseph in Maurice Maeterlinck's *The Miracle of St. Anthony* (1921), Dymba in Anton Chekhov's *A Wedding* (1921), and Pantalone and Truffaldino in the celebrated presentation of Carlo Gozzi's *Princess Turandot* (February 1922), Vakhtangov's final production.

After Vakhtangov's death in May 1922, the theatre continued to operate under the supervision of his widow, and by 1924, Simonov had directed his first play, *Lev Gurych Sinichkin* by D. T. Lensky. During his tenure as artistic director of the theatre from 1924 to 1939, and then as chief director from 1939 until his death in 1968, he directed over three dozen productions. Simonov was succeeded at the Vakhtangov Theatre by his son, Evgeni Rubenovich Simonov.

Simonov's devotion to Vakhtangov's directorial approach is evident in his enthusiastic memoir, *Stanislavsky's Protege: Eugene Vakhtangov*. As did Vakhtangov, Simonov strived to suit the production style to the play, employing varied means to approach everything from operettas to socialist realism. Although Simonov engineered several significant socially oriented and patriotic productions (*The Man with a Gun*, by N. Pogodin, 1937, revived 1954; *The Front*, by A. Korneichuk, 1942; *Big Kirill*, by Illa Sel'vinsky, 1957), his true gift was a strong sense of musicality, which served him best in larger-than-life comedies. Simonov received the title of People's Artist of the USSR in 1946.

ADDITIONAL PRODUCTIONS: 1926: *Marion Delorme* (Victor Hugo); 1930: *The Front Page* (Ben Hecht and Charles MacArthur); 1933: *Intervention* (Lev Slavin); 1944: *Mam'zelle Nitouch* (F. Herve); 1956: *Foma Gordeev* (based on Gorky); 1967: *Warsaw Melody* (Leonid Zorin).

SELECTED BIBLIOGRAPHY: Houghton, Norris. *Moscow Rehearsals*. New York: Harcourt, Brace and Company, 1936; Pimenov, Vladimir. *Zhizn i Stsena*. Moscow: Iskusstvo, 1971; Simonov, Ruben. *Stanislavsky's Protege: Eugene Vakhtangov*. Trans. Miriam Goldina. New York: Drama Book Specialists, 1969; *Teatr imeni Vakhtangova 1921–1971*. Moscow: Iskusstvo, 1971.

Lurana Donnels O'Malley

ALF SJÖBERG [b. June 21, 1903, Stockholm, Sweden; d. April 17, 1980, Stockholm, Sweden]. Swedish director, Alf Sjöberg found his way to the Royal Dramatic Theatre at an early age. In 1923, he was accepted as a drama student; two years later, he was employed as an actor, and from 1930 until his death, he was active as a director at the Swedish National Theatre. During these fifty years, Sjöberg mounted 138 productions which were recognized for their aesthetically detailed scenic form and their ideologically aware interpretation of the text.

Fascinated at an early stage by the idea of a folk theatre, Sjöberg worked to attract a new audience to the National Theatre. During his first two decades, he also worked for the Swedish Broadcasting Company, for whose enormous audience he created roughly 250 productions. Mostly during the forties and the fifties, he was also active as a film director and produced a total of eighteen films, of which *Frenzy*, *Miss Julie*, and *Barabbas* aroused international attention. *Miss Julie* won the Grand Prix at Cannes in 1951.

The foundation of Sjöberg's work as a director can be seen in his credo: "living stage poetry is for me a work in which there is a powerful tension between what is and what appears to be." For Sjöberg, dramatic art, with its potential for using a variety of sign systems simultaneously, both realized and conveyed the many different levels at which the action took place. This applied to both classical texts and contemporary plays. During his early years, Sjöberg preferred to produce recently written Swedish or Scandinavian dramas, but he soon realized that his main task was to introduce Swedish audiences to international drama. Sjöberg's choice of repertoire was also motivated by his determination to make the theatre into a forum for contemporary criticism.

During the 1930s and 1940s, Sjöberg's imaginative interpretations of American plays, such as Eugene O'Neill's *Desire under the Elms*, Clifford Odets's *Clash by Night*, and Arthur Miller's *Death of a Salesman*, aroused a positive response from critics and audiences alike. His early, highly nuanced, and remarkable interpretations of Federico García Lorca's *Blood Wedding*, Jean-Paul Sartre's *The Flies*, and Paul Claudel's *The Tidings Brought to Mary* rendered these landmark experiences. The influence of surrealism on Sjöberg, in his early years, later found mature expression in his 1960s production of the drama of Stanisław Witkiewicz and Witold Gombrowicz. During the same decade, he also presented five plays by Bertolt Brecht,* a series that was crowned with the highly acclaimed production of *Galileo* in 1974. By emphasizing equally the sociocritical nature of the text and the positive sensualism of the characters, Sjöberg's dramatic presentation of the lives and fortunes of the characters in *The Good Soldier Schweik*, *Mother Courage*, and *Galileo* served as an indirect opposition to the contemporary ascetic productions of the Berliner Ensemble.

Sjöberg maintained that dramatic art always functions in the present, a contention that in no way prevented him from reinterpreting the classics. What is wonderful about the theatre, Sjöberg has claimed, "is that the really great works are never out of date: you go back to them and re-work them on a completely different basis." He tackled Shakespeare early, but his definitive directorial breakthrough came in 1938 with a colorful, music and rhythm-filled production of *As You Like It*, which he interpreted as a sensuous, rococo dream. This was followed by a series of Shakespearean productions which added further depth to Sjöberg's textual interpretation and developed his ability to create dramatic characters.

Sjöberg's final production was Molière's *School for Wives* in 1980, a tribute to a man of the theatre with whom Sjöberg felt a spiritual affinity. He was also passionately interested in August Strindberg, Sweden's only *klassiker*, which led to a distinguished production of *Miss Julie* in 1949, and also to a deeper understanding of many of Strindberg's lesser-known dramas.

Sjöberg was unique in his ability to break free from shallow illusionism and, partly in connection with expressionist and surrealist aesthetics, to illuminate instead the multidimensional in the dramatic conflict. In later years, his modernist craftsmanship gained in depth from contact with French structuralism. Another quality which distinguished Sjöberg's productions was their visual beauty and sensuality. Sjöberg possessed a talent for persuading established painters and sculptors to work for the stage. They were able to collaborate very closely, as Sjöberg himself, an excellent draftsman, made the initial sketches for the sets. On the basis of these ideas, the artists were able to provide the settings with form and color. Aesthetic effect was not, however, allowed to become its own criterion, but was fully integrated into the total effect of the production. This was partly achieved with the help of Sjöberg's own sensitive lighting schemes, which always reinforced the rhythm of the play.

For Sjöberg, theatre was more than fine art; it was an invocation of life. In an absurd world, in which people readily became passive, it was essential that theatre portray alternative forms of existence. The task of Sjöberg's theatre was therefore to shake the audience to its depths; to provide pictures and counter-pictures of reality which would provoke audiences into consciously taking sides. In Sjöberg's theatre, the cooperation of the individual spectator was a fundamental requirement for the creation of each dramatic work.

SELECTED BIBLIOGRAPHY: Ek, Sverker R. *Spelplatsens magi (The Magic of the Stage). The Creative Art of Alf Sjöberg 1930–1957*. Hedemora: Gidlund, 1988; Lundin, Gunnar. *Filmregi Alf Sjöberg (Film Direction, Alf Sjöberg)*. Lund: Wallin and Dalholm, 1979; Lundin, Gunnar, and Jan Olsson. *Regtssörens roller (The Roles of the Director: Conversations with Alf Sjöberg)*. Lund: Cavefors, 1976; Sjöberg, Alf. *Teater som besvärjelse* (The Theatre as Invocation). Ed. Sverker R. Ek, Ulla Åberg, et al. Stockholm: Nordstedt, 1982.

Sverker E. Ek

BERNARD (ROTHSTEIN) SOBEL [b. January 10, 1936, Paris, France]. Bernard Sobel's personal identity as a stage director emerged from the collaborative atmosphere he fostered within the Ensemble Théâtral de Gennevilliers, a theatrical collective he has directed since its inception in 1964. Sobel's directing accomplishments, some fifty productions to date, reflect a broad repertory responsible for introducing the French public to a number of formerly unfamiliar or uncelebrated authors and works such as Ludvig Holberg's *Jeppe de la montagne* (1967) or Jakob Lenz's *Le Précepteur* (1974).

A member of the new generation of French Brechtian directors, which includes Patrice Chéreau* and Jean-Pierre Vincent,* Sobel advocates a conception of the theatre as a place of historical and dramaturgical research. Described repeatedly as "rigorous" and "didactic," Sobel's directing style, which earned him a reputation as an "orthodox Brechtian," repudiates gratuitous emotionalism and illusionism in favor of an aesthetic often accused of elitism. Artist and militant communist, he rejects the populist/elitist dichotomy in art, envisioning the theatre as a tool for comprehending reality and recognizing the mechanisms ordering our daily lives. This fundamental understanding is requisite to confrontation and change. The Ensemble's dedication to critical reflection is extended beyond the theatre in its monthly review entitled *Théâtre/Public*.

Sobel's production of *Don Juan* (1973) demonstrated a reorientation in his approach to the theatrical text, a change which corresponded to concomitant developments in structuralist criticism in the 1970s. While remaining aesthetically loyal to Brecht, Sobel abandoned "Brechtian realism," with its insistence upon the fable's content, and developed a kind of "formalist realism," accentuating the production of the text itself in order to unveil the author's ideological biases consciously or unconsciously inscribed in the work. Concern for content was thus replaced by a concern for the dialectical relation governing form and content.

In addition to directing, Sobel is also a producer of television films and documentaries. Under the name Rothstein, he has filmed several of his theatrical productions for television, among these Ludvig Holberg's *Jeppe, des collines* (1973) and Isaac Babel's *Marie* staring Maria Casarès (1980).

ADDITIONAL PRODUCTIONS: 1970: *Man Is Man*; 1972: *Madame Legros* (H. Mann; adapted by Sobel); 1973: *Round Heads and Peaked Heads* (Brecht); 1974: *The Tempest*; 1975: *Marie* (Babel); 1976: *The Jew of Malta* (Christopher Marlowe); 1981: *Edward II* (Christopher Marlowe); 1983: *Maria Stuart* (Schiller); 1984: *La Cruche cassée* (Heinrich von Kleist); 1985: *The School for Wives*; 1987: *Nathan the Wise* (Lessing); 1988: *Hecuba* (Euripides); 1990: *The Good Woman of Setzuan*; 1991: *Life of the Revolutionary Pelagie Vlassova of Tver* (adaptation of Brecht's *Mother*).

SELECTED BIBLIOGRAPHY: Sandier, Gilles. *Théâtre en crise*. Grenoble: Edition La Pensée Sauvage, 1982; Temkine, Raymonde. *Mettre en scène au présent*. Lausanne: La Cité/l'Age d'Homme, 1977; Temkine, Raymonde. *Le Théâtre au présent*. Lectoure, France: Pezin, 1987.

Constance Spreen

LUIGI SQUARZINA [b. February 18, 1922, Livorno, Italy]. After graduating as a theatre director from the National Academy of Dramatic Art in Rome in 1947, Squarzina started a long and active career as playwright, translator, critic, and, above all, as theatre director. As a director, he is best known for staging some of the most notable Italian productions of the 1960s and 1970s. At the beginning of his career, his interest was mainly in contemporary dramaturgy (especially American), but he later shifted to a more traditional, "classical" repertoire.

After his initial experimental productions of John Steinbeck's *Of Mice and Men* (1944) and *All My Sons* (1947), Squarzina sought to find a more balanced staging technique through study in the United States. The recipient of a Fulbright Fellowship in 1951–52, he attended the Yale Drama School, where he was profoundly influenced by Professor Alois Nagler's method of teaching the history of theatre. After returning to Italy, relying upon Nagler's methodology, Squarzina served as a principal supervisor for the comprehensive *Theatre Encyclopedia* for many years, while continuing to direct and write plays.

Squarzina is responsible for introducing Italian audiences to Sidney Kingsley's *Detective Story*, Herman Wouk's *Caine Mutiny*, Michael V. Gazzo's *A Hatful of Rain*, and Archibald MacLeish's *J.B.* As co-director of the Teatro Stabile of Genoa from 1962 until 1976 (when he moved to the Teatro di Roma, where he remained until 1983), Squarzina became known for his innovative productions of Bertolt Brecht,* whom he championed in Italy. He was equally renowned for producing Luigi Pirandello* and Carlo Goldoni (*One of the Last Evenings of Carneval*, 1968; *I rusteghi*, 1969; *The New House,* 1973), and revived both playwrights' work on the Italian stage.

While Squarzina's name is most frequently attached to Brecht's, Pirandello's, and Goldoni's work, he has also had an impact by directing his own plays— *Universal Exposition* (1949), *A Three-Quarter Moon* (1953), *Her Part in History* (1955), *The Woman from Romagna* (1959), and *Five Days at the Port* (1969). Most of his productions were staged with the Teatro Stabile of Genoa (1962– 76) and the Teatro Stabile of Rome (1976–83) while he was its director.

Squarzina's productions reflect a leftist ideology and the Italian cultural climate of postwar Italy. Influenced by Brecht, who was one of the most significant influences on the Italian stage in the late forties and fifties due to his social imperatives which appealed to a society ripe for reform, Squarzina staged some of the most innovative productions of the fifties.

Brecht's influence extended to the plays Squarzina wrote and then produced and directed. Their historical nature indicates Squarzina's intent of presenting the shifting social mechanisms which the dialectical view of history seems to reveal. Such dialectics, while expressing the "flow of things," show that history, like any human manifestation can never be treated as static and that all causes, all effects, all relationships are essentially dynamic. Thus, Squarzina, like Brecht, views history as a never-ending series of clashes or contradictions between opposing forces, and this belief remains at the center of his art. In representing this view onstage, Squarzina's characters are never portrayed simply as individuals but also represent the dynamics of their particular historic moment. Squarzina's conviction that historical process is shaped by man, or more precisely by a collective body of men, and that individual psychological states are thus also subject to change and correction, determines not only the treatment of his characters as written, but the shape of his productions as well.

Critics generally consider *The Woman from Romagna* to be Squarzina's major play. Written in 1957 and produced in 1959, it presents a tragic love story set against a tapestry of historical events in Romagna during the last fifteen years of fascism. Its thirty episodes and large cast emphasize Squarzina's tendency to stage scenes of mass social action, and his employment of songs and popular music further illustrates his use of Brechtian techniques.

ADDITIONAL PRODUCTIONS: 1957: *The Daughter of Jorio* (Gabriele D'Annunzio); 1960: *The Miracle Worker* (William Gibson); 1961: *Each in His Own Way* (Pirandello), *Man and Superman*; 1962: *The Devil and the Good Lord* (Sartre); 1970: *Mother Courage*; 1972: *Tonight We Improvise* (Pirandello); 1974: *The Caucasian Chalk Circle*.

SELECTED BIBLIOGRAPHY: Squarzina, Luigi. *Da Dionisio a Brecht*. Bologna: Il Mulino, 1988; Poli, Gianlli, ed. *Spettacolo teatral del Novecento*. Turin: Marietti, 1979.

Mario B. Mignone

KONSTANTIN SERGEIVICH STANISLAVSKY [b. Konstantin Alekseyev, January 5, 1863, Moscow; d. August 7, 1938, Moscow]. Long acknowledged as the most influential personality of Russian theatre, Konstantin Stanislavsky pioneered a system of actor training that is still widely accepted throughout the world. In addition, the Moscow Art Theatre (MAT), which he founded with Vladimir Nemirovich-Danchenko* in 1897, is regarded as one of the outstanding companies internationally. In the early part of his career, however, Stanislavsky made his reputation as an innovative and resourceful director.

The son of a wealthy Moscow manufacturer, Stanislavsky was denied little in the form of financial backing for his amateur theatrical ventures. In 1891, after fifteen years of training and apprenticeship as an actor, he tried his hand at directing as well. Using the semiprofessional Society of Art and Literature, which his family supported financially, Stanislavsky mounted over one dozen productions, including Tolstoy's *The Fruits of Enlightenment*, *The Polish Jew*, *Twelfth Night*, and *Much Ado about Nothing*.

Inspired by the leading foreign practitioners of the day, Stanislavsky presented Moscow with the newest West European theatrical styles. Most notable among Stanislavsky's influences were the Duke of Saxe-Meiningen,* the inventor of scenic "time-machines," which naturalistically conjured up the world of Shakespeare's Rome and the medieval cities of German Romantic texts, and the aging Tomasso Salvini, who enacted a shockingly passionate and physical Othello. Attentive to the smallest historical detail, each Art and Literature Society production unveiled a breathtaking spectacle of realism and verisimilitude. Yet the movement of the sets and performers pulsated with the aesthetic vigor of circus and popular theatre, Stanislavsky's first loves.

In 1897, Vladimir Nemirovich-Danchenko, a playwright and dramaturg, joined with Stanislavsky to create the MAT, Russia's first completely ensemble, professional theatre. Supported by private patronage and general subscription, the MAT could offer a yearly season of high-quality drama, independent of box-office uncertainties and conservative tastes. Also, a stable of eager young performers working without the debilitating pressures of time and money allowed Stanislavsky the luxury of experimentation and slow, artistic growth.

Set in sixteenth-century Russia, the MAT's first production, *Czar Fyodor* (1897), resembled a Saxe-Meiningen production but with a more believable style of acting. The performers adapted their movements to the heavy costumes and oversized furniture. They studied the drawings and paintings of the period to intuit their characters and acting choices. The use of real objects like church bells and food-laden plates further convinced the audience of the production's authenticity.

Similar MAT presentations followed. But the next important success signaled a change in Stanislavsky's approach to directing. Nemirovich-Danchenko managed to secure the rights to Anton Chekhov's *The Sea Gull* (1897), a contemporary play about Russia's intelligentsia. Stanislavsky exploded the simple stage directions into a carnival of tiny details and moody effects. What may have taken another company a few minutes to stage was stretched out endlessly into real time with long pauses and gloomy stares. Instead of boring the spectators, however, these concentrated activities drew them deeply into Chekhov's invisible universe of frustration and regret. The secret desires and monotony of daily life were finally exposed in the truthful emotions and actions of the performers. Stanislavsky called this "psychological realism."

Sensing something novel, Moscow audiences flocked to Stanislavsky's productions. Foreigners, especially Germans, were stunned by the intensity of the players and pronounced them the leading theatre of Europe. But after seven triumphant years of acting and directing, Stanislavsky once again changed the course of his MAT activities. He added symbolist and fantasy plays to the repertoire. His early failures to wed psychological realism to nonrealistic dramas led him to reinvestigate the source of great acting.

From 1907 until his death in 1938, Stanislavsky devoted himself to the development of a revolutionary System of actor training. His productions were, by and large, experiments in this process. What he learned in studio settings was quickly applied to mainstage work. Stanislavsky discovered that actors who substituted personal experiences and remembered feelings for those of their characters were able to achieve a special link with the audience. In addition, when used properly, this difficult mental technique allowed the performer to repeat his scenic work without the vagaries of nightly inspiration. Therefore, the superficial reality or truthfulness of the script became immaterial to the emotional reality of the actor.

In fact, after Stanislavsky began his search for a teachable System, he directed relatively few productions that were not classical or avant-garde ın design. His association with turn-of-the-century realism was mostly historic. Even the socialist realist plays that he was required to produce in the late twenties sparked with imagination and verve.

In the teens and the period after the Revolution, Stanislavsky explored the possibilities of a totally improvised theatre. Later, he attempted to give the performer the artistic means of breaking down a text according to the motivations of the character and beliefs of the playwright. This was formerly the strict domain of the director. At the end of his life, however, Stanislavsky experimented with a formula that once again gave the director total intellectual control over the rehearsal process. He called this ''the theory of physical action.''

ADDITIONAL PRODUCTIONS: 1895: *Uriel Acosta*; 1896: *Othello, The Polish Jew*; 1899: *Uncle Vanya*; 1900: *Enemy of the People*; 1901: *Three Sisters*; 1902: *Lower Depths*; 1904: *The Cherry Orchard*; 1908: *The Blue Bird*; 1909: *A Month in the Country*; 1911: *Hamlet*; 1924: *Burning Heart*; 1926: *The Days of the Turbins*; 1927: *Armored Train 14– 69*; 1931: *Othello*.

SELECTED BIBLIOGRAPHY: Benedetti, Jean. *Stanislavski*. London: Routledge, 1988; Gordon, Mel. *The Stanislavsky Technique: Russia*. New York: Applause Theatre Books, 1988; Magarshack, David. *Stanislavsky*. London: Macgibbon and Kee, 1950; Polyakova, Elena. *Stanislavsky*. Trans. Liv Tudge. Moscow: Progress Publishers, 1982; Stanislavsky, Konstantin. *My Life in Art*. Trans. J. J. Robbins. Boston: Little, Brown, and Company, 1924; Stanislavsky, Konstantin. *Selected Works*. Trans. Vladimir Yankilevsky. Moscow: Raduga Publishers, 1984; Toporkov, Vasily Osipovich. *Stanislavski in Rehearsal*. Trans. Christine Edwards. New York: Theatre Arts Books, 1979.

Mel Gordon

PETER STEIN [b. October 1, 1937, Berlin, Germany]. Peter Stein began his career in the theatre as an undergraduate at Munich University. In 1964, he joined the prestigious Munich Kammerspiele as a dramaturge and directorial assistant, and was hailed as one of Germany's most important young directors for his 1967 debut with Edward Bond's *Saved*, in a Bavarian-dialect version by Martin Sperr. His 1969 Bremen production of Goethe's *Torquato Tasso* exemplified a new generation's approach to classical plays; it remains one of the quarter-century's most influential productions.

In 1970 Stein formed a new ensemble at Berlin's Schaubühne am Halleschen Ufer. The ensemble's core included *Tasso* actors Bruno Ganz, Jutta Lampe, Edith Clever, and Werner Rehm, the dramaturges Dieter Sturm and Frank-Patrick Steckel (now a major director in his own right), and the designer Karl-Ernst Herrmann, with whom Stein had first worked on a Kammerspiele production of Brecht's *In the Jungle of Cities* (1968), and with whom he continues to work frequently. These and other ensemble members proved to be among their generation's leading talents, and they helped the Schaubühne secure a reputation as Germany's important theatre that it sustained for over a decade.

Although Stein's artistic vision dominated the Schaubühne during these years, the theatre was organized along lines of communal responsibility. All major decisions were made or approved by the company. On the level of individual productions, company members worked together first to conduct exhaustive research into a play and its historical context, then to find the contemporary connections which would allow an old play to speak afresh to a modern audience. Such research also allowed the actors to participate in Stein's extremely precise directorial approach, which extends to composing an interpretational score at the level of individual gesture and vocal inflection. Stein has twice mounted evenings demonstrating the results of the company's dramaturgical investigations and the exercises developed to implement them: in 1974, the *Antiquity Project I* showed the company's preparatory work for Klaus Michael Grüber's production of the *Bacchae*; *Shakespeare's Memory* in 1976 was a kind of Renaissance fair filled with curiosities the company had unearthed in its work toward a production of *As You Like It* that premiered the next year. This stress on the importance of dramaturgy in individual productions has redefined the role of the literary manager in Germany, England, and the United States.

Stein began his career as it became clear that the generation controlling Germany's major theatres had outlived its artistic potency. He became the leading figure of the new generation that now controls these theatres, and he has helped pass on the influence of the older generation's two most enduring directors: Bertolt Brecht* and Fritz Kortner, whom Stein assisted at the Kammerspiele. Stein also belonged to the generation that radicalized German politics in the 1960s. His work into the late 1970s was marked by an exploration of the ways in which a particular social configuration can condition the individual psyche. His 1971 *Peer Gynt*, in which he exposed the bourgeois myth of an autonomous individuality free from such social influence, became a signature production for the German theatre of the 1970s. As befits his directorial style, Stein made this influence visible in the characters' gestures and speech. He has been praised for this work's clarity of detail, but also criticized for dominating the actor in order to accomplish it. His drive for formal perfection has also won both praise and blame, particularly in his work since the early 1980s, when he turned away from a political aesthetics, even going so far as to disavow his earlier *Tasso* and *Gynt*. His 1984 Schaubühne production of Anton Chekhov's *Three Sisters*, for example, became famous throughout Europe, but struck some observers as so internally perfect that there was no room left for the spectator.

Stein resigned from the Schaubühne's directorial collective in 1985. Since then, he has continued to direct regularly at the Schaubühne, but has also directed outside Germany, including productions for the Paris and Welsh National operas. In 1992 he became *Schauspieldirektor* (director of theatre) for the Salzburg Festspiele.

ADDITIONAL PRODUCTIONS: 1968: *Vietnam Discourse* (Peter Weiss); 1969: *Early Morning* (Edward Bond), German-language premiere, in Zurich; 1970: *The Mother*, which opened the new Schaubühne; 1972: *Optimistic Tragedy* (Vsevolod Vishnevsky), *The Prince of Homburg*; 1974: *Summerfolk*; 1976: *Rheingold*, with Georg Solti, musical director; 1978: *Big and Little* (Botho Strauß), world premiere; 1980: *The Oresteia*; 1981: *Class Enemy* (Nigel Williams); 1983: *The Blacks* (Genet); 1986: *Otello* (Verdi); 1986: *The Hairy Ape*; 1987: *Phèdre*; 1988: *Falstaff* (Verdi).

SELECTED BIBLIOGRAPHY: Patterson, Michael. *Peter Stein: Germany's Leading Theatre Director*. New York: Cambridge University Press, 1981; Rorrison, Hugh. "Berlin's Democratic Theatre and Its *Peer Gynt*." *Theatre Quarterly* No. 13 (1974): 15–36; Rouse, John. *Brecht and the West German Theatre: The Practice and Politics of Interpretation*.

Ann Arbor: UMI Research Press, 1989: 149–67; Stein, Peter. "The Collective Impulse." Interview by Jack Zipes. *Performance* 4 (1972): 69–72; Zipes, Jack. "Ends and Beginnings: West German Theatre Now." *Performance* 4 (1972): 54–62; Zipes, Jack. "The Irresistible Rise of the Schaubühne am Halleschen Ufer: A Retrospective of the West Berlin Theatre Collective." *Theatre* 9 (Winter 1977): 7–49.

John Rouse

LEE STRASBERG [b. November 17, 1901, Budanov, Austria-Hungary; d. February 17, 1982, New York, New York]. An emigré to New York's Lower East Side, Lee Strasberg, a former ladies' wigs manufacturer, was a self-taught scholar of the theatre. He read extensively in theatrical history and biography and was greatly influenced by the work of Gordon Craig, Jacques Copeau,* and most fundamentally, Konstantin Stanislavsky* and Evgeni Vakhtangov.* His introduction to the famous Russian system of actor training came when he enrolled in the American Laboratory Theatre in 1923. The director, Richard Boleskavsky,* developed a training program based on the technique of emotion memory and the analytical pursuit of specific dramatic action. Directors were encouraged to deconstruct and then score the script, a process known as spine work.

Strasberg experimented with these theoretical principles at the Chrystie Street Settlement House between 1924 and 1931. Each of his productions investigated a particular directorial style. For example, Racine's *Esther* (1926) explored Stanislavsky's ideas on psychological characterization, while the constructivist ideals of Vsevolod Meyerhold* were examined in Anatole France's *The Man Who Married a Dumb Wife* (1927). His final production at Chrystie Street was Copeau's *The House into Which We Are Born* (1927), dedicated to its author.

In 1931, Strasberg, Harold Clurman,* and Cheryl Crawford formulated plans for the Group Theatre, which serves as the model for the American theatrical collective. The triumvirate stressed a unified approach to production and performance grounded in the principles of the Russian System legacy. Strasberg rehearsed the Group's first production, Paul Green's *The House of Connelly* at Brookfield Center, Connecticut. The company of twenty-eight actors included Franchot Tone, Stella Adler, Robert Lewis,* Sanford Meisner, and Morris Car novsky. The important experimental elements to emerge from rehearsal were improvisational approaches to the text and the use of affective memory to connect the actor's life experience to the character's intention. Actors were directed to discover imaginative adjustments that would spontaneously lead them to the specific intellectual and emotional life of the character. Strasberg's subsequent directorial efforts with the Group continued this innovative exploration. From the strictly psychologically realistic *The House of Connelly* (1931), his next productions of *Success Story* (1932) and *Men in White* (1933) displayed increasing theatricality. His last production, the musical play *Johnny Johnson* (1936), was characterized as a blend of Hogarth, the Marx Brothers, and Charlie Chaplin.

As the Group Theatre dissolved for political, philosophical, and financial reasons, Strasberg used the next thirteen years to establish his professional directing career. Of the sixteen plays he staged between 1938 and 1951, Ernest Hemingway's *The Fifth Column* (1940) and Strasberg's collaborations with Clifford Odets on *Clash by Night* (1941) and *The Big Knife* (1949) best exemplify his gifts for complexity of emotional layers, acute sensitivity to rhythm, and solid ensemble playing.

In 1951, a former student of Strasberg, Elia Kazan,* invited his mentor to become the artistic director of the Actors' Studio. Strasberg had conducted classes at the Studio as early as 1948, but under his directorship this laboratory became a focal point in American actor training as he developed his famous Method.

Strasberg's work with actors has been a much discussed, often misunderstood, and well-documented phenomenon. What is not as widely emphasized is his impact on American directorial technique. Frank Corsaro, Martin Fried, Jack Garfein, Arthur Penn,* Alan Schneider,* John Stix, and José Quintero* actively participated in Studio productions and training under Strasberg's tutelage. By 1960 a Directors Unit was formed to encourage exploration of form and style apart from the commercial arena. Among the directors who attended sessions were Michael Bennett,* André Gregory,* Michael Kahn,* Nikos Psacharopolous, Lloyd Richards,* Gene Saks,* and Arthur Storch. Strasberg's influence on the American directing heritage is further illustrated by the seventeen Academy Award nominations for Best Director earned by Studio directors between 1947 and 1983.

Harold Clurman, in his definitive history *The Fervent Years*, aptly describes Strasberg's directorial contributions. Strasberg "is the director of introverted feeling, of strong emotions curbed by ascetic control. . . . Above everything, the feeling in Strasberg's production is never stagy. Its roots are clearly in the intimate experience of complex psychology, an acute awareness of human contradiction and suffering, a distinguished though perhaps too specialized sensibility" (61).

ADDITIONAL PRODUCTIONS: 1932: *Night over Taos* (Maxwell Anderson); 1933: *Hilda Cassidy* (Henry Lieferant); 1934: *Gentlewoman* (John Lawson), *Gold Eagle Guy* (Melvin Levy); 1936: *Waiting for Lefty*; 1937: *Roosty* (Martin Berkeley), *All the Living* (Hardie Albright); 1939: *Summer Night* (Vicki Baum and Benjamin Glazer); 1942: *R.U.R.* (Čapek); 1951: *Peer Gynt*; 1964 (1965 in London): *The Three Sisters*, with Geraldine Page, Shirley Knight, and Kim Stanley.

SELECTED BIBLIOGRAPHY: Clurman, Harold. *The Fervent Years*. New York: Hill and Wang, 1958; Garfield, David. *A Player's Place: The Story of the Actors Studio*. New York: Macmillan, 1980; Hethman, Robert H. *Strasberg at the Actors Studio*. New York: Viking Press, 1965; Hirsch, Foster. *A Method to Their Madness: The History of the Actors Studio*. New York: W. W. Norton, 1984; Hull, S. Loraine. *Strasberg's Legacy*. Woodbridge, CT: Ox Bow, 1985; Strasberg, Lee. *A Dream of Passion*. New York: Plume, 1988; Strasberg, Lee. "Acting and the Training of the Actor." *Producing the Play*. Ed. John Gassner. New York: Dryden Press, 1941: 128–62.

Richard Warner

GIORGIO STREHLER [b. August 15, 1921, Barcola (Trieste), Italy]. Born into a musical family, Giorgio Strehler dreamed of becoming a conductor, but after attending his first play in 1936 in Milan, his devotion to the theatre was unswerving. He entered the claque of the Milan Odeon and enrolled as a drama student at the Accademia dei Philodrammatica. Graduating with honors, he served with several companies and published major critical articles on theatre in the monthly *Palcoscenio* showing a strong influence from such theatre artists as Jacques Copeau,* Louis Jouvet,* and Jean Cocteau.

In 1945, he founded in Geneva the French-inspired Compagnie des Masques with actors of various languages, whom he had directed in *Our Town, Murder in the Cathedral*, and the world premiere of Albert Camus's *Caligula*. Following the war, he returned to Milan to direct and serve as drama critic for the *Milano Sera*. In 1947, he founded the only permanent public theatre in Italy, the Piccolo Teatro, which he headed until 1968, making it into one of the most famous houses in Europe.

Although Strehler has directed works ranging from naturalist dramas to grand opera and from Euripides to Genet, those dramatists with whom his career has been most associated and who have most defined his style have been Carlo Goldoni, Shakespeare, and Bertolt Brecht.* A major success of his first season at the Piccolo was Goldoni's loving recreation of the *commedia, Arlecchino servitore di due padroni* (1947). Strehler's physically dazzling production became the best-known Piccolo work. It was revived many times and toured throughout the world. Shakespeare also fascinated Strehler from the first, providing a mixture of early realism and dazzling fantasy that accorded extremely well with Strehler's theatrical gifts. As early as 1948, he mounted *Richard II, The Tempest*, and *Romeo and Juliet*. Eventually the Piccolo produced fourteen Shakespearean plays, all but two of them directed by Strehler.

During this first period at the Piccolo, which lasted until the mid–1950s, Strehler offered a series of brilliant productions which displayed his enormous visual imagination and theatrical zest; but he remained tied to realism and to social concerns which he exhibited in works like Maxim Gorky's *Lower Depths*, another major production of the opening season. Both tendencies were reinforced during the next period of the Piccolo's work, especially in Strehler's production of modern Italian works (most notably Carlo Bertolazzi's *El nost Milan*, 1955) and in a series of widely acclaimed Brecht productions crowned by *Galileo* in 1963. Brecht's influence could also be seen in the *Coriolanus* of 1957 and in the monumental *Il gioco dei poteni* (1965), based on Shakespeare's *Henry VI* trilogy. The last great work of this period was Pirandello's *Giganti della montagna* (1966), a dark and moving exploration of theatrical artifice and Strehler's farewell to his twenty years at the Piccolo.

In 1968, Strehler left the Piccolo to found the Gruppo Teatro e Azione, dedicated to developing a theatre more directly involved with social questions. There he directed a new, more politicized *Lower Depths* and such new works as Peter Weiss's anticolonialist *Song of the Lusitanian Bogey*. In 1972, he returned to the Piccolo, where he produced his monumental *King Lear*, combining his familiar interest in realism with insights from Samuel Beckett and Jan Kott. At a period when most Italian stages were emphasizing stars, the Piccolo remained notable for its artistic and social vision, most notably in productions of Strehler's favorite dramatists, Brecht (*The Threepenny Opera*, 1973) and Shakespeare (*The Tempest*, 1978).

In 1982, Strehler became director of the new Théâtre de l'Europe, with a combined home in Paris and Milan. This new venture opened with *The Tempest* (1978), inaugurating a major trilogy on illusion and theatricality that continued with *The Comic Illusion* (1984), by Pierre Corneille, and concluded with *La grande magia* (1985), by Eduardo De Filippo.* In 1986, this directorship was renewed for three years, and Strehler developed a new bridge with the Centro Dramático Nacional of Madrid. Its director, Lluis Pasqual, became director of the Théâtre de l'Europe in 1989, allowing Strehler to oversee the construction of a new home for the Piccolo in Milan and to develop the major new project which crowned his half century of theatre work: Goethe's *Faust*, part one opening in 1989, part two in 1991.

ADDITIONAL PRODUCTIONS: 1944: *Murder in the Cathedral*; 1947: *The Lower Depths*; 1950: *Richard III*; 1951: *Electra*; 1953: *Six Characters in Search of an Author*; 1955: *The Cherry Orchard*, *The House of Bernarda Alba*; 1956: *The Threepenny Opera*; 1964: *Mahagonny*; 1977: *The Good Woman of Setzuan*; 1980: *The Thunderstorm*.

SELECTED BIBLIOGRAPHY: Aslan, Odette, et al. *Strehler: Les vois de la création théâtrale*. Paris: Centre National de la Recherche Scientifique (CNRS), 1991; Battistini, Fabio. *Giorgio Strehler*. Rome: Gremese, 1980; Fechner, Eberhard. *Strehler Inszeniert*. Hannover, Germany: Friedrich Verlag, 1963; Gaipa, Ettore. *Giorgio Strehler*. Documenti di Teatro 4. Bologna: Cappelli, 1959; Moscati, Italo. *Strehler*. Milan: Camunia, 1985; Strehler, Giorgio. *Io, Strehler: Conversazioni con Uao Ronfani*. Milan: Rusconi, 1986; Strehler, Giorgio. *Per un teatro umano*. Milan: Feltrinelli, 1974; Strehler, Giorgio, et al. "Le Piccolo Teatro de Milan." *Theatre en Europe* 4 (October 1984): 44–114.

Marvin Carlson

TADASHI SUZUKI [b. 1939, Japan]. While studying political and economic sciences at Waseda University during the 1960s, Tadashi Suzuki belonged to a student theatre group called the Waseda Free Stage. The productions were staged in the contemporary Japanese tradition (Shingeki), but employed a realistic, Stanislavsky-based, Western performance style. Along with a group of other artists, Suzuki moved the company off the university campus and, calling themselves the Free Stage and later the Waseda Little Theatre, began to explore post-Shingeki/avant-garde theatre.

Suzuki soon came to the realizations that it was futile for the Japanese actor to perform within a style that was not consistent with his own communication process and that the nature of the Japanese language was violated by the imposition of foreign gesture. Suzuki therefore adopted as his mission the restoration of "the wholeness of the human body in the theatrical context." To this end, he has employed the ideas of the traditional Japanese theatre forms of Kabuki and Noh.

Between 1966 and 1970, the Waseda Little Theatre produced *On the Dramatic Passions I, II and III*. This collage of scenes drew from both Japanese and Western drama and laid the foundation for the company to bridge the gap between traditional and modern theatre. Suzuki was able to display the power of this synthesis when the company was invited by Jean-Louis Barrault* to perform at the 1972 Théâtres des Nations Festival in Paris. This highly successful trip abroad, which featured performances in Nancy, Paris, and Amsterdam, not only motivated Suzuki to continue work in this direction, but gave him additional inspiration to create a spiritual and physical home for his company. Upon returning to Japan, he moved the group to the remote village of Toga-Mura, 400 miles from Tokyo, and with the help of architect Isozaki Arata, renovated several farmhouses into what is now the training and performance center of the Suzuki Company of Toga (SCOT) and the site of International Toga Festival.

The ideology that informs Suzuki's training system is also present in his productions. He encourages actors to reclaim their heritage of mystical power—the tradition of the shaman and spiritual possession. In an attempt to restore the modern actor to a place of spiritual power and physical strength, Suzuki trains his performers in a series of disciplines (known as the Suzuki Method) that address the voice and body as holistic unit. The relationship between the actor and the ground—the feet with the earth—is essential to the disciplines. The performance area is viewed respectfully as a meeting place where ensemble and audience enter into communal conversation. Little scenery and few properties are used, allowing the performance of the text to maintain focus.

Suzuki's aim is to communicate the essence of the drama. He has taken liberties with texts, creating his own adaptation of classics. The power of these performances has brought him world recognition as a director and an acting teacher. Suzuki and his company have participated in many cross-cultural projects, especially with American acting companies and training programs.

ADDITIONAL PRODUCTIONS: 1974: *The Trojan Women*; 1978: *The Bacchae*; 1981: *The Bacchae* (a bilingual production with American students from the University of Wisconsin–Milwaukee and Japanese students); 1984: *The Tale of Lear* (an English language production with American actors from Arena Stage, Berkeley Rep, Milwaukee Rep, and StageWest), *Clytemnestra*; 1990: Toga Festival (fourteenth year), Mito Festival, Mitsui Festival (three international performance festivals organized by Suzuki).

SELECTED BIBLIOGRAPHY: Beeman, William O. "Tadashi Suzuki: The Word Is an Act of the Body." Trans. Kadogami Rosho. *Performing Arts Journal* 6 (1982): 88–92; Beeman, William O. "Tadashi Suzuki's Universal Vision." *Performing Arts Journal* 6 (1982): 77–87; Brandon, James R. "Training at the Waseda Little Theatre: The Suzuki Method." *The Drama Review* 22 (Dec. 1978): 29–42; Myerscough, Marie. "East Meets West in the Art of Tadashi Suzuki." *American Theatre* Jan. 1986: 4–10; Suzuki, Tadashi. *The Way of Acting: The Theater Writings of Tadashi Suzuki*. Trans. J. Thomas Rimer. New York: Theatre Communications Group, 1986.

Colleen Kelly

KONRAD SWINARSKI [b. July 4, 1929, Warsaw, Poland; d. August 20, 1975, Damascus, Syria]. Although Swinarski's career was tragically cut short in an airplane crash, he nevertheless had established himself as one of the leading practitioners (along with Erwin Axer,* his mentor and compatriot) of directing in the "literary" tradition in postwar Polish theatre. His methodology greatly respected both the letter and the textual structure of the playscript by seeking to discover and develop theatrical equivalents for each nuance in the drama. Although not reluctant to use striking production elements, Swinarski always conceived their use in terms of their contribution toward greater understanding of the playwright's textual imagery.

Swinarski's most prominent directorial work focused on the landmarks of Polish drama. In works such as Zygmunt Krasínski's *Un-Divine Comedy* (1965) and Adam Mickiewicz's *Forefather's Eve* (1967, 1971, 1972), historical as well as mystical elements central to much of Polish culture were reexplored in light of the need to reestablish a national identity and sensibility in the aftermath of 160 years of occupation and repression by invaders (with only the twenty-year interim between the world wars as temporary respite). At the same time, Swinarski was highly sensitive to the social contexts and topical connotations that performances of the classical Polish repertory invariably suggested to an audience. In this vein, he devised productions that consciously looked at the past in order to come to terms with the present.

An apprenticeship with Bertolt Brecht* at the Berliner Ensemble in the 1950s was tellingly revealed by the overt emphasis Swinarski placed on movement and gesture as well as the frequent introduction of music to subvert any illusionary sense of a performance's onstage reality. In a Brechtian manner, Swinarski's productions encouraged a critical distance and objectivity to the themes and values presented through the drama. By means of a deliberately undisguised technique, the spectator typically witnessed historical imagery juxtaposed within recognizably contemporary circumstances. The effective application of these techniques in his staging of the premiere production of Peter Weiss's *Marat/ Sade* in Berlin (1963) firmly established Swinarski's international reputation.

Swinarski's productions of *Forefather's Eve* presented the inner moral and ideological struggles of the drama's hero—Konrad, a poet and revolutionist on trial after the failed November 1830 uprising against the Russian occupation—as a battle between angels and devils, costumed respectively as winged spirits from an old-fashioned operatic spectacle and proletariat thugs itching for a fight. With his staging of *Liberation* by Stanisław Wyspiański (1974), a play originally set in 1902 in which a production of "Poland Today" is being prepared by a local troupe, Swinarski conceived of the drama's hero (shrewdly named Konrad in reference to Mickiewicz's hero) as an individual caught up in the difficulties not only of seeking the truth about himself and his society, but also of openly admitting the errors and deceptions of his age. It is to Swinarski's credit that this effect was accomplished without recourse to historically oblique symbolism; instead, it was effected by rendering Konrad's plight in terms of strictly contemporary conditions of the 1970s. By producing the play in the exact same theatre in Cracow where Wyspiański had set the action seventy years earlier, a stunningly ironic effect was achieved, as current events and past history were fused into a unitary experience, something unprecedented at that time in Communist Poland.

ADDITIONAL PRODUCTIONS: 1964: *Caucasian Chalk Circle* in Berlin; 1966: *The Three-penny Opera*; 1968: *Kordian* (Juliusz Słowacki).

SELECTED BIBLIOGRAPHY: Drozdowski, Bohdan, *Twentieth Century Polish Theatre*. London: John Calder, 1979; Filler, Witold. *Contemporary Polish Theatre*. Warsaw: Interpress, 1977; Grodzicki, August. *Polish Theatre Directors*. Warsaw: Interpress, 1979; Szydłowski, Roman. *The Theatre in Poland*. Warsaw: Interpress, 1972. Also, see *The Theatre in Poland* (monthly journal). Warsaw: Institute International du Théâtre, 1958– .

Thomas Leff

JÓZEF SZAJNA [b. 1922]. Like so many Central European artists born in the first third of this century, Józef Szajna's artistic vision has been permeated by the tragedy of two world wars. For Szajna this catastrophic atmosphere was underscored by his incarceration as a young man in the Auschwitz death camp. After his rescue and recovery in 1945, Szajna studied painting in Krakow, Poland, and took an interest in stage design, following in the footsteps of Andrzej Pronaszko, one of Poland's leading designers in the postwar period. Szajna quickly established a distinctive visual style that emphasized a non-illusionistic, anti-aesthetical crudeness. Simple compositions using rags, junk, and grotesquely stylized costumes became his signature. These designs generated tremendous interest among younger Polish directors including Jerzy Grotowski,* who asked him to collaborate on *Akropolis* (1962), for which Szajna set the action in a concentration camp of stove pipes, wire, and burlap. Gradually, Szajna assumed greater directorial control over his productions, and in 1964 he was appointed director of the Ludowy Theatre in Nowa Huta. Later he was to direct at Katowice, and ultimately took over the directorship of the Classic Studio in Warsaw, where he continued to work into the 1980s.

Szajna's directorial work (he continued to design as well) always favored visual effects over dramatic text and conventional acting. While sometimes using a well-known text (e.g., Goethe's *Faust*, Cervantes' *Don Quixote*, Dante's *Inferno*) as a point of departure, Szajna invariably composed a living picture that selectively drew upon textual imagery while creating its own theatrical autonomy. *Replique* (1973), a deeply personal meditation upon Szajna's experiences in Auschwitz which juxtaposed found objects and actual mementos with frighteningly mutilated manikins, is regarded as a modern masterpiece. In method and style Szajna's work anticipated the Performance Art movement of the 1970s and 1980s.

ADDITIONAL PRODUCTIONS: 1964: *Revizor*; 1965: *Puste pole*, a play set in Auschwitz many years after the war (Hołuj); 1968: *Regarding November* (Bryll) at Katowice; 1969: *Faust* at the Polski Theatre in Warsaw; 1972: *Witkacy,* a piece using the writing of S. I. Witkiewicz at the Classic Studio, Warsaw; 1974: *Dante*; 1976: *Cervantes.*

SELECTED BIBLIOGRAPHY: Drozdowski, Bohdan. *Twentieth Century Polish Theatre.* Dallas: Riverrun Press, 1980; Grodzicki, August. *Polish Theatre Directors.* Warsaw: Interpress, 1979; Szydłowski, Roman. *The Theatre in Poland.* Warsaw: Interpress, 1972.

Thomas Leff

T

GEORGE TABORI [b. May 24, 1914, Budapest, Hungary]. Born to Jewish parents and educated in Germany, Tabori emigrated to England in 1933, where he became a war correspondent and a spy for the British army during World War II. His father was murdered at Auschwitz, but his mother managed to escape. These incidents informed many of Tabori's later dramatic works. Originally a novelist, Tabori became involved in theatre in 1947, when Metro Goldwyn Mayer hired him to write screenplays. After meeting Bertolt Brecht* in California, Tabori began writing plays himself and also played a major role in disseminating Brecht's works in the United States, translating and directing several of Brecht's plays, including a collage entitled *Brecht on Brecht* (1962), which ran Off-Broadway for three years.

In 1966,Tabori and actress Viveca Lindfors founded the Strolling Players, an acting company in New York. In 1968, he was invited to Germany to direct, and he introduced techniques and philosophies of the New York experimental theatre scene to German audiences, particularly in his work from 1975 to 1978 at the Bremen Theater Laboratory, where he emphasized consciousness-raising, personal experience, movement, and improvisation, combining the Konstantin Stanislavsky* focus on the actor's inner life with Brecht's call for social change. During the 1970s and 1980s, Tabori directed throughout Germany, becoming well-known for his controversial adaptations of classics and for his satiric and surrealistic original plays, many dealing with contemporary anti-Semitism. From 1987 to 1990, Tabori directed a theatre in Vienna, Der Kreis (The Circle), which he modeled after the Actors' Studio directed by Lee Strasberg.* Since 1990, he has worked at the Burgtheater in Vienna. His unique style, which combines black humor with concern for social justice, has earned him a devoted following among actors and audiences.

ADDITIONAL PRODUCTIONS: 1968: *The Cannibals*, with Martin Fried, first original play about the Holocaust (New York; Berlin, 1969); 1971: *Pinkville*, Vietnam War protest drama (New York, Berlin); 1978: *Shylock-Improvisations*, collective work based on *The Merchant of Venice*; 1979: *My Mother's Courage*; 1983: *Waiting for Godot, Jubilee*; 1987: *Mein Kampf, The Book of the Seven Seals*, based on Book of Revelation, banned from Salzburg music festival; 1988: *Masada*; 1990: *Whiteman and Redface*, a Jewish Western; 1991: *Goldberg Variations*.

SELECTED BIBLIOGRAPHY: Elsom John. "Nightmare Memories in Viennese Theater." *The World and I* April 1989: 148–53; Honegger, Gitta. "Tales from the Imperial City." *Performing Arts Journal* 11.2 (1988): 45–61; Patraka, Vivian. "Contemporary Drama, Fascism, and the Holocaust." *Theatre Journal* 39 (March 1987): 65–77; Russell, Susan. " 'Beyond All Tears': The Holocaust Plays of George Tabori." M. A. thesis, U of Wisconsin–Madison, 1989; Skloot, Robert. *The Darkness We Carry: The Drama of the Holocaust*. Madison: University of Wisconsin Press, 1988; Tabori, George. "Hamlet in Blue." *Theatre Quarterly* 5 (Dec. 1975–Feb. 1976): 116–32.

Susan Frances Russell

ALEKSANDR JAKOVLEVICH TAIROV [b. Aleskandr Kornblit, June 24, 1885, Romny, Poltava, Ukraine; d. September 25, 1950, Moscow]. Aleksandr Tairov began his career as an actor at the Komissarzhevskaya Theatre in St. Petersburg in 1906 under the direction of Vsevolod Meyerhold.* Rejecting Meyerhold's emphasis on the director and designer over the actor, Tairov left after less than a year, joining small companies in the provinces as an actor and director. In 1913, he briefly joined the Free Theatre in Moscow, where he met his wife, leading lady, and collaborator, Alisa Koonen. In 1914, Tairov and Koonen opened the Kamerny (Chamber) Theatre with a production of Kalidasa's *Sakuntala*, designed by Alexandra Exter.

At the Kamerny, Tairov created a unique production style called "synthetic theatre." This theatre would combine the elements of music, design, and movement into a single statement to serve the actor. Tairov believed the actor must become a highly trained artist, versed in all aspects of performance, and he opened a school in 1920 to develop actors who were as well-trained and disciplined as ballet performers. Equally important, this new actor would recognize the collective nature of theatre and submit voluntarily to the guidance of the director's vision. In design, Tairov used major artists of the avant-garde to create the production elements in a unified, usually cubist, style. His most important artistic collaborators were Alexandra Exter, Aleksandr Vesnin, Natalie Goncharova, Georgi Yakulov, and the Sternberg brothers. Musical accompaniment was created for each play, and movement was choreographed to follow the demands of the aural and visual elements. Tairov believed that he could best demonstrate his methods through classics and fairy tales, and his production of Racine's *Phèdre* (1922) became the culmination of synthetic theatre.

The Kamerny was named an "Academic" (State) Theatre in 1920, but Tairov was coming under increasing criticism for formalism, for lacking contemporary works in his repertory, and for believing that art was independent of politics.

In response, Tairov wrote *Notes of a Director* (1921), in which he outlined and defended his practices. Meanwhile, the Kamerny became the most prominent Soviet theatre in the West because of its tours in 1923, 1925, and 1930.

After his first tour, Tairov began to stage contemporary works, beginning with G. K. Chesterton's *The Man Who Was Thursday* (1924). Throughout the 1920s, Tairov became the greatest exponent of Western drama in the Soviet Union, staging among other plays, Bernard Shaw's *Saint Joan* (1924), Eugene O'Neill's *The Hairy Ape* (1926) and *Desire under the Elms* (1926), and Walter Hasenclever's *Antigone* (1927). In 1930, he staged the first production of Bertolt Brecht* outside of Germany, producing *The Threepenny Opera*. Tairov was unfortunate in his choices of Soviet works, however, and except for his production of Alexander Ovstrovsky's *The Storm* (1924), plays such as Mikhail Levidov's *The Conspiracy of the Equals* (1927) and Mikhail Bulgakov's *The Crimson Island* (1928) were roundly condemned.

During the 1930s, Tairov directed numerous unsuccessful Soviet plays, but achieved success with Vsevelod Vishnevsky's *An Optimistic Tragedy* (1933). It became the most successful socialist-realist play, and won the title "People's Artist" for Tairov. But with the staging of Alexander Borodin's *The Epic Heroes* (1936) and growing criticism of Tairov's formalism, the Kamerny was merged for an unsuccessful year with the Realistic Theatre of Nikolai Okhlopkov* in 1937. In 1939, the Kamerny went on an extended tour of the Far East, missing the worst of the purges that claimed Meyerhold. Returning to Moscow briefly in 1940, the Kamerny had tremendous success with *Madame Bovary*, but was evacuated to Siberia during the war. In 1945, Tairov received the Order of Lenin and staged Vishnevsky's new play, *At the Walls of Leningrad*. After the war, Tairov's last major production was Maxim Gorky's *The Old Man* (1946), staged with Lukyanov. In 1949, the Kamerny was closed, and Tairov was assigned as an assistant director at the Vakhtangov Theatre. He was awarded a pension in 1950 and began his autobiography, but he died soon after.

ADDITIONAL PRODUCTIONS: 1913: *Pierrette's Veil* (Schnitzler), *The Yellow Jacket* (Hazelton-Benrimo); 1916: *Famira-Kifared* (Annensky); 1917: *King Harlequin* (Lothar), *Salomé*; 1918: *The Exchange* (Claudel) staged with Meyerhold; 1919: *Adrienne Lecouvreur* (Scribe), *Princess Brambilla* (Hoffman); 1920: *The Tidings Brought to Mary* (Claudel); 1921: *Romeo and Juliet*; 1922: *Giroflé-Girofla* (Lecocq); 1925: *Kukirol* (revue); 1929: *All God's Chillun Got Wings*; 1933: *Machinal* (Treadwell); 1934: *Egyptian Nights* (Shakespeare, Pushkin, and Shaw); 1939: *Bridge of Devils* (A. N. Tolstoy); 1945: *An Inspector Calls* (Priestley).

SELECTED BIBLIOGRAPHY: Carter, Huntly. *The New Spirit in the Russian Theatre*. 1929. reprint New York: Benjamin Blom, 1970; Glover, J. Garrett. *The Cubist Theatre*. Ann Arbor: UMI Research Press, 1983; Gorchakov, Nikolai. *The Theatre in Soviet Russia*. 1957. Trans. Edgar Lehrman. Freeport, NY: Books for Libraries Press, 1972; Slonim, Marc. *Russian Theater*. New York: Collier Books, 1962; Tairov, Alexander. *Notes of a Director*. Trans. William Kuhlke. Coral Gables: University of Miami Press, 1969; Torda, Thomas. "Tairov's *Phaedra*: Monumental, Mythological Tragedy." *The Drama Review*

29 (Winter 1985): 76–90; Worral, Nick. *From Modernism to Realism on the Soviet Stage*. Cambridge: Cambridge University Press, 1989; Zelikson, Michael, comp. *The Artist of the Kamerny Theatre: 1914–1934*. Moscow: Ogiz, 1935.

Edward Dee

BEN TEAL [b. 1855; d. April 20, 1917, New York, New York]. The first American to adopt stage directing as a vocation, Ben Teal began directing in the early 1880s during the period of transition of the stage manager into the modern stage director. In fact, Teal was the prototype of the "model" stage director: an authoritarian, dictatorial taskmaster.

A lawyer in California before entering the theatre, Teal began his stage career as an actor and stage manager. In 1883, he migrated to New York where he began staging farces and melodramatic spectacles. This phase of his career culminated in 1899 with his best-known production, *Ben Hur*. Its success stamped him as the "ablest" stage director in America. Beginning with *The Algerian* in 1893, Teal increasingly devoted himself to musical comedies and also staged a string of hits for the Rogers Brothers ("Dutch" comics) and for Joe Weber and Lew Fields.

Known as "*Mr*. Ben Teal," he had a forceful and energetic personality, an important element of his directorial style. His caustic and biting qualities were legendary, for Teal was strict, abrupt, and demanding with everyone from stars to chorus members. Being a practical, disciplined director, Teal used a systematic approach that resulted in several directorial innovations. He usually rehearsed four to six weeks, setting a schedule in which each actor knew when he or she would rehearse. He instituted the practice of rehearsing the principals and the chorus separately, until each was perfect, and then bringing them together. Further, he rehearsed actors for no more than four hours at a time. Viewing actors as *units* who served the purpose of securing the desired effect, Teal evidently had difficulty in molding a cast into a unified whole and in coaching individual actors. Uneven acting was a recurring happenstance in his productions.

Teal's success in musicals stemmed from his giving them the same attention that he gave serious drama. His productions exhibited taste in costuming; they were sumptuous; they had pleasing color schemes; the groupings and stagings were beautiful; and the choruses were carefully trained. Vivacity, color, harmony, and humor were the hallmarks of his work, and without question, Teal set the standards for others to follow.

During his thirty-four year career, Teal produced over eighty New York productions. While not important today as dramatic literature, these plays encompassed almost every style of the time: melodrama, spectacle, tragedy, travesty, farce, comedy, comic opera, and musical comedy. A martinet who was castigated for his style of working with actors, Teal had the pragmatic aesthetic of a commercial Broadway director. Nevertheless, he was so successful at producing commercial fare that in 1910, Robert Grau called him "the representative general stage director in the country."

ADDITIONAL PRODUCTIONS: 1883: *Passion's Slave*; 1886: *Held by the Enemy* (William Gillette); 1888: *Hamlet*; 1890: *A Tale of a Coat* (Boucicault); 1898: *The Bride Elect* (John Phillip Sousa); 1899: *Ben Hur*; 1900: *The Rogers Brothers in Central Park*; 1901: *The Sleeping Beauty and the Beast* (Teal's most successful musical); 1903: *Whoop-Dee-Doo* (Weber and Fields production); 1905: *The Rollicking Girl*; 1906: *The Little Cherub, The Rich Mr. Hoggenheimer*; 1908: *The Queen of the Moulin Rouge*; 1913: *Adele*; 1914: *The Midnight Girl*; 1915: *The Girl Who Smiles*; 1917: *The Wanderer*.

SELECTED BIBLIOGRAPHY: Grau, Robert. *The Business Man in the Amusement World.* New York: Broadway Publishing Co., 1910; Shelton, Lewis E. "Mr. Ben Teal: America's Abusive Director." *The Journal of American Drama and Theatre* 2 (Spring 1990): 55–80.

Lewis E. Shelton

BARBARA ANN TEER [b. June 18, 1937, East St. Louis, Illinois]. In 1968, after trying her hand at dancing, acting, and teaching, Barbara Ann Teer founded the National Black Theatre (NBT) in Harlem. A neighborhood and cultural mainstay since its founding; the NBT has been Teer's primary tool for rediscovering African culture and traditions. With a fierce commitment to her culture and her community, Teer has fused these traditions with the political realities of everyday life in Harlem to form a theatre of community.

Teer received a B.A. in dance education from the University of Illinois and began her career as a dancer, performing with the Alvin Ailey, Louis Johnson, and Alwin Nikolais companies before a leg injury forced her to stop. She then studied acting with Sanford Meisner, Paul Mann, Phillip Burton, and Lloyd Richards.* She also worked with Robert Hooks and his Group Theatre Workshop, which later became the Negro Ensemble Company. In 1961, she made her Broadway debut in the musical *Kwamina*.

In the mid–1960s, Teer taught dance and drama in the New York public schools. In the workshops she ran with young people, she found that the acting techniques she had learned—techniques that relied on external elements, rather than internal feelings—didn't provide the proper outlet for her students' emotions, nor could they be used to articulate the black experience. Searching for a more relevant theatre, Teer moved to Harlem and became founder, producing director, and playwright of the National Black Theatre in 1968. She stated, in an interview in *Black Creation*, that the intent behind the NBT was to "house what we think of as the Black experience. . . . [to be] a multi-faceted institution, [an] educational institution [that] uses theatrical experience to decrude ourselves and to help reverse the process of negative thinking" (Jones, 19).

Like many experimental theatre artists and groups in the late 1960s and early 1970s, such as the Living Theatre and the Performance Group, Teer found traditional Western theatre too narrow, too confining, and too neat. These groups were looking for ways to break the conventional arrangements and involve the audience more actively as participants. Rituals, therefore, became an important part of a theatrical presentation. With productions such as *The Believers: The Black Experience in Song* (1968), *A Revival: Change/Love Together/Organize* (1972), and *Soljourney into Truth* (1975), Teer blended ritualistic elements from Africa and America to entertain and educate. One of the first attempts to chronicle the black experience in American song and dance, *The Believers* was a seminal piece for Teer. She employed a half dozen composers who utilized tribal chants, slave songs, blues, revival tunes, and jazz street cries. More than just elements to further or illustrate plot, the songs functioned as historical documents, tracing the roots of the African-American experience from Africa through slavery to northern migration. *Soljourney into Truth* was an example of a "ritualistic revival," blending African ceremonies, music, dance, song, and poetry to eliminate the distance between audience and performer. There was no separate stage, no audience, only participants.

The "ritualistic revivals" grew out of NBT workshop techniques for liberating the minds and spirits of individuals, often through improvisations. These techniques were then worked into a new structure that allowed Teer and company to share them with the public in a way that was both educational and entertaining. Beside the performances and workshops, Teer developed other programs, such as symposiums and Sunday afternoon "Blackenings," to reach out to the community. Teer firmly believes that all presentations by NBT (plays, musicals, rituals, "revivals") must achieve five goals: they must raise the level of consciousness, address political issues, educate, illuminate, and entertain.

ADDITIONAL PRODUCTIONS: 1968: *The Believers: The Black Experience in Song* (Book by Josephine Jackson, Sylvia Jackson, Joseph A. Walker. Composers and Lyricists: Benjamin Carter, Dorothy Dimroe, Josephine Jackson, Amje Ray, Ron Steward, Jospeh A. Walker); 1969: *Five on the Black Hand Side* (Charlie L. Russell); 1969–72: *A Revival: Change/Love Together /Organize* (Teer); 1975: *Soljourney into Truth* (Author and Choreographer Teer).

SELECTED BIBLIOGRAPHY: Barbour, Floyd B., comp. and ed. *Black Power Revolt*. Boston: Porter Sargent, 1968; Jones, Martha M. "Barbara Ann Teer's Black National Theater." *Black Creation* 3 (Summer 1972): 18–20; Harris, Jessica B. "The National Black Theatre: The Sun People of 125th St." *The Drama Review* 16 (December 1972): 39–45; Mapp, Edward. *Directory of Blacks in the Performing Arts*. 2nd ed. Metuchen, NJ: Scarecrow Press, 1990; Porter, Curtiss F. "Interview." *Black Lines: A Journal of Black Studies* 2 (Spring 1973): 22; Teer, Barbara Ann. "We Can Be What We Were Born to Be."*New York Times* 7 July 1968: sec. 2; Woll, Allen. *Dictionary of the Black Theatre: Broadway, Off-Broadway, and Selected Harlem Theatre*. Westport, CT: Greenwood Press, 1983.

Mark C. Maniak

SHUJI TERAYAMA [b. December 10, 1935, Aomori Prefecture, Japan; d. May 4, 1983, Tokyo, Japan]. Shuji Terayama, avant-garde Japanese poet, stage director, playwright, filmmaker, screenwriter, and essayist, was born in Aomori Prefecture in northern Japan. Following the death of his father, Terayama was raised alternately by his mother, who worked on American army bases after

Japan's defeat, and his granduncle, who ran a movie theatre. There, he became a passionate fan of American gangster movies, reveling in the performances of James Cagney, George Raft, and Humphrey Bogart and immersing himself in the exploits of Al Capone, the Cincinnati Kid, and others, a pastime some feel led to Terayama's attraction to gambling, horse racing, boxing, and the Yakuzu (the Japanese underworld) later in his life. Terayama's education at Waseda University ended in 1955 when he was hospitalized with nephritis, during which time he read such writers as Comte de Lautreamont, Antonin Artaud, and the Japanese Gothic novelist Izumi Kyoka. Thereafter, he spent most of his time watching movies and hanging around the Shinjuku district, Tokyo's equivalent to Greenwich Village.

In 1967, after having achieved success and fame as a poet and a screenwriter, Terayama founded the Tenjo-Sajiki (translated as "cheap seats" or "peanut gallery" to connote Terayama's preference for an audience of commoners), an underground theatre company which had, as one of its stated purposes, "to whip the world with our imagination and theatricalize revolution" (Mellen, 275). The company has variously been lionized for its audacity, stylistic innovation, unapologetic iconoclasm, and revolutionary fervor, and vilified for its obsession with sexual perversity, violence, and physical deformity, its misogynist tendencies, and its militaristic discipline and attitudes which have resulted in several attacks upon or fights with audiences.

Terayama's work has been characterized as multiplex, nondiegetic, flagrantly antagonistic to both Eastern and Western bourgeois sensibilities (*Jashumon*, 1971, for example, is a violent condemnation of the family unit, which includes a son's physical assault upon his mother, and prominently features a song titled "Please Die, Mother"), and wildly eclectic, freely intermixing and juxtaposing elements from Western icons and forms like happenings, guerilla theater, Hollywood, European "art" films, and sports. Terayama also expressed an ongoing fascination with masks, puppets, role-playing, transformations, and camp, and an almost perverse attraction to dwarves, hunchbacks, and enormously fat women. Spectators at *La Marie Vision* (*Mink Marie*, 1967), for example, watched a grossly fat cook hacking at a victim's body with a meat cleaver (in the kitchen), while in the bathroom a "hairy fairy" examined his ugly face in a mirror and speculated whether or not he was lovelier than Snow White. Nearby, a dwarf imitated the actions of the "hairy fairy."

Terayama's theatre, throughout his career, remained highly personal and he claimed repeatedly in interviews that he was unable to distinguish between "the theater and real life." His production of *Throw Away the Books and Get Out in the Streets* (1968), which one critic labeled "a kind of carnival for runaways and fairies," was a Living Theater-esque collage of poems, confessions, and political preachments of teenagers who delivered them from the stage.

"Despite displays of iconoclastic bravura," as Carol Fisher Sorgenfrei has noted, "the works of Terayama maintain[ed] profound links with Japanese tradition. The structural patterns and performance techniques of *noh*, *kabuki*, *bun-*

raku, and such popular entertainments as *naniwabushi* (a form of story-telling to music), *kakubejishi* (street tumblers wearing lion masks), mediums, fortune tellers, circus-acts, and other elements of folk theater emerge[d] in startling contexts'' (Sorgenfrei, 119).

Participation at major theatre festivals—Experimenta 3 in Germany, Shiraz, Nancy, Belgrade International Theatre Festival (BITEF)—and at famous avant-garde venues like New York's Cafe LaMama ETC brought Terayama international notoriety. In 1983, he succumbed to the nephritis which had plagued him throughout his life. He was forty-seven years old.

ADDITIONAL PRODUCTIONS: 1967: *The Hunchback of Aomori*; 1969: *The Crime of Dr. Galigari*, *We're All Riding on a Circus Elephant*; 1970: *Baron Bura Bura* (Rock Musical), *The Man-Powered Airplane, Solomon*; 1973: *Origin of Blood*; 1974–75: *Blind Man's Letter*; 1975: *Knock*; 1977: *Directions to Servants*. **Films:** 1970: *The Emperor of To-matocatsup*; 1971: *Throw Away the Books and Get Out in the Streets*; 1975: *Pastoral Hide-and-Seek*; 1977: *The Boxer*.

SELECTED BIBLIOGRAPHY: Lester, Elenore. "There Will Be No Audience." *New York Times* 5 July 1970; Mellen, Joan. *Voices from the Japanese Cinema*. New York: Liveright, 1975: 275–88; Merin, Jennifer. "Terayama's *Jashumon*." *The Drama Review* 16 (September 1972): 103–14; Myers, Maria. "Terayama's *Directions to Servants*." *The Drama Review* 25 (March 1981): 79–94; Sorgenfrei, Carol. "Showdown at Culture Gap: Images of the West in the Plays of Shuji Terayama." *Modern Drama* 35 (March 1992): 116–26.

John W. Frick

VIVIANE THÉOPHILIDÈS [b. September 29, 1940, Paris, France]. Like the gypsy ancestors from whom she claims her fierce intensity, Viviane Théophilidès has moved, physically and aesthetically, throughout her career. She began as an actress in Marseilles in the early 1960s, committed to the movement to decentralize theatrical production in France. There, she worked with other neo-phytes, including Antoine Vitez,* learning "by doing" how to adapt, produce, and direct theatre texts. A year in Burgundy and five years in Aquitaine brought her a fruitful collaboration with Armand Gatti, whose one-woman show, *L'In-firmière* (which she created and toured in 1967–68), garnered her a national reputation.

Through her contact with regional publics, Théophilidès developed an idea of theatre—to encourage spectators to confront critically their reality by exposing the way reality is constructed—which, despite her peregrinations, has under-scored all her directorial work. This interest has led her, since the mid–1970s, to examine the reality of women's lives. In 1975, in collaboration with actress-director Anne-Marie Lazarini, with whom she also animated the Parisian Association des Athévains, Théophilidès targeted the baby-selling racket. To undercut the potential melodrama in Denise Bonal's muckraking *Légère en août*, Théophilidès stylized the actresses' movements and constructed pauses in the "pregnant women's" confessions, thus building in moments for the spectators to take their distance. Again with Lazarini, in 1978 Théophilidès adapted and directed *La Fortune de Gaspard* from the edifying tales of the Countess of Ségur. This production provided a satirical look at how learning tales function to reinforce the capitalist system.

In 1980, Théophilidès founded (with Micheline Uzan) Des femmes dans le texte, a theatrical project which explored how a female subject might be portrayed onstage. In their 1980 production *Une fille à brûler* (after Joseph Delteil's novel), Théophilidès used quick cutting, storybook images, and broad choreographic strokes to decenter a mythic Joan of Arc, establishing in her place a character both human and female. She evoked a similar nurturing image in her 1979 adaptation of Hélène Cixous's *Là*, but as a departure from her usual style, she employed highly ritualized movements and rhythms throughout the production.

Théophilidès's penchant for arresting stage pictures and vivacious changes served to foreground and valorize the female characters in her productions of Alfred de Musset's *No Trifling with Love* (1986) and Denise Boucher's musical review *Gémeaux croisées*, starring popular singers Pauline Julien and Anne Sylvestre. The latter show toured France and Canada from 1987 to 1989.

From 1983 to 1989, Théophilidès taught acting at France's National Conservatory, but later left to strike out again on her own. In 1991, she was awarded a writer-in-residence grant at the Chartreuse in Villeneuve-lès-Avignon in order to write her first play, *Joë Bousquet: Rue de Verdun*, in which the paralyzed poet Joë Bousquet, the powerful publisher Jean Paulhan, and the mystic philosopher Simone Veil ruminate over questions concerning the future of the world and the place of art within it on the eve of World War II. Like Théophilidès, her characters only find answers in never-ending discussion.

ADDITIONAL PRODUCTIONS: 1979: *L'Arrivante* (adaptation of Hélène Cixous); 1981: *Les Mystères de l'amour* (Roger Vitrac); 1982: *Ida* (Gertrude Stein); 1984: *Adiedi* (Yelena Kohout); 1990: *François d'Assis* (adaptation of Joseph Delteil).

SELECTED BIBLIOGRAPHY: Moss, Jane. "Women's Theatre in France." *Signs* 12 (Spring 1987): 549–67; Temkine, Raymonde. *Le Théâtre au présent*. Paris: Bouffoneries/ Contrastes; 1987.

Judith G. Miller

BORIS (BARUCH AARON) THOMASHEFSKY [b. ca. 1868, Kiev Province, Ukraine; d. July 9, 1939, New York, New York]. Like many stars of the early Yiddish theatre, Boris Thomashefsky got his musical training as a boy by serving as a *meshoyrer* (cantor's apprentice). When the family immigrated to the United States, Thomashefsky got a job singing in a synagogue on New York's Lower East Side, where he befriended a wealthy saloon-keeper and convinced him to bring to New York a troupe of Yiddish actors who were playing in London. They arrived in 1882, and that year Thomashefsky performed with them in Avrom Goldfadn's *Koldunya*, the first professional Yiddish play on an American stage.

Thomashefsky and his actors led a peripatetic existence for the next few years, performing seasons or parts of seasons in Philadelphia, Baltimore, Boston, and

Chicago before returning to New York at the behest of Jacob P. Adler, with whom Thomashefsky formed a short-lived partnership in 1890. They opened the Adler-Thomashefsky Theatre with Moishe Hurwitz's *The Johnstown Flood*, but the partners soon quarreled and went their separate ways. Thomashefsky and Adler would unite again in the middle of the 1896–97 season, this time with rival actor David Kessler, but the trio stayed together for just a few weeks.

While Adler would make a name for himself as the star of numerous plays by Jacob Gordin, Thomashefksy became known as the matinee idol of the Yiddish theatre. He directed and starred in numerous melodramas and operettas; the latter genre included Joseph Lateiner's *Alexander or The Crown Prince of Jerusalem* (1892) and *Yudele* (1896); Jacob Ter's *Di yidishe neshome* (*The Jewish Soul*, 1908); his adaptation of Moishe Zeifert's *Dos pintele yid* (*The Essential Spark of Jewishness*, 1909); and his own *Di grine kuzine* (*The "Green" Cousin*, 1922). In such spectacles, Thomashefsky revelled in elaborate patriotic effects, celebrating both Jewish and American values. His character waved an American flag at the end of *Di Yidishe neshome*, and during the finale of *Dos Pintele yid*, a Star of David electrically lit with the words "dos pintele yid" descended from the ceiling.

Yet in spite of his reputation for promoting elaborate spectacles and sentimental melodramas, Thomashefsky also supported dramas by playwrights who sought to reform the Yiddish stage by introducing elements of Ibsenesque realism. Such works included Jacob Gordin's *Di litvishe brider Luria* (*The Lithuanian Luria Brothers*, 1894), Leon Kobrin's *Mina* (1898) and *Breach of Promise* (1912), and Osip Dimov's *Shma Yisroel* (*Hear, O Israel*, 1907) and *Der eybiker vanderer* (*The Eternal Wanderer*, 1913). Thomashefsky also appeared in a number of adaptations of the classics, including *Hamlet* (1893), *Faust* (1902), *Othello* (1903, under the title, *The Blind Musician or the Jewish Othello*), and *The Taming of the Shrew* (*The Pretty American*, 1910).

But such deference to high art was always tempered by Thomashefsky's business sense; the health of the box office always determined whether he would take risks, and he continually returned to the plays that had made him popular in the first place. In such works, he went for the grandiose *coup de théâtre*, whether visual, aural, or both. In 1916, in his own operetta *Dos tsebrokhene fidele* (*The Broken Little Fiddle*), he staged a ballet for the first time on the American Yiddish stage; Joseph Rumshinsky's score was played by a twenty-four piece orchestra, unusually large for the time. In 1922, he directed his own operetta, *Der goldener fodem* (*The Golden Thread*), in which he played both himself and Avrom Goldfadn, "the Father of the Yiddish Theatre."

In 1924, Thomashefsky brought another group of European Yiddish performers to New York, this time on a temporary basis; he invited the Vilna Troupe to perform in his theatre for several months. Thomashefsky maintained close ties to European Yiddish companies throughout his career. He performed on several European tours, and frequently traveled to London and Eastern Europe at the end of a season to lure the top actors to the United States. Thus, in the tradition of the nineteenth-century actor-manager, Thomashefksy continued to make his mark on the Yiddish theatre both onstage and behind the scenes. He also wrote numerous articles on theatre for the Yiddish press, and published a theatre newspaper, *Di Yidishe bine* (The Yiddish Stage) for a few months in 1909–10. He also left living legacies; his sons Milton and Harry occasionally collaborated with him, and Harry headed the Yiddish Drama Unit of the Federal Theatre Project.

ADDITIONAL PRODUCTIONS: 1891: *Ezra, oder der eviger yude* (*Ezra, or the Eternal Jew*, written by Lateiner for Thomashefsky and his wife Bessie); 1893: *Bathsheba* (Lateiner); 1895: *Kuzri* (Moishe Hurwitz); 1901: *Di goldene medine* (*The Golden Land*, by Nahum Meier Shaikevitch); 1907: *The Weavers, Ben-Ami* (Avrom Goldfadn's last play); 1908: *Dementia Americana* (Jacob Gordin's last play); 1909: *Dos tsveyte vayb* (*The Second Wife*, by Isidore Zolatarevsky); 1914: *Di poilishe khasene* (*The Polish Wedding*, by Boris Thomashefsky); 1919: *Di tsvey khazonim* (*The Two Cantors*, by Harry Kalmanovitch, starring Thomashefsky and Kessler); 1920: *Parlor Floor and Basement* (Harry Thomashefsky); 1923: *Dos odeser Yidl* (*The Little Jew of Odessa*, by A. Kartozhinsky).

SELECTED BIBLIOGRAPHY: Gorin B. *Di geshikhte fun yidishn teatre* [*The History of Yiddish Theatre*]. Vol. 2. New York: Max N. Mayzel, 1923; Howe, Irving. *World of Our Fathers*. New York: Harcourt Brace Jovanovich, 1976: 460–96; Kobrin, Leon. *Erinerungen fun a yidishn dramaturg* [*Recollections of a Yiddish Dramatist*]. Vol. 2. New York: Committee for Kobrin's Writings, 1925; Perlmutter, Sholem. *Yidishe dramaturgn un teater-compozitors* [*Yiddish Dramatists and Theatre Composers*]. New York: Yiddisher Kultur Farband (YKUF), 1952: 98–110; Sandrow, Nahma. *Vagabond Stars*. New York: Limelight Editions, 1986; Thomashefsky, Bessie. *Mayn lebns-geshikhte* [*My Life Story*]. New York: Varhayt Publishing, 1916; Thomashefsky, Boris. *Mayn Lebnsgeshikhte* [*My Life Story*]. New York: Trio Press, 1937; Zylbercweig, Zalmen. *Leksikon fun yidishn teater* [*Lexicon of Yiddish Theatre*]. Vol. 2. New York: Hebrew Actors Union of America, 1931: 804–40.

Joel Berkowitz

PAUL THOMPSON [b. 1940, Charlottetown, Prince Edward Island, Canada]. Widely considered to be the major and most iconoclastic director of the alternative theatre movement that defined an indigenous Canadian theatrical style in the 1970s, Paul Thompson has had a profound influence on playwriting and acting in Canada. After working as a university teacher of French, he apprenticed under Roger Planchon* in Avignon and returned to Canada determined to create a popular theatre in a country he (along with many others in the nationalist 1970s) perceived as deeply colonized by American and British theatrical models. In 1971 Thompson joined Theatre Passe Muraille (TPM), a small radical theatre in Toronto, and began using the techniques of collective creation and documentary drama to explore Canadian mythologies and regional culture. His period as artistic director of TPM was a decade of furious creativity that gave birth to dozens of new playwrights as well as a distinct acting style that emphasized storytelling, gestural theatricality, and the actor's literary creativity. His work at Passe Muraille inspired numerous collective theatres across Canada, many of which began as TPM seed projects.

Thompson's first foray into documentary theatre was the 1971 *Dhoukobors*, a collage about the Russian religious sect that emigrated to Canada in the late nineteenth century, which the ensemble identified as a model of anti-establishment pacifism. The following year, Thompson took a group of actors to a rural Ontario farming community to improvise a play about their meetings with farmers. The result was *The Farm Show*, which premiered in an auction barn in 1972 and went on to become the legendary prototype of the collective documentaries that revolutionized Canadian theatre. In the ensuing decade, *The Farm Show* was followed by literally hundreds of similar ventures across the country. For many young artists, Thompson's collective creation methods enabled them to recover local culture and compensate for the paucity of Canadian playwrights. These companies in turn, like Passe Muraille, created an outlet for novice playwrights and contributed to a remarkable increase in Canadian drama.

Although committed to collective creation, Thompson was also fascinated with the power of the written word, and began working with writers in his collectives in 1973 when Rick Salutin co-wrote *1837: The Farmers' Revolt*. One of the most important plays of the decade, *1837* dramatized a populist rebellion against British autocracy in nineteenth-century Toronto, with an explicit thematic reference to contemporary American cultural domination in Canada.

Thompson's interest in regional culture took him to the prairie provinces of Manitoba, Saskatchewan, and Alberta, where he created a series of plays on local themes in collaboration with novelists: Rudy Weibe on *The West Show* (1976) and *Far As the Eye Can See* (1978), Robert Kroetsch on *The Studhorse Man* (1982). In Toronto he encouraged his actors to extend their creativity into playwriting; the most significant example is that of Linda Griffiths, who began as an actor in several collective shows and later wrote and performed in her solo play *Maggie and Pierre* (1980), about the tempestuous marriage of Prime Minister Pierre Trudeau and his young wife Margaret Sinclair, under Thompson's direction.

Thompson enjoyed risk-taking in his productions, often to the discomfort of critics, and always relished controversy. *Dhoukobors* excited much comment because of its use of nudity, which in 1971 was still rarely seen on Toronto stages, and in 1975, *I Love You, Baby Blue*, inspired by the soft-core porno films shown on a local television station, shocked and delighted audiences with its extremely graphic portrayal of sexual mores in Toronto. After a three-month run it was closed by the police, but the theatre, which won its court case, made sufficient profit from the show to buy a new building. No less controversial were Thompson's attempts to breach the cultural wall that separates English Canada from Francophone Québec. In 1978, he directed *Les Maudits Anglais*, a collective play about English Canadian attitudes to Québec, which was then performed in French in Montréal by its Anglophone creators. In 1991 he brought about a storm of controversy with his Montréal production of David Fennario's *The Death of René Levesque*, a left-wing critique of the late Québecois separatist premier, produced at a time of volatile nationalist sentiment in Québec.

After leaving Theatre Passe Muraille in 1982, Thompson free-lanced across Canada until 1987, when he accepted the position of director general of the National Theatre School in Montréal.

ADDITIONAL PRODUCTIONS: 1971: *Notes from Quebec* (Jean-Claude Germaine); 1973: *Under the Greywacke*; 1975: *Them Donellys*; 1978: *Les Maudits Anglais*; 1982: *The Studhorse Man* (Frank Moher/Robert Kroetsch); 1984; *School for Immigrants* (with 7/84 England), *Torontonians, Nathan Cohen: A Review* (Salutin); 1987: *The Games of Winter*.

SELECTED BIBLIOGRAPHY: Filewod, Alan. *Collective Encounters: Documentary Theatre in English Canada.* Toronto: University of Toronto Press, 1987; Johnston, Denis. *Up the Mainstream: The Rise of Toronto's Alternate Theatres.* Toronto: University of Toronto Press, 1991; Nunn, Robert. "The Meeting of Actuality and Theatricality in *The Farm Show*." *Canadian Drama* 8.1 (1982): 42–54; Salutin, Rick. "*1837*: Diary of a Canadian Play." *This Magazine* 7 (1973); Usmiani, Renate. *Second Stage: The Alternative Theatre Movement in Canada.* Vancouver: University of British Columbia Press, 1983; Wallace, Robert, and Cynthia Zimmerman. *The Work: Conversations with Canadian Playwrights.* Toronto: Coach House Press, 1982.

Alan Filewod

THÓRHILDUR THORLEIFSDÓTTIR [b. March 25, 1945, Isafjørdur, Iceland]. Within the last generation, the Icelandic theatre has produced a number of vital and imaginative women directors. These include Gudrún Ásmundsdóttir, Brynja Benediktsdóttir, Bríet Hédinsdóttir, María Kristjánsdóttir, and Thórunn Sigurdardóttir. With her work since the mid–1970s, Thórhildur Thorleifsdóttir has established herself, not only within this group, but as one of the most original stage directors in Iceland. Her productions have often been interpreted in a political light, and they have gathered even more attention that way since she entered Iceland's political arena. She has directed works ranging from children's plays to Lerner and Loewe, and from classic and modern Icelandic works to Ibsen, Chekhov, Lorca, and Brecht. She has worked regularly at Iceland's three major professional theatres and with the Opera Company of Iceland, Icelandic State Television, and in feature films as well.

Thorleifsdóttir studied ballet in the school formerly housed in the National Theatre of Iceland, and later at the Royal Ballet School in London. Her early exposure to dance is a formative element in a directing style marked by largeness of vision, logistical complexity, and kinesthetic energy. In these respects, she has challenged the traditional literary affinities of the Icelandic theatre and the more static and pictorial stagings that preceded hers. She also helped found the experimental theatre groups PlayForge and the People's Theatre. Indeed, her earliest experience as a director came with these groups during the late 1960s and early 1970s at a time when many younger people in the Icelandic theatre set out to challenge the methods and values of the established companies.

Later in the 1970s, she helped found the Akureyri Theatre Company in the north of Iceland, and this group eventually established itself along with the National Theatre in Reykjavík and the Reykjavík City Theatre among Iceland's ongoing professional companies. Thorleifsdóttir was also instrumental in founding the Icelandic Women's Party in the early 1980s, boosting it to prominence through a series of political demonstrations and advertisements which she helped devise. She was elected in 1987 to serve a four-year term in her country's Parliament as a representative of the Women's Party.

Her production of *My Fair Lady* in 1983–84 made persistent and surprising reference to contemporary feminist concerns. When her term in Parliament ended in 1991, she directed Ibsen's *Peer Gynt* to reopen the National Theatre after its extensive renovation. This production was notable for its radical adaptation which split Peer into a younger and older self (played by two actors), its use of modern Icelandic music instead of Edvard Grieg's classic score, and its final tableau showing the young Peer in Solveig's arms, the old one in his mother Asa's, and the troll-prince in his mother's, too. Such features added to the controversy punctuating Thorleifsdóttir's career, and on which she seems to have thrived.

ADDITIONAL PRODUCTIONS: 1978–79: *Steal a Tiny Million* (Arrabal); 1979–80: *Blind Man's Bluff* (B. Gudmundsson); 1979–81: *The Shepherdess and the Outlaws* (S. Gudmundsson and Thorgeirsson); 1980–81: *The Taming of the Shrew* (costumes by Una Collins); 1983–84: *Schweyk in the Second World War* (Brecht); 1984–85: *Agnes of God* (John Pielmeier); 1985–86: *Wild Honey* (Chekhov/Frayne); 1986–87: *Yerma* (Lorca); 1987–88: *Don Giovanni* (designed by Una Collins).

SELECTED BIBLIOGRAPHY: Programs from the National Theatre of Iceland and the City Theatres of Reykjavík and Akureyri; "Theatre in Iceland," three pamphlets covering 1975–80, 1980–85, and 1985–88 (Reykjavík: Association of Icelandic Actors et al., 1982, 1985, and 1988).

Leigh Woods

GEORGY ALEKSANDROVICH TOVSTONOGOV [b. September 9, 1915, Tbilisi; d. May 24, 1989, Leningrad]. Tovstonogov began his career as an actor and assistant director in Tbilisi's Children's theatre. After graduating from the Moscow State Theatre Institute (GITIS), he worked at the Tbilisi Russian Theatre as artistic director, in the Moscow Children's Theatre, and as artistic director of the Leningrad's Komsomol Theatre. In 1956 he was appointed artistic director of the Leningrad Bolshoi Dramatic Theatre, which became known as one of the best theatres in the Soviet Union for more than two decades. Tovstonogov also directed productions in Poland, Bulgaria, Finland, Hungary, Germany, and the United States. Throughout his long artistic career, he also taught a directing class at the Leningrad Institute of Theatre, Music and Film.

Like two other noted Russian directors of his time, Anatoly Efros* and Yuri Lyubimov,* Tovstonogov talked about the curses, pain, and sufferings of Russian life in his work. Tovstonogov was never explicit or didactic; he spoke through images and metaphors. His productions were marked by a combination of fantasy and intellect, temperament and logic, passion and strong ideas. His main themes were the pettiness that threatens free will, the complacency and satiety that slowly kill individuals, and the fate of an individual in the society of slaves.

Tovstonogov's productions were built like symphonies: many different instruments and themes merged together, united by one dominant idea. In *The*

Idiot (with Innokenty Smoktunovsky), adapted from Dostoyevsky's novel in 1957, Tovstonogov showed an incompatibility between spiritual life and active pettiness; a kind, credulous person and rude and cynical reality. Smoktunovsky's movements symbolized the spiritual, the abstract, the vulnerable about his character: he walked lightly, as if he were afraid to hurt the ground. His palms looked flat; they could stroke human beings or animals, but they could not hold the arms. However, he could stretch his hands to the sky, which created an image of spears, thus making a wall between two people who wanted to hurt each other. The mental illness of the main character was the result of his hopes being shattered, his realization that kindness cannot change complacent society, where talent is doomed to be stifled.

Alexander Griboyedov's *Woe from Wit* (1962) started with a lit curtain, on which a famous Pushkin saying was displayed: "Why on earth did the Devil have me, with my wit and talent, condemned to be born in Russia?" (Party officials forced Tovstonogov to remove this curtain after opening night.) Tovstonogov stood an intellectual, intelligent, and truthful man against an entire society that didn't need and actually feared wit and intellect. Tovstonogov challenged and blamed contemporary Soviet society for wasting Russian talent, for sending talent into exile, and for closing its ears against the truth. Chatsky, the main character, played by Sergei Yursky, stood alone in the corner, against a hateful crowd wearing masks. Theatrical masks revealed that society consisted of swine, foxes, and wolves, rather than human beings.

In Maxim Gorky's *Petty Bourgeoisie* (1966), Tovstonogov lit an oval portrait on the curtain with the actors' faces. In the background of the portrait was a decorative volcano. The image of explosion revealed the hypocrisy of the participants, and mocked their unity. The strongest ones killed the hopes of the weakest ones. At the end the main character of the play, Tatyana, played by Emma Popova, walked onstage trying to catch invisible moths, as if fighting with ghosts. However, she was unable to win, and just stood alone on an empty stage, hopelessly raising her hands. In Nikolai Gogol's *Inspector General* (1972) one of the main images of the production was the fear that possessed the governor. Frightening shadows hung over him, flew along the big walls of his house, and turned into a horrible phantom that wore a black overcoat, gloves, and glasses. The musical *The Story of a Horse* (1975, known in the United States as *Strider*), taken from Tolstoy's story, was a philosophical fable designed by Kochergin with Evgeny Lebedev. Tovstonogov used the Brechtian method which allowed the actors to be transformed into their characters and to be alienated from them, to imitate horses' habits and humanize them, to show an animal in a human being and a human in an animal.

In his work, Tovstonogov synthesized the theatrical methods of Konstantin Stanislavsky* and the metaphorical images of Vsevolod Meyerhold*; the festivity of Evgeni Vakhtangov* and the alienation between an actor and his character of Bertolt Brecht.* The images and metaphors Tovstonogov created in his productions became part of textbooks and lectures for Russian theatre professionals and for theatregoers. Tovstonogov, with a few other Russian directors, created the Golden Age of the Russian theatre.

ADDITIONAL PRODUCTIONS: 1959: *Barbarians* (Gorky, with Tatyana Doronina); *Five Evenings* (Aleksander Volodin); 1961: *My Elder Sister* (Volodin, with Doronina); 1965: *Three Sisters*; 1968: *The Price*; 1974: *Last Summer in Chulimsk* (Vampilov, designed by E. Kochergin); 1980: *Wolves and Sheep* (A. Ostrovsky, designed by Kochergin); 1984: *Tarelkin's Death* (adapted from Sukhovo-Kobylin).

SELECTED BIBLIOGRAPHY: Berkovsky, N. "Dostoevsky on Stage. *Idiot* directed by G. A. Tovstonogov." *Literature and Theatre.* Moscow: Iskusstvo, 1969; *Directors' Portraits.* Moskva: Iskusstvo, 1972: 97–144; Ribakov, U. *Tovstonogov and Problems of Directing.* Leningrad: Iskusstvo, 1977; Tovstonogov, G. *Conversations with Colleagues.* Moskva: Soyuz teatral'nykh deyateley (STD) RSFSR, 1988; Tovstonogov, G. *The Profession of a Stage Director.* Moskva: Iskusstvo, 1965, published in English in 1972; Tovstonogov, G. *The Stage's Mirror.* 2 vols. Leningrad: Iskusstvo, 1980.

Paulina Shur

TOMMY TUNE [b. February 28, 1939, Wichita Falls, Texas]. In 1944 at the age of five, Tune enrolled in tap, acrobatic, and ballet classes. As a teenager, he realized that his lengthy body was not suited to ballet, and he began to turn his attention to the dance styles of Fred Astaire and Gene Kelly. After seeing a production of *The King and I*, he fell in love with musical comedy. After two years at Lon Morris College in Jacksonville, Texas, Tune transferred to the University of Texas at Austin and earned a B.F.A. in drama, and then a master's degree in directing from the University of Houston. After his first professional dancing job, in *Redhead* at the State Fair of Texas, he moved to New York in March 1961 and was immediately cast in the chorus of *Irma La Douce*. He also appeared in the choruses of *Baker Street*, *A Joyful Noise*, and *How Now, Dow Jones*, and in the films of *Hello, Dolly!* and *The Boy Friend*.

In 1973, Michael Bennett* gave Tune a featured role in *Seesaw* for which he won his first Antoinette Perry Award. When other roles were not forthcoming, Tune turned his attention to choreographing and directing. His first directing job—an Off-Broadway play entitled *The Club* in 1976—received critical acclaim and he received an Obie. In 1977, he directed and choreographed his first Broadway musical, *The Best Little Whorehouse in Texas*. That was followed in 1980 by his work as co-choreographer and director of *A Day in Hollywood, a Night in the Ukraine*. In 1981, he directed the highly acclaimed *Cloud 9* Off-Broadway. He received another Tony for his direction of the Broadway hit *Nine* in 1982, which was also named Best Musical. He returned to the stage the following year as both performer and director in *My One and Only*, for which he, again, won a Tony, this time for Best Actor in a Musical. His direction and choreography of *Grand Hotel* in 1989 brought him two more Tony Awards for choreography and direction. He followed that up in 1991 with Tony Awards again for direction and choreography for his work on *The Will Rogers Follies*, while the show won the Tony for Best Musical.

It is interesting that while Tune is primarily recognized for his direction of traditional Broadway musicals, he received high praise for his direction of two very nontraditional straight plays. His direction of musicals is noted for its Broadway showmanship. While many critics do not feel that he has advanced the style, he has certainly captured the expected energetic, flashy dancing associated with Broadway musicals. With the early deaths of Gower Champion,* Michael Bennett, and Bob Fosse,* Tommy Tune is currently reigning as Broadway's most noted director-choreographer.

PRODUCTION HISTORY: 1976: *The Club*; 1977: *The Best Little Whorehouse in Texas*; 1980: *A Day in Hollywood, a Night in the Ukraine*; 1981: *Cloud 9*; 1982: *Nine*; 1983: *My One and Only*; 1989: *Grand Hotel*; 1991: *The Will Rogers Follies*.

SELECTED BIBLIOGRAPHY: Clarke, Gerald. "A Dude from Another Planet." *Time* 28 June 1982: 66; Gottfried, Martin. *More Broadway Musicals: Since 1980*. New York: Harry N. Abrams, 1991: 94–124; Guthrie, Constance. "A Tall Texan Stretches Out." *Newsweek* 24 May 1982: 74; Kalem, T. E. "Skyscraper and Swizzle Stick." *Time* 16 May 1983: 76; Linton, Gregg. *Musical Comedy in America*. New York: Theatre Arts Books, 1981; Pikula, Joan. "Tommy Tune." *Dance Magazine* September 1982: 53–57; Rich, Frank. "Tune's Swirling Vision of a *Grand Hotel*." *New York Times* 13 November 1989: C13; "Tune, Tommy." *Current Biography* January 1983: 38–42; Wetzsteon, Ross. "Broadway's Triple Threat." *Saturday Review* May 1982: 31–35.

Reagan Fletcher

JOUKA TURKKA [b. April 17, 1942, Pirkkala, Finland]. Since 1981, Jouka Turkka has served as director at several Finnish theatres, as a drama professor (1981–82), as a college president (1982–85), and as professor of directing at Teatterikorkeakoulu (Theatre College, 1985–88). During the same period, Turkka has received accolades as a leading Finnish director and playwright, and has been credited with modifying the Finnish school of acting through the use of physical expression.

Turkka has directed primarily Finnish scripts, many of them world premieres. Between 1966 and 1981, only fifteen of his sixty one productions were foreign dramas. Most of Turkka's productions, such as *Runar ja Kyllikki* (*Runar and Kyllikki*, Kylatasku, 1974), *Viisas neitsyt* (*Smart Virgin*, Lassila, 1979) and *Murtovarkaus* (*Burglary*, Canth, 1981), focused on the deserted countryside and the hypocrisy of the country folk, but were nevertheless endowed with a passionate erotica. In addition, Turkka has chosen to portray and examine contemporary marriage and close friendships as well. Strindberg's *Ghost Sonata* (1978), for example, emphasized human depression brought on by guilt and lack of will power.

While passionate feeling and actors' enthusiasm have been typical of Turkka's theatre (which has been labeled "sensual" and "physical"), his directing is ever changing, with the meanings of objects forever shifting. Turkka's method of physical action differs from the naturalistic system of Konstantin Stanislavsky,* approximating more closely the biomechanics of Vsevolod Meyerhold.* Turkka's works have, in a unique way, crystallized the most important new theatrical approaches. He uses the author's language to theatrically actualize terms which are somewhere between thought and expression, the performances emphasizing "substantive words," actors' movements, expressions, gestures, and sounds, rather than the interpretation of the script.

Turkka has added to his stature as a director by writing his own manuscripts for the plays he directs. Turkka's manuscripts *Kott och Karlek* (*Flesh and Love*, 1985), produced in Göteburg's city theatre, and *Hvpnoosi* (*Hypnosis*, 1985) represent attempts to bring provocative subjects to the stage.

ADDITIONAL PRODUCTIONS: 1969: *Hvvasti Mansikka* (*Goodbye Mansikka* by Puhakka); 1976: *Siina tekija missa nakija* (*There Is the Doer Where Is the Seer* by Salama); 1979: *Tuntematon sotilas* (*Unknown soldier* by Linna); 1980: *Kohti toista tasavaltaa* (*Toward Second Republic* by Salama); 1984: *Nummisuutarit* (*Meadow Shoemakers* by Kivi); 1983: *Tuhat ja vksi yota* (*Thousand and One Nights*); 1985: *Jeppe Niilonpoika* (Holberg); 1990: *Valheita* (*Lies* by Turkka), *Seitseman veljesta* (*Seven Brothers* by Kivi, TV).

SELECTED BIBLIOGRAPHY: Ollikainen, Anneli. *Lihat ylos. Muistiinpanoja Jouko Turkan opetuksesta* (*Flesh Up, Notes About Jouko Turkka's Directing*). Helsinki: Valtion painatuskeskus, Teatterikorkeakoulu, 1988; *Turkan pitka juoksu. Jouko Turkan ohjaukset* (*Turkka's Long Run, Jouko Turkka's Directing*). Helsinki: Gaudeamus, 1986; Turkka, Jouko. *Aiheita* (*Subjects*). Keuruu: Otava, 1983.

Hanna-Leena Helavuori

V

EVGENI VAKHTANGOV [b. February 1, 1883, Vladikavkaz; d. May 29, 1922, Moscow]. Evgeni Vakhtangov staged less than a half-dozen major productions before his death of cancer at thirty-nine, but he remains one of the most influential and beloved figures in the Russian theatre. At once a disciple and critic of the Konstantin Stanislavsky* System, he added an ingenious layer of theatricalism to his scenic work that has never been matched. That actors could be both wholly truthful and nonrealistic was a central tenet of Vakhtangov's beliefs. And through his final productions—manifestations of the grotesque—he proved that Stanislavsky's theories had much wider applications than even the master knew.

Accepted into the Moscow Art Theatre in 1911, Vakhtangov found himself being groomed as a teacher of Stanislavsky's System of acting. He appeared in numerous plays and was selected to be a member of the experimental First Studio, Stanislavsky's acting laboratory. Guided by the Tolstoyan Leopold Sulerzhitsky, the First Studio pupils pioneered new psychophysical methods, such as exercises in relaxation and concentration, to achieve what Stanislavsky had called "the Creative State of Mind." Among them, Vakhtangov excelled.

In 1913, as a test of the System, Vakhtangov staged two intimate chamber productions: Gerhart Hauptmann's *The Festival of Peace* at the First Studio and Boris Zaitsev's *The Lanin Estate* with an amateur group. The hysterical power of his actors and overly intense—and even morbid—atmospheres that he created in his direction caused Vakhtangov to reconsider certain aspects of Stanislavsky's techniques. Set in the unfamiliar American West, *The Deluge* (by Henning

Berger, 1915) allowed Vakhtangov to next emphasize the grotesque psychology of his exotic characters and their odd, mechanical rhythms.

The Russian Revolution seemed to release Vakhtangov from old loyalties and adherence to the System's most cherished ideals. Not the aesthetic unity of a drama but the audience's perception of a play mattered most. Working in ill health almost around the clock, Vakhtangov also developed his own formulations on acting technique. How to maintain the performer's inner reality and sense of creativity within a perfectly choreographed stage picture became Vakhtangov's newest problem. For this, Vakhtangov invented the notion of justification: every movement and sound of the actor must have an inspired, personal motivation, even if that motivation is totally removed from the circumstances of the play.

At the First Studio, the Hebrew-speaking Habima, and his own theatre, Vakhtangov proved his thesis with spectacular results. Basing his production of August Strindberg's *Erik XIV* (1921) on the contrasting effects of colors, lights, gestures, and sounds, Vakhtangov demonstrated that the depth of his performers' feelings could be communicated to the spectator even in the most stylized mise-en-scène. According to Vakhtangov, the constructs of human behavior are only opposing emotions held in balance. The theatre of the grotesque, when wedded to the actor's reality, can expose that.

The amateur Habima's production of the mystical *The Dybbuk* (by S. Ansky, 1922), a play about possession in a Jewish village, further revealed Vakhtangov's skill and unsurpassed talents. Asking the mostly untrained performers to find both personal substitutions and imaginative embodiments, like animals or objects, for their fantasy characters, he quickly gave emotional and physical shape to a difficult play. With every twisted step and prolonged syllable justified, *The Dybbuk* exploded with unexpected emotional power and range. It remained in Habima's repertoire in Russia and in exile for over four decades.

Vakhtangov's final production, the comic *Turandot* (by Carlo Gozzi, 1922), convinced Stanislavsky that his rebellious student had made crucial theatrical discoveries. In fact, as *Turandot* unfolded, its audience experienced the entire spectrum of Vakhtangov's pioneering work. What Vakhtangov called "the festive spirit" manifested itself in a showy barrage of acting techniques. Conventional narration, improvisation, Moscow Art emotional realism, satirical dance, ridiculous clowning, and melodrama all mixed in a delirious cocktail of undisguised theatricality. Yet throughout, the actors maintained a curious truthfulness that the audience could not forget.

ADDITIONAL PRODUCTIONS: 1918, 1921: *Miracle of St. Anthony* (Maeterlinck); 1918: *Rosmersholm*, Opening of the Habima: *The Elder Sister* (Shoslem Asch), *The Fire* (J. L. Peretz), *The Sun! The Sun!* (Yitzhak Katznelson), *The Nuisance* (J. D. Berkowitz); 1920, 1921: *The Wedding* (Chekhov).

SELECTED BIBLIOGRAPHY: Gorchakov, Nikolai. *The Vakhtangov School of Stage Art.* Trans. G. Ivanov-Mumjiev. Moscow: Foreign Languages Publishing House, 1965; Gordon, Mel. *The Stanislavsky Technique: Russia.* New York: Applause Theatre Books, 1988; Simonov, Ruben. *Stanislavsky's Protege: Eugene Vakhtangov.* Trans. Miriam

Goldina. New York: Drama Books Specialists, 1969; Vendrovskaya, Lyubov, and Galina Kaptereva, eds. *Evgeny Vakhtangov*. Trans. Doris Bradbury. Moscow: Progress Pubishers, 1982; Worrall, Nick. *Modernism to Realism on the Soviet Stage*. Cambridge: Cambridge University Press, 1989.

Mel Gordon

LUIS VALDEZ [b. June 26, 1940, Delano, California]. Luis Valdez is a leading Chicano director and playwright who founded the Teatro Campesino (Farm Workers' Theatre) and went on to gain international recognition as a playwright, director, and filmmaker. His creative output includes plays, poems, books, essays, films, and videos, all of which deal with the Chicano and Mexican experience in the United States. Through his Teatro Campesino, Valdez inspired a national movement of Chicano theatre troupes dedicated to the exposure of sociopolitical problems within the Mexican-American communities of the United States.

Following a year with the San Francisco Mime Troupe, Valdez founded the Teatro Campesino in 1965, becoming the artistic director as well as resident playwright for this ragtag troupe of striking farm workers. Under Valdez's guidance, the troupe collectively created brief sketches, called *actos*, about the need for a farm workers' union. The *acto* became the basic style adapted by the scores of Chicano theatre groups that followed Valdez's example.

After two years of performing for farm workers and the general public, Valdez left the ranks of the union in 1967 in order to focus on the development of his theatre. He began to explore issues relevant to the Chicano beyond the fields as he simultaneously developed a core of theatre artists no longer dedicated to one cause and one style alone. The Teatro began to tour nationally and internationally, attracting attention to the hitherto ignored Chicanos.

In 1968, the Teatro was awarded an Obie, and the following year Valdez and his troupe gained international exposure at the Theatre des Nations at Nancy, France. Three years later, the troupe moved to its permanent home in San Juan Bautista, California. During his period, Valdez moved from the *acto* to the *mito*, or myth, exploring the Chicanos' roots in Mayan philosophy while the group continued to work collectively under Valdez's guidance. During the same period, he developed what he terms the *theater of the sphere* which, he claims, integrates "the physical dynamism of the human body with the emotional power of the human spirit to engender a balanced universal vision of humanity."

In 1973, Valdez wrote and directed *La carpa de los Rasguachis* (*The Tent of the Underdogs*), an epic mito which follows a Mexican character from his crossing of the border into the United States to the subsequent indignities to which he is exposed. This production brought together a Valdezian aesthetic that could be defined as raucous, lively street theatre with deep sociopolitical and spiritual roots. The style combined elements of the *acto, mito,* and *corrido* with an almost constant musical undertone. This was the apogee of Valdez's "poor theater."

In 1978, Valdez wrote and directed *Zoot Suit* in a co-production with the Center Theatre Group of Los Angeles. This play was based on the events surrounding the "Sleepy Lagoon Murder Trial" in Los Angeles in the early 1940s which exposed the court's discrimination against a group of young Chicanos accused of killing another Chicano. *Zoot Suit* was the director's first collaboration with a major non-Chicano regional theatre company which employed professional theatre artists, and the production broke all records for a Los Angeles run while a second production at New York's Winter Garden Theatre became the first Chicano play on Broadway.

Zoot Suit combined elements of the earliest Teatro Campesino street theatre aesthetic with Living Newspaper techniques, professional choreography, and Brechtian narrative. Although the play did not win critical acclaim in New York, it continued to run in Los Angeles and was subsequently adapted and directed as a film by Valdez. In 1980, Valdez's core company disbanded as a resident theatre, and the Teatro began hiring its artists on a per-production basis. In 1982, Valdez wrote and directed *Corridos*, a program of dramatized and choreographed Mexican folk ballads which had always been a part of Valdez's aesthetic. The songs tell tales of love, revenge, death, and revolution through musical narrative intertwined with dialogue and action to reveal their stories. After a record-breaking six-month run in San Francisco, the play moved to San Diego and Los Angeles.

Valdez's next major production was *I Don't Have to Show You No Stinking Badges*, which he wrote, directed, and coproduced (with the Los Angeles Theatre Center) in 1986. This play took the audience into the world of the television sitcom as it explored the lives of two "Hispanic extras" who lived a middle-class life portraying stereotypical Latinos for Hollywood. This play also ran successfully in San Diego and Florida.

Valdez's reputation as a film director was secured in 1987 with the success of his first major motion picture, *La Bamba*, about the life and death of 1950s rock star Richie Valens. Valdez continues to head the nation's leading Chicano theatre company as he also continues to develop stage, television, and film projects.

ADDITIONAL PRODUCTIONS: [Unless otherwise noted the playwright is Valdez]: 1965: *Las dos caras del patroncito*; 1968: *Los vendidos*; 1970: *Bernabe*; 1971: *Dark Root of a Scream, Soldado razo*; 1975: *El fin del mundo*; 1983: *Zoot Suit* (the film); 1987: *Corridos: Tales of Passion and Revolution* (PBS); 1991: *La Pastorela* (Spanish folk play, PBS).

SELECTED BIBLIOGRAPHY: Bagby, Beth. "El Teatro Campesino: Interviews with Luis Valdez." *Tulane Drama Review* 4 (1967): 71–80; Diamond, Betty. "The Brown Eyed Children of the Sun: The Cultural Politics of El Teatro Campesino." Diss. U of Wisconsin, 1977; Harrop, John, and Huerta, Jorge. "The Agitprop Pilgrimage of Luis Valdez and El Teatro Campesino." *Theatre Quarterly* 5 (1975): 3–39; Huerta, Jorge. *Chicano The-*

ater: Themes and Forms. Tempe, AZ: Bilingual Press, 1982, 1991; Kelley, Ken. "The Interview: Luis Valdez." *San Francisco Focus* September 1987: 51–53; Kourilsky, Francoise. "Approaching Quetzalcoatl: The Evolution of El Teatro Campesino." *Performance* 2 (1975): 37–46; Valdez, Luis. *Early Works: Actos, Bernabe and Pensamiento Serpentino.* Houston: Arte Publico Press, 1990; Valdez, Luis. *Zoot Suit and Other Plays.* Houston: Arte Publico Press, 1992.

Jorge Huerta

JOSE LUIS VALENZUELA [b. May 23, 1953, Los Mochis, Sinaloa, Mexico]. Jose Luis Valenzuela is a director whose work is deeply rooted in and inspired by his Mexicano-Chicano heritage. He studied at Universidad Technologica in Mexico City and came to the United States during the height of the Chicano theatre movement to become an actor. In 1973, he joined El Teatro de la Gente of San Jose, California, and acted in the company until 1977. Between 1978 and 1984 he was a member of El Teatro de la Esperanza, a company notorious for collective creations of full-length plays dealing with social issues. Valenzuela joined the company as an actor, but eventually became the voice that gave productions their final form. Serving as an in-house director, he assisted in the development of several collective works including *La Victima*, *The Octopus*, *And Death Comes Singing*, and *Loteria de Pasiones*.

Valenzuela left the company in 1984 to pursue a career as a free-lance director. In 1985, he directed a production of *Hijos* (collectively created by El Teatro de la Esperanza while he was a member) at Teatro Jorge Negrete in Los Angeles. The production was successful, receiving Drama-Logue Awards for Best Direction, Best Ensemble, and Best Actor. Later that year, Valenzuela was hired by Bill Bushnell, who had opened the Los Angeles Theatre Center (LATC), to plan and develop a Latino theatre laboratory.

While at LATC, Valenzuela assisted Norwegian director Stein Winge,* who directed a production of *Barabbas* in 1986. Later that year, Valenzuela served as assistant director on Winge's productions of Michel de Ghelderode's *Pantagleize* at Det Norske Teatret in Oslo, Norway, and the following year Wagner's *Die Walküre* in Geneva. Valenzuela returned to Oslo in late 1989 to direct a production of Manuel Puig's *Kiss of the Spider Woman* that opened at Det Norske Teatret in early 1990.

The Latino Theatre Lab under the direction of Valenzuela has been successful in developing original work as well as producing works of prominent Latino writers. At least two full-length plays produced by LATC were collectively developed in the Latino Theatre lab under Valenzuela's direction, the most recent being the critically acclaimed *August 29* (1990). Other plays directed by him at LATC include M. Sanchez-Scott's *Roosters* (1988) and Jose Rivera's *The Promise* (1988), two visually rich productions in the vein of magical realism.

ADDITIONAL PRODUCTIONS: 1989: *A Burning Beach* (Eduardo Machado); 1990: *The Mission* (Culture Clash), *August 29* (Violetta Calles).

Tony Curiel

NINA VANCE [b. October 22, 1914, Yoakum, Texas; d. February 18, 1980, Houston, Texas]. Regarded as a matriarch of American regional theatre, Nina Vance was the founder and artistic director of Houston's Alley Theatre from 1947 until her death. She produced all 245 Alley Theatre productions during that period and directed 102 of them. Although she occasionally directed elsewhere, notably at Washington's Arena Stage and Philadelphia's Playhouse in the Park, Vance's reputation as a passionate director of both the classics and new works was established at the Alley.

Born Nina Eloise Whittington, she received a B.A. in speech arts from Texas Christian University in 1935. She did graduate work in theatre at the University of Southern California (1936), Columbia University (1937), and the American Academy of Dramatic Art in New York before returning to Houston to teach high school and work as assistant to Margo Jones* at the Houston Community Players.

After Jones left for Dallas, Vance began teaching and directing for Houston's Jewish Community Center and mounting productions in a dance studio in an alley off Main Street. At her instigation, the group of amateurs soon evolved into the Alley Theatre. With $2.14 in her pocket, Vance sent 214 postcards to theatre enthusiasts announcing a new theatre for Houston. The hundred people who attended formed the core of the new theatre, which premiered November 18, 1947, with Vance's production of Harry Brown's *A Sound of Hunting*.

Vance produced and directed six productions that first season which included Lillian Hellman's *Another Part of the Forest* and Clifford Odets's *Clash by Night*. During the sixth production, Norman Krasna's farce, *John Loves Mary*, the fire marshal declared the venue unsafe, but allowed the show to complete its run. The Alley reopened in a converted fan factory February 8, 1949 with Hellman's *The Children's Hour*.

Like the dance studio, the factory had arena seating which served Vance's unconventional stagings, many of which were forerunners of environmental theatre. An example was her production of *Desire under the Elms* (1949), which consisted of rock piles, multilevel platforms, and a small realistic sitting room, all delineated by light. The square dance scene was played in and through the audience. The production was considered typical of her best work, tightly focused and emotionally charged.

The second Alley Theatre housed 149 productions from 1949 to 1968 and realized significant strides for the theatre and for Vance. The Alley became an Equity theatre in 1954 with her production of *Death of a Salesman* starring Albert Dekker, the first of many noted actors hired as guest artists. In 1959, Vance received the first of three Ford Foundation grants which would allow the theatre to hire professional resident companies and expand its operations. A $2.1 million grant awarded in 1962, the largest ever made to a theatre at that time, supported construction and development over the following ten years. As a result, in 1968 the Alley moved to its permanent home, a dual theatre complex called the Nina Vance Alley Theatre.

ADDITIONAL PRODUCTIONS: 1955: *All My Sons* with Joseph Calleia; 1964: *The Three Sisters*; 1965: *The Effect of Gamma Rays on Man-in-the-Moon Marigolds* (world premiere); 1977: *Mary Stuart*.

SELECTED BIBLIOGRAPHY: Beeson, William. *Thresholds: The Story of Nina Vance's Alley Theatre*. Houston: Alley Theatre Monograph, 1969; Chinoy, Helen Krich, and Linda Walsh Jenkins, eds. *Women in American Theatre*. New York: Theatre Communications Group, 1987; Robinson, Alice M., Vera M. Roberts, and Milly S. Barranger, eds. *Notable Women in the American Theatre*. Westport, CT: Greenwood Press, 1989.

Martha Schmoyer LoMonaco

STUART (JOHN WALKER) VAUGHAN [b. August 23, 1925, Terre Haute, Indiana]. Known primarily for his association with the New York Shakespeare Festival, Stuart Vaughan represents the merging of academic theatre experience with professional theatre practice. With an M.A. in theatre from Indiana University, he taught speech and drama at Indiana State Teacher's College in 1947–48. After he had acted and directed in various stock companies and community theatres, he achieved his first critical directing success in New York with a series of staged readings of Sean O'Casey's autobiographical *Pictures in the Hallway* (1956). In 1956, Vaughan became artistic director of the New York Shakespeare Festival and then in 1958 of the faltering Phoenix Theatre in New York, where he planned to launch a repertory company. His *Henry IV, Pt. I* received such popular success that it revived the Phoenix Theatre's finances. He received an Obie Award for Best Director of 1957–58.

Pursuing his commitment to a classical repertory company, he joined the Seattle Repertory Theatre as director in 1963, but his refusal to relinquish artistic control to its Board of Directors caused him to leave in 1965. Shortly thereafter, he became director of the Repertory Theatre of New Orleans. In 1969, he resigned his position there and rejoined the New York Shakespeare Festival, for which he edited and directed *The Wars of the Roses* (1970), an eleven-hour marathon, combining the two parts of *Henry IV* and *Richard III*. Vaughan's approach to the classics, combining broad humor and fast-paced action and dialogue, has sometimes been faulted by critics accustomed to more traditional staging. Vaughan's offbeat casting also has received both praise and blame; he has used actors better known for contemporary American film acting than for classical roles. American audiences, however, have appreciated his revitalization of the classics.

ADDITIONAL PRODUCTIONS: 1956: *The Taming of the Shrew*; 1960: *Henry IV, Pt. I*; 1963: *The Lady's Not for Burning*; 1988: *Julius Caesar, Ghosts*; 1990: *Twelfth Night*.

SELECTED BIBLIOGRAPHY: Funke, Lewis. "Theatre: Self Portrait." *New York Times* 17 September 1956: 23, Herbert, Ian, ed. *Who's Who in the Theatre*. Vol. 1. New York: Gale Research Co., 1981: 679; Keating, John. " 'New' Man of the Arts." *New York Times* 21 May 1961: sec. 2: 3; Levey, Stanley. "Director on the Move." *New York Times* 20 March 1960: sec. 2: 1; Zeigler, Joseph Wesley. *Regional Theatre: The Revolutionary Stage*. New York: Da Capo Press, 1977.

Ann Demling

JEAN VILAR [b. March 25, 1912, Sète, France; d. May 28, 1971, Sète, France].
Jean Vilar, one of France's great actors, directors, and producers, founder of
the world-famous Avignon Festival, and director of the Théâtre National Populaire (TNP) from 1951 to 1963, is especially remembered for his success in
advancing the cause of people's theatre in postwar France.

The son of small-town shopkeepers in Sète, Vilar had not prepared for a career
in the theatre. When he moved to Paris in 1932, it was to study literature, not
to become an actor, but a chance exposure to Charles Dullin* rehearsing *Richard
III* led him to study at the Atelier school and eventually to become an actor and
director in his own right. He perfected his training as a member of the Roulotte
traveling theatre company which played the provinces during the war (1940–
43).

Vilar was first noticed critically for his performances in August Strindberg's
The Storm in 1943 and *The Dance of Death* in 1945. Critics praised his subtle
use of silences to underscore the unspoken suggestions of the plays. In 1945,
Vilar's production of T. S. Eliot's *Murder in the Cathedral* at the Vieux Colombier (in which he played Becket) was his first major success as director and
actor.

Invited by art critic Christian Zervos to bring his award-winning production
to Avignon in September 1947 as part of a rare exhibition of modern art, Vilar
characteristically proposed an entirely different program: Shakespeare's *Richard
II*, never before presented in France; *Tobie and Sara*, a little-known work by
Paul Claudel; and a new play by an unknown young author, *La Terrasse de
Midi* by Maurice Clavel. Even though the program was too expensive, the
municipality of Avignon contributed monies and in-kind services so that Vilar's
bold program could be presented.

Vilar staged *Richard II* (1947) in the vast open-air Honor Court of the Pope's
Palace, a "theatre" that would eventually draw over 3,000 spectators a night.
It was in Avignon (and thanks to the open-air) that Vilar came to understand
the validity of the lessons of the great, unadorned stages of the past. His stage
thereafter would be an immense raised platform reaching far out into the audience,
bare but for a few props and small decorative elements. He wanted no wings,
curtains, footlights, or unnecessary sets to separate or distract audiences from
the play. On such a bare stage, defined only by masts flying colorful banners,
the spectacle would be born of the imaginative use of light, music, color, and
choreography.

Vilar was helped in the realization of his concept by a team of outstanding
artists and technicians: Léon Gischia, whose bright, bold costumes delineated
and magnified the players against a dark background; Maurice Jarre, whose
music perfectly set the climate; and lighting designer Pierre Saveron, who mag-
ically created evocative sets out of light. Together with a first-rate young acting
company—Jeanne Moreau, Michel Bouquet, Jean-Paul Moulinot, and Jean Né-
groni among them—they created the style that became the trademark of Avignon
and TNP performances.

In 1948, Vilar changed festival dates to July and continued his courageous programming, adding Georg Büchner's *Danton's Death* in a translation by Arthur Adamov, and in 1949, Pierre Corneille's *Le Cid*, rarely played at the time. Thus the Avignon Festival was born. Success came relatively quickly as young people flocked to the festival and critics praised the importance of the event. When Gérard Philipe, the popular film and stage actor, joined the company in 1951, playing Rodrigue in *Le Cid* and the title role in Heinrich von Kleist's *Prince of Homburg*, the Festival definitely became an important summer rendezvous, drawing "pilgrims," as they were frequently called, from far and wide to celebrate great art.

The success of Avignon led to Vilar's appointment in 1951 as director of the government-subsidized Théâtre National Populaire, established in 1920 and housed in the cavernous Palais Chaillot at the Trocadéro in Paris. His mission, as he defined it, was to make the TNP a public service as readily available as gas, electricity, and water. Everyone, especially the economically disadvantaged and the culturally deprived, would have easy access to first-rate plays and flawless performances at low prices. This was Vilar's ideal.

The endeavor was fraught with difficulties. How, for example, would he bring the working classes to Chaillot in the chic part of Paris even if ticket prices were the lowest in town? How would he recruit and develop a new, broader-based audience of students, shopkeepers, civil servants, workers, teachers, and magistrates—people of all classes and all professions?

Vilar and his team tackled the job with great imagination. They took the TNP to the working-class suburbs of Paris where they created mini-festival weekends of theatre including two TNP productions, music and an evening of dancing. They made theatregoing at Chaillot a relaxed, informal affair. Performances conveniently began earlier than usual; tipping and coatroom charges were eliminated: inexpensive food and drink were made available. But more importantly, they enlisted the trade unions in setting up *Associations populaires* to educate audiences about the TNP repertory and organize block bookings, and they made student matinees a priority.

Vilar's repertory choices reflected the TNP's dual mission—to entertain, but also to educate—and included serious plays debating man's moral and political responsibilities (*Tiger at the Gates*, *Antigone*, *A Man for all Seasons*); enlightening comedies of the human condition (*L'Avare*, *Ubu*, *Les Précieuses Ridicules*); plays about human relationships, good and bad (Marivaux's *Triumph of Love*, or Musset's *Les Caprices de Marianne*, and of course *Le Cid*). Vilar directed thirty-five of the fifty-seven plays he produced during his twelve-year tenure at Chaillot and starred in twenty.

Through such a repertory, post-performance discussions, monthly letters to the *Associations populaires,* and visits to schools and trade union groups, Vilar established an ongoing dialogue with workers and students who came to understand that the TNP was their theatre.

In 1963, Vilar resigned from the TNP as a protest against the inadequacy of his contract with the government, a contract the government refused to renegotiate. He returned to Avignon—a return to the source, as he put it—where he programmed and directed the Festival until his death.

ADDITIONAL PRODUCTIONS: 1951: *Mother Courage*; 1952: *L'Avare*; 1953: *Don Juan* (Molière); 1955: *Le Triomphe de l'Amour* (Marivaux); 1956: *The Marriage of Figaro* (Beaumarchais), *La Ville* (Claudel); 1957: *Henry IV* (Pirandello); 1960: *Antigone* (Sophocles), *The Resistible Rise of Arturo Ui*; 1961: *Red Roses for Me* (O'Casey), *La Paix* (Aristophanes, adapted by Vilar); 1962: *Tiger at the Gates*, *A Man for All Seasons* (Bolt); 1964: *The Oppenheimer Dossier* (adapted by Vilar).

SELECTED BIBLIOGRAPHY: Bardot, Jean-Claude. *Jean Vilar*. Paris: Armand Colin, 1991; *Jean Vilar; diapolivre*. (text by Melly Puaux and 84 slides); Leclerc, Guy. *Le T.N.P. de Jean Vilar*. Paris: Union générale d'éditions, 1971; Roy, Claude. *Jean Vilar*. 1968. Calmann-Levy, 1987; Serrière, Marie-Thérèse. *Le T.N.P. et nous*. Paris: José Corti, 1959; Valogne, Catherine. *Jean Vilar*. Presses universitaires de France, 1954; Vilar, Jean. *De la tradition théâtrale*. Paris: L'Arche, 1955, Gallimard, 1963; Vilar, Jean. *Le théâtre service public et autres textes*. Paris: Gallimard, 1975, 1986; Vilar, Jean. *Mémento*. Paris: Gallimard, 1981; Wehle, Philippa. "Model for an Open Stage: A Study of Jean Vilar's Theater for the People." Diss. Columbia U, 1974; Wehle, Philippa. *Le théâtre populaire selon Jean Vilar*. 1981. Actes Sud, revised 1991.

Philippa Wehle

JEAN-PIERRE VINCENT [b. August 26, 1942, Juvisy-sur-Orge, France]. Part of an astonishingly promising high-school drama group, which included Patrice Chéreau,* Jean-Pierre Vincent has been in the forefront of theatrical practice in France for a quarter of a century. He first acted under Chéreau's direction in the mid-sixties; then began a collaboration with Brechtian dramaturg Jean Jourdheuil which led to several reinterpretations of Brecht's earliest plays (1968–74). Their 1972 production of *In the Jungle of Cities*, for example, emphasized the play's stylistic discontinuities while underlining the Marxist critique of consumerism already embedded in the play's anarchic excesses. In 1973, Vincent and Jourdheuil took on Vishnevsky's *An Optimistic Tragedy*, and through lengthy study sessions with the actors, a hallmark of Vincent's approach, evolved a critique of the Manichean interpretation of the Bolshevik revolution, superimposing layers of meaning on the play's final image of collective death.

From these formative years, Vincent developed a style and a theatrical goal from which he has never wavered. A master at choreography in concentrated spaces, Vincent insists that theatre, like a rugby match, be based on lines of force, with all players concentrating on a moving center. He also insists that theatrical expression include a critical commentary on contemporary history, a clue as to how history is built.

These two notions resulted in a series of exemplary collective creations which Vincent "supervised"—a term he deems well suited to the dramaturgical and scenographic teamwork characteristic of his productions during his tenure as head (1975–83) of the Théâtre National de Strasbourg (TNS). Under Vincent, the TNS, with the four research components he nurtured (East European theatrical expression, feminist reportage, quotidian theatre, theatre in nontheatrical spaces), provided the critical moment of 1970s French theatre.

The TNS's collective adaptation of Emile Zola's novel *Germinal* (1975) not only evoked the stark material conditions of French miners' lives through carefully selected images, but also, by adopting the narrative voice of the novel, ironically critiqued Zola's patronizing attitude toward the working class. Their collective work on *Le Palais de Justice* in 1981 was built on direct observation of the Strasbourg court in action. Vincent called this experience "critical hyperrealism," theatricalizing the reality of the justice system in such a way that it became horrifyingly unacceptable. In *Vichy-Fictions* (1980), a two-part piece by Bernard Chartreux and Michel Deutsch, the company successfully exploded the myth of the omnipresence of the French Resistance by showing the self-delusions of Vichy collaborators.

For *Vichy*, as for all his later outstanding productions (*The Marriage of Figaro*, 1987; *Oedipus and the Birds*, 1989; *That Scoundrel Scapin*, 1990; and *Princesses*, 1991), Vincent called on the talents of painter Jean-Paul Chambas, whose stage designs combine acute realism in selected details with vast frontal spaces. Vincent breaks the potential stasis of Chambas's frontal designs by the concentrated energy he demands of his actors.

His desire to experiment with new forms and his demand that actors be creative team members marred Vincent's three-year appointment (1983–86) to the directorship of La Comédie Française. At the Théâtre National des Amandiers, which he has headed since 1990, he will again be able to work on taking apart theatre texts until they can be read from fresh angles.

ADDITIONAL PRODUCTIONS: 1968: *The Wedding* (Brecht); 1971: *Pots of Money* (Labiche), *Capitaine Schelle. Capitaine Eçço* (Rezvani); 1973: *Woyzeck*; 1977: *The Misanthrope*; 1983: *Félicité* (Jean Audureau), *Dernières Nouvelles de la Peste* (Chartreux); 1984: *The Suicide* (Erdmann); 1992: *Fantasio, The Caprices of Marianne* (Musset).

SELECTED BIBLIOGRAPHY: Bradby, David. *Modern French Drama 1940–1990*. Cambridge: Cambridge University Press, 1991; Büchner, Georg. *Woyzeck*. Paris: Stock, 1971; Dort, Bernard. "L'Age de la représentation." *Le Théâtre en France II*. Ed. Jacqueline de Jomaron. Paris: Armand Colin, 1989: 452–534; Dort, Bernard. *Théâtre en jeu 1970–1978*. Paris: du Seuil, 1979; Gunthert, André. *Le Voyage du T.N.S. 1975–1983*. Paris: Solin, 1983; Rezvani, Serge. *Capitaine Schelle. Capitaine Eçço*. Paris: Stock, 1971; Temkine, Raymonde. *Mettre en scène au présent II*. Paris: La Cité/L'Age d'homme, 1979; Temkine, Raymonde. Le Théâtre au présent. Paris: Bouffoneries/Contrastes, 1987.

Judith G. Miller

LUCHINO VISCONTI [b. November 2, 1906, Milan, Italy; d. March 17, 1976, Rome, Italy]. Luchino Visconti was one of Italy's most famous directors of opera, theatre, and film. His family, one of the oldest noble families in Italy, was long connected with opera and theatre production, particularly at La Scala. He began working in the theatre, and only turned to opera much later in his successful career as a director, a career which began in Italy and earned Visconti international recognition.

Visconti's name is often associated with that of Maria Callas because he directed many of her most famous performances, particularly at La Scala. This famous collaboration began with Spontini's *La Vestale* at La Scala in 1954, a production that made Callas an international star, and continued through such La Scala productions as *La Sonnambula* (1955), *La Traviata* (1955), and *Anna Bolena* (1957), which Visconti also staged expressly for Callas. In 1958, he staged Verdi's *Don Carlo* at London's Covent Garden, his first opera production outside Italy.

Visconti is particularly famous for reintroducing the bel canto operas of the early nineteenth century into the international operatic repertory. After World War II, the bel canto composers Rossini, Donizetti, and Bellini were virtually unproduced, but both Callas and Visconti helped to revive these composers' work. Subsequent generations of singers and directors (including Franco Zeffirelli,* Visconti's most famous pupil) have followed Visconti's lead.

Visconti's directorial style emphasized a neo-Romanticism that combined a realistic vision for theatrical and operatic production along with a visual splendor which excited audiences because of its graphic intensity and dramatic appropriateness. While most famous for opera production, Visconti also directed films and theatre and wrote librettos. He composed the libretto for Mannino's opera *Il Diavolo in Giardino* and Mannino's ballet *Mario e Il Mago* (based on a Thomas Mann short story), and he also wrote the libretto for Hans Werner Henze's ballet *Maratona di Danza*.

ADDITIONAL PRODUCTIONS: 1945: *Antigone* (Anouilh); 1946: *Crime and Punishment*, *The Glass Menagerie*; 1948: *As You Like It*; 1949: *A Streetcar Named Desire*; 1951: *Death of a Salesman*; 1952: *The Three Sisters*; 1955: *Uncle Vanya*; 1966: *Falstaff* (Vienna). **Films:** 1942: *Ossessione*; 1946: *La Terra Trema*; 1960: *Rocco and His Brothers*; 1963: *The Leopard*; 1969: *The Damned*; 1971: *Death in Venice*.
SELECTED BIBLIOGRAPHY: Baldelli, Pio. *Luchino Visconti*. Milan: G. Mazzotta, 1982; DiGaetani, John Louis. "Visconti." *An Invitation to the Opera*. New York: Doubleday, 1991; Nowell-Smith, Geoffrey. *Luchino Visconti*. New York: Doubleday, 1968; Servadio, Gaia. *Luchino Visconti: A Biography*. London: Weidenfeld and Nicolson, 1982; Stirling, Monica. *A Screen of Time: A Study of Luchino Visconti*. New York: Harcourt Brace Jovanovich, 1979; Tonetti, Claretta. *Luchino Visconti*. Boston: Twayne, 1983; Visconti, Luchino. *Il Mio Teatro*. Bologna: Cappelli, 1979; Weaver, William. "Luchino Visconti." *The New Grove Dictionary of Music and Musicians*. Ed Stanley Sadie. London: Macmillan, 1980.

John Louis DiGaetani

ANTOINE VITEZ [b. December 20, 1930, Paris, France; d. April 30, 1990, Paris, France]. Antoine Vitez began his directing career at regional theatres in Marseilles and Caen in the 1960s, but it was not until he founded his own theatre and school in 1972 in the Parisian suburb of Ivry that he became a significant presence in French theatre. Vitez remained at the head of the Théâtre des Quartiers d'Ivry until 1981, when he was appointed artistic director of the Théâtre National de Chaillot in Paris. (He had earlier served as Jack Lang's co-director at the Théâtre National de Chaillot in 1972–74.) In June 1988, he was appointed general administrator of the Comédie Française, a position he occupied until his sudden death in 1990.

Vitez was thirty-five years old when he directed his own translation of Sophocles' *Electra* in 1965 at the newly established Maison de la Culture at Caen in Normandy. It was his first mise-en-scène although he had committed himself to a life in the theatre at the age of nineteen when he began his training at Théâtre du Vieux Colombier, which at that time offered training that had scarcely changed since the time of Jacques Copeau,* creator of both the theatre and the school. (He was refused admission to the Conservatoire National d'Art Dramatique. Ironically, he became one of its most celebrated teachers of acting during the 1970s.) According to Vitez, his most influential teacher was Tania Balachova, who exposed him to Konstantin Stanislavsky.* Although in later years Vitez embraced the aesthetic of Vsevolod Meyerhold,* he never entirely rejected the lessons of Stanislavsky (particularly his ideas about physical actions).

Vitez experienced great difficulties finding work as an actor in the early years of his career. He studied Russian and began to work as a translator, an activity that later enormously influenced his ideas about directing. His early translations include Anton Chekhov's *Ivanov* (1958) and Mikhail Sholokov's *Le Don paisible* [*And Quiet Flows the Don*] (1959–64). Other translations from Russian include works by Mikhail Bulgakov, Maxim Gorky, and Vladimir Mayakovsky. He published his translation of *Electra* in 1971, a version that included interpolated passages from the modern Greek poet Yannis Ritsos, also translated by Vitez. Vitez staged his translation in 1971 and again in 1986 at Chaillot. In addition, Vitez translated the poetry of Bertolt Brecht* into French. During the 1950s and 1960s, Vitez also contributed to *Bref*, the journal published by the Théâtre National Populaire, directed by Jean Vilar*; *Cité-Panorama*, the journal published by the Théâtre National Poulaire at Villeurbanne under the direction of Roger Planchon*; and *Théâtre Populaire*, which energetically championed Brecht and was perhaps the most influential periodical of the period (for a time, Vitez was one of the editors). In addition, he traveled to Russia to research the history of the Soviet Union on behalf of the poet Louis Aragon, whose patronage finally solved Vitez's chronic unemployment problem. Vitez himself published a history of Soviet theatre in 1966.

When he began to direct in the 1960s, Vitez was already a person of significant literary and scholarly accomplishments, intimately familiar with modern Russian theatre as well as with the work of Brecht. His work as a director bore witness to these early influences. Combining Stanislavsky's physical actions with Meyerhold's biomechanics, Vitez developed a manner of working that privileged the actor's body as the site of theatricality. In a Vitez mise-en-scène, the actors' bodies offered narratives and gave expression to ideas that appeared to be unsupported by the text, which Vitez frequently directed to actors to deliver in an unorthodox manner. In his productions of Racine, for example, he asked them to pronounce the mute vowels of poetic dialogue composed in twelve-syllable alexandrines, thus calling attention to the poetic conventions used by the dramatist. Following Meyerhold, Vitez emphasized the "conventionality" of a particular mise-en-scène, asking his audience to recognize that they were dealing with a simulacrum, not with an actual event.

ADDITIONAL PRODUCTIONS: 1966: *The Bathhouse* (Vladimir Mayakovsky); 1968: *The Dragon* (Yevgeny Schwarz); 1969: *The Parade* (Loula Anagnostaki); 1970: *Sea Gull* (Vitez translation); 1972: *Faust*; 1973: *Mother Courage, Vendredi, ou la Vie Sauvage* (*Friday, or the Savage Life*, adaptation by Vitez from the novel by Michel Tournier); 1974: *Le Pique-nique de Claretta* (*Claretta's Picnic*, René Kalisky); 1975: *Phèdre, Catherine* (based on Aragon's *Les Cloches de Bâle*), *Partage de Midi* (Paul Claudel); 1977: *Iphigénie-Hôtel* (Michel Vinaver); 1978: *The School for Wives, Tartuffe, Don Juan, The Misanthrope* (performed as a tetralogy); 1979: *Dave au bord de la mer* (*Dave at the Seaside*, Kalisky); 1980: *Bérénice*; 1981–82: *Faust, Britannicus, Tombeau pour 500,000 soldats* (*A Tomb for 500,000 Soldiers*, Pierre Guyotat, performed in repertory, scenography by Yannis Kokkos); 1982: *Hippolyte* (Robert Garnier); 1982–83: *Hamlet*; 1983–84: *The Sea Gull*; 1984–85: *Hernani* (Victor Hugo); 1985–86: *Lucrèce Borgia* (Hugo); 1987–88: *The Misanthrope, Le Soulier de satin* (Claudel); 1989: *The Marriage of Figaro*; 1990: *Galileo*.

SELECTED BIBLIOGRAPHY: *L'Art du théâtre* 10 (1989) [A retrospective on Vitez's work at Chaillot]; Benhamou, Anne. *Antoine Vitez: Toutes les mises en scène*. Paris: Godefroy, 1981; Dizier, Anna. *Antoine Vitez: Faust, Britannicus, Tombeau pour 500,000 soldats*. Paris: Solin, 1982; Vitez, Antoine, and Emile Copferman. *De Chaillot à Chaillot*. Paris: Hachette, 1981.

James Carmody

RAFFAELE VIVIANI [b. January 10, 1888, Castellammare di Stabia, Italy; d. March 22, 1950, Naples, Italy]. Raffaele Viviani, Italian actor-manager, playwright, poet, and composer, began his theatrical career as an actor-singer doing multiple-character sketches (macchiette) in variety theatres, or caffe-concerti. By 1908, his "Street Urchin" sketch had made him famous throughout Italy, placing him on a par with Nicola Maldacea and Ettore Petrolini. When variety theatres were temporarily closed in 1917, he formed a company in Naples, of which his sister Luisella Viviani was an integral part for many years. There, he directed and acted in plays for which he often wrote both dialogue and music.

In his depiction of the Neapolitan lower classes and his fidelity to the Neapolitan dialect as an important stage language, Viviani was following the lead of Italy's greatest Pulcinella, Antonio Petito (1822–76), and Neapolitan playwrights such as Pasquale Altavilla, Eduardo Scarpetta, Salvatore Di Giacomo, and Ferdinando Russo. What was unique in Viviani's vision was the nonromantic, nonsentimental depiction of the lives of the Neapolitan poor—a bitter, yet comic, vision that would later catch the attention of Maxim Gorky and Vladimir Nemirovich-Danchenko.* Although his stage world included aristocrats, the upper-bourgeoisie, shopkeepers, and policemen, Viviani's focus was principally upon the needy proletariat, the marginals: vagabonds, urchins, traveling street merchants, prostitutes, gypsies, pimps, racketeers, migrant workers. The epic aspect of his plays and their middle European overtones led to comparisons with Bertolt Brecht.*

Viviani's company became well-known throughout Italy, and in 1929, he toured South America. He also adapted several Luigi Pirandello* plays into Neapolitan. At the height of their power, the Fascists obstructed Viviani's productions because his theatre was not *in lingua* and because they considered his dramatic vision demeaning to Italians. His work has often been performed abroad. Giuseppe Patroni-Griffi* presented several Viviani works at the Aldwych Theatre, London, for the 1968 International Festival.

In addition to directing, Viviani wrote over sixty-five plays. Between 1917 and 1919 alone, he wrote seventeen plays, mostly one-act musical pieces drawn from his *macchiette*. Often considered his liveliest work, they were usually named after their Neapolitan settings (i.e., *Via Toledo di notte*), which were more important than the dramatic event. The protagonists were the public places themselves and the collectives that inhabited them. The people and situations changed quickly in an almost cinematographic rhythm. These early plays, replete with *lazzi*, jokes, songs, comic duets, and choral actions, often had no dramatic resolution.

Viviani's plays of the 1920s and 1930s were longer, more complex, with stronger dramatic threads as he shifted focus to the individual, necessitating a more psychological approach. He wrote two tragedies during this period: *I pescatori* (1925) and *Gli zingari* (1926). In the 1930s, he turned toward more obvious social commentary.

ADDITIONAL PRODUCTIONS: 1917: *Lo vico*; 1918: *Scugnizzo* or *Via Partenope*, *Scalo martittimo*, *Via Toledo di notte*, *Porta Capuana*, *Santa Lucia Nova*; 1919: *Caffe di notte e giorno*, *Lo Sposalizio*, *Eden teatro*, *Piazza Municipio*, *Festa di Piedigrotta*; 1921: *Circo equestre Sgueglia*; 1922: *Fatto di cronaca*; 1923: *Don Giacinto*; 1924: *La figliata*; 1927: *La musica dei ciechi*; 1931: *Mastro di forgia*; 1932: *L'ultimo scugnizzo*, *Guappo di cartone*; 1936: *La tavola dei poveri*; 1937: *Padroni di barche*.

SELECTED BIBLIOGRAPHY: Angellini, F. *Il teatro del novecento da Pirandello a Fo*. Roma-Bari: Laterza, 1976; De Simone, R. *Appunti di regia per "Festa di Piedigrotto" di Raffaele Viviani*. Napoli, 1979; Rao, Angela Maria. *Raffaele Viviani: O della miseria coatta*. Poggibonsi: Antonio Lalli Editore, 1981; Ricci, Paolo. *Ritorno a Viviani*. Roma: Editori Riuniti, 1979; Rosa, A. Asor. *Scrittori e popolo*. Roma: Samona e Savelli, 1965; Viviani, Raffaele. *Dalla vita alle scene*. Napoli: Guida, 1977; Viviani, Raffaele. *Poesie*. Firenze: Vallecchi, 1956; Viviani, Raffaele. *Teatro*. Vols. 1–5. Napoli: Guida, 1987.

Jane House

W

ANDRZEJ WAJDA [b. March 6, 1926, Suwalki, Poland]. Initially, Andrzej Wajda studied painting, but he eventually abandoned it in favor of a career in film. He made his debut as a film director in 1955 and directed such well-known films as *Kanał* (1956) and *Popiół i diament* (1958), which gained him recognition as one of the most important filmmakers in Europe, a position he occupies to this day. He is perhaps best known as the director of such films as *Ziemia obiecana* (1974), *Człowiek z marmuru* (1976), *Człowiek z zelaza* (1981), and *Korczak* (1990), which gained international success. At the same time, since 1959 he has worked as a theatre director, gaining international acclaim mainly for producing plays based on Dostoyevsky's novels (*Biesy*, 1971; *Nastazja Filipowna*, based on *Idiota*, 1977; and *Zbrodnia i kara*, 1984), as well as the visionary staging of Polish dramas *Noc Listopadowa* (*November Night*, 1974) by St. Wyspiański, *Sprawa Dantona* by St. Przybyszewska (1975), and numerous productions of *Hamlet* (the last one staged in 1989).

As both a film and theatre director Wajda has covered a broad spectrum of themes and authors ranging from classical dramas like Sophocles' *Antigone* (1984) to contemporary Polish authors (e.g., *Emigranci* by S. Mrożek, 1976). Individual productions differ considerably as to aesthetics and the range of theatrical forms Wajda employs, earning him a reputation of possessing an eclectic mind; however, one can definitely notice a mark of individual style which is clearly visible, first of all, in the role Wajda gives to the visual elements of his productions. He is also identified by the high emotional pitch of his productions as well as his personal interpretation of the most important contemporary events in Poland and the world. As a result of the political considerations in Wajda's productions (e.g., *Wieczernik* by E. Bryll, 1985), both his theatre work and his films have been instrumental in the struggle of the Polish nation to free itself from communism, a freedom gained only in 1990. Wajda's participation in the spiritual and political life of the nation, as well as his usage of particular theatre forms which appealed to the emotions of the spectators, is attributed to the tradition of romanticism, which Wajda more than anyone else represents. In Poland, the romantic tradition manifests itself through the strong patriotic themes in culture and the prevalence of poetic and epic forms, both of which are visible in Wajda's theatre.

Wajda's film and theatre debuts both fall within the period when Polish theatre was freeing itself from the rigid norms of socialist realism. At that time, the impetuosity of Wajda's early productions (e.g., *Kapelusz pełen deszczu* by M. V. Gazzo, 1959) seemed to be a reaction to the rigors of this poetics. A period of experimentation, during which Wajda searched for his own directorial style was followed by a series of "grand" productions (*Biesy*, *Noc Listopadowa*, *Sprawna Dantona*) that expressed Wajda's unique version of "total theatre" and displayed the main features of his individuality—lavishness of productions; use of a wealth of theatre forms (music, acoustic effects, stage sets); and an ability to extract outstanding performances from his actors.

Wajda works mostly in Teatr Stary in Kraków, but many of his productions have been staged at other Polish theatres as well as in the United States, Germany, Italy, and Japan. His most outstanding theatre work has been the trilogy of plays based on Dostoyevsky's *Biesy* (*The Devils*), *Nastazja Filipowna*, and *Zbrodnia i kara*. In each of the three, he offered an original and deep interpretation of the Russian writer and presented Dostoyevsky's philosophical and psychological timelessness, while at the same time capturing the spiritual atmosphere of the literary piece (although with time he moved away further from the literal faithfulness to the original work). The entire action of *Biesy* was performed to haunting music, and the stage set consisted mainly of mud and sets which were changed by masked "helpers" modeled after the Japanese theatre. In *Nastazja Filipowna*, based on *Idiota*, Wajda selected only two characters and limited his play to the last part of Dostoyevsky's work which, due partially to the actors' improvisation, became something of a psychodrama. Wajda also limited the number of characters in *Zbrodnia i kara* and selected one theme (ideological crime) to represent the contemporary world. Recently, Wajda has continued to limit the stage space, forcing the audience into the role of "peepers," and actors to the highest degree of truth of expression. He used a similar approach in his latest version of *Hamlet* which, in a sense, created a unique summary of Wajda's theatre experiences.

ADDITIONAL PRODUCTIONS: 1959: *Kapelusz pełen deszczu* (M. V. Gazzo); 1960: *Hamlet*; 1970: *Play Strindberg* (F. Dürrenmatt); 1976: *Gdy rozum śpi* (A. Buero Vallejo), *Emigranci* (S. Mrożek); 1981: *Hamlet*; 1985: *Wieczernik* (E. Bryll); 1989: *Dybbuk* (S. Ansky); 1991: *Wesele* (St. Wyspiański).

SELECTED BIBLIOGRAPHY: Karpiński, Maciej. *Dostojewski—Teatr Sumienia*. Warszawa: Pax Publishers, 1989; Karpiński, Maciej. *Teatr Andrzeja Wajdy*. Warszawa:

Wydawnictwa Artystyczne i Filmowe (WAiF), 1991; Karpiński, Maciej. *The Theater of Andrzej Wajda*. Cambridge: Cambridge University Press, 1989.

Maciej Karpiński

DOUGLAS TURNER WARD [b. May 5, 1930, Burnside, Louisiana]. Douglas Turner Ward began his career in theatre as a writer and actor after working as a journalist. He studied playwriting and acting at the Paul Mann Workshop in New York in the mid–1950s and appeared in the critically acclaimed José Quintero* production of *The Iceman Cometh* at Circle in the Square (1956). In 1959 he appeared in *A Raisin in the Sun*, understudying Sidney Poitier and then starring in the national tour.

Ward's earliest plays are *Day of Absence* (1965), a parody of Southern manners performed by African-American actors in whiteface makeup, and *Happy Ending* (1965), a comedy that reveals the way in which a savvy African-American maid makes America's unjust social system work for her and her family. Although Ward has written other plays, these two companion pieces remain his best-known work. He writes for an African-American audience and acknowledges the influence of the absurdist work of Jean Genet.

Ward's directing gained national attention through the Negro Ensemble Company (NEC), which he co-founded with actor Robert Hooks and manager Gerald S. Krone in 1968. At this time, the Black Arts Movement, which insisted that African-American playwrights write for and about African Americans and that their works be presented in African-American neighborhoods, was well underway. By producing works at its original home in Greenwich Village instead of Harlem, by working with a white manager, and by accepting funds from the Ford Foundation, the NEC often found itself at odds with the most organized African-American artistic movement of the time. Neither the NEC nor Ward was a part of Amiri Baraka's "revolutionary theatre," though Ward had his own African-American theatre institution in mind. As stated in the *New York Times* of August 8, 1966, Ward was interested in providing "a center where Black creative talent would be nurtured and a Black audience built" even if that meant alienating those artists who did not have similar institutional aspirations.

Ward generally works with new scripts which requires a close relationship with playwrights. Because he believes his role as director is to help a writer see what he or she has created, Ward does not immediately cut problem areas of the play. While preparing to direct Charles Fuller's *Zooman and the Sign* (1980), Ward recorded the play combining two of the three versions Fuller had submitted. After listening to the tape, Fuller was able to create a draft of the play that solved the play's structural problems. In this way, when directing, Ward is able to use his own playwriting skills to advance the playwright's creation. Through this collaborative process, Ward has premiered the works of Samm-Art Williams, Charles Fuller, Gus Edwards, Paul Carter Harrison, Judi Ann Mason, Leslie Lee, and Joseph A. Walker.

Ward's trademark is his use of nonrealistic sets that allow for a fluidity of scenes. His use of platforms, boxes, door frames, and pools of light in his productions of *Home* (Williams, 1980), *Zooman and the Sign* (1980), and *The Offering* (Edwards, 1978) established the visual iconography now firmly attached to each work and reflect his admiration for the work of Bertolt Brecht.* Another hallmark of Ward's productions is the use of music to serve as a connective device between the frequently episodic work he directs. For Ward, the music exists not only to establish mood, but also to serve as the climax to a previous scene and comment on an upcoming one.

In the rehearsal of contemporary plays, Ward prefers not to analyze the structure and content of the plays. Ward memorizes most of his director's notes and shares them with all actors present so everyone is working with the same information. He will often allow an actor to discover what is missing from a scene without telling the performer explicitly. Actors who have worked regularly with Ward recognize his technique of stuttering until the actor fills in the word with the appropriate quality missing from the performance. These rehearsal methods allow Ward to mount a production with as little as two weeks of rehearsal. The short rehearsal period became increasingly common as funding constraints were imposed on the NEC.

Ward has worked nationally and internationally. In addition to directing for NEC in New York, Ward has mounted NEC productions at the Guthrie, the Mark Taper Forum, the Goodman Theatre, and the Shubert Theatre in Philadelphia. In 1979, Ward traveled to Zambia to assist in a two-week project that combined theatre craft with educational techniques on the need for water sanitation. He continues to direct for NEC and to premiere the work of some of America's best African-American playwrights.

ADDITIONAL PRODUCTIONS: 1968: *Daddy Goodness* (Richard Wright); 1970: *Brotherhood/Day of Absence*; 1972: *The River Niger* (by Joseph A. Walker; Ward received Tony nomination for Best Supporting Actor); 1974: *The Great MacDaddy* (Harrison); 1975: *The First Breeze of Summer* (Leslie Lee); 1976: *Livin' Fat* (Mason); 1981: *A Soldier's Play* (Fuller); 1984: *Ceremonies in Dark Old Men* (Lonne Elder III), *District Line* (Walker); 1986: *The War Party* (Lee), *Louie and Ophelia* (Edwards). Television: 1976: *The First Breeze of Summer*, *Black Pride*.

SELECTED BIBLIOGRAPHY: Bartow, Arthur. "Douglas Turner Ward." *The Director's Voice*. New York: Theatre Communications Group, 1988: 300–308; Bigsby, C.W.E. "Three Black Playwrights: Loften Mitchell, Ossie Davis, Douglas Turner Ward." *The Theatre of Black Americans*. Ed. Errol Hill. New York: Applause Theatre Book Publishers, 1987: 148–67; Foreman, Ellen. "The Negro Ensemble Company: A Transcendent Vision." *The Theatre of Black Americans*. Ed. Errol Hill. New York: Applause Theatre Book Publishers, 1987: 270–82; Mapp, Edward. *Directory of Blacks in the Performing Arts*. Metuchen, NJ: Scarecrow Press, 1978; Ward, Douglas Turner. "American Theatre: For Whites Only?" *New York Times* 8 August 1966; Williams, Mance. *Black Theatre in the 1960s and 1970s*. Westport, CT: Greenwood Press, 1985; Woll, Allen. *Dictionary of the Black Theatre*. Westport, CT: Greenwood Press, 1983.

Joni L. Jones

DEBORAH WARNER [b. May 1959, Burford, Oxfordshire, England]. Trained as a stage manager at London's Central School of Speech and Drama, Deborah Warner at age twenty founded her own theatre, the Kick Theatre Company. For Kick, she directed a series of small-scale, powerfully concentrated Shakespeare productions that, over the next six years, developed and defined her distinctive style. Influenced by the work of Peter Brook* and Steven Berkoff, as well as by the intimate studio conditions of Kick, that style is characteristically compact and highly focused, aiming for utter clarity of storytelling. Working with sparse stage environments, Warner melds a spartan simplicity of staging with stunning dramatic effects and darkly comic flashes, so that the focus of each production becomes the intensity of the emotional experience, the humanness of the characters, and the purity of the narrative line. Exposure at the Edinburgh Festival brought attention to several Kick productions, also winning for the company the *Drama* Special Achievement Award in 1985 and a *Time Out* Theatre Award for Warner for *King Lear* (1985).

Warner left Kick in 1987. She directed *The Tempest* in Bangladesh, courtesy of the British Council, and devoted the next two years to the Royal Shakespeare Company (RSC), staging productions in both Stratford and London. Her Kick projects, which Warner has said "taught me Shakespeare practically, not through the world of the academic," provided the model for her taut, critically acclaimed RSC interpretations—a Lear-like *Titus Andronicus*, an imaginative *King John*, and an intimate, powerful *Electra*. Performed in small spaces, the richly austere RSC productions have been described as "almost religious celebrations of classic texts"; and Warner's sharp, uncluttered directorial approach has been praised for its "guts, energy and bravado." In 1989, Warner was named an associate director of the Royal National Theatre, initiating her tenure at this institution with a moving production of Brecht's *The Good Woman of Setzuan* (1990) and amplifying Warner's customary compactness with a wider comic range and epic scope.

Warner has been described by colleagues as a strong ensemble leader who draws performances from her actors by offering them full opportunity for creative contribution in rehearsal. Her process is unusual in that she believes in working with a cast beyond previews, remaining with a production for its full term whenever possible. Her tenacity, attention to detail, and economy of expression, as well as the dynamic imagination and palpable intensity of her productions, have confirmed Deborah Warner, in the space of a decade, as one of the most gifted directors of her generation.

ADDITIONAL PRODUCTIONS: **Kick Theatre Company, 1980–86:** *The Tempest*, *Measure for Measure*, *Woyzeck*, *Coriolanus*.

SELECTED BIBLIOGRAPHY: Gore Langton, Robert. "Kick for Coriolanus." *Plays and Players* 396 (September 1986): 18–19; Morley, Sheridan. "Leading Lady Moves Centrestage." *The Times* 5 January 1989: 8; Wolf, Matt. "Britain's Bright New Directors Are Women." *American Theatre* 7 (April 1990): 60–61.

James DePaul

NED WAYBURN [b. Edward Claudius Wayburn, March 30, 1874, Pittsburgh, Pennsylvania; d. September 2, 1942, New York, New York]. From vaudeville to early television, Ned Wayburn was the leading dance director in early twentieth-century American popular entertainment. Trained as an architectural engineer, he pioneered ways to manipulate perspective and direct the audience's view with lighting, scenery, and live performance. After a short career as an adolescent pianist, Wayburn made his directing debut in *By the Sad Sea Waves* (1899), in which he also played the Rag-time Butler. He staged individual and feature vaudeville acts, combining precision dance numbers with spectacular lighting and stage effects which he invented.

Most of his over 300 full-evening directing/dance directing credits were for musicals with plots into which he integrated comedy and dance production numbers. He created annual productions for the Rogers Brothers comedy team and the Shubert Brothers, and with Lew Fields. Each had memorable scenes based around onstage effects, such as trains, circuses, or nightclubs, in which dancers did their specialities. Wayburn's work in revues also integrated individual specialties with special effects. He became famous for displaying comic as well as dance specialties at their best within the context of a plotted musical. In *The Honeymoon Express* (1914), for example, Al Jolson and Fannie Brice burst into fame with their small specialty numbers in a musical created to focus attention on an exhibition ballroom team. Wayburn's continuous manipulation of the routine format could be seen in the first Shubert *Passing Shows* (1912, 1913), most notably in the "Capitol Steps" scene (Act I finale, 1913), a parody of Hazel MacKaye's Suffragist pageant in which fourteen individual comic and dance routines were staged on a revolving sixty-four-step staircase. Wayburn's work became even more spectacular on the extra-wide stages of the London Hippodrome, *Hullo Tango* (1913) and *Zig Zag* (1917), and at New York's Century Theatre, *The Century Girl* (1916) and *Miss* (1917).

He remains best known for his direction and dance direction of Florenz Ziegfeld, Jr.'s two annual series—the full stage *Follies* (1915–19, 1922–23) and intimate roof garden *Frolics* (1915–19). With Ziegfeld, he codified the dance specialties and choruses into gradations of size (from pony to show girl) and into five technical systems, of which four (Tap and Stepping, Music Comedy Dance, Acrobatics, and Exhibition Ballroom dance) are still in common use. Among his many innovations were pony precision choruses, non-erotic audience participation numbers, precision toe dancing, movable stages, and many individual lighting effects.

In the 1920s, Wayburn switched from extravaganzas to intimate social musicals, trading in his large choruses for flirtation songs and ballroom-based dances. These ranged in length from full-evening productions for the Dolly Sisters or the Fairbanks Twins to seventeen-minute vaudeville acts for the very young Fred and Adele Astaire. He also worked extensively in radio in the 1920s and 1930s and staged dance numbers for Cosmopolitan Pictures. He directed and hosted four variety shows for the television link-up from the World's Fair in

1939–40. A series, "Search for Beauty," was set to premiere on December 7, 1941; it was never rescheduled due to his failing health.

ADDITIONAL PRODUCTIONS: 1901: *The Governor's Son*; 1907: *The Time, the Place and the Girl*; 1909: *The Midnight Sons*; 1911: *Hullo Paris, The Wife Hunters*; 1912: *The Passing Show of 1912*; 1913: *The Passing Show of 1913*; *Ziegfeld Follies* of 1915–19, 1922–23; *Ziegfeld Midnight Frolics* of 1912–15; 1921: *Two Little Girls in Blue*; 1924: *The Great White Way* (Cosmopolitan Pictures); 1930: *Smiles*.

SELECTED BIBLIOGRAPHY: Cohen-Stratyner, Barbara. "The Dance Direction of Ned Wayburn." Diss. New York U, 1984; Cohen-Stratyner, Barbara. "Welcome to Laceland." In *Musical Comedy in America*. Ed. Glen Loney. Westport, CT: Greenwood Press, 1983; Wayburn, Ned. *The Art of Stage Dancing*. New York: Ned Wayburn Studio; 1923, 1925, 1931.

Barbara Cohen-Stratyner

MARGARET WEBSTER [b. March 15, 1905, New York, New York; d. November 13, 1972, London, England]. Margaret Webster was the last theatrical notable in a family whose stage careers spanned four generations. B. N. Webster, her great-grandfather, was a prominent actor-manager in early nineteenth-century London and her father Benjamin performed on the stage and in early silent films. Born in New York while her parents were on tour from London, Webster maintained dual citizenship throughout her life, a choice that proved fortunate during the McCarthy era. She made her first professional appearance on the stage in 1924 as a chorus member in Euripides' *The Trojan Women* and spent the next decade acting in London, joining the Old Vic in 1929.

Her career turned to directing in 1934 with a mammoth outdoor production of *Henry VIII*. Her directorial success was firmly established when she directed Maurice Evans in *Richard II* (1937) and *Hamlet* (1938) in New York. Evans and Webster also collaborated on productions of *Henry IV, Part I* (1939), *Twelfth Night* (1940), *Macbeth* (1941), and *The Taming of the Shrew* (1951). Although her career would include contemporary plays, modern classics, and opera, Webster's primary contribution as a director was the revitalization of popular interest in Shakespearean production in the United States. Other notable Shakespearean efforts include the 1942 *Othello* with Paul Robeson (Webster played Emilia), *The Tempest* (1945) with Eva Le Gallienne,* and a two-year tour that took the Bard to high schools and small towns in thirty-six states and four Canadian provinces between 1948 and 1950. She also presented excerpts from various Shakespearean texts at the 1939 New York World's Fair and in 1946 founded the American Repertory Theatre with Cheryl Crawford and Eva Le Gallienne.

Webster's desire to bring Shakespeare before the public in an accessible and unfettered fashion underlies her directorial precepts. A firm believer in the primacy of the text, she had little patience for auteurs. Firmly opposed to "bardolatry," she also refused to contemporize the setting and characters: "We shall not need to dress Hotspur in the uniform of the R.A.F. in order to invest him with life" (*Shakespeare without Tears*, 297).

Although she occasionally made significant alterations to the text (eliminating the clown in *Othello* and placing Prospero's Act IV "revels" speech in *The Tempest* at the end of the play as an epilogue), Webster generally kept textual modifications to a minimum. Because she felt Shakespeare was both a great poet and a great craftsman, she thought a director of Shakespeare should trust the text and produce it honestly and simply.

Webster also lectured extensively on Shakespeare and wrote more than forty articles. Many of her lectures and solo performances are available on audio cassette. Her papers are at the Library of Congress.

ADDITIONAL PRODUCTIONS: 1934: *Henry VIII*; 1937: *Richard II*; 1938: *Hamlet*; 1939: *Henry IV, Part 1*; 1940: *Twelfth Night*; 1941: *Macbeth*; 1942: *Othello*: 1945: *The Tempest*; 1948–50 (on tour through United States and Canada with the Margaret Webster Shakespeare Company): *Hamlet, Macbeth*; 1951: *The Taming of the Shrew*; 1956: *The Merchant of Venice*; 1960: *Waiting in the Wings* (Noel Coward).

SELECTED BIBLIOGRAPHY: Cole, Toby, and Helen Krich Chinoy. *Directors on Directing*. Indianapolis: Bobbs-Merrill Co., 1963; Hassencahl, Fran. "Margaret Webster." *Notable Women in the American Theatre*. Ed. Alice Robinson, Vera Mowry Roberts, and Milly Barranger. Westport, CT: Greenwood Press, 1989: 908–13; Heggie, Barbara. "We" (Profile of Webster). *The New Yorker* 20 May 1944: 32–36 + ; Leiter, Samuel L. *From Belasco to Brook: Representative Directors of the English-Speaking Stage*. Westport, CT: Greenwood Press, 1991: 109–46; Silverman, Ely. "Margaret Webster's Theory and Practice of Shakespearean Production in the United States (1937–1953)." Diss. New York U, 1969; Webster, Margaret. *Don't Put Your Daughter on the Stage*. New York: Alfred A. Knopf, 1972; Webster, Margaret. "Producing Shakespeare." *Theatre Arts Magazine* 26 (January 1942): 43–48; Webster, Margaret. *The Same Only Different*. New York: Alfred A. Knopf, 1969; Webster, Margaret. *Shakespeare without Tears*. New York: McGraw, 1942, revised 1957, published in Great Britain as *Shakespeare Today*; Worsely, Ronald Craig. "Margaret Webster: A Study of Her Contributions to the American Theatre." Diss. Wayne State U, 1972.

Stephen Nelson

G. ORSON WELLES [b. May 6, 1915, Kenosha, Wisconsin; d. October 9, 1985, Los Angeles, California]. Known primarily as an actor with a mellifluous and sonorous voice and as an innovator in directing radio drama and films, Orson Welles gained a reputation as the "Boy Genius of the American Theatre" by the time he was twenty-two years old. The most important of his productions, in which he usually took a starring role, were executed under the auspices of the Federal Theatre Project and the Mercury Theatre Company between 1935 and 1941 with the support of his partner, John Houseman.*

Influenced by his predilection for popular entertainments and by the Federal Theatre Project mandate to bring classical plays to the "people," Welles radically edited and rearranged the play texts in order to emphasize action and to make them more accessible to his audience. More interested in heightening the spectacle than creating consistent interpretations of the characters and themes, he relied upon dazzling lighting effects (executed by lighting designers Abe Feder and Jean Rosenthal) against a permanent, adaptable setting, carefully staged crowd scenes, and an integrated sound score. The eerie visual and sound effects created by the African drumming and lighting of his Harlem Federal Theatre Project "voodoo" *Macbeth* (1935), the magical appearance and disappearance of characters achieved by focusing and limiting lighting against the black velvet drapes cloaking the Federal Theatre's stage in *Dr. Faustus* (1936), and the lighting effects on a series of rising platforms against a bare, red brick wall evoking Mussolini's Italy in the Mercury Theatre's modern-dress *Julius Caesar* (1937) won Welles critical acclaim as the most innovative director of his time.

Although Welles's earliest works owed a great deal to the aesthetics of New Theatre, this was merely a result of Welles's ability to assimilate all production concepts available to him. Continuously searching for other ways to create theatre, he utilized techniques from other entertainment media. He borrowed acts from magic shows and circus, and vaudeville and burlesque turns to give his comedies popular appeal. From radio, he took the technique of music as a linking device between scenes for his successful 1941 production of *Native Son*. Fascinated with movies, he experimented in his productions of *Too Much Johnson* (1938, by William Gillette), *Green Goddess* (1939, by William Archer), and *Around the World* (1946, adapted by Welles from Jules Verne's novel with music by Cole Porter) with using film interspersed with live action to replace exposition. Driven to find a way of portraying continuous action in the theatre, in 1939 he staged *Five Kings*, his adaptation of Shakespeare's *Henry IV, Parts I and II* and *Henry V*, on a revolving stage so that characters could actually walk from one London locale to another and the battle scenes of Harfleur, Salisbury, and Agincourt could be presented realistically. These experiments failed because there was not enough money to overcome technical difficulties. Yet their significance as the training ground for Welles's extraordinary filmmaking career is indisputable.

ADDITIONAL PRODUCTIONS: 1936: *Horse Eats Hat* (adapted by Welles and Edwin Denby from *An Italian Straw Hat*) with Joseph Cotten, Arlene Francis, Paula Lawrence and Edgerton Paul; 1937: *The Cradle Will Rock* (Marc Blitzstein) with Will Greer and Howard da Silva; 1938: *The Shoemaker's Holiday* with Edith Barrett, Ruth Ford, Alice Frost, John Hoyt, Whitford Kane, Joseph Cotten, and Vincent Price; *Heartbreak House* with Geraldine Fitzgerald, Mady Christians, Vincent Price, and George Coulouris; *Danton's Death* (songs by Marc Blitzstein) with Martin Gabel, Arlene Francis, Vladimir Sokoloff, and Joseph Cotten; 1955: *Moby Dick—Rehearsed* with Patrick McGoohan and Joan Plowright; 1956: *King Lear*; 1960: *Chimes at Midnight*, *Rhinoceros* (Ionesco) with Laurence Olivier and Joan Plowright.

SELECTED BIBLIOGRAPHY: Brady, Frank. *Citizen Welles*. New York: Charles Scribner's Sons, 1989; Flanagan, Hallie. *Arena: A History of the Federal Theatre*. New York: Duell, Sloan and Pierce, 1940, reprinted by Benjamin Blom, 1965; France, Richard. *Orson Welles on Shakespeare*. Westport, CT: Greenwood Press, 1990: France, Richard. *The Theatre of Orson Welles*. Lewisburg, PA: Bucknell University Press, 1977; Houseman, John. *Run-Through*. New York: Curtis Books, 1972; Leaming, Barbara. *Orsen Welles: A Biography*. New York: Viking Penguin, 1985; Wood, Bret. *Orson Welles: A Bio-Bibliography*. Westport, CT: Greenwood Press, 1990.

Andrea J. Nouryeh

CLIFFORD WILLIAMS [b. December 30, 1926, Cardiff, Wales]. A broad-based director with extraordinarily varied training and production credits, Clifford Williams has been highly successful in both the subsidized and the commercial sectors of the British theatre. Since his Arts Theatre, London production of *Yerma* brought him to prominence in 1957, Williams has directed everything from *Volpone* (1967) to *Sleuth* (1970); and from Shakespearean tragedy to *Oh! Calcutta!* (1970). His productions at the Royal Shakespeare Company (RSC), where he was made an associate director in 1963, have been hailed as among the troupe's finest work. His famous all-male interpretation of *As You Like It* for the National Theatre in 1967 was one of the decade's most discussed productions.

Although most of Williams's work has been in Britain, touring productions of his RSC work have frequently been seen in New York, and commercial productions like *Aren't We All* (1984), *Pack of Lies* (1984), and *Breaking the Code* (1986) were well received on Broadway. In 1968, Williams was named artistic director of Theater Toronto, where he recruited an all-Canadian company to form an ambitious resident troupe. His other international contributions include directing at the Finnish National Theatre, the Bulgarian National Theatre, and the Yugoslav National Theatre. He has also directed for the Mexican National Theatre and the Royal Danish Theatre, and his work has appeared in venues as disparate as Cleveland, Ohio; Madrid, Spain; and the Yale School of Drama.

As well as working with the British subsidized companies, Williams directed twenty mime plays for the Mime Theatre Company, which he founded in 1950. He has also served as director of productions at the Marlowe Theatre, Canterbury, and the Queen's Theatre, Hornchurch. Provincial directing credits include the Edinburgh Festival, Coventry's Belgrade Theatre, and the Arena Theatre, Birmingham. His commercial Shakespearean productions (coproduced by Washington's Kennedy Center) at London's Phoenix in the late 1980s challenged the assumption that classical theatre had no place in the modern West End.

Williams's repertoire is so extensive, it is difficult to classify his directorial approach or taste, although he is generally regarded as possessing remarkable clarity, fluidity and insight, along with a populist perspective. He once told the *New York Times* that, for a classical play to interest him, it must be one "which doesn't seem to want to be a classical play; it wants to be a modern play." Williams's productions have always been willing to take risks. Reviewers of *The Representative* (1963) celebrated Williams's ability to bludgeon reality into the face of his audience. In 1965, Williams opened *The Jew of Malta* and *The Merchant of Venice* at Stratford within sixteen hours of each other, and the two productions, which shared designers and leading actor, brilliantly compared and contrasted the two Elizabethan Jews. Five years later, Williams was shattering sexual taboos with the revue *Oh! Calcutta!*, replete with nudity and sadomasochism and assuredly aimed at those who did not usually frequent the RSC. Back with the classics, in 1977, he collected the Society of West End Theatres (SWET) Best Director award for *Wild Oats* (1976).

Since then, Williams has directed innumerable times in a number of countries. Williams wrote in 1968 that he aimed to capture "new, fresh audiences." He has been so doing ever since.

ADDITIONAL PRODUCTIONS: 1959: Dürrenmatt's *The Marriage of Mr. Mississippi*; 1960: *A Moon for the Misbegotten*; 1962: *Afore Night Come* (David Rudkin); 1963: *The Comedy of Errors*, *The Tempest*; 1964: *The Jew of Malta*, *Our Main Crichton*; 1966: *Twelfth Night*; 1968: *Dr. Faustus*, *Othello*; 1969: *A Winter's Tale*; 1971: *The Duchess of Malfi*, *The Taming of the Shrew*; 1973: *A Lesson in Blood and Roses*; 1974: *Henry IV* (Pirandello), *Cymbeline*, *What Every Woman Knows*; 1975: *The Mouth Organ* (also co-devisor); 1977: *The Old Country*, *Rosmersholm*, *Man and Superman*; 1978: *The Tempest*; 1979: *Threepenny Opera*, *Born in the Gardens*; 1980: *Lord Arthur Saville's Crime*; 1981: *The Love-Girl and the Innocent* (Solzhenitsyn), *Overheard* (Peter Ustinov); 1984: *The Happiest Days of Your Life* (John Dighton); 1988: *Richard II*; 1989: *Richard III*; 1991: *It's Ralph*.

SELECTED BIBLIOGRAPHY: Beauman, Sally. *The Royal Shakespeare Company: A History of Ten Decades*. Oxford: Oxford University Press, 1982; French, Philip. "Winston Carve-Up." *The Best of Plays and Players: 1953–1968*. Ed. Peter Roberts. London: Methuen, 1988; "Green Room." *The Best of Plays and Players: 1953–1968*; Novick, Julius. "A New Troupe Talks to Our Time." *New York Times* 4 February 1968; Williams, Clifford. "Two Jews at Stratford." *The Best of Plays and Players: 1953–1968*.

Chris Jones

ROBERT WILSON [b. October 4, 1941, Waco, Texas]. From the beginning of his career Robert Wilson has always shown a distinctive affinity for the scenic, typically manifested in "operatic" productions conceived and directed by himself. In fact, many have come to see Wilson's work as the acme of "scenic writing," achieving Gordon Craig's dream of the super-artist of the theatre who assumes complete control over production as auteur, designer, and stage manager. Others see Wilson's work as the fulfillment of surrealism, while all generally categorize it as the "Theatre of Images." Formal, aesthetical, and generally apolitical, Wilson's work has been mostly produced in Europe, where he is lionized, but only occasionally performed in his homeland.

Wilson's education as an architect and his love of sketching and painting, along with his work as a movement therapist for the mentally disturbed, provided material for his first productions, especially *The King of Spain* (1969), a collection of visual and verbal fragments deliberately juxtaposed in order that their phenomenological qualities might be experienced independent of any naturalistic or linear narrative. Participating in these early productions were a number of Wilson's patients who were encouraged to work out their inner visions during workshops. Later this material was transferred directly (if innocently but honestly) into performance. Wilson's collaboration with Raymond Andrews, a deaf child, in *Deafman Glance* (1971), and with Christopher Knowles, a brain-damaged youth, in *A Letter for Queen Victoria* (1974) and *Einstein on the Beach* (1976 at the Metropolitan Opera House), offered audiences not only strikingly fragmented imagery, but the challenge of relating to and accepting the prerational, non-narrative, multilinear forms of perception that these performers experienced in everyday life. Ironically, Wilson's stage visions are "natural" at the deeper levels of subconscious experience even as their surface representation appears disrupted and alogical.

Space, time, and action are manipulated by Wilson to the fullest extent possible within the available stagecraft of the proscenium theatre. Trap doors, elaborate lighting effects, trapezes, arcane mechanical devices, huge manikins, live animals, artificial animals, and oversized costumes are mixed with perfectly ordinary looking objects to create a tension of signification that requires a reassessment of normal representational values. Time and action are likewise attenuated, sometimes egregiously: *The Life and Times of Joseph Stalin* (1973) lasted twelve hours, while *KA MOUNTAIN and GUARDenia TERRACE* (1972), set in the ruins of Persepolis, Iran, was performed without interruption over a period of seven days and nights. Often scenes involve deliberately monotonic devices such as an hour-long raising of an actor's arm or the repetitive chanting of the same phrase with only subtle variations. These effects are intended to produce a state of revery (some claim it's excruciating boredom) in the spectator that opens the way to a different and refreshing theatrical experience. Wilson's work as director-auteur culminated in his creation of the *CIVIL warS* (1984), a six-part, multinational work finished in pieces which was to have been performed complete at the opening ceremonies of the Los Angeles Olympics but regrettably cancelled for lack of funding.

Wilson typically draws material from many sources: biographies of famous people, myth, other dramatic writing, and popular films, as well as the autobiography and "automatic" writing of his collaborators. He has also developed excellent relationships with choreographers such as Andrew de Groat and Lucinda Childs, as well as musicians Philip Glass and Tom Waits, and authors Heiner Müller, William S. Burroughs, and Darryl Pinckney. Recently, Wilson has undertaken to direct more conventional dramas and operas including Euripides' *Alcestis* (1986), Müller's *Hamletmachine* (1987, New York University), Chekhov's *Swan Song* (1989), and *King Lear* (1990), but always with his distinctive manner of visual and temporal manipulation.

ADDITIONAL PRODUCTIONS: 1969: *The Life and Times of Sigmund Freud*; 1974: *DIA LOG* with Christopher Knowles, *I Was Sitting on My Patio* . . . with Lucinda Childs; 1979: *Death Destruction and Detroit*; 1982: *The Golden Windows, Great Day in the Morning* with Jessye Norman; 1987: *Salomé* (Strauss); 1990: *Alceste* (Gluck) with Jessye Norman at the Chicago Lyric Opera; 1992: *Danton's Death* (Büchner) with Richard Thomas, Alley Theatre, Houston, Texas.

SELECTED BIBLIOGRAPHY: Bradbey, David, and David Williams. *Director's Theatre*. New York: Macmillan, 1988; Cole, Susan Letzler. *Directors in Rehearsal: A Hidden World*. New York: Routledge, 1992: 145–70; Glass, Philip. *Music by Philip Glass*. New York: Harper and Row, 1987; Marranca, Bonnie, ed. *The Theatre of Images*. New York: Drama Book Specialists, 1977; Nelson, Craig, ed. *Robert Wilson: The Theatre of Images*.

New York: Harper and Row, 1984; Rockwell, John. "Staging Painterly Visions." *New York Times Magazine* 15 November 1992: 22–26, 61; Shyer, Laurence. *Robert Wilson and His Collaborators.* New York: Theatre Communications Group (TCG), 1990.

Thomas Leff

STEIN WINGE [b. November 10, 1940, Oslo, Norway]. In 1969, four years after his acting debut at Oslo's Nationaltheatret playing Paris opposite Liv Ullmann in *Romeo and Juliet*, Stein Winge began directing. Since then, after staging over ninety productions, he has earned a reputation in Europe and the United States as an irreverent, brilliant director of classical plays and opera. In 1990, he began as artistic director of Nationaltheatret and instituted an annual International Ibsen Festival, bringing the most exciting, iconoclastic Ibsen productions to Norway's main stage. Winge wants the classics to brutally confront the present. Consequently, his productions are disturbing, visceral, raw, and profane.

Although Winge has been one of the most castigated directors in Norway, in a personal letter Ingmar Bergman* called him a "genius." Winge's *enfant terrible* reputation began at Trøndelag Teater in Trondheim with *Antigone* (1970), which was designed by his father, the famous Norwegian expressionistic artist Sigurd Winge. A staff director at Nationaltheatret by 1971, he was soon defying traditions of staging Mozart, Verdi, Strindberg, Brecht, Ibsen, and Shakespeare on main as well as experimental stages throughout Norway. After 1979, as artistic director at Torshov, Nationaltheatret's experimental space, his productions became more blasphemous, controversial, and popular. His *Shakespeare Project* ("poor theatre" productions of *King John* and *Richard II*, 1983–84) played to packed houses.

Earlier, Winge had begun collaborating with designers Tine Schwab and Timian Alsaker and composer Ketil Hvoslef. He has continued building a collaborative team which includes designer Pavel Dobrusky and actors Espen Skjønberg, Kari Onstad, and Bjørn Sundquist. Boldly theatrical scenography, original music, nontraditional casting, and radical use of space and style place Winge among the best European auteur directors, artists the calibre of Giorgio Strehler,* Peter Brook,* and Ariane Mnouchkine.*

In 1984, Winge began his most ambitious productions at Oslo's Norske Teatret, and the following year, he launched his international career with a wacky *Three Sisters* at the Los Angeles Theatre Center. He returned to Los Angeles yearly with a series of uncompromising productions including a violent, pornographic *King Lear* with Espen Skjønberg (1987). Winge's reputation for *gesamtkunstwerk* led to productions of *Die Walküre* in Geneva (1987) and *The Persians* (Frederic Rzewski) in Wiesbaden (1989). In 1991, besides the successful Ibsen Festival, Winge opened Malersalen (the Paint Shop), a second experimental space within Oslo's Nationaltheatret.

ADDITIONAL PRODUCTIONS: 1972 and 1987: *Hamlet*; 1974: *The Farm* (David Storey); 1975: *Oedipus*; 1977: *A Dream Play*; 1979: *Ubu Roi*; 1980: *Othello*; 1981: *Mother Courage*; 1981 and 1986: *Barabbas*; 1984: *Galileo*; 1985: *Faust*; 1986: *Pantagleize* (Ghelderode); 1987 and 1989: *King Lear*; 1988: *The Inspector General*, *Merlin* (Tankred Dorst); 1990: *Richard III*; 1990 and 1991: *The Wild Duck*; 1991: *Carmen* (Bizet and Prosper Mérimée).

SELECTED BIBLIOGRAPHY: Christon, Lawrence. "A Change of Climate for Norwegian Director." *Los Angeles Times* 19 September 1985; *Store Norske Leksikon* 14. Oslo: Kunnskapsforlaget, 1989: 559.

Susan Vaneta Mason

ROBERT E. WOODRUFF [b. March 18, 1947, Brooklyn, New York]. In the late 1970s and early 1980s, Robert Woodruff was known as Sam Shepard's director. Since then, he has moved into an arena of his own making and is considered one of the leading avant-garde directors of the early 1990s.

Woodruff was born and raised in New York. He earned a B.A. in political science from the University of Buffalo in 1968, undertook graduate study in theatre at the City College of New York, and taught theatre classes in Washington Heights and Harlem. Eventually tiring of New York, he relocated to San Francisco in the early 1970s.

Much of Woodruff's most significant early career work was done in the Bay Area. He co-founded the Eureka Theatre in 1972, serving as its artistic and resident director until 1978, and in 1976 he founded the Bay Area Playwrights Festival, a venue for developing new works for the stage. It was during the first Festival that Woodruff began his collaboration with Sam Shepard by directing *The Sad Lament of Pecos Bill* (1976). Forming an alliance with Shepard and the Magic Theatre in San Francisco, Woodruff went on to direct the premieres of *Buried Child* (1978) and *True West* (1980). He also directed the American premiere of *Curse of the Starving Class* (1978), and the Shepard/Joseph Chaikin* collaborations, *Tongues* (1980) and *Savage/Love* (1980).

As the definitive interpreter of Shepard's later plays, Woodruff seemed to recede into the text, allowing and encouraging the raw, visceral poetry to support the productions. In 1983, however, a shift occurred in Woodruff's directing while he collaborated with the Flying Karamazov Brothers on a production of *The Comedy of Errors* at the Goodman Theatre. Woodruff's direction of this production was bold and imagistic. A second collaboration with the Karamazovs, *The Three Moscowteers* (1984), and Woodruff's 1985 production of *Man Is Man* at the La Jolla Playhouse solidified his shift away from language-oriented texts to visually and aurally aggressive works. Since then, Woodruff's directing no longer recedes into the text, and he has produced a series of dynamic, visual works, as evidenced by his frequent collaborations with scenic designer Douglas Stein. Woodruff enjoys the creative freedom of working with a team of artists on an established script, and he strongly believes that, while directing a new play requires a director to respect the playwright's voice, staging an established script demands that every collaborator's voice be heard. Woodruff actively encourages the "disharmony" these simultaneous, strong voices often produce.

Although Woodruff has been an artistic associate at the Mark Taper Forum since 1989, he has remained unaffiliated with any one theatre. The regional theatres (including the Guthrie Theatre, Trinity Repertory Company, Alliance Theatre, Northlight Repertory Theatre, and the Goodman Theatre) provide his primary directing forum. In New York City, he has directed for Circle Repertory Company, the Phoenix Theatre, the Brooklyn Academy of Music, and the New York Shakespeare Festival. Woodruff does not work in the commercial theatre.

ADDITIONAL PRODUCTIONS: 1979: *Ice* (Michael Cristofer), *Suicide in B Flat*; 1980: *The Death of Von Richthofen as Witnessed from Earth* (Des McAnuff*); 1984: *The Comedy of Errors* (recreation of the 1983 production for the 1984 Olympic Arts Festival in Los Angeles), *In the Belly of the Beast* (adapted by Adrian Hall*); 1986: *Figaro Gets a Divorce* (Odon von Horvath), *L'Histoire du Soldat* (Paul Magid/Len Jenkins adapt.); 1987: *The Tempest*; 1988: *A Lie of the Mind*, *Struck Dumb*, and *The War in Heaven* with Joseph Chaikin; 1990: *The Skin of Our Teeth*, *Baal* (Bertolt Brecht*).

SELECTED BIBLIOGRAPHY: Bartow, Arthur. "Robert Woodruff." *The Director's Voice*. New York: Theatre Communications Group, 1988: 309–24; Cummings, Scott. "Robert Woodruff" (interview). *Theater* 15 (Spring 1984): 60–66; Shewey, Don. "A Boot in Two Camps." *American Theatre* 3 (October 1986); 12–17, 45.

Andrea Urice

GARLAND WRIGHT [b. April 18, 1946, Midland, Texas]. Raised in a small Texas oil town, Garland Wright began his formal artistic training at Southern Methodist University, studying graphics before transferring to theatre midway through his academic career. In 1969 he moved to New York City and became a journeyman actor at the American Shakespeare Theatre, Stratford, Connecticut, where he made his directorial debut with *Julius Caesar* (1973). The following year Wright, with several members of the Stratford acting ensemble, cofounded the Lion Theatre Company, in New York City, mounting productions which included Len Jenkin's *Kitty Hawk* (1974), *The Tempest* (1975), and *Marathon '33* by June Havoc (1976). In 1977 the company moved to an abandoned airline terminal in New York City's red-light district and developed *K: Impressions of the Trial* by Franz Kafka. This piece, which earned the first of Wright's two Obie Awards, contained all of the elements that epitomized Wright's early career: precise ensemble playing, collaborative development of script, and minimalist staging.

Wright gained national attention in 1976 with three highly successful commercial ventures: Jack Heifner's *Vanities* (one of the longest running nonmusical Off-Broadway productions), *Lone Star* and *Private Wars* (James McLure) at the Century Theatre and *New Jerusalem* by Len Jenkin at the Public Theatre.

In 1980, Wright was appointed associate director of the Guthrie Theatre, serving for three years in this position under Liviu Ciulei.* In 1987, he became the artistic director of the Guthrie. During the 1980s, Wright's productions at the Guthrie included *Camille* (1980), *Anything Goes* (1985), *The Misanthrope* and Eugene Labiche's *The Piggy Bank* (1987), *Richard III* and *Hamlet* (1988) and, with associate Charles Newell, *Richard II*, *Henry IV (Parts I & II)*, and *Henry V* (1990).

Wright's eclectic range was also evident in his work at other regional theatres during the same decade. At the Arena Stage, Washington, D.C. (where he was an artistic associate in 1985–86), he staged *The Imaginary Invalid* (1983), *Happy End* (1984), *The Tempest* (1984), *The Good Woman of Setzuan* (1985), and *Old Times* (1986). He also directed for the Denver Theatre Center, Seattle Repertory, and the Acting Company, where he won his second Obie Award in 1987 with his production of Eric Overmyer's *On the Verge or The Geography of Yearning*.

Garland Wright's extensive regional career has established him as a proto-typical American director of the 1980s. His work shows a fascination with the classics as well as modern American authors, an innovative sense of ensemble with the actor as the primary artist, a preference for long-standing collaborations with designers, and a heightened sensibility for the aural and visual aspects of a play.

The visual elements are important in Wright's productions. Color and tone, varying intensities of light, and objects in high relief are essential characteristics of his directorial palette. He considers himself someone who sculpts a foreground of sound, color, and action in an imagistic background where the interaction of isolated objects will provoke thought and emotion.

ADDITIONAL PRODUCTIONS: 1980: *Das Lusitania Songspiel* (Sigourney Weaver and Christopher Durang), Chelsea Theatre Center; *Mary Stuart* (Schiller), Guthrie Theatre; 1982: *Candide* (adapt. by Len Jenkin); 1983: *Guys and Dolls*, Guthrie Theatre; 1984: *The Importance of Being Earnest*, Guthrie Theatre and national tour; 1987: *The Misanthrope*, Guthrie Theatre; 1992: *Iphigenia in Aulis, Agamemnon, Electra*.

SELECTED BIBLIOGRAPHY: Bartow, Arthur. "Garland Wright." *The Director's Voice*. New York: Theatre Communications Group, 1988: 325–42; Bennetts, Leslie. "A Director's Odyssey through Time and Space." *New York Times* 22 February 1987: sec. 2: 5, 21; Bly, Mark. "Garland Wright" (interview). *Theater* 15 (Spring 1984): 67–73; Copelin, David. "From Texas to the Taper." *Performing Arts: California's Music and Theatre Magazine* November 1976: 29–31; Shewey, Don. "Getting Acquainted with Mr. Wright." *American Theatre* 4 (November 1987): 23–28.

Richard Warner

Y

OLEG NIKOLAYEVICH YEFREMOV [b. October 1, 1927, Moscow]. Yefremov's long association with the Moscow Art Theatre (MAT) began in 1945, when he entered the MAT academy. While studying there, he saw plays in stagings created by Konstantin Stanislavsky* and Vladimir Nemirovich-Danchenko* and performances by members of the original MAT ensemble, such as Knipper-Chekhova. However, when he completed his studies in 1949, he was not invited to join the MAT company, and he accepted a position with Moscow's Central Children's Theatre.

At the Children's Theatre, Yefremov not only proved his exceptional abilities as an actor, but also directed for the first time. Moreover, the theatre's innovative director, Konstantin Shakh-Azizov, brought together many of the actors, directors, and writers who were to transform Soviet theatre in coming decades. Yefremov thus had an opportunity to form important professional relationships, most notably with the writer Victor Rozov.

In 1956, Yefremov and several colleagues, in loose affiliation with the Moscow Art Theatre, formed the Young Actors' Studio Theatre. This theatre, which soon changed its name to the Sovremenik (Contemporary), leapt to fame with its first production, *Eternal Life* (1957) by Rozov. Yefremov both directed and performed in the production, which set the tone for the Sovremenik's work during its first decade: contemporary plays offering unadorned views of everyday Soviet life in a style which has been described as Soviet neo-realism. The theatre soon became a popular symbol of the post-Stalin "thaw." During 1966 and 1967 Yefremov expanded the company's repertory with a series of plays, such as Leonid Zorin's *The Decembrists* and Mikhail Shatrov's *Bolsheviks*, which reexamined Russian history from a contemporary perspective. The Sovremenik was less successful with its occasional ventures into the classics, such as Yefremov's 1970 staging of *The Sea Gull*.

For fourteen years, Yefremov was the dominant force in the Sovremenik. He served as artistic director while acting in and directing dozens of plays, often performing in the plays he himself staged. Nevertheless, his turn toward Anton Chekhov in 1970 was prophetic, for in the same year the Moscow Art Theatre invited him to become its new artistic director, and he accepted the offer.

Yefremov's first few seasons at the Art Theatre were stormy, as he sought to introduce more contemporary plays to the repertory and to trim the size of the acting company. In time, however, he seemed to achieve a compromise between the old and the new. While introducing the works of controversial young playwrights, such as Alexander Gel'man, to the MAT repertoire, he continued to stage Chekhov, and produced plays designed to showcase MAT's elder stars. Ironically, by the late 1980s, Yefremov—the radical of the previous decade— was being criticized by some members of his company for excessive conservatism and his supposed favoritism toward a small group of middle-aged actors. The tensions at MAT came to a head during the 1986–87 season, with a bitter division of the company into two separate organizations: one headed by Yefremov, the other by Tat'yana Doronina.

The schism at MAT is only one aspect of the challenge to Yefremov's leadership in a Soviet theatre freed of censorship and open to a wide range of experimentation. Unlike many of his contemporaries, he has eschewed the fantastic, the grotesque, the avant-garde, and most of the classical repertory. As his 1989 production of Ludmilla Petrushevskaya's *Moscow Choir* demonstrates, his strength as a director continues to be his ability to draw strong performances from actors in modern realistic dramas of the type he introduced at the Sovremenik. The place of such drama in the changing Soviet theatre remains to be seen.

However he may be judged as a director, Yefremov's accomplishments as an actor-manager are impressive. He has revitalized the legacy of Stanislavsky, led two of the most influential Soviet theatre companies, and furthered the careers of many of the playwrights who shaped the contemporary Soviet repertory.

ADDITIONAL PRODUCTIONS: 1955: *Dimka the Invisible* (Korostylev and L'vovsky); 1959: *Two Colors* (Zaka and Kuznetsov); 1961: *The Fourth* (Simonov); 1967: *A Traditional Gathering* (Rozov); 1972: *Steelworkers* (Bokarev); 1973: *Solo for a Clock with Chimes* (Zagradnik); 1976, 1990: *Ivanov*; 1977: *Feedback* (Gel'man); 1979: *Duck Hunting* (Vampilov); 1980: *The Sea Gull* (at Moscow Art Theatre); 1981: *Thus We Conquer!* (Shatrov); 1985, 1989: *Uncle Vanya*; 1985: *Silver Wedding* (Masharin).

SELECTED BIBLIOGRAPHY: Ben'yash, R. "Oleg Yefremov." *Teatr* 6 (1967): 82–94; "MXAT—vchera, segodnya i zavtra." *Teatr* 4 (1988): 24–42; Smelyansky, Anatoly Mironovich. *Oleg Yefremov: teatral'ny portret*. Moscow: Soyuz teatral'nykh deyateley (STD) RSFSR, 1987.

Cheyanne Boyd

Z

PETER ZADEK [b. May 19, 1926, Berlin, Germany]. Although raised and educated in England with a theatre career already established (1933–58), returning Jewish emigré Peter Zadek soon became a major force in the postwar theatre of West Germany. Sustaining influences during his formative years included studying Shakespeare under Neville Coghill at Oxford University and directing at the Old Vic School. There, the work of Michel Saint-Denis* and of the visiting American director, Elia Kazan,* helped to shape Zadek's approach to his craft. *Salomé* (1947), Zadek's first professional production, demonstrated his lifelong interest in movement as the primary communicator of human contradictory behavior. Sources for that expression of movement in this production included Kurt Jooss, Martha Graham, and Rudolf Laban.

In 1958 Zadek began directing in Germany. Even though he soon had offers to direct in major theatres, Zadek chose to join the experimental ensemble of young theatre artists assembled by Intendant Kurt Hübner in Ulm. In this small city and later in Bremen, Hübner, Peter Palitsch, a former director from the Berlin Ensemble, and Zadek, along with stage designer Wilfried Minks, changed the course of German theatre history. With their experiments in dramaturgy, staging, acting, movement, and scenography, they sought to reform the deeply entrenched mode of theatre expression in vogue in Germany since the early 1930s. Each man approached the creation of a new theatre language very differently; however, it was Zadek, with Minks, who provided the definition of the first phase of the "Bremen style" (1962–67). Zadek directed plays in an aggressively anti-intellectual manner. Placed in Minks's cool, abstract spaces, Zadek evoked a chaotic atmosphere of vitality and spontaneity in which serious subjects were treated with irony or irreverence. Zadek's productions, then and now, provoke audiences to question their previous assumptions on subject matter and aesthetic form.

Zadek's major contributions to the contemporary West German theatre can be categorized into three major genres. Best known for his innovative work with Shakespeare, Zadek overturned German traditions of Shakespearean production. His production of *Measure for Measure* in Bremen (1967) explored the potential of movement as nonverbal communication set against the language of the text. Then in the 1970s Zadek took a small group of actors away from the premir es and pressures of German public theatre to spend four to five months at a time rehearsing *King Lear* (1974), *Othello* (1976), and *Hamlet* (1977). These productions grew out of group study, improvisation, and rehearsal of the text. The company developed a direct, naive, even vulgar theatre which focused on the actor finding extremes of character expression and relationships between characters. The actors chose "theatrical" costumes and props from theatre storage areas. The resulting anarchistic ahistorical performances placed in nontraditional and relatively bare theatre spaces triggered a rich field of associations from contemporary memory. The productions were heralded as revolutionary in terms of content and form.

The musical/revue genre which disappeared following the emigration or extermination of independent producers in the Nazi era has been reintroduced in the public theatres by Zadek. In 1972, Zadek first transformed Hans Fallada's novel, *Kleiner Mann, was tun?* (*Little Man, What Now?*) into revue material. Since then Zadek has used other serious twentieth-century novels of a political or social nature for musical/revue material.

Throughout his career, Zadek has directed subtle, detailed studies of the dramas of Henrik Ibsen and Anton Chekhov. Divorced from social history, the productions focus on the characters. Each of these productions has been acclaimed for its enlightening perceptions on human behavior.

Twice in his carer Zadek has held the position of Intendant, or head of a theatre—Bochum (1972–77) and Deutsches Schauspielhaus/Hamburg (1985–89). Whether on the staff of a theatre, or as a free-lance artist, Zadek has remained a major director on the German theatre scene for over three decades.

ADDITIONAL PRODUCTIONS: 1957: *The Balcony*, London; 1962: *The Hostage*, Bremen; 1964: *Held Henry* (*The Chronicle History of King Henry the Fifth*, Shakespeare), *The Quare Fellow*; 1965: *Frühlings Erwachen* (*Spring's Awakening*), (Wedekind); 1966: *Die Räuber* (Schiller); 1972: *The Merchant of Venice*, Bochum; 1973: *The Sea Gull*, Bochum; 1975: *The Wild Duck*, Deutsches Schauspielhaus/Hamburg; 1977: *Hedda Gabler*, Bochum; 1978: *The Winter's Tale*, Deutsches Schauspielhaus; 1983: *The Master Builder*, Munich; 1984: *Ghetto* (Sobol), Freie Volksbühne/Berlin; 1988: *Lulu* (the first version), Deutsches Schauspielhaus; 1990: *Ivanov*, Burgtheater/Vienna.

SELECTED BIBLIOGRAPHY: Berry, Ralph, and Christian Jauslin. *Shakespeare inszenieren: Gesprächte mit Regisseuren*. Basel: Ulrike Jaulsin Verlag, 1978: 109–24; Canaris, Volker. *Peter Zadek: Der Theatermann und Filmemacher*. Munich: Carl Hanser Verlag, 1979; Höfele, Andreas. "The Erotic in the Theater of Peter Zadek." *New Theatre*

Quarterly 7.27 (1991): 229–37; Kässens, Wend, and Jörg W. Gronius. "Peter Zadek." In *TheaterMacher*. Frankfurt am Main: Athenäum Verlag, 1987: 175–97; Lange, Mechthild. *Peter Zadek*. Frankfurt am Main: Fischer Taschenbuch Verlag, 1989; Riddell, Richard V. "Wilfried Minks and the 'Bremer Stil': Study of a Contemporary German Stage Designer." Diss. Stanford U, 1978: Scheidler, Gisela. *Hamlet in Hamme*. Frankfurt am Main: Suhrkamp Verlag, 1977; Scheidler, Gisela. *Das Wintermärchen*. Bremen: J. H. Schmalfeldt Verlag, 1978; Sucher, C. Bernd. *Theaterzauberer 2—Von Vondy bis Zadek: 10 Regisseure des deutschen Gegenwartstjheaters*. München: Piper Verlag, 1990. Zadek, Peter. *Das Wilde Ufer: Ein Theaterbuch*. Ed. Laszlo Kornitzer. Cologne: Kiepenheuer and Witsch Verlag, 1990; Zadek, Peter. "Hoping for the Unexpected: The Theater of Peter Zadek," interviewed by Roy Kift. *New Theatre Quarterly* 1 (November 1985): 323–37.

Marna King

BORIS YEVGEN'YEVICH ZAKHAVA (b. May 24, 1896, Moscow; d. November 25, 1976, Moscow). Zakhava began his acting career when he was just eighteen, appearing in the first production of the Vakhtangov Studio, *The Lanin Estate* (Zaitsev) in 1914. He later performed major roles in such Vakhtangov productions as *The Miracle of St. Anthony* (1918) and *Princess Turandot* (1922). For two seasons, from 1923 to 1925, he had the unique distinction of performing at both the Vakhtangov Theatre and the Meyerhold Theatre, appearing in Meyerhold's productions of *The Forest*, *D.E.*, and *Teacher Bubus*. He took extensive notes on his experience acting with Evgeni Vakhtangov* and Vsevolod Meyerhold* and later published studies of the two directors (see below).

Zakhava's own directing career began in 1923, with the Vakhtangov Theatre's production of Alexander Ostrovsky's *Truth Is Good but Happiness Is Better*. Thereafter, he was one of a staff of directors (including Aleksey Popov* and Ruben Simonov*) who shared the stage of the Vakhtangov. His most famous productions were stagings of two plays by Maxim Gorky: *Yegor Bulychov and Others* (1932, revived 1951) and *Dostigayev and Others* (1933). *Yegor Bulychov*, with Boris Shchukin in the title role and Zakhava himself in the supporting role of Dostigayev, was especially popular with both audiences and critics. In the production, Zakhava achieved a unique synthesis of the realist and anti-realist trends in Soviet theatre of the 1920s. While the acting style was consistent with Stanislavskian psychological realism, the set was a cross section of a house which allowed various scenes to be presented simultaneously, and the action was interrupted from time to time by political declarations which actors delivered to the audience from the forestage.

In many respects, Zakhava's career peaked in the mid–1930s. Despite his respect for Vakhtangov and Meyerhold, his own work was increasingly confined by the narrow interpretation of realism under Stalin. While Zakhava often succeeded in injecting a degree of taste and humanity into propaganda dramas such as Nikolai Pogodin's *Aristocrats* (1935), his later productions adhered to a conventional, realistic presentational form.

After 1935, Zakhava directed only rarely, devoting most of his time to teaching acting and directing at the Vakhtangov Theatre School (later, the Shchukin Theatre Institute) and GITIS (the State Institute of Theatre Arts).

ADDITIONAL PRODUCTIONS: 1939: *Inspector General* (Gogol); 1945: *The Great Sovereign* (Solov'yëv); 1947: *The Young Guard* (Fadeyev).

SELECTED BIBLIOGRAPHY: Cinel'nikova, M. "Zakhava." *Teatr* 5 (1976): 35–39; Rudnitsky, Konstantin. *Russian and Soviet Theater, 1905–1932*. Trans. Roxane Permar. New York: Abrams, 1988; Zakhava, Boris. *Sovremenniki: Vakhtangov, Meyerkhol'd*. Moscow: Iskusstvo, 1969; Zakhava, Boris. *Vakhtangov i yego studiya*. Moscow: Teakinopechat', 1930.

Cheyanne Boyd

JERRY ZAKS [b. September 7, 1946, Stuttgart, Germany]. A string of hit productions, an Obie Award, and four Tony Awards for Best Director have confirmed Jerry Zaks's position as one of the most successful directors in New York during the 1980s and 1990s. Zaks specializes in twentieth-century American comedy, notably the work of Christopher Durang and John Guare, and musical comedy. Zaks won Tony Awards for his direction of two Guare plays: the 1986 revival of *The House of Blue Leaves* and *Six Degrees of Separation* in 1990. His production of *Anything Goes* (1987) and *Guys and Dolls* (1992) both received Tonys for Best Revival, and he received another Tony for his direction of *Guys and Dolls*.

Zaks was born in Germany, the son of Holocaust survivors. The family moved to the United States in 1948, eventually settling in Paterson, New Jersey, where Zaks grew up. He entered Dartmouth College in 1963 as a premed student but quickly switched to theatre after witnessing a Dartmouth Players production of *Wonderful Town* during his sophomore year. He began acting almost immediately and spent the first decade of his theatrical career as an actor, appearing in the Broadway productions of *Grease, Tintypes*, and *The 1940's Radio Hour*, among others, and Off-Broadway and regionally in such shows as *Isn't It Romantic?, Talley's Folly*, and *Fiddler on the Roof* with Zero Mostel.

Zaks dates his transformation from actor to director to Christopher Durang's decision to let him direct *Sister Mary Ignatius Explains It All for You*, a script he found in a pile of submissions at Ensemble Studio Theatre in 1979. The show was presented at Playwrights Horizons in 1982 along with a companion piece, *The Actor's Nightmare*.

From the start, Zaks's directorial style showed a close rapport with actors, a commitment to the playwright's vision as expressed through dialogue and action, and the importance of building an ensemble. Over the years, many actors in his productions, such as Stockard Channing, Swoosie Kurtz, Patti LuPone, and John Mahoney, have been cited for outstanding acting, but their performances are never star turns. Particularly in directing comedy, Zaks concentrates on the emotional truth of the situation and the connections between characters. The characters must be grounded in reality and focused on their own desperate needs and the way these needs affect the characters around them. He feels that no matter how outrageous the situation, the show will work if the audience cares about the characters and feels that their needs are real. There is no need to play for the humor; in a real situation with real characters, the comedy, he believes, will take care of itself.

Along with this basic philosophy, Zaks is heralded for his attention to detail. Admittedly a nitpicker, Zaks will work a piece of business or moment for weeks until it's right. Consequently, he casts only malleable, committed actors who are willing to try anything. In addition, he insists on closed rehearsals, initially even to the playwrights, in order to create an unthreatening atmosphere for experimentation and discovery.

Zaks was director in residence at the Lincoln Center Theatre from 1985 until 1990 when he left to accept a position with Jujamcyn Theatres as a developer of plays and musicals for the company's five Broadway theatres.

ADDITIONAL PRODUCTIONS: 1982: *Gemini* and *The Contest*, Philadelphia Drama Guild, Philadelphia, Pennsylvania; 1983: *Baby with the Bathwater*, Playwrights Horizons; 1984: *The Foreigner*, Astor Place Theatre; 1985: *The Marriage of Bette and Boo*, New York Shakespeare Festival, Public Theatre (1985 Obie Award as Best Director for both); 1988: *Wenceslas Square*, Public Theatre; 1989: *Lend Me a Tenor* (Tony Award, Best Director); 1991: *Assassins* (Stephen Sondheim/John Weidman musical), Playwrights Horizons.

SELECTED BIBLIOGRAPHY: Hubbard, Linda S., and Owen O'Donnell, eds. *Contemporary Theatre, Film, and Television*. Vol. 6. Detroit: Gale, 1989; Primus, Francesca. "Directors on Comedy: A Serious Business, Part One, Jerry Zaks and John Tillinger." *Back Stage* 20 June 1986; Wetzsteon, Ross. "Zaks Appeal." *New York* 28 May 1990.

Martha Schmoyer LoMonaco

YURI ALEKSANDROVICH ZAVADSKY (b. July 12, 1894, Moscow; d. April 5, 1977, Moscow). Zavadsky joined the Vakhtangov Studio in Moscow in 1915 as a scenic designer, but in 1916 Evgeni Vakhtangov* cast him in the title role in *The Miracle of St. Anthony*. Thereafter, Zavadsky performed in several of Vakhtangov's productions, including the legendary *Princess Turandot*. In 1924, following Vakhtangov's death, he joined the Moscow Art Theatre (MAT), where he remained until 1931, performing such leading roles as Chatsky in *Woe from Wit* and the Count in *The Marriage of Figaro*. He also took copious notes on the teaching and rehearsal methods of Konstantin Stanislavsky,* which were later published.

Also in 1924, Zavadsky formed his own acting studio. He continued to perform for the MAT, but he and other Vakhtangov protégés carried on their own staging experiments at his studio. From 1932 to 1935, he was artistic director of the Red Army Theatre. In 1936, the Zavadsky Studio was invited to become the Gorky Theatre of Rostov-on-Don. Zavadsky directed this new theatre until 1940, when he returned to Moscow to head the Mossovet Theatre, a position he held until shortly before his death. In 1940 he also joined the faculty of GITIS (the State Institute of Theatre Arts), where he was an influential teacher to two generations of Soviet actors, and numbered Jerzy Grotowski* among his foreign pupils.

Throughout his career, Zavadsky sought to integrate the teachings of his early mentors, Vakhtangov and Stanislavsky. As an acting teacher, he stressed the importance of combining psychological truth with virtuoso theatrical technique, insisting that his students master a broad range of styles, from classical tragedy to slapstick comedy. As a director, his tastes were conservative. In the 1920s and 1930s, he avoided both the avant-garde and socialist realism, building his reputation primarily on the classics. Subsequently, like most Soviet directors, he incorporated a number of Stalinist epics into his repertoire. His speciality, however, continued to be classic dramas enlivened by a lyrical, playful theatricalism reminiscent of Vakhtangov. Zavadsky sometimes designed his early productions, and his design experience was evident throughout his career in the emphasis he placed on striking visual compositions.

ADDITIONAL PRODUCTIONS: 1932: *Volpone*; 1933: *The Devil's Disciple*; 1934: *Wolves and Sheep* (Ostrovsky); 1935: *School for Debtors* (Verneuil); 1938: *Taming of the Shrew*; 1940: *Mistress of the Inn* (Goldoni); 1946: *Brandenburg Gate* (Svetlov); 1957: *Merry Wives of Windsor*; 1960: *The Cherry Orchard* and *The Wood Demon* (Chekhov); 1963: *Masquerade* (Lermontov); 1967: *The Storm* (Bill-Belotserkovsky); 1969: *Dreams of St. Petersburg* (adaptation of *Crime and Punishment*).

SELECTED BIBLIOGRAPHY: Lyubomudrov, M. *N. Simonov/Yu. Zavadsky*. Moscow: Molodaya gvardiya, 1988; Rudnitsky, Konstantin. *Russian and Soviet Theater, 1905–1932*. Trans. Roxane Permar. New York: Abrams, 1988; Slonim, Marc. *Russian Theatre from the Empire to the Soviets*. New York: Collier, 1962; Zavadsky, Yuri. *Rezhisserskiye ekzempliyary K. S. Stanislavskogo, 1898–1930*. 2 vols. Moscow: Iskusstvo, 1980.

Cheyanne Boyd

FRANCO ZEFFIRELLI [b. February 12, 1923, Florence, Italy]. Franco Zeffirelli, Italian director and producer, began as the student of Luchino Visconti.* His first interest was theatre, but he also directed opera and film. More recently, he has combined film and opera, first staging an opera, and then directing a film version of the same opera.

Zeffirelli began his theatre career as an actor, but quickly changed to directing and became internationally famous as an opera director. His first major assignment was at La Scala in Milan in 1953, directing Rossini's *La Cenerentola*, which was a major success and provided international publicity for Zeffirelli. He directed Donizetti's *Lucia di Lammermoor* at Covent Garden in 1959, his first major assignment outside Italy. That production also introduced Joan Sutherland in the title role and made both Sutherland and Zeffirelli international stars.

The same year, he also staged *Cavalleria Rusticana* and *I Pagliacci* for the Royal Opera at Covent Garden, followed by *Falstaff* in 1961 and the famous *Tosca* in 1964 with Maria Callas as the fiery heroine and Tito Gobbi as Scarpia. In 1961, he directed *L'Elisir D'Amore* for Glyndebourne. His first major production in America was a successful *La Traviata* (with Callas) for the Dallas

Opera, followed in 1960 by Handel's *Alcina* for the Dallas Opera with Joan Sutherland in the title role.

Following his success in Dallas, Zeffirelli moved in 1963 to the Metropolitan Opera in New York, producing a series of controversial, but generally popular, operatic productions including a beautiful production of Verdi's *Falstaff*. In 1966, his production of Samuel Barber's *Anthony and Cleopatra* opened the Met's new house at Lincoln Center. His *Otello* (for the Met) appeared in 1972, followed by *La Boheme* (1985), *Tosca* (1988), and *La Traviata* (1990). Zeffirelli not only directed these productions, but also designed both sets and costumes.

Franco Zeffirelli's directing has become synonymous with mammoth productions featuring a realistic but spectacular approach. Though generally popular with audiences, his productions have also caused some critics to express reservations about the very size of his operatic productions. Nevertheless, Zeffirelli clearly feels that theatrical performance must be an event which combines realism, spectacle, and excitement for the audience. His use of color and choral directing remain especially impressive for their dramatic excitement, while his directing of the principals has improved the general quality of operatic acting.

ADDITIONAL PRODUCTIONS: 1953: *L'Italiana in Algeri* (La Scala); 1954: *La Cenerentola* (La Scala); 1955: *Il Turco in Italia* (La Scala); 1958: *La Traviata* (with Callas); 1959: *Tosca* (with Callas); 1960: *Romeo and Juliet* (Old Vic); 1965: *La Lupa*; 1975: *Tosca*; 1976: *Otello* (La Scala); 1990: *La Traviata* (Metropolitan Opera). **Films:** 1967: *Romeo and Juliet*; 1968: *Taming of the Shrew*; 1971: *Brother Sun, Sister Moon*; 1976: *Jesus of Nazareth*; 1979: *The Champ*; 1981: *Endless Love*; 1982: *La Traviata*; 1985: *Otello*.

SELECTED BIBLIOGRAPHY: DiGaetani, John. "Zeffirelli." *An Invitation to the Opera*. New York: Doubleday, 1991; Sheren, Paul. "Franco Zeffirelli." *The New Grove Dictionary of Music and Musicians*. Ed. Stanley Sadie. London: Macmillan, 1980; Zeffirelli, Franco. *The Autobiography of Franco Zeffirelli*. New York: Weidenfeld and Nicolson, 1986; Zeffirelli, Franco. *Franco Zeffirelli's Jesus: A Spiritual Diary*. San Francisco: Harper and Row, 1984.

John Louis DiGaetani

Appendix A
Chronological List of Directors

Director	Country of Birth	Born	Died
Georg II, Duke of Saxe-Meiningen	Germany	1826	1914
Henry Irving	England	1838	1905
Augustin Daly	United States	1838	1899
Steele MacKaye	United States	1842	1894
William Edvard Bloch	Denmark	1845	1926
William Poel	England	1852	1934
Eugene Presbrey	United States	1853	1931
David Belasco	United States	1853	1931
Julian Mitchell	United States	1854	1926
Ben Teal	United States	1855	1917
Otto Brahm	Germany	1856	1912
André Antoine	France	1857	1943
Eleonora Duse	Italy	1858	1924
Vladimir Nemirovich-Danchenko	Russia	1858	1943
Bjørn Bjørnson	Norway	1859	1942
Konstantin Stanislavsky	Russia	1863	1938
Clyde Fitch	United States	1865	1909
Luigi Pirandello	Italy	1867	1936
Johanne Dybwad	Norway	1867	1950

Director	Country of Birth	Born	Died
Jaroslav Kvapil	Bohemia	1868	1950
Boris Thomashefsky	Ukraine	c.1868	1939
Firmin Gémier	France	1869/70	1933
Aurélien-François Lugné-Poe	France	1869	1940
Richard H. Burnside	Scotland	1870	1952
Winthrop Ames	United States	1871	1937
William George Fay	Ireland	1872	1947
Betty Nansen	Denmark	1873	1943
Max Reinhardt	Austria	1873	1943
Vsevolod Meyerhold	Russia	1874	1940
Ned Wayburn	United States	1874	1942
Nigel R. Playfair	England	1874	1934
Filippo Tommaso Marinetti	Egypt	1876	1944
Harley Granville Barker	England	1877	1946
Leopold Jessner	Germany	1878	1945
George M. Cohan	United States	1878	1942
Arthur Hopkins	United States	1878	1950
Jacques Copeau	France	1879	1949
Nikolai Evreinov	Russia	1879	1953
Philip Moeller	United States	1880	1958
Maurice Browne	England	1881	1955
Evgeni Vakhtangov	Russia	1883	1922
Georges Pitoëff	Russia	1884	1939
Charles Dullin	France	1885	1949
Gaston Baty	France	1885	1952
Samuel Hume	United States	1885	1962
Juliusz Osterwa	Poland	1885	1947
Alexsandr Tairov	Ukraine	1885	1950
Karel Hugo Hilar (Bakule)	Bohemia	1885	1935
Brock Pemberton	United States	1885	1950
Leon Schiller	Poland	1887	1954
Les Kurbas	Ukraine	1887	1942
Louis Jouvet	France	1887	1951
Raffaele Viviani	Italy	1888	1950
Oskar Schlemmer	Germany	1888	1943
Richard Boleslavsky	Poland	1889	1937

Director	Country of Birth	Born	Died
Aleksey Diky	Ukraine	1889	1955
George Abbott	United States	1889	
Barry Jackson	England	1889	1961
Anton Giulio Bragaglia	Italy	1890	1960
Maurice Schwartz	Ukraine	1890	1960
Aleksei Granovsky	Russia	1890	1937
Michael Chekhov	Russia	1891	1955
Aleksey Popov	Russia	1892	1961
Nikolai Foregger	Russia	1892	1939
Sergei Radlov	Russia	1892	1958
Olof Molander	Finland	1892	1966
Guthrie McClintic	United States	1893	1961
Erwin Friedrich Piscator	Germany	1893	1966
Jindřich Honzl	Bohemia	1894	1953
Yuri Zavadsky	Russia	1894	1977
Jürgen Fehling	Germany	1895	1968
László Moholy-Nagy	Hungary	1895	1946
Boris Zakhava	Russia	1896	1976
Michel Saint-Denis	France	1897	1971
Hans Jacob Nilsen	Norway	1897	1957
Sergei Eisenstein	Russia	1898	1948
Bertolt Brecht	Germany	1898	1956
Eva Le Gallienne	England	1899	1991
Ruben Simonov	Russia	1899	1968
Jed Harris	Austria	1900	1979
Nikolai Okhlopkov	Russia	1900	1967
Eduardo De Filippo	Italy	1900	1984
Tyrone Guthrie	England	1900	1971
Nikolai Akimov	Russia	1901	1968
Harold Clurman	United States	1901	1980
Lee Strasberg	Austria	1901	1982
John Houseman	Romania	1902	1988
Alf Sjöberg	Sweden	1903	1980
Natalia Sats	Russia	1903	
Jiří Frejka	Bohemia	1904	1952
John Gielgud	England	1904	

Director	Country of Birth	Born	Died
Emil František Burian	Bohemia	1904	1959
Jean Dasté	France	1904	
Margaret Webster	United States	1905	1972
Émile Legault	Canada	1906	1983
Laurette Larocque-Auger	Canada	1906	1965
Luchino Visconti	Italy	1906	1976
Roger Blin	France	1907	1984
Alfred Emmet	England	1908	
Joshua Logan	United States	1908	1988
André Barsacq	Crimea	1909	1973
Robert Lewis	United States	1909	
Elia Kazan	Turkey	1909	
Jacques Huisman	Belgium	1910	
Jean-Louis Barrault	France	1910	1994
George Devine	England	1910	1966
Orazio [Giovangigli] Costa	Italy	1911	
Margo Jones	United States	1911	1955
Jean Vilar	France	1912	1971
Lárus Pálsson	Iceland	1914	1968
George Tabori	Hungary	1914	
Joan Littlewood	England	1914	
Nina Vance	United States	1914	1980
Owen Dodson	United States	1914	1983
Alfred Radok	Bohemia	1914	1976
Jean-Marie Serreau	France	1915	1973
Tadeusz Kantor	Poland	1915	1990
Orson Welles	United States	1915	1985
Georgy Tovstonogov	Russia	1915	1989
Erwin Axer	Austria	1917	
Claude Etienne	Brussels	1917	1992
Yuri Lyubimov	Russia	1917	
Alan Schneider	Russia	1917	1984
Ingmar Bergman	Sweden	1918	
Jerome Robbins	United States	1918	
Gower Champion	United States	1919	1980
Michael Langham	England	1919	
Paolo Grassi	Italy	1919	1981

Director	Country of Birth	Born	Died
Jean Gascon	Canada	1920	1988
Giuseppe Patroni-Griffi	Italy	1921	
Giorgio Strehler	Italy	1921	
Gene Saks	United States	1921	
Otomar Krejča	Czechoslovakia	1921	
Luigi Squarzina	Italy	1922	
Vinnette Carroll	United States	1922	
Vittorio Gassman	Italy	1922	
Arthur Penn	United States	1922	
Józef Szajna	Poland?	1922	
Lloyd Richards	Canada	c.1922	
Franco Zeffirelli	Italy	1923	
Pierre Dagenais	Canada	1923	1990
Liviu Ciulei	Romania	1923	
Kazimierz Dejmek	Poland	1924	
Zelda Fichandler	United States	1924	
José Quintero	Panama	1924	
Jan Grossman	Czechoslovakia	1925	
Peter Brook	England	1925	
Julian Beck	United States	1925	1985
Anatoly Efros	Russia	1925	1987
John Dexter	England	1925	1990
Stuart Vaughan	United States	1925	
Albert Marre	United States	1925	
Rene Augusto Buch	Cuba	1925	
Andrzej Wajda	Poland	1926	
Dario Fo	Italy	1926	
Peter Zadek	Germany	1926	
Judith Malina	Germany	1926	
George Luscombe	Canada	1926	
Paul Buissonneau	France	1926	
Clifford Williams	Wales	1926	
Bob Fosse	United States	1927	1987
Oleg Yefremov	Russia	1927	
James Roose-Evans	England	1927	
Paul Sills	United States	1927	
Harold Prince	United States	1928	

Director	Country of Birth	Born	Died
John Barton	England	1928	
Adrian Hall	United States	1928	
Ulu Grosbard	Belgium	1929	
Heiner Müller	Germany	1929	
Ronald Eyre	England	1929	
Peter Coe	England	1929	1987
Jerzy Jarocki	Poland	1929	
Konrad Swinarski	Poland	1929	1975
Franca Rame	Italy	1929	
Wilford Leach	United States	1929	1988
Jean-Pierre Ronfard	France	1929	
Antoine Bourseiller	France	1930	
John Hirsch	Hungary	1930	1989
Douglas Turner Ward	United States	1930	
Maria Irene Fornes	Cuba	1930	
William Gaskill	England	1930	
Peter Hall	England	1930	
Antoine Vitez	France	1930	1990
Jorge Lavelli	Argentina	1931	
Augusto Boal	Brazil	1931	
William Ball	United States	1931	1991
Pierre Laroche	Belgium	1931	
Roger Planchon	France	1931	
Mike Nichols	Germany	1931	
Peter Cheeseman	England	1932	
Ralf Runar Långbacka	Finland	1932	
Lucian Pintilie	Moldavian SSR	1933	
Luca Ronconi	Tunisia	1933	
Gordon Davidson	United States	1933	
Jerzy Grotowski	Poland	1933	
André Gregory	France	1934	
David Hugh Jones	England	1934	
Peter Schumann	Germany	1934	
Jonathan Miller	England	1934	
Richard Schechner	United States	1934	
Sveinn Einarsson	Iceland	1934	
Miriam Colón	Puerto Rico	1935	

Director	Country of Birth	Born	Died
Bill Glassco	Canada	1935	
Harold R. Scott	United States	1935	
Joseph Chaikin	United States	1935	
Shuji Terayama	Japan	1935	1983
Bernard Sobel	France	1936	
Kazimierz Braun	Poland	1936	
Margarita Galban	Cuba	1936	
Eugenio Barba	Italy	1936	
Patrick Garland	England	1936	
Lee Breuer	United States	1937	
Richard Foreman	United States	1937	
Barbara Ann Teer	United States	1937	
Joanne Akalaitis	United States	1937	
Max Ferrá	Cuba	1937	
Woodie King, Jr.	United States	1937	
Carmelo Bene	Italy	1937	
Peter Stein	Germany	1937	
Marcel Louis-Noel Maréchal	France	1937	
Simone Benmussa	Tunisia	1938	
Michael Bogdanov	Great Britain	1938	
Tommy Tune	United States	1939	
Jerzy Grzegorzewski	Poland	1939	
Ariane Mnouchkine	France	1939	
Tadashi Suzuki	Japan	1939	
Memé Perlini	Italy	1940	
Paul Thompson	Canada	1940	
Leo de Berardinis	Italy	1940	
Trevor Nunn	England	1940	
Marshall W. Mason	United States	1940	
Claude E. Purdy	United States	1940	
Arvin Brown	United States	1940	
Luis Valdez	United States	1940	
Pina Bausch	Germany	1940	
Michael Kahn	United States	1940	
Viviane Théophilidès	France	1940	
Stein Winge	Norway	1940	
Tisa Chang	China	1941	

Director	Country of Birth	Born	Died
Jürgen Flimm	Germany	1941	
Robert Wilson	United States	1941	
Robin Phillips	England	1942	
Jouka Turkka	Finland	1942	
Jérôme Savary	Argentina	1942	
Jean-Pierre Vincent	France	1942	
Jorge Huerta	United States	1942	
Meredith Monk	United States	1942	
Richard Eyre	England	1943	
Michael Bennett	United States	1943	1987
Charles Ludlam	United States	1943	1987
Andrei Serban	Romania	1943	
Michael Gates	United States	1944	
Elizabeth Lecompte	United States	1944	
Martha Clarke	United States	1944	
Patrice Chéreau	France	1944	
Jürgen Gosch	Germany	1944	
Glenda Dickerson	United States	1945	
Thórhildur Thorleifsdóttir	Iceland	1945	
Howard Davies	England	c.1945	
Valery Fokin	Russia	1946	
Mark Lamos	United States	1946	
Garland Wright	United States	1946	
Henri Ronse	Belgium	1946	
Brigitte Jaques	Switzerland	1946	
André Brassard	Canada	1946	
Jerry Zaks	Germany	1946	
Lynne Meadow	United States	1946	
Ruben Sierra	United States	1946	
Jo (Georges) Lavaudant	France	1947	
Robert Woodruff	United States	1947	
Gildas Bourdet	France	1947	
Gilles Maheu	Canada	1948	
John Caird	Canada	1948	
Gregory Dean Mosher	United States	1949	
Adrian Noble	England	1950	
Benny Sato Ambush	United States	1951	

Director	Country of Birth	Born	Died
Lorraine Pintal	Canada	1951	
Anne Bogart	United States	1951	
Emily Mann	United States	1952	
Des McAnuff	United States	1952	
Jose Luis Valenzuela	Mexico	1953	
Declan Donnellan	England	1953	
Robert Falls	United States	1954	
Tony Curiel	United States	1954	
Bernard de Coster	Belgium	1954	1991
Richard Rose	Venezuela	1955	
Nicholas Hytner	United States	1956	
Peter Sellars	United States	1957	
Robert Lepage	Canada	1957	
Deborah Warner	England	1959	

Appendix B
Directors Listed by Country in Which Primary Work Was Done

Director	Born	Died
Argentina		
Sats, Natalia	1903	
Austria		
Fehling, Jürgen	1895	1968
Reinhardt, Max	1873	1943
Stein, Peter	1937	
Tabori, George	1914	
Belgium		
De Coster, Bernard	1954	1991
Etienne, Claude	1917	1992
Huisman, Jacques	1910	
Laroche, Pierre	1931	
Ronse, Henri	1946	
Brazil		
Boal, Augusto	1931	

Director	Born	Died
Bulgaria		
Tovstonogov, Georgy	1915	1989
Canada		
Brassard, André	1946	
Buissonneau, Paul	1926	
Dagenais, Pierre	1923	1990
Gascon, Jean	1920	1988
Glassco, Bill	1935	
Hirsch, John	1930	1989
Larocque-Auger, Laurette	1906	1965
Legault, Émile	1906	1983
Lepage, Robert	1957	
Luscombe, George	1926	
Maheu, Gilles	1948	
Phillips, Robin	1942	
Pintal, Lorraine	1951	
Ronfard, Jean-Pierre	1929	
Rose, Richard	1955	
Thompson, Paul	1940	
Czechoslovakia		
Burian, E. F.	1904	1959
Frejka, Jiří	1904	1952
Grossman, Jan	1925	
Hilar, Karel Hugo	1885	1935
Honzl, Jindřich	1894	1953
Krejča, Otomar	1921	
Kvapil, Jaroslav	1868	1950
Radok, Alfred	1914	1976
Denmark		
Bloch, William	1845	1926
Nansen, Betty	1873	1943
Finland		
Långbacka, Ralf	1932	
Tovstonogov, Georgy	1915	1989
Turkka, Jouka	1942	

Director	Born	Died
France		
Antoine, André	1857	1943
Barrault, Jean-Louis	1910	1994
Barsacq, André	1909	1973
Baty, Gaston	1885	1952
Benmussa, Simone	1938	
Blin, Roger	1907	1984
Bourdet, Gildas	1947	
Bourseiller, Antoine	1930	
Chéreau, Patrice	1944	
Copeau, Jacques	1879	1949
Dasté, Jean	1904	
Dullin, Charles	1885	1949
Gémier, Firmin	1869/70	1933
Jaques, Brigitte	1946	
Jouvet, Louis	1887	1951
Lavaudant, Georges	1947	
Lavelli, Jorge	1931	
Lugné-Poe, A.	1869	1940
Maréchal, Marcel	1937	
Mnouchkine, Ariane	1939	
Pitoëff, Georges	1884	1939
Planchon, Roger	1931	
Saint-Denis, Michel	1897	1971
Savary, Jérôme	1942	
Serreau, Jean-Marie	1915	1973
Sobel, Bernard	1936	
Théophilidès, Viviane	1940	
Vilar, Jean	1912	1971
Vincent, Jean-Pierre	1942	
Vitez, Antoine	1930	1990
Germany		
Bausch, Pina	1940	
Brahm, Otto	1856	1912
Brecht, Bertolt	1898	1956
Chekhov, Michael	1891	1955
Fehling, Jürgen	1895	1968

Director	Born	Died
Flimm, Jürgen	1941	
Gosch, Jürgen	1944	
Granovsky, Aleksei	1890	1937
Jessner, Leopold	1878	1945
Moholy-Nagy, László	1895	1946
Müller, Heiner	1929	
Piscator, Erwin	1893	1966
Reinhardt, Max	1873	1943
Sats, Natalia	1903	
Saxe-Meiningen [Georg II, Duke of]	1826	1914
Schlemmer, Oskar	1888	1943
Stein, Peter	1937	
Tabori, George	1914	
Tovstonogov, Georgy	1915	1989
Zadek, Peter	1926	

Great Britain

Barker, Harley Granville	1877	1946
Barton, John	1928	
Bogdanov, Michael	1938	
Brook, Peter	1925	
Caird, John	1948	
Cheeseman, Peter	1932	
Coe, Peter	1929	1987
Davies, Howard	ca.1945	
Devine, George	1910	1966
Dexter, John	1925	1990
Donnellan, Declan	1953	
Emmet, Alfred	1908	
Eyre, Richard	1943	
Eyre, Ronald	1929	
Garland, Patrick	1936	
Gaskill, William	1930	
Gielgud, John	1904	
Guthrie, Tyrone	1900	1971
Hall, Peter	1930	
Hytner, Nicholas	1956	

Director	*Born*	*Died*
Irving, Henry	1838	1905
Jackson, Barry	1889	1961
Jones, David	1934	
Littlewood, Joan	1914	
Miller, Jonathan	1943	
Noble, Adrian	1950	
Nunn, Trevor	1940	
Phillips, Robin	1942	
Playfair, Nigel	1874	1934
Poel, William	1852	1934
Roose-Evans, James	1927	
Warner, Deborah	1959	
Williams, Clifford	1926	
Zadek, Peter	1926	

Iceland

Einarsson, Sveinn	1934	
Pálsson, Lárus	1914	1968
Thorleifsdóttir, Thórhildur	1945	

Israel

Lyubimov, Yuri	1917	

Italy

Barba, Eugenio	1936	
Bene, Carmelo	1937	
Bragaglia, Anton Giulio	1890	1960
Costa, Orazio	1911	
De Berardinis, Leo	1940	
De Filippo, Eduardo	1900	1984
Duse, Eleonora	1858	1924
Fo, Dario	1926	
Gassman, Vittorio	1922	
Grassi, Paolo	1919	1981
Marinetti, Filippo Tommaso	1876	1944
Patroni-Griffi, Giuseppe	1921	
Perlini, Memé	1940	
Pirandello, Luigi	1867	1936

Director	Born	Died
Rame, Franca	1929	
Ronconi, Luca	1933	
Squarzina, Luigi	1922	
Strehler, Giorgio	1921	
Visconti, Luchino	1906	1976
Viviani, Raffaele	1888	1950
Zeffirelli, Franco	1923	

Japan

Suzuki, Tadashi	1939	
Terayama, Shuji	1935	1983

Norway

Bjørnson, Bjørn	1859	1942
Dybwad, Johanne	1867	1950
Nilsen, Hans Jacob	1897	1957
Winge, Stein	1940	

Poland

Axer, Erwin	1917	
Braun, Kazimierz	1936	
Dejmek, Kazimierz	1924	
Grotowski, Jerzy	1933	
Grzegorzewski, Jerzy	1939	
Jarocki, Jerzy	1929	
Kantor, Tadeusz	1915	1990
Osterwa, Juliusz	1885	1947
Schiller, Leon	1887	1954
Swinarski, Konrad	1929	1975
Szajna, Józef	1922	
Wajda, Andrzej	1926	

Romania

Ciulei, Liviu	1923	
Pintilie, Lucian	1933	
Serban, Andrei	1943	

Director	*Born*	*Died*
Russia		
Akimov, Nikolai	1901	1968
Chekhov, Michael	1891	1955
Diky, Aleksey	1899	1955
Efros, Anatoly	1925	1987
Eisenstein, Sergei	1898	1948
Evreinov, Nikolai	1897	1953
Fokin, Valery	1946	
Foregger, Nikolai	1892	1939
Granovsky, Aleksei	1890	1937
Kurbas, Les (Ukraine)	1887	1942
Lyubimov, Yuri	1917	
Meyerhold, Vsevolod	1874	1940
Nemirovich-Danchenko, Vladimir	1858	1943
Okhlopkov, Nikolai	1900	1967
Popov, Aleksey	1892	1961
Radlov, Sergei	1892	1958
Sats, Natalia	1903	
Simonov, Ruben	1899	1968
Stanislavsky, Konstantin	1863	1938
Tairov, Aleksandr	1885	1950
Tovstonogov, Georgy*	1915	1989
Vakhtangov, Evgeni	1883	1922
Yefremov, Oleg	1927	
Zakhava, Boris	1896	1976
Zavadsky, Yuri	1894	1977

(*Tovstonogov also directed productions in Poland, Bulgaria, Finland, Hungary, Germany, and the United States.)

Sweden		
Bergman, Ingmar	1918	
Molander, Olof	1892	1966
Sjöberg, Alf	1903	1980

United States		
Abbott, George	1889	
Akalaitis, Joanne	1937	
Ambush, Benny Sato	1951	

Director	Born	Died
Ames, Winthrop	1871	1937
Ball, William	1931	1991
Beck, Julian	1925	1985
Belasco, David	1853	1931
Bennett, Michael	1943	1987
Bogart, Anne	1951	
Boleslavsky, Richard	1889	1937
Breuer, Lee	1937	
Brown, Arvin	1940	
Browne, Maurice	1881	1955
Buch, Rene Augusto	1925	
Burnside, R. H.	1870	1952
Carroll, Vinnette	1922	
Chaikin, Joseph	1935	
Champion, Gower	1919	1980
Chang, Tisa	1940	
Chekhov, Michael	1891	1955
Ciulei, Liviu	1923	
Clarke, Martha	1944	
Clurman, Harold	1901	1980
Cohan, George M.	1878	1942
Colón, Miriam	1935	
Curiel, Tony	1954	
Daly, Augustin	1838	1899
Davidson, Gordon	1933	
Dickerson, Glenda	1945	
Dodson, Owen	1914	1983
Falls, Robert	1954	
Fay, W. G.	1872	1947
Ferrá, Max	1937	
Fichandler, Zelda	1924	
Fitch, Clyde	1865	1909
Foreman, Richard	1937	
Fornes, Maria Irene	1930	
Fosse, Bob	1927	1987
Galban, Margarita	1936	
Gates, [Thomas] Michael	1944	

Director	*Born*	*Died*
Gregory, André	1934	
Grosbard, Ulu	1929	
Guthrie, Tyrone	1900	1971
Hall, Adrian	1928	
Harris, Jed	1900	1979
Hirsch, John	1930	1989
Hopkins, Arthur	1878	1950
Houseman, John	1902	1988
Huerta, Jorge	1942	
Hume, Samuel	1885	1962
Jones, Margo	1911	1955
Kahn, Michael	1940	
Kazan, Elia	1909	
King, Woodie, Jr.	1937	
Lamos, Mark	1946	
Langham, Michael	1919	
Leach, Wilford	1929	1988
LeCompte, Elizabeth	1944	
Le Gallienne, Eva	1899	1991
Lewis, Robert	1909	
Logan, Joshua	1908	1988
Ludlam, Charles	1943	1987
MacKaye, Steele	1842	1894
Malina, Judith	1926	
Mann, Emily	1952	
Marre, Albert	1925	
Mason, Marshall	1940	
McAnuff, Des	1952	
McClintic, Guthrie	1893	1961
Meadow, Lynne	1946	
Mitchell, Julian	1854	1926
Moeller, Philip	1880	1958
Monk, Meredith	1942	
Mosher, Gregory	1949	
Nichols, Mike	1931	
Pemberton, Brock	1885	1950
Penn, Arthur	1922	

Director	Born	Died
Piscator, Erwin	1893	1966
Presbrey, Eugene	1853	1931
Prince, Harold	1928	
Purdy, Claude	1940	
Quintero, José	1924	
Richards, Lloyd	1922	
Robbins, Jerome	1918	
Saks, Gene	1921	
Schechner, Richard	1934	
Schneider, Alan	1917	1984
Schumann, Peter	1934	
Schwartz, Maurice	1890	1960
Scott, Harold	1935	
Sellars, Peter	1957	
Serban, Andrei	1943	
Sierra, Ruben	1946	
Sills, Paul	1927	
Strasberg, Lee	1901	1982
Suzuki, Tadashi	1939	
Teal, Ben	1855	1917
Teer, Barbara Ann	1937	
Thomashefsky, Boris	c.1868	1939
Tune, Tommy	1939	
Valdez, Luis	1940	
Valenzuela, Jose Luis	1953	
Vance, Nina	1914	1980
Vaughan, Stuart	1925	
Ward, Douglas Turner	1930	
Wayburn, Ned	1874	1942
Webster, Margaret	1905	1972
Welles, Orson	1915	1985
Wilson, Robert	1941	
Woodruff, Robert	1947	
Wright, Garland	1946	
Zaks, Jerry	1946	

Selected Bibliography

Ball, William. *A Sense of Direction: Some Observations on the Art of Directing*. New York: Drama Book Publishers, 1984.

Barton, John. *Playing Shakespeare*. London: Methuen, 1984.

Bartow, Arthur. *The Director's Voice: Twenty-one Interviews*. New York: Theatre Communications Group, 1988.

Benedetti, Robert. *The Director at Work*. Englewood Cliffs, NJ: Prentice-Hall, 1985.

Berry, Ralph. *On Directing Shakespeare: Interviews with Contemporary Directors*. New York: Barnes and Noble, 1977.

Bradby, David, and David Williams. *Director's Theatre*. New York: St. Martin's Press, 1988.

Braun, Edward. *The Director and the Stage: From Naturalism to Grotowski*. New York: Holmes and Meier, 1982.

Brustein, Robert. "The Limits of the Auteur." *New Republic* 27 June 1988: 26–27.

Carra, Lawrence. "The Influence of the Director (Directing: 1920–1969)." *The American Theatre: A Sum of Its Parts*. New York: Samuel French, 1971.

Chekhov, Michael. *To the Director and Playwright*. New York: Harper, 1962.

Chinoy, Helen Krich. "The Professional and the Art (Directing: 1860–1920)." *The American Theatre: A Sum of Its Parts*. New York: Samuel French, 1971.

Chinoy, Helen Krich, and Linda Walsh Jenkins, eds. *Women in American Theatre*. New York: Theatre Communications Group, 1987.

Clurman, Harold. *On Directing*. New York: Macmillan, 1972.

Cole, Susan Letzler. *Directors in Rehearsal: A Hidden World*. New York: Routledge, 1992.

Cole, Toby, and Helen Krich Chinoy, eds. *Directors on Directing: A Sourcebook of the Modern Theatre*. Indianapolis: Bobbs-Merrill Company, 1963.

Cook, Judith. *Director's Theatre*. London: Holden and Stoughton, 1989.

Dickinson, T. H. *The Theater in a Changing Europe*. New York: Henry Holt, 1937.

Gaskill, William. *A Sense of Direction*. London: Faber and Faber, 1981.

Houseman, John. "On Directing Shakespeare." *Theatre Arts* 33 (April 1951): 52–54.

Itzen, Catherine, ed. *Directory of Playwrights, Directors, Designers*. Eastbourne, England: John Offord, 1983.

Jones, David Richard. *Great Directors at Work: Stanislavsky, Brecht, Kazan, Brook*. Berkeley: University of California Press, 1986.

Jouvet, Louis. "The Profession of the Producer." *Theatre Arts Monthly* 20 (December 1936): 942–49.

———. "The Profession of the Producer." *Theatre Arts Monthly* 21 (January 1937): 57–64.

Kommisarjevsky, Theodore. "The Producer in the Theatre." *Drama* 13 (November 1934): 19–21.

———. "The Producer in the Theatre." *Drama* 13 (December 1934): 35–37.

Leiter, Samuel L. *From Belasco to Brook: Representative Directors of the English-Speaking Stage*. Westport, CT: Greenwood Press, 1991: 51–76.

———. *From Stanislavsky to Barrault: Representative Directors of the European Stage*. Westport, CT: Greenwood Press, 1991.

Pemberton, Brock. "The Director." *Our Theatre Today*. New York: Samuel French, 1936: 185–95.

———. "The Making of a Play-Producer." *Theatre Magazine* 49 (March 1929): 13 + .

The Drama Review 16 (June 1972). Directing Issue.

The Drama Review 25 (Fall 1981). Actor/Director Issue.

Webster, Margaret. "Credo of a Director." *Theatre Arts Monthly* 22 (May 1938): 343–48.

Wetzsteon, Ross. "The Director in Spite of Himself: An Interview with Jonathan Miller." *American Theatre* November 1985: 4–9, 40–41.

Whitton, David. *Stage Directors in Modern France*. Manchester, England: Manchester University Press, 1987.

Wills, J. Robert, ed. *The Director in a Changing Theatre: Essays on the Theory and Practice, with New Plays for Performance*, Paio Alto, CA: Mayfield Publishing Co., 1976.

Name Index

Note: Page numbers in **boldface** type refer to the main entry for each theatrical director.

Play, Film, and Television Title Index

About the Advisors
and Contributors

ADDELL AUSTIN ANDERSON is an Assistant Professor and Director of the Black Theatre Program at Wayne State University. President of the Black Theatre Network, she serves as the compiler and editor of the *Black Theatre Directory*. Her articles on Black Theatre have appeared in such publications as *Contemporary Dramatists*, *Masterplots II*, *Cyclopedia of Literary Characters*, *Theatre Journal*, *The Drama Review*, *The Chronicle of Higher Education*, and *CLA Journal*.

SETH BAUMRIN teaches acting and theatre at Queensborough Community College and at Hunter College. He has studied theatre at the City University of New York Graduate Center and also at the International School of Theatre Anthropology, Holstebro, Denmark, which is directed by Eugenio Barba. He has worked extensively as a director in New York and has had a number of his own plays produced in the New York City area.

JANA O'KEEFE BAZZONI is Assistant Professor of Speech at Baruch College of the City University of New York. She has published articles on Pirandello, Dario Fo, Luca Ronconi, and other artists in *Modern Drama*, *Western European Stages*, *Review of National Literatures*, *Theatre Three*, *Performing Arts Journal*, *Ridotto*, and *Sipario*.

HÉLÈNE BEAUCHAMP has contributed numerous articles to books and journals in Canada, France, Belgium, Morocco, and the United States. She has published *Les Enfants et le jeu dramatique* (Brussels, 1984), *Le Théâtre pour enfants au*

Québec: 1950–1980 (Montréal, 1985), *Théâtre et Adolescence* (UQAM, 1988), *Travail théâtral en cours* (Montréal, 1992) and *Le Théâtral dans L'école* (Montréal, 1992), and is currently on the editorial boards of *l'Annuaire Théâtral* (Montreal) and *Recherches théâtrales au Canada/Theatre Research in Canada* (Toronto). She teaches in the Theatre Department of Université du Québec à Montréal.

GUY BEAULNE is a lecturer, drama critic, actor, director, and teacher. He has directed for the stage and produced radio and television in Canada. He is also former Director General of Le Grand Théâtre (Quebec) and le Conservatoire d'art dramatique de Montréal.

JOEL BERKOWITZ is finishing his dissertation on "Shakespeare on the American Yiddish Stage" in the Ph.D. Program in Theatre at the City University of New York.

GEORGE BLACK is Professor of Drama and Head of the Directing Program at the University of Virginia. A member of the Society of Stage Directors and Choreographers, he has acted and directed professionally in New York, Washington, and in regional theatres and is currently the Artistic Director of The Heritage Repertory Theatre. He is the author of articles on acting and directing and a directing text, *Contemporary Stage Directing*.

CHEYANNE BOYD received a Ph.D. in Theatre and Drama from the University of Wisconsin–Madison in 1991. Her dissertation dealt with environmental stagings at Moscow theatres between 1928 and 1934. Previously, she received an M.F.A. from Trinity University's Dallas Theatre Center Program. She has worked as an actress in regional theatre and as an arts administrator for regional and national organizations and has taught English and Drama at several colleges. She has held fellowships from the International Research and Exchange Board (IREX) and the Department of Education. Her articles and reviews have been published in *Slavic and East European Journal*, *Theatre Survey*, *Theatre Studies*, and *Theatre Insight*. She teaches at Trenton State College.

KAZIMIERZ BRAUN, a leading director in Poland during the 1960s, 1970s, and 1980s, is the author of eleven plays and nine scholarly books including *The Great Reform of the Theatre*, *The Second Reform of the Theatre*, and *Cyprian Norwid's Theatre Without Theatre*. He emigrated from his native Poland to the United States in 1985 and he is currently on the faculty of the Department of Theatre and Dance at the University of Buffalo, SUNY. A 1991 Guggenheim Grant enabled Professor Braun to return to Poland to conduct research.

SUZANNE BURGOYNE is Associate Professor of Theatre at the University of Missouri–Columbia and is a former Visiting Professor of Directing at the Belgian

National Theatre Institute. She has had articles published in *Theatre Journal*, *Theatre Topics*, *The Kenyon Review*, *The Bloomsbury Review*, *Studies in American Drama, 1945–Present*, *Twentieth-Century American Dramatists*, *American Playwrights Since 1945*, and is the editor and translator of two plays in the forthcoming *Dreams and Reflections: Plays of Paul Willems*. Professor Burgoyne is a former recipient of a Fulbright Fellowship to Belgium and of a Kellogg National Fellowship.

JARKA M. BURIAN is Professor of Theatre at the University of Albany, SUNY. He has published books and articles dealing primarily with Czechoslovak theatre and international scenography.

SHIRLEY VENDRASCO BURKE is a doctoral student in the Ph.D. Program in Theatre at the City University of New York Graduate Center. Her area of specialization is modern Italian drama with a particular emphasis upon the work of Ugo Betti. She has taught theatre at Hunter College and is an actress and director.

MARVIN CARLSON is Sidney E. Cohn Distinguished Professor of Theatre and Comparative Literature and Chair of the Theatre Program at the Graduate Center, City University of New York. He is the author of numerous articles and books on the theatre, including *Theories of the Theatre*, *Places of Performance*, *Signs of Life: Semiotics of the Theatre*, and *The Play's the Thing: An Introduction to Theatre* (with Yvonne Shafer).

DAVID CARLYON is a Ph.D. candidate at Northwestern University where he is conducting research on "Dan Rice and Middle Class Formation: The 19th Century Circus Clown as Aspiring Gentleman." A former professional actor with membership in AEA, SAG, AFTRA, and AGVA and a former clown with Ringling Brothers and Barnum & Bailey Circus, Mr. Carlyon has taught at University College of Northwestern University, at Act One School of Performance, and at the Virginia Shakespeare Festival. He has given clowning workshops and seminars at numerous colleges and universities including Brown University, Temple University, University of Illinois, Boston University, and the University of North Carolina.

JAMES CARMODY is an Assistant Professor in the Department of Theatre at the University of California in San Diego, where he leads the MFA Program in Dramaturgy. He has recently completed a study entitled *Rereading Molière: Mise en scène from Antoine to Vitez*, and is currently working on a project exploring the intersections of photography and the theatre.

ROBERT CHAPEL is Professor of Drama and Chair of the Department of Drama at the University of Virginia. A professional director, he has acted and directed in New York, Los Angeles, and in regional theatres throughout the country, has served as Artistic Director of Music Theatre North in Potsdam, New York, and has served on the faculties of New York University, the University of Michigan, California Institute of the Arts, the University of Alabama, and San Diego State University. In addition to his positions at UVA, he is also Managing Director of the Heritage Repertory Theatre. Professor Chapel has recently finished a book, *The Arena Stage, 1951–1991: Productions and Personnel in Profile*, which will be published by Greenwood Press in 1993.

DEBRA BRINEGAR CHARLTON is a Ph.D. candidate in Theatre History/ Criticism with a specialization in Shakespearean Drama at the University of Texas–Austin. She has published in *Theatre Insight* and is a former member of the Alley Theatre Young Company.

DAN M. CHURCH is Associate Professor of French at Vanderbilt University. He has published studies of the theatre of Camus, Gide, and Jarry and of the popular theatre movement in France and elsewhere in *Drama Survey*, *The French Review*, and *PMLA*. He spent a sabbatical working with the Théâtre de la Commune d'Aubervillers in the working-class suburbs of Paris and has directed numerous French-language plays.

JAN COHEN-CRUZ, Assistant Professor of Drama at New York University, has taught and directed in prisons, schools, psychiatric facilities, migrant camps, and parks. She has performed at the Edinburgh Festival Fringe, New York's Playwrights' Horizons, the National Theatre of Israel, and with the New York Street Theatre. She co-produced Augusto Boal's workshops in New York and in Rio in 1989–91 and co-directed (1982–91) the Experimental Theatre Project, which created and/or presented experimental and activist performances in rural and urban settings. She is co-editor with Mady Schutzman of the forthcoming *Playing Boal: Theatre, Therapy, Activism* and has been published in *The Drama Review*, *Women and Performance*, and *Urban Resources*.

BARBARA COHEN-STRATYNER, Ph.D., currently serving as Curator of Exhibitions for the New York Public Library for the Performing Arts, has developed over a dozen major exhibitions on theatre, film, music, and urban history. She is a member of the faculty of the City University of New York graduate program in Dance and of the Parsons School of Design. She is the Editor of *Performing Arts Resources*.

MILES COINER is Associate Professor of Performing Arts at Emerson College. In 1968–69, Professor Coiner was a Fulbright Scholar at the Institute of Theatre and Cinematography, Bucharest, Romania. His publications appear in *Modern Drama*, *The Antioch Review*, and *Literature/Film Quarterly*.

CANDICE M. COLEMAN is Chair of the Department of Theatre and Dance at Principia College in Elsah, Illinois. She has presented papers at various conferences including the Association for Theatre in Higher Education and the Speech Communication Association. Coleman has also worked as an archival assistant for the Shubert Archive and was on the editorial staff of *The Passing Show*.

ROBERT CONNOLLY is the former curator of the Paterno Library of the Casa Italiana, the Italian cultural center of Columbia University. He has taught at Hofstra University, Queens College, the American Studies Center (Naples), and the English Institute (Naples) and is a regular contributor of articles on Italian film, theatre, and opera to *Film Comment*, *Opera News*, *Stereo Review*, and the British *Opera*. Recently, he translated an Italian novel, *Fosca*, by a little-known nineteenth-century writer, Tarchetti.

TONY CURIEL teaches acting, directing and Chicano Theatre at the University of California–San Diego. Professor Curiel has directed at El Teatro Campesino (which he also served as Assistant to the Artistic Director), the Los Angeles Theatre, the Burt Reynolds Jupiter Theatre, and the Public Theatre, among others.

MIMI GISOLFI D'APONTE is Professor of Speech at Baruch College and teaches in the Ph.D. Program in Theatre at the City University of New York Graduate Center where she has also served as Acting Director of the Center for Advanced Study of Theatre Arts. Professor D'Aponte has translated numerous plays from Italian and her articles have been published in *Western European Stages*, *The Journal of Dramatic Theory and Criticism*, *Commonweal*, *Other Stages*, *Performing Arts Journal*, and *The Drama Review*. Currently, Professor D'Aponte is writing a book on Street Festivals in New York City.

EDWARD DEE is assistant editor of *Soviet and East European Performance*. He is a doctoral candidate at the Graduate Center of the City University of New York.

ANN DEMLING is Associate Professor and Director of Theatre at Northern Montana College. A 1987 recipient of a National Endowment for the Humanities grant to attend a Summer Seminar for College Teachers at Columbia University, Professor Demling's publications have appeared in *The Southern Quarterly*, *Theatre Southwest*, and *CHOICE*.

JAMES DePAUL is a director and Assistant Professor of Theatre in the Meadows School of the Arts, where he teaches in Southern Methodist University's professional actor training program. In the past decade, Mr. DePaul has directed a wide range of plays for professional and educational theatre and has given master workshops in improvisation and acting. For four years, he served as artistic director of the Oberlin Repertory Company in Ohio. He is a member of SSDC, SAG, and AFTRA.

JOHN LOUIS DiGAETANI is Associate Professor of English at Hofstra University. He has published in *The Drama Review*, *Studies in American Drama: 1945–Present*, *Modern Fiction Studies*, *The Opera Quarterly*, *Opera News*, *The New Orleans Review*, and *Opera Monthly*. Professor DiGaetani is the author of *A Companion to Pirandello Studies*, *Puccini the Thinker*, *Carlo Gozzi: Translations of "The Love of Three Oranges,"* *"Turandot"*, and *"The Snake Lady"* with a Bio-critical Introduction, *An Invitation to the Opera*, *Richard Wagner and the Modern British Novel*, *Penetrating Wagner's Ring: An Anthology*, and the forthcoming *A Search for a Postmodern Theater: Interviews with Contemporary Playwrights*.

SVERKER E. EK is Professor and Head of the Department of Comparative Literature at the University of Umeå, Sweden. He has written extensively on Hjalmar Bergman, Funnar Ekelöf, Peter Weiss, Georg Büchner, Olof Molander, and Knut Ström. He has also conducted research on the repertoires of Swedish theatres.

THOMAS-WHIT ELLIS teaches theatre at California State University at Fresno. He has also taught at the University of Georgia and other universities. A member of the Screen Actors Guild, Mr. Ellis has a long list of stage, film, and television credits.

HARLEY ERDMAN is a doctoral candidate in Theatre History at the University of Texas–Austin with a specialty in Spanish-language drama. His translation of Lope de Vega's *La gallarda toledana*, which was performed at the Chamizal and Texas Hispanic Theatre Festivals in 1991, won a special award for excellence for Hispanic Classical Theatre.

JON ERICKSON is Assistant Professor of Drama in the Department of English at Ohio State University. His essays on performance and culture have been published in *Journal of Dramatic Theory and Criticism*, *Theatre Journal*, *Psychiatry and the Humanities*, *Discourse*, and *Boundary 2*. In addition to performance theory, Professor Erickson has written about and lectured on painting, conceptual art, and poetry.

ALAN FILEWOD is Associate Professor of Drama at the University of Guelph and Editor of *Canadian Theatre Review*. He was elected President of the Association for Canadian Theatre Research in 1991 and has written numerous articles on contemporary Canadian theatre, with a special interest in political theatre. He is the author of *Collective Encounters: Documentary Theatre in*

English Canada (University of Toronto Press, 1987) and editor of two anthologies of Canadian plays.

CHRIS FLAHARTY is Assistant Professor of Theatre and Dance and a designer-director currently in residence at Oberlin College Conservatory, where he teaches design and creates costumes for theatre, dance, and opera. He has designed costumes or sets for a variety of classical and contemporary works in the Midwest and southern California.

REAGAN FLETCHER is finishing a Ph.D. at New York University's Department of Performance Studies. He is an archivist at the Shubert Archive and has also directed many shows in the New York area.

MARCEL FORTIN is a teacher of French Literature at Collège de Valleyfield and researching at the Université du Quebec à Trois-Rivières. He has published articles in *Cahiers de Théâtre Jeu*, *Canadian Theatre History* and *L'Annuaire Théâtral*.

JOHN W. FRICK teaches Theatre History, Dramatic Literature and Criticism at the University of Virginia. He is the author of *New York's First Theatrical Center: The Rialto at Union Square*, the co-editor of *The Directory of Historic American Theatres*, and has published articles and reviews in *The Drama Review*, *Theatre Journal*, *The Journal of American Drama and Theatre*, *The Yearbook of Interdisciplinary Studies in the Fine-Arts*, *Performing Arts Resources*, *Southern Theatre*, *Marquee*, *American National Biography*, and *The Encyclopedia of New York City*.

MEL GORDON is Professor of Dramatic Art at the University of California at Berkeley. A director and writer, he is the author of many books and articles on American, French, German, Italian, Soviet, and Yiddish theatre. His most recent books are *The Stanislavsky Technique: Russia* (New York: Applause Books, 1988) and *The Grand Guignol* (New York: Amok Press, 1988).

RENÉE N. GURIK, set and costume designer, teaches History, Set, and Costume Design at the Lionel-Groulx's Option-Théâtre. She has published articles in *Jeu*, *Annuaire Théâtral*, *Les Veilleurs de nuit*, and *Les Cahiers de la N.C.T.*

KAI HAMMERMEISTER studied German literature, rhetoric, and philosophy at the University of Tübingen, Germany, and received an M.A. from the Department of Germanic Languages and Literature at the University of Virginia. He is currently writing his dissertation on Metaphor, Social Change and Gay Studies.

JAMES V. HATCH teaches in the Theatre Program at the Graduate Center, City University of New York. His book *Sorrow Is the Only Faithful One, a Biography of the Life of Owen Dodson* was published in 1993 by the University of Illinois Press. He has also published *The Roots of African American Drama* with Leo Hamalian (Wayne State University Press, 1991) and edited *Black Theatre U.S.A.* (The Free Press, 1974), as well as numerous articles. Professor Hatch also runs the Hatch-Billops Collection.

HANNA-LEENA HELAVUORI has taught at Turku University and is currently the Director of the Theatre Museum, Finland. Her articles and reviews have been published in *Nordiska spelplatser. Studier i nordisk teaterverksamhet fran sekelskifte mot sekelslut*, *Nordic Theatre Studies*, *Yearbook for Theatre Research in Scandinavia*, *Theatre Studies Publications in association with FIRT/IFTR*, *Journal of Scandinavian Studies*, and *Nordisk kvindellitteraturhistorie*.

JOHN H. HOUCHIN holds a Ph.D. from New York University and has taught at the University of Texas at Dallas, Richland College, Berry College, the University of Houston at Victoria, and St. Francis College. His articles have appeared in *The Drama Review* and he has presented papers at ATHE, Popular Culture Association, and Southwest Theatre Conference conventions. In addition, he had directed numerous productions and served as general manager of Dancers Unlimited Repertory Company and the Plaza Theatre in Dallas.

JANE HOUSE is former Director of the Theatre Project at Columbia University's Institute on Western Europe and has taught theatre at New York University, Vassar College, Lehman College, Baruch College, and Queens College. She has published in *Theatre Theory/Theory Theatre*, *Anthology of Twentieth-Century Italian Drama*, *Western European Theatre*, *The Blackwell Companion to 20th-Century Theatre*, and *Political Theatre Today*. A professional actress as well as a scholar, Dr. House has appeared on Broadway and Off-Broadway, and in regional theatres as well as on television and in films.

JORGE HUERTA is a professional director and Professor of Theatre at the University of California, San Diego. He is editor of three anthologies and author of numerous articles about Chicano theatre as well as the book *Chicano Theatre: Themes and Forms*. Professor Huerta has lectured and conducted workshops on Chicano Theatre throughout the United States, Latin America, and Western Europe.

PAUL KEITH JACKSON is the chair of Spelman College's Department of Drama, where he has taught since 1986. He is currently editing *Woman in Metamorphosis: A Collection of Critical Essays on Adrienne Kennedy*. He has delivered papers at the Southeast Theatre Conference and ATHE conventions. He received his Ph.D. from the University of Wisconsin–Madison.

SHERRY ENGLE JOHNSON will receive a Ph.D. in Dramatic Text and Criticism from the University of Texas–Austin in 1993. A playwright (*Adrianna's Muse*, *A Kind of Offering*), her specialties are playwriting and American women playwrights.

STEPHEN BURGE JOHNSON teaches theatre and directs at McMaster University in Hamilton, Ontario. He is the author of *The Roof Gardens of Broadway Theatres, 1883–1942*, Associate Editor of *The Oxford Companion to Canadian Theatre*, and has published articles and reviews in *The Drama Review*, *Theatre Research in Canada*, and *Nineteenth Century Theatre Research*. Dr. Johnson is currently Co-editor of *Theatre Research in Canada* and a member of the executive board of the International Federation for Theatre Research.

DENIS W. JOHNSTON teaches theatre history at the University of British Columbia. He is the author of *Up the Mainstream*, a history of Toronto's alternative theatres, and many articles on Canadian drama and theatre.

CHRIS JONES is Assistant Professor in the Department of Theatre Arts at Northern Illinois University. As a theatre critic for *Variety*, Jones reviews new plays throughout the Midwest, and his work has also been published in *Popular Culture Review* and *Theatre Studies*. He is currently working on a reader's guide to the plays of Willy Russell.

JONI L. JONES is an Assistant Professor at the University of Texas at Austin with a joint appointment in the Departments of Theatre and Dance and Speech Communication where she teaches History of African-American Theatre and Performance of Literature. As part of the completion of her doctoral degree from New York University, Jones is developing a dramatic structure based on African performance practices.

MACIEJ KARPIŃSKI is a drama critic who has collaborated with the Polish director, Andrzej Wajda on a number of productions and is the author of *The Theatre of Andrzej Wajda* which was published by Cambridge University Press, in 1989.

COLLEEN KELLY is Assistant Professor and movement specialist in the Department of Drama at the University of Virginia. She is a Certified Teacher with the Society of American Fight Directors and recently staged fights for Joanne Akalaitis's production of *'Tis Pity She's a Whore* at the Public Theatre. Professor Kelly has published in *Fight Journal* and is editor of the SETC/ATHE movement periodical *Connections*.

MARNA KING is Professor of Costume Design for the Theatre at the University of Wisconsin–Madison. She has researched and written about theatre in the

Federal Republic of Germany, and in 1989 received a Fulbright Senior Professor Research Award to study German Theatre.

MICHAL KOBIALKA is McKnight-Land Professor of Theatre at the University of Minnesota. His articles and reviews have been published in *Journal of Dramatic Theory and Criticism*, *Theatre History Studies*, *Medieval Perspectives*, *The Drama Review*, *Theatre Journal*, *Performing Arts Journal*, *Stages*, *Theatre Annual*, *Theatre Nordic Studies*, *Slavic and East European Journal*, and *Soviet and East-European Drama, Theatre and Film*. Dr. Kobialka has recently finished a book on Tadeusz Kantor and his Cricot 2 Theatre.

ALAN KREIZENBECK teaches theatre at the University of Maryland Baltimore County. He received his Ph.D. from New York University and has published articles in *The Drama Review*, *The Journal of Popular Culture*, and *The New England Theatre Journal*.

KELA KVAM teaches at the Institute for Theatre Studies, University of Copenhagen, and has published books on August Strindberg, Max Reinhardt, theatre during the interwar years, and avant-garde theatre. Professor Kvam is Editor-in-Chief of *Nordic Theatre Studies, Yearbook for Scandinavian Theatre Research*, 1–4; Co-Editor of *A History of the Danish Theatre*; and Chairman of The Society of Danish Theatre Scholars.

JEAN-MARC LARRUE is Professor of Theatre at the Collège de Valleyfield in Quebec. He has published articles on theatre and theory and is the author of *Le Théâtre à Montréal à la fin du XIXe siècle*, *Le Théâtre au Québec: mémoire et appropriation*, *Le Théâtre au Québec: repères et perspectives*, *Les Nuits de la Main* et *le Monument-National de Montréal*. He is editor of *L'Annuaire théâtral—revue québécoise d'études théâtrales*, a journal of theatre research.

THOMAS LEFF is an independent scholar, director, and designer who has taught at Colgate University, the University of Notre Dame, and Swarthmore College. His published writings have appeared in *Theatre Journal*, *The New England Theatre Journal*, *Theatre Topics*, and the *Swarthmore Bulletin*. *Originary Space*, a book in which Leff explores the phenomenology of theatrical space, will be published in the near future.

STUART LENIG teaches at Columbia State Community College. He is the former Artistic Director of the Mariner Theatre project in Payson, Arizona, and has taught theatre at the University of Richmond, Adelphi Junior College, and Los Angeles City College. Professor Lenig has published in *The Journal of Theory and Criticism*, *Occulus*, *Cableday Magazine*, and various trade publications.

MARTHA SCHMOYER LoMONACO is Assistant Professor of Fine Arts and Resident Theatre Director at Fairfield University in Connecticut. She has contributed articles to *The Drama Review*, *MicroTheater*, *Performing Arts Resources*, *Princeton University Library Chronicle*, *Women & Performance*, and the forthcoming *Encyclopedia of New York City*. Her first book, *A Broadway Revue Every Week: The Tamiment Playhouse, 1921–1960*, was recently published by Greenwood Press.

FELICIA HARDISON LONDRÉ is Curator's Professor of Theatre at the University of Missouri–Kansas City. She has published numerous articles on the theatre, is the author of *The History of World Theater: From the English Restoration to the Present*, *Tennessee Williams: Life, Work, and Criticism*, *Federico Garcia Lorca*, *Tom Stoppard*, and *Tennessee Williams*, and Associate Editor of *Shakespeare Around the Globe: A Guide to Notable Postwar Revivals*. Professor Londré also serves as resident dramaturg for the Missouri Repertory Theatre, has been guest dramaturg for Great Lakes Theatre Festival, dramaturg at the Nebraska Shakespeare Festival, has worked with Actors Theatre of Louisville, and is Co-founder and Associate Director of the Missouri Shakespeare Festival.

JULIE MALNIG holds a Ph.D. in Performance Studies from New York University, where she is an Adjunct Assistant Professor. She is the author of *Dancing Till Dawn: A Century of Exhibition Ballroom Dance* (Greenwood Press). Dr. Malnig is also an editor of *Women & Performance Journal* and has written on feminist performance and popular theatre and dance.

MARK C. MANIAK works as an actor in New York. He received a B.A. in Theatre from SUNY Geneseo and an M.A. in theatre history from the Department of Performance Studies at New York University.

GERALDINE MASCHIO is Chairperson of the Department of Theatre at the University of Kentucky. She has published in *Performing Arts Resources*, *Women and Performance*, *Journal of Popular Culture*, *Studies in Popular Culture*, and other periodicals. She is currently writing a book on cross-dressing during the nineteenth century.

SUSAN VANETA MASON teaches Dramatic Literature and Theatre History at California State University, Los Angeles. She is Literary Associate and Publications Coordinator at the Los Angeles Theatre Center, where she also serves as a director and dramaturg of the Women's Project. Professor Mason has worked as a dramaturg at Lincoln Center's Newhouse Theatre, for the American Place Theatre, and the Yale School of Drama and has published in *Theater*, *American Theatre*, *Theatre Journal*, and *Ibsen News and Comment* and is Review Editor for *Theatre Journal*.

LINDA J. K. MASSON, who holds a Ph.D. in Drama/Performance Studies, is an associate director of Riverside Shakespeare Company, where she has directed Austin Pendleton in *Hamlet*, F. Murray Abraham in *Othello*, and Ralph Williams in *The Miser*. She previously co-directed Joseph Papp's parks tour of *Merry Wives*, as well as directed new plays at the Women's Interart, Quaigh, and American Globe at the Writers Theatre. She teaches acting and drama in New York City.

M. CLARE MATHER is Assistant Professor of French at Saint Olaf College. Her area of specialization is twentieth-century French theatre and Professor Mather has a special interest in Francophone African theatre and the integration of Francophone literacy into the French language and literature curriculum.

MARIO B. MIGNONE is Chairman of the Department of French and Italian at SUNY Stony Brook, where he also has served as Director of the Summer Program in Rome and Director of the Academic Year in Rome Program. Professor Mignone is the author of *Il teatro di Eduardo De Filippo: Critica sociale, Anormalita e angoscia nella narrativa di Dino Buzzati, Eduardo De Filippo*, and *Pirandello in America* as well as numerous articles on Italian theatre.

TOM MIKOTOWICZ, who received his doctorate in Performance Studies from New York University in 1985, is an Assistant Professor of Theatre in the Department of Theatre/Dance at the University of Maine and supervises the directing program. He has published articles and delivered papers on such varied topics as street performers, puppetry, postmodern directing, and design in such publications as *TD&T*, *The Puppetry Journal*, *Theatre Topics*, *Contemporary Designers* (London: St. James Press and Macmillan), and *The Cambridge Guide to World Theatre*. In addition, he has directed and designed more than 75 major productions at community, educational, and professional theatres in Pennsylvania, Texas, Illinois, New York, and Maine. Dr. Mikotowicz is the editor of *Theatrical Designers: An International Dictionary*.

JUDITH G. MILLER is the author of *Theatre and Revolution since 1968, François Sagan*, and, with Christine Makward, *Out of Bounds: Women's Theatre From the French: A Critical Anthology*. She has written extensively on French theatre and directs and adapts plays for her students at the University of Wisconsin–Madison.

JUNE MIYASAKI is a Ph.D. candidate in the Department of French and Italian at the University of Wisconsin–Madison. A former preparatory school teacher, she is currently studying the problems of representation in French postcolonial theatre.

PAMELA MYERS-MORGAN is Associate Artist Director of the Dallas Theatre Center. An experienced director, she has also been associated with the Portland (Maine) Stage Company (for whom she directed *Cowboys #2*); the Southern Appalachian Repertory Theatre (where she staged the world premiere of *Echo 4 Mi.*); Piccolo Spoleto; Charleston Theatreworks; and Center Stage in Charleston, SC.

PAUL NADLER is an adjunct lecturer in the Hunter College Department of Theatre and Film. He has an M.A. in Theatre and Film from Hunter College and is currently completing his Ph.D. in Theatre at the City University of New York. He won the 1991 Shuster Award for his theatrical history of the Brooklyn Academy of Music, the 1990 and 1991 John Golden Awards for Playwriting, and the 1992 Association for Theatre in Higher Education (ATHE) Graduate Student Playwriting Award. He is also a contributor to *Contemporary Dramatists*, *The Bloomsbury Theatre Guide*, and *Black Women in America*.

STEPHEN NELSON has taught at New York University, Hunter College, and the University of Delaware. He has written a full-length study of Billy Rose, *Only a Paper Moon: The Theatre of Billy Rose* (UMI Research Press).

ANDREA J. NOURYEH is Assistant Professor of Theatre at St. Lawrence University. Professor Nouryeh's publications have appeared in *Theatre Topics*, *Shakespeare on Film Newsletter*, *Broadside*, *The Cambridge Guide to World Theatre*, *Theatre Design and Technology*, *Black American Literature Forum*, and *Theatrical Designers: An International Dictionary*.

JUDY LEE OLIVA teaches theatre at the University of Tennessee. Professor Oliva is the author of the book, *David Hare: Theatricalizing Politics*, and has contributed articles and reviews to *Casebook on Howard Brenton*, *Theatre Journal*, *Theatre Studies*, and *Theatre Three*.

TOM J. A. OLSSON is Curator of the Archives and Library at the Royal Dramatic Theatre in Stockholm and serves as the international secretary (for Europe) of the Eugene O'Neill Society. An experienced actor and director, Dr. Olsson has worked at the Municipal Theatre, Gothenburg; the People's Theatre, Gothenburg, where he was Assistant Director to Erwin Piscator; and his own experimental theatre in Stockholm.

LURANA DONNELS O'MALLEY teaches in the Department of Theatre and Dance, University of Hawaii at Manoa. She received her Ph.D. from the University of Texas at Austin, and traveled to Moscow in 1989–90 on an International Research and Exchange Board (IREX) Arts Exchange grant to study Soviet Theatre.

M. ELIZABETH OSBORN is a free-lance writer, editor and dramaturg who specializes in contemporary theatre. Her anthology *The Way We Live Now: American Plays and the AIDS Crisis* (New York: Theatre Communications Group) won the Lambda Award for the best AIDS book published in 1990. She is working on a book on John Hirsch.

ZBIGNIEW OSIŃSKI is a historian and Professor at the Institute of Polish Culture at the University of Warsaw and the Director of the Center for Studies on Jerzy Grotowski's Work and of Cultural and Theatrical Research in Wroclaw. Professor Osiński's writings have been published in many languages, and he is the author of *Grotowski and His Laboratory* which has been translated into English.

LILIANE PAPIN teaches at the University of Tohoku, Japan. Professor Papin is the author of *L'autre scène: le théâtre de Marguerite Duras* and has published articles in *Modern Drama*, *The French Review*, *Stanford French Review*, *Cincinnati Romance Review*, and *Remains To Be Seen*. She is currently writing a second book, *Black Holes and Literature*, a study of modern representation.

DAVID J. PASTO has taught at the University of Massachusetts, Mount Holyoke College, Kent State University, and Hollins College. An experienced actor and director, Dr. Pasto has served as an acting instructor at the Drama Studio (Springfield, MA) and has worked at the Berkshire Theatre Festival, Mill Mountain Theatre, Salt City Center for the Performing Arts, and the Westfield Theatre. His articles and reviews have been published in *Estreno*, *Theatre Journal*, *Nineteenth Century Theatre*, *Theatre Survey*, and *The Hollins Critic*.

DAVID PAYNE CARTER taught at New York University's Undergraduate Drama Department, the University of Delaware, Oberlin, and Hofstra. He received his Ph.D. from the Performance Studies Department at New York University, and his book on Gower Champion is forthcoming. Dr. Payne Carter died in 1991.

ELIZABETH RAMIREZ is Assistant Professor of Performance Studies and Director of the Master of Arts Program at the University of Arizona. She is a former Fellow in Dramaturgy at the American Repertory Theatre Institute for Advanced Theatre Training and is the author of *Footlights Across the Border: A History of Spanish-Language Professional Theatre in Texas*. Dr. Ramirez is a contributor to *The Cambridge Guide to American Theatre* and has published articles and reviews in *Theatre History Studies*, *Handbook of Texas History*, *Choice*, and *American Repertory Theatre Newsletter*.

MAARTEN A. REILINGH teaches and directs at McNeese State University (Lake Charles, LA). He wrote the chapter on William Inge in *American Play-*

wrights Since 1945: A Guide to Scholarship, Criticism, and Performance and has entries in *Shakespeare Around the Globe: A Guide to Notable Postwar Revivals*, *The Cambridge Guide to World Theatre*, and the upcoming *Cambridge Guide to American Theatre*. Professor Reilingh is a Field Bibliographer for the *International Bibliography of Theatre*.

JANNE RISUM is an Associate Professor at Institut for Dramaturgi, Aarhus University, Denmark. Professor Risum has published widely on acting and theatre history, has written on Kierkegaard in *Nordic Theatre Studies*, Volume 1, and is Co-editor of *Dansk teaterhistorie*.

WILLIAM H. ROUGH is the coauthor of the recently published history, *Step Right Up! The Adventure of Circus in America*, and author of numerous articles in the field of drama education. His playscripts include *Ladybird, Ladybird*, a 1991 winner of the Festival of Emerging American Theatre, *Ringmaster*, *Second Shepherds' Play*, and *Blackout*. Mr. Rough holds degrees from the University of Virginia, Columbia, and Princeton universities. A founder and co-president of the American Alliance for Theatre and Education, Mr. Rough is the recipient of several awards and commendations honoring his work in secondary school theatre education.

JOHN ROUSE is Assistant Professor and Head of the M.A. program at Tulane University. He is the author of *Brecht and the West German Theatre: The Practice and Politics of Interpretation* (UMI Research Press, 1989) and articles on Brecht, the German theatre, Robert Wilson, and theatre semiotics in *Theatre Journal*, *Theater*, *The Brecht Yearbook*, and other journals. He is the Vice-President of the International Brecht Society and is currently at work on a book about the German playwright Heiner Müller.

JEAN-LOUIS ROUX was cofounder (1951) and Artistic Director (1966–82) of Le Théâtre du Nouveau Monde; Co-Founder (1960) and Director General (1982–87) of The National Theatre School of Canada. Since then, he has been a free-lance writer, director, and actor. He has published many articles in various Canadian periodicals.

CYNTHIA RUNNING-JOHNSON is Associate Professor of French at Western Michigan University. Professor Running-Johnson's articles and reviews have been published in *Romantic Review*, *Theatre Journal*, *French Review*, *Women in Theatre*, *Journal of Dramatic Theory and Criticism*, *Romance Quarterly*, and *South Central Review: The Journal of the South Central Modern Language Association*.

SUSAN FRANCES RUSSELL is completing her doctoral thesis on Gender Ideology in Twentieth Century German Theatre at the University of Washington.

She has published articles on George Tabori, Oskar Kokoschka, and German Theatre, and received a Fulbright/Hayes grant to study German theatre in 1985–86.

ERIC SAMUELSEN is Assistant Professor of Theatre at Brigham Young University. He received a Ph.D. in Dramatic History from Indiana University in 1991. His dissertation dealt with Ibsen's *Brand* and interpretations in production history.

TIMOTHY SCHEIE is a Ph.D. candidate in French at the University of Wisconsin–Madison and is writing a dissertation on *Roland Barthes and the Body on Stage*.

HELEN SHEEHY, a writer-biographer, is the author of a textbook *All About Theatre, Margo: The Life and Theatre of Margo Jones* (Southern Methodist University Press, 1989), and is working on a biography of Eva Le Gallienne to be published by Alfred A. Knopf. A resident of Connecticut, Sheehy worked as a dramaturg for the Hartford Stage Company, has written a number of articles and essays, and has taught theatre for over twenty years.

LEWIS E. SHELTON is Associate Professor and Director of Theatre at Kansas State University where he teaches acting, directing, and dramatic literature. His articles on Alan Schneider, Ben Teal, and others have been published in *The Journal of American Drama and Theatre*, *The Midwest Quarterly*, and *A&S, the Magazine of the College of Arts and Sciences, Kansas State University*.

PAULINA SHUR holds a Ph.D. in Theatre and Film Criticism from the Institute of Theatre, Music and Film, Leningrad, and an M.F.A. in directing from the University of Virginia. She has translated a number of plays from Russian, and directed plays in Minnesota and Virginia.

MARC SILBERMAN is Associate Professor of German at the University of Wisconsin–Madison, specializing in twentieth-century German literature and culture, German cinema and East German literature. He has published *Literature of the Working World: A Study of the Industrial Novel in East Germany* (Bern/Frankfurt: H. Lang, 1976), *Heiner Müller*, Forschungsberichte zur DDR-Literatur 2 (Amsterdam: Rodopi, 1980), and edited and wrote an introduction for *Interpretationen zum Roman in der DDR* (Stuttgart: Klett Verlag, 1980), as well as numerous journal articles.

HENRIK SJÖGREN is a drama critic and author of books on Ingmar Bergman (*Ingmar Bergman: på Teatern* and *Regi: Ingmar Bergman*), as well as a book on Swedish theatre, *Stage and Society in Sweden*.

LYNN SOBIESKI is Assistant Professor of Theatre History and Criticism at the University of Texas–Austin where she also heads the Dramaturgy program. A past recipient of a Hays-Fulbright Grant to West Germany, Dr. Sobieski has worked at theatres in Germany, England, and the United States. Her articles and reviews have been published in *The Drama Review*, *Other Stages*, and *The Villager*.

LARRY SOLLER teaches directing, acting, cinema, and humanities at Phoenix College and has directed over 50 major productions from Shakespeare to Ibsen to Joe Orton. A professional actor, Dr. Soller has worked with the Arizona Theatre Company in *American Dreams: Lost and Found*, *The Middle Ages*, and *Tales of the Lost Formicans* and was recently in an episode of ABC's "Young Riders."

CONSTANCE SPREEN is currently a Ph.D. candidate in French Literature at the University of Chicago. Her work is concerned with the "vision mélodramatique au XIXe et XXe siècles," a historically and philosophically oriented study of the rise and continuation of the melodramatic world view since the French and American revolutions. Ms. Spreen is also Assistant Manuscript Editor for the journal *Montaigne Studies*.

RÉMI TOURANGEAU is Professor of Literature and Theatre at Université du Québec à Trois-Rivières. He is author of *L'Eglise et le Théâtre au Québec*, *Trois-Rivières en Liesse*, *125 ans de Théâtre au Seminaire de Trois-Rivières* and *Fêtes et Spectacles du Québec*, etc. He has published many articles in such journals as *L'Annuaire Théâtral*, *Le Théâtre Canadien Français*, *Theatre History in Canada*, *The Oxford Companion to Canadian Theatre*, and *Les Cahiers de Cap-Rouge*. He was co-founder and president of the Society of Theatre History in Quebec.

ANDREA URICE is a free-lance director based in Chicago. A former Arts Programming administrator at Luther College and Jacob K. Javits Fellowship recipient, Ms. Urice has been associated with Actors Theatre of Louisville, the Guthrie Theatre, the Source Theatre in Washington, D.C., and the Northlight Theatre in Chicago.

STEPHEN M. VALLILLO is Assistant Professor of Speech at St. John's University. He has published articles in *The Drama Review*, *Black American Literature Forum*, *Theatre History Studies*, *Musical Theatre in America*, *Dictionary of Literary Biography*, and *Performing Arts Resources*.

LOUISE VIGEANT is a professor in the French Department at Collège Edouard-Montpetit, in the Montreal area. She is a theatre critic on Radio-Canada, and has written articles for *Canadian Theatre Review*, *Theatre Research Interna-*

tional, *L'Annuaire Théâtral*, *Veilleurs de nuit*, and most frequently, *Les Cahiers de théâtre Jeu*. She is also the author of *La Lecture du spectacle théâtral*, an introduction to a semiotic approach to theatre.

CARLA WAAL is Professor of Theatre at the University of Missouri–Columbia. She has been the recipient of grants from the Fulbright program, the Norwegian Foreign Ministry, the George C. Marshall Fund, the Swedish Foreign Ministry and the University of Missouri which have allowed her to conduct research in Scandinavia. She is the author of numerous articles on theatre past and present and two major biographies, *Johanne Dybwad* and the award-winning *Harriet Bosse*.

RICHARD WARNER is Head of the Acting Program at the University of Virginia. He has worked in New York at the Manhattan Theatre Club, the Chelsea Center, W.P.A. Theatre, and the Douglas Fairbanks Theatre; and his regional credits include the Genesse Valley (GEVA) Theatre, Florida Studio Theatre, Paper Mill Playhouse, Heritage Repertory Theatre, and the Performing Arts Foundation (PAF) Playhouse. He was recently seen in the film *Toy Soldiers*, and he directed the inaugural production of *Her Great Match* at New York's Pearl Theatre Company, where he was a founding member.

DANIEL J. WATERMEIER is Professor of Theatre and Drama at the University of Toledo. He is the author of two book-length studies of the actor Edwin Booth, and his articles and reviews concerned with American theatre and drama and Shakespearean stage history have appeared in leading scholarly journals and reference works.

PHILIPPA WEHLE is Professor of Language, Culture and Drama Studies at SUNY Purchase. For the past eleven years, she has been actively involved in the Avignon Performing Arts Festival in France and has served as advisor to the festival's director in selection of American artists. Dr. Wehle is the author of numerous scholarly articles on contemporary European and American theatre, dance, and performance and the author of three books: *Le Théâtre Populaire selon Jean Vilar*, *Jimmy's Blues* (a translation of James Baldwin's poetry into French), and *DramaContemporary: France*.

MARK S. WEINBERG is Associate Professor of Communications at the University of Wisconsin Center–Rock County where he is also Director of Theatre. Professor Weinberg's articles and reviews have appeared in *Journal of Dramatic Theory and Criticism*, *Theaterwork*, and *Theatre Journal*, and he is the author of *Challenging the Hierarchy: Collective Theatre in the United States*.

SULLIVAN WHITE is on the staff of Actors Guild of Lexington (Kentucky) and works as a free-lance director and stage manager.

DON B. WILMETH, Professor of Theatre and English and Curator of the H. Adrian Smith Collection of Conjuring Books and Magicana at Brown University, is the author, editor, or co-editor of nine books, including the award-winning *George Frederick Cooke: Machiavel of the Stage*. A contributing, advisory editor of *The Cambridge Guide to World Theatre*, he is co-editor of *The Cambridge Guide to American Theatre*. He is a past book editor for *Theatre Journal* and has written for many journals and publications including *The Dictionary of American Biography*, *World Book Encyclopedia*, and *Prospects*. Professor Wilmeth is on the editorial board of a half dozen journals and is currently President of the American Society for Theatre Research.

STACY WOLF is a Ph.D. candidate in Dramatic Theory and Criticism at the University of Wisconsin–Madison. She has published articles and reviews in *Theatre Studies*, *Women and Performance*, and *Journal of Dramatic Theory and Criticism*.

LILA WOLFF-WILKINSON is completing a D.F.A. in Dramaturgy and Dramatic Criticism at Yale School of Drama. She is a past officer of the Association of Theatre in Higher Education and was formerly Director of Theatre at the University of New Haven.

LEIGH WOODS is Associate Professor and Head of Theatre Studies at the University of Michigan. His articles have appeared in *Biography*, *Essays in Theatre*, *Scandinavian Review*, *Shakespeare Quarterly*, *Theatre Journal*, and *Theatre Survey*. He has written two books for Greenwood Press: *Garrick Claims the Stage* (1984) and *On Playing Shakespeare* (1991). Also a professional actor, he was last seen as Lenin in the American premiere of Mikhail Shatrov's *Onward! Onward! Onward!*.

ELZBIETA WYSIŃSKA is a theatre critic and theatre historian. For the past thirty years, she has been associated with the Polish theatre magazine, *Dialog*, and has been published in *Teatrze* and *Theatre in Poland*. Ms. Wysinska is co-author of *Slownik wspolczesnego teatru*.